THE DREAM ENDURES

B — You lived through some of this.

H.

Christmas 2002

AMERICANS AND THE CALIFORNIA DREAM

Americans and the California Dream, 1850–1915

Inventing the Dream
California Through the Progressive Era

Material Dreams
Southern California Through the 1920s

Endangered Dreams
The Great Depression in California

The Dream Endures
California Enters the 1940s

THE DREAM
ENDURES

California Enters the 1940s

KEVIN STARR

OXFORD
UNIVERSITY PRESS

OXFORD

UNIVERSITY PRESS

Oxford   New York
Auckland   Bangkok   Buenos Aires   Cape Town   Chennai   Dar es Salaam
Delhi   Hong Kong   Istanbul   Karachi   Kolkata   Kuala Lumpur   Madrid   Melbourne
Mexico City   Mumbai   Nairobi   São Paulo   Shanghai   Singapore
Taipei   Tokyo   Toronto

and an associated company in Berlin

Copyright © 1997 by Kevin Starr

First published by Oxford University Press, Inc., 1997
198 Madison Avenue, New York, New York 10016
First issued as an Oxford University Press paperback, 2002

Oxford is a registered trademark of Oxford University Press

Library of Congress Cataloging-in-Publication Data
Starr, Kevin.
The dream endures : California enters the 1940s
Kevin Starr.
p. cm.
Includes bibliographical references and index.
ISBN 0-19-510079-4 (cloth) ISBN 0-19-515797-4 (pbk.)
1. California—Civilization—20th century.
2. Depression—1929—California
I. Title.
F866.S78   1997   979.4'052—dc20   96-17087

1 3 5 7 9 8 6 4 2
Printed in the United States of America
on acid-free paper

for Sheldon Meyer

Preface

The previous volume of the *Americans and the California Dream* series, *Endangered Dreams: The Great Depression in California*, focused on social, political, and economic history. While some attention was paid to such compelling artists as Dorothea Lange and John Steinbeck, so important to the documentation of the Great Depression, as well as to the imaginative dimension of public works, *Endangered Dreams* had as its primary concern the *noir* aspects of the period. Yet the worst of times can be the best of times as well, often for the same person or group. Even as Californians were absorbing the thousand natural shocks of the Great Depression—unemployment, strikes, Communist agitation, reactionary conspiracies—they were also, simultaneously, exploring ranges of value, lifestyle, and creativity that would establish paradigms for the rest of the nation in the post-war era. In so many inter-related pursuits—sport, leisure, fashion, architecture, urban and suburban lifestyles—the creativity of pre-war California defined and broadcast a message of great social significance to the rest of the nation: California had arrived and, in arriving, had achieved the good life for increasing numbers of Americans. The problems and challenges of this era, moreover, inspired a level of response in fiction, film, painting, sculpture, photography, design, and the writing of history that added even further intensity to the image of California being communicated to the rest of the nation.

Even in the matter of the impending war, and after 1939 the war in Europe, and after 7 December 1941 the world war that now involved the United States, California played an interpretive and supportive role that further added to its identity as a mediating American place. As war clouds loomed, Californians pondered the great issues of war and peace from the perspectives of philosophy, poetry, anthropology, psychoanalysis, and archival documentation. Southern California emerged as the energizing refuge for Europeans in exile, Jews and Christians alike. From this rapidly formed Euro-Southern California were launched many of the most enduring responses—in film and the novel, in music, philosophy, and social science—to the possible end of European civilization itself.

As is the case with all volumes of the *Americans and the California Dream* series, *The Dream Endures* is concerned primarily with the intersection of social and imaginative experience, public and private. The narrative rests on the assumption that idea, ideal, and metaphor as well as economic and political forces have shaped the past and remain equal parts of a recoverable history. The method and approach of *The Dream Endures*—eclectic narrative seeking to convey analysis and symbolic interpretation through concrete event—has its risks. Among them is the temptation to succumb to variety for its own sake, which results in a mere taxonomy of experience. Properly structured, however, an encyclopedic narrative such as *The Dream Endures* can also suggest the fullness, the complexity, the interrelatedness of human culture in its personal and social vitality.

Ever focused on the human dimension, *The Dream Endures* is also shaped and enlivened by my profession, librarianship, and my formation in literary and American studies thirty years ago at Harvard under the tutelage of such scholars as Douglas Bush, Lewis Mumford, Howard Mumford Jones, Harry Levin, Walter Jackson Bate, and Alan Heimert. From librarianship, I have absorbed a passion for the multiplicity of evidence, for the highways and byways one must travel in pursuit of interpretation. At Harvard, I absorbed a conviction that interpretation was a process essential to the development of culture, especially in these United States, where the process of selecting and arranging the imaginative materials of identity serves a society constantly running out ahead of itself. As in the case of previous volumes in the *Americans and the California Dream* series, *The Dream Endures* seeks to identify and dramatize a usable past. What was achieved by Californians in the decade before Pearl Harbor and into the early war years in the matter of value, lifestyle, and creativity went into the making of contemporary American culture. In my next volume, a study of the war and post-war era into the 1960s, I hope to chronicle the flowering of the California Dream challenged and accelerated by the war and the boom that followed. Today, as California reassembles and revitalizes itself, it is more important than ever to remember that encountering adversity, a Great Depression and a world war, Californians achieved a direct connection with the best possibilities of themselves and the society they were seeking to create.

Los Angeles, San Francisco, Sacramento   K.S.
October 1996

Contents

III   REFRACTIONS

IV WAR AND RUMORS OF WAR

together, part of a single émigré community. How could or would Jewish civilization reconstitute itself? asked Lion Feuchtwanger. What demonic urges lurked in the Faustian center of the German soul? asked Thomas Mann. How, asked Franz Werfel, could Jews and Christians ever again find each other after the enormity, the horror, of what had happened?

I

THE SEARCH
FOR THE GOOD LIFE

1

Good Times on the Coast

Affluence and the Anti-Depression

IN a three-part series published in *Westways* in the fall of 1936, Los Angeles journalist Farnsworth Crowder assessed the California temperament as a matter of sunshine, physicality, and the pleasure principle. Because of the California climate, Crowder claimed, an unapologetic pursuit of pleasure had emerged as a driving force in daily life among Californians. This preference manifested itself through an intensified relationship to the environment and life in the outdoors. "Your Californian," Crowder claimed, "seeks snowbanks, beach sands, channel islands, pine forests, desert inns, in preference to museums, theatres, birthplaces, tombs, and historic landmarks. He feels that there is a distinct appropriateness about a concert under the stars, a graduation-out-of-doors, a supper in a patio, in preference to anything under a roof; he will even suffer chilblains in defense of this preference."

The relative lack of a history, Crowder argued, served this obsession with nature. True, California had a Spanish and Mexican past, and before that a Native American heritage; but few traces of these eras had survived, and their relationship to the cultural consciousness of contemporary California was virtually nil. ("Almost any square block of London is more drenched with flavors of the past than the whole of Los Angeles.") Unburdened by history, Crowder speculated, Californians related directly to the here and now and to the physical. "This cult of the body snubs tradition, formality, and dignity," Crowder maintained. "Sun-bathing, nudity, bare heads, open-necked shirts are not imposed by cranks; they are dictated by the sun. Health consciousness is extreme and is reflected in the medical profession and in the prevalence of quackery, pseudo-science and cultism. The climate is so entirely congenial to the American athletics mania that sports flourish and champions are a major product. Body-awareness is, of course, heightened among women by the presence of the movies, and one sees glamour attempted in the most unexpected corners on the most improbable faces and figures, until as one draws closer and closer to Hollywood and Vine the effect becomes positively bizarre."[1]

Crowder's thesis, like all such synthetic speculations, was at once overstated— and correct. As a matter of social experience and self-perception, Californians did glory in athletics, outdoor living, and the festive pageantry of life in a manner that did not differ in kind, but rather in intensity, from patterns of enjoyment in other regions. Nor did the Depression totally interrupt the fun. Amidst the stories of poverty, labor strife, and urban and rural wretchedness, which are so much a part of the California story in the 1930s, there must also be chronicled the emergence of a pleasure-seeking, leisure-oriented society that contained within itself the formula for post-war America. What affluent Californians and in many cases the middle classes could enjoy in the 1930s—swimming, golf, tennis, country clubs, horseback riding, resort life, backyard barbecues, musical entertainment— decisively shaped America's conception of the good life in the post-war era. If California tested alternatives of Far Left and Far Right in its political culture during this period, it also was testing, triumphantly, a Hedonistic Middle based on the desire of ordinary people to get a little more out of life, to have more fun: a motivation, however commonplace in its formulation, that would bring millions to the Golden State after World War II.

Already, by the 1930s, the California lifestyle had discovered its first premise and most sustaining metaphor in the automobile. From the automobile came tourism: not just in terms of visitors from out of state, but intra-California tourism as well. By the mid-1930s the tourist business in California represented three-quarters of a billion dollars in assets and employed more than a hundred thousand Californians. More than a million tourists arrived each year between early May and late October. In 1935 alone, Southern California, which accounted for three-quarters of the tourist business in the state, reported 459,000 winter and 810,000 summer visitors. Most of them arrived by automobile, at an average rate of some six hundred thousand cars per year. Internal tourism was equally important. At a time when an estimated 75 percent of the American population never traveled more than five hundred miles from home, Californians were showing themselves addicted to the weekend or holiday getaway—almost always by automobile. Organizations such as the Automobile Club of Southern California and the California State Automobile Association trumpeted statistics asserting that the roads and highways of California were traveled, twelve months a year, by a greater number of cars per person than those in any other state.

Motoring implied a psychological relationship to California as a landscape in motion, unfolding as a lavish pageant across the windshield, and to the automobile as a source of well-being and personal identity. One sees this relationship developing in the 1910s as motor tourism, initially an elite activity, became popular enough to warrant its own manual, *On Sunset Highways: A Book of Motor Rambles in California*, by Thomas D. Murphy, first published in 1915 and reissued in 1921. Meticulously illustrated with photographs and color reproductions of California paintings, *On Sunset Highways* represents an early and powerful presentation of California to itself and to the rest of the nation as a source of moral, spiritual, and psychological uplift via the automobile. Whereas John Muir and his counterparts in the Sierra Club might consider the hiking trek, or at most the horseback ride, as the only politically correct mode of encountering California as a source of beauty and inspiration, Murphy and the other motor tourist writers of the period (who remained, after all, touched by the high-mindedness of their era) saw in the automobile a comparable source of improving experience. The very linkage of motoring and art in Murphy's guide spoke for itself in an era that viewed landscape painting as an intrinsically uplifting medium. The automobile, to their way of thinking, in California and elsewhere, but in California especially, turned Everyman and Everywoman into secular pilgrims en route to the California equivalents of Canterbury and Compostela.

As in the case of so many other leisure activities, the aesthetic formulations of the 1910s regarding motoring began to move into more middle-class directions in the 1920s as more and more tourists embarked on motor pilgrimage throughout the state in the long, sleek, and shiny black Auburns, Chandlers, Hupmobiles, Nashes, Peerlesses, Pontiacs, Rickenbackers, Roosevelts, Stutzes, Whippets, Willyses, Buicks, Packards, Cadillacs, and Fords of that era. On 12 December 1925 a new American institution, the motel, made its debut with the opening of the Milestone Motel outside San Luis Obispo. Designed by Pasadena architect Arthur Heineman, the Milestone Motel featured the near-mandatory Mission Revival bell tower, in this case a replica of the Santa Barbara Mission, and red-tiled roof. Behind the Spanish romance, however, was a no-nonsense bungalow court, with a garage in back of each cabin. It took another twenty five years for the word *motel* to be accepted into Webster's dictionary, but by that time this California-invented institution had long since further wedded America to highway culture.

In December 1935 Basil Woon, writing in *Westways*, noted how motels and motor lodges were competing effectively against hotels in the city for the tourist traffic. The urban hotel, Woon pointed out, tended to be situated near the downtown railway stations. Since most tourists now arrived in California by automobile, motels and motor lodges—clean, efficient, inexpensive, conveniently located near highways for a late arrival or early getaway—were proving competitive. Most air terminals were also located outside of cities, so motels and motor lodges were competing for elite air travelers as well, thanks to even yet another variation of automobile culture, the rent-a-car. To his delight, travel writer Jim Tully discovered in January 1934 that he could be sitting at the bar at the Algonquin in New York and, some seventeen hours of flying time later—via stops and plane changes in Cleveland, Cheyenne, Salt Lake City, and Las Vegas—could be busy about his business in Los Angeles, having been impressed by the efficiency of Miss Angelina Butkiewicz, a registered nurse serving as stewardess, and her equally adept replacements on the flight west.

The 1930s witnessed the automobilization not only of the hotel via the motel, but of the home via the house trailer and of the restaurant via the drive-in. Between 1935 and 1937, the number of car-drawn house trailers in the United States tripled to three hundred thousand. A new facility, the trailer camp, a development of the earlier auto camp, emerged to meet the needs of the estimated one million Americans who either spent their leisure time or lived permanently in house trailers. In Southern California, with its excellent climate, trailer camps, courts, and parks began in 1939 and 1940 to emerge as a significant form of permanent housing for the first wave of newly arriving defense workers. By 1940 an automobile culture was in place in California that anticipated how Americans would live in the post-war era. Fast food, drive-ins, the motel, the automobile as home and habitat: the road culture of America was not exclusively invented in California, yet California did intensify the paradigms.

Emergent regions and lifestyles require explanations, instructions, and celebrations, which is the appointed task of the American magazine. California was no exception. The 1930s witnessed the emergence of *Sunset*, one of the most successful regional lifestyle magazines in the country. Founded in 1898 by the Southern Pacific as a magazine to promote West Coast tourism, *Sunset* began its existence oriented to an East Coast market. In 1914 a group of employees led by *Sunset* editor Charles Field purchased the magazine from the Southern Pacific and made every effort to transform it into a California-based *Harper's* or *Atlantic Monthly*, while keeping its orientation toward tourism and lifestyle. Writers for *Sunset* in this era included such California-based literati as Stewart Edward White, William Rose Benét, George Sterling, Peter Kyne, Kathleen Norris, Herbert Hoover, Sinclair Lewis (in his Carmel phase), John Muir, Stanford president David Starr Jordan, Zane Grey, Dashiell Hammett, Joseph Henry Jackson, and other regional writers of reputation. The *Sunset* magazine of 1914 through 1928, in fact, was the single most distinguished literary magazine on the West Coast. Its bold and chromatic covers were striking, with San Francisco artist Maynard Dixon, who also wrote poetry for the magazine, doing a notable series.

As excellent as it was, however, *Sunset* was on the verge of bankruptcy by late 1928, yet one more among the numerous literary periodicals that have failed in California. Enter Larry Lane, advertising director of the Des Moines–based Meredith Publications, which owned the highly successful *Better Homes and Gardens*. With the help of six other Des Moines investors, Lane purchased *Sunset* in September 1928 for $65,000 and immediately laid down a new editorial policy. *Sunset* would no longer seek to rival *Harper's* and the *Atlantic* as a writer-driven literary review. It would become, rather, a staff-written magazine, no bylines, no well-known writers, focusing on the West Coast lifestyle, meaning homes, gardens, cuisine, travel, and leisure. Liquor and tobacco advertising were forbidden.

Lane also pioneered the concept of regional editions, differing in story content and advertising, within a single format, with bureaus being maintained in Tacoma for the Northwest, Palo Alto for California, and Palm Springs for the desert Southwest. Overnight, the intellectually ambitious magazine of the 1920s became exclusively focused on matters of regional lifestyle.

Like all successful magazine editors, Larry Lane used *Sunset* to define first to himself, and then to his readership, why California and the West had so enchanted him in the years he had traveled there on behalf of Meredith Publications. To review the files of *Sunset* from 1929 to 1941 is to miss completely any suggestion that a Depression was happening. As a business, *Sunset* might have been struggling along with everyone else. (Not until 1938 did *Sunset* experience an operating profit.) But within the pages of the magazine there unfolded a panoramic pageant of gardening, architecture, regional cuisine, patio dining, golf, tennis, horseback riding, and other leisure pursuits, which represented, in its own way, a cunning strategy for economic success. *Sunset* fought the Depression by ignoring it, by holding before the middle classes an image of the good life as it was surviving even in dire times and would be even more joyously repossessed in times to come. In presenting the West as suburban paradise, *Sunset* flattered the taste and expectations of middle-class Westerners as it chronicled a lifestyle, increasingly available by the late 1930s, that in the post-war era would provide the blueprint for the way Westerners conceived of, and lived, the good life.

An experience central to that lifestyle, covered extensively by *Sunset*, which tested each recipe in its own kitchens, was the cuisine of California and the Far West. The beginnings of an indigenous California cuisine can be seen in such frontier items as piñon nut soup and acorn biscuits. In each case, a Native American staple, the food of the land itself, was transmuted into a parallel American dish. Mid- to late nineteenth-century California recipes show a decided proclivity for indigenous (one is tempted to say Native American) foods: rabbit, venison, wild fowl seasoned with local herbs; the use of acorns in muffins, breads, and breakfast porridge. At the same time, Mexican-Californian dishes survived the transition from Mexican to Yankee occupation. There was never a time, in fact, when Mexican cuisine was absent from the Yankee-Californian diet, which in and of itself suggests larger social and cultural realities. Barbecued meats, chili peppers, tortillas and enchiladas, tamale pie (corn meal, meat, olives, peppers, and tomato sauce, roasted in a casserole), and other corn-meal dishes, together with the delicate Mexican custards and *aguardiente*, a fiery local brandy, held their own through the nineteenth century.

French *haute cuisine* flourished in San Francisco from the 1850s onward, and the turn of the century witnessed an interest in Italian cooking, again in San Francisco especially, with its large Italian community and many Italian restaurants. In 1904 the Telegraph Hill Neighborhood Association issued a collection of Italian recipes compiled by Linie Loyall McLaren under the title *High Living: Recipes from Southern Climes*. The eclectic *fin de siècle* was framed by two San

Francisco books, Daniel O'Connell's *The Inner Man: Good Things to Eat and Drink and Where to Get Them* (1891) and Clarence Edgar Edwords's *Bohemian San Francisco: Its Restaurants and Their Most Famous Recipes* (1914). Especially strong in the cuisine of San Francisco was seafood, as might be expected, with an elegant local white fish, the sand dab, emerging as a special favorite, along with the redoubtable oyster loaf (a long loaf of heated sourdough French bread stuffed with oysters and appropriate sauces), a favorite late-night meal of the sporting set.

Meanwhile, there were Quaker cookbooks, a spiritualist cookbook, a number of cookbooks from the ladies' auxiliaries of Jewish temples, Japanese cookbooks, a Chinese cookbook, Swedish cookbooks, and a French cookbook, the stunning 307-page *Hotel St. Francis Book of Recipes and Modern Menus* (1910) by the hotel's executive chef Victor Hiertzler. Emphasizing fresh fruits and vegetables and a limited use of meat, the Japanese cookbook, *Entree and Salad Cookery* by Aoki Taiseido, published in San Francisco in 1909, might be said to have foreshadowed, if only indirectly, the Japanese-Californian cuisine of the 1980s, but it was printed in Japan in Japanese, with the exception of its English preface, and was used only in the Japanese community, whose cuisine would ultimately exercise such an important influence on the eating habits of Californians. Already, since the turn of the century, Californians were eating more fresh fruits and vegetables than the rest of the nation, and enjoying an abundance of citrus, for obvious reasons; yet the plenitude of such fruit and produce cannot be said to have substantially modified the meat-and-potato-oriented American diet, although visitors to California did note, among other things, the prevalence of fresh seafood, a rarity in so much of the nation, and the luxuriant salads served as a first course.

Ethnic groups—Chinese, Japanese, Armenians, Italians, and others—continued to prefer their national dishes; and ordinary Californians continued to dine through the 1930s on meat loaf and potatoes, tuna-noodle casserole, peanut butter and jelly sandwiches, Jell-O, tapioca pudding, macaroni and cheese, and other dishes typical of mid-America in this penny-stretching period. The privileged classes, however, revived the barbecue of the rancho era. *Early California Hospitality* (1933) by Mrs. A. B. de Packman, published in Pasadena, indicated a growing preference in the 1930s for the reconstituted, one might say reimagined, cuisine of early California, which meant the barbecue. A preference for barbecuing was strongest among the upper middle classes and the wealthy, for whom the outdoor barbecue became a rite of celebration of their identity as heirs to the dons of Old California. Elaborate outdoor grills became increasingly characteristic of the patios and backyards of affluent California: great stone constructions, many of them possessed of architectural distinction, equipped with iron spits and other utensils fashioned in a style to suggest Mexico, set beneath oak trees, surrounded by stone or redwood tables. Group excursions among the affluent—organized horseback rides, special celebrations at country clubs, large-scale entertainments at the ranch-estates of the wealthy—frequently ended in pit barbecues for a hundred or more, in which a whole carcass—a heifer, a pig, a lamb stuffed with rice and raisins—was simmered among buried coals for twenty-four hours, beneath a covering of earth. Disinterred, the meat was served piping hot with baked beans, green peppers, sliced onions, cole slaw, sourdough French bread, and red wine.

The use of wine as an ordinary beverage was also a growing characteristic of affluent California in the 1930s. Wealthy Americans had always enjoyed wine as part of formal dining. In post–Volsted Act California, however, locally produced reds and whites appeared frequently on even the luncheon table. It was the abundance of red wine, in fact, that differentiated the California barbecue from its Texas counterpart, at which cold beer was usually served. Like so much else in the 1930s, California dining preferences expressed elite values that would become mainstream after the war. By the 1950s even middle-class Californians had learned to drink the wines of Italian Swiss Colony, Petri, Christian Brothers, Gallo, Sebastiani, and Foppiano, red and white, along with their meals. While a great backyard barbecue, and certainly a pit barbecue feeding a hundred, might be beyond the means of an ordinary Californian, the near-ritual cooking of meat in the outdoors, so strongly associated with the vanished Spanish or Mexican way of life, so promotive of group identity and well-being, so celebratory of family, friends, and community, anticipated the post-war mania for the outdoor barbecue, which became an almost universal symbol of well-being in the Golden State.

For a smashingly successful pit barbecue, it helped to have a ranch. The 1930s witnessed an intensification of resort ranching and dude ranching among the affluent. William Randolph Hearst's San Simeon was obviously the biggest resort ranch of them all; but the lifestyle magazines of the period showcased many lesser, even more authentic, ranch-estates, in Carmel Valley outside Monterey, in the Santa Ynez Valley and the Ojai Valley in Santa Barbara County, and in Rancho Santa Fe in northern San Diego County. Two forces were at work: either the wealthy had acquired working ranches that previous owners had lost to the Depression or, as in the case of the Carmel Valley and Rancho Santa Fe especially, ranch-estates were developed by part-time Californians from the East who preferred the central and south coastal climate and a ranch-oriented lifestyle to the resort amenities of Palm Springs. In any event, such Californians as Mr. and Mrs. Bing Crosby of Rancho Santa Fe were spending a good part of the year as lady and gentleman ranchers, ensconced in architect-designed or architect-renovated ranch houses—adobe walls, red-tiled roofs, flagstone patios, exposed beam ceilings, oversized fireplaces—the whole emanating an idealized mood of a gracious, spacious Spanish/Mexican California.

Once again, the trickle-down theory asserted itself. Discovered by the wealthy, leisure clothes in a cowboy-Western idiom became the rage by late 1939, as no-nonsense working clothes—jeans, flannel shirts, cowboy boots and hats—became increasingly stylized for the leisure market. At the Billy Rose Aquacade Theater at the Golden Gate International Exposition on Treasure Island, Levi Strauss and Company introduced an extensive line of stylized Western resort and leisure wear at a gala showing in early September 1940. (The most popular event on Treasure

Island, incidentally, was the Cavalcade of the West, a musical pageant involving cowboys, Indians, covered wagons, and an early railroad train.) The Levi line as well as other California-produced Western leisure wear caught on immediately in California and the national market.

As early as the 1890s, Southern Californians were showing an intense relationship to the stunning shoreline that fronted their mountain-and-desert-guarded enclave. Middle-class families would spend an entire month on the beach (Redondo Beach was a favored site) living in tents. Putting aside late Victorian and Edwardian taboos, young women, wearing bathing suits that would raise eyebrows in the East, plunged into the surf alongside the men. Elsewhere, a pale complexion was prized in a woman through the First World War. In Southern California, a new phenomenon, the deliberate suntan, became a badge of beauty and health. The seaside villages and summer tent cities of the 1910s developed in the 1920s into a string of beach towns running from Laguna Beach in Orange County to Malibu north of Santa Monica, where a sea-and-shore-oriented lifestyle, as yet free of over-population and suburban sprawl, flourished with a special charm. The very roll call of these Southern California beach towns—Malibu, Santa Monica, Venice Beach, Hermosa Beach, Manhattan Beach, Redondo Beach, Long Beach, Seal Beach, Sunset Beach, Huntington Beach, Newport Beach, Balboa, Laguna Beach, Oceanside, Encinitas, Del Mar, Coronado—bespoke long days on the sand, a bracing plunge into the surf, the smell and taste of food and drink in the outdoors, splendid sunsets and party-happy nights.

In the 1930s the rather casual, even haphazard beach cabins of an earlier era showed signs, among the affluent, of stylization. Architects such as Winchton Risley and Roland Coate entered the beach house business, designing vacation homes that avoided the pretensions of the Santa Monica mansions as well as the scruffy rusticity of Laguna Beach in favor of deliberately contrived complexes—informal, picturesque, serviceable—keyed to the long weekend. In one prototype Risley suggested two dormitories, one for women and one for men, as part of a beach house complex, so as to make the house compatible to large gatherings. On Martha's Vineyard, a beach house might contain a formal dining room. The Southern California beach house of the late 1930s, by contrast, tended to substitute a half-covered patio for outdoor dining.

For the younger crowd, the beach itself was habitat enough. No beach house was necessary, only sleeping bags and a station wagon. At San Onofre Beach just south of the Orange County–San Diego County line, near San Clemente, a new sport, surfing, was taking hold. The surfboards of the 1930s were long, ten to fifteen feet, and heavy, weighing up to sixty pounds in that pre-fiberglass era; and surfing was enjoyed more by young men in their twenties and early thirties, the college crowd and young professionals, as opposed to the later dominance of the sport by teenagers. At San Onofre, Hermosa, Palos Verdes, or Malibu, perhaps a hundred surfers and their wives and girlfriends, representing a variety of surfing clubs or informal circles, would converge on a weekend in their wood-paneled station wagons of the era (later revered as woodies, a prime element of the surf cult) and proceed to erect tents or lean-tos of driftwood and palm fronds. While surfers were on shore, they would plant their tall surfboards, twice the length of ordinary human height, upright in the sand in rows and circles, thereby creating a surfers' Stonehenge, each board bearing its name in block letters. (Surfing screen star Jackie Coogan called his board *Opuu*, the Hawaiian word for stomach, poking fun at his ability to stand upright.) Entering the surf, dozens of surfers would advance on-line into the water, paddling on their stomachs, then break formation as they caught a wave into the shore. At San Onofre, where the waves broke far out, a surfer could catch a quarter-mile ride. By night, there were campfires and beach parties into the late hours, with singing and ukelele music. Surfers had a reverence for things Hawaiian—Hawaiian shirts, Hawaiian names for their surfboards, ukelele music, Hawaiian chants—since the islands were *fons et origo* of surfing in the Southland.

Among beach towns, each had its orientation. Laguna Beach, for example, was an art colony, the Carmel of Southern California, slightly raffish and affordable. A handful of galleries selling the works of local artists lined the Pacific Coast Highway as it passed through Laguna Beach, and each year beginning in 1932 the town sponsored a Festival of the Arts, which attracted large crowds of amateur artists and collectors. In 1933 Laguna Beach residents organized the first annual Pageant of the Masters as part of the festival, with locals arranging themselves into elaborate *tableaux vivants* of Old Master paintings.

Sailing-oriented Balboa had once been the preserve of the upper middle classes. The Depression removed some of Balboa's pretensions, transforming it to a more accessible beach resort. Hollywood dominated shorefront development at Malibu, although a more modest lifestyle prevailed in the canyons. Hollywood had a stake in Santa Monica as well. Marion Davies, mistress of William Randolph Hearst, maintained her official residence there. Santa Monica also served as the Riviera of inland Los Angeles. The downtown Jonathan Club operated a beach club there, and in the nearby Santa Monica Mountains the Uplifters sponsored a ranch resort where polo players could enjoy playing fields created for the 1932 Olympics. There was also, in Santa Monica, in the hundreds of cottages just up from the shore, and in the canyons, a flourishing middle-class life. In its Art Deco shoreline—restaurants, hotels, dancing pavilions—Santa Monica epitomized Southern California as suburban seaside; and on Sundays, as had been the case since the 1890s, the beach teemed with the middle classes of the region. Nearby Venice, by contrast, was a Coney Island kind of place: popular, demotic, its great boardwalk teeming with working families of a Sunday, drawn there as much by the arcades, shooting galleries, roller coasters, mirror mazes, fun houses, hot dog stands, and merry-go-rounds as by the good weather and the seashore.

Further south, Long Beach was, in one glorious jumble, an oil boom city, an industrial center, Des Moines by the Sea (ground zero for the Iowa Society, the

Kansas Society, the Missouri Society, and similar organizations), the geriatric capital of the United States (never before in human history had so many people over
sixty-five been assembled in one place), a busy port, a naval base—and, amidst it
all, a seaside resort. The industry came from the oil derricks, pumping since 1921
when the gushers began to spout on nearby Signal Hill, peaking at sixty-eight
million barrels in 1923. The port of Long Beach and the ship repair facilities of
the Navy, based there since 1919, added to the industrial character. Soon, Douglas Aircraft would open a plant adjacent to a newly constructed municipal airport,
the most modern airport in the Far West, Streamline Moderne in style and graced
with WPA murals.

In the early 1900s, Long Beach was the most important beach resort in Southern California, its accessibility enhanced by direct streetcar service to the rest of
the Los Angeles Basin. Constructed in 1905 at the base of the Pike Pier, the first
Municipal Auditorium hosted Chautauqua meetings, Shriners' conventions, song
fests, and church gatherings. In 1908 the upscale Virginia Hotel opened, and
Long Beach began to attract a national clientele. Photographs from the period
show Long Beach teeming with well-dressed men and women, promenading or
sitting beneath striped canvas awnings on the sand. In the 1920s Long Beach
became a popular resort for the Folks. The annual Iowa picnic held in Bixby Park
attracted more than a hundred thousand former Iowans and their descendants.

By the 1930s the popular character of the Folks' Long Beach was memorialized
in three oceanside constructions: an eight-acre Municipal Auditorium, opened in
1932, which also functioned as community center; the Pike, an amusement zone
extending for nearly a mile along the beach west of Pine Avenue and Ocean
Boulevard; and the Silver Spray Pier, which extended midway from the Pike into
the ocean. Its great indoor salt-water plunge was dubbed (with appropriate Iowa
corn) the Million Dollar Bathhouse. Each facility served a bustling democratic
life, the sort of scene Reginald Marsh loved to paint on Coney Island. In the case
of Long Beach, artistic celebration came from a spectacular tile mosaic mural in
the Municipal Auditorium entitled *Recreation in Long Beach*, completed by forty
artists and craftsmen of the Los Angeles Federal Art Project: the largest tile mosaic
in the world. By night it was illumined by powerful floodlights. Designed in an
Italian Renaissance style by the firm of MacDowell and Austin, the Municipal
Auditorium was available for a variety of activities: concerts by the municipal
band, meetings on Sunday morning of the world's biggest Bible class, symphony
concerts, an annual art festival, community sings, plays, square dancing, the annual Navy Ball. Day and night, the Pike teemed with comparable vitality as people enjoyed roller coaster rides, shooting galleries, penny arcades, a merry-go-
round, sideshows, and miniature automobile races; ate ice cream cones and cotton
candy; or stood as spectators as such annual events as the Baby Parade, the Pet
Parade, the Doll Fiesta, or the Bathing Beauty Contest. On Halloween, the
Fourth of July, and New Year's Eve, the Pike and the Silver Spray Pier were
thronged like Times Square with celebrating sailors and civilians.

From the Long Beach airport or the port, pleasure-seekers might fly or take a steamer to Avalon on the island of Santa Catalina, twenty-six miles offshore, where in the 1920s Chicago chewing gum magnate William Wrigley Jr., owner of the Chicago Cubs, was developing a resort city on the shores of Avalon Bay. Wrigley owned the island in its entirety, having purchased it for $3 million in 1919 from the Banning family. He intended to transform Avalon, so he said, into a resort for Everyman that avoided the excesses of Coney Island. Wrigley devoted the 1920s to the construction of, eventually, twenty-five hundred "bungalettes," which housed two to three people for between $12 and $17.50 a week. To bring them over and back, Wrigley purchased and had sailed through the Panama Canal a sixteen-hundred-passenger Great Lakes steamer, which he renamed the *Avalon*, augmenting it with the construction of a brand-new ship, the *Catalina*, which carried two thousand. By the late 1920s more than four hundred thousand people each year were visiting Avalon and the interior island, where boars, wild goats, and buffalo, left over from the filming of *The Vanishing American* in 1925, roamed, and where *Captain Blood*, *Mutiny on the Bounty*, and *Sadie Thompson* were filmed and such Hollywood personalities as Stan Laurel, Oliver Hardy, Gloria Swanson, Wallace Beery, Victor McLaglen, Ward Bond, Jean Harlow, Dolores Del Rio, Mickey Rooney, Errol Flynn, and David Niven were wont to frolic in the sun.

Founded early in the century by Charles Frederick Holder of Pasadena, the Tuna Club on Santa Catalina was the center of sport fishing in the Southland. The tuna is a gallant antagonist, capable of battling an angler for up to five hours. When the tuna went elsewhere, as they did for four to five years at a time, there were always marlin or swordfish on hand. Hooked, such fish leapt from the sea and appeared to walk across the waves on their tails. To a later generation, the fishing of these great creatures might seem barbaric; but through the 1930s, photographs of victorious anglers, rod and reel in hand, standing alongside a suspended gigantic fish, provided a dramatic emblem of the good life, Santa Catalina style.

As the capstone of his development, Wrigley built the Casino at Sugarloaf Point on the northern tip of Avalon Bay, designed by Sumner Spaulding and variously described as Moorish-Venetian, Spanish Colonial, or Adriatic. Opening on 29 May 1929, the Casino was, and remains, a glorious structure: a fantasy Xanadu on Avalon Point with a 1,250-seat motion picture theater on the first floor (one of the first theaters in the country to be acoustically engineered for the new talkies) and on the second floor a fifteen-thousand-square foot ballroom, circular in form, its maple, white oak, and rosewood surface resting on a supportive sub-floor of pine and cork to cushion the shock of thousands of dancers. Innumerable Southern Californians danced innumerable weekend and summer evenings of the 1930s to the music of Irving Aaronson and His Commanders, the resident orchestra in the first half of the decade. CBS Radio carried these dance sessions live to a national audience, and millions of Americans who had never been to Southern California felt themselves almost there as the announcer intoned: "From the beautiful Casino Ballroom overlooking Avalon Bay at Catalina Island, we bring you the music of Irving Aaronson and His Commanders . . . " As the Casino gained in popularity, better-known groups—the orchestras of Jimmy Dorsey, Harry James, Alvino Rey, Glenn Miller, and Tommy Dorsey; Kay Kyser and the College of Musical Knowledge; Bob Crosby and the Bobcats; the Freddie Martin Band; the Ted Weems Band, featuring Perry Como—crossed the channel. The daily arrival of the steamer on Avalon Bay was a big event. An announcer greeted celebrities over a loudspeaker system, and musicians led the passengers off the ship in parade to the hotels.

William Wrigley Jr., alas, was not on hand for the fun. He might have been uncomfortable with it all anyway, being of a shy and retiring nature. Wrigley passed away in 1932. At his memorial service in the Avalon Theater, the organist played "Beautiful Isle of Somewhere." Two years later, Wrigley's remains were interred in one of the most ambitious one-person mausoleums in the country: an eighty-foot concrete tower rising from a massive base set on a hilltop in the center of a thirty-eight-acre botanical garden, which soon became yet another tourist amenity.

Californians loved their mountains as much as their seashore; indeed, the mountains of California had inspired such figures as William Brewer, Thomas Starr King, Clarence King, John Muir, J. Smeaton Chase, George Wharton James, and Joseph Le Conte to produce much notable literature. Founded in San Francisco in 1892, the Sierra Club served the species of high-minded mountaineering represented by these writers, with its emphasis upon a purist relationship to the mountain wilderness, a conservation-oriented ethos, and an upper-middle-class aesthetic. Such a Progressive response was edging into a more democratic preference by the 1920s. The city of San Francisco, for example, maintained a public camp on its Hetch Hetchy water preserve, Camp Mather, named in honor of Stephen Mather, the first director of the national parks system. The fact that a city should maintain a public camp in the mountains, where families might vacation on the American plan at most reasonable rates, testified to the love of the mountains characteristic of that city and the rest of Northern California as well. Not surprisingly, both the University of California (the Bear's Lair) and Stanford University (Fallen Leaf Lake Lodge) also maintained mountain camps in the Sierra for alumni. Southern Californians also loved their highlands, the Tehachapis, the Santa Monica Mountains, the San Gabriel and San Bernardino ranges, and other montane spurs. In the late 1910s and early 1920s the Los Angeles *Times* ran a popular column by Pasadena writer, photographer, and landscape painter Frederick Roland Miner concerned almost exclusively with the pleasures of mountain life—mule packing, hiking, fishing, camping, and cabin craft—which the Times Mirror Press published as a book in 1923. Miner was writing for a statewide audience that included hundreds of thousands of urban and suburban Californians, even those of moderate income, who maintained a mountain retreat, if only a remote cabin.

Next to New England, California had emerged as the skiing capital of the nation by the 1930s, and there were those, such as Berkeley chemistry professor Joel Hildebrand and Wendell Robie, president of the Auburn Ski Club, the oldest ski club in California, who believed that California had surpassed Vermont and New Hampshire as skiing centers. A charter member of the Auburn Ski Club, Hildebrand was invited to manage the United States Winter Olympic team at Garmisch-Partekirchen, Germany, in 1936. His son Alex won the intercollegiate cross-country American championship. Another son, Milton, was a leading downhill skier, as was Hildebrand's daughter Louise. Located near Cisco in the Truckee-Lake Tahoe region, the Auburn Ski Club was not only the oldest and most prestigious of the twenty-three winter sports club in California, it was also the most developed skiing facility in the state, with a lodge and three-hundred-foot ski jump. Ski club president Wendell Robie brought a number of well-known jumpers—Roy and Harvor Mikkelsen, Sig Weterstaad, Rolf Wigaard, and Andrew Blodjer, among others—from Europe to work as instructors. With champions such as these in their midst, the young skiers of California, many of them college students, acquired an expertise that the United States Army would soon be utilizing in its Tenth Mountain Division.

Other popular winter resorts were located in Truckee, where the Truckee Ski Club rivaled the Auburn Ski Club in facilities; in Grass Valley, where the Grass Valley–Nevada City Ski Club was located on the Tahoe-Ukiah Highway; in Shasta City and the Yosemite; at Shaver Lake in the Sierra Nevada foothills, fifty-five miles east of Fresno; at the nearby General Grant National Park, the Giant Forest Winter Camp in Sequoia National Park, and a number of sites in the San Bernardino Mountains. As usual in matters Californian, a high level of amenities prevailed in many of these lodges, where fine food and warm drink before a roaring fire ended an exhilarating day on the slopes. At the Ahwahnee Hotel in the Yosemite, skiers and other winter visitors enjoyed each Christmas a festive Bracebridge Hall dinner re-creating the procession of dishes—the fish, the boar's head, the peacock pie, the baron of beef, the flaming pudding, the wassail bowl—described by Washington Irving in the Christmas sketches of *Bracebridge Hall* (1822).

Polo, golf, and tennis were other avid California pursuits and were also showing the same progress from elite to middle-class usage as motoring and skiing. In the mid-1930s the City and County of San Francisco used PWA and WPA funds to clear a polo field in Golden Gate Park, adjacent to the St. Francis Riding Stables. One scans in vain the newspapers of the period in an effort to detect signs of community opposition or complaining letters to the editor regarding the use of public monies to facilitate this most elite of elite sports. Polo came early to California, with the formation of a California Polo Club in 1876. In the 1890s polo was especially popular in the Anglo-Canadian community centered in Riverside in Southern California and, a little later, in the Burlingame Country Club south of San Francisco. The *California Polo Annual* for the 1913–14 season lists a busy schedule with matches held at the Hotel Del Coronado, at the Hotel Del Monte on the Monterey Peninsula, at Riverside, Pasadena, the Midwick Country Club in Monterey Park in the San Gabriel Valley near Los Angeles, Santa Barbara, and Burlingame. The San Francisco Peninsula sustained a polo culture mature enough to support its own publication, the *Peninsula Polo Annual*, which chronicled the well-attended matches of the region.

Central to the success of polo in California was a father-and-son team: William Pedley of Riverside and the Midwick Country Club, who had taken up polo in India while working there as an irrigation engineer, and his son Eric, a Stanford undergraduate just before World War I, who learned the game from his father and the great English player Hugh Drury, when Drury was living in Riverside. In 1921 Drury and Eric Pedley played for the Del Monte Polo Club and set new standards for the sport on the West Coast. By 1924 Pedley, then playing for Midwick, was leading a strong California team in the National Open of the United States Polo Association in Long Island. For the first time California polo made an impression in the polo-savvy East. In September 1930 Pedley played for the United States against England, perhaps the high point of his career. Throughout the Depression, polo continued to thrive in California, with such celebrities as Will Rogers, who played at the Uplifters Ranch near Santa Monica, becoming prominent advocates of the sport. In San Francisco the Army polo team from the Presidio—for whose benefit the Polo Field in Golden Gate Park was largely created—continued to set high standards of sportsmanship throughout the decade. Once again, there was the elite-popular connection so typical of the 1930s, as crowds gathered on Sundays in Golden Gate Park to watch cavalry officers from West Point ride against their equally privileged competitors.

Golf in California ran true to form, moving from elite to more popular circumstances. Established in March 1894, the Riverside Polo and Golf Club pioneered both golf and polo in the United States; indeed, the Riverside Golf Course was one of the first in the country. In the next few years, golf courses were laid out in Santa Barbara, Santa Monica, Redondo Beach, Pasadena, and Los Angeles. In the 1920s California witnessed the rise of a number of elite golf and tennis clubs as golf became the sport of preference for the upper middle classes. The courses of the San Francisco Golf Club and the Olympic Club of San Francisco, fronting the Pacific on the southwest corner of the city, were among the most beautiful golf courses in the world, as was the Army-sponsored Presidio Golf Course on an equally dramatic site approaching the Golden Gate.

Perhaps the most beautiful course in the state belonged to the Monterey Peninsula Club at Pebble Beach, a privileged residential community on the famed Seventeen Mile Drive fronting Monterey Bay, which the Del Monte Hotel had been serving as a center of elite social life since the 1890s. Throughout the late teens and 1920s, a Riviera row of ambitious mansions had been abuilding amidst the Monterey cypress trees lining the Seventeen Mile Drive, winding along the dramatic palisade fronting the Pacific. Samuel F. B. Morse, a direct descendant of the painter-inventor and an artist in his own right, was active in the development of Pebble Beach as a principal in the Pacific Improvement Company and, later, Del Monte Properties. In February 1919 Del Monte Properties purchased a strategically situated watershed tract on the Seventeen Mile Drive for development as a golf and country club. Morse brought golf course architects Charles MacDonald and Seth Raynor out from the East to design the fairways and retained architect Clarence Tantau of San Francisco to design an elegant Spanish Colonial–style building set amidst a grove of pine and cypress. When the new club was granted a charter by the State of California in January 1919, Samuel F. B. Morse, president and general manager of Del Monte Properties and the social leader in the affluent circles that had roosted on Pebble Beach, was elected president. Photographs from the period show golfers, resplendent in knickers and cardigans, golfing their way amiably through the 1930s. Very soon, the club developed a national champion, Lawson Little Jr., who won both the United States and British Amateur Championships in 1934 and 1935.

Like polo, golf was edging into greater availability, and not just as a spectator sport. Once again, San Francisco took the lead as the city continued to develop its municipally owned Lincoln Park course on Land's End overlooking the Golden Gate. If the Monterey Peninsula Country Club had any competition as far as scenic grandeur was concerned, it came from the Lincoln Park course, which ordinary San Franciscans might use for a modest fee. PWA and WPA funds were used both to improve the Lincoln Park course and to develop a second and third municipal golf course, the Harding Park course in the center of the city and a nine-hole course on the rolling dunes fronting Ocean Beach. Somehow, despite the Depression (or was it because of the Depression?), San Francisco was finding it appropriate to use federal funds on behalf of an elite game that demanded expensive park-like facilities but could now be enjoyed by the general public for whom the cost of a country club membership was out of the question. In the post-war era, both municipal and county golf courses would proliferate throughout California, together with innumerable private country clubs, as golf approached the condition of a social obsession.

As in the case of other sports, tennis as well went popular in the 1930s. True to pattern, tennis first emerged as an elite pursuit among the various clubs belonging to the Southern California Lawn Tennis Association organized in 1887. Good weather, together with the ease with which tennis courts could be laid out, soon made Southern California, along with Long Island, one of the two tennis capitals of the United States. In 1904 a seventeen-year-old from Los Angeles, May Sutton, astonished the tennis world by winning the Wimbledon women's singles, the first American to achieve championship status in this international contest. Although most tennis in Southern California was played in private clubs through the 1920s, many Southern California cities, Los Angeles included, were initiating an ambitious construction of public courts. By the late 1930s thousands of free courts were available to the urban middle classes.

A tennis champion from Berkeley, Helen Wills, led the parade. Wills began her career while still a high school student. By 1940 she had won eight Wimbledon singles championships and two Olympic gold medals. She remained undefeated in national and international matches between 1927 and 1933. At once muscular and feminine, the epitome of the California Girl, Helen Wills melded the genres of athlete and Hollywood star. The toast of London, Paris, and the Long Island tennis circuit, she made the cover of *Time* twice, on 26 July 1926 and 1 August 1929. When she played in England, she drew crowds of ten thousand and more. A crowd of four thousand gathered to see her play at Stanford. When she agreed to write a book for Scribner's, Maxwell Perkins was assigned as her editor. When Mexican muralist Diego Rivera arrived in San Francisco in 1929 to paint a mural in the San Francisco Stock Exchange Club, he persuaded Wills, whom he met at a reception, to pose as California. Rivera made daily trips to the California Club on Bush Street, where Wills was practicing, to observe his subject prior to painting her as the essence, in Rivera's words, of "all that was beautiful in California womanhood."[2] In December 1929 she married Frederick Moody, a San Francisco stockbroker, in an Episcopalian ceremony at St. Clement's Chapel in Berkeley in which Helen Wills, now Helen Wills Moody, explicitly did not promise to obey her husband. Socialite banker-lawyer Cyril Tobin lent the couple his yacht *Galeta* for a honeymoon cruise to Mexico.

Tennis, in other words, as represented by Helen Wills, had sex appeal and a distinctive California-oriented cachet, although women tennis players were required to wear calf-length tennis skirts until Helen Hull Jacobs broke the barrier by appearing on court in shorts at the Sea Bright Lawn Tennis Club Invitational Tennis Tournament in New Jersey in 1933. In the late 1930s, tennis became more and more a celebrity-oriented event, with large crowds of non–tennis players following the action or reading about it in the newspapers, just as they would read movie magazines about the stars who were also wont to make guest appearances on the court. Active on the Southern California tennis circuit in the 1930s as players and presenters of trophies were Gilbert Roland, Joan and Constance Bennett, Norma Shearer, Robert Taylor, Gary Cooper, Johnny Weissmuller, and an Errol Flynn, ever so splendid in white flannels, not yet debilitated by an off-court pursuit of wine, women, and song.

What to wear while pursuing the California lifestyle, how to furnish one's home, indeed, the design of the house itself also emerged as pressing questions. Throughout the 1930s regional designers increasingly stylized the consumer environment to reflect the casual, leisure-oriented values of California, which emerged as an increasingly important design premise for leisure clothes, tableware, and household furnishings. By the late 1930s, California leisure and sports wear—slacks for women, open-neck polo shirts for men, women's sunsuits, swimming suits for men and women, golf and tennis attire, even evening wear with a casual accent—was gaining a national reputation. Whether casual shoes from Joyce, sportswear and accessories from Louella Ballerino, Margery Montgomery, or Irene Bury, an afternoon frock from Violet Tatum, an evening dress from Patricia Perkins, a swimsuit from Gantner and Mattern, or sportswear from Koret, the one characteristic California fashions had in common was color: bright color, new colors, citrus colors—orange, lemon, lime, tangerine—newly introduced into American apparel. In the post-war era, such colors would be commonplace in American sportswear, but in the mid- to late 1930s, their introduction represented an innovation that bespoke the lifestyle of the Golden State.

The same was true of pottery and tableware. Pacific Clay Products of Los Angeles issued glazed settings in Apache red, canary yellow, silver green, royal blue, and mocha white. Like California cuisine, California-designed tableware frequently invoked the Spanish-Mexican past, blending Latin motifs with Moderne and Art Deco. The Gladding McBean Company of San Francisco issued Franciscan Ware, which managed to Art Deco–ize the Mission era. Another line, Fiesta Ware, fused Old California and Streamline Moderne with a bright-hot California palette and the heavy solidity of hand-thrown pottery. Fifty-five and more years later, Fiesta Ware remains a collector's item as it continues to emanate the self-confident mood of California 1940.

By November that year, *House and Garden* was reporting on the emergence of Asian and Hawaiian motifs in California interior decoration and household design. The Gump's look, of course—a juxtaposition of Asian screens, vases, and other objets d'art and traditional European furniture—had long characterized the San Francisco style; but Hawaiian motifs, stylized rattan and bamboo furniture especially, at once reflected the long-standing relationship between California and Hawaii and, one suspects, the growing involvement of the United States in the South Pacific and Far East. California-Hawaiian was an informal look. Those with developed taste used it sparingly, mostly in beach homes. It was also a favorite in bars and darkly lit restaurants such as Trader Vic's in Oakland and San Francisco, having, one supposes, suggestions of the mystery and adventure, and possible escapes from restraint, in exotic atmospheres. The Gump's look, by contrast, was decidedly upper-end, yet possessed as well of that Asia Pacific connection ever on the subliminal frontier of the California consciousness.

And now the most basic design challenge of them all—housing! In what domestic circumstances should the California Dream be pursued, even if a Depression were raging? How should the Californian build the ideal home, for private purposes most obviously, but also as a means of influencing national taste? In the mid- to late 1930s, California architects and developers and their middle-class clientele began to assemble the affordable dream house of the post-war era.

As far back as the 1870s the Southern Pacific Railroad, anxious to promote immigration to the Golden State, ballyhooed California as Land of Homes. Here, it was suggested, ordinary Americans in large numbers might experience the joys and consolations (and social stabilization) of home ownership. While this dream of owning one's own home came true for many, the concept of mass home ownership gained renewed intensity in the second half of the 1930s with the entry of the federal government into the home-loan business. The challenge now became to bring the amenities of the California dream house to the widest possible audience. Already, from the 1910s onward, a formula was in place: the patio; a reversed floor plan, with the living area opening onto a rear garden or patio enclosure; the facilitation of an indoor/outdoor lifestyle through wall-length glass-pane doors opening onto the interior patio or back garden; a designated sun room, which was in effect an indoor solarium; a breakfast nook adjacent to the kitchen, distinct from the dining room; an attached first-floor garage, directly accessible to the house.

In the 1920s and 1930s, the quest for the perfect California home regained strength as a regional preoccupation. Where one chose to live, place and house alike, together with the style one chose to live in, asserted itself as a substantive element in the discussion of what it meant to be a Californian. Madame Ernestine Schumann-Heink, for example, and novelist Kathleen Norris consciously saw themselves as paradigms of an achieved home-style, Southern and Northern California versions respectively. For Madame Schumann-Heink home was a rose-covered villa on Coronado, Late Prairie in style, to which she moved in the early 1920s after donating her former home at Grossmont in San Diego to the Disabled Veterans of the United States. "Above all, what I love is the spirit of the place—like no other in the world," she told a reporter from *Sunset* in October 1928. "Such a spirit, this of California! Once you have come under the spell, you never care to throw it off, nor do you care to be long away from it."[3] As the highest-paid writer in the United States, making more than $300,000 a year through the Depression, Kathleen Norris could afford the perfect California home, which in her case meant La Casa Abierta, the Open House, in Palo Alto, where she and her husband novelist Charles Norris (Frank Norris's younger brother) lived from October to May, when they repaired to their summer home at Saratoga in the foothills of the Santa Cruz Mountains. Designed and built in 1929, La Casa Abierta demonstrated the hold of Spanish Revival on upper-middle-class California through the 1930s, although fewer and fewer such homes were built as the 1930s progressed.

Spanish Revival did not translate automatically into mass housing, as Arts and Crafts and Prairie had so effectively lent themselves to downsizing in the early 1900s. The Sunstream Corporation, on the other hand, made a valiant (and generally successful) attempt to reproduce Spanish Revival on a mass basis in its creation of the Sunset district in San Francisco in the 1920s and 1930s. By 1940 avenue upon avenue of mini-villas, Spanish in inspiration, stood side by side on the once shifting sand dunes of westside San Francisco. In Southern California, the most successful suburbs of the 1920s—Bel Air, Brentwood, Beverly Hills,

Flintridge–La Canada, Palos Verdes Estates, San Clemente, Rancho Santa Fe, and La Jolla—were predominantly Spanish. Architect Lillian Jennette Rice, one of the first women to graduate (in 1910) from the School of Architecture at Berkeley, designed and supervised the development of Rancho Santa Fe on behalf of the well-known San Diego firm of Richard Requa and Herbert Jackson and the Santa Fe Land Improvement Company. Rice both designed the homes and civic center structures and did the landscaping for this elegant and tasteful planned development, which was set amidst groves of eucalyptus trees planted by the Santa Fe in the 1910s as a source of railroad ties. "Every environment there," noted Rice of the site, "calls for simplicity and beauty—the gorgeous natural landscapes, the gently broken topography, the nearby mountains. No one with a sense of fitness, it seems to me, could violate these natural factors by creating anything that lacked simplicity in line and form and color."[4] Under development at the same time by La Jolla Properties was the La Jolla Hermosa Tract designed by architects Edgar Ullrich, Thomas Shepherd, Herbert Palmer, and Cliff May. Rancho Santa Fe was inland, and La Jolla was coastal; yet each development emanated an ambience of dignity and tasteful restraint within the Spanish Revival idiom so congenial to San Diego County.

A native San Diegan, Cliff May, the youngest of the La Jolla architects, took Spanish Revival into the 1930s (the 1940s, 1950s, and 1960s, for that matter) after detaching it from archeological fussiness, streamlining it, and running it parallel to more contemporary styles. May refocused the Spanish Revival movement away from Andalusia and baroque Mexico and returned it to the more simple prototypes of frontier California in the 1820s and 1830s. Best described as California Spanish, a Cliff May house—heavy walls suggesting adobe, visible timbers in construction, sweeping horizontal lines, slate (not tile) roofs, oversized stone pavements—remained a style of choice thirty years after Spanish Revival peaked as a regional preference. May paid special attention to such interior details as built-in drawers, electric outlets, and ultra-modern kitchens. (The kitchen, noted real estate and architecture writer Jack Courtney in the February 1937 Westways, had become the most technically and aesthetically dynamic component of the California home, with the possible exception of the bathroom.) In the penultimate phase of his career, May was given the commission to design the holy of holies of the California lifestyle, the headquarters of Sunset magazine in Menlo Park. He finished his career with another cultural icon, the Robert Mondavi Winery in Napa.

At the same time, in Southern California, architects Richard Neutra and Rudolph Schindler were evolving a regional version of the International Style, which detached California from its largely imaginary Spanish and Mexican past in favor of designs that were clean and functional, aerodynamic even, and built in the materials of the machine age. In 1937 Neutra won the House Beautiful competition for the Palm Springs home he designed for Grace Lewis Miller, a physical fitness instructor, which featured solid concrete floors, large panels of glass as wall replacements, sliding doors, and an exterior of sheet steel. Simple, functional, possessed of compelling compositional logic, the 1930s homes of Richard Neutra and Rudolph Schindler established prototypes that remained influential for fifty years. The house Schindler designed in 1934 for Elizabeth Van Patten in the Silver Lake district of Los Angeles, or the 1936 Los Angeles house of Ralph Walker, together with the parallel work of Neutra and other masters of the International Style, Southern California version—Gregory Ain, Harwell Harris, Raphael Soriano, and Kem Weber (also an innovative designer of furniture)—foreshadowed the Case Study movement of the post-war era, which sought to devise an architecture that was aerodynamic, industrial in materials, and thoroughly functional, bringing taste and convenience to a middle-class market.

Not that the work of Schindler, Neutra, Ain, Harris, Soriano, Weber, and others working in this mode was then, in the 1930s, the preference of mass taste. Clients who chose the International Style tended to come from an affluent liberal intellectual elite. Yet these homes, so inexpensively a matter of skin over structure, with structure determining design, could be mass-produced—and were, with variations, in the post-war era. Neutra's Palm Springs house for Grace Miller, for example, cost $7,000, which put it $500 less than the $7,500 figure Jack Courtney of *Westways* believed to be the acceptable price for an architect-designed house in the Southland. Los Angeles architect Theodore Pettit, meanwhile, was designing five-room homes in the Spanish style to sell for $4,000. Remarkably, Pettit kept all elements of the Spanish style, including a twenty-by-thirty-foot interior patio or court. As furnishing for Pettit's low-cost Spanish bungalow, consulting decorator Edgar Harrison Wileman suggested the Fiesta Monterey line carried by Barker Brothers in Los Angeles, a style inspired by Monterey in the 1830s and 1840s. Barker Brothers had an entire department on the eighth floor of its store dedicated to Monterey Fiesta and other furniture lines in the Spanish-Mexican style. By 1940 small concrete homes ("Thermo-Crete" the concrete was called, poured to resemble adobe and given sculptural effects) were selling in Glendale for $2,650. Thus the decade ended with the mass production, even the democratization, of the Spanish style, a process true to the general drift of the 1930s. What could be enjoyed in Montecito and Santa Barbara in the 1920s could be enjoyed in Glendale by 1940.

In November 1940 *House and Garden* praised this Southern California trend of incorporating a full range of amenities into smaller homes. "It is not unusual," noted the magazine, "to find even a small suburban lot planned with marvelous skill to include not only the house but a tennis court, badminton court and the ubiquitous barbecue besides."[5] *House and Garden* noted another California trend: the development of the home as an outdoor recreation center. By 1937 sporting goods retailer A. G. Spalding and Brothers was doing a land-office business in ping-pong tables, badminton racquets and nets, croquet sets, and a strictly local game called Lawn Hi-Li, a backyard adaptation of the Basque game *jai-alai*. While the swimming pool remained an expensive amenity, a number of $4,000 to $5,000 homes covered by magazines in the 1937–40 period proudly showcased a backyard swimming pool. The war delayed this trend, but like so much else in the 1930s it was already there—the private swimming pool as a middle-class amenity—and by the end of the 1950s Southern California had become, as Oscar Levant would put it, a pool's paradise.

Nor was Southern California ungraced by those two most urban of living arrangements, the apartment building and the penthouse. Los Angeles and Long Beach featured a number of large New York City–style apartment complexes. The El Royale apartments on North Rossmore featured a duplex penthouse, as did the Chateau Elysee in Hollywood and the Chateau Marmont on Sunset Boulevard. For such a democratic city, Long Beach sustained a large number of elite apartment buildings on Ocean Boulevard, most notably the Villa Riviera, the Cooper Arms, and the apartment-hotel Breakers, each of them impressive structures. In Los Angeles the George Pepperdine Foundation owned and operated twelve apartment buildings, with monthly rentals ranging from $35 to $135. Located at 570 North Rossmore (a street promoted as the Park Avenue of the West), the Ravenswood, the flagship Pepperdine property, offered valet parking, housekeeping, laundry, dry cleaning, and room service from a restaurant on the property. Monthly rates ranged from $60 to $350. Income from the Ravenswood was channeled to George Pepperdine College, as well as to a boys' home and a home for underprivileged girls.

For the less affluent urbanite, there was always the bungalow court. Few urban housing forms have proven so successful in serving, simultaneously, density, privacy, and community as the bungalow court. Sylvanus Marston designed the first bungalow court in Pasadena in 1909, eleven freestanding full-sized bungalows arranged around a common courtyard. In the 1920s the bungalow court became more completely adapted to urban land use patterns, with units becoming smaller in size and larger in number. Bungalow courts proved ideally suited to single young women flocking into the city as office help, younger couples, and older couples without children, although there is plenty of evidence that families with children did equally well in this housing environment. The interior court provided a safe play space, and the other residents functioned as an extended family. Almost by definition, bungalow courts were situated on major streetcar lines. Bungalow court residents were not the type to own their own automobile. Yet many units came provided with a rear garage or outdoor parking area. Private yet communal, convenient, landscaped, highly affordable, the bungalow court constituted an important contribution by Southern California to urbanism, and the 1930s was its high point. Very few were built in the suburbanizing post-war era, yet surviving bungalow courts remained the housing of choice for a post-war and post-post-war generation of singles, the elderly, the bohemian, and the odd private eye.

Leisure, the outdoors, a distinctive architecture, the good life: it was the California formula, and Palm Springs had it all. The story of the emergence of Palm Springs recapitulates the entire development of California as pleasure principle, as resort.

Like so much else in California during this period, Palm Springs was entering its first golden age of maturity. The population of the Village of Palm Springs (it became an incorporated city of the sixth class in the spring of 1938) doubled between 1929 and 1934, then doubled again between 1934 and 1939. "I have heard Palm Springs discussed in China, Manchuria, in Australia and all over Europe," observed Los Angeles *Times* columnist Harry Carr.[6] A cluster of Mediterranean-style hotels and winter cottages, Palm Springs stood centered on a Spanish-style plaza, planted with orange, eucalyptus, cottonwood palm, and pepper trees. Just beyond the town was the desert, its rolling dunes sculpted by the winds into stilled sea waves. Everything—structures, plaza, desert, and mountains—was suffused in a persistent golden haze, with runs of lavender created by the ever-present verbena blanketing the desert floor and hillsides, and streaks of cinnamon, umber, salmon pink, scarlet, and royal purple in the mountain ridges guarding the plain on which Palm Springs was centered. Nearby, protecting Palm Springs from the desert winds, Mount San Jacinto rose straight from the desert floor. San Jacinto had no time for foothills. This twelve-thousand-foot mountain peak was, in geological terms, an adolescent that had reached its height overnight. Its canyons were still grinding and settling, and making a sound like growling, which the Cahuilla Indians attributed to an evil spirit named Tahquitz.

In the early 1900s, a generation of writers and poets—Charles Fletcher Lummis, George Wharton James, Mary Austin, Theodore Van Dyke, J. Smeaton Chase, and others—discovered the desert; but their perspective was literary and aesthetic. This first Progressive generation of writers did not come to the desert to play, which would have been impossible in that time of non-development. They traveled into the desert, rather, either alone or in small groups, to experience its grandeur and solitude and to create upon their return a distinguished body of descriptive literature. From its beginnings as an American settlement, however, Palm Springs showed signs of becoming a resort. The first Anglo resident of Palm Springs, John Guthrie McCallum, a San Francisco attorney, took up residence alongside the Agua Caliente band of the Cahuilla Indians in March 1885 in an effort to help his son John, stricken in the typhoid epidemic of 1879, regain his health. McCallum built a home on 320 acres, planted orchards, constructed a stone-lined ditch from Whitewater River nineteen miles away—and began to interest others in settling in the desert, a novel idea in the mid-1880s. The very next resident, Welwood Murray, a Scotsman who moved to Palm Springs from Banning at the suggestion of McCallum, went immediately into the resort business. With the help of local Native Americans, Murray built a charming hotel of wood and adobe and began to promote business. Rather soon, Murray decided he needed an image, an angle, a way of marketing an environment still considered hostile by most Americans. Deciding upon an Arab metaphor, Murray bought a camel. (Camels had been intermittently in use in the deserts of California since the 1850s and could still be locally purchased.) Next, he hired a local Native American, Willie Marcus, to stand with said camel at the train station at Seven

Palms, dressed in Arab robes and headgear, and hand out brochures promoting Palm Valley, as it was then called, and Murray's Palm Springs Hotel.

Right from the start, then, there was in the Palm Springs experience an element of promotional glitz, even hokum. Murray's well-run hotel (his wife was an accomplished cook) flourished. In 1909 Dr. Harry Coffman, his wife Nellie, and their two sons, previous visitors to Palm Springs, moved there permanently and built a second hostelry, the Desert Inn, which Nellie Coffman managed. It flourished as well and had to be augmented with tent cabins. Then, in 1912, came another physician, Franilla White of New York, and her two sisters, Cornelia and Isabel, who purchased the Palm Springs Hotel from Welwood Murray. The presence of two physician-hoteliers, Drs. Coffman and White, indicated that Palm Springs was entering the twentieth century as a health spa in the nineteenth-century style, organized around the dry desert climate and the hot springs in the center of the village that had provided Palm Springs with its first name, Agua Caliente. This image of Palm Springs as a dignified health resort, a place for physical and spiritual refreshment, pervades J. Smeaton Chase's *Our Araby: Palm Springs and the Garden of the Sun* (1920), the final literary response from a desert writer of the old school.

The 1920s witnessed the transition of Palm Springs from health resort to a winter resort for the affluent. In 1924 a young couple, Pearl and Austin McManus, commissioned Los Angeles architect Lloyd Wright, the talented son of a very famous father, to design a hotel, the Oasis. In and of itself, the intense stylization of Wright's scheme for the Oasis—white concrete walls, a Secessionist exterior playing off against gigantic cottonwood trees and an orange grove, an irregularly shaped swimming pool, a patio court, lush lawns and a great fountain, a ninety-foot dining room heated by exposed charcoal braziers, an exquisite use of copper and leather for lamps, wall decorations, and other finishes—bespoke a dramatic transition from an earlier era of rustic inns and tent cabins. Here was a hotel clearly keyed to the stylization of the environment, in this case the desert: a stylization that must be at the core of every successful resort. During the twenties as well, a new kind of resident, the celebrity, began to make connection with Palm Springs: artist and cartoonist Jimmy Swinnerton, for example, and Rudolph Valentino, who had become acquainted with Palm Springs during the filming of *The Sheik*.

In the 1930s Hollywood discovered Palm Springs and made it its own special place, centered in an even more stylized hotel, El Mirador, which catered to a movie clientele. Actor Charles Farrell, meanwhile, a top-ranked amateur tennis player, and his wife Virginia, desiring a change of residence and career, moved to Palm Springs permanently, where they developed the Racquet Club, which soon became the tennis epicenter of Southern California, with champions such as Gene Mako and Alice Marble seen frequently on the courts. By 1938 visitors to Palm Springs had the choice of five resorts—the Desert Inn, the Oasis, El Mirador, and two dude ranches, Smoke Tree and Deep Well—and a fully developed program of golf, tennis, swimming, horseback riding, buckboard treks into the desert, polo, skeet shooting, bicycling, lazing by the side of a proliferating number of swimming pools, and a luxuriant night life. Around the pool at El Mirador of an afternoon, or on the courts at the Racquet Club, or on the links of the O'Donnell Desert Golf Course, or at the firing line of the Palm Springs Skeet Club, or watching the polo matches at the Field Club, or favorably seated at one or another of the nightclubs that flourished in the hotels, one might catch sight of Marlene Dietrich, Leslie Howard, Melba Bennett, Gilbert Roland, Don Ameche, George Arliss, the ever-present Farrells, Bob and Dolores Hope, together with assorted producers, directors, and writers such as Leslie Charteris, creator of the Saint detective series, who had a distinctively British love of the Palm Springs sun, together with such captains of industry as Major Reuben Fleet, president of Consolidated Aircraft, who liked the Hollywood glamour as much as the clear air and winter sunshine. E. F. Hutton maintained an office on the plaza, with a direct connection to the New York Stock Exchange. "In a way of speaking," noted Frank Condon in December 1936, "Palm Springs might be regarded as the dude in the family of desert towns. For where else can you purchase perfume among the dunes at eighty dollars a bottle? Where else would you find the latest New York and Parisian models, white flannels, snake skin belts with silver buckles, and a broker's office with a direct wire into New York?"[7]

By day, Palm Springs was a casual place. Women appeared on the streets in the brightly patterned one-piece sunsuits of the era, or in flimsy ensembles known as day pajamas, or in bell-bottomed slacks. Palm Springs later claimed to have, if not invented shorts, then at least to have made them acceptable public attire. Jeans, cowboy hats, shirts, boots, bandannas, and Western fringed jackets were also the fashion, especially at riding events such as the Circus Day Rodeo at the Field Club. In the evenings, Palm Springs got dressy, with black tie *de rigueur* at nightclubs, especially on weekends and in the busy social season from Christmas through New Year's. "Nothing is sadder," laments an issue of *Palm Springs Life* from 1938, "than the week-end visitor who didn't bring a thing to wear after dark, because the desert is supposed to be so simple."[8] Those caught short could rush to Bullock's of Los Angeles, which maintained a full-service clothing boutique at the Desert Inn.

The social year got off to its start in late October with the annual five-day ride of the Vaqueros del Desierto, a group of some hundred horsemen who trekked through the desert by day and by night enjoyed sumptuous meals and campfire entertainment. In early November, Palm Springs hosted a number of statewide swimming and diving meets. By Thanksgiving, winter residents from the East began to arrive. The Palm Springs Kennel Club gave its annual dog show in early December. By Christmas time, the season was at its height, with the full influx of winter visitors from Hollywood and the East, arriving by Santa Fe Super Chief or on special Sun Land flights from New York via Chicago on TWA, together with an array of Hollywood celebrities seeking to avoid the enforced religiosity of the Christmas season. Hotels and nightclubs made much of New Year's Eve, with most hotels and the Racquet Club featuring large orchestras bused in from Hollywood. In January there was the two-day Midwinter Rodeo, followed by a second rodeo in Circus Week, which occurred in March and was the best-publicized event in the Palm Springs social cycle. In March as well, the thoughts of Palm Springs turned to Polo Week, with matches held at the Field Club, and to golf, with invitational tournaments held for men in March and for women in April.

Among other things, the Palm Springs of the late 1930s anticipated the post-war emergence of California as affluent resort. The paradoxes of the capitalist system stood fully revealed in the contrast between this playground for the rich and famous and the living conditions of farm workers during this period in the Imperial Valley, just a short drive away. As a stylized urban environment, Palm Springs anticipated the post-war planned suburb, followed by the gated community: enclaves into which the affluent might retreat, not just for a winter vacation, but for the entire year. Palm Springs bespoke the privileged privacy of the California Rich, Hollywood branch, a style that would one day enter the White House itself when President Ronald Reagan spent each New Year's Eve in Palm Springs in what had by then become a half-century-old Hollywood ritual.

Like Hollywood films in the 1930s, Palm Springs offered ordinary Americans, so many of them still beset by Depression difficulties, opportunities for gawking and vicarious satisfaction. "Los Angeles simply goes desert daffy on Sundays," noted Frank Condon in December 1936, "and the gasoline parade crawls along eastward through San Bernardino, Colton, Redlands, Beaumont, and Banning, and slowly slides down the long hill into the valley. . . . The city slickers bring along their own lunches in cardboard boxes, some bottled beer in a tin pail, and do not spend a dime with the town merchants, so, as Palm Springs enquires, what good are they? Upon arriving in the general vicinity of the desert resort, the Los Angeles hordes pull up on side roads, or out on the desert, or in a ravine, or anywhere, look admiringly at the purple mountains, ask eagerly where the movie stars may be seen, dig out the pickles, jam and sandwiches, and loaf around happily until five in the afternoon. The parade then starts for home, fourteen miles an hour, bumpers touching and everyone contented. The next Sunday they do it all over again."[9] Every weekend, by 1939, the plaza and streets of Palm Springs teemed with thousands of daytime visitors, hoping to see a movie star. "The town," noted Max Miller of Palm Springs on a crowded weekend, "with its boiled egg sandwiches, its paper plates, its babies, its fat women in slacks, its portable radios, its cameras, has become of a weekend nothing more than a beach town slightly transplanted."[10] Like motoring, barbecuing, wine drinking, surfing, golf, tennis, lazing by the swimming pool, and so many other California pursuits—and places—of the 1930s, Palm Springs had made the transition from elite to democratic. Everyone could now wear polo shirts and slacks.

2

Arcadian Shores

College Towns and Other Rusticated Enclaves

WHEN it came to college towns, the California of the 1930s, north and south, offered an abundance of settings for the good life— Berkeley, Palo Alto, Pasadena, Pomona, Claremont, and Redlands most conspicuously—for academics and those who preferred to live in the vicinity of a university. John Kenneth Galbraith, a graduate student in agricultural economics at Berkeley in the early 1930s, later described this decade as the golden age of Cal Berkeley, and there is much to justify this opinion. In Galbraith's case at least, it was the best of times. As of 1930 he enjoyed an annual stipend of $720, a room in the newly completed International House, and the congenial company of such fellow graduate students as Robert Merriman of Nevada, later commanding officer of the Abraham Lincoln Brigade. "Coming up Bancroft Way to the International House of an evening," Galbraith later remembered, "one saw the fraternity men policing up the lawns of their houses or sitting contentedly in front. Walking along Piedmont at night, one heard the shouts of laughter from within, or occasional bits of song, or what Evelyn Waugh correctly described as the most evocative and nostalgic of all the sounds of an aristocracy at play, the crash of breaking glass."[1]

By then, the 1930s, the Berkeley campus stood complete in gleaming granite and marble splendor, as first called for by the master plan submitted by Paris architect Emil Bernard in 1899 and realized over the next three decades by supervising architect John Galen Howard. In 1930 Robert Gordon Sproul, an Old Blue who had worked his way up from the accounting office, was elected president of the statewide system. Not being a professor, Sproul turned over the academic development of the campus to Vice President and Provost Monroe E. Deutsch, a classicist, who proceeded to transform the state university into a leading center of research in physics, history, law, and the social sciences. Surveying the reputation of UC Berkeley by 1937 in *The Golden Book of California*, a history of the first seventy-five years of the university, Deutsch reported that according to the American Council on Education, California had twenty-one distinguished departments, second only to Harvard, which had only two more, and tied with Columbia and Chicago. Deutsch also cited an article in the *Atlantic Monthly* for June 1935 that rated the leading five universities in the United States as Harvard, Chicago, Columbia, California, and Yale, in that order. The University of California had twenty-two members in the National Academy of Sciences, Deutsch announced, out of a total of 250 academy members; once again, California stood second only to Harvard. Of scientists listed in the latest edition of *American Men of Science* (1933), Harvard had sixteen on its faculty, with California in second place with fifteen. When it came to Guggenheim fellowships, the University of California led the pack with thirty-two, with Chicago, Harvard, and Minnesota each receiving twenty. Certainly with such Cal professors as Alfred Kroeber, anthropology, Herbert Bolton, history, Joel Hildebrand, chemistry, Ernest Lawrence, physics, and the astronomers Robert Aitken, William Campbell, Joseph Moore, Robert Trumpler, and William Wright on staff, Deutsch was not stretching the truth in his concluding assertion that Berkeley stood at the forefront of American university life—second only to Harvard.

The 1930s was a good time to be a faculty member at Berkeley. The university had emerged into national prominence without losing the genteel intimacy of an earlier era. Professors could easily afford large houses, many of them rambling Craftsman structures that had survived the Berkeley fire of 1923. Many such homes enjoyed commanding views of the Golden Gate or were tucked into wooded glens through which streams bubbled part of the year. Two Berkeley professors, historian Herbert Eugene Bolton and physicist J. Robert Oppenheimer, embodied the present and soon-to-be post-war lifestyles of the Berkeley professorate.

In terms of the researching and writing of regional history, the 1930s belonged to Herbert Eugene Bolton, director of the Bancroft Library. Never before or since would one historian so dominate a department, a library, a university, a state even; for Bolton became among the half dozen most representative Californians of his era, a living landmark—the Californian as heroic historian, the Francis Parkman of the Spanish Borderlands. Bolton had arrived in Berkeley as a young scholar in 1911, animated by nothing less than a determination to do for the story of Spain in North America what Francis Parkman had done for the French in Canada—memorialize it, that is, through a vastly envisioned, heroically researched and energetically written historical epic, volume after volume. Ensconced in Library 426, his study on the fourth floor of the Doe Library, six, sometimes seven, days a week, from early morning to midnight, with breaks for lunch at the rustic faculty club designed by Bernard Maybeck and dinner with his family at home in the Berkeley hills, Bolton was in the process of singlehandedly creating a library of historical works while directing scores of theses and teaching brilliantly on the undergraduate and graduate levels. Library 426 was usually blue with cigarette smoke, and occasionally the wastebasket erupted into flames when Bolton carelessly emptied an ashtray of still-smoldering cigarettes onto a pile of paper. Because he maintained an open-door policy, interruptions—from students, colleagues, the Bancroft staff, the university administration—were frequent; and it was mainly in the evening, returning to campus after dinner with his wife, his six daughters, and his son, or on the weekends that Bolton managed uninterrupted stints of writing.

Bolton stories from this era (and they are legion, if not always true) usually revolve around his obsession with work and the resulting fits of absentmindedness: the time, for example, his daughter drove up to him as he waited at the North Gate and Bolton refused to get into the car with the remark that he was waiting for one of his daughters to pick him up; or the time when Bolton, mistaking another car for his own and its lady driver for his wife, slammed himself into the front seat. Fortunately, another professor's wife, a friend of the Boltons, was at the wheel, and she good-naturedly drove him home. They were halfway there, the story goes, before Bolton noticed the difference.

While many Bolton stories concerned his automotive ineptitude, Bolton nevertheless managed to vary his schedule with Sunday drives with his family in his Hupmobile or, during the academic vacation, with longer treks (with someone else doing the driving) retracing the route of this or that Spanish explorer. Thus Bolton retraced part of the route of the De Anza expedition during the Christmas vacation of 1925, did the Escalante trail in the summer vacation of 1926, spent the summer of 1927 in Utah and Arizona, and made a trip into Mexico in 1930 to explore the western slope of the Sierra Madre. Despite the long hours he spent at his desk, Bolton disdained the armchair historian and only wrote after he had personally explored a route, guided by the maps that he considered an essential tool of his historian's calling.

If Bolton represented an older and aging generation of WASP academics at Cal—local men, strongly rooted in California and the West—J. Robert Oppenheimer prefigured the post-war flourishing at Berkeley and the other Cal campuses of East Coast academics, many of them Jewish, in the process of becoming Californians. Educated at Harvard and the University of Göttingen in Germany, where he took his doctorate in physics in 1927, Oppenheimer was offered assistant professorships by ten universities at the commencement of his career. He chose a joint appointment in physics at Berkeley and Cal Tech in Pasadena. While Oppenheimer enjoyed his Cal Tech appointment, he was essentially an outsider there, regarded by his boss Robert Millikan as too much the bohemian in lifestyle and too much the academic generalist. Oppenheimer, Millikan openly stated, would never win a Nobel Prize. He was a brilliant synthesizer but would never originate a new theory. Millikan had a point: Oppenheimer was as much a philosopher, a poet even, of protons and particles as he was an original investigator. Academics of this type, however, charismatic generalists, provide excellent ful-

crum points around which great departments can build themselves; and this became the case with the physics department at Berkeley. Blocked by Millikan from
any influence at Cal Tech, Oppenheimer poured his institution-building efforts
and his considerable leadership skills into the establishment at Berkeley of the
finest school of theoretical physics in the nation.

In appearance and lifestyle, J. Robert Oppenheimer anticipated in the 1930s a
kind of offhand elegance, touched by hauteur, which would eventually emerge as
the academic demeanor of the 1960s. Berkeley professors in the 1930s wore
tweedy suits, white shirts, and neckties. Mixing Santa Fe chic with Ivy League
insouciance, Oppenheimer wore jeans, a Mexican silver buckle on his belt, loaf-
ers with no socks, a blue denim shirt open at the neck. He knew fine food and
wine and maintained an excellent cellar of European and California vintages then
only beginning to come into notice. Traditional academic culture rewarded researchers who stayed within their specialties. Oppenheimer ranged through San-
skrit, medieval French poetry, and European literature in the original languages,
including a knowledge of Dutch. He read Marcel Proust's A *La Recherche du
temps perdu* in a single summer on Corsica.

Like so many newcomers from the East Coast, Oppenheimer relished the aesthetics of outdoor life in California and the Southwest. He purchased a small
ranch called Perro Caliente in the Sangre de Cristo Mountains of New Mexico,
where he spent much of his free time. In Berkeley he lived in a Craftsman aerie
on the edge of a steep canyon on Tamalpais Road surrounded by live oak trees
and affording a breathtaking view of San Francisco Bay and the two great bridges
under construction. Oppenheimer kept the redwood-paneled rooms in pristine
condition. He scattered brightly colored Navajo rugs across the polished hardwood
floors. In his well-equipped kitchen, he entertained the coterie of graduate students that was always gathered around him, preparing combinations of European
and Santa Fe cuisine with skill, mixing congenial martinis, serving notable wines.
Graduate students, including Luis Alvarez and Glenn Seaborg, later Nobel laureates, went so far as to imitate his style of dress and manner, including Oppenheimer's use of a rhythmic "Ja, ja," spoken with a slight German accent, a holdover
from his graduate days. Detractors of Oppenheimer spread the rumor that the
group had a homosexual underpinning, citing its worship of its handsome young
leader who gave students dinner in his apartment and brought them down to his
ranch for vacations. Untrue: one would have to understand the intensity of the
mentor-student relationship at Oxford and Cambridge, or the European universities, or the Harvard Society of Junior Fellows, or elsewhere in the Ivy League, to
understand this bonding of young men around the figure of a brilliant, charismatic professor who embodied their own hopes for achievement.

And yet, the minute one notes this, one must note as well a strong undercur-
rent of magnetism that Oppenheimer emanated in these years, a charisma speaking to men and women equally and containing within itself a strong element of
authority and submission. "He looked like a young Einstein," remembered his

friend from these days Haakon Chevalier, a member of the French department, "and at the same time like an overgrown choir-boy. There was something both subtly wise and terribly innocent about his face. It was an extraordinarily sensitive face, which seemed capable of registering and conveying every shade of emotion. I associated it with the faces of apostles, either imagined or remembered from Renaissance paintings. A kind of light shone from it, which illuminated the scene around him."[2]

Like all college towns, Berkeley nurtured a community that, while not formally academic, depended upon the university for ambience and identity. In certain cases, this relationship could be rather desperate, as Clarkson Crane dramatized in his novel *The Western Shore* (1925), which included the portrait of a UC graduate who could never bear to leave the scene of his happy college days. Julia Cooley Altrocchi, by contrast, belonged to a now almost vanished genre, the faculty wife who was productive as a writer in her own right, a role in which she would later be followed by two other Berkeley faculty wives, Theodora Kroeber and Doris Muscatine. A graduate of Vassar, with post-graduate work at the University of Perugia, Altrocchi had already published a book of poetry before she moved to Berkeley from Chicago in 1928 when her husband accepted the chairmanship of the Italian department. Ensconced in a spacious hilltop aerie at 129 Tamalpais Road (Oppenheimer lived nearby) filled with Italian books and paintings, Altrocchi turned to California history. In 1936 she produced a two-hundred-page narrative poem on the Donner Party, *Snow-Covered Wagons: A Pioneer Epic*, later followed by the highly credible *The Old California Trail* (1938), *Wolves Against the Moon* (1940), and *The Spectacular San Franciscans* (1946). Socially, the Altrocchis made 129 Tamalpais Road ground zero of the good life, Berkeley style, with an emphasis on research and writing, a knowledge of fine food and wine, good talk at dinner parties, and soirees that brought together the academic and non-academic intelligentsia of the Bay Area.

Guests at the Altrocchi table included the two leading literary journalists of the region, Chester Rowell and Joseph Henry Jackson, each on the staff of the San Francisco *Chronicle*. A Ph.D. in philosophy from Germany at the turn of the century, Rowell had been part of the original Lincoln-Roosevelt League of Progressives who had gained control of state government in 1910. From 1932 to 1935 he served as editor of the *Chronicle* and was after 1935 its chief editorial writer and political columnist. Joseph Henry Jackson had left Lafayette College in Pennsylvania during the First World War to serve as a lieutenant in an ambulance unit in France and moved to San Francisco after his demobilization. Joining the staff of *Sunset* in its literary phase, Jackson went on to become book editor of the San Francisco–based *Argonaut* before moving on to the *Chronicle*. Neither before nor since has there been such an influential book reviewer and literary journalist on the West Coast. Meticulous about nurturing his East Coast connections, Jackson wrote frequently for the *Herald Tribune* and served on Pulitzer Prize committees. He was among the first to praise the work of John Steinbeck and William

Saroyan. By turns a journalist, a historian, an anthologist, a radio broadcaster, and an indefatigable reviewer, appearing in the *Chronicle*, the *Saturday Review*, *Harper's*, the *Atlantic Monthly*, and the *Herald Tribune*, Jackson demonstrated by his success that a Berkeley-based career as a man of letters with national connections was possible. His *Anybody's Gold: The Story of California's Mining Towns* (1941), the first of his many books, remains the best guide to the subject.

More regionally focused but equally productive were the Sierra Clubbers, men and women for whom Berkeley was the premise of a combined outdoor-intellectual life. Many of them, professionals working in San Francisco, were, aside from their mountaineering and Sierra Club activities, productive researchers and writers as well, such as the Massachusetts-born Francis Farquhar, a San Francisco–based CPA living in Berkeley since 1909. In 1914, as a young mountaineer, five years out of Harvard, Farquhar had climbed Mount Olympus in Greece and experienced its power as landscape and mythic statement. So too, Farquhar decided, was the Sierra Nevada a *mise-en-scène* of natural and human forces, including the human imagination. Farquhar determined that he would write the history of the Range of Light. A mountaineer of distinction, Farquhar pursued a busy life in accountancy, public service (the National Park Service, the California Academy of Sciences), international mountaineering, journalism (for twenty years he edited the *Bulletin* of the Sierra Club), and writing the history of the Sierra Nevada. He brought to his self-appointed task of writing the interactive natural and human history of the Sierra Nevada the instincts of an informed naturalist and mountaineer. His was the sensibility of the Sierra Club, whose founder John Muir had been alive and well when Farquhar arrived from Harvard: a combination of naturalist learning, poetic reverence, and intense physical involvement, the spirit of such nineteenth-century California scientist-writers as William Brewer and Clarence King, whose masterpieces Farquhar carefully edited and introduced for publication. As he pursued his history of the Range of Light, increment by increment, his research appearing over the years in the Sierra Club *Bulletin* and the *Quarterly* of the California Historical Society, Farquhar climbed the mountains he chronicled with equal gusto. In addition to his unfolding history, which appeared in its final book form in 1965, Farquhar produced some one hundred scholarly and popular essays on mountaineering, on aviation (Farquhar flew over the North Pole in 1949 and around the world in 1951 on exploratory treks for the California Academy of Sciences), and on alpine trees and flora and wrote the Yosemite, Sequoia, and Sierra Nevada entries in the *Encyclopedia Britannica*.

Farquhar's overt, expressive environmentalism, so characteristic of Berkeley culture since the nineteenth century, set the theme for *Ordeal by Hunger* (1936), a history of the Donner Party, written by Professor George Stewart of the English Department. The Range of Light could be dangerous, as the Donner Party had found in late October 1846, caught by an early snow. Occasionally, the Sierra Nevada reasserted its dangerous dimension, keeping the Berkeley Sierra Clubbers on their guard, as it did in August 1933 when the gallant young mountaineer

Walter A. Starr Jr. was lost in the Range of Light. Starr left behind the perennially best-selling Sierra Club tote book *Starr's Guide to the John Muir Trail and the High Sierra Region*, posthumously published in 1934 and kept in print ever after. Before he died researching this book, Walter A. Starr Jr. had walked and surveyed, seen and enjoyed, fixed and measured every geographical feature on the John Muir Trail. Designed and bound to fit into a knapsack and to withstand the rigors of backpacking, *Starr's Guide* soon won its place as the Baedeker of the High Sierra: a concise and accurate annotation of every trail, pass, and approach, every mountain meadow and declivity, every creek, lake, and stream in the High Country, precisely presented, fixed in elevation and accurate distance to what precedes it and what comes after. For generations of mountaineers, whether members of the Sierra Club or not, *Starr's Guide*, a product of the distinctive connection between the Bay Area and the Sierra Nevada, quickly became near-scriptural in affection and authority.

Like Francis Farquhar, Franklin Dickerson Walker, another Berkeley-based outdoorsman who taught at Mills College in Oakland, had been led to California as an intellectual preoccupation largely through the influence of Europe: in Walker's case, by the dons at Saint Edmund Hall, Oxford, where Walker studied on a Rhodes scholarship, and by the landscapes of England and the Continent, which he toured by motorcycle in the late 1920s. Raised in Southern California and Arizona, Dickerson had gone to Oxford with an interest in that classic Far Western pursuit, geology. While at Oxford, his interests shifted from geology and mining engineering to literary history. Not only did Walker, a skilled out-doorsman, rediscover by imaginative contrast the landscapes of the western United States, so vast, so unsettled, as he motorcycled through the storied landscapes of Europe, he was also delighted to discover the interest his British mentors at Oxford had in the history and writing of the Far West, especially California. While the scenery of Europe evoked its complementary opposite in the young Rhodes scholar's mind, the approving interest of Oxford dons and fellow students helped dispel the notion that only the literary history of New England, with some reference to the Middle and Southern Atlantic states, was worth studying.

Returning to California with an honors degree, Walker presented himself to the graduate school at Berkeley after a few years of teaching. For his doctoral dissertation Walker had in mind a great big subject inspired by his Oxford experiences, England and the California literary frontier; but his advisor, the Americanist T. K. Whipple, cautioned him to save that spacious topic for a later day and to write a biography of Frank Norris instead. Helped by Norris's widow Jeannette Black, whose courtship Norris had so charmingly portrayed in the novelette *Blix* (1899), and by Norris's brother Charles Gilman Norris, Walker commenced a series of interviews, backed by library research, which gave to his biography, published as a book in 1932, an authority that still lasts.

Settled in as a professor at Mills College in Oakland, often called the eighth of the Seven Sisters, Walker returned in the mid-1930s to the theme he had first brought to Berkeley, Anglo-Californian literary relations and influences. Only now his focus centered more strongly on the literary life of frontier San Francisco. In doing so, Walker subtly rebuffed Frederick Jackson Turner's contention that the frontier as a benevolent stimulus to American creative effort was essentially rural or agrarian in nature. The frontier depicted in Walker's *San Francisco's Literary Frontier*, issued by Knopf in 1939, was a maritime colony mushroomed overnight into urbanism. Despite its remoteness and raw beginnings, San Francisco possessed churches, schools, libraries, scientific academies, art galleries, clubs, and literature. It was also linked directly in its imaginative life to Boston, still the literary capital of the nation, and to London, epicenter of Anglo-American consciousness. Establishing these associations, catching that brief moment when, as Harry Levin has pointed out, San Francisco became the literary capital of the nation, Walker suggested interactions and relationships between frontiers and cities, high culture and undeveloped environments, which immeasurably enriched the American formula.

Every fall, Berkeley geared itself for the Big Game against Stanford, which had been alternating between Berkeley and Palo Alto since the early 1900s. When the game was at Berkeley, Stanford students came by special train to San Francisco on Friday afternoon, and Cal students poured over to the city by ferry boat. The previous evening, the Stanford student body held a bonfire rally around the Big Game Pyre in Lagunita Field on its spacious campus. (Bonfires were *verboten* in the densely residential Berkeley, which had already burned down once.) Yell leaders such as the legendary Paul Speegle and Al Peache whipped undergraduates to a frenzy as to whether or not the Stanford Indians, coached by Claude (Tiny) Thornhill, would hold the Axe trophy for another year or be forced to relinquish it to the Golden Bears of UC Berkeley, under the able coaching of Stubb Allison. The Axe was fiercely guarded by whichever student body had it in its possession. Stealing the Axe before the Big Game represented the apogee of an undergraduate prank. Also part of Big Game Week on the Stanford campus: the Big Game Gaieties, a musical comedy revue of epic proportions.

On the Friday before the Big Game, there were impromptu rallies throughout downtown San Francisco all afternoon and a rally in Union Square in the evening, followed by the parading of both university bands through the hotel lobbies of the city. Both Cal and Stanford alumni held banquets in San Francisco on the Friday evening before the game. In November 1936 Stanford alumni, dining in the Palace Hotel, were entertained by the Stanford Glee Club, who later left the hotel to sing on a Big Game Rally program being broadcast by NBC throughout Northern California. After dinner, there were Big Game dances in a number of San Francisco hotels, with the Williams-Walsh Orchestra in the Peacock Court of the Hotel Mark Hopkins being a special favorite. Less affluent undergraduates might avail themselves of the advantageously priced Bal Tabarin on Columbus at Chestnut, where for the mere cover charge of a dollar the college crowd might dance to the music of Kay Kyser, who boasted that his college-oriented orchestra (a College of Musical Knowledge, Kyser called it) included members of Phi Gamma Delta, Kappa Alpha, Sigma Alpha Epsilon, Sigma Alpha Nu, Sigma Chi, and Sigma Phi. More accessible to financially challenged undergraduates was Roberts-at-the-Beach, where Bears and Indians might dance to the music of aspiring bands and later assuage their late-night munchies with drippy, delicious pork or beef sandwiches from Fat Boy Barbecue. According to the *Stanford Quad* yearbook for 1933, the dean of women advised each Stanford coed to keep a five-dollar bill tucked into her purse so as to be able to make a strategic getaway by taxicab if things got dicey.

Saturday morning, students, alumni, and fans converged on Berkeley by ferry boat and streetcar, or on Palo Alto by train and automobile, for a forenoon of reunions and luncheon parties at fraternities, sororities, and restaurants. Each campus represented a perfection of its own: the Stanford quadrangle in the buff brown, rough-cut stone, and red tile of Spanish Romanesque; Berkeley in the gleaming white neo-classical grandeur of marble and granite. Over each campus swayed horizon-high treescapes of soaring eucalyptus, their silver-green leaves shimmering in the clear sunlight of autumn. While the automobiles of the era precluded tailgating, an early version of this art, trunk-gating it could be called, from wicker baskets in open trunks, was receiving some notice in the newspaper social pages. Then the Big Game itself, with former president Herbert Hoover in front-line attendance and the bands of Cal and Stanford marching at halftime. Stanford destroyed California on 23 November 1935, 13 to 0; but no matter, two years later, 20 November 1937, the Bears returned the compliment with their own 13 to 0 victory. Card stunts on either side of the stadium grew progressively more intricate through the decade. With its two days of festivities, its reflection of other Big Games in the more established East, the UC versus Stanford clash, like the annual USC–Notre Dame game and the Rose Bowl in Pasadena, very much signaled the coming of age of California as a football culture.

Interestingly enough, it was not UC or even Stanford, or even USC or UCLA, that took this football message most powerfully to the nation in the 1920s and 1930s. It was the much smaller St. Mary's College of California in the nearby Moraga Valley and the St. Mary's coach, Edward Patrick (Slip) Madigan, who received most attention from the national media. Like the Holy Cross Fathers at Notre Dame (and the Methodists at USC for that matter), the Christian Brothers at St. Mary's College determined in the early 1920s upon a simple strategy of development: football. Wanting the best football team in the nation but lacking the financial resources to hire a big-name coach, the brothers recruited in 1921 a young high school coach from Portland, Oregon, Slip Madigan, who, coached by the legendary Knute Rockne, had won All-American honors as a lineman at Notre Dame. In and of itself, Madigan's connection to Rockne and Notre Dame constituted, the brothers hoped, a form of apostolic succession, for the Notre

Dame paradigm was ever on their mind. By the late 1920s, the Galloping Gaels of St. Mary's had become one of the best-known football teams in the nation. Miraculously, Slip Madigan had taken a haphazard collection of Irish, Italian, Polish, and Slovakian boys from the Mission district in San Francisco or the blue-collar neighborhoods of Los Angeles, recruited them to a college barely large enough to support a football team, and fashioned them into one of the best teams to take to the field in the golden age of college football.

As brilliant a promoter as he was a coach, Madigan knew that if St. Mary's wanted to earn a national reputation, it would have to play in New York City, where the important sportswriters of the day—Grantland Rice, Damon Runyon, Arthur Daley—hung their battered hats. Taking St. Mary's on the road, Madigan scheduled games against the most logical opponents for an unknown California Catholic college, the East Coast Catholic independents—Boston College, Holy Cross, Georgetown, Fordham—with special attention paid to Fordham, then coached by the World War I hero Frank Cavanaugh, the legendary Iron Major. The Fordham rivalry paid off. Starting in 1927, the annual St. Mary's–Fordham game at the Polo Grounds in New York drew huge crowds, fascinated by the New York–San Francisco aspects of the rivalry.

The press loved Slip Madigan, and he returned the compliment. Madigan knew scores of sportswriters by their first names, and when they came into his office or into the locker room for an interview, Slip made sure that their favorite adult beverage was at hand. A handsome Irishman in the dark Irish style, with thick hair and beetle brows, Madigan dressed, especially when in New York, with the flair of Jimmy Walker: tailored double-breasted suits, a swash of pocket handkerchief, a gold tie-bar keeping his necktie in place, French cuffs on his finely striped shirt, a sumptuous camel-colored polo overcoat, its belt draped with nonchalance, a dashing silk scarf against the New York wind, a fedora hat tilted at just the right angle. After New York games, Madigan did the town—Leone's, Dinty Moore's, Leon & Eddie's, the Cotton Club, the Stork—where he was frequently recognized. When Madigan entered Dinty Moore's after the Fordham game one November night in the mid-1930s, the emcee stopped the show, called Slip onto the stage, and led the audience in singing "The Bells of St. Mary's," the school song that Bing Crosby and Tony Martin made an American pop standard.

The 1930s opened with Herbert Hoover inviting the Galloping Gaels to the White House and posing with them in the Rose Garden. By then, Madigan was scheduling the big California teams—Berkeley, Stanford, USC—which had previously found St. Mary's beneath their notice. When Knute Rockne died in a plane crash in the spring of 1931, Madigan began to garner even more ink from sportswriters, now bereft of their most colorful figure. The annual St. Mary's–UC Berkeley game commonly drew more than eighty thousand spectators. The annual Little Big Game between St. Mary's and the Jesuit University of Santa Clara drew huge crowds to Kezar Stadium in San Francisco over the Thanksgiving weekend. In 1933 eighty-three thousand fans jammed the Los Angeles Coliseum to watch what many considered the two best football teams in the country, St. Mary's and USC. It was the second largest crowd USC had ever attracted. In the latter part of the decade, the broadcasting of St. Mary's games over NBC and CBS brought it an even larger national constituency. When St. Mary's played Texas Tech in the Cotton Bowl at Dallas in 1938, Jimmy Dorsey led an augmented band in the halftime concert.

Madigan's *Doppelgänger* at St. Mary's College of California, his reverse paradigm, was Francis Meehan, Brother Leo in religion, professor of English and chancellor of the college in the early 1930s. If Slip Madigan represented Catholic America in its passionate devotion to sport, Brother Leo embodied the aspirations of Catholic America in another direction. A noted man of letters in Catholic circles, Brother Leo taught literature at St. Mary's and wrote hundreds of articles, four plays, and a college textbook in English literature, together with fiction and poetry under the pseudonyms Leslie Stanton and Will Scarlet. He was also a brilliant lecturer, capable of filling the newly constructed Opera House in San Francisco for a lecture on Dante, speaking on educational and literary subjects on the national NBC network, offering classes through the University of California Extension that attracted up to a thousand students, and conducting oversubscribed summer school courses at UC Berkeley, UCLA, and the College of the Pacific. As in the case of another Catholic orator of the era, Monsignor Fulton Sheen of the Catholic University of America, it was an equal matter with Brother Leo between what he was discussing—Dante, Shakespeare, the great tradition— and how he said it: his handsome Irish face (the face of William Butler Yeats, perhaps, or some minor poet from the Celtic Twilight), his sonorous voice, mystic and musical, his piercing blue eyes, the ecclesiastical elegance of his black cassock and starched white neckbands.

Brother Leo dreamed of fashioning St. Mary's College into, as he put it, a white-walled academic city, a cathedral campus of European civilization in the Moraga Valley. In the 1920s, thanks in part to the notoriety brought to the college by football, the architectural aspects of Brother Leo's dream came true as St. Mary's developed an imposing Spanish Revival quadrangle. The soaring churrigueresque chapel of the new campus (where the Abbé Jean Ribeyron, an émigré French priest, conducted the liturgy with the highest standards of vestments and music), its white-walled cloisters and arcades, its red-tiled roofs, its landscaping and gardens, its black-robed brothers moving between chapel and classroom, its curriculum organized around the Great Books that Brother Leo revered—all perfectly expressed the Chancellor's vision of St. Mary's as a translation of high European Catholic consciousness to California. In the fall of 1930, Brother Leo and faculty member James Hagerty launched the *Moraga Quarterly*, an ambitious scholarly journal that lasted until the Navy took over St. Mary's College as a preflight school in 1942.

Alas, like his alter ego Slip Madigan, Brother Leo grew too grand for St. Mary's and for the restrictions of his order. Already, his tailored black suits with satin lapels, the chauffeured limousine that took him to and from his speaking engagements, the more or less permanent suite that he maintained in the Clift Hotel in San Francisco, and his private bank account bespoke the fact that Francis Meehan was growing restive with life as a simple Brother of the Christian Schools. So few of his colleagues, after all, pious, hard-working, practical-minded classroom teachers, shared his dreams for St. Mary's, most of them preferring, if the truth be told, something closer to the image of the college being advanced by Slip Madigan and the Galloping Gaels. In August 1941 Francis Meehan slipped back into lay status and continued his writing career under his own name. He moved to Southern California, where he gave lessons in elocution to aspiring actors and actresses, and married the attractive hostess at the Redwood Room of the Clift Hotel.

No matter: Brother Cornelius (Hermann Braeg) was toiling on, pursing the vision of St. Mary's as a center of scholarship as well as football that Brother Leo had envisioned and exemplified before returning to secular life. A Swiss by birth, Brother Cornelius had studied architecture and German literature at Berkeley after entering the brotherhood. He planned to do a doctorate under Bolton with a thesis on the pioneer California artist William Keith, but Bolton, aware of Cornelius's age (he was born in 1877) and his heavy teaching schedule at St. Mary's, told the middle-aged brother to "forget the degree and write the book," which Cornelius proceeded to do with a religious ardor not surprising in a man of his calling. For more than a decade Cornelius immersed himself in the Keith papers in the Bancroft, tracked down hundreds of Keith paintings (establishing in the process a permanent Keith gallery at St. Mary's), retraced Keith's journeys to Europe, the eastern United States, and Alaska, and interviewed and reinterviewed his widow (Keith died in 1911), his niece, and surviving friends and colleagues. Empathetically, a brother in religion yoked to his teaching duties in a small college (which he loved) and to the observances of his calling found an energizing release for his inner life in pursuing down to the last detail the studio and literary environments of nineteenth-century Dusseldorf, Dresden, Paris, Boston, New York, and San Francisco as these places impinged on the life of William Keith, along with John Muir the most representative California artist in the nineteenth century. Brother Cornelius's biography, *Keith: Old Master of California* (1942), sweeps forward with Balzacian amplitude. Rich in its web of connections and influences, the biography also constitutes one of the first full-fledged cultural histories of nineteenth-century California. St. Mary's College of California had a great football team. Through Brother Cornelius, along with Franklin Walker at Mills College, this small school also helped establish the academic study of California as an instance of American civilization.

William Keith delighted in capturing on canvas the scenic sweep, the landscape drama of Northern California. Through the 1930s, the top tier of California—mountainous, rich in lakes and rivers, graced in its coastal regions with forests of redwood and pine—continued to flourish, as Jack London had predicted it would a quarter of a century earlier, as the Switzerland of North America. Already, as early as the 1860s, Clear Lake in Lake County had become a favored summering spot, along with Calistoga in Napa County, a resort town founded in 1859 by pioneer developer Samuel Brannan along the lines of the New York spa Saratoga. The three counties that most impressed London in 1910 for their resort potential—Mendocino, Lake, and Humboldt—remained twenty-five years later relatively undeveloped, with the exception of the lumbering industry on the coast; yet the two dominant cities of the area, inland Ukiah in Mendocino County and Eureka on Humboldt Bay, preserved their Victorian charm. The rambling Carson Inn in Eureka, the most ambitious hostelry north of San Francisco, continued to emanate the ambience of the late nineteenth century when Eureka served as the lumbering capital of the Pacific Coast and a fishing port second only to San Francisco. Ukiah had its ornate Palace Hotel, and its streets were lined with ornate Victorians equally suggestive of the well-being of an earlier era.

Near Ukiah, in the Anderson Valley, an Ozark world of rural whites with their own special patois, Boontling, brought added color to the region. Boontling had emerged at the turn of the century among the hardscrabble ranchers, lumberjacks, hop growers, and sheep herders of Anderson Valley centered on the hamlet of Boonville. It was, in its heyday, a joyous Li'l Abner world, free, frank, exuberant, given to barn dances, baseball games, moonshine liquor, and linguistic and sexual gusto, all of it accompanied, day and night, by fiddles, banjos, and harmonicas. Scholars would later see in Boontling an argot possessed of a rather high degree of inclusiveness and flexibility. Not surprisingly, given the lifestyle of the Anderson Valley, a significant percentage of the vocabulary was devoted to liquor, sex, fiddle music, baseball, local feuds, and putting it over on outsiders. Bits and pieces of Boontling seeped into the general Northern California vocabulary: *horn*, for example, meaning a drink, or *hoot* meaning a laugh.

From Willits north of Ukiah, tourists could take a picturesque Mack rail bus, gasoline- (later diesel-) driven on standard gauge railroad tracks, through the Noyo Valley to Fort Bragg on the coast. Operated by the California Western Railroad, the Skunk, so called because its snout-like engine hood gave a skunkish appearance to the vehicle, passed through beautiful redwood country, including the exquisite Noyo Valley, through which ran the Noyo River, where redwood forests gave way, suddenly, exhilaratingly, to mountain orchards of pear and apple, planted in the nineteenth century. Boy Scout and school camps, together with the camp of the San Francisco Boys Club and a number of adult camps, lined the California Western route, with the Skunk stopping twice daily at open-air redwood depots that were themselves masterpieces of vernacular architecture. To get the Skunk safely across any number of steep gorges, the California Western constructed a series of redwood trestles Gothic in soaring grace. To cross these trestles by foot (as I did as a boy) looking down between the railroad ties to the flowing river below, hearing its steady roar, was to experience the grandeur of

Northern California in its Noyo Valley dimension. To hear and see the Skunk, yellow with a silver roof, blast its horn from the distance, then approach the station with a flourish was to have proof positive that somewhere out there, inland or on the coast, was a great world that began at places called Willits and Fort Bragg and extended southwards to San Francisco, Monterey, Los Angeles along the magic coast of California. The Depression did not see any important growth in this region, either in permanent or resort settlements; yet Clear Lake continued as a popular summer resort, and further north, in the counties of Trinity, Shasta, and Siskiyou, the rich maintained baronial mountain ranches and retreats, the best known being Wyntoon, a lodge complex on the McCloud River designed for Mrs. Phoebe Hearst earlier in the century by Berkeley architect Bernard Maybeck and used throughout the thirties by her son William Randolph.

If the wealthy had Lake Tahoe, still a remote and elite resort, the blue-collar and middle classes could enjoy the Russian River seventy miles north of the city, the Catskills of working-class San Francisco. Each side of the lazy Russian River was lined with summer cabins. Further offshore were a number of affordable family resorts, including Rio Nido, where each night there was an outdoor dance illumined by a great Japanese lantern, which inspired the song "It's Only a Paper Moon." The Rio Nido Hotel charged $4.50 a night for two persons, European plan. Further north in Lake County was Hoberg's: $8 for a single, $14 for a double room, meals included, which put Hoberg's in a slightly more expensive range than Rio Nido, midway between Rio Nido and the Laurel Dell Lodge on Laurel Lake in the Blue Lakes region twenty miles east of Ukiah, or the Agua Caliente Springs Hotel in the Valley of the Moon, or the Sonoma Mission Inn at the village of Boyes Springs north of the Spanish settlement of Sonoma, where a single room could cost as much as $12 a night.

On the Russian River as well, at Monte Rio some fourteen miles in from the coast, the Bohemian Club of San Francisco maintained a redwood grove retreat purchased in the 1890s. Each July, hundreds of Bohemians and their guests converged on the Grove for the annual Cremation of Care ceremony in which the corpse of Dull Care was incinerated before a druidical owl shrine designed by San Francisco sculptor Haig Patigian and constructed in the 1920s. Two weeks of revelry in the redwoods followed the Cremation of Care ceremony: with days and nights filled with an exhausting schedule of lectures, musical performances, a Low Jinks musical comedy review, and a High Jinks opera-pageant (productions in the 1930s included *St. Patrick of Tara*, *Ivanhoe*, and *Saul*) in which hundreds of Bohemians would perform an original work, together with much good dining and consumption of spirits. The Bohemian Grove was but one of many such communal encampments on the Russian River. Others included the Odd Fellows Park and the Christian Alliance Camps, each carrying on the nineteenth-century tradition of group vacations in camp settings by church and fraternal organizations. With so much resort activity in this area, an exuberant road culture of bars, restaurants, and roadhouses developed. The Union Hotel in Occidental, for example, a lumbering town just south of Monte Rio, served gargantuan chicken and roast beef dinners that attracted hundreds of hungry customers each evening during the summer season.

Roadside dinners were far from *de rigueur* south of San Francisco in Burlingame and Hillsborough, where the financial and social elite of San Francisco had been seeking the haven of the Burlingame Country Club since the 1890s. "As the populace followed the older San Franciscans to Burlingame," wrote Lawrence Rising in his San Francisco novel *Proud Flesh* (1924), "that little group of social favorites separated themselves, forming a township of Hillsborough, and no longer allowed the public access. Even those who lived at the lodge gates of the privileged never saw more than a glimpse of a shrouded figure under the bonnet of a foreign car that flashed in and out beneath the arch."[3] In terms of luxury and taste, the Filoli estate, designed in 1915 by Willis Polk, with landscaping by Bruce Porter (Henry James's nephew-in-law), represented the culmination of this rusticating trend. Built for William Bourn, owner (among many other holdings) of the Spring Valley Water Company, which held a monopoly in San Francisco, and acquired by the shipping magnate William Roth in the spring of 1937, Filoli epitomized the life the San Francisco financial elite had been busy creating for itself in the 1890–1920 era, as it retreated further and further into its estates: a life modeled as closely as possible to that of upper-class England in its devotion to sport and socializing, centered on the Burlingame Country Club. By the 1920s a number of these Burlingame–San Franciscans had acquired connections with the French, Spanish, English, and Anglo-Irish aristocracy through marriage. Having made the transition from middle-class entreprenuer to self-proclaimed aristocrat in one generation, the Burlingame elite grew increasingly self-conscious in matters of lineage, as their counterparts on the Atlantic Coast had become a generation or two earlier.

Further south on the Peninsula in Palo Alto near Stanford University, Charles and Kathleen Norris were at the center of another, more literary social circle quite distinct from the Burlingame crowd; and former president Herbert Hoover, living near the Stanford campus, presided like a doge in exile over the city-state of Stanford–Palo Alto. Hoover was providing the rallying point for a regrouping of former Progressives, first *en route* to, then arrived at, a Bourbon conservativism destined to dominate the Republican Party after the war. The Palo Alto or Deep Peninsula circle extended south to Los Altos and Saratoga, where yet a third and decidedly more bohemian circle grouped itself around such figures as Charles Erskine Scott Wood and his wife Sara Bard Field, Fremont and Cora Older, Ruth Comfort Mitchell, and the Menuhins. Most members of this third circle—with the exception of John Steinbeck of Los Gatos, who kept to himself anyway—were rusticated San Franciscans.

Born in San Francisco in 1880, Kathleen Norris scored her first big success in 1914 with the novella *Mother.* A steady stream of best-selling fiction followed.

Norris's *Mother* remains a minor classic; *Saturday's Child* (1914) and *Little Ships* (1925) are equally masterful. Writing for the magazines, yet with disciplined sentiment, Norris attained more than financial success. She achieved a direct connection with the concerns of ordinary, everyday life. One of the reasons she so thrived in the Depression was her knowledge of that most prosaic and most powerful fact of human life, especially in hard times—money. So many of her plot ideas in the 1930s, Norris later remembered, came to her in agitated, heartfelt letters, written by embattled housewives on lined paper from the Big Chief tablets sold in dime stores, telling her the story of how they were trying to keep their families together. Critics will one day rediscover Kathleen Norris, one suspects; for like so many popular women novelists, only with considerably more literary skill, she understood the vulnerabilities, the secrecies, the dependencies, and the necessity of self-actualization, often in a world of weak or vacillating men, which are so often a woman's lot.

Kathleen Norris knew of what she spoke, for her husband Charles Gilman (Cigi) Norris, the younger brother of the late great Frank Norris, had broken off sexual relations with her after the birth of their son Frank. Handsome, dashing, a devotee of the cocktails, red wine, rare roast beef, and cigarettes (three packs a day) that carried him off via a stroke in his early sixties, Major Norris (this, his wartime rank) not only managed his wife's career with great shrewdness, but also managed to produce a series of well-crafted novels of his own. Although distanced from his wife sexually, Charles Norris, a closet homosexual, was in every other respect a model husband. When Kathleen's sister Teresa Frances died in the influenza epidemic of 1919 and her husband William Rose Benét was unable to care for their three children, Kathleen and Cigi raised them as their own. The Norrises entertained frequently and had Casa Abierta, the Open House, designed accordingly. Its Spanish-style kitchen featured a built-in barbecue and looked out onto a garden landscape of royal palm, yucca, rhododendron, azalea, daphne, several varieties of cactus, aucuba, thuya, junipers, Italian cypress, magnolia, lilac, and flowering banana. The story-and-a-half open-beamed living room showcased an oversized fireplace and a wrought-iron Spanish-style chandelier. The dining room was long, refectory-like; and on Sunday evenings, when Stanford University was in session and the Norrises at home in Palo Alto, up to twenty-five might sit down for dinner, many of them guests of their son Frank and their nephew and two nieces, all of them undergraduates at Stanford.

Cigi Norris also pursued an ardent bon vivantism at the Bohemian Club in San Francisco and the Bohemian Grove in Sonoma each summer, for which he wrote two Grove Plays and served as Sire (master of ceremonies) for many a merry evening. His friend Dr. Russell Lee, director of the Palo Alto Clinic, admonished Norris to lose weight, exercise daily, stop smoking cigarettes, forgo rare roast beef, and drink only one glass of white wine a day if he wished to make it through his sixties. He could not envision life in such a style, Norris replied; and a few years later, in the spring of 1944, in the Persian Room of the Plaza Hotel in New York, cheering on his favorite cabaret singer, the incomparable Hildegarde, the Major fell back to his seat with a stroke that left him paralyzed for the remaining eighteen months of his life. Dr. Russell Lee, incidentally, who tried so hard to get Cigi to change his ways, was the perfect college-town physician: a medical savant with rather advanced ideas regarding group practice, which he pursued in the Palo Alto Clinic, an early precursor of the HMO.

A few miles south of Palo Alto, on their Woodhills Ranch in Cupertino, Santa Clara County, Fremont and Cora Baggerly Older stood at the center of a third Peninsula circle, in left-liberal contrast to the Norris circle, which tended to be conservative Republican. (Kathleen Norris herself was active in the isolationist America First movement.) Fremont Older, as he was then, can best be described as a Tolstoyan anarchist, which is to say, a onetime Progressive reformer, the scourge of graft in San Francisco, who in mid-life, like St. Paul arriving in Damascus, had the scales of Progressivism fall from his eyes. This is not to say that Older became cynical, merely that he had come to the realization that intelligence, good will, the best of intentions, and all the other Progressive premises were frequently not enough: that there is an innate capacity for evil in human beings, that society institutionalizes power and corruption, and that those who live on the margins—burglars, prostitutes, San Francisco political boss Abraham Ruef, whom Older had helped to send to prison—frequently penetrate the inner arrangements, hence the inner landscape and meaning of society, more deeply than do the proper and the just: especially when such sinners reform themselves and come back from the underworld to tell the tale. In the aftermath of the graft trials in San Francisco following the Earthquake, Fremont Older became keenly aware that many of the biggest crooks in San Francisco lived on Nob Hill and lunched at the best clubs. This insight, so powerful in a self-made man who had hoisted himself into the establishment, could have moved Older in the direction of cynicism, even nihilism; yet in the Tolstoyan side of his being, Older sought the specific redemptive act—the rescuing of one prostitute, the rehabilitation of one ex-con—as the best that he or anyone could do in a confused and muddled world.

"To understand Fremont Older," Bruce Bliven of the New Republic remarked shortly after Older's death, "is to understand San Francisco."[4] Bliven knew of what he spoke, being himself one of the finest journalists to emerge from San Francisco, or any other city for that matter, in the 1930s. In Fremont Older, Bliven and others beheld a self-educated frontier journalist of an almost vanished sort: the counterpart of Samuel Clemens, William Dean Howells, Hamlin Garland, and so many others. Born in 1856 in a log cabin in rural Wisconsin, Older went out on his own at the age of thirteen, working as a printer's devil (Howell started this way), and as a cabin boy on some sort of a Mississippi steamer on which Clemens served as a pilot, before arriving in San Francisco at age sixteen in 1873, after taking to heart the admonition of New York editor Horace Greeley to go west, young man, go west and grow up with the country! Like Samuel

Clemens, Older moved to Virginia City, where he set type on the *Territorial Enterprise* before returning to San Francisco in 1875 and rising to foreman in the composing room of the *Daily Mail*. Like another San Francisco pressman in the leather apron of his trade, Henry George, or like Harrison Gray Otis in Los Angeles, Older made the transition from compositor to reporter to editor. By the early 1900s, when Older was editing the *Bulletin*, Lincoln Steffens, impressed with Older's commitment to muckraking and reform, considered him the greatest newspaperman in the nation.

After his conversion en route to Damascus, when he recognized that only Abraham Ruef, of all the corrupt people in San Francisco, was going to San Quentin, Older focused his efforts on the underdog. Almost alone, he editorialized against the railroading of Tom Mooney; and when Charles Fickert, the district attorney who was prosecuting Mooney with perjured testimony, encountered Older at the bar of the Palace Hotel, Fickert, a notorious drunk, swore at Older and struck him to the floor with the full force of a onetime Stanford football player still in half-decent shape. Years later, when Fickert was a disgraced alcoholic down on his luck, Older lent him money.

Until 1914, Older and his wife Cora Baggerly Older, a writer in her own right, lived in a suite at the Palace Hotel, where they entertained lavishly. Gertrude Atherton considered them the handsomest couple in San Francisco. After 1914 the Olders began to spend more time on their Woodhills Ranch near Cupertino, where they lived with their ward Mary d'Antonio, a half dozen dogs, assorted convicts on parole, prostitutes trying to reform, and visiting celebrities, including Edward Albert Filene, the Boston department store owner and reformer, Andrew Furuseth, president of the Sailors Union of the Pacific, Har Dyal, the Hindu independence activist, and Lincoln Steffens, the grandest muckraker of them all, who frequently came up from Carmel to talk shop with his favorite journalist. Also living with the Olders was Jack Black, on parole from San Quentin for burglary. Under Older's guidance, Black wrote the best-selling anti-crime book *You Can't Win* (1916). Intelligent and laconic, looking life square in the face, Jack Black epitomized the wisdom Older believed was special to reformed criminals. Photos from the 1920s and early 1930s show Older and Black, pals, an Odd Couple if ever there was one, with Black looking alert and self-contained, part dapper urbanite, part savvy con in the San Quentin yard, and Older with the walrus mustache of an earlier generation, an ever-present cigar jutting from his clenched teeth.

Older could afford his Woodhills estate in the Depression, commuting to San Francisco on the Southern Pacific during the work week, meticulously catching the four P.M. train back to Cupertino, because in 1918 William Randolph Hearst had hired him to edit the *Call* after Older was fired from the *Bulletin* for protesting the Mooney case. Hearst considered Fremont Older the last of the great frontier journalists, the kind of reporter and editor he himself had hired in the late 1880s when as an irrepressible youngster he was making journalistic history at the *Examiner*. Hearst started Older at the munificent salary of $325 a week plus a share of profits and continued to remain generous. In 1929 Hearst acquired the *Call* and organized the *Call-Bulletin*, arguably the best newspaper San Francisco has ever had: a New York–style afternoon daily, vibrant with the excitement of city life, superior in its comics, sports, lively columnists, including a number of women writers, race results, radio and movie reviews, a breezy but intelligent format, together with the continuing Older tradition of standing up for the little guy.

On Sunday, 3 March 1935, Fremont and Cora Older and their ward Mary d'Antonio were driving to Sacramento for the annual Camellia Show. As Cora and Mary were enjoying the flowers, Older sat in his car, writing a column on Montaigne's essay "Thoughts on Death." Driving home to Cupertino, Older had a heart attack near Stockton. With his usual concern for others, he managed to pull the car over to the side of the road before expiring. That Monday, funeral services were held at Woodhills. Cops, ex-cons, ex-prostitutes, would-be ex-prostitutes, Francis Heaney, the prosecutor who had sent Abe Ruef to San Quentin, Abe Ruef himself—the usual celebrities—all came down from the city to hear the Reverend Henry Ohloff, rector of St. Mary the Virgin Episcopal Church in San Francisco, praise Fremont Older for being what he truly was: a living reminder into the 1930s of that distinct blend of self-education, robust appetites, compassion for the human condition, abhorrence of snobbery, grand style, and good bourbon and cigars that had helped make the West.

With the death of Fremont Older, Charles Erskine Scott Wood of Los Gatos, a town a few miles south of Cupertino, where Wood lived with his wife the poet Sara Bard Field, now survived as the most conspicuous literary Deep Peninsulan with authentic frontier roots. With John Steinbeck, Charles Erskine Scott Wood and Sara Bard Field, Ruth Comfort Mitchell, and the Menuhin family all living there at overlapping times in the late 1930s, Los Gatos enjoyed some reputation as a literary and musical center, although in political terms Wood, Field, and Steinbeck were on the left, Mitchell was on the far right, and the Menuhins were apolitical. Wood and Field lived at The Cats, a thirty-acre hilltop estate in Los Gatos named in honor of the two granite felines guarding its entrance. Carey McWilliams visited them there in August 1929, driving past the cats, then up a corkscrew road that led to a Roman villa perched on a hillside and commanding a panoramic view of the Santa Clara Valley. McWilliams found the Colonel (a militia title from Oregon) at home, attired in toga and sandals, looking the perfect embodiment of Zeus, with his piercing eyes, white hair, and flowing beard. The Colonel went to fetch Sara, who also appeared in Roman dress. Opening a bottle of burgundy, the two aging writers spent several hours with McWilliams, drinking wine, eating cheese, discussing the verities. Los Angeles bookseller Jacob Zeitlin had a similar experience. Wood looked like a Sunday school–book version of God, Zeitlin later remembered. After lunch, Wood took Zeitlin into his library where he showed him his books, including a Shakespeare second folio that had once belonged to David Garrick.

Charles Erskine Scott Wood had begun his career as a professional Army officer, West Point Class of 1874. In the spring of 1877, he served as an aide to the commanding general, Oliver Howard, in the campaign against the Nez Percé. When Howard was named superintendent of West Point in 1880, Wood returned to his alma mater as adjutant. Shortly thereafter, he went on leave from the Army to take a law degree at Columbia. Wood resigned his commission in 1884 and moved to Portland, Oregon, where he pursued a dual career as attorney and man of letters.

Charles Erskine Scott Wood embodied the paradox of bourgeois radicalism that was to become increasingly characteristic of the Left after World War II. He practiced law with sagacity, a lucrative career climaxed in 1918 by a million-dollar fee received for conducting long-term negotiations for the sale of a wagon road grant. On the other hand, Wood was increasingly radical in his political opinions, a Populist-Progressive with strong leanings toward the single tax theory of Henry George and a foe of organized religion. By the early 1900s, his satirical sketches against Christianity and on behalf of birth control and women's rights were appearing in *The Masses*, the New York radical journal edited by Max Eastman and Floyd Dell. Today, Wood's satires seem pedestrian and heavy-handed, yet in their day they were considered daring, although even by 1927, when they appeared in book form as *Heavenly Discourse*, they possessed the rapidly dated ambience of Greenwich Village radicalism in the pre–World War I period.

A practicing poet as well as a short story writer and a satirist, Wood formed a literary association with the Portland proto-feminist poet Sara Bard Field, thirty years his junior, then the wife of a Baptist minister. Mentorship yielded to passion, and the literary couple lived together for a number of years before the appropriate divorces could be arranged. When Wood made his million in 1918, he and Sara moved to San Francisco, where they ensconced themselves on Taylor Street atop Russian Hill, before acquiring The Cats in 1923, which soon became their primary residence. The Colonel and Sara loved every tree, bush, flower, bird, and animal on their estate. They chronicled their lives there in a large cloth-bound journal, into which they entered naturalist observations, a diary of visitors, bits of poetry. The journal reveals them as aging radicals playing Héloïse and Abelard, had those thwarted medieval lovers been allowed a life together and old age, or what John Reed (another radical from Portland, Oregon) and Louise Bryant might have wanted for themselves, had they been able to return to the West and live in autumnal splendor, had Reed not died of typhus in Russia and been buried in the Kremlin. The Colonel and Sara had defied convention, each of them, not just the political or social pieties of the day but the conventions of the bourgeois life, which, paradoxically, they also relished. Casting the rules aside and living outside wedlock for so many years, they remained for all this bourgeois to the core: the Colonel with his earned fortune, the two of them puttering about The Cats in toga and sandals, and entertaining *New Masses* alumni when they passed through the Bay Area, or Robinson and Una Jeffers and Lincoln Steffens up from Carmel, or the brilliant young photographer Ansel Adams, or their Los Gatos neighbors John Steinbeck and Yehudi Menuhin. In November 1936 the eighty-four-year-old Colonel galvanized the newly organizing League of Western Writers meeting in San Francisco with a stirring call to social action. More than two hundred delegates—John Steinbeck, Nathanael West, Upton Sinclair, and Irwin Shaw among them—gave Wood a standing ovation and elected him the first president of the league.

Wood's Los Gatos neighbor Ruth Comfort Mitchell shuddered at the very thought of the Colonel and Sara's politics. Yet they were neighbors, after all, and charming in their eccentric way, and one should always try to get along. Like the other Deep Peninsulans, Ruth Comfort Mitchell was a rusticated San Franciscan. Born in the city in 1883, the daughter of a prosperous hotel operator, she published her first book of poems in 1916 and her first novel in 1921. She and her husband Sanborn Young, a conservative rancher and state senator from Santa Clara County, moved in ultra-conservative circles. They loathed the New Deal, and Ruth was very active in Pro-America, a conservative Republican women's organization. All in all, she wrote sixteen novels, several books of poetry, and innumerable short stories and magazine articles, while assisting her husband in running his ranch and his political career.

Aside from their ultra-conservative politics, Ruth Mitchell had something else in common with her fellow Peninsulite Kathleen Norris: an unerring intelligence when it came to plots and a powerful sympathy for women in their daily lives and vulnerabilities, which dramatically mitigated the impression of hard-heartedness that could have been created by their hard-right political opinions. Along with Norris, Comfort filled her novels with California women embarked upon lives that were at once compelling in their private dimension but illustrative as well of the contemporary social situation. Like Norris, Mitchell belonged to an era in which fiction had an array of outlets in popular magazines and hence, almost of necessity, kept its connection to ordinary experience. Taken cumulatively, Mitchell's sixteen novels illustrate the social development of Northern California in the 1920s and 1930s, with a special emphasis on the social context of women's lives in such matters as career, sexual choice, and class and ethnic barriers.

Also in Los Gatos, adjacent to the Jesuit Novitiate of the Sacred Heart, the Moshe Menuhin family was spending a year of rustication, from October of 1936 to October of 1937, which Mrs. Menuhin felt absolutely necessary for her son Yehudi, now twenty, who for the past ten years had been ceaselessly touring the world as a violin prodigy. The Menuhins were a tightly knit family from San Francisco, where Moshe Menuhin served as the superintendent of the seven Bay Area Hebrew Schools sponsored by the Pacific Hebrew Orphan Asylum, one of the oldest philanthropies in the state, at the princely salary of $350 a month.

Living at 1043 Steiner Street near Alta Plaza Park in a paradigm of that well-being that characterized Jewish San Francisco in this era—strong family bonds, wonderful cooking, lively conversation at the dinner table, books, music, a pride in being Jewish in a significantly Jewish city—the Menuhins discovered in the mid-1920s that two of their three children were prodigies: Hephzibah on the piano, Yehudi on violin.

As a boy of three, Yehudi heard violinist Louis Persinger as concertmaster at the Curran Theater on Geary Street. Yehudi asked his parents if he could have a violin for his fourth birthday and if Persinger could give him lessons. The Menuhins agreed, and after a period of instruction at Persinger's studio on Hyde Street, brought there each day by one or another of his parents on the streetcar, Menuhin made his first public appearance in November 1921 at a recital at the Fairmont Hotel. On 29 February 1924 he formally debuted at the Oakland Auditorium, followed by a solo performance with the San Francisco Symphony under the direction of Alfred Hertz and a recital at the Scottish Rite Hall. Their son's genius revealed, the Menuhins withdrew Yehudi from school and began to educate him at home in music and primary and secondary subjects. Yehudi Menuhin's California reputation preceded him to New York for his debut there on 17 March 1926 at the Manhattan Opera House.

Like Helen Wills, Yehudi Menuhin soon found himself a civic symbol. The San Francisco Police Department made him an honorary officer, presenting him with a gold badge, which he treasured. Sensitive yet strong, talented but devoid of narcissism, Yehudi grew into a lively young man, manly in manner, yet capable of displaying deep emotion without embarrassment. He adored his parents, whom he called Aba and Mammina, and his sisters Yaltah and Hephzibah, and the three adults who had meant so much to his development: his teacher Louis Persinger, whom he loved as a second father; his patron, the San Francisco lawyer Sidney Ehrman, Uncle Sidney, living in a grand home on Broadway at Lyon with a clear view of the Golden Gate Bridge (the patron of historian Herbert Bolton as well); and Willa Cather, Aunt Willa, whom Yehudi met in Pasadena on tour in 1931 and to whom he confided in person or by letter his rich and resonant emotional life—two great artists, close friends across barriers of gender and half a hundred years.

As a teenager, Yehudi fell in love with Esther Ehrman, Uncle Sidney's daughter, a young woman ten years his senior, who broke Yehudi's heart when she married (in a Roman Catholic ceremony, testimony to the ecumenism of San Francisco) Claude Lazard of the distinguished French banking family, then living in San Francisco and in the process of ousting Herbert Fleishhacker from control of the Anglo-French Bank. As an internationally feted prodigy, Yehudi had ample opportunity to become infatuated yet again with a number of young women whom he met on his travels—which was why Mammina Menuhin insisted in the fall of 1936 that the whole family take a year away from the concert scene, so that Yehudi, so lively in his emotional life, might have a space in which to move into manhood unbuffeted by the stimulations, indeed the temptations, of the concert circuit. And besides: Yehudi had been practicing and performing constantly for sixteen of his twenty years and needed a break, a time to be away from it all, a time to be just another prosperous young Californian in the year 1936, when life was so sweet for the privileged few.

The family called this year of rustication in Los Gatos Mother's Year, but it was Yehudi's year as well. He left San Francisco in an open Cadillac V-12 convertible with white sidewall tires ("I had a sense of style in motorcars," he later admitted) and settled into a year of tennis, swimming, impromptu concerts, and amateur theatricals in a lovely villa backed by oak trees, with a terrace commanding a view of the Santa Clara Valley and San Francisco Bay. Yehudi was an inveterate hiker: up Mount Hamilton to the Lick Observatory, or, more close at hand, through the vineyards of the adjacent Jesuit novitiate, where the rector had given the Menuhins freedom of the property, including full use of the tennis courts. Yehudi and his sisters, with whom he often hiked, found themselves enchanted by the golden sunlight, the clumps of bay and manzanita, the sudden discovery of a shrine in a hidden copse, an impromptu snack of raisinated grapes left behind by the Jesuit novices who had harvested the vines. The impressions of this year resonated with impressions of earlier Northern Californian excursions to Uncle Sidney's estate on Lake Tahoe, with its great Central European–style chateau looming on the shoreline, and of excursions into the nearby Santa Cruz Mountains. Despite his international career and his eventual British citizenship and life peerage, Lord Menuhin would later claim that because of the first twenty years of his life, he remained most fundamentally a citizen of the Bay Area. "California laid ideal landscapes in my mind which nothing later was to overlay," he would write; "it sowed the seed of adult enthusiasms for a world embracing all creation, human, animal, vegetable, mineral; it prompted the first awed responses to my American heritage." [5]

During the 1930s, as always, the artists' colony at Carmel constituted its own autonomous place. Developed by Frank Powers and J. F. Devendorf after the earthquake and fire of 1906 had rendered San Francisco uninhabitable, Carmel began as a development keyed to the artistic lifestyle. Shrewdly, Powers and Devendorf realized that if they brought the right people into Carmel, they could establish a tone, a style, that would become self-reflecting and self-perpetuating; hence lots were virtually given away in the early phases of development (for a few dollars down, pay the balance when you can) to such preeminent figures as Stanford president David Starr Jordan, San Francisco poet George Sterling, short story writer James Hooper, literary regionalist Mary Austin, and other assorted creative folk. Later, Robinson and Una Jeffers arrived, with Jeffers building Tor House, stone by stone, on an elevation overlooking the sweep of shore where the Carmel River runs into the Pacific.

By the 1930s, Carmel-by-the-Sea had become a flourishing colony of artists and writers and art-loving folk living on a combination of royalties, gallery sales, and inherited or elsewhere-earned income: Robinson Jeffers included, for it was a modest legacy, carefully nurtured, that allowed Jeffers to remove himself from the world while sitting in judgment of it from his rock-fast aerie. Rather self-consciously, if the truth be told, Carmel made a cult of being above it all, which was another way of being safe from it all, especially during the Great Depression. In the 1920s, seeking to fashion Carmel as a privileged and protected enclave, the Nantucket of the West, Carmelites had practically invented the no-growth revolt of a later era with the election of journalist Perry Newberry to the Board of Trustees on a draconian platform of anti-development. A zoning law passed in 1929 decreed that business development should be forever subordinate to residential character. Residents passed a bond issue to buy the dunes and cliffs along the shoreline so as to keep hotels away from the seafront.

Carmelites, as they called themselves, liked things the way they were: the lack of doorbells or addresses on their cottages, so many of them in English Country or Hansel and Gretel style; the absence of sidewalks; the community bulletin board; the pickup post office (nothing as vulgar as postmen on Carmel streets!); the row of boutiques on Ocean Avenue: Cabbages and Kings for sportswear, the Cinderella Shop for women's clothes, the Eliot and Marian weaving shop for scarves and homespun, the Seven Arts Court for books and artist's supplies, the Tuck Box Tea Room. Shopkeepers, butchers, and grocers, it was rumored, read Proust between customers. Each summer, Carmelites of all conditions, gentry and tradesmen alike, joined to produce play pageants in the outdoor Forest Theater that rivaled in sets, lighting, and spectacle the annual Midsummer Jinks at the Bohemian Grove. The very elaborateness of these productions, which called for the cooperative effort of hundreds of Carmelites, testified to the coherence of the Carmelite identity among its permanent and summer residents. Carmel, one and all believed, was magic in its beauty and enchanting in its commitment to life lived for art. How many other villages, after all, could say that the local plumber had a featured part at the Forest Theater or that the owner of the hardware store also taught dance? Even the dogs of Carmel possessed cachet, especially the several who belonged to the town at large, fed by the butchers and grocers, sleeping on cold nights in the post office. The best known of these in the 1930s was an airedale-bulldog mongrel (if such can be imagined) by the name of Pal, who was given his own tombstone at public expense when he passed away in December 1942.

It is easy to fall into irony when discussing Carmel, for there was much to it that was recherché, even precious. Carey McWilliams once constructed a taxonomy of Carmel cottage names in his "Tides West" column in *Westways*. There were oceanic names, McWilliams noted: Driftwood, White Caps, Hi-Tide, Surf Echoes, Sea Urchin, Periwinkle, Breakers, and Barnacle. There were California Sunshine names: Sunbeam, Sunaround, Sunny Nook, Maison du Soleil. There were flora and fauna names: Fairy Lantern, Footsteps of Spring, Twin Pines,

Dancing Oaks, Ye Oaks, Grey Oaks, Whispering Pine, Sheltering Pine, Pine Log, Pinecroft, Pinemere, and Port o' Pines; and Spanish and Hawaiian names: Laguna Vista, Olas Verdes, Leialoha and Aloha; and whimsy names: Kozee, Mee Too, Cookie Jar, Out' n' Inn, Cuddledoon, Elves House, Friar Tuck, Bide-a-Wee, and Three Sheets in the Wind. Certain names—Hob Knobs, the Secret Door, Next Door, Green Lantern, Green Dragon, Green Lattice—defied classification. In its basic identity, Carmel was a fantasy resort for the affluent, cozy and comforting in its Hansel and Gretel thatched-cottage cuteness. Carmel paralleled Palm Springs as a stylization of experience. Beach walks, abalone and mussel bakes, bonfires and community sings, reading circles, amateur theatricals in the Forest, Golden Bough, and Arts and Crafts theaters, and gardening clubs replaced the dude ranch and desert activities of its Hollywood-oriented counterpart further south. From this perspective, Carmel was most fundamentally a resort—a stylized community operating twelve months a year for many of its residents, who possessed the financial wherewithal to withdraw from the bloody strife into a storybook village.

Yet this was only part of the story; for Carmel had in its heyday sustained a resident community of writers and artists that included some of the best talent in the state. At one time or another, a number of creditable writers—in the first generation, Mary Austin, Jack London, and George Sterling, followed by a transient second generation that included William Rose Benét, Sinclair Lewis, Van Wyck Brooks, Theodore Maynard, and Michael Williams—had sojourned in Carmel. Under the influence of Mission Carmel, Michael Williams converted to Roman Catholicism. Williams and Theodore Maynard became two of the best-known American Catholic writers of their generation. Organized around the mission basilica, where Father Junipero Serra lay buried, Catholic Carmel had its own intensity and symbolic valence. Carmel had been among the most prominent of the missions, and its ambience was further reinforced in the 1920s by the construction in nearby Carmel Highlands of a monastery and church for contemplative Carmelite sisters, the gift of Noel Sullivan in honor of his sister, Sister Agnes of Jesus, prioress of the community.

Neither Robinson Jeffers nor Lincoln Steffens could be expected to have much sympathy for such a variant kind of Carmelite as Sister Agnes of Jesus, with her vows in an order that its members traced back to its founding in ancient Israel atop Mount Carmel. Twinned in their vast differences—Steffens a man of the Left and Jeffers an anarcho-conservative who considered himself beyond politics—the poet and the muckraker were the best known of the literary Carmelites, with Steffens taking up residence in Carmel after one of the most influential careers in American journalism. There he devoted himself to raising his son Peter, born to him late in life, finishing his tumultuous career as a doting father and inveterate letter writer in a safe and cozy haven, from which he and his radical left wife Ella Winter might survey, at a distance, the upheavals of the Depression. Visiting the Steffenses in Carmel in the mid-1930s, travel writer Charles Brooks wondered whether the file cabinets contained the names of those who were prepared to flock to the revolution, once it broke out. Returning from the Soviet Union, Steffens had told one and all that he had seen the future and it worked. He himself, however, preferred to await the revolution and the future amidst the rusticated certainties of Carmel.

When it came to art, Carmel owed no apologies to anyone. Francis McComas, an important Monterey painter along with Charles Rollo Peters, had settled in rather early; William Merritt Chase conducted a successful summer school; and in the years just after the war, a number of artists who would eventually win national rank—among them, William Ritschel and John O'Shea—had cast their lot with Carmel. Sculptor Joseph Mora, meanwhile, continued to excel in heroic representative sculpture and to supervise the restoration of Carmel Mission. Finn Haakon Frolid (a name right out of Tolkien!), an artist destined to keep Carmel on the cutting edge of California sculpture, made his home there. Another Carmelite in the visual arts, photographer Edward Weston, was, along with Dorothea Lange and Ansel Adams, among the leading photographers of the state.

South of Carmel, in Big Sur, the contrivances and postures of the aesthetic bourgeois gave out in favor of the elemental life of backcountry ranchers and homesteaders whose Homeric existence Robinson Jeffers drew upon for the setting and protagonists of his narrative poems. Until the late 1930s, Big Sur, the rugged coastline and backcountry extending a hundred miles from Point Sur south of Carmel to Morro Bay north of San Luis Obispo, had for all practical purposes been absent from the history and consciousness of California, there being so few people in this region and barely a settlement worthy of the name village. With the completion of the Rainbow Bridge across Bixby Landing and the opening of the Pacific Coast Highway in 1937, however, Big Sur became accessible to the general public, although the emergence of Big Sur as the psychic and spiritual center of the higher consciousness, California-style, awaited the post-war era. Yet there were already indications by the late 1930s that Big Sur was en route to becoming the psychic center of California: an American Mount Athos, an American Tibet, Shangri-La for a generation of holistic healers and the transcendentally minded. A Tibetan lama visiting the Panama Pacific International Exposition in 1915 had insisted on making a pilgrimage to Point Lobos, telling reporters that it was a tradition at Lhasa that the Monterey cypress tree was a direct descendant of seeds brought to California a thousand years earlier by wandering Buddhist monks who had reached California via China and Japan. Visiting the cypress groves on Point Lobos, the monk verified the tradition: these were trees from the monastery garden at Lhasa. They stood, he said, as a living link between the Buddhism of Tibet and the mystical future of Point Lobos and its hinterlands.

In his long poems of the 1920s, Robinson Jeffers likewise seeded Big Sur with myth, and already there lived in the region a personality prophetic of things to come, Jaime de Angulo, a medical doctor turned anthropologist, who had been ranching in Big Sur since 1914. Born in Paris in 1887 of aristocratic Spanish parents who had fled Spain for political reasons, Jaime de Angulo had been educated by the Jesuits before emigrating to the United States at the age of eighteen and going to work as a cowboy in the Far West. In 1907 he secured admission to Johns Hopkins, where he acquired an M.D. degree and a wife before buying a ranch in Big Sur and devoting himself to cattle raising and the study of Native American languages. Dressing habitually in the attire of an Old California *vaquero*—black chaps, black shirt, a black sombrero from which flowed his shoulder-length hair, a turquoise-studded silver conch belt around his waist—Jaime de Angulo was for all his posing and Big Sur bohemianism a serious scholar of Indian anthropology and linguistics. When World War I broke out, he joined the Army as a physician and was assigned to care for victims of shell-shock. After the war, he spent time studying psychiatry with Freud in Vienna and was among the first to bring Freudian theories back to the United States. His second wife was Carl Jung's translator.

As a scholar and a clinician, de Angulo was interested in that intersection point of Native American anthropology, with its emphasis upon environmental living, holistic health, and mythic narrative as a probe of the subconscious; modern psychiatry, with its insight into contemporary neurosis; and California, specifically Big Sur, as an arena in which the insights of European psychiatry and Native American anthropology might coalesce to establish new premises for art and a creative connection with the subconscious. Meanwhile, Jaime de Angulo wrestled with his own demons. He drank too much and brooded over his family's exile from Spain. For Van Wyck Brooks, de Angulo, with his Arab horse, red sash, and El Greco face and beard, seemed a figure from the golden age of Spanish letters, a Don Quixote in exile, capable, when in his cups, of breaking into Indian chants and dances or howling at the moon in imitation of Brother Coyote.

If Jaime de Angulo saw in Big Sur the intersection of Freud and Native America, another and equally prophetic figure, Ella Young, envisioned Big Sur as the enchanted coast of a second Celtic Twilight. Robinson and Una Jeffers were equally obsessed with the Celtic past and the correspondences between Carmel–Big Sur and the western Irish coast. Jeffers spent a year in Ireland studying Celtic anthropology and folklore and found in Celtic culture what Jaime de Angulo was finding in Native America: a corroboration of spiritual experience rooted in place. Ella Young helped foster this Celtic consciousness in the Jefferses and in other Carmelites. In Ireland Young had associated with Yeats, Lady Gregory, George Russell, John Millington Synge, and Maud Gonne in the revival of Celtic culture; but she decided to migrate to the United States during the Irish Civil War, believing that violence had driven all enchantment from the Emerald Isle.

Learned in Celtic culture, Young was also a mystic with strong folkloric beliefs. (She had been briefly detained at Ellis Island as a probable mental case when the authorities learned that she believed in the existence of fairies, elves, and pixies.) Point Lobos near Carmel, Young believed, was the psychic center of the Pacific

Coast. "When the force of Lobos is released," she claimed, "a great thing will happen in America—but Lobos is not ready to make friends yet."[6] Carmelite Noel Sullivan endowed a professorship in Celtic studies at UC Berkeley on Ella Young's behalf. Big Sur native Rosalind Sharpe encountered Young at Berkeley in 1936, lecturing on Cuchulain and other figures from Irish mythology, attired in the purple robes of a Druid bard. Despite being in her early eighties, Sharpe later remembered, Ella Young exuded a supernal beauty, at once Celtic and Carmelite-Californian.

At the southern entrance to Big Sur nestled the coastal enclave college town of San Luis Obispo, home of the California State Polytechnic College, Cal Poly for short, flourishing since 1901 as a center for engineering, industrial, and agricultural education. Concerned with such practical no-nonsense studies and being equally remote from San Francisco and Los Angeles, neither Cal Poly nor San Luis Obispo, despite their dramatic settings on the coast, attracted much of an affiliated community. No matter: at nearby San Simeon, north of Morro Bay, William Randolph Hearst was more than taking up the slack. Each Thursday afternoon, automobiles packed with Hollywood celebrities would arrive from Southern California for the long weekend at Hearst Castle, which W.R. had been developing since 1919 with the assistance of his architect, Julia Morgan. Whatever his faults, Hearst had always given women more than a fair chance on his newspapers, and in Julia Morgan's case both he and his mother, the late Phoebe Apperson Hearst, had been long since offering steady patronage to the first woman to win an architect's license in California. A graduate of UC Berkeley and L'Ecole des Beaux Arts, Julia Morgan might have been the first among women architects in the state, but from another perspective she was the youngest of a brilliant turn-of-the-century generation of San Francisco–based architects—George Applegarth, Ernest Coxhead, Albert Pissis, Willis Polk, Bernard Maybeck, and others—who from the 1890s onwards had been creating and pacing the architecture of California. Into the 1930s Morgan carried on the distinctive reconciliation of classical and Craftsman, scholarship and innovation, formalism and whimsy of the *fin de siècle*.

Rising from its hilltop site like a Spanish Xanadu, Hearst Castle remains an enigma, as it was in the 1930s. What did all this mean, visitors asked themselves as they were shown to their rooms by a silently efficient staff, who briefed them on protocol: one drink before dinner, no smoking at table, no political discussions, no philandering, early to bed and early to rise? Of what significance beyond hyper-plutocratic display were these great galleries with their European art and statuary, the ninety-foot-long library with its Spanish-Moorish ceiling and ascending shelves of rare editions, the soaring refectory in Spanish Gothic, the oversized swimming pool in Roman classic, the gardens everywhere, the zoo, the zebras grazing on the coastal hills? Was this the last gasp of another era, the twilight of an even earlier twilight of splendor? Or was there something more personal involved in the old man's mania to create a world of beauty beyond perishability or pain, even if it meant, as it did on one occasion, that an entire Spanish monastery be bought, disassembled, crated, and shipped to California, stone by stone?

More than anyone else in the world—more than his editors, his lawyers, his mistress even—Julia Morgan understood William Randolph Hearst. This was her genius. She always understood her clients, women clients especially. Having worked for Phoebe Apperson Hearst and known from first hand the powerful bond between Phoebe and her erratic genius of a son, Morgan also sensed that Hearst himself had a strong feminine streak in his nature (his compulsive aestheticism, his intuition, his love of costume parties and female company in platonic circumstances) and that his relationship with his mother, even after her death in 1919, the year he began San Simeon as a memorial to her, was the most important point of reference in his emotional life. When he was a boy of ten, an only child, his mother, absenting herself from her strong-willed, frequently cranky husband, took young Willie on a two-year tour of Europe. Her letters from Europe survive in the Bancroft Library in Berkeley. In them Phoebe Hearst makes constant reference to her son and to the galleries and architectural monuments they are visiting together. William Randolph Hearst discovered the art of Europe in the context of his mother's love and companionship, a half world away from a dominating father. Theirs was a mother-son idyll to be remembered, and recovered, across a lifetime. Together, mother and son had achieved a place apart, a castle of the imagination, and when she was gone Hearst began to translate that interior castle into reality with Julia Morgan's guidance.

As in the case of just about everything Hearst did, psychological motivation linked itself to social experience and symbol. Hearst Castle was not only Rosebud, the remembered idyll of childhood, it was also an architectural icon of the California the Hearst family had helped to create. On a bare hillside in south-central coastal California arose a treasure trove of European art housed within a re-created Spanish castle. San Simeon was materializing the daydream California had of itself as a second Mediterranean shore, another Europe. Like the hills of San Simeon, California had only recently been, in European terms, a *tabula rasa*, an Italy awaiting its history, as Henry James phrased it. Throughout the 1920s William Randolph Hearst feverishly filled in the void—his lost mother, the emptiness of the California hills—with an orgy of acquisition and construction. Even as it rose, Hearst Castle had its *retardaire* dimensions. Americans had not been building residences on such a scale since the passage of the income tax. And yet, from the perspective of the 1920s, Hearst Castle was not totally out of date. It was a time of Spanish Revival—a revival that Morgan herself had helped launch with the Spanish fantasy headquarters of Hearst's Los Angeles *Examiner*, constructed in 1915—and here was the ultimate castle in Spain. It was a time of lavish materials, the 1920s, and here was the most lavish residence in the state. Here was California as castle in Spain.

Incongruities were everywhere. At dinner, unadorned bottles of Heinz catsup, suitable to a downtown lunch counter, topped a refectory table from Renaissance Spain set with fine china and antique silver. Movies were shown in a library lined with rare books. Guests played parlor games in a soaring Spanish Gothic hall. Yet neither Hearst Castle nor WR himself is to be taken to task for these dissonances. So much of California, so many of the college towns and the other rusticated enclaves where imagination was the first premise of lifestyle, where the resort impulse materialized itself almost effortlessly, represented an over-reaching for Arcadia. Despite the Depression, the search for Arcadia was continuing through the 1930s, and it would continue unabated for the next half century. It represented, after all, a persistent American quest for a place called California that existed, first and foremost, in the imagination.

II

URBAN AND SUBURBAN
PERSPECTIVES

3

Unto the Stars Themselves

Astronomy and the Pasadena Perspective

O N New Year's Day 1931, Albert and Elsa Einstein arrived in Pasadena, where Professor Einstein was scheduled to take up a winter appointment as a Visiting Fellow at the California Institute of Technology, more commonly known as Cal Tech. Like any visitors to Southern California in mid-winter, the Einsteins relished the opportunity to escape the bitter cold, in their case, the chill of Oxford, where Einstein held an appointment at Christ Church, or the even more challenging climate of New York, where he had been feted upon his arrival in a minor version of Lindbergh returning from Paris. During their two-month stay in Southern California, ensconced in a snug Craftsman bungalow near the campus, the Einsteins behaved like typical, if privileged, tourists. They had dinner with Charlie Chaplin. Upton Sinclair took them to a preview of Sergei Eisenstein's new film on Mexico, and there was a special showing of *All Quiet on the Western Front*, which was banned in Germany. The Einsteins went sailing off Long Beach to Santa Catalina and spent time in Santa Barbara.

But Albert Einstein, the presiding genius of the twentieth century, had come to Pasadena—which is to say, to Cal Tech—not merely to enjoy the sunshine, but to learn as well as to teach. Until recently, Einstein had believed that the universe, while relative, was fixed and constant, spherical and closed. The universe might be relative, but it was possessed of form and limit. Of late, however, Einstein had been studying the theories of two Cal Tech professors, mathematical physicist Richard Chase Tolman and astronomer Edwin Hubble, who were painting a dramatically different portrait of the cosmos. The universe, Hubble argued from his observation of red shifts in the outer galaxies, was expanding. Tolman, in turn, bolstered Hubble's notion of an expanding universe with appropriate mathematics, which drew upon the previous calculations of the Abbé G. E. Lemaitre, a Harvard-trained Catholic priest from Belgium who in 1927 had offered

61

calculations asserting that the world according to Einstein could not be fixed but had to be unstable. Lemaitre's calculations, Hubble's observations through the hundred-inch Hooker Telescope atop Mount Wilson next to Pasadena, and Tolman's mathematical refinements coalesced to bring Albert Einstein to Pasadena with a very pressing question on his mind.

Throughout his winter visit, Einstein had ample opportunity to consult with Hubble, Tolman, and the other distinguished scientists assembled at Cal Tech by its executive director, Robert Millikan. (Millikan, Einstein noted in his diary, presided over his faculty like God himself.) Even before he left Pasadena in March, Einstein was admitting grave doubts regarding the fixed state of the universe. Three months later, back in Berlin, Einstein wrote Millikan that, thanks to his visit to Cal Tech, which had included a crucial conference with Hubble at the Mount Wilson Observatory, he now had changed his view of the universe to bring it into conformity with Hubble's observations and Tolman's mathematics. Shortly thereafter, Einstein announced that he had been converted to the notion that the universe was expanding and that such a notion was thoroughly in conformity to the theory of relativity.

The fact that Cal Tech, a small new scientific institute in a suburban Southern California township, had helped the master of contemporary physics refine his theories was not lost on either the international and American scientific community, the faculty of Cal Tech, or boosters of Cal Tech and Pasadena. Einstein's visit—which was repeated in the winters of 1932 and 1933, and was preceded and followed by similar visits from Neils Bohr, Max Born, and Werner Heisenberg— brought to culmination three decades of effort to establish Pasadena as a world center of scientific research.

At Cal Tech Einstein encountered an institution emanating a near-religious dedication to science and to the priesthood of scientists. (Not until after the Second World War would women be admitted.) The very buildings of Cal Tech were monastic in inspiration: a series of Romanesque Revival cloisters, gargoyle-guarded, grouped around arcaded gardens where one might expect to find monks strolling in meditation. Bertram Grosvenor Goodhue, master of Spanish Revival (the California Building in San Diego, the Los Angeles Public Library), had supervised the establishment of the new campus in 1916, assisted by local architects Elmer Grey and Myron Hunt, who drew up a master plan incorporating elements of the medieval cloister and Jefferson's plan for the University of Virginia. Each cloister quadrangle featured a residential house system with a resident faculty master, based on the colleges of Oxford and Cambridge: Ricketts House, Blacker House, Dabney House, Fleming House, representing, according to Millikan, "one of the first successful attempts to introduce into American undergraduate life the essential advantages of the English house or college system as opposed to the fraternity and commons system."[1] Here, in an atmosphere akin to that of a monastic novitiate, a generation of distinguished scientists—including many of the preeminent scientists of the Second World War and post-war era—was being trained by an outstanding faculty. Only UC Berkeley would surpass Cal Tech in the production of notable scientists in the first four decades of the twentieth century.

No Oxford or Cambridge senior common room, moreover, no chapter house of an endowed religious order in the high Middle Ages could equal the aesthetic self-regard emanating from the Athenaeum, the Cal Tech faculty club designed by Gordon Kaufmann, completed in 1930, where Albert Einstein lunched and frequently dined during his three winter visits. For the better part of a decade the English-born Kaufmann had been giving the cultural dreams of affluent Anglo-American Pasadena a local habitation and a name in a series of handsome Tudor and Jacobean homes worthy of Old England itself. For the Athenaeum, Kaufmann turned to Spanish-Italian Romanesque Revival: creamy surfaces without, red-tiled roofs, arched arcades enveloping olive trees; within, dining areas and lounges embellished with modillions, pateras, rosettes, and embellished moldings suggestive of the Italian Renaissance. An oversized fireplace dominated one wall of the faculty lounge. Oriental rugs were everywhere; so were polished refectory tables, lit by soft lamplight, piled high with a mixture of general interest and scientific periodicals. Even to enter the Athenaeum, an architectural critic would later say, made one feel like a Nobel Prize winner.

Which was precisely the point. Having recruited potential Nobel Prize winners in the 1920s, Cal Tech was now in the process of training its own first generation of Nobel laureates. In 1923, for work done at the University of Chicago, Robert Millikan, the *de facto* president of Cal Tech (Millikan refused the title), won the Nobel Prize in physics. In 1933 Cal Tech geneticist Thomas Hunt Morgan, whom Millikan recruited from Columbia in 1928, won the Nobel Prize in physiology and medicine for his research into chromosomal transmission in fruit flies. In 1936 Cal Tech received its first fully home-grown Nobel Prize when Carl Anderson was honored in physics for ascertaining in 1932 the first empirical evidence of anti-matter, using a magnetic cloud chamber in the Guggenheim Aeronautical Laboratory on campus. During his three visits, Einstein might also encounter members of the up and coming generation: J. Robert Oppenheimer in physics, who held a joint appointment with Berkeley; the Russian-born geneticist Theodosius Dobzhansky, recruited to Cal Tech by Thomas Hunt Morgan; Linus Pauling, a Cal Tech product (Ph.D., 1925), a full professor in chemistry at the age of thirty. As a graduate student, Pauling had written revolutionary papers on the quantum mechanics of the chemical bond, moving this subject from theoretical physics, where it had previously been, into chemistry. By 1935 Pauling had already achieved research that would be recognized nineteen years later by a Nobel prize in chemistry.

Nor was Cal Tech devoid of a creative connection to its immediate situation in Southern California; indeed, Millikan claimed that Cal Tech's relationship to Southern California represented a classic case study of what British historian Arnold Toynbee described as challenge and response. Early civilizations, Toynbee had argued and Millikan further emphasized, found their best energies in coping with the gradual desiccation of Mesopotamia, Asia Minor, North Africa, and northwest India. So too, Millikan believed, would Southern California—a semi-arid wasteland with only the desert for a hinterland—require a high degree of applied science and engineering to reach its social and cultural goals; and Cal Tech was on hand to provide such service. In a region vulnerable to geological upheavals, Cal Tech became a world center of seismological research with its recruitment of Beno Gutenberg, Harry Wood, and Charles Richter, whose scale for measuring the order of magnitude of earthquakes would eventually make his name one of the best known in American science.

After agriculture, tourism, and the motion picture industry, aviation held a leading place in the Southern California economy. Empowered by funds from the Guggenheim Foundation, Cal Tech built a state-of-the-art wind tunnel in 1929, capable of testing model aircraft in winds up to two hundred miles per hour. Millikan contacted aircraft designer and manufacturer Donald Douglas for assistance in this project. Douglas sent over his assistant chief engineer Arthur Raymond. In 1930 the distinguished Hungarian-born engineer and applied mathematician Theodore von Karman, the most gifted aerodynamicist of the period, joined Cal Tech as professor of aeronautics and first director of the Daniel Guggenheim Graduate School of Aeronautics. A golden age of aeronautics ensued, which witnessed the design and testing of the Douglas DC-1, a prototype for a two-engine all-metal passenger plane, followed by the issuing of one production model, the DC-2, followed in 1935 by the manufacturing of the twenty-one-passenger DC-3, which ushered the world into its modern era of air travel. Shortly thereafter, von Karman and his colleague Frank Malina turned their attention to rocketry and jet propulsion, with experiments beginning as early as 1936. In the spring of 1939, General H. D. (Hap) Arnold awarded Cal Tech a contract to research the application of jet propulsion for assisted take-offs of aircraft from both land and sea. During World War II Cal Tech spearheaded the nation's rocket research program, a task carried on after the war by the Jet Propulsion Laboratory at the institute.

Despite such applied research, Millikan always insisted that Cal Tech serve, first and foremost, scientific research in the purest sense of the term. Cal Tech, he asserted, was not a university, with its myriad connections to business, public service, education, law, medicine, and the arts. Cal Tech was a more focused entity, an institute, oriented to scientific and engineering teaching and research. Much of the focus of Cal Tech, Millikan argued, its precision, its single-mindedness, came from the fact that its development had been stimulated by the Mount Wilson Observatory, a research institution devoted to one of the purest of pure scientific pursuits, astronomy. "As I read values," Millikan later stated, "the Mount Wilson Observatory has already been the greatest asset possessed by Southern California, not excluding the Los Angeles Chamber of Commerce, for it began to demonstrate the possibility of making this climatically favored Southwest region a center for the development of great scientific, intellectual, and cultural activities and values."[2] The Mount Wilson Observatory, in other words, had boosted Cal Tech into prominence; and Cal Tech, in turn, had put not only Pasadena, but all of Southern California as well, on the cultural map.

No one bore greater responsibility for the emergence of Pasadena than Cal Tech astronomer emeritus George Ellery Hale, whose mind, imagination, aspirations, strengths, weaknesses, and inconsistencies fully embodied the Pasadena perspective. Hale's efforts on behalf of the Mount Wilson Observatory, Cal Tech, the Huntington Library, and a number of important civic projects stimulated and shaped, indeed refounded, Pasadena in the first two decades of the century. If Pasadena had any single founder, it was George Ellery Hale.

Hale was a Chicagoan, which is not surprising. Turn-of-the-century and early twentieth-century Southern California, Los Angeles especially, had noticeably been the creation of men and women from Chicago and its suburbs. Progressive in politics, upper middle class in lifestyle and preferences, such Chicagoans sought in Southern California at first a resort, relief from winter, or in many cases an opportunity to heal damaged lungs, then later, by the early 1900s, an opportunity to give Midwestern Progressivism a new colony on the Pacific. Before moving to California in 1903, Hale had been serving since 1892 as professor of astrophysics and director of the Yerkes Observatory of the University of Chicago, located at Williams Bay, Wisconsin. With its three domes designed by Daniel Hudson Burnham rising in neo-classical splendor in a profile suggestive of the Great White City itself (Burnham had served as planning director and architect-in-chief of the World's Columbian Exposition held in Chicago in 1893), its forty-inch refractor telescope (the largest in the nation), and its state-of-the-art use of photography as well as direct observation, the Yerkes Observatory expressed both the ambitions of astronomy in America, as embodied in its leading astronomer, George Ellery Hale, and the ambitions of Chicago itself as reflected in its rising university.

Why, then, would Hale even think of moving to Southern California? Even after all the evidence is taken into account, the answer to this question remains mysterious. First of all, it must be emphasized that Hale initially saw Southern California as a field of colonization: a place where the Yerkes Observatory might find better altitudes and atmospherics. Only later did the necessity of a new and independent institution, linked to the rise of Southern California, become a separate goal in Hale's mind. A more subtle cause can also be argued. George Ellery Hale moved to Southern California in 1903, it can be said, because he instinctively understood that in terms of topography, atmospherics, and an already flourishing astronomical tradition, California held the lead, not just in observation, but in a more subtle assent to astronomy as the cutting edge, the purest form, of science. Maria Mitchell might have done her pioneering work on the island of

Nantucket, and certainly the Naval Observatory in Washington, the Harvard Observatory, and the Yerkes Observatory were formidable institutions; but only California had cohered around astronomy as a regional way of life.

Three San Franciscans—George Davidson, James Lick, and Richard Samuel Floyd—played major roles in the establishment of this astronomical tradition. Coming to maturity in Philadelphia, a center of scientific interest since the eighteenth century, the English-born Davidson arrived in San Francisco in 1850 as director of the Coast Survey. Becoming interested in applied astronomy as a means of establishing coastal longitudes, Davidson in 1879 built the first astronomical observatory on the West Coast atop a hill in San Francisco subsequently developed as Lafayette Park in the Pacific Heights district. Although the instrumentation of the Davidson observatory was not particularly impressive, the pioneer astronomer used his 6.4-inch refracting device and auxiliary instruments to make a valuable series of astronomical observations keyed to geodetic research, which he published in the *Proceedings* and *Bulletin* of the San Francisco–based California Academy of Sciences and the *Annual Reports* of the Coast Survey. As president of the California Academy of Sciences, Davidson evangelized constantly regarding the preeminence of astronomy as a pure and practical science in which California might assume national leadership, given its superb atmospherics.

One person hearing Davidson's message was the eccentric millionaire James Lick, and from Lick came the bequest that created the Lick Observatory, which overnight put California in the forefront of astronomical research. A Pennsylvanian of Dutch descent, James Lick was the sort of quirky self-made millionaire abundantly found in American history. A piano repairer and furniture maker by trade, Lick spent his youth and middle years buying, selling, and repairing pianos and making furniture in Latin America, based out of Lima. By 1847 he had moved his operation to Valparaiso, where he became friendly with chocolate broker Domingo Ghirardelli. In late 1847 Lick decided to try his luck in California. He arrived in San Francisco on 7 January 1848 with $30,000 in Peruvian gold doubloons and six hundred pounds of Guatemalan chocolate on consignment from Ghirardelli. The $30,000 nest egg expressed not only Lick's industry but his obsessive frugality as well. Poor, uneducated, Lick had been as a young man denied the right to marry a young woman of higher station; even with his daughter pregnant by Lick, the girl's father had not considered him good enough to marry her. Sorely wounded, Lick sustained an ambivalence toward wealth throughout his entire life. He worked hard, made money, saved most of it, and pursued frugality with an obsession born of that ambivalence, as if no amount of wealth could compensate for an earlier hurt and hence the fruits of wealth were to be kept at an anorexic distance. For a number of years, even a bed seemed too great a luxury. Lick slept atop a piano or in a furniture packing case, wrapping himself in delivery blankets.

In Latin America Lick had worked with his hands. In California he prospered in real estate, although he did express his artisan's instincts in building a state-of-the-art flour mill in San Jose. It is astonishing to contemplate just exactly how much real estate James Lick amassed in a few short years: vineyards in the Santa Clara Valley, property at Lake Tahoe and Virginia City, the entire Rancho Los Feliz in Los Angeles County (the present North Hollywood, Griffith Park, and Glendale), and, for a time, the entire island of Santa Catalina. In 1861 Lick built the Lick House at the corner of Sutter and Montgomery streets in San Francisco, which remained the leading hotel in the city until the Palace opened in 1876.

In his lifetime, James Lick had gone from poverty and humiliation to regal wealth and civic prominence as the wealthiest man in San Francisco. He had done this, moreover, with a minimum of formal culture. Not surprisingly, when he began to search for the meaning of his life as he entered his mid-seventies in the 1870s (an Uncle Sam figure, tall, lanky, a long white beard but no mustache) and to seek a way to memorialize his success, he did so with a clumsy naiveté that is tempting to satirize. For a while, he considered constructing a marble pyramid larger than the Great Pyramid of ancient Egypt on the shores of San Francisco Bay. He also spoke of building three heroic statues, himself and his parents, in the North Beach district, so as to be visible to incoming and outgoing ships.

Fortunately, George Davidson was also having conversations with James Lick about the construction of an astronomical observatory on Market Street. Lick's growing interest represented not only his own experience but the experience of an entire generation. Lick had always been interested, in a Masonic sort of way, in ancient Egypt and its mysteries; hence his idea of reconstructing the Great Pyramid on the shores of San Francisco Bay. Astronomy dovetailed with this interest in Egypt. Lick was fascinated by the way the priests of the ancient world, in Egypt and Babylon especially, deciphered the mystery of the heavens. In 1860 Lick attended a lecture in San Jose given by George Madera, an itinerant astronomer, and looked through Madera's telescope. He never forgot the experience, and undoubtedly it fueled his receptivity to Davidson's lobbying efforts. When Lick died in October 1876 at the age of eighty and was interred in the Masonic vault in San Francisco after a huge civic funeral, his executors announced a series of bequests: an industrial school for the youth of San Francisco, a new museum for the Academy of Sciences, an endowment for the Society of California Pioneers—and funds to construct what Lick insisted must be an observatory supporting the most powerful telescope on the planet. Two years prior to his death, Lick had established a trust to supervise the construction of the observatory, which when completed would be turned over to the University of California.

It took twelve years to find the site—Mount Hamilton in Santa Clara County, 4,250 feet above sea level—build the necessary roads to the summit, construct the observatory and attendant buildings, and, most important, cast and grind the thirty-six-inch lens, the largest in the world, and design and build not only the telescope but its supporting mechanical structures. In a manner totally suggestive of the appeal of astronomy to the lay people of California as well as to its scientists, a non-scientist, Captain Richard Samuel Floyd, saw the construction of the Lick Observatory to its conclusion. A Georgian who had resigned from Annapolis to serve in the Confederate Navy, Floyd had arrived in San Francisco in December 1865 and entered the merchant service. Captain Floyd was smooth, dashing, handsome—an ex-Confederate corsair who had sunk his share of Union shipping. As such, he found acceptance in the wealthier circles of San Francisco, and in September 1871 he wed a daughter of privilege, Cora Lyons, in much-noted nuptials at Trinity Church. The newly married Captain and Mrs. Floyd almost immediately took their place at the forefront of San Francisco society.

If opposites attract, Captain Floyd, the dashing socially prominent gentleman, was just the sort of man to attract James Lick, for whom nothing came easy, who had lived in a self-imposed isolation for most of his life. Well before his death, Lick chose Floyd to be the person who would get his observatory built. As in most of his business dealings, James Lick was not mistaken. Richard Floyd devoted what turned out to be the last twelve years of his life to seeing the great enterprise to a successful conclusion. He and Cora traveled to the East Coast and to Europe, visiting the great observatories, consulting with eminent astronomers, mastering the details of optics and mechanical engineering associated with great telescopes. It is startling to think of this amateur layman, with only his abbreviated instruction at Annapolis for guidance, taking personal responsibility for the design and construction of the greatest astronomical observatory on the planet.

The blank disc of flint glass intended for the Lick Observatory was cast by Feil and Company of Paris in 1882. Discouragingly, the disc cracked in the initial casting. No one had ever attempted a lens of this size. The most minuscule impurity would make it useless for astronomical purposes. The Feil brothers were being asked by Captain Floyd to do the work of nature herself: to cast a lens of a purity comparable to crystalline structures formed over millennia by the unreproduceable heat of Earth's magma core. Assisted by their elderly father, who came out of retirement, the Feil brothers spent two more years and twenty more attempts before a new crown disc, weighing 375 pounds, devoid of even microscopic impurities, was successfully cast and shipped to the Clark Factory in Cambridge, Massachusetts, for grinding and polishing. When the polished lens arrived atop Mount Hamilton in November 1887, the dome, telescope, and supporting mechanical structures, as intricate as the finest watch, were ready to receive the thirty-six-inch lens, ten inches larger than that of the Naval Observatory in Washington, its nearest competitor. On 10 January 1887, James Lick was disinterred from his Masonic vault in San Francisco and reinterred in a sealed tomb at the base of the great telescope.

The power of the Lick Telescope, aided by the exquisite atmospherics of Mount Hamilton, soon became apparent. On 9 September 1892, on his very first night on the telescope, astronomer Edward Emerson Barnard discovered the faint fifth satellite of Jupiter, which a number of historians of astronomy have described as the greatest astronomical discovery of the nineteenth century. The opening of the

Lick Observatory also encouraged the formation of the Astronomical Society of the Pacific in February 1889, with Edward Holden, director of the Lick Observatory, as president. In a manner typical of the wider interest in astronomy in California, the society included both professional and amateur astronomers, together with businessmen such as William Alvord, president of the Bank of California, an early director of the society, who were interested in funding astronomical research. On 25 May 1889 the newly organized Astronomical Society of the Pacific met at the Lick Observatory atop Mount Hamilton, where the telescope was made available to the membership from seven until ten o'clock. Thus thirty-five amateur astronomers and interested lay people had the opportunity to gaze upon the heavens and to see sights that had never been seen before. For years to come, the Lick Observatory continued this policy of making the great telescope available to qualified amateurs and observatory patrons.

An early visitor to Lick Observatory, reaching there on 10 July 1890, was the twenty-two-year-old George Ellery Hale, a recent graduate of the Massachusetts Institute of Technology. Hale was on his honeymoon, having married Evelina Conklin, his childhood sweetheart, two days after graduation. After touring San Francisco and the Yosemite, the newlyweds journeyed to Mount Hamilton by stagecoach from San Jose, arriving at the summit on the hottest day of the year. Hale was welcomed by astronomer S. W. Burnham. Eight years earlier, back in Chicago, Burnham had provided the fourteen-year-old Hale with his first instruction. After the day's visit, during which Hale discussed his work on the solar corona with members of the Lick Observatory staff, astronomer James Keeler invited Hale to join him at the great telescope. For the rest of his life, Hale never forgot the sight of the gigantic apparatus balanced on its massive pier, guided by its intricate machinery, peering through the great dome to the heavens beyond.

It would be difficult at this point, his first visit to the West Coast, to say whether George Ellery Hale was an amateur or a professional, if such a distinction even mattered in California at that time. The next morning, in fact, Lick director Edward Holden, impressed by Hale's research into solar prominences, invited the young man to stay on as a volunteer, with access to the great telescope. In one side of his nature, Hale was, and remained throughout his life, the brilliant amateur. He had come to astronomy early, as a fourteen-year-old boy in search of a hobby, the privileged if frail son of a wealthy Chicago elevator manufacturer and real estate developer. (Among other notable projects, William Hale developed the Rookery, designed by Daniel Hudson Burnham, one of the great office buildings of the golden age of Chicago architecture.) After trying unsuccessfully to make his own telescope, George Ellery Hale sought out the assistance of S. W. Burnham, a talented Chicago astronomer then doing important research in twin stars. Burnham encouraged the boy's interest in astronomy and advised him to ask his father to buy him a secondhand four-inch Clark refractor telescope, which he could use to observe the transit of Venus on 6 December 1882. William Hale bought the telescope for his son, and George set it up in his backyard and observed the transit. His career as an astronomer began that simply.

Even as a teenaged hobbyist, however, George Ellery Hale showed a restlessness propelling toward the professional. Dissatisfied with mere observation, he constructed a spectroscope to attach to his telescope and began observing spectral lines. His delighted father bought him a professionally constructed spectroscope to replace the homemade device. "I shall never forget my delight," Hale later wrote, "when as a boy, I first learned of the spectroscope. Its extraordinary achievements, and the endless possibilities, vaguely imagined, of its further applications in astronomical research, filled me with enthusiasm, and kindled the strong desire for immediate work."[3] Hale continued to observe and to devour books and articles on astrophysics. In the summer of 1886, while on a tour of Europe with his parents, Hale secured an interview with the noted astronomer Jules Janssen, a pioneer in the field of solar spectroscopy, at the Meudon Observatory near Paris. In London, Hale's ever-supportive father bought him a Browning spectroscope.

Returning from Europe, Hale enrolled at MIT, where he concentrated in physics, chemistry, and mathematics, while giving his best energies to astronomy as a volunteer assistant at the Harvard Observatory. During vacation, he worked in his own laboratory in the attic of the family mansion on Drexel Boulevard in Chicago. For his senior thesis at MIT, a study of solar prominences, Hale invented a photographic device, later named the spectroheliograph, which allowed him to map solar tornados by capturing their spectral patterns on a photographic plate.

After Hale's graduation in May 1890, his marriage, and his honeymoon, he returned to Chicago, where his father, ever the backer of his brilliant son, presented him with an observatory designed by the distinguished architectural firm of Burnham and Root, located on family property in the Chicago suburb of Kenwood. Equipping the Kenwood Observatory with a twelve-inch lens and a telescope mounting sturdy enough to support an attached spectrograph, George Ellery Hale put aside thoughts of graduate study at Johns Hopkins and got to work, a talented and fully supported amateur. Within the year, he was elected a Fellow of the Royal Astronomical Society of Great Britain for his invention of the spectroheliograph and his study of solar prominences. In 1892 the University of Chicago offered him an associate professorship, to which Hale was initially ambivalent, not wishing to lose his independence. Even as a faculty member, however, Hale remained in his father's debt; for William Hale agreed with President William Rainey Harper to underwrite his son's research and to maintain the Kenwood Observatory as part of the university. Hale Senior also presented his son with a sixty-inch blank disc. Fourteen years later, Hale would have it ground and polished and mounted in a telescope atop Mount Wilson in Pasadena.

The psychological dynamics of the young astronomer's development are fascinating. William Hale, a self-made millionaire, did not demand that his son go into the elevator or real estate business; instead, he nurtured his son's interest in astronomy with gift after gift; and George Hale in turn met each gift with an even more brilliant level of performance. The Hales had lost two children before George was born, and George had been weak and sickly as a child. This would suggest one line of explanation: grateful parents, a powerful and highly endowed father especially, clearing a pathway for the cherished son. But was it all so clear? Were there no shadows against the light? George Ellery Hale's later breakdowns, so prolonged and debilitating, would seem to argue otherwise.

The cultural dynamics of the Hale relationship, father and son, by contrast, are more clear-cut and paradigmatic. The Hale relationship, self-made father, academically accomplished son, epitomized a process that fascinated Henry Adams: the ability of Chicago in the 1880s to move from frontier to high culture within a decade. Visiting the Columbian Exposition in 1893, Adams noted with a mixture of snobbery and awe that the most astonishing thing about Chicago, this grand city set in the middle of the prairies, was that it was there in the first place. Had Adams met George Ellery Hale at the time of his visit, he would have encountered a perfect Chicago paradigm: an astronomer barely in his twenties, working out of his attic and backyard, and already a Fellow of the Royal Society.

In Hale's swift ascent, his Mozartian creativity, there are even larger implications. The Hales were New Englanders by background, the very type of New Englanders then in the process of creating Pasadena. Research by Stephen Sargent Visher in the 1940s has revealed a number of interesting patterns regarding the most creative scientists of the 1860–1920 era. Despite the fact that the first American Nobel laureate, Albert Michelson, was of Prussian-Jewish immigrant stock, a disproportionate number of outstanding scientists in the early twentieth century— starred scientists, in Visher's terminology—were of British descent. Within this category, an even larger number traced their ancestry to East Anglia, the region that had peopled most of New England in the Puritan era. More immediately, a disproportionate number traced their immediate origins to New England, followed by the Middle Atlantic states, dominated by New York. Because of its size, New York produced the most starred scientists in this period; yet Massachusetts, the seventh most populous state in the nation, ranked second. Even within that second place, Boston and its suburbs produced the highest yield. The majority of these starred scientists, moreover, came from business or professional families, with a disproportionate number being the children of Episcopalian, Presbyterian, Congregational, and Unitarian clergy. New Hampshire, Vermont, and Massachusetts, ground zero of the old Puritan ascendancy, led the nation in the production of astronomers.

The creativity of George Ellery Hale—Anglo-American in origin, affluent, urban and suburban in upbringing—fits into this larger American pattern. In the 1880s and 1890s a generation of Anglo-Americans, many of them children of ministers or otherwise possessed of family roots in the Puritan past, turned to science, with astronomy as a strong option, and university-based careers. High-minded Protestants who might have worked on behalf of abolition in the pre–Civil

War period or entered seminaries tended by the end of the nineteenth century to regard careers in pure science as comparable goals. Within this genre, moreover, astronomers represented the highest of the high-minded; for astronomy was, and remains, a discipline akin to philosophy and theology in its emphasis upon the pursuit of truth for its own sake. Like psychoanalysis, then being pioneered by Hale's brilliant contemporary Sigmund Freud, astronomy offered Hale's generation the chance for a long voyage into the unknown, for encounters with mysteries only dimly dreamed of in the past: the explosion of novas, the spinning of galaxies, endless spaces without, equally endless spaces within.

Given the New Englandism of science, as Visher has documented it, the intensely Anglo-American city of Pasadena would seem by the early 1900s to be in an excellent position to support a first-rate scientific institution. Astronomy, in fact, had already come, indirectly, to Pasadena with the opening of the Lowe Observatory in 1894 under the direction of Lewis Swift, the famed comet seeker. Thaddeus Lowe, the civilian head of the Balloon Corps in the Union Army during the Civil War, left his native New Hampshire for Pasadena in the early 1880s and prospered as a real estate investor and developer. Among Lowe's projects: the Mount Lowe Incline Railway, which lifted passengers to the top of nearby Echo Mountain, where Lowe built Echo Mountain House, an alpine hostelry that entertained some three million guests—food, refreshments, an overnight stay—in the forty-one years of its operation. As a boy in New Hampshire, Lowe had fallen in love with the stars; indeed, had he been born twenty years later, he might have joined Hale's generation of astronomers. As it was, Lowe decided to build and staff his own observatory.

With the help of Harvard president Charles Eliot, who was wont to spend the winter vacation in Southern California during this period, Lowe searched for the best location on Echo Mountain. Interestingly enough, one of Eliot's professors, William Pickering of the Harvard Observatory, had visited Pasadena in 1889 and surveyed Mount Wilson as a possible satellite site. Pickering was enthusiastic about Mount Wilson and had a telescope installed on its summit. It took a month to get the twenty-seven-hundred-pound telescope to the top of the peak via horse, sled, and block and tackle. Harvard later abandoned its plans for a satellite observatory atop Mount Wilson, however, and shipped the telescope back to Cambridge.

George Ellery Hale first explored Mount Wilson in the spring of 1903 in the company of W. W. Campbell, director of the Lick Observatory and later president of the University of California. The Lick Observatory had already sent astronomer W. J. Hussey to Australia and New Zealand to scout possible sites for a satellite observatory, but to Hale's way of thinking, Southern California offered all the advantages of the Southern Hemisphere without the necessity of establishing operations on the other side of the globe. Hale returned to Pasadena in the winter of 1903–4, bringing along his wife and children. He spent most of this second visit scouting Mount Wilson, a mile-high promontory overlooking the Los Angeles Basin and the San Gabriel Valley, with a clear view of the Pacific Ocean fifty miles in the distance.

Two trails led to the summit: an ancient Indian pathway from the town of Sierra Madre via the canyon of the Little Santa Anita stream, and a road from the mouth of Easton's Canyon in Altadena, cut by the Pasadena and Mount Wilson Toll Road Company and zigzagging up the craggy southern face. Atop Mount Wilson, Hale found the Casino, a rambling structure built of cedar logs in 1893 as a mountain resort but subsequently abandoned. Delighted by this haphazard observatory, Hale spent his first night atop Mount Wilson lying on his cot, gazing through the partially fallen roof of the Casino at the stars overhead, thinking of the observatory to come.

On the last day of February in the leap year 1904, Hale and a hired carpenter winterized the Casino, with Hale, a skilled craftsman, doing his fair share of the work. In early March, Hale returned to the Casino with a colleague and a small coelostat ground telescope and began systematic observations. Two more Yerkes staff members joined the Casino in May. Was Hale establishing a colony of the Yerkes Observatory or raiding its personnel for a new institution? By the spring of 1904, he had already sunk $35,000 of his own money into the venture. Running ahead of any formal support or authorization, Hale secured a ninety-nine-year lease in his own name from the Pasadena and Mount Wilson Toll Road Company for acreage on the peak, rent free. Delighted with the prospect of a busy observatory atop Mount Wilson, the toll road company was more than willing to subsidize the Chicago astronomer. (In Southern California, everything, even astronomy, had a way of getting down to questions of real estate development.)

Meanwhile, Hale was in dialogue with the newly established Carnegie Institution in Washington for formal support of a sixty-inch reflector telescope on Mount Wilson. He had already secured permission from patron Helen Snow to borrow from the Yerkes Observatory the Snow Telescope, a coelostat mirror that reflected its image horizontally to a photographic lens through a tube sixty-one and a half feet in length. Disassembled, the Snow Telescope was shipped by rail to Pasadena, then carried piece by piece to the peak by pack mules, block and tackle, and a horse-drawn dray wagon designed at a tilt for mountain ascent. Hale had the Snow Telescope operational by early 1904 and began a study of sunspots. In October the Carnegie Institution awarded him $150,000 (soon increased to $310,000) for the construction of a sixty-inch reflector. The date of this grant, 20 December 1904, constituted the founding of Mount Wilson Observatory as a freestanding observatory under the auspices of the Carnegie Institution. Two weeks later, Hale resigned the directorship of the Yerkes Observatory and his University of Chicago professorship. He was now a full-time Pasadenan.

Next came the challenging task of mounting the sixty-inch reflector lens William Hale had presented to his son a decade earlier. Ever resourceful, Hale persuaded the city of Pasadena to donate to the observatory two lots on Santa Barbara

Street for an optical laboratory designed by the promising young Pasadena architect Myron Hunt. There, the blank disc was laboriously polished into the largest
astronomical lens in the world, while its intricate mounting was designed for construction by the Union Iron Works in San Francisco. The finished steel, all 150
tons of it, was shipped from San Francisco to Pasadena by rail, then hauled up
Mount Wilson, piece by piece, by mule train, block and tackle, and mountain
truck, a task completed by late November 1907. By 7 December 1908 the sixty-
inch mirror was at last installed in its telescope, which was itself mounted in a
150-foot tower. On 20 December 1908, four years after Mount Wilson was established, George Ellery Hale was taking photographs of the Orion Nebula through
what was now the most powerful telescope on the planet.

But what of Pasadena on the plain below? Of what relevance to this city of fifteen
thousand inhabitants, with its vineyards and orange groves, were the stargazers
atop Mount Wilson? There might have been no connection whatsoever. Academic history offers numerous examples of remote research centers that had little
effect on surrounding communities. Thanks to George Ellery Hale, however, the
Mount Wilson Observatory would soon, very soon, be boosting Pasadena into a
new level of civic maturity. First of all, unlike the Lick Observatory, the astronomers and staff of Mount Wilson did not establish a separate mountaintop community. They lived with their families, rather, in Pasadena, and became integrated
into the daily life of the town. When on duty at Mount Wilson, the astronomers
went into bachelor's digs at the Monastery, a dormitory designed by Myron Hunt
and sited on a ridge next to a sheer precipice, with a stunning view of canyons
and mountains.

George Ellery Hale loved Pasadena from the first: its sweeping boulevards, its
stately homes, its sunshine and mountain vistas, the orange blossoms and flowers
whose scent rose from the valley floor halfway up Mount Wilson. On New Year's
Day, the city turned out for a Tournament of Roses parade of floral floats, followed by chariot races, a college football game, and a grand reception in the
evening. Hale, a bibliophile, loved the bookishness of Pasadena people and their
continuing connection to New England ways. In their lingering Yankeeness, Pasadenans loved projects of community improvement, no matter how quirky. In the
1890s, for example, the city constructed an elevated wooden cycleway from Colorado Street to the Raymond Hill, so that residents might ride their bicycles safe
from horse-drawn traffic. Then there was the Throop Polytechnic Institute,
founded in 1891 by Amos Throop, a Chicago businessman with a passion for
crafts. Throop offered a high school and junior college curriculum, with instruction in the practical arts.

As might be expected, the Hales were immediately accepted into the upper
reaches of Pasadena life. Evelina Hale joined the Visiting Nurse Society, the
Pasadena Hospital Guild, the Coleman Chamber Music Society, the Pasadena
Garden Club, and the Pasadena Playhouse. George joined the Valley Hunt Club

and the Twilight Club, a dining society that met monthly to hear scholarly essays. He formed a close friendship with Charles Frederick Holder, the naturalist-sportsman formerly on the staff of the Museum of Natural History in New York, who had played a prominent role in the founding of the Tournament of Roses, the Valley Hunt Club, and the Tuna Club on Santa Catalina Island. (It was in the course of a conversation one evening in Holder's book-lined study that the idea first surfaced of transforming the Throop Polytechnic Institute into a more ambitious institution.) Hale also became active in the Pasadena Board of Trade, the equivalent of a Chamber of Commerce. In the fall of 1907, he exchanged his first home for the home in South Pasadena of his physician, James McBride. Called Hermosa Vista, the Comely View (all Pasadena and South Pasadena manses had names), the large shingle-style structure on Bellefontaine Street emanated a sense of well-being and taste, Pasadena style. Hale devoted the floor of one wing of the rambling mansion to his large personal library, where he did his research, wrote his many books, and continued to read widely in English, American, and European literature. In another room, he installed an 8.5 inch telescope, through which he could monitor current construction at the Mount Wilson Observatory.

In the course of promoting funds from the Carnegie Institution (and dissuading it from backing an alternate observatory in the Southern Hemisphere), Hale had used Pasadena as part of his argument, making much of its wealth and gentility and future prospects as an educational center. He now became the prime catalyst of his adopted community. Over the next decade, he spearheaded the virtual refounding of the city via a fourfold line of attack: the continuing success of the Mount Wilson Observatory, the transformation of the Throop Polytechnic Institute into a first-rate scientific institution, the upgrading of Henry Huntington's private library into a humanities research center open to scholars, and the master-planning and construction of a new Civic Center.

When Theodore Roosevelt visited Pasadena in March 1911, he specifically praised Hale as a noted scientist who was an equally impressive man of affairs. What Roosevelt had in mind, among other things, was the role Hale was playing in the refounding of the Throop Polytechnic Institute. As early as January 1904, barely a week or two after his arrival in Pasadena, Hale was lecturing on the evolution of the stars to a large audience at Throop in an effort to gain the good will of Pasadenans for the proposed observatory and, of equal importance, to enlist local oligarchs as donors. Hale quickly perceived that the fortunes of his observatory, the fortunes of Pasadena, and the fortunes of Throop Polytechnic were intertwined. Almost immediately upon his arrival, he became a trustee of the institution.

In January 1907, in a speech at Throop, Hale went public with his dream of transforming Throop into a nationally ranked college of science and technology. That meant shedding the preparatory department, putting aside the emphasis on manual arts, and reforming the curricula. That June, under Hale's leadership, the

Throop trustees issued a series of rigid new requirements emphasizing mathematics, basic sciences, and electrical engineering. The next year, Hale engineered the appointment of James Scherer, a literary scholar whom he had met at Andrew Carnegie's castle in Scotland, to the presidency. Although not a scientist, Scherer was a proven fundraiser and administrator. As a Chicagoan, Hale thoroughly understood the relationship between institutional excellence and fine architecture. At his prompting, architects Myron Hunt and Elmer Grey were invited to commence a campus plan, which by the 1930s had guided the development of one of the most beautiful academic complexes in the nation. In the spring of 1910 the entire student body of Throop, five hundred strong, was asked to attend other institutions. The preparatory department was separated into the Polytechnic High School. Astonishingly, Hale, Scherer, and the other like-minded trustees under Hale's influence had the temerity, the courage, to detach Throop from its clientele, hence its cash flow, and begin anew. That fall, Throop reopened its doors to a select thirty-one students.

At this point, Throop almost became a public institution. In 1911 a bill was introduced into the legislature calling for the establishment of a California Institute of Technology as part of the state university system. The Board of Trustees of Throop, Hale included, feared that such an institution, with an initial budget of a million dollars, ten times the budget of Throop, would swamp their fledgling institute. The board offered to turn Throop over to the state and make it a public campus. Fearing competition from a publicly supported Throop Institute, David Starr Jordan, president of Stanford, and Benjamin Ide Wheeler, president of the University of California, lobbied for the defeat of the bill in the state senate in March 1911. This left Throop on its own, a private institution, but it also prevented the creation of a publicly supported science-oriented university in Southern California until the rise of UCLA following the Second World War. Thus Throop had both pure science and Southern California to itself from 1911 until the 1950s. Whatever there was of scientific ambition in Southern California would of necessity be focused on this Pasadena institution. Acknowledging its flagship status, the trustees voted in 1920 to rename their institution the California Institute of Technology.

Sitting next to Henry Huntington at a banquet soon after his arrival in Pasadena, Hale broached the idea to the arch-oligarch of transforming his private library and art collection located in San Marino in a building designed by Myron Hunt into a full-fledged research institution comparable to the Mount Wilson Observatory: a pure research institution, that is, whose fellows and visiting scholars would have no teaching duties. Hale continued the conversation with Huntington at a subsequent luncheon at the California Club in Los Angeles, taking the opportunity to interest Huntington in Mount Wilson as well. (For a while, Huntington was considering the possibility of linking Mount Wilson with Mount Lowe via a second incline railway.) Huntington took his time mulling over Hale's proposal, but in May 1927, a few weeks before his death, Huntington signed a legal instrument organizing and endowing his collection on the lines suggested by Hale, who must thus be given some credit for the creation of this third (after Mount Wilson and Cal Tech) Pasadena institution.

For the planning and architectural improvement of Pasadena, Hale showed equal energy. Hale, after all, had come of age in the golden age of Chicago architecture and planning. Daniel Hudson Burnham had not only designed the Rookery for Hale's father but had become a close family friend. Burnham would eventually design the dome for the hundred-inch Hooker Telescope atop Mount Wilson, bringing the classicism of the Chicago World's Fair to a remote mountaintop in Southern California, and would work closely with Hale in planning the new headquarters building in Washington, D.C., for the National Academy of Sciences. Visiting Greece in the summer of 1913, encountering its grand ruins, thinking of Burnham and Chicago as well, Hale resolved to involve himself in planning for a new and better Pasadena: a Pasadena that would cohere around a grand city hall and civic center in the style of the City Beautiful, while at the same time preserving the sequestered suburbanism of its manse-lined boulevards. Thanks in significant part to Hale's work on the Pasadena Civic Improvement Committee, a spectacular classical-Iberian city hall, designed by Bakewell and Brown of San Francisco, together with attendant gardens and boulevards, was planned and built in the late 1920s.

What was this affinity, this synergy, between George Ellery Hale and his adopted city? Why was he able, especially in the early years, to stimulate so much high-minded development, to refashion Pasadena into a scientific Athens amidst the orange groves? Pasadena, first of all, was ready for development, as was the rest of Southern California. This was a time—and a place!—when men and women were able to translate their dreams and ambitions into reality with an apparent ease that makes subsequent generations envious. In a city that prized social status, Hale epitomized the Anglo-American upper middle class at a time of its most expansive activity as, among other things, it was creating the modern American research university between 1880 and 1920. For Hale and his colleagues, astronomy in general, Mount Wilson in particular, were offering a generational challenge to young men (and some women) of their class and caste in a meridian period of achievement. Atop Mount Wilson, they attired themselves in bush jackets, jodhpurs, puttees, Baden-Powell hats, pistols, and hunting knives as if they were officers on campaign. Theodore Roosevelt would have found them a bully group, Gibson Men, Stovers from Yale, stepping from the pages of a novel by Richard Harding Davis. Hale considered his colleagues a fraternity, a brotherhood, with almost a mystical dimension to their association in the service of pure science.

Fascinated by George Curzon's accounts of the monasteries of the Levant, poised on their rocky peaks, Hale chose a comparable site for his Mount Wilson Monastery, with a stunning view of the San Gabriel Mountains. To design it, he retained the services of no less than Myron Hunt, architect *par excellence* of Anglo-America in its exuberant yet tasteful Southern California identity. Hunt designed a residence suggestive of the sort of monastery to which such Renaissance humanists as Pico della Mirandola and Marsilio Ficino (or their chronicler John Addington Symonds, for that matter!) might ensconce themselves to discuss neo-Platonic theory. Hunt embellished the walls and door with mystic insignia, much of it Egyptian in inspiration, and within, at Hale's suggestion, he emplaced an oversized fireplace of local granite. On their first night in the new facility, Hale and his astronomers dedicated the building with monastic rituals. Lighted candles in hand, they walked down from the Casino at nightfall and stoked a great fire in the Monastery, before which they sat talking late into the night. The Monastery soon became an international senior common room, an elite fellowship, for those who qualified. Here, before the great fire, the best astronomers of the world talked shop, whether the specifics of optics, photography, mechanical engineering—or the profound question of where the universe came from and how it evolved.

Hale sought to create a college of astronomy in direct succession to those of ancient Mesopotamia, Egypt, or Greece, with all that such mystic associations implied for Hale and his entire generation. With a touch of obscurantism, Hale described himself as a sun-worshipper and was delighted when the New York *Times* called him "Priest of the Sun, Zoroaster of our time." One of Hale's closest friends was the University of Chicago Egyptologist James Breasted, with whom Hale and his family visited Egypt in January 1911. Through Breasted and through his own researches, Hale became especially sensitive to the linkage between religion and astronomy in Egyptian culture. In the spring of 1923, Hale and Breasted returned to Egypt for a second visit. In London, Breasted purchased from an antique dealer an Egyptian device for measuring the transit of planets and stars: a rectangular strip of ebony wood, ten and a half inches long, with astronomical designations, used in conjunction with a plumb line. Breasted believed the instrument to have been made by Tutankhamen himself.

After he retired from the active direction of the Mount Wilson Observatory in March 1922, Hale commissioned Myron Hunt to design for him a private Solar Laboratory on the grounds of his new home in Pasadena. The structure was completed in March 1925. Hale furnished it with the twelve-inch lens, spectroheliograph, lathe, milling machine, circular saw, and grinder from the Kenwood Observatory where he had begun his career, borrowing this equipment back from the Yerkes Observatory. After a brilliant public career, George Ellery Hale was once again the gentleman amateur and the Solar Laboratory a fitting refuge for the Priest of the Sun. A bas-relief of the Egyptian pharaoh Ikhnaton driving his chariot toward the sun god Aton was emplaced above the fireplace, along with a bust of Nefertiti. Above the front door was another Aton image: sun rays flowing into hands grasping the symbol of life, an image copied from a Theban tomb. The Priest of the Sun had become a monk in his cell. There, Hale gave himself fully to the poetry and mysticism of astronomy as well as to its science in a series of books directed toward the general reader: *The New Heavens* (1922), *The Depths of the Universe* (1924), *Beyond the Milky Way* (1926), *Signals from the Stars* (1931).

Hale belonged to a generation of academics nurtured on the classics who seemed incapable of writing a bad sentence. In his scholarship, with its ever-present linkages to history and religion, Hale became the very paradigm of Protestant Pasadena: the most accomplished general intellectual that Pasadena would ever produce—and in no instance more typically Pasadenan, more linked to the high-minded culture of the city, than in his efforts to integrate religion and science. Hale did not equate astronomy with religion. He knew the difference. He praised the Greeks, for instance, for detaching astronomy from religion and putting it on a systematic scientific basis. On the other hand, Hale did not consider science to be locked in opposition to religion either. (The MIT of Hale's era was not anti-religious. Phillips Brooks gave the baccalaureate sermon in Trinity Church for Hale's graduating class.) Astronomy, Hale believed, led toward, not away from, divinity.

Fluent in Italian (Hale could quote Italian poetry flawlessly), Hale revered Dante as a poet who brought into conjunction high theological ambitions with the best astronomical knowledge of his time. Ascending Mount Wilson in the company of the Italian astronomer Giorgio Abetti, director of the Arcetri Observatory above Florence, Hale quoted a string of astronomical passages from the *Divine Comedy*. He revered John Milton for similar reasons, as well as Galileo, who had served both science and religion, in the higher sense of that term, throughout his career. In *The Depths of the Universe* (1924) Hale praised Galileo as the model for his own professional quest. One of the high points of his life, Hale wrote, came in the spring of 1923 when he and Breasted, returning from Egypt, were allowed by the rector of the Royal Astrophysical Observatory in Florence to observe the moon, Saturn, and Jupiter and its four satellites through two of Galileo's telescopes. Hale loved the moment Galileo described in his *The Sidereal Messenger* (1610) of his first glimpse through the newly invented telescope at the Milky Way. "Thus arose a new and vast conception of an ordered cosmos," Hale writes in *Signals from the Stars*, "involving the countless spiral nebulae far beyond our own galactic island, in which the solar system is as a grain of sand. In this conception we may glimpse the imprint of a creator, infinitely above the tribal deities of early man, whose immutable laws it is our first duty and greatest advantage to discover and to obey."[4]

Hale, moreover, was a staunch stellar evolutionist. The very same year, 1908, that the sixty-inch reflector went into operation on Mount Wilson, the University of Chicago Press published Hale's monumental *The Study of Stellar Evolution*, its introduction bearing a "Pasadena, November 1907" dateline, making this the first important scientific work to take Pasadena as its point of origin. Aligning himself with Charles Darwin, Hale probed questions only then emerging in the speculations of astronomers and astrophysicists: how did the universe evolve, and where did stars come from? The spiral nebulae, Hale wrote, now visible through the great telescopes, offered the best empirical clues. Thanks to the power of the James Lick Telescope, astronomer James Keeler had discovered at the close of the century that fully half of the 120,000 nebulae strewn across the heavens were spiral in form. The universe was disclosing its genesis, its founding pattern. These vast star spirals suggested cosmic shapings and condensations over the eons, a dance to the music of time, orderly and progressive, through which the elements of the universe were continuing to arrange themselves into galaxies.

The dream of a hundred-inch telescope kept Hale in Southern California, kept him from relocating permanently in the East as the *de facto* doge of American science. In 1902, at the age of thirty-three, Hale was elected to the National Academy of Sciences, the youngest scientist to be elected since the academy was founded during the Civil War. Hale soon rose to leadership in the academy and over the next thirty years played a key role in turning it from a loosely organized honor society into a major force in American science, headquartered in an impressive Washington building, planned by Burnham, designed by Bertram Grosvenor Goodhue, catalyzed by Hale himself, with a portrait of Hale by Seymour Thomas eventually holding the place of honor in the atrium. In January 1904, when Hale was camping out atop Mount Wilson, he was awarded the Gold Medal of the Royal Astronomical Society of Great Britain for his pioneering work in photographing the surface of the sun, an astonishing honor for an astronomer barely into his thirties. In 1906 he was all but offered the secretaryship of the Smithsonian Institution, but he turned away from that possibility in favor of continuing to develop the Mount Wilson Observatory. In the early 1920s, he would turn down the presidency of the Carnegie Institution. In July 1908 Albert Michelson lobbied the Nobel Committee in Sweden for a Nobel Prize for Hale in physics, since no Nobel Prize had been established in astronomy. (In his will Alfred Nobel had explicitly excluded astronomy from his bequest, having once bitterly quarreled with an astronomer.) Eventually, the Nobel Committee would make awards in astrophysics, but for the time being it regarded Hale's work as too purely astronomical in character. In 1910 Hale was elected to membership in the Royal Society of London, and Oxford awarded him an honorary doctorate. A survey conducted in 1914 determined that Hale was one of the twelve best-known scientists in the United States.

Beginning in the spring of 1916, Hale began to spend increasingly more time in Washington, where he stimulated the creation of the National Research Council under the auspices of the National Academy of Sciences to coordinate the scientific effort necessary once the United States entered the war, which Hale saw as inevitable. Working closely with Robert Millikan, professor of physics at Chicago, and Arthur Noyes, professor of chemistry at MIT and Hale's undergraduate mentor, Hale used the National Research Council, energized by wartime urgency, to create, for the first time, a national scientific establishment, linked to government and the university world, fueled by public spending. For the rest of the century, this establishment held itself in place.

Clearly, George Ellery Hale was needed in the East; yet despite long sojourns in Washington and frequent trips to New York, he remained in Pasadena, for it was there that the crowning achievement of his career, the hundred-inch telescope, was edging toward fulfillment. In the summer of 1906, two years before the sixty-inch telescope was in place, Hale was already launching his hundred-inch venture in a series of conversations with John Hooker of Los Angeles, a hardware and steel pipe millionaire then serving as president of the Western Union Oil Company. Hooker lived in a mansion on West Adams, then the district of fashion and wealth. An amateur astronomer, he maintained his own telescope in his back garden and invited Hale for lunch at the California Club to talk shop. With Evelina Conklin Hale resting in a sanitarium in the summer of 1906 (trouble in paradise?), Hale was spending a lot of time at the Hooker mansion, attracted there, if the truth were told, by the company of Katherine Putnam Hooker, Hooker's charming wife, and Katherine's friend Alicia Mosgrove. With these two attractive and accomplished women, Hale formed a kind of Hearts of Three intimacy, which John Hooker barely, just barely, tolerated.

Blue-blooded and blue-stockinged, the two women might have stepped out of a novel by Henry James, William Dean Howells, or Francis Marion Crawford. Katherine Putnam Hooker was of New England descent. She adored Italian culture, like Hale, and had written a travel book, *Wayfarers in Italy* (1902), whose philo-Italianizing dovetailed perfectly with the current concept of Southern California as, in Henry James's phrase, an Italy awaiting its history. Alicia Mosgrove, to whom Hale was especially attracted, was like Hale an energetically engaged personality. Active in the park and recreation movement, she had climbed Mount Whitney with John Muir, sailed to Tahiti by yacht, and traveled a thousand miles down the Nile in an Egyptian boat with a native crew. When Hale met her, Alicia, whom Hale called Ellie, was serving as a director of the California Institution for Women in Tehachapi and was opening a progressive school in Los Angeles.

Hale was thirty-six years old at the time, a handsome if slight man, Henry Adams–ish in appearance, holder of the Gold Medal of the Royal Academy of Astronomy, independently wealthy, the very paradigm of Progressive culture colonizing the Southland. One sees the three of them in the Hooker garden on West Adams, close in conversation, in the soft focus of a Merchant-Ivory film. The camera moves to close-ups of John Hooker and Evelina Hale as they, from a distance, view the magic circle from which they are excluded. To structure their relationship through playful narrative, Hale, Katherine, and Ellie sustained the running conceit that the three of them owned a saloon on the Embarcadero in San Francisco, with Alicia playing the gal behind the bar. It was all very harmless, a Pasadena–Los Angeles version of the Queen of Hearts Circle of Henry Adams,

Clarence King, John Hay, and their spouses. Yet Marian Adams had committed suicide, hadn't she? And out in Southern California, Mr. Hooker grew progressively estranged. And what did Mrs. Hale think, observing her husband and his two friends at parties, drawn off in their special circle, enjoying their private jokes?

Overhearing Hale talking animatedly with his wife and Alicia Mosgrove one weekend in the summer of 1906 regarding the possibilities of a hundred-inch telescope, John Hooker saw an opportunity to bring himself into the conversation, which continued after dinner. Hale informed Hooker that a hundred-inch telescope would be two and a half times more powerful than a sixty-inch—and seven times more powerful as a means of stellar spectroscopy. Hooker asked the obvious question. How much would such an instrument cost? Twenty-five thousand dollars, Hale replied, just to cast the disc. Four days later, Hooker contacted Hale, saying that he would donate $45,000 to the venture, provided the telescope be the largest in the world.

That September, Hooker ordered the casting of a hundred-inch disc from the the Plate Glass Company of St. Gobain in France. Never before had a disc of this magnitude been cast. The sixty-inch mirror for the Mount Wilson reflector was eight inches thick and weighed a ton. A hundred-inch disc would have to be thirteen inches thick and weigh five tons. Could this much glass be cast and annealed to the necessary purity? It was an open question. After repeated experiments, the St. Gobain Company achieved the impossible: a disc so large and so perfect as to rival the diamonds and crystals of nature. When it was being shipped to New York aboard the steamer St. Andrew, the New York Times described the lens as the single most valuable piece of merchandise ever to cross the Atlantic. From the docks of Hoboken, the disc was routed to New Orleans, then slowly by special freight train to Pasadena. The very day the sixty-inch reflector was set in place on Mount Wilson, 7 December 1908, the hundred-inch disc arrived in Pasadena for polishing.

It took nine years to polish the disc and design its unprecedented reflecting telescope, fifty feet in focal length, and attendant infrastructure, which was, in effect, a gigantic ultra-precise watch set inside the observatory designed by Daniel Hudson Burnham. Every piece of the mechanism had to be carted up Mount Wilson (fortunately, motorized trucks had come to the assistance of the mules) for an equally delicate assembly process. The smallest errors of weight or calibration could make the entire instrument useless.

On the night of 2 November 1917, joined by astronomer Walter Adams and the British poet Alfred Noyes, Hale took the first look through the Hooker telescope. Disaster! Six Jupiters in view! A sick feeling in the pit of everyone's stomach. Silence. More silence. What to do? The loss of ten years and hundreds of thousands of dollars stared everyone in the face. At long last, someone on the staff mentioned that workmen had left the dome open that day. The heat of the sun might have distorted the mirror! Hale and the others must now wait three or four hours while the mirror cooled. It was the longest wait of Hale's life. He tossed on his bed in the Monastery for three hours, fully dressed. Shortly after two-thirty in the morning, he and Adams reconvened at the telescope, which they focused on the brilliant blue star Vega. Cooled from the direct heat of the Southern California sun, the Hooker Telescope worked perfectly. Five years later, in *The Torch-Bearers* (1922), a history of astronomy in narrative verse that begins and ends on Mount Wilson with the setting into operation of the Hooker Telescope, Noyes suppressed the frightening first view of six Jupiters and the three-hour wait as the great disc cooled.

Receiving nearly three times as much light from the stars as its sixty-inch predecessor, the Hooker Telescope increased the observable universe by a factor approaching 300 percent. Turning the Hooker to the moon, Hale and his associates could practically walk on its surface, like characters in a Jules Verne novel. The Ring Nebula in Lyra and the Great Nebula in Orion presented themselves with a clarity never before known in human history. Galaxy M 81 in Ursa Major came into view; then Crab Nebula $\lambda6300-\lambda6700$, a gigantic configuration five light years in extent, formed by gases flung into space by a supernova star observed to have exploded in A.D. 1054. In *Beyond the Milky Way* Hale published a sequence of three photographs to demonstrate the power of the Hooker. The first showed a drawing by Sir John Herschel of the spiral Nebula M 51, followed by a more clarified drawing made by Lord Rosse in the nineteenth century, followed by a photograph made with the Hooker Telescope. Thanks to this mighty instrument, what was only dimly glimpsed now stood forth magnificently clarified.

Thanks, furthermore, to the observations, calculations, and theorizing of Mount Wilson astronomer Edwin Powell Hubble, the Hooker Telescope also helped make possible a startling new insight: the universe was in a state of constant expansion; and it was this discovery that brought Albert Einstein to Pasadena.

If, as the Visher study shows, science in general, and astronomy in particular, attracted Anglo-Americans to their ranks during this period, then Edwin Powell Hubble represented the perfection of the type. A champion boxer and a Rhodes scholar, Hubble had turned from the law to astronomy, finishing his doctorate at Chicago just before the United States entered the war. Rising to the command of an infantry battalion in the Eighty-sixth Division, Hubble joined the Mount Wilson staff at Hale's invitation upon his release from the Army as a lieutenant colonel. The very year Hubble took his degree at Oxford, 1912, Henrietta Leavitt, a Radcliffe College graduate working in the Harvard Observatory, made a simple but profound discovery. Examining photographs of the Lesser Magellanic Cloud taken by Harvard astronomers in Arequipa, Peru, Leavitt discovered that the large and brighter Cepheids were fluctuating more slowly than their smaller and fainter counterparts. The large Cepheids, moreover, took a longer time to reach their greatest brightness, then receded in luminosity. Intrigued by the brightness of the larger Cepheids and the duration of their pulsation, Leavitt closely examined hundreds of Harvard Observatory photographs and in the end formulated the law of period-luminosity. The apparent brightness of a star, Leavitt theorized, was not necessarily its intrinsic brightness. Stars at a further distance might very well be intrinsically brighter but seem dimmer from the perspective of Earth due to the factor of distance. It all sounded so simple—but for thousands of years astronomers had missed the point now being grasped by Henrietta Leavitt: intensities of light provided a measuring rod for distance.

As yet, these distances remained constant, at least as far as general astronomy—and Albert Einstein!—were concerned. Enter Edwin Powell Hubble. At Mount Wilson, Hubble took up the study of Cepheids. In 1923 he discovered a Cepheid variable in the Great Nebula in Andromeda. The Cepheid in question, Hubble established, was far beyond our own galaxy. Continuing his search, Hubble discovered Cepheids in numerous other nebulae, which he also established as extra-galactic. He then studied the patterns of distribution of extra-galactic nebulae from photographs of thirteen hundred selected areas of the heavens. The distribution of these extra-galactic nebulae was uniform. Hubble began to map the universe in terms of its galaxies. (Eventually, there would be a *Hubble Atlas of Galaxies*, with Hubble having placed his name, a cosmic Amerigo Vespucci, on the universe itself.)

Having established distribution and distance, Hubble began to pursue the question of movement. Using spectrograms of the galaxies obtained by V. M. Slipher at the Lowell Observatory at Harvard and M. L. Humason at Mount Wilson, Hubble studied red shifts in the spectra of extra-galactic objects and determined that they indicated recessional velocities directly proportional to distance. Now the big payoff, the next step, the leap beyond the observations of Henrietta Leavitt and the mathematics of Abbé Lemaitre! The galaxies, Hubble discovered, were receding from an original starting point, and they had been doing so for seven thousand million years at a constant rate—the Hubble Constant it would soon be called—at the speed of 500 km/sec per million parsecs, a velocity only mathematicians might comprehend.

Hubble's discovery of the constant and uniform expansion of the universe set the agenda for astronomy in the second half of the twentieth century. How could the universe be expanding, for one thing, and not run down? Would it eventually expand to a point of stasis and remain constant? Would it then die? Or would it collapse back upon itself? If it collapsed back on itself, would that be the end? Or would the process begin all over again in an infinitely repeated diastolic dance? Or was the universe expanding infinitely, as some would eventually theorize, constantly bringing new matter and energy into being? Was the universe eternal?

Profound questions, pushing astronomy and mathematics, as well as philosophy and theology, to new limits. Thanks in great part to George Ellery Hale, Pasadena had now become the world capital of astronomical observation and theory. Yet all this—Mount Wilson, the Hooker Telescope, Cal Tech, the Huntington, the Pasadena improvements, the national and international involvements, the whole vast enterprise—had not come without its cost for Hale, whose dramatic breakdowns constituted the dissonant counterpoint, the chiaroscuro, of his brilliant achievement. As a child, Hale had suffered from typhoid, dysentery, and colitis, the latter being especially indicative of his nervous temperament. Evelina Conklin Hale was of comparably delicate constitution and suffered her first breakdown in the summer of 1906, at a period when her husband was becoming increasingly involved in a friendship circle with Katherine Putnam Hooker and Alicia Mosgrove. In 1910 Evelina Hale suffered a second breakdown, followed by a relapse. In late March 1910 it became Hale's turn. He broke down and was advised by his physician to take a long outdoor vacation near Klamath Lake, followed by a leisurely visit to London and a tour of the Continent in the company of his friend Daniel Hudson Burnham. In the late summer of 1911, Hale suffered a relapse and was referred to a sanitarium in Bethel, Maine, where the psychiatrist put him to work sawing wood, gardening, and undergoing daily massages. John Hooker died in 1911, and the Hales summered in Santa Barbara near the widowed Katherine and her daughter Marian. Was Alicia Mosgrove on hand as well? In any event, Hale suffered a third relapse in March 1913 and returned to the Bethel sanitarium. In 1927 he returned to Bethel for his third stay and was there when he was awarded the gold medal by the Franklin Institute and offered the presidency of the National Academy of Sciences.

In the midst of it all, Hale remained wedded to his various Pasadena agendas. His genius, after all, was to provoke, to stimulate, to guide, and not necessarily to administer. As an undergraduate at MIT, Hale had studied chemistry under Arthur Noyes, a University of Leipzig Ph.D. who had helped produce the first generation of physical chemistry doctorates at MIT. In the spring of 1913 Hale recruited Noyes to spend part of each year at Cal Tech. After the war, the appointment became permanent. Hale also recruited his Chicago colleague Robert Millikan, the son of a Congregationalist minister, who, after majoring in physics and Greek at Oberlin, had taken his doctorate in physics at Columbia and done postdoctoral work under Max Planck at the University of Berlin, followed by further research in physical chemistry at Gottingen, before joining the physics department at the University of Chicago at the invitation of its chair, Nobel laureate Albert Michelson. At Chicago Millikan conducted experiments verifying Einstein's photoelectric equations and determining the numerical value of Planck's Constant, research that won him the Nobel Prize in 1923. In July 1916 Hale took Millikan to dinner at the Biltmore Hotel in New York (Millikan was teaching summer school at Columbia) and broached the idea of Millikan spending three months a year in Pasadena, where Hale wanted him to establish a laboratory of experimental physics. When James Scherer resigned as president of Cal Tech in February 1920, Millikan finally agreed to leave his beloved Chicago and come to Cal Tech on a permanent basis.

At Cal Tech, Millikan refused the title of president; indeed, he loathed the way the office of university president was developing in the United States, overloaded, in Millikan's opinion, with pomp, prerogatives, bureaucracy, and expense. He preferred instead the German system in which the faculty designated one of its more distinguished members to serve as rector, which is to say, chief spokesman for the faculty. Millikan believed that the strong university presidency as it was developing in the United States under the influence of the American corporation would stifle colleagueship and ultimately reduce the status of faculty to mere employees. In accepting the Cal Tech offer, Millikan expressly stipulated that he would continue as a research scientist in the department of physics, with the title of professor, while chairing the Executive Council. Within the Executive Council, the triumvirate of Hale, Noyes, and Millikan (memorialized today in an oil-painting group portrait in the atrium of the Athenaeum) exercised preeminent authority during the growth years of the 1920s and 1930s.

Like Hale, Robert Millikan was a man of upper-middle-class style, given to sweeping into the physics laboratory late at night in formal wear after an event at one or another club to check on his graduate students. Only one photograph of Millikan, Hale, and Noyes standing together at Cal Tech is known to exist. The photograph exudes the assurance of academic scientists at the dawning of a golden age. Each man wears a carefully tailored suit, a starched white shirt, a carefully tied necktie. Here is a new kind of American, the research scientist, the scientific administrator, senators and satraps of a new establishment, their assured presence bespeaking their equality to their counterparts in diplomacy, banking, and the law.

Nor was this triumvirate of Hale, Noyes, and Millikan reluctant to reach out and involve laymen, many of them Pasadenans, and to confer on them an equally distinctive mode of authority. Non-scientist businessmen such as Allan Balch, Henry Robinson, Harvey Mudd, and James Page sat confidently on the Executive Council, side by side with the scientists, in a model that melded faculty and trustee authority. Had Millikan followed the lead of Arthur Fleming, chairman of the board and chief benefactor of Cal Tech, in fact, he might have been able to recruit Albert Einstein on a permanent basis. In the spring of 1931, Fleming—impulsive, growingly erratic, heading for a breakdown, but still no one's fool—unilaterally offered Einstein $20,000 a year, together with an annuity for Mrs. Einstein, if Einstein would agree to accept the title of professor and visit Cal Tech annually for ten weeks. While shocked at the impulsiveness of this offer, the other trustees went along with it, sensing no doubt that no one better than Albert Einstein could symbolize the fact that Cal Tech was now playing in the major leagues. Millikan traveled to Berlin to discuss the offer with Einstein. Prompted by his wife, who loved the winter climate of Southern California, Einstein agreed to accept the offer of another winter at Cal Tech and continue discussions on the matter of a permanent appointment. But when Millikan finalized the offer, it was for a more prudent salary of $7,000, not the lavish $20,000 Fleming had promised. The newly established Institute of Advanced Studies at Princeton, meanwhile, had opened negotiations with Einstein with suggestions of being willing to outbid any other offer. In October 1933 Albert Einstein accepted a tenured appointment at the Institute of Advanced Studies at a salary of $15,000 a year.

No man deserved more credit for the creation of Cal Tech, Robert Millikan later claimed, than Henry Mauris Robinson, who joined the trustees of Throop Polytechnic in 1907 and served until his death thirty years later. Robinson was a typical Pasadenan of his sort: a lawyer from Ohio who had prospered in the general rise of the Far West as a merger specialist; a mining investor in Arizona; an investor in lumber (the Pacific Lumber Company); public utilities (Southern California Telephone, Pacific Light and Power, Southern California Edison, San Antonio Light and Power), the oil business (Union Oil), banking (First National Bank of Los Angeles), and shipbuilding (at Newport News, Virginia). Settling in 1906 into a beautiful Greene and Greene home in Pasadena just off Orange Grove Avenue, Robinson spent the rest of his life in various forms of public service, including an assignment to the Supreme Economic Council at the Paris Peace Conference, a stint in 1924 as American economic representative in Berlin, and membership on his friend Herbert Hoover's task force against the Depression. Robinson bore equal responsibility with Hale in persuading Henry Huntington to transform his private library into a research institution. When Huntington's right-hand man, attorney George Patton Sr. (father of the general), died a mere eighteen days after Huntington, Robinson succeeded to the chair of the Huntington trustees, a body that would include by the late 1930s Herbert Hoover, Edwin Hubble, Robert Millikan, and William Munro, Harkness Professor of History and Government at Cal Tech, thus further cementing the relationship between the two institutions.

It was the creation of the Cal Tech Associates by Robinson, investor Allan Balch, lawyer Henry O'Melveny, *Times* publisher Harry Chandler, physician Norman Bridge, and Millikan, meeting for lunch at the California Club in Los Angeles on 25 March 1925, that Millikan later considered the jumping-off point of the institute. Very shortly, the campus in its modern form began to take shape on twenty-two acres at Wilson Street and California Boulevard, property donated to Throop by Canadian-born Pasadenan Arthur Fleming, who for some years had been paying President Scherer's salary out of his own pocket. Fleming donated $4 million to build Millikan his research laboratory. In February 1928 Allan Balch and his wife turned over more than $1 million in Southern California Gas Company bonds, paid for the construction of the Athenaeum, and endowed a graduate school in geological sciences, for which Colonel Seeley Mudd and Charles Arms donated laboratories. In the decade to come, Mr. and Mrs. Joseph Dabney built a hall for humanities instruction, and Edward Harkness endowed the division of humanities. Mr. and Mrs. William Kerckhoff donated a biological laboratory for Professor Thomas Hunt Morgan. When Henry Mauris Robinson died in 1937, he left his entire estate to the Henry M. Robinson Laboratory of Astrophysics.

George Ellery Hale, meanwhile, was embarking on his last great project, the two hundred-inch telescope that would bear his name. Having been primarily responsible for the forty-inch refractor at Yerkes, and the sixty- and one hundred-inch reflectors on Mount Wilson, Hale devoted the 1920s—despite the headaches, the ulcerated cornea, the imminence of yet another breakdown!—to the two-hundred-inch telescope, a heroic venture to cap a heroic career. As early as 1919, thrilled by the success of the Hooker Telescope, Hale and Mount Wilson astronomer Francis Pease were discussing an even larger instrument. Pease went so far as to design a three-hundred-inch reflector. In the April 1928 *Harper's*, Hale went public with his plans in an essay, "The Possibilities of Large Telescopes," in which he discussed, in some technical detail, the astronomic possibilities—and the technical difficulties—of such an instrument. Once again, Hale showed his skill in marshaling a larger audience behind astronomy as a venture on the cutting edge of human development. Sending an advance copy of the essay to Wickliffe Rose, president of the Rockefeller Foundation, Hale began the laborious process of lobbying funds. In the fall of 1928, the International Education Board of the Rockefeller Foundation came through with a $6 million grant for construction purposes only. Trustee Henry Mauris Robinson pledged $3 million to the establishment of an operating endowment and to the creation of a program in astronomy and astrophysics at Cal Tech.

Now began the epic of design and construction of the new observatory, to be operated jointly by Cal Tech and the Carnegie Institution. Despite his shaky health, Hale chaired the Observatory Council responsible for the project. Once again, Hale did what he did so well, select staff: Mount Wilson astronomer John Anderson to be executive officer, the renowned Russell Porter of Vermont to serve as chief designer, Navy Captain Clyde McDowell to serve as supervising engineer. The Rockefeller grant included three buildings on the Cal Tech campus, an astrophysics laboratory, and machine and optical shops. The buildings were operative by the summer of 1933, and it was there, on the Cal Tech campus in Pasadena, that the most powerful lens in the history of the human race was pushed toward completion during the Depression years: yet another instance of the astonishing creativity of California during these economically troubled times. On 21 September 1934, after a number of surveys, an observatory site was selected atop the 6,126-foot Mount Palomar in north central San Diego County in the center of the Cleveland National Forest.

As in the case of the Hooker Telescope, or the telescopes at the Lick and Yerkes observatories for that matter, the casting and polishing of the disc presented the greatest challenges. Initial plans called for the two-hundred-inch mirror to be cast in quartz, despite the fact that the largest quartz disc previously made had only been twenty-two inches. By the end of 1929, however, with the cracking of a sixty-inch experimental quartz disc at the laboratories of General Electric in upstate New York, Hale began negotiations with the Corning Glass Works of New York regarding the possibilities of a Pyrex disc. General Electric, meanwhile, succeeded in casting a sixty-inch quartz disc but informed Hale that a two-hundred-inch disc in quartz could cost as much as $2.5 million, and even then the outcome remained chancy. Hale resumed negotiations with Corning Glass. By January 1932 the Observatory Council had finalized discussions with Corning Glass regarding a Pyrex reflector that would be evolved through 30-, 60-, 120-, and 180-inch stages before a two-hundred-inch disc was cast. Corning put the price tag for the two hundred-inch Pyrex disc at approximately $300,000.

Because a two-hundred-inch Pyrex reflector would weigh forty-two tons and thus would bend or crack under its own weight when rotated, Francis Pease recommended that its non-reflecting side be hollowed in geometric proportions like a waffle or a honeycomb. Successfully poured at the Corning factory on Sunday, 25 March 1934, and annealed in an igloo-like structure of silica brick and cement, the two-hundred-inch disc was followed by the pouring of a second backup disc on 2 December 1934. By January 1936 the first disc had annealed—the work of eons, the fusing of a crystal, the making of a diamond over geological time, done in less than two years—and was ready for shipment by rail to the air-conditioned optical laboratory at Cal Tech. Wrapped in felt, cushioned with sponge rubber, protected by a steel-plated crate, the disc began its transcontinental train journey on 26 March 1936 and arrived in Pasadena on 10 April. The opticians began their grinding. Two imperfections were discovered just below the surface but disappeared as the grinding continued. By 1938 more than five tons of glass had been ground away from the twenty ton blank. Site preparation and preliminary construction, meanwhile, was underway on Mount Palomar. The great dome was finished by 1938, yet one more impressive public work in a miraculous decade of construction.

George Ellery Hale, meanwhile, had reentered Las Encinas sanitarium and was there as the polishing of the Pyrex disc continued and the Westinghouse engineers were busy completing the tube, the yoke, and the bearing parts of the Palomar telescope. In April 1937 Albert Einstein was on hand to celebrate the completion of the fifty-five-foot, 125-ton tube. In mid-February 1938 Hale looked out of his window at the Las Encinas sanitarium and said: "It is a beautiful day. The sun is shining, and they are working on Palomar."[5] A few days later, 21 February 1938, at one thirty in the afternoon, George Ellery Hale made his final journey to the light. Ten years later, after a wartime delay, the Hale Telescope was dedicated at the Mount Palomar Observatory. The Hale Telescope brought a thousand million galaxies within range of observation. Each of these galaxies contained some hundred thousand million planetary systems. With the Hale telescope, astronomers might now observe a near-infinity of new worlds. From a remote hilltop in the backcountry of San Diego County, the human race now enjoyed a visual connection to one half the observable universe. For nearly seventy years, Californians had been seeking such a connection through astronomy. George Ellery Hale had brought them there: had led them from a hilltop in Pasadena unto the stars themselves.

4

Gibraltar of the Pacific

San Diego Joins the Navy

*I*N early 1931 literary journalist Edmund Wilson visited San Diego. Wilson jotted into his notebooks specific instances of the suicide epidemic gripping the city and later fashioned these notes into an article for the *New Republic* entitled "The Jumping-Off Place," which he included in his Depression panorama *The American Jitters: A Year of the Slump* (1932). Between January 1911 and January 1927, Wilson pointed out, more than five hundred people had committed suicide in San Diego, giving that remote urban enclave (population 148,000 in 1930) the highest suicide rate in the United States. Much of this, Wilson admitted, could be explained by the fact that so many critically ill people had come to San Diego in a desperate last-ditch effort to recover their health and committed suicide when they lost all hope. But the Depression was an even more important factor. While there were fifty seven suicides in San Diego in 1926, there were seventy-one in the first nine months of 1930, and the toll had reached thirty-six by the end of the first quarter of 1931, when Wilson was writing. "These coroner's records in San Diego are melancholy reading," Wilson wrote. "You seem to see the last blind feeble futile effervescence of the great burst of the American adventure. Here this people, so long told to 'go West' to escape from poverty, ill health, maladjustment, industrialism and oppression, discover that, having come West, their problems and diseases still remain and that there is no further to go."[1]

Without fudging or distorting his facts, Edmund Wilson was being highly selective, as is always the case when reporters focus their story. In its *noir* dimension, San Diego might very well be what Wilson found it, the jumping-off point, the end of the line, persistently unfulfilled beneath an empty California sun. On the other hand, the majority of people living in San Diego, city and county alike, were finding it—even in the Depression—the best possible place to be. Between

1930 and 1940, San Diego County experienced a 38 percent growth rate, from 209,700 to 289,300, and the City of San Diego a growth rate of 37.3 percent, from 148,000 to 203,300. California, meanwhile, was growing by 21.6 percent and the nation by a mere 7.2 percent. Even such a skeptical observer as Wilson could not equate all this growth, a total of 134,900 new San Diegans, with the unhealthy, the losers, the people on the verge of jumping off to oblivion.

A depressed city, after all, would not have been able, as San Diego was, to pass a city bond issue to provide $300,000 for a municipal golf course and tennis courts in Balboa Park, or to authorize $150,000 a year to improve its harbor, or issue $3.6 million in bonds to improve its water system, or construct an impressive Spanish-style campus for San Diego State College, or restore Mission San Diego, or enlarge Lindbergh Field, where Pacific Air Transport, later part of United Air Lines, and American Airways, predecessor of American Air Lines, were even then connecting San Diego to Phoenix, Los Angeles, and Seattle—all of which happened in the early 1930s. Nor, toward the end of the decade, to build with federal assistance a $2 million administration building in the Civic Center, dedicated on 16 July 1938 by no less than President Roosevelt himself, just before FDR boarded the USS *Houston* for an equatorial cruise. Despite the Depression, San Diegans continued to flock to the Fox Theater in the downtown, the third largest movie palace on the Pacific Coast; and, after its opening on 3 July 1937, to flock to the Del Mar Race Track owned and developed by Rancho Santa Fe resident Bing Crosby, his Hollywood pal Pat O'Brien, and William Quigley of La Jolla. The very next year, before an electrified crowd, Seabiscuit won over Ligaroti in a $25,000 winner-take-all race that—along with the presence of Crosby, O'Brien, Loretta Young, Mickey Rooney, Gary Cooper, and a score of other turf-loving Hollywood stars—put Del Mar on the racing map.

Eleven San Diego banks were back in operation by the end of 1933. The Navy and the Army, meanwhile, were pumping millions of dollars into construction projects. Then came the most brilliant coup of all: the wholesale removal of the Consolidated Aircraft Corporation of Buffalo, New York—eight hundred employees, $9 million in back orders—to San Diego, where the new plant commenced operation in October 1935. Consolidated president Reuben Fleet had earned his wings as an Army aviator at Rockwell Field during the First World War and had dreamed ever since of returning, which he now did with a flourish, pointing to such advantages as an excellent airport and harbor, an aviation-friendly climate, and, most important, a city peopled by an intelligent, well-motivated work force. Located in a grand new assembly plant adjacent to Lindbergh Field, Consolidated got busy building for the Navy a fleet of PBYs, the famed Catalinas, graceful flying boats capable of great speed and distance. By the end of 1936 the Consolidated work force had grown to three thousand; and Major Reuben Fleet (his Army Reserve rank) was discussing the possibility of building gigantic flying boats capable of carrying up to one hundred passengers across the Pacific. Meanwhile, orders at the Ryan Aeronautical Company had tripled by 1937, and the Solar Aircraft Company was doing equally well in the manufacturing of exhaust manifolds and other airplane parts.

The central expression of this sense of civic well-being, so resistent to Edmund Wilson's scenario of San Diego as an end-of-the-line dead-end city, was the California-Pacific International Exposition, held in Balboa Park in 1935 and 1936 and attracting 7.2 million visitors. Two forces—the end of the Chicago Century of Progress Exposition and the need to refurbish the buildings left behind in Balboa Park by the Panama California Exposition of 1915—served as catalysts for the San Diego Fair. In 1915 Bertram Goodhue had designed the Panama-California Exposition as a series of temporary structures; but so successful was his scheme, so powerfully did Goodhue's Spanish City speak to San Diego's conception of itself as capital of the Spanish Southwest, the buildings (including Goodhue's California Building, the energizing archetype for the Spanish Revival of the 1920s) were kept standing. Matters came to a head early in 1933 when the San Diego City Council made a move to tear down the crumbling structures. A citizens' group organized by Scripps-Howard newsman Frank Drugan successfully promoted the idea of bringing to San Diego from Chicago portions of the Century of Progress Exposition for a fair that would restore the Spanish City in Balboa Park. In September 1934 the City Council went along with the scheme, and the duly organized directors of the California-Pacific International Exposition commenced the restoration of the 1915 buildings. As an expression of San Diego's flourishing garden culture, three new garden courts were installed replicating the gardens of the House of Moorish Kings in Ronda in southern Spain, the Alcazar garden in Seville, and a patio garden from Guadalajara, Mexico.

On 29 May 1935, the exposition—four hundred exhibitors from twenty-three nations—opened with a grand parade led by a Marine color guard across Cabrillo Bridge to the Plaza del Pacifico. Like its predecessor in 1915, the California-Pacific International Exposition celebrated San Diego as the capital, the crossroads city, of Mexico, the Spanish Southwest, and the Pacific Basin. Under the direction of supervising architect Richard Requa, a mélange of pre-Columbian and Spanish Revival styles were integrated with modern structures, Art Deco and Streamline Moderne, to suggest San Diego past, present, and future. The Federal Building replicated the Mayan Palace of the Governors in Uxmal, Yucatán. The Ford Building, by contrast, was a pure instance of industrial-futurist Moderne. Because Edsel Ford enjoyed vacationing in San Diego, Ford maintained a noticeable presence at the Fair and sponsored the construction of the Ford Bowl, a counterpart to the Hollywood Bowl in Los Angeles, for well-attended public concerts by such groups as the symphony orchestras of San Diego, Los Angeles, San Francisco, Portland, and Seattle and the Mormon Tabernacle Choir. The Ford Bowl came equipped with a five-thousand-watt electronic organ, which could be heard in Mission Hills three miles away. Hollywood set designer Juan Larrinaga created stunning lighting and decorative effects. By night the exposition glowed with the luminosity of a Maxfield Parrish painting.

As in the case of all expositions, high-brow, middle-brow, and low-brow comingled in a typically American manner. Symphony orchestras performed in the Ford Bowl, and the legendary contralto Madame Ernestine Schumann-Heink, a San Diego resident, sang "The Star-Spangled Banner." At the Old Globe Theater, a replica of the Elizabethan structure constructed next to Goodhue's California Building, there were six performances daily (forty cents for adults, weekday matinees for a quarter, children under twelve fifteen cents) of Shakespearean plays edited down to an hour for popular consumption. At the Indian Village some 150 Native Americans conducted dances and craft displays. There was also a Mickey Mouse Circus, with midget actors attired as Mickey and his friends. In the risqué Gold Gulch section of the fairgrounds, some fifty denizens of a semi-nude nudist camp, their attire personally supervised by San Diego police chief George Sears, offered mid-America a mild shock as, reading in deck chairs, playing softball and handball, dining on vegetables, they demonstrated the possibilities of life beneath the San Diego sun. In the second year of the fair, fan dancer Sally Rand brought her artistry to San Diego, two shows daily in the Palace of Entertainment, and two shows each evening in the Plaza del Pacifico. Miss Rand expressed some hostility to the nudists, contrasting their naive exhibitionism with her more studied artistry. There was also the Le Moulin Rouge cabaret review. After the show, the dancers were quite generous in posing for photographs with young bluejackets from the fleet.

As usual, this being San Diego, the Navy played an important role in the proceedings. In June 1935 the entire Pacific Fleet assembled in the San Diego Harbor for Fleet Week: forty-eight battleships, cruisers, carriers, and other vessels; four hundred naval aircraft; fifty-five thousand enlisted men and three thousand officers under the command of Admiral Joseph Reeves, an early naval aviator who was also a courtly Joseph Conrad look-alike in his precisely trimmed Van Dyke beard. Never before in the history of the United States had such a fleet assembled in one place under one command, as if to finalize once and for all the ongoing love affair between San Diego and the United States Navy. Thousands of sailors poured ashore to visit the fair and other favored waterfront places, and an even greater number of San Diegans were offered tours of the anchored ships. Two months later, 115 warships of the Pacific Fleet, returning from a cruise off Alaska, passed off San Diego between La Jolla and Point Loma in a column fifteen miles long. More than fifteen thousand schoolchildren gathered to watch the great fleet steam once again into San Diego Bay. Unfortunately, film star Mae West, arriving in San Diego on 9 June 1935, missed the first visit of the fleet by a day. "I'm sorry I didn't know the Fleet was coming in tomorrow," Miss West told a reporter from the San Diego *Union*, "as I certainly would have come down then. I'm very patriotic that way."[2]

Among other celebrity visitors to the exposition were former president Herbert Hoover, Los Angeles evangelist Aimee Semple McPherson, Jack Dempsey, Dr. Francis Townsend, and the number one San Diego booster in the United States,

Franklin Delano Roosevelt. Having served as Assistant Secretary of the Navy in the First World War, Roosevelt had a special fondness for both the Navy and the headquarters city of the Pacific Fleet. Arriving by train on 1 October 1935, the President stayed overnight at the Hotel del Coronado and on the next day was driven along a thirty-mile route lined with spectators for a visit to the fair. After lunch in the House of Hospitality, Roosevelt gave a speech to fifty thousand people gathered in the stadium of the San Diego High School, using the occasion to link the Latin American themes of the fair to his own Good Neighbor Policy. Boarding the cruiser *USS Houston*, Roosevelt reviewed the fleet at sea, then returned to Washington via the Panama Canal. Roosevelt's delight in his San Diego visit, together with his concern for the ongoing well-being of the Navy in that town, had some strong connection, one speculates, with the $6 million in WPA projects that subsequently flowed into the city.

San Diego joined the Navy in the early 1920s as a matter of economic policy and social choice. Earlier San Diego identities, still continuing in the naval era, included resort, sanitarium, art colony, and agricultural captial. Climate and topography made all these options and identities possible; and in pre-European times the four dominant peoples of the region—the Diegueño, Luiseño, Cupeño, and Cahuilla—had each explored a specific range of possibilities as they settled by the sea, harvested the yields of the canyons and arroyos, or bathed themselves in healing springs. Coastal San Diego began in salt marshes, then rose to coastal sage, then higher still, to the chaparral and oak parklands of the foothills, ascending to the oak and pine forests of the mountain ranges, then descending once again to chaparral on the eastern edge of the mountains before ending, abruptly, in desert. Two great mesas, Kearny Mesa in the north, Otay Mesa in the south on the Mexican border, together with Mission Valley and El Cajon Valley extending to the northeast, evoked the possibility of an advantageously sited riviera of urban and suburban settlements: a situation reinforced by a rather formidable mountainous backcountry—the Cuyamaca, the San Miguel, the Jamul mountain ranges—which would eventually function as the natural eastern containment for coastal urban settlement. Then further east came the great flatlands of the Imperial Valley and the Salton Sea, which irrigation would eventually rescue for agriculture. If climate were destiny, San Diego was determined by the sun. Seventy three percent of the year, San Diego enjoyed sunshine. On the coast the climate was classified as cool Mediterranean, perfect for urban settlement, with a warm Mediterranean belt immediately adjacent. Each of these Mediterranean zones suggested the health and sanitarium culture, as well as the tourist culture to come.

　　Two figures, Alonzo Erastus Horton and William Ellsworth Smythe, each a dreamer and doer in his respective way, first conceptualized the American San Diego experience. As the *de facto* founder—more correctly, as the refounder—of American San Diego, Alonzo Horton envisioned San Diego as a coastal metropolis connected to great cities on either side of the Pacific in maritime travel and trade. Smythe, by contrast, looked eastward into the hinterlands and envisioned San Diego as the capital of an irrigated Southwest.

Alonzo Horton was fifty-four years of age in 1867, an upstate New Yorker by birth, of seventeenth-century Connecticut Yankee stock, owning and operating a furniture store in San Francisco, when he attended a lecture on the urban possibilities of the Pacific Coast. The speaker began with the recently established Seattle, then proceeded southwards down the coast. When he came to San Diego, the speaker extolled the harbor and the climate, saying that here surely should one day rise up a great city. Returning home to bed, Horton tossed and turned through a sleepless night, obsessed by the sudden idea, so he later tells us, of giving form and meaning to his fragmented life (lumberjack, grocer, hardscrabble farmer in east central Wisconsin, storekeeper in the Mother Lode) by founding a great city. Rising from his restless bed at two in the morning, Horton got out a map and began studying the port of San Diego. In the morning, so he later claimed, he said to his wife: "I am going to sell my goods and go to San Diego and build a city."[3]

Liquidating his assets, Alonzo Horton took the paddle-wheel steamer *Pacific* to San Diego. Stepping ashore on 15 April 1867, he found two settlements, the inland Old Town, three miles to the north at the mouth of Mission Valley, and a dispirited coastal settlement whose first promoters had already gone bust. Determining that the Old Town "doesn't lie right," and that the New Town, by contrast, was the "best spot for building a city I ever saw," Horton set about to persuade the state-appointed San Diego Board of Trustees to sell him 960 acres in 160-acre lots along what is today the harbor and downtown of the city. Horton paid $265, for an average of twenty-seven and a half cents per acre, for the tract. He then retained the services of L. L. Locking, the deputy county surveyor, to survey and subdivide the proposed development. Surveyor Locking did even more. He integrated Old Town and New Town into one survey scheme, and a map of the entire plan was published in San Francisco. Like Jasper O'Farrell's 1847 map of San Francisco, the Horton-Locking map evoked a San Diego that existed only in the mind—but existed nevertheless as a vision of a complete and fully urban city, arrayed on its spectacular site.

Horton commenced to sell off his lots and, having sparked the interest of other investors, to build a hundred-room hotel, Horton House, completed in October 1870 at the cost of $150,000. The ambitious urbanism of the entire Horton venture stood revealed. Remote San Diego, a town of three thousand residents, lacking a railroad connection and poorly served by rural roads, with an unimproved port and irregular passenger ship service, was suddenly graced by one of the largest and finest hotels on the Pacific Coast. The size and elegance of the Horton House bespoke the future of San Diego as a commercial center and destination resort. If we build it, Horton was saying, they'll come.

And come they did, beginning with the settlers who bought Horton's lots. On 4 March 1882, on the side-wheeler *Orizaba* arriving from Santa Barbara, came perhaps the most important visitor in this first era, from the point of publicity at least, the writer Helen Hunt Jackson, on assignment from Richard Watson Gilder of *Century* magazine. Based out of the Horton House, Jackson toured the region by buckboard in the company of Father Anthony Ubach, pastor of San Diego Mission. Known as the Last of the Padres, Ubach had a special care for the Native Americans of the region and interested Mrs. Jackson in their cause. Later, in April 1883, Mrs. Jackson and Abbott Kinney of Los Angeles returned to San Diego as Special Commissioners of Indian Affairs in Southern California. The results of Jackson's sojourn—descriptive journalism, later reprinted as *Glimpses of Three Coasts* (1886), and the best-selling novel *Ramona* (1884), set in great part in San Diego County—promoted the region to a national audience and provided not just San Diego, but all of Southern California, with a promotional image of itself as Ramona-land, successor to Spanish California.

What Jackson helped begin with *Ramona*, the California Southern Railroad, a spur line of the Santa Fe, arriving that same year, 1884, continued: the booming and the boosting of the San Diego region. By 1887 San Diego had forty thousand residents, including retired lawman Wyatt Earp, survivor of the gunfight at the OK Corral, who raised thoroughbred race horses and operated three gambling parlors. Earp's wife was Jewish, as was Samuel Fox, who had fled the anti-Semitism of his native Hungary as a young man of eighteen for New York and, after he had learned English, for San Francisco, where he worked for Raphael and Son, clothiers. Twenty-four years of age at the time of his arrival in San Diego, Fox went into real estate, then back into haberdashery, joining his brother-in-law in the Lion Clothing store, which passed to his ownership entirely when the brother-in-law died. Raised in Hungary in a rigidly Orthodox community, Fox made the transition to Reform Judaism in the United States. Two years after his arrival in San Diego in 1886, Fox joined other Reform Jews in the organization of Congregation Beth Israel, which constructed the city's first synagogue in 1889.

One promoter, Colonel Thomas Fitch, predicted a million people moving to San Diego County before the boom peaked. The newly founded University of Southern California in Los Angeles planned a second campus for University Heights, a subdivision to the north of the city park. Promoter Daniel Choate, a Maine man, purchased and subdivided sixteen hundred acres for the proposed university-oriented development, with the proceeds of every other block scheduled for donation to the Methodist Episcopal Church, which operated USC. While this campus did not materialize, many of its supporters were among those who brought club life to San Diego, with the organization in May 1887 of the Cuyamaca Club, which completed its own building in the downtown in August 1888.The boom went bust, as booms frequently did in the 1880s. By 1890 the City of San Diego had dropped to slightly more than sixteen thousand in population, with another thirty-five thousand settled in the county. The financial panic of 1893 hit San Diego especially hard, closing five of its eight banks. Yet the urban formula established by Alonzo Horton had taken hold once and for all. San

Diego had internalized an urban identity that would see it developed, if not now, then over the next century, into the second largest city in California.

Nothing symbolized these aspirations better than the 399-room Hotel del Coronado, the grandest tourist hotel on the Pacific Coast, which opened in 1888. Like the Horton House, the Del Coronado had two purposes. On the one hand, it was intended to attract tourists, which it did with great success, including a visit by Henry James in 1905, who praised the hotel for its spectacular seaside site and exquisite gardens. The hotel also served as a stimulus to subdivision of Coronado Island in San Diego Bay, in much the same way that the Horton House had stimulated the growth of downtown San Diego, and the Hotel Virginia was stimulating the growth of Long Beach, and the Beverly Hills Hotel would later stimulate the rise of Beverly Hills. All great hotels are utopias of a sort. As an idealizing statement, the Del Coronado suggested to Eastern visitors the urban possibilities and lifestyles the San Diego region might afford permanent residents.

William Ellsworth Smythe, meanwhile, was looking not to the sea but to inland San Diego as the source and symbol of the future. In the early 1900s this brilliant irrigation advocate saw the entire County of San Diego as a network of irrigated farms and townships, linked to each other and to the City of San Diego by an interruban electric railway. For San Diego to be great, Smythe argued, it needed developed hinterlands. Taken together, an irrigated and settled Imperial Valley, an interurban electric system, and a direct railroad connection to the East provided the proper formula. Smythe envisioned more than ten thousand new homes on two hundred thousand acres of San Diego hinterlands, the entire region irrigated by publicly owned water projects. Although his advocacy of public water and power initially put Smythe at odds with the John D. Spreckels interests that ran the town (Spreckels owned the Hotel del Coronado and other properties, the San Diego Electric Railway, the San Diego *Union* and *Evening Tribune*, the Southern California Water Company, and the San Diego and Arizona Railroad), Smythe eventually won acceptance as the leading spokesman for the Chamber of Commerce, so compelling was his vision of San Diego as the capital of an agricultural region peopled by educated irrigationists linked to the metropolis by swiftly traveling interurban electrics. And besides: Smythe also spoke powerfully for the city of San Diego, whose beauty engendered in him, as he put it, "a nameless exaltation no one can describe."[4] Larger than the states of Delaware and Rhode Island combined, San Diego County had become by the 1920s, as Smythe predicted, a rich and varied agricultural region—livestock, poultry, citrus (the best lemon groves in the state), bees, honey, strawberries, flowers, olives, and olive oil: crops and enterprises touched by Virgilian associations appropriate to lady and gentleman farmers of the middle classes who combined ranch life with a high degree of personal culture.

Personal culture, as a matter of health and aesthetics, helped shape the San Diego experience in terms of its values, lifestyle, and urban form. From the perspective of health and beauty, the emergence of San Diego ran parallel to that other coastal enclave and health resort, Santa Barbara. With tuberculosis such a scourge in the nineteenth century, it is no surprise that San Diegans would seek almost immediately to capitalize on the restoratative aspects of the local climate. The Horton House set aside twenty specially equipped suites for invalids on its first floor. The Reverend Charles Russell Clarke, a graduate of Princeton College and Theological Seminary, wrote a series of articles in the national press regarding the healthfulness of San Diego for those suffering from consumption.

Unfortunately, Clarke died of tuberculosis in San Diego in 1872, the same year that Dr. Peter Remondino arrived in search of renewed health. A native of Torino, Italy, Remondino had been brought to the United States as a boy and raised on the Minnesota frontier, where he grew up in the outdoors, adding Sioux and French to his Italian and English. Graduating from the Jefferson Medical College in Philadelphia, Remondino served as a physician in the Union Army during the Civil War before contracting malaria in Virginia. In 1870 he joined the French army as a physician in the Franco-Prussian War and suffered a relapse. Studying maps and geographies and various analyses of climates, Remondino determined that the best place for him to regain his health was far-off San Diego. Moving to San Diego from France, Remondino recovered his health. He became, in fact, city physician of San Diego in 1875 and president of the San Diego Board of Health. He also became a tireless propagandist for San Diego as a health resort. In 1879 Remondino and another San Diego physician, Thomas Stockton, built the city's first private sanitarium. In 1886 Remondino went into the hotel business, buying and renovating the Santa Rosa Hotel, which he renamed the St. James, having refurbished its 250 rooms in the most modern manner. Working with a traveling salesman, Alfred Huntington Isham, Remondino promoted the sale of bottled mineral water from the Rancho Jamacha in southern San Diego County under the label Isham's California Waters of Life. The doctor also began to produce a steady stream of articles regarding the healthfulness of the San Diego climate. In 1892 Remondino gathered his articles into *The Mediterranean Shores of America*, a book that, following closely upon Charles Dudley Warner's *Our Italy* (1891), in which the Hartford, Connecticut, journalist reported on the extraordinary longevity of Native Americans in San Diego County, fixed in the national consciousness, especially the health care community, the image of Southern California as a Mediterranean shore, a region of sparkling blue skies and water, sunshine and health, and San Diego as the Naples-sanitarium of the Pacific.

Opening in 1896, the Kneipp Sanitarium offered a treatment based on baths (vapor baths, steam baths, cold water baths, herb baths) and herbal packs. In 1903 the hundred-bed Agnew Sanitarium opened, adding electrical treatments and Swedish massage to bath therapy. Under the direction of J. A. Parks, M.D., the Parks Sanitarium in La Mesa specialized in diseases of the lungs and throat, which Dr. Parks treated in a program of outdoor life, housing his patients in tent cottages. Another physician, William Edwards, offered a mixed program of diet, baths, exercise, and outdoor life at the Edwards Sanitarium on the outskirts of the city. In 1913 Rest Haven, an outdoor camp for children in pre-tubercular stages of anemia, opened; reorganized and reopened in 1920 by the English-born Florence Mead, it flourished through the 1920s and 1930s with a program of diet, rest, exercise, and sunshine for children in danger of TB. Even the Hotel del Coronado got into the health care business with special programs for invalids. Bottling its local water, the hotel promoted Coronado Mineral Water as the equivalent of the most healthful waters of the best spas in Europe.

Emerging as a health resort, San Diego also appealed to those in search of aesthetic well-being. Literary journalist Harr Wagner, for example, moved to San Diego in 1887 from the Mother Lode, bringing with him the *Golden Era*, a literary magazine to which Mark Twain and Bret Harte had contributed in the 1860s. San Diego now had a literary publication as well as a literary circle, for around Wagner gathered such figures as poet Rose Hartwick Thorpe ("Curfew Shall Not Ring Tonight") and the Spiritualist writer Jesse Shepard, who was also a concert pianist.

Spiritualism was strong in San Diego at the time, with no less than Mrs. Alonzo Horton herself active in the First Spiritualist Society. Delighted with the presence among them of an internationally known concert artist, who was also a medium and might bring great distinction to both their city and the Spiritualist movement, a group of wealthy San Diego Spiritualists raised $19,000 on Jesse Shepard's behalf and built for him a mansion in the Queen Anne style at 1925 K Street, which Shepard named the Villa Montezuma. As brief as it was, Jesse Shepard's two-year sojourn in San Diego was at the time, and remained, a cultural reference point. Why were the locals so mesmerized? Was it because Shepard had played the major cities and some of the courts of Europe? Was it because his candlelight concerts cast a special spell in a remote enclave? Yes, but such explanations do not go far enough. Shepard's hyper-aestheticism and Spiritualism also represented a ratcheting up, an intensification, of the San Diego formula. Sunshine led to Spiritualism as well as to health and aesthetics. The belief that the other world was the more real offset the terrible knowledge that so many who came to San Diego came there only to die and so many who came there to prosper in the boom of the mid-1880s went bust.

In 1897 Theosophy arrived in San Diego in the person of Katherine Tingley, Madame Blatavsky's successor as leader of Theosophy in the United States. Founded by the renowned Russian occultist Madame Helena Petrovna Blavatsky in New York in 1875, Theosophy held to a broadly syncretic melange of Egyptian, neo-Platonic, Gnostic, Cabalist, Vedic, Yogic, Buddhist, Brahmanical, and Swedenborgian teachings. Purporting to represent the wisdom of the Ancients, Theosophy postulated the existence of a World Soul, immanent in nature, with Which one might make connection through meditation, the arts, and mystical experience. Theosophy also taught a doctrine of reincarnation, in which individual souls passed through progressively higher stages of awareness in succeeding lives.

In conversation in 1896 with the frail and elderly John Charles Frémont, the

Pathfinder who fifty-four years earlier had helped bring California to the consciousness of the nation, Mrs. Tingley—a robust and commanding woman in her forties, thrice married but childless, every inch the successful executive, skilled in money management as well as the arcane lore of Theosophy—told the aged General of a dream she recently had of building "a white city in a golden land by the sundown sea."[5] The General said that her dream reminded him of Point Loma on San Diego Bay. Without seeing the site, Tingley had her agents purchase a 132-acre tract atop Point Loma adjacent to a Navy station, where she planned to construct what she was then calling her School for the Revival of Lost Mysteries of Antiquity. Soon, within five years, the shining walls and stained-glass domes of an otherworldly Xanadu, the national headquarters of Theosophy in America, rose atop Point Loma. On the grounds as well was an outdoor Greek Theater oriented on a Doric stoa, modeled on a surviving Greek theater at Taormina, Sicily. Tingley also purchased the Fisher Opera House in downtown San Diego, renaming it the Isis.

School, commune, art academy, theater company: Point Loma sustained a rich and complex community. Theosophists from England and the Atlantic Coast, including a number of noted artists, converged on the city. Photographs of Point Loma reveal elegantly furnished public rooms, rich with Oriental rugs, statuary, paintings, European and Asian objets d'art, Chinese and Japanese vases, screens, and pottery. Private quarters are more austere, yet everywhere there is taste, with an emphasis on Craftsman, Art Nouveau, and Symbolist-decorated furnishings. From the in-house press of Point Loma Publications issued a steady stream of well-written and -designed books and magazines, translated into a number of languages. Over it all presided Madame Tingley with the aplomb and assurance of Hildegard of Bingen in medieval Germany.

Central to the mission of Point Loma was the Raja Yoga School, which had three hundred pupils by 1910. Using methods that greatly resembled Montessori techniques, the Raja Yoga School (the phrase meant "kingly union") sought to teach children through physical, emotional, and intellectual involvement. Children were taught only three hours a day, but very intensely. More controversially, they were required to wear uniforms and to maintain silence at meals. In terms of reading, writing, and computational skills, the system yielded impressive results; but the silence and the uniforms made an unfavorable impression on a number of visitors. The Los Angeles *Times* blasted Point Loma in October 1901 as a cult gone awry, with forced labor and nighttime lock-ups. The children, the *Times* claimed, were forbidden to speak and kept on the verge of starvation, and there were strange midnight processions by mixed groups in their nightrobes.

The criticism, especially the midnight processions, gained national press attention; and when Madame Tingley sought to bring nine boys and two girls from her school in Cuba to Point Loma, the Immigration Service detained them at Ellis Island at the request of the New York Society for the Prevention of Cruelty to Children. Assisted by the wealthy sporting goods manufacturer Albert Spalding, whose children were in the Raja Yoga School, Madame Tingley made a spirited defense of the institution. With her full cooperation, the governor, the state board of health, the state board of examiners, and the San Diego Chapter of the Society for the Prevention of Cruelty to Children sent inspection teams to the school. Each of them wound up praising the institution: its cleanliness and order, its teaching techniques, the health and welfare of the children, even the lessons in patriotism taught by the school and the American flags flying in each classroom. Ellis Island released the children, and with the help of Spalding they were transported by train to San Diego, where they were welcomed with a parade up Broadway from the Santa Fe Depot, led by the City Guard Band, followed by a rally at the Isis Theater. San Diego was equally joyous when Madame Tingley won her libel suit against the Los Angeles *Times*, a paper given to trashing San Diego on any possible occasion.

The Point Loma Theosophical community, in other words, had become mainstream. To understand fully the inner landscape of San Diego, one must grasp this fact: a white Protestant city, mid-American in so many respects, accepted, indeed took pride in, an institution that by most mid-American standards would be considered exotic. Something in the Point Loma community—its eerily beautiful buildings, its nature-based mysticism, its ambitious program in the arts, its sense of the Other Side shimmering on the horizon of the Pacific—spoke to the collective San Diego identity in a way that leavened an otherwise ordinary American city with the mystical and the aesthetic.

The strongest connection between the Point Loma Theosophists and San Diego was the fine and performing arts. As early as 1902, Madame Tingley was producing plays at the Isis Theater in the downtown. Later, in April 1911, she opened the Greek Theater to the public for pageants and productions of Greek and Shakespearean plays, each of them directed by Madame Tingley herself: *The Aroma of Athens* in 1911 (a Theosophical play depicting the feelings of the Greek philosophers at the outbreak of the Peloponnesian War in 431 B.C.E.), *Midsummer Night's Dream* in 1915, *As You Like It* in 1917, *Twelfth Night* in 1918, *The Tempest* in 1926. Lavishly costumed, professionally staged, incorporating dozens of well-directed actors, these plays constituted a welcomed amenity for theater-starved San Diego.

In the matter of painting, the Theosophical community in and of itself established San Diego as a serious art center. Like Swedenborgianism, Theosophy, with its sense of spirit in nature and nature in spirit, held great appeal for many artists, especially in England, where painting had already been spiritualized by the Pre-Raphaelites. A number of promising English painters—among them, Joseph Fussell Sr., Leonard Lester, Reginald Machell, and Charles James Ryan—joined the Theosophical movement in London and migrated to Point Loma in the early 1900s. The background of Reginald Machell can be taken as representative of these English artists. Educated in art and classics, Machell had studied at the Academie Julien in Paris in 1876 and began exhibiting at the Royal Academy upon his return. In 1893 he was elected to the Royal Society of British Artists. Joining the Theosophical Society of London, Machell did the interior decorations in Madame Blavatsky's home in Regents Park. Matchell was forty-six when he arrived in Point Loma with his son Montague: courageously making the abrupt transition from London, where he had flourished as a painter, book illustrator, furniture designer, and woodcarver, to far-off San Diego, where artistic activity was just beginning.

At Point Loma, the English artists were joined by a number of American artists who were also Theosophists: most conspicuously Edith White, a graduate of Mills College and the San Francisco School of Design, recently practicing in a studio in the Green Hotel in Pasadena, and the Hungarian-born Maurice Braun, then in his early thirties, whom Madame Tingley provided studio space in the Isis Theater Building downtown. Arriving in 1909, Braun was destined to become by the 1930s the leader of the San Diego art community and one of the best-known painters working in California.

While Theosophy might not be for everyone in San Diego, even skeptics admitted that Madame Tingley had assembled in their rather remote enclave an extraordinary group of talented and aspiring folk. Given the institutional thinness of San Diego, Point Loma released reverberations that further defined the distinctive brand of Californianism, with its emphasis on community aesthetics, that was accumulating beside the Silver Gate. Point Loma, from this perspective, led to the Spanish City of the Panama-California Exposition of 1915 atop Balboa Park and to the greater City of San Diego engendered by both institutions.

Just exactly how San Diego should grow, however, and in what ways, constituted the central debate of the city in the first two decades of the 1900s. As the debate emerged, there were two opposing camps: those favoring smokestacks and those favoring geraniums. Smokestacks versus geraniums, industrial growth versus an aesthetic environmentalism, San Diego as a resort enclave versus San Diego as a metropolitan rival of Los Angeles and San Francisco—so the debate was framed. Joining the Navy appeased both camps.

In the aftermath of the bust of the 1880s boom and the even more severe depression and financial panic of 1893, there were some, such as John Diedrich Spreckels and Ulysses Simpson Grant Jr., whose deep pockets enabled them to acquire commanding positions at a time of stress. The son of Claus Spreckels, the German-born, San Francisco–based Hawaii sugar king, John D. Spreckels inherited his father's genius for business. While still in his twenties, he founded the Oceanic Steamship Company, operating between New Zealand, Hawaii, and the Pacific Coast. A skilled yachtsman, Spreckels discovered San Diego while cruising off Southern California in 1887 and determined to create there what his father had created in Hawaii: a diversified fiefdom, which eventually included a water company, a waterfront warehouse, choice parcels of downtown real estate, the Hotel del Coronado, a streetcar line, and the San Diego *Union*.

If Spreckels shared the limelight with anyone, it was with the Exeter- and Harvard-educated second son of Julia Dent and Ulysses Simpson Grant. Just before his assassination, Abraham Lincoln made a casual reference to moving to California when he stepped down from the presidency and resuming the practice of law. What Lincoln was tragically prevented from doing, General Grant's widow and children did in earnest after the former president died in July 1885. U. S. Grant Jr.'s younger brother Jesse led the exodus, moving to San Diego in 1892, about the same time that his sister Nellie Grant Sartoris began wintering in Santa Barbara. President Grant's widow was in poor health, and so, like so many others, Mr. and Mrs. U. S. Grant Jr., their three children, two nurses, the family governess, and the former president's widow entrained for San Diego from New York in October 1893 in a privately chartered railroad car.

Entering a depressed real estate market, the Grants purchased a three-story Queen Anne mansion at 8th and Ash Streets on Prospect Hill, designed by the Reid brothers, James and Merritt, who had designed the Hotel del Coronado, for a quarter of what it had cost the original owner to build and furnish. As a young man, Grant Junior had been badly shaken in 1884 by the collapse of his Wall Street firm, Grant and Ward, Bankers and Brokers. Partner Ferdinand Ward went off to the state penitentiary, and the Grants, including the former president, were plunged into poverty and humiliation. Now, in San Diego, Ulysses Simpson Grant Jr. regained his business reputation through a series of astute real estate investments and developments. San Diego, in turn, was flattered to have the son of a national hero in its midst; and the Grants became the most socially distinguished family in the city.

Among the properties acquired by Grant was the Horton House, the originating text of San Diego as an American city. Grant planned to replace the Horton House with a hotel that would serve as a monument to his father. On the evening of 12 July 1905 Alonzo Horton himself, now well into his eighties and known as Father Horton, Founder of the City, was on hand to bless the dismantlement of the Horton House and the construction of the U. S. Grant Hotel on Horton Plaza. Designed by Harrison Allbright, the U. S. Grant Hotel featured 437 rooms, a roof garden, a palm court, a spacious dining room, and a grand ballroom on the ninth floor. A portrait of General Grant hung in the lobby. Like the Horton House that it replaced, the U. S. Grant Hotel suggested an even greater San Diego to come.

Alonzo Horton died in 1909. That same year, the pro-growth wing of the San Diego oligarchy set in motion a development scheme, the Panama-California International Exposition, that would not only fill the U. S. Grant Hotel but boost San Diego into a new phase of development. At a meeting of the San Diego Chamber of Commerce on 9 July 1909, banker G. Aubrey Davidson proposed that San Diego develop itself through an international exposition celebrating the forthcoming completion of the San Diego and Arizona Railway, connecting San Diego to the East, and the also-scheduled completion of the Panama Canal, which would, at long last, stimulate San Diego properly to develop its harbor, since San Diego was the first important port of call north of the isthmus. On 4 September 1909 twenty-one members of the oligarchy signed the articles of incorporation of the Panama-California Exposition Company, with U. S. Grant Jr. as chairman of the board and John D. Spreckels and Davidson as vice presidents. The directors of the company pledged themselves to sell a million dollars in stock, with Spreckels pledging an upfront purchase of $100,000.

As a place, a focus of planning debate, and an expression of opposing philosophies of development, the site chosen for the exposition, the fourteen-hundred-acre City Park (renamed Balboa Park in October 1910 in honor of the Spanish explorer Vasco Nuñez de Balboa, who crossed the Isthmus of Panama and discovered the Pacific Ocean in 1513) centered the debate as to just exactly what kind of place San Diego would become: a controlled Progressive enclave or a booming, wide-open city, or something in between. It is to point to something distinctive in the San Diego formula to note that the citizens of the city framed the debate over growth in terms of park aesthetics. For nearly twenty years, the question of how best to develop Balboa Park bore the burden of an even larger issue: how best to develop San Diego.

First of all, it was remarkable that in February 1868 the remote frontier town of San Diego, with a population of only 2,310 people, set aside by vote of its Board of Trustees nine pueblo lots, or 1,440 acres, for a public park. The trustee most responsible for this measure was Ephraim Morse (the first of a number of horticulturally-minded Yankees to involve themselves in this project), a former Boston teacher who had grown up on a Massachusetts farm, loved plants and flowers, and wanted San Diego someday to have its own Boston Common or Central Park. It took until February 1870 for the state legislature to confirm San Diego's parkland set-aside, this after the first of many attempts by private developers to acquire park properties for their own use. Even as a reserved wilderness, which it remained for most of the nineteenth century, the City Park, as it was called, implied a future comparison of San Diego to Boston, New York, and San Francisco, which had set aside its Golden Gate Park preserve in the mid-1850s. For the time being, the canyons and mesas of City Park remained a wild chaparral inhabited by lingering Native Americans given permission to live there alongside the wildcats and coyotes. American residents used a remote part of the park as a city dump. After the winter rains, the chaparral would bloom in a profusion of yellow, white, and blue flowers, which promised the park to come.

In December 1884 a group of San Diegans volunteered to plant eucalyptus trees at their own expense. Two years later, the park came close to being abandoned in favor of establishing a smaller park on the site of some former Army barracks near the waterfront. Not only developers but the non-profit sector as well had designs on the property. In November 1887 a number of philanthropists, including Bryant Howard and Ephraim Morse, originator of the park idea, petitioned the city trustees for permission to develop a hundred acres of the City Park on a promontory between Cabrillo and Florida canyons for an orphanage, boarding school, kindergarten, and industrial school complex. On 2 December 1887 the city trustees authorized the so-called Howard Tract and granted another five acres to the Woman's Home Association for a hostel serving indigent women. The state confirmed the transfer, and in the spring of 1890, Bryant Howard and his associates began to grade roads, lay down irrigation pipes, and plant the grounds of the Howard Tract (or Charities Tract or Orphan's Tract, as it was also called) with some ten thousand eucalyptus, pepper, acacia, fan palm, and cypress trees. A three-story Children's Home and an equally impressive Woman's Home were then constructed.

From one perspective, the development of the hundred-acre Howard Tract represented a welcomed appearance of philanthropy, hence civic maturity, in San Diego. For George White Marston, however, the Howard Tract represented the beginning of the end: the first of many giveaways, he believed—today to philanthropy, tomorrow to private developers. Marston had a much more pure ideal in mind: the development of City Park according to the standards established by Calvert Vaux and Frederick Law Olmsted in Central Park. A man of means (he owned the largest department store in San Diego), Marston brought to this conviction the full force of his devoutly Presbyterian and Progressive temperament. To his way of thinking, the struggle for the purity of City Park touched upon, indeed advanced, the very notion of San Diego as a distinctive American city.

Enter Kate Sessions, a remarkable woman in a city in which women, from Madame Tingley to Joan Kroc and Helen Copley, would play conspicuous public roles. Born in San Francisco in 1857, Sessions studied agriculture at UC Berkeley, the first woman to achieve such professional training on the Pacific Coast. Arriving in San Diego in 1883, she opened a nursery on Coronado Island, which prospered. In January 1892 Sessions sought permission to transfer her nursery to thirty-two acres of leased land in the northwest corner of City Park. Not only would she pay rent, Sessions promised, she would plant a hundred trees a year for free and provide another three hundred trees for city streets, plazas, and playgrounds. Over the next ten years, drawing upon her stock of twenty thousand plants, Kate Sessions planted thousands of eucalpytus, palm, pepper, acacia, elm, oak, torrey pine, and Monterey cypress trees, together with such exotics as bamboo, kuki trees from Hawaii, and banyans from Fiji, throughout the park and the streets and boulevards of the city. Sessions wanted San Diego to be nothing less than the most beautifully landscaped city in the nation, not just with trees but with strategically placed clumps of poinsettias, cacti, bougainvillea, and other flowering plants as well. Like George Marston, Sessions adhered to the Olmsted philosophy of park development, with its emphasis upon romantic naturalism, picturesque vistas, and no commercial development.

With the arrival of the twentieth century, City Park at long last received the attention it deserved. In July 1901 publisher Edward Scripps offered to donate enough trees and shrubs from his Miramar ranch north of San Diego to develop the entire tract. In August 1902 a Park Improvement Committee was formed by the Chamber of Commerce. It included Kate Sessions, George Marston, and banker Julius Wangenheim. In order to have a comprehensive plan for City Park, Marston donated $10,000 to bring out Samuel Parsons Jr., landscape architect for the State of New York, president of the American Society of Landscape Architects, former superintendent of Central Park, and a friend and disciple of Frederick Law Olmsted, to whom Parsons stood in direct succession. Marston also hired Mary Coulston, the former editor of *Garden and Forest* magazine, to serve as secretary and publicist to the committee. Parsons arrived in San Diego on 21 December 1902. Working with Kate Sessions and T. S. Brandagee, an expert in cacti, he roamed the canyons and mesas of City Park, thrilled with the opportunity to create on this fourteen-hundred-acre site one of the great parks of the nation. Parsons's partner George Cooke presented the final plan to San Diego in July 1903.

Kate Sessions, meanwhile, was organizing an annual Arbor Day each spring in which thousands of schoolchildren and their parents turned out to plant trees according to the Parsons Plan. In 1907 Sessions joined a number of other like-minded San Diegans to found the San Diego Floral Association, which was soon publishing *California Garden*. Before the rise of the Bay Area–based *Sunset* magazine, *California Garden* put San Diego at the forefront of garden theory and practice throughout the Far West.

In 1907 George White Marston brought to San Diego the noted city planner John Nolen of Cambridge, Massachusetts, to prepare a comprehensive plan for the city. Just as the Parsons Plan for City Park saw the park in its purest possible terms, so too did the Nolen Report of 1908 envision San Diego as a city capable of replicating on its spectacular site the best of the City Beautiful and the Mediterranean city, with special reference to Naples, Nice, Seville, and Rio de Janeiro. Nolen encouraged San Diego to orient itself to two all-important entities, the Bay and City Park. With the Parsons Plan and the Nolen Plan submitted, with George Marston now serving as president of a newly established Park Commission, and with Parsons's partner George Cooke now a full-time San Diegan and park consultant, the stage seemed set for a golden age of Progressive planning.

Unfortunately, Cooke died the next year from injuries sustained in a road accident; the business community dismissed the Nolen Plan as too idealistic and expensive; and the Panama-California International Exposition ran roughshod over the Parsons proposals. The exposition, first of all, planned to develop buildings in the park, a concept abhorent to the Olmsted-Parsons vision. Then there was the question of where these buildings should be located. Initially, it was proposed to put them in the southwest corner, thus preserving the best aspects of the Parsons Plan. The landscape architects for the exposition, in fact, John and Frederick Law Olmsted Jr., of Brookline, Massachusetts, whom Marston had personally hired in his capacity as chairman of the Buildings and Grounds Committee, insisted that the Parsons Plan, so directly inspired by their father, should be preserved. But

John D. Spreckels wanted the exposition buildings centrally located so as to be serviced by the streetcars of the Spreckels-owned San Diego Electric Railway Company, with service through the park connecting downtown San Diego with the newly developing suburbs of Normal Heights and North Park. The exposition, in other words, would be used as a means of penetrating the park with the streetcar line so necessary to real estate development in the suburbs. Disgusted by these proposals, the Olmsted brothers resigned as landscape architects to the exposition, followed by the resignation of George Marston as the chair of the Buildings and Grounds Committee. The battle for City Park as a protected sylvan enclave had been lost.

Likewise, the rejection of San Diego architect Irving Gill as architect-in-chief of the exposition in favor of the better-known, more commercially successful Bertram Grosvenor Goodhue of New York bespoke a victory of one San Diego over another. No one better embodied the pursuit of San Diego as an aesthetic ideal, at once Progressive and beautiful, than did Irving Gill, whose work had forged a distinctive San Diego–based style blending modernity and Mediterraneanism, graciousness and efficiency. The Gill style, so evident in the Bishop's School for Girls (1909) and dozens of other San Diego houses, businesses, and institutions, incorporated elements of Secessionist minimalism, the horizontalism and arches of North Africa and southern Spain, and the domesticity of the Prairie School, harmonized and unified by a modesty, a restraint, that one might consider typical of San Diego Progressivism as either an architectural style, a political or planning program, or a way of life. Had George Marston had his way, Gill would have produced an ensemble of buildings notable for their unadorned modernity, their orchestrations of mass, arch, and wall: a larger Bishop School, in short, showing strength through restraint.

The Spreckels crowd, however, having glimpsed the larger development possibilities of the exposition, wanted a bigger name and a flashier style; and the bigger name, Bertram Grosvenor Goodhue of New York, very much wanted the job. Goodhue lobbied Marston and the other members of the Buildings and Grounds Committee through a number of Los Angeles architects. The committee also consulted Sylvester Baxter's twelve-volume *Spanish Colonial Architecture of Mexico* (1901), in which Goodhue, as illustrator, had shown his mastery of Spanish Colonial. For San Diego, Goodhue and his associates produced not so much pure architecture, as Gill would have produced it, but a romantic text, immediately comprehensible to the general public and eminently saleable in terms of future development. Goodhue's San Diego buildings did more than any other factor to determine the look of Southern California residential neighborhoods and suburbs into the 1940s.

The loss of the Parsons Plan, the Nolen Plan, and the Gill scheme for the exposition represented more than a mere question of design alternatives. Here was being played out a clash between the Progressivism of the George White Marston clique, based on a conviction of public interest detached from economic motive, and the more profit-motivated schemes of John Spreckels and his associates. Despite the best efforts of the Marston wing of the oligarchy, San Diego would be no Progressive City on a Hill. It would be a go-ahead business town. Smokestacks would prevail over geraniums.

In the mayoral elections of 1913 and 1917, George Marston made two last-ditch efforts to keep San Diego focused on a Progressive program of planned and orderly development. In 1913 Marston ran on a platform advocating the implementation of the Nolen Plan and was defeated. The 1917 campaign introduced a slogan, Smokestacks versus Geraniums, which remained for the rest of the century as a proposition for local debate. It was especially difficult for Marston, a cultivated Progressive patrician, to run in the 1917 campaign against his polar opposite, banker-businesman Louis Wilde, a former Texas oilman and Babbitt booster. Outspoken, flamboyant, Wilde pilloried Marston as Geranium George, an elitist interested in maintaining San Diego as a non-industrialized enclave. In reality, Marston was not anti-development. He had served, after all, as president of the San Diego and Eastern Railroad Company in early efforts to secure a direct connection to the East. As mayor, Marston told the San Diego Union on 21 January 1917, he would "encourage the industrial development of the city and country along the lines of manufacturing, commerce, and horticulture." It was the horticulture that got Marston into trouble. "San Diego needs a mayor who will bring prosperity," ran a campaign song published in The Daily Smokestack, a throwaway from the Wilde campaign,

> Who will help to build up factories in this city by
>   the sea.
> Oh, we love to have the tourists come, in our
>   sunshine to bask.
> But we need some smokestacks:
> Give us work: a chance is all we ask.[6]

Naturally, labor backed Wilde; and even John Spreckels, ostensibly a Marston supporter (Marston's department store being the biggest advertiser in Spreckels's two newspapers), kept his distance.

Louis Wilde wanted San Diego to be less like San Diego according to the Nolen Plan and more like Los Angeles, which seemed to have no plan at all: an ambitious, go-ahead, boosterish city. Los Angeles and San Diego ran parallel to each other through the 1880s. With the dredging of a deep-water port in Los Angeles in 1900, however, followed by the annexation of Hollywood in 1910, the successful completion of the Los Angeles Aqueduct in 1913, and the annexation of the San Fernando Valley in 1914, Los Angeles boosted itself into the status of a city-state complete unto itself, with its port, water and electricity, even its agriculture (the San Fernando Valley) under a unified municipal jurisdiction. Los Angeles, smokestack candidate Louis Wilde argued, was "full of youth, vision, imagination, optimism, curiosity, boosters, and brains." San Diego, by contrast, was filled with "old tight-wads, pessimists, vacillating, visionary dreamers."[7]

Wilde won the election and did his best to make San Diego a second Los Angeles. In two terms, he experienced only minimal success. Tiring of San Diego, Wilde moved to Los Angeles in 1921, having lost hope in transforming San Diego into Booster Town. For a former mayor of San Diego to move to Los Angeles was like Benedict Arnold going over to the British; for by this time, the 1920s, San Diego had developed a full-blown obsession with Los Angeles as a city representing everything it did not want to become (despite the fact that it had voted for smokestacks over geraniums in 1917). Since that time forward, fear of Los Angelesization (Max Miller described it as a fear of being gobbled by the City of Southern California encroaching southwards from the north) became a fixed point of San Diego identity and a constant call to vigilance and action.

To prevent such Los Angelesization, and yet to ensure a proper balance of smoke-stacks and geraniums, and hence to experience industrial growth while remaining a privileged urban enclave, the City of San Diego upped and joined the Navy. The possibilities of enlistment were there from the start, given the location of San Diego Bay as a strategically located Pacific port of call commanding the southwest-ern edge of the North American continent. In the 1830s and 1840s, San Diego Bay served the hide, tallow, and fur trade conducted by ships of the Bryant and Sturgis company out of Boston. Connecting Boston with Valparaiso, Lima, San Blas, the California coast, the Sandwich Islands, Canton, and the South Pacific, the hide and tallow trade pointed in the direction of the United States as a Pacific nation, and this in turn pointed to San Diego: which was why the twenty-two-gun American corvette USS *Cyane*, Captain Samuel F. du Pont commanding, sailed into San Diego Bay on 29 July 1846, clearing the bar of the unimproved harbor by a mere six inches. At 3:40 in the afternoon, the launch *Alligator*, under the command of Lieutenant Stephen Rowan, with a contingent of Marines under the command of Marine Lieutenant William Maddox, was rowed by its white-jacketed crew to the shore for the ceremony of raising the American flag in the plaza near the Casa Estudillo. The possession of San Diego and its port, together with the possession of the Bay of San Francisco to the north, officially transformed the United States into a naval power on the Pacific.

It took more than a half century for this naval relationship to be developed. The Navy initially chose Mare Island in San Francisco Bay as its Navy Yard; yet even during these neglected years, ships of the Navy passed frequently in and out of the San Diego harbor. In one instance, tragedy struck: the explosion of Boiler B aboard the patrol gunboat USS *Bennington*, just in from Honolulu, on 21 July 1905, killing sixty-four enlisted men and one officer. Acting Secretary of the Navy Charles Darling called it the most terrible explosion aboard an American vessel since the USS *Maine* exploded in Havana Harbor seven years earlier and precipi-tated the Spanish-American War. On Sunday the 23rd, San Diego held a mass burial service in the post cemetery at Fort Rosecrans atop Point Loma: a Book of Common Prayer rite conducted by the Reverend J. A. M. Richey, rector of St. Paul's, and a Catholic mass celebrated by Father Anthony Ubach.

The tragedy bonded San Diego to the Navy in a powerful and enduring way. Scalded and maimed sailors were cared for in city hospitals. San Diegans kept vigil in funeral parlors of the city before the caskets of young men who had died far from home and family. Young women seemed especially touched, obsessed even, by the mass death of so many young men, laid out in their blue jackets in the funeral parlors of the city. A huge crowd turned out for the burial service, and three years later a soaring granite obelisk was dedicated at the Fort Rosecrans cemetery in honor of the *Bennington* dead.

When the Great White Fleet steamed into San Diego Bay on 5 December 1908, the relationship between San Diego and the Navy became even more solidified. The fleet had been sent on its round-the-world cruise by President Theodore Roosevelt expressly to announce the advent of the United States as a naval power. Already the idea had been growing in the minds of many San Diegans that their city might capture the Pacific Fleet as its own. The Navy had other ideas, having invested fifty years and millions of dollars in its Mare Island Navy Yard in San Francisco Bay. The newly developed deep-water Port of Los Angeles at Wilmington/San Pedro, together with the adjacent Port of Long Beach, also offered serious competition.

Two figures, aviator Glenn Curtiss and Congressman William Kettner, played key roles in positioning San Diego eventually to capture the Pacific Fleet. In 1911, a mere eight years after Kitty Hawk, Curtiss established an aviation school on North Island in San Diego Bay, lured there by the San Diego Aero Club and the Spreckels-owned Coronado Beach Company, which offered Curtiss the use of the island, rent free, for three years as a promotional device. Just a few miles to the south of North Island, at Otay Mesa on the Mexican border, Santa Clara College professor John Montgomery had in 1883 conducted what was most likely the first heavier-than-air glider flight in history; and now the aviation identity of the region was further unfolding with the establishment of the Curtiss school.

Curtiss was interested in the military application of heavier-than-air flight. On 18 January 1911, a pilot in his employ, Eugene Ely, made the first airplane take-off from a ship: this from a wooden deck on the cruiser USS *Pennsylvania* at anchor in San Francisco Bay. Eight days later, Curtiss sponsored another demonstration, landing and taking off from the waters of San Diego Bay on a newly devised hydro-aeroplane equipped with a pontoon float. When the USS *Pennsylvania* anchored in San Diego Bay in mid-February, Curtis landed his hydro-aeroplane alongside the cruiser and was hoisted aboard, then lowered back into the water for a return flight to North Island. Thus within the space of a month Curtiss had demonstrated to the Navy that an airplane could take off from a ship and—of immediate importance—that a hydro-aeroplane might serve as an aerial scout for the fleet.

The connection had been made between sea power and the airplane. The next step: military pilots. At the specific invitation of Curtiss, the Secretary of the Navy assigned Lieutenant Theodore Ellyson, a submariner, to take a course of instruction at the Curtiss school. Graduating in 1911, Lieutenant Ellyson won his wings of gold as Navy Pilot Number One in an as yet unorganized Naval Air Corps. Also graduating were First Lieutenant Paul Beck of the Army and Signal Corps and Infantry Second Lieutenants G. E. M. Kelly and John Walker Jr., the first pilots of Army Air.

Even as the newly established Pacific Fleet began its operations, and as Glenn Curtiss was pioneering naval aviation, the Panama Canal was nearing completion. The intent of the Panama-California Exposition of 1915 was to identify and promote San Diego as the first American port of call north of the canal. Did this location not have military implications as well? Decidedly yes, believed San Diego's go-getting Congressman William Kettner and the oligarchy he represented. In April 1908 Kettner, a San Diego insurance man, had served as chair of the reception committee for the Great White Fleet, an experience that had left him convinced that San Diego had a chance to compete with San Francisco as a naval port. In 1912 Kettner went to Congress, a conservative Democrat representing a Republican constituency, swept into office by the Wilson landslide. In a brilliant coup for a freshman congressman, Kettner, over the objections of the Navy, won a $249,000 appropriation from the Senate Commerce Committee for the dredging of San Diego Harbor, followed by appropriations to complete the naval coaling station on Point Loma, to construct a naval radio station on Chollas Heights, to strengthen the coastal defenses at Fort Rosecrans, and to resurvey and remap the harbor and offshore waters. Kettner also persuaded the Navy to rename the cruiser USS *California* the USS *San Diego*, a rechristening ceremony held in San Diego Harbor on 16 December 1914. Not surprisingly, Kettner soon became known as the "gettinist" congressman thus far to represent the Golden State.

Kettner and the oligarchy he represented used the Panama-California Exposition as an opportunity to alert such visiting dignitaries as Secretary of the Navy Josephus Daniels and Assistant Secretary Franklin Delano Roosevelt to the advantages of San Diego not only as a deep-water port but as a place to train naval recruits. (For Assistant Secretary Roosevelt, his first visit to San Diego was the beginning of a lifelong love affair with the city.) Going even further, Kettner expressed the willingness of San Diego officials to lease buildings at a dollar a year to the Navy as temporary training facilities when the exposition closed. In less than two years, the Navy had some four thousand sailors quartered in Balboa Park: a far cry from the purism of the Parsons Plan! Kettner also pointed out to Commandant of the Marine Corps Major General George Barnett and Marine Colonel (later General) Joseph Pendleton the advantages of North Island as a Marine Corps training center. Returning to Washington, General Barnett joined Assistant Secretary Roosevelt as a convinced and vocal San Diego booster. Kettner, meanwhile, by then a member of the Naval Affairs Committee, introduced a resolution into the House on 5 Janaury 1916 providing for the purchase of properties on North Island for the use of the Marine Corps and the Army Signal Corps, which ran Army aviation. Concurrently, the San Diego Chamber of Commerce created a fund of $280,000 to purchase strategic properties for donation to the Navy. The City Council expressed its willingness to make available some seventy-nine acres of equally strategic tidelands. Deeds to these sites were sent to Kettner in Washington, and the congressman had the pleasure of presenting them to Secretary Daniels, who placed them in escrow.

The strategic importance of San Diego received a further boost in February 1915 when the Japanese cruiser *Asama* went aground on unchartered rocks at Puerto San Bartolomé in Baja California, also known as Turtle Bay. The *Asama* belonged to the North American Squadron of the Japanese Imperial Navy and had been operating off the coast of California and Mexico under the direct tactical command of the British in hopes of intercepting German shipping entering or leaving neutral American ports. When the Imperial Japanese Navy dispatched a squadron to conduct rescue operations on the *Asama*, and these operations stretched out over a two-month period, a Yellow Peril scare, fanned by an especially inflammatory article in the Los Angeles *Times*, which depicted the rescue operation as a Japanese reconnaissance in force, captured the headlines. The Japanese fleet, it was now recognized, was fully capable of conducting operations off the United States and Mexico; and that, as far as San Diego was concerned, reemphasized the necessity of a second naval base on the Pacific. The entrance of the United States into the war in April 1917 pushed these plans to fulfillment. Very soon, Secretary Daniels was recommending the creation of major Navy, Marine, and Army aviation facilities throughout greater San Diego.

The second city plan, which John Nolen completed in late 1925, depicted a city that had encompassed a naval presence into its core identity. San Diego had reinvented itself as the Gibraltar of the Pacific: the city as garrison and fortress, as naval port. The Naval Training Center and Marine Corps Recruit Depot fronting the Bay, the Naval Station and Repair Facility on the donated tidelands, the Naval Air Station on North Island, the Naval Hospital in Balboa Park, the Naval Radio Stations at Point Loma and Chollas Heights, and, later, the Naval Air Station at Miramar, the Naval Amphibious Base on Coronado, the Marine Corps Aviation Base at El Toro, and the Marine Corps Training Center at Camp Pendleton: truly the City of San Diego and its hinterlands had joined the Navy with a vengeance. Interestingly enough, Bertram Grosvenor Goodhue, architect of the Panama-California International Exposition, was chosen to design the Naval Training Station and Marine Corps Recruit Depot on North Island. For these facilities, Goodhue devised a Spanish Revival scheme more campus than barrack, which linked the Navy and the Marine Corps to the utopianism of the Spanish City in Balboa Park.

Joining the Navy, San Diego created a sustainable industrial economy that could be kept under control. Becoming the Gibraltar of the Pacific, San Diego found a way to develop its economy while remaining a resort. As in the case of all resorts, the money was coming from elsewhere, specifically the Department of the Navy in Washington. While the Navy did not demand an excess of local control, it must be admitted that in very short order, certainly by 1923, the rear admiral serving as Commandant of the Eleventh Naval District functioned as the Doge of San Diego: a ceremonial figure at public gatherings, resplendent in blue and gold or dress whites, a sword at his side, a Marine color guard in attendance. Like the Doge, the Commandant embodied the economy and consciousness of San Diego in a way that no mere mayor, no mere member of the City Council, no mere oligarch (not even John D. Spreckels, who passed away in June 1926) might ever hope to do.

Like all negotiated settlements, joing the Navy had its trade-offs. Was there, one might fairly ask, a postponement of civic maturity in such a dependent relationship? Could San Diego ever develop into a truly distinguished city now that it had become a direct dependent of Washington? However colorful it might be, after all, Gibraltar was in its basic identity a garrison, an outpost, and not a vital urban center. But then again: San Diego had always been a city that sustained within itself an anti-urban impulse, a city that wanted to be urban and suburban-pastoral at one and the same moment. Transforming itself into a military theme park, San Diego found a Progressive middle way between the untrammeled capitalism of Los Angeles and the restrictive aestheticism that was even then relegating Santa Barbara to the permanent status of a semi-resort. Selective, socially structured through rank and protocol, the Navy brought an idealized industrial presence to San Diego. Ship repair and aviation involved sophisticated levels of industrial engineering and technology; and aviation technology especially stimulated its civilian counterparts, as the construction and testing of the *Spirit of St. Louis* in San Diego soon proved. Aviation, military and civilian, brought to San Diego a high concentration of technologically astute Americans, from pilots and engineers to aircraft designers; and the very density of such talent helped establish a distinctive urban culture that would eventually render San Diego highly receptive to science and technology at its most innovative.

In 1925 T. Claude Ryan organized Ryan Airlines linking San Diego and Los Angeles, the first regularly scheduled air passenger service in the United States. By 1929 four airlines—Maddux, Western Air Express, Pickwick, and Continental Air Express—had made the air corridor between San Diego and Los Angeles the busiest in the nation. Under special contract, Ryan Airlines designed and built the *Spirit of St. Louis* for Charles Lindbergh in March and April of 1927; and when Lindbergh returned to San Diego on 21 September, having completed his epic flight to Paris, sixty thousand San Diegans packed City Stadium to celebrate, not just Lindbergh, but the San Diego–based aviation expertise that the *Spirit of St. Louis* represented. Two months later, voters passed a $650,000 bond issue to redeem tidal and submerged flatlands, as recommended by John Nolen in his second plan, for the construction of a metropolitan airport named in Lindbergh's honor, which was dedicated on 16 August 1928.

The Navy and Marine officer corps mingled easily with the local oligarchy, and enlisted sailors and Marines did not go out on strike or riot on the docks as the IWW did in 1912. In fact, young officers in dress whites made perfect escorts for the daughters of the oligarchy, as San Diego discovered to its delight on 7 April 1920 when His Royal Highness Edward, the Prince of Wales, attired in the uniform of a naval captain, stepped ashore from the steam tender of the British battleship HMS *Renown* and was greeted by Governor William Stephens, Mayor Louis Wilde, Rear Admiral Roger Welles, and assorted congressmen and state, county, and city officials.

Just as the San Diego oligarchy had wooed the Navy and the Marine Corps, it also wooed, arm-twisted even, the twenty-six-year-old heir to the throne, then en route to Australia and New Zealand. Initially, the HMS *Renown* was scheduled to touch only briefly in San Diego for refueling and refurbishment; but Mayor Louis Wilde, embroiled at the time in a financial scandal, knew a good opportunity when he saw it. Appointing a reception committee of oligarchs and military notables, Wilde persuaded the British liaison officer, Air Commodore L. E. O. Charlton, air attaché to the United States, to entreat the Prince and his entourage, which included the Prince's twenty-year-old cousin Sub-Lieutenant Louis Mountbatten, to spend a day and a half in San Diego. Events included a reception for British war veterans at dockside, a sightseeing motorcade through the city, an appearance before twenty-five thousand in the city stadium (the Prince was fascinated by the Magnavox sound system), a round of golf at the Coronado County Club, and a dinner and ball at the Hotel del Coronado, at which the mayor's daughter Lucille made her debut, together with a reception aboard the HMS *Renown* the following day for four hundred selected guests. As brief as it was, the visit represented a public relations triumph for San Diego: proof positive of its new status as Gibraltar of the Pacific.

In the years to come, San Diego showed a distinct partiality for ceremonial events, as they pertained to the Navy and military aviation. To celebrate the opening of Lindbergh Field, for example, the Navy and Army assembled more than four hundred airplanes. Bad weather reduced the flight to 222 aircraft, but it was still an impressive show. Four years later, on 28 July 1932, the Navy, Marine Corps, and Army organized a flight of 420 airplanes over San Diego in honor of visiting newspaper editors and reporters in Southern California for the opening of the Tenth Olympiad. Never before had so many military aircraft, including twenty eight flying boats and a dozen torpedo bombers, flown in one formation. For San Diego, the flight, like the visit of the Prince twelve years earlier, was a celebration of identity. Others might see in it a chilling forecast of the death that soon would be raining from the sky in Europe and the Far East. San Diego, in any event, was safe. San Diego had joined the Navy.

5

One Man's Family

Localism and Well-Being in Pre-War San Francisco

IKE other successful provincial cities, San Francisco had a way of promoting a sense of well-being and self-esteem in its citizenry. Take, for example, the Barbour family of Seacliff, the neighborhood fronting the Golden Gate. From 1932 to 1956, some 3,256 episodes in all, this fictional San Francisco family appeared daily on a national radio show called *One Man's Family*, written by San Franciscan Carleton Morse and originating from San Francisco radio station KPO for the NBC network.

The Barbours embodied what later became known as family values—in an unmistakably San Franciscan context. The program was filled with local references, including the stunning vista of the Golden Gate, which the Barbours could see from their rear living room window or gaze at from their garden wall, where members of the family were wont to take refuge for meditation at times of perplexity. *One Man's Family* postulated San Francisco as a unified, prosperous, middle-class city, struggling through the Depression in a middle-American way, sustained in significant measure by the city the Barbours called home. A decade later, San Francisco writer Kathryn Forbes successfully attempted similar themes in *Mama's Bank Account* (1943), which went to Broadway as *I Remember Mama*: the story of a Norwegian immigrant family coming of age in San Francisco, sustained by a similar sense of well-being.

For the previous two decades, the mayor of San Francisco, James (Sunny Jim) Rolph Jr., had been making a specialty of promoting this sense of identification and well-being that Carleton Morse was now using as the psychological and social context of *One Man's Family*. Partly out of necessity, Rolph had made himself the master of making San Francisco feel good about itself. A Republican of Progressive inclinations, Rolph performed brilliantly in his first term, 1912–16. Virtually every achievement of his long tenure in office, from 1912 to 1932, when he became governor of the state—the many public works, the Civic Center, the Panama-Pacific International Exposition, the publicly owned Municipal Railway—dates from this first term. As a Progressive, Rolph believed in the gospel of efficiency. He even went so far as to establish a Bureau of Efficiency to monitor city government. Believing in experts, he appointed such preeminent civil servants as City Engineer Michael O'Shaughnessy to supervise millions of dollars of public works, and he reappointed landscapist John McLaren Superintendent of Parks and backed McLaren's efforts to finish William Hammond Hall's master plan drawn up in the late 1870s. For a few wonderful years, Rolph's combination of personal charm and mayoral diplomacy perfectly fit the bill for San Francisco. During the exposition year of 1915, the ebullient mayor led innumerable groups in parade from Civic Center down Van Ness Avenue to the fair, perfectly embodying the aspiring civility of the city he governed—a civility kept genial and robust by a certain Western flair, unpretentious and direct—as he greeted former presidents Roosevelt and Taft, Secretary of State William Jennings Bryan, composer Camille Saint-Saens, Marine Band master John Philip Sousa, and other visiting dignitaries.

As impressive as its legacy in architecture, civic design, and public works might be, the Panama-Pacific International Exposition of 1915 led not to an era of good feeling, but to the most bitter and paranoid period in San Francisco history since the sandlot demonstrations of the late 1870s. Already exhausted by the frantic pace of his life (he was quietly hospitalized for exhaustion, possibly a breakdown, in January 1916), Rolph was devastated by the fierce class warfare that led up to the Preparedness Day bombing on 22 July 1916 and the revengeful mood of the oligarchy and the bitter response of labor in the aftermath of this terrible event. For the ensuing decade and a half of Rolph's mayoralty, the oligarchy remained paranoid and prosecutorial in its attitude toward labor. From within Rolph's own circle of shippers, in fact, his Pacific Union clubmates who controlled the Industrial Association of San Francisco, came the fiercest resistance, culminating in the maritime strike of 1934. Torn asunder by the conflict, Rolph found himself identifying, simultaneously, with his colleagues in the shipping business and other assorted oligarchs, such as banker Herbert Fleishhacker (who held approximately a million dollars in promissory notes from Hind, Rolph, and company) and the average voter, including labor unionists, from whom, election after election, he received continuing support at the ballot box.

Rolph solved his dilemma by drifting quietly into the camp of the oligarchy throughout the 1920s while doing everything possible in the ceremonial side of his office to make every San Franciscan feel good about his or her place in the city. Through the sheer genius of his healing presence, Rolph managed to smooth over, on the surface at least, the class antagonisms that were waiting to erupt in 1934. When he is recalled today, whether by historians or journalists, Rolph is perceived from the perspective of his genial colorfulness as mayor or from his increasingly conservative performance as governor, climaxed by his ultra-right approval of the vigilante lynchings in San Jose in 1934: a controversy that cost Rolph his life through a stroke. Historians frequently criticize Rolph for abandoning the effort to govern or manage San Francisco in preference to becoming, in urban historian Moses Rischin's wonderful phrase, the Constitutional Caliph of the City. Rarely mentioned, however, is the deliberate, self-conscious effort at healing and reconciliation Rolph made as mayor amidst the subeval class tensions of San Francisco. Virtually on his own, as mayor and public performer, Rolph sought to establish a shared realm of values and identity among San Franciscans of all classes and backgrounds. True, he was becoming progressively more under the control of the oligarchy—men such as William H. Crocker, M. H. de Young, and his personal banker Herbert Fleishhacker—although in 1917 he did veto a bill giving donors to an opera house proposed for the Civic Center proprietary rights to boxes and seats as smacking of too much aristocratic pretension. For most of the 1920s, however, Rolph, the perfervid Progressive of the previous decade, preferred to go along to get along. Appearing variously in an Eskimo parka, the apron of a master Mason, the war bonnet of an Indian chief, the fez of a Shriner, the plumed hat of a Knight of Columbus, the yarmulke of B'nai B'rith, or the regalia of Odd Fellows, Elks, the Ancient Order of Hibernians, or one or another of the unions in which he held honorary membership—Rolph perfected the art of seeming Mayor of all the People, which is the way he preferred to describe his role. "Only New York's very different Fiorello H. La Guardia," notes Moses Richin, "has rivaled Rolph as a symbol of the human and communal possibilities of the modern great city."[1]

Rolph, it must be remembered, was a self-made millionaire, a banker and a shipper. Much of the sense of well-being that Rolph was able to foster arose from the prosperity of San Francisco in the 1920s: a sense of well-being that continued after his departure for Sacramento due to the relative good fortune with which San Francisco went through the Great Depression. With the exception of the Dollar Steamship Company, whose fleet of passenger ships purchased from the government reverted to federal control in 1938, no significant company with deep San Francisco roots was forced to declare bankruptcy in the 1930s. The strength of business in San Francisco came from its diversity and the time-tested nature of its key companies, many of them with origins in the Gold Rush. The diversity of the San Francisco economy came from the isolated yet populous and strategically placed location of San Francisco itself.

Like frontier Chicago, San Francisco was a self-actualizing market and marketplace, which very soon found itself either supplying or orchestrating the trade of a vast inland and maritime region. It was also a manufacturing center. By 1860 San Francisco could build a locomotive. By 1875 it could repair ships in the dry docks at Hunter's Point. By the late 1880s, at the Union Iron Works, it could build such impressive ships-of-the-line as the cruisers USS *Charleston* (1889), *San Francisco* (1890), and *Olympia* (1892), Admiral Dewey's flagship at the Battle of

Manila Bay, and the battleships USS *Wisconsin* (1902), *Ohio* (1904), and *California* (1904). San Francisco repaired its own ships with parts manufactured in San Francisco. It also loaded and reloaded them, insured them, and orchestrated the buying and selling of their cargos. San Francisco manufactured its own cordage, paint, and bricks and brewed its own beer—and by the 1880s scores of breweries in San Francisco were slaking the thirst of the Far West.

Because it functioned as the most notable urban center west of Chicago and east of Hong Kong, San Francisco not only became an industrial city, it also bought and sold what it manufactured and hence became an important center of commercial exchange. Through its banks and insurance companies, San Francisco financed and insured what was made and traded and thus emerged as the financial center of the Far West. Having developed its own gas plant and delivery system in the mid-1850s, San Francisco electrified itself at the turn of the century through a series of locally financed hydro-electric projects. Thus by the early 1900s, San Francisco was playing yet another economic role, energy capital of Northern and Central California.

Ships, import-export, insurance, blue jeans, gas and electricity, paint, or beer: most of the companies of San Francisco tended to be family owned and operated, and, most important, many of these family executives, some of them in the third generation of ownership, tended to be professionally educated and competent in the latest technology and managerial techniques. Walter Haas, for example, president of Levi Strauss, in his forties in the 1930s, had studied economics and business at UC Berkeley and interned in New York with the Guarantee Trust Company following his graduation before entering the family business of manufacturing jeans.

At the Golden Gate International Exposition of 1939 and 1940, the number of flourishing San Francisco–based companies that mounted exhibitions testified to the durability of the San Francisco economy through the Depression. Obviously, such San Francisco–based giants as the Southern Pacific, Levi Strauss, Crown Zellerbach, Wells Fargo, the Bank of America, I. Magnin & Company, Lucky Stores, Simmons Mattress, Stauffer Chemical, S & W Fine Foods, and Fireman's Fund Insurance had a dominant presence, but the full variety of San Francisco business showed its best self as well. First of all, there were the port-related companies: Crowley Maritime, with its great fleet of tugboats operating up and down the Pacific Coast; Matson Lines, developing travel and trade with Hawaii and the South Pacific; and the American Hawaiian Steamship Company, headed by the redoubtable Roger Lapham. Next came the companies dependent upon docks and shipping, most notably Schilling, Hills Brothers, Folgers, and MJB. The presence of such national coffee, tea, and spice companies constituted a prime expression of San Francisco as international port of call, for the products that were imported, processed, and packaged by these companies came from Latin America, Southeast Asia, and the Arab states. Along the docks of San Francisco, when the breezes were right, you could smell the aroma of coffee beans being roasted, that fragrance so pleasing to the senses and so suggestive of the great world, rich and exotic, unfolding beyond the Golden Gate.

Founded by Austin and Reuben Hills in 1878, Hills Brothers successfully projected its image by means of an innovative packaging and logo, which engendered another San Francisco industry: the design and printing of commercial labels, most noticeably by the Schmidt, Schwabacher-Fry, Stecher-Traung, and Union lithograph companies, which printed the orange crate labels of California for two generations. In the late 1890s Hills Brothers first employed the figure of a turbaned, bearded Arab in flowing caftan, sipping coffee, an image destined to become one of the best-known trademarks in American packaging history. Like Betty Crocker, the Morton Salt girl, Uncle Ben, or Aunt Jemima, the coffee-sipping Arab of Hills Brothers would change subtly over the years yet persist into the 1960s. In 1901 Hills Brothers joined with the San Francisco–based American Can Company to pioneer vacuum packing, which soon became another flourishing industry. Headquartered in an Italian Renaissance palazzo facing the Embarcadero, Hills Brothers in 1926 introduced the concept of a key attached to each coffee can, another of many patented innovations from San Francisco in this era.

By 1939 the San Francisco–based Bank of America had become the second largest bank in the nation, after Chase Manhattan of New York. Presiding over the Bank of America, headquartered at One Powell at Market, was its founder and chairman A. P. Giannini, then nearing seventy. Founded in the Italian-dominated North Beach district in October 1904, Giannini's Bank of Italy, as it was then called, had 276 branches through the state by 1927. Yet Giannini wanted more. He wanted a banking network covering the nation and key foreign markets. In October 1928 Giannini organized the Transamerica Corporation, a holding company chartered in Delaware, and rechartered the Bank of Italy, which he renamed the Bank of America, as the first step in establishing his goal. The move temporarily cost Giannini his bank when Elisha Walker, a young Wall Street investment banker, gained control of Transamerica in January 1930 and pushed Giannini from the scene. It took two years for Giannini's friend Charles Fay to organize a proxy counter-attack against the Eastern forces led by Walker, now chairman of the board of Transamerica. Had Fay lost the battle, California would have entered the 1930s as a financial colony of the East, rather than its own center of finance. In July 1933 the Bank of America resumed paying dividends, having made an early recovery from the Depression.

The economic history of California cannot be written without constant reference to the Bank of America. Giannini financed Hollywood. He bought the bonds that financed the Hetch Hetchy and the Golden Gate Bridge. Through subsidiary corporations, the Bank of America refinanced California agriculture at a time when it was on the verge of collapse. On the political scene, Giannini helped broker the nomination of his friend FDR in 1932, a fact FDR never forgot. During the bank crisis of 1933, FDR depended heavily on Giannini for advice. Although Giannini was by the late 1930s one of the most powerful bankers in America, the friend of FDR and a frequent guest at the White House, his personal style remained unpretentious, still touched by his boyhood and young manhood spent among Italian ranchers. He refused to use his private office, preferring instead to sit at an open desk on the main floor, as if he were a loan officer ready for business. Although he belonged to the Pacific Union and Bohemian clubs, he preferred to lunch with his cronies at Louis Fasion's restaurant on O'Farrell just west of Powell Street. Most of Giannini's lunch gang were fellow Italian-Americans, as was the cuisine. After lunch, Giannini loved to roll dice to see who would pay the check. When he won, Giannini laughed joyfully: this great financial mogul, happy to have bested his cronies at dice! Living comfortably in the suburb of San Mateo, Giannini seemed uninterested in creating a personal fortune. His net worth never amounted to more than a million dollars, and he eventually gave away almost half of what he had acquired.

Located on Bayshore Boulevard on the southern edge of the city, the Schlage Lock Company asserted in no uncertain terms that San Francisco remained a hands-on manufacturing town. San Franciscan Charles Kendrick had gotten involved in Schlage Lock as an investor in the early 1920s, at the same time he was investing in another San Francisco product, SOS scouring pads, invented by William Smith, an advertising solicitor with the San Francisco *Examiner*. Kendrick eventually moved the SOS operation to Chicago but kept Schlage Lock in San Francisco, refinancing and reorganizing it in 1926–27, and being elected president by stockholders in March 1927. The first years of the Depression were difficult, but by 1933 Schlage Lock was back in full operation, creating hundreds of blue-collar and clerical jobs.

Financial success allowed Charles Kendrick to take a leadership role in civic affairs. A self-made man who never had the opportunity to attend college, Kendrick was very much the self-created gentleman, well read, impeccable in articulation and enunciation, a nighttime elocution school having served as his college. During the war, he served as a captain, later major, in the Remount Service, responsible for the horses of the Yankee Division. Wounded and gassed at Saint-Mihiel, Captain Kendrick discharged himself from the hospital and returned to the front. Two months later, Major Kendrick was wounded a second time while serving as remount officer for V Corps. Returning to San Francisco with the Silver Star and a Purple Heart with cluster, Kendrick remained Major Kendrick for the rest of his life, the center of a dozen civic activities. In the fall of 1928, he spearheaded the drive to persuade San Francisco voters to pass a bond issue to build a War Memorial complex, including an opera house, in honor of San Franciscans who had lost their lives in the Great War. He helped design and implement the financing of the last phase of the Hetch Hetchy project. In the early 1930s Kendrick spearheaded the San Francisco Emergency Relief Committee, which fed seventeen thousand people a day in the four years of its operation.

Despite the Depression, which they were weathering with comparative success, the elites who controlled San Francisco—which is to say, the elites who organized the Golden Gate International Exposition of 1939 and 1940—led the clubby, almost inbred life characteristic of provincial urban elites in the United States prior to the Second World War. Many, in fact, such as Templeton Crocker, grandson of Charles Crocker of the railroad Big Four, were in the third generation of wealth. Born in San Francisco in 1884, Charles Templeton Crocker attended Yale, where he palled around with Cole Porter, and returned to San Francisco to pursue a Cole Porter–ish sort of life, based out of a thirty-seven-room Italian villa on a 118-acre estate in Hillsborough. Crocker collected rare books, refounded the California Historical Society in the early 1920s, and wrote the lyrics for an opera, *The Land of Happiness*, a Chinese fantasy-extravaganza that premiered on the evening of 4 August 1917 as the fifteenth annual Grove Play production in the Bohemian Grove, with music by Joseph Redding, a San Francisco lawyer-composer who had already collaborated with Victor Herbert on the Broadway operetta *Natoma*, a tale of Indian love in the forest, which also had its origins as a Bohemian Club production. In February 1925 Crocker and Redding traveled to Monte Carlo, where their opera, renamed *Fay Yen Fah*, had its European pre-miere at the Monte Carlo Opera House, with choreography by a youthful George Balanchine and Diaghilev's Ballet Russe and sumptuous costumes and sets by Herbert Julian Stowitts. In mid-January 1926 Gaetano Merola, founding director of the San Francisco Opera Company, gave *Fay Yen Fah* its American debut at the Columbia Theater. In 1930 Crocker turned his attention to yachting, building the *Zaca*, a double topsail schooner, 118 feet in length, costing a quarter of a million dollars and rated as one of the finest yachts in the nation. Crocker pro-ceeded to sail around the world, which he considered a reasonable way to live through the Depression.

Returning to San Francisco, Templeton Crocker devoted himself intermittently to the management of the St. Francis Hotel on Union Square, which the Crocker family had financed and built just before the Earthquake. Crucial to the success of the St. Francis was its restaurant and nightclub, the Mural Room, named in honor of the Pageant of Nations mural painted along one wall in 1913 by Santa Barbara artist Albert Herter (his son Christian would be Secretary of State in the Eisenhower administration), including a striking depiction of San Francisco writer Gertrude Atherton as California. In 1935 Crocker moved the Mural Room from its opening on Powell Street to the interior of the hotel and placed Swiss-born maître d' Ernest Gloor in charge, with Jan Garber and His Orchestra on hand for luncheon and dinner music. At the Monday luncheons favored by prominent women, maître d' Gloor seated guests according to an intricate system that consti-tuted its own form of Social Register. Gloor knew, among other things, never to seat a De Young next to a Spreckels since in the previous generation gunfire had been exchanged between the two families.

In May 1937 reality caught up—briefly!—with Templeton Crocker when the workers of the St. Francis Hotel went out on strike, closing the St. Francis for eighty-seven days until Crocker recognized the union and accepted arbitration. Sobered by this brief but painful brush with reality, Crocker hired Dan London, the thirty-two-year-old general manager of the rival Sir Francis Drake, to take the helm of the St. Francis, which London did with great panache for the next thirty-two years, living on the premises with his wife and children: the perfect hotelier, six feet, two inches tall, clipped mustache, impeccable British tailoring. Drawn to his profession as a young man in Seattle after reading the hotel novels of Arnold Bennett, London epitomized San Francisco's growing sense of itself as a hotel and convention city. He became, in fact, the official greeter of the city, welcoming three decades of royalty, presidents, statesmen, and assorted celebrities to the city by the Golden Gate.

Among other things, San Francisco was a sports-minded town. The city supported a consistently popular Pacific Coast League baseball team, the Seals, whose home ballpark at 16th and Bryant sat some forty thousand fans on a sold-out day in the Mission district sunshine. Seals manager Frank (Lefty) O'Doul, a Butchertown native (the stockyard and meat-packing district of the city) embodied the Irish-American urban style to a T. The Seals recruited three brothers from North Beach, Joe, Dom, and Vince DiMaggio. Destined to share honors with Babe Ruth and a handful of other players in the upper pantheon of baseball greats, brother Joe, a quiet kid, had dropped out of Galileo High School to work in a box factory and sell the *Call-Bulletin* in North Beach. He also acquired a reputation as the best pool and card player hanging out at LaRocca's on Columbus. Joe played basketball and football with equal aplomb, but it was his skills as a shortstop and slugger that brought him to the Seals. All three DiMaggio brothers went on to the major league, which meant leaving San Francisco and moving to the East Coast. Joe DiMaggio's thirteen years with the New York Yankees made him the best-known San Franciscan in the nation.

Perhaps because of its proximity to the water, San Francisco was a swimming city as well as a baseball town. Built in the late 1890s, Sutro Baths adjacent to the Cliff House on the western edge of the peninsula was the largest indoor plunge in the world, a steel and glass palace arching over a number of parallel pools, all of it the gift of millionaire mayor Adolph Sutro to the city where he had grown wealthy in real estate. San Francisco sustained the largest outdoor swimming pool in the world as well: Fleishhacker Pool, southwards down the Great Highway from Sutro Baths at the western edge of Golden Gate Park, 220 yards in length, so large that the lifeguards patrolled it in rowboats. In the private sector there were the Neptune Baths on Lombard, the Crystal Plunge in North Beach, the Lurline Baths at Bush and Larkin, catering to the downtown, the Women's Athletic Club on Sutter, the Olympic Club on Post, perhaps the most beautiful indoor swimming pool in the country, the YWCA on Sutter, and the YMCA on the Embarcadero. All these pools, together with the pool of the Concordia Argonaut Club on Van Ness, were fed with ocean water by the pipeline of the Olympic Salt

Water Company, set up in 1892 by the Olympic Club to pipe salt water via an eleven-inch cast-iron aqueduct from Ocean Beach. (Barber shops subscribed to the salt water service as well.) For those who preferred to plunge into the salt water directly, the Dolphin Club and the South End Rowing Club had been accommodating bay swimmers and oarsmen since the 1870s.

In the matter of public recreation, the WPA was very good to San Francisco. In August 1939 assistant city engineer Clyde Healy, coordinator of WPA projects in San Francisco, filed a report chronicling an impressive record: $2.8 million of improvements in Golden Gate Park, including new tennis courts, the refurbishment of Kezar Stadium, where high school football games were played, the construction of a fly-caster's pool and clubhouse, the completion of two clubhouses at the Harding Park and Lincoln Park municipal golf courses, and a bathhouse at Aquatic Park on the Bay (designed in the shape of an ocean liner) intended to facilitate bay swimming, together with numerous other improvements in the city's park and recreation system.

Public transportation was equally flourishing. Cable cars ran on Powell, Hyde, and California streets. Streetcars of the Market Street and the Municipal Railway systems connected every sector of the city with the downtown. Thanks to the tunnel completed beneath Twin Peaks in 1917, connection between the downtown and the developing southwestern districts of the city—the West Portal, the Sunset, St. Francis Wood, Forest Hill, Miraloma Park, Sherwood Forest—took no more than twenty minutes and cost only a nickel.

When it came to connecting with Marin County or the East Bay, ferry boats continued to compete against the two recently completed bridges into the 1940s. On a weekday, fifty thousand commuters came and left through the Ferry Building at the foot of Market Street. This heavy traffic made the Ferry Building, a stately replica of the Giralda Tower of Seville, the busiest terminal in the world outside London's Charing Cross Station. Ferry boat amenities included coffee and donut bars, food counters (the corned beef hash on the Key System ferries was in a league of its own), newsstands, a cocktail service in the evening (after 1933!), shoeshine stands, and other conveniences. Passengers sat in loosely organized circles by habit, with an informal system of assigned seats. There were book-reading, sewing, card-playing, and checkers circles. Age groups had varying preferences. The younger crowd, for example, favored the restaurants on the upper deck of the Southern Pacific ferry *Sacramento*, a newer ferry, constructed in 1924, which had seats for nineteen hundred passengers. During the Christmas season, volunteer committees would decorate the ferries and organize parties. Carolers in costumes would stroll the decks singing. In April, straw boaters replaced felt fedoras on the men, and the decks were crowded with commuters enjoying the sunshine. With forty million passengers being transported each year, the ferry boat system constituted a city afloat at peak commuter hours.

More important, the ferry system was linked directly with Market Street and Municipal Railway streetcars in front of the Ferry Building and Key System Interurban Electrics in the East Bay. Founded in the early 1900s by entrepreneur Frank (Borax) Smith, who had made his fortune in borax ore, the Key System served the East Bay. A commuter railroad, the Key System swept through the East Bay from Richmond to Hayward, with spur lines extending into the hills of Berkeley and Oakland. The Key System was a real railroad. Its drivers and conductors wore dark blue uniforms with gold buttons and standard driver or conductor hats, squared off with a blunted leather visor. Like a real railroad, the Key System Interurbans were capable of linking up to four cars in one train at peak hours. Powered from overhead lines, Key System Interurbans were objects of beauty. They conferred on the sub/urban network of East Bay communities an almost European ambience. Cars were well designed, possessing the boxy self-assurance of the 1910s and 1920s, followed by the Streamline Moderne models of the 1930s. The Key System also ran its own ferry boats and maintained a sixteen-thousand-foot-long pier at Emeryville, serviced by a neo-Gothic terminal breathtaking in the sweep of its interior spaces. On 6 May 1933 the terminal burned and was later replaced with unpretentious sheds.

The Golden Gate International Exposition inspired an even better idea: the running of the Key System across the San Francisco–Oakland Bay Bridge directly into San Francisco. This connection came into service in January 1939. Now passengers could embark on Key System Interurbans at the Transbay Terminal in the city for a speedy trip across the Bay. This first-rate public transit system kept San Francisco at the economic and entertainment center of the ever-growing metropolitan Bay Area through the 1960s. Because of the efficiency and inexpensiveness of the public commute to San Francisco, companies continued to maintain their headquarters and many of their other operations as well in the downtown.

Public education was in comparably excellent shape. Through the flush years of the later 1910s and 1920s, San Francisco constructed an array of architecturally distinguished grammar and high schools, including Timothy Pflueger's Roosevelt Junior High School on Geary Street. With the exception of the parochial school system and private girls' schools (Sarah Dix Hamlin and Katherine Delmar Burke), San Francisco was a public school–oriented city, from K-12 through UC Berkeley. (With the UC Berkeley campus a mere thirty minutes away by streetcar and ferry, the university remained, for an entire generation of San Franciscans, a commuter school.) The city supported a number of fine high schools—Mission High School on Dolores Street in the Mission district, Commerce High School at Grove and Van Ness, Galileo between Francisco and Bay in North Beach, Polytechnic on Frederick Street near Kezar Stadium in Golden Gate Park.

Of these public high schools, Lowell High School held a most favored position. An amalgamation of two pioneering San Francisco institutions, Boys' High School and Girls' High School, Lowell represented the San Francisco equivalent of Boston Latin or of Peter Stuyvesant or Horace Mann high schools in New York: an elite urban academy with exacting standards within a public school format. In the 1860s philosopher Josiah Royce attended Boys' High School, along with Albert Michelson, the first American to win the Nobel Prize. Located since 1913 in a sprawling red brick complex at the corner of Hayes and Masonic in the Panhandle district of the city, Lowell offered near automatic acceptance to Berkeley. Lowell teachers enjoyed a high esprit de corps. Graduates of good universities taught at Lowell and tended to keep their positions for a lifetime. The Jewish community especially favored Lowell, putting it into friendly competition with the nearby St. Ignatius, a Jesuit institution peopled in the main by Italian and Irish. The business elite of San Francisco were by and large Lowell graduates, while St. Ignatius graduates dominated the bench and bar and civil service.

In its own proper and provincial way, San Francisco was a Jewish city: not like New York was a Jewish city, alive with the tumultuous energies of recent immigration, but a Jewish city nonetheless, cohesive and understated. Sephardic Jews of multi-generational American standing, together with more recent German Jewish immigrants, played an important role in the establishment of San Francisco in the 1850s; and Jewish culture flourished in San Francisco through the nineteenth and early twentieth centuries. By 1940 there were approximately forty thousand Jews in San Francisco, out of a total population of 634,536, or roughly 6 percent of the population. From one perspective, sheer numbers, San Francisco was not an intensely Jewish city; yet from other perspectives—prosperity, a sense of well being, a philanthropic commitment to Jewish and non-Jewish causes alike, leadership in business and the arts—the Jewish community of San Francisco more than held its own. Since the turn of the century, moreover, Eastern European Jews had been migrating in some numbers to San Francisco, settling in the Western Addition. Fillmore Street and Fulton Street, which crossed Fillmore, comprised San Francisco's Lower East Side, with a wonderful array of bakeries, delicatessens, clothing and furniture stores, bookstores, and shops selling every manner of reconditioned furniture and bric-a-brac.

Although the Jewish community had not made politics a priority, it showed a small but steady presence, mostly Republican, on the Board of Supervisors from 1900 onwards. One Jewish supervisor, Jessie Colman, a Republican, served on the Board for twenty-six years, from 1921 until 1947. In 1898 Republican Julius Kahn won election to Congress, where he remained, with only one two-year interruption, until his death in 1924, when he was succeeded by his wife Florence, who represented San Francisco until 1937. Two other Jewish Republicans, B. J. Feigenbaum and Jefferson Peyser, represented San Francisco in the state assembly through the 1930s.

Ensconced with his family in a grand Victorian at 1735 Franklin Street, Edward Bransten, a partner in the MJB coffee, tea, and spice company, epitomized the solidarity, the regularity, the sense of well-being of German-Jewish San Francisco as it moved into the 1930s. In later years, Bransten's daughter Frances would write a charming memoir of her family life in the late 1930s with its mingled mood of San Francisco and Thomas Mann: her father's early rising, the fine array of brushes and combs on his dressing table, the conservative suits and starched white shirts with French cuffs and separate collars, the white linen handkerchief tucked ever so precisely in the breast pocket ("I never saw Father without a tie or jacket," Frances remembered), breakfast and the morning paper, a few well-chosen words to wife and children, the daily walk or cable car ride to the Olympic Club for a morning shave just before the office, lunch almost inevitably at the Concordia-Argonaut, and an equally ceremonial meal, formally served, with wife and scrubbed children in the evening. Had Thomas Mann visited San Francisco from Pacific Palisades, where he had taken up his exile, and met the Branstens, he would have encountered a German-Jewish Buddenbrooks in its San Francisco variation.

Like Jewish thought itself, Jewish philanthropy cut two ways: to the larger city and to the Jewish community. The Steinhart Aquarium and Strybing Arboretum in Golden Gate Park, the Sigmund Stern Grove—any number of city-wide bene-factions came from the Jewish community. Internally, Jewish philanthropy and self-help organizations—the Emanu-El Sisterhood, the Hebrew Free Loan Association, the Hebrew Home for the Aged Disabled, the Jewish Family Service Agency, the Hebrew Orphan Asylum and Home Society, Mt. Zion Hospital—had deep roots in the frontier era. The Jewish Family Service Agency, for example, known until 1937 as the Eureka Benevolent Society, was founded in the 1850s to care for one solitary orphan whose parents had perished in the explosion of a Sacramento steamer. The agency handled more than six hundred cases a year: coming to the aid of a family whose household furniture was on the verge of repossession, helping a student through Berkeley, providing care for an emotionally disturbed child. In 1937 Bernstein's Fish Grotto on Powell Street contributed free Thanksgiving dinners to needy Jewish families recommended by the agency. After 1936 the attention of Jewish philanthropy turned to refugees from Nazi Germany through its San Francisco Committee for Service to Emigrés. Beginning in 1938, the Pacific Hebrew Orphan Asylum and Home Society inaugurated a program with German-Jewish Children's Aid to resettle German-Jewish children in the city. Eleven boys and six girls safely arrived before the Nazis blocked the program.

The business and professional classes of the Jewish community belonged to the Argonaut Club at 421 Powell just off Union Square and the Concordia on Van Ness Avenue at Post. Patrician and exclusive, the Argonaut offered a parallel to the Pacific Union, serving primarily as a downtown luncheon club frequented by the older Jewish families: the Haases, Koshlands, Branstens, Slosses, Gunsts, Gerstles, and others. The Concordia, by contrast, had a more inclusive membership among aspiring merchants and middle-class professionals. In 1931 the Concordia remodeled its basement swimming pool and other athletic facilities and launched an ambitious sports program, fielding teams against the largely Irish Catholic Olympic Club. Taking office as the president of the Concordia in 1935, Dr.

Franklin Harris, chief of staff of Mt. Zion Hospital, warned the membership not to become too assimilated: not, that is, to lose contact with the Ishmaelites on McAllister Street, as Dr. Harris put it, and detach themselves from the world of Eastern European Jewry that was also part of the larger Jewish community. In 1939 the Argonaut merged with the Concordia as a matter of financial necessity, but also as a way of fusing the upper-class nineteenth-century families of the Argonaut with their more aspiring confreres at the Concordia.

Through the 1920s and into the early 1930s, the Fleishhacker brothers, Herbert and Mortimer, were the most prominent Jews in the city. The San Francisco–born sons of Aaron and Delia Stern Fleishhacker, the Fleishhacker boys joined their father's paper business as teenagers in 1887. While yet in their mid-twenties, they financed the transmission of hydro-electricity to San Francisco. Herbert spent his twenties and early thirties in the field in Oregon and Northern California. Next up: banking, specifically the London, Paris, and American Bank of San Francisco, later renamed the Anglo and London Paris National Bank, where Herbert served as president from 1911 to 1932. Other Fleishhacker involvements included the Fireman's Fund Insurance Company, the Natomas Company, the Pacific Steamship Company, the Realty Syndicate Corporation, the San Francisco Remedial Loan Association, Tyler Island Farms, the Yosemite Chemical Company, Del Monte Properties, the Crown Zellerbach Corporation, Occidental Insurance: a roll call of prosperous San Francisco–based enterprises in the first three decades of the century. Mortimer became a UC regent, and Mayor James Rolph appointed Herbert to the Park and Recreation Commission in 1918, where he served as president for thirty years, guiding the development of the city's zoo and outdoor swimming pool that bore his name. In 1932, however, Herbert lost control of the Anglo and London Paris National Bank to Lazard Frères in Paris and the Anglo California Trust Company of San Francisco. The controlling partners in the new bank, the Anglo California National Bank, did not like the way that Herbert Fleishhacker was keeping his books. There was a court case, and when it was over, Herbert's brother Mortimer had been forced to honor from his own resources a crushing number of unsecured loans. Herbert Fleishhacker lost his home at 2418 Pacific and moved into the St. Francis Hotel, where he lived the rest of his life, supported by his brother.

San Francisco Jewry was equally divided between two temples: Sherith Israel, Conservative, located since 1906 in a great domed structure at Webster and California designed by Albert Pissis, the leading architect of turn-of-the-century San Francisco; and Temple Emanu-El, Reform, whose neo-Byzantine dome at Lake and Arguello commanded the northeast skyline. Completed in 1925, this splendid edifice had been ecumenically designed by the Protestant Arthur Brown Jr., who had followed Pissis to the Beaux Arts, and Gustave Albert Lansburgh, a prominent Jewish architect responsible, among other projects, for the Orpheum Theater on Market Street.

Throughout the second half of the nineteenth century, the frontier urban Jewish tradition, be it located in Pittsburgh, Cleveland, Cincinnati, or Chicago, was Reform, and San Francisco was no exception. Established in 1851, Temple Emanu-El had gathered unto itself three generations of German Jewish San Franciscans. The sensibility at Emanu-El, while not assimilationist, was not isolationist either. For the Reform German Jews of San Francisco, Judaism was a religion, an ethical heritage, a range of cultural values, a style of living totally commensurate with American (read San Franciscan) life. As rabbi, the trustees of Emanu-El in 1930 chose Irving Reichert, who in his cultural ecumenism, his anti-Zionism, and his sense of Judaism as a species of Unitarianism within a Mosaic framework represented the beliefs and attitudes of at least half of San Francisco Jewry. Born in New York City in 1895, Reichert had earned his bachelor's in Hebrew literature at that citadel of the Reform movement, the Hebrew Union College of Cincinnati, followed by further study at Columbia. Ecumenical in his tastes, Reichert did not eliminate Jesus from the roll call of Hebrew prophets. On the other hand, he was no patsy either. In 1933 he led efforts to remove religious references from Christmastime celebrations in public schools, and he persuaded local radio stations not to carry Father Charles Coughlin, the anti-Semitic radio evangelist. Outspoken in his support of the cotton strikers in 1933 and the striking longshoremen in 1934, Reichert blasted Governor Rolph for countenancing the San Jose lynchings and agitated ceaselessly for the release of Tom Mooney.

In 1933 Reichert traveled into the belly of the beast itself, to Germany, where he saw the problem as hopeless. His solution: Jews from around the world should finance the escape of as many European Jews as possible. Late that year, Reichert helped organize the Campaign for the Relief of Victims of Nazi Oppression. Anti-Zionism, in Reichert's opinion, did not imply blindness to Naziism, merely opposition to the necessity of a Jewish state. In 1937 Reichert braved the gorgon yet one more time, returning to Nazi Germany as part of an investigative team. Despite such involvements, he remained a fervid anti-interventionist until Pearl Harbor: a conviction, he argued, arising from his distrust of war as a solution to anything, even the Nazi menace. Not surprisingly, Reichert's outspoken anti-Zionism and anti-interventionism cost him his pulpit after the war. By then, the horror of the Holocaust hand rendered him a figure from the past: naive, overly optimistic, too much the assimilated San Franciscan.

Assimilation was always an issue for upper-middle-class Jewish San Franciscans. Here, after all, was a city in which they were in so many respects the establishment; where Christmas trees appeared without apology in living rooms during the holiday season; where the best-known Jew in the city, Albert (Micky) Bender, had been born in Dublin, the son of a rabbi, spoke with a Dublin accent, and celebrated St. Patrick's Day. Arriving in San Francisco in his teens, Bender prospered as an insurance broker, first in partnership with his uncle William Bremer, then later on his own, headquartered in the Robert Dollar Building at California and Battery. Bender kept bachelor's digs at the Studio Building at 1369 Post between Franklin and Gough, a slightly raffish and bohemian establishment just west of

Auto Row on Van Ness, favored by aspiring painters, with Betty Horst's Studio of the Dance on the first floor. As a young man, Micky Bender adored his first cousin, artist Ann Bremer, whose father, Micky's uncle, had been his first employer and, later, his business partner. Ann Bremer developed into an artist of great promise, keeping her studio–living space also in the Studio Building on Post. When she died suddenly in 1923, the bottom fell out of Micky's life. To his dying day, he maintained her studio as a shrine. Having lost Ann, Micky Bender rebuilt himself around her memory—and the service of San Francisco. An astute insurance broker, independently employed, Bender possessed the income and the personal freedom to put himself at the service of these two ideals, which fused as the new premise of his emotional and psychological life.

By the 1930s, when he was in his mid-sixties, Micky Bender had become a living institution. Already, he had donated important rare book collections to Stanford, UC Berkeley, Mills College, Trinity College (Dublin), the San Francisco Public Library, and the San Francisco Art Institute, where he established the Ann Bremer Memorial Library. Stanford and Mills named their rare books rooms in his honor. To Trinity College he made a gift of books and manuscripts in honor of his parents. He followed this with a collection of Asian art (this, the San Francisco touch, the preoccupation with the aesthetics of Asia), given in his mother's name to the National Museum in Dublin. The President of the Republic, Eamon de Valera, personally dedicated the Augusta Bender Memorial Room of Far Eastern Art in June 1934, with Bender on hand. Bender also donated important collections of art to UC, the de Young Museum, and the California Palace of the Legion of Honor. Along with Albert Gerstle, Bender put the San Francisco Museum of Art in the forefront of collecting Diego Rivera. When Rivera had trouble getting a visa, Bender fixed the matter through his connections with the State Department. He commissioned and underwrote Gottardo Piazzoni's landscape murals on the grand staircase of the Main Library.

Concurrent with this impressive work of patronage was Bender's other role as the acknowledged greeter of the city, now that Mayor Rolph was no longer on the scene. Elegantly attired in his tailored double-breasted suit with extra-wide and finely pointed lapels, his tie impeccable against a gleamingly white starched shirt, his hat at a jaunty angle (the right brim raised, the left brim rakishly lowered), Bender negotiated the streets of the city as if on a family visit. He knew everyone and they knew him. To walk with him in the downtown en route to the Robert Dollar Building was to have the opportunity to experience San Francisco as a cohesive community, even a small town. Micky Bender loved parties, his own and others. His annual St. Patrick's Day gala, with its mixed Irish and Jewish guest lists, was a civic institution, covered in the press like opening day at the races. For these occasions, Bender dressed in the robes of a cardinal. Despite a slight speech impediment, he could recite heroic quantities of verse from memory, a legacy of his Dublin boyhood. An inveterate letter writer, he maintained extensive connections with the Irish literary establishment, as well as the writers, artists, and fine printers of San Francisco: Robinson and Una Jeffers at Carmel, J. B. Priestley in London, Otis Skinner, Margaret Anglin, Will Irwin, Ruth Chatterton, Katherine Cornell, and Ruth St. Dennis in New York.

History has a way of forgetting greeters. Their art form is evanescent. Bender achieved his moment, and when he passed away in March 1941 an overflow crowd spilled out into the courtyard of Temple Emanu-El for the services. Other greeters took his place. Not until the post-war emergence of merchant prince Cyril Magnin, however, would any single figure offer a better probe into the well-being of San Francisco, with special reference to its Jewish dimension.

If San Francisco was a distinctively Jewish city, it was a distinctively Roman Catholic city as well; indeed, many Jewish families sent their sons and daughters to St. Ignatius and the Convent of the Sacred Heart for their educations, including, a little later, young Dianne Goldman [Feinstein], later mayor of the city and senator from California. The 1930s represented a turning point for the Roman Catholic community in the United States. Already, the popularity of Notre Dame as a football power and the success of a number of Catholic-oriented movies suggested that the previous rejection of Roman Catholics by Protestant America was softening around the edges. Nowhere was this golden age of American Catholicism more palpable than in New York, Boston, Chicago, and San Francisco, where the Spanish-Mexican colonial heritage, together with the large number of Irish, French, and German Catholic residents, gave a special intensity to the overall sense of well-being characterizing Catholic America in 1930.

The Official Catholic Directory for the Year of Our Lord 1935 testifies to the flourishing condition of the Archdiocese of San Francisco, established by Rome in July 1853. Catholics numbered more than four hundred thousand in an archdiocese that extended from San Jose to the Oregon border. Six hundred and sixty-seven priests, 1,612 nuns, and 167 brothers served this population through a network of 222 churches, seventy-one parochial grammar schools, twenty-five high schools or private academies, seven colleges and universities, eleven seminaries, twelve novitiates, eight hospitals, ten day care facilities and orphanages, twelve resident facilities for single men and women, three homes for the aged, and an array of supportive welfare, counseling, and catechetical agencies and of young-single and teenaged youth groups.

Presiding over this flourishing ecclesiastical barony until he stepped down in March 1935 was the Most Reverend Edward Joseph Hanna, the third Archbishop of San Francisco, a kindly, compassionate man, popular with Catholics and non-Catholics alike. Hanna had come to his office not through the usual route of administration but from an academic career, although his appointment as archbishop had been delayed by Rome for a decade when articles he wrote while teaching at St. Bernard's Seminary in Rochester, New York, probing the human psychology of Jesus Christ attracted the suspicion of the Curia. This ten-year ordeal made Archbishop Hanna a champion of the underdog, eager to celebrate mass at San Quentin and other jails and prisons, judicious as a moderator in labor strikes.

By 1935 an aging Hanna had his own Co-Adjutor Archbishop with right of succession, the Most Reverend John Joseph Mitty, a no-nonsense New Yorker, formerly chaplain at West Point, whose administrative exactitude contrasted dramatically with the hands-off style of Hanna, who turned the day-to-day affairs of the archdiocese over to Monsignors Charles Ramm and James Cantwell while he was out visiting the sick or tramping through the cotton fields of the San Joaquin interviewing strikers. The senior priest of the archdiocese, the Right Reverend Monsignor Charles Ramm, administrator of the cathedral, dean, and *officialis*, was a converted Protestant of affluent background, an 1880s graduate of the University of California, where he excelled in athletics, and to which he later returned as regent. As such, Ramm moved with assurance in both Catholic and WASP milieus, proof positive to many that a Catholic priest could also be a gentleman, provided he be born an upper-class Protestant and earn his varsity letter at Cal.

Monsignor Ramm was a brilliant preacher, as was the Jesuit Dennis Kavanagh of St. Ignatius Church, a native San Franciscan who had entered the Society of Jesus at the tender age of fifteen. When Kavanagh preached the Three Hours devotion on Good Friday at St. Ignatius, the largest church structure west of the Mississippi, there was standing room only, and large crowds listened via loudspeakers on the sidewalks. The Jesuits at St. Ignatius—Kavanagh, the poet Alexander Cody, the historian Peter Dunne, the bibliophile Richard Gleeson, the saintly Aloysius Stern—specialized in preaching, confessions, and personalized spiritual direction in addition to their duties as professors and chaplains at the adjacent University of San Francisco. Priding themselves on being available to any caller twenty-four hours a day, seven days a week, the Jesuits made a point of walking in the garden adjacent to the church while reading their breviaries, attired in black cassocks and birettas, figures from the Counter-Reformation, always there, always available. Of comparable cachet was St. Dominic's Church in Pacific Heights. Established in 1878, St. Dominic's was staffed by white-robed Dominicans, the Order of Preachers, who rivaled the Jesuits in learning and savoir faire. In 1928 the Dominicans built an ambitious Gothic Revival church, impeccable in its detail, designed by architect Arnold Constable, a disciple of Gothic *meister* Ralph Adams Cram. In October 1935 the Dominicans established the Shrine of St. Jude at St. Dominic's. By the 1940s, the annual novena conducted at the shrine had become a nationally popular Catholic devotion.

Whereas other churches and denominations tended to encompass a majority of one or another class—the Episcopalian upper class, the Congregationalist and Presbyterian professional and middle classes, the middle to lower-middle Lutheran, Methodist, and Baptist communities—Catholic San Francisco, like Catholic communities elsewhere in the United States, showed more ethnic and sociological diversity. If St. Dominic's and St. Brigid's on Van Ness (a Celtic Revival structure donated in 1900 by the Phelan-Sullivan family) served the carriage trade, the Franciscans at St. Boniface in the Tenderloin were there for the poor, and the diocesan clergy attached to St. Peter's and St. Paul's parishes in the Mission district ministered to flourishing blue-collar congregations. Union leaders, most of them Catholic, served naturally as leaders in such communities, along with ranking police and firemen and civil service administrators.

The bar and bench of San Francisco were significantly Catholic as well, peopled by graduates of the law school of the Jesuit University of San Francisco. As the attorney of the archdiocese, Garret McEnerney functioned as tetrarch of the San Francisco Catholic bench and bar. Then in his sixties, distinguished in mien, with thick waves of silver hair flowing back from a Roman brow, McEnerney had held a leading position in San Francisco legal circles since the 1890s. Like Monsignor Ramm, he was a UC regent, serving for forty-one years. In Catholic terms, McEnerney's credentials were impeccable. He was related by marriage to Hilaire Belloc, the well-known English Catholic historian and controversialist, who, like McEnerney, had also married into the Hogan family of Napa. In 1902 McEnerney represented the bishops of California before an international tribunal at The Hague in what turned out to be a successful effort to regain control of the impounded Pious Fund established in Mexico in the colonial era for the support of the California missions. The fund was by then pushing $1.5 million in accrued value. In the aftermath of the April 1906 catastrophe, McEnerney devised a special court proceeding in which land titles could be proved by secondary evidence and drafted the act that would make it law, which the legislature passed and named in his honor.

It is doubtful that Garret McEnerney ever met legal secretary Margaret Collins, who since 1932 had been working for attorney Vincent Hallinan in the Mills Building; but Margaret certainly knew who Garret McEnerney was, everyone did, and her own employer was equally well known in the less genteel calling of criminal defense. Margaret lived with her widowed mother Mollie Norton Collins, her sisters Marian, Pat, and Clair, and her brother Johnny in a rented two-floor Victorian, $60 a month, on the 600 block of Waller Street in the Hayes Valley section of the city, Sacred Heart Parish, where Erich von Stroheim had a decade earlier filmed *Greed*, his version of Frank Norris's *McTeague*, a story of turn-of-the-century San Francisco. Hayes Valley, Stroheim discovered, had the feel of pre-1906 San Francisco because so many Victorians in this neighborhood had survived the Earthquake and Fire.

The Collins family was an all-female household, with Margaret serving as the co-supporter of her sisters and the *de facto* link between them and the outside world, given the fact that Mollie Collins, born in San Francisco in 1888 and widowed since 1925 when her Irish-born husband Thomas Patrick, a fireman, died in the line of duty, belonged to a generation and class of Irish women who remained secluded homemakers. The oldest Collins boy, Elliott, had already left home to marry Ursula Rajeski, a Polish girl from the Noe Valley neighborhood, and was working at Eppler's Bakery on Sutter Street and living at 24th and Diamond in Eureka Valley. The second son, Thomas Patrick, was studying for the priesthood with the Catholic Foreign Mission Society of America, more popularly known as Maryknoll, in Ossining, New York. A third son, Johnny, had dropped out of high school in mid-decade and shipped out with the merchant marine. Work for Margaret and Marian, school for Pat and Clair, household tasks for Mollie, mass on Sunday morning at the Sacred Heart Church, a commanding Lombardesque structure at Hayes and Fillmore, summer vacations at Calistoga in Napa County or Hoberg's Resort in Lake County: the rhythms of life among the Collins women continued at a steady pace through the Depression, no major setbacks, no tragedies.

Already, Margaret was seeing Dennis Joyce, a Canadian-born Irishman working as a mechanic with the Municipal Railway. She, Denny, her sister Marian, and Marian's boyfriend Owen Starr, a San Francisco shipyard worker, would double-date in the late 1930s, dining in North Beach for a dollar each, or at the Old Grotto on Washington for fifty to seventy-five cents, or at Neptune's at Fisherman's Wharf, dancing at the Isadore Gomez Cafe at 848 Pacific. Margaret had met Denny in 1938 at the Firemen's Ball in Civic Auditorium, where Mayor Angelo Rossi led the opening dance. By late 1939 Marian and Owen Starr were married, as were Margaret and Denny; and Mollie Collins entered the 1940s with only two girls at home, and Johnny now and then back from sea. She was looking forward to Tom's ordination in New York, which would occasion in June 1942 her first trip beyond the immediate environs of San Francisco.

Irish Catholics dominated the Olympic Club, founded in 1860, and hence among the oldest athletic clubs in the United States. The Olympic Club survived through the Depression, maintaining its downtown facility on Post Street and its golf course and tennis courts on the southern edge of the city, and sponsoring a full program of not just the expected sports—swimming, basketball, handball, track and field, tennis, golf—but ambitious programs in crew, fencing, cycling, football, ice hockey, water polo, and Greco-Roman wrestling. True to the spirit of the times (San Francisco, after all, had recently constructed a polo field in Golden Gate Park with PWA funds), the Olympic Club maintained a fully complemented polo team, captained by Will Tevis. The Olympic Club rugby team, which had sent five men to the Olympics in 1924, dominated rugby, a popular Bay Area sport. Its boxing program was likewise a nursery of amateur champions, with James (Spider) Roche holding the coaching post in pugilism once held by James (Gentleman Jim) Corbett, heavyweight champion of the world in 1892 and the most famous athlete ever to wear the Winged-O into competition. The fully uniformed Olympic Club marching band performed each year at San Quentin when Olympic Club athletes traveled across the Bay to that formidable penitentiary for a day of competition and games with the inmates. As much a carnival as an athletic competition, the Olympic Club–sponsored Field Day at San Quentin also included a costume competition. Photographs of this event reveal an intricacy of drag outfits that suggest to the anthropological eye some revealing insights into San Quentin culture in this period.

If Catholic San Francisco was strongly Irish, it was noticeably Italian as well. The Salesian Fathers at Sts. Peter and Paul Church in North Beach ministered to the Italian community. Directed by the charismatic Angelo Fusco, the Salesian Boys' Club attached to the parish offered an array of cultural and athletic programs designed to introduce North Beach youngsters, many of them growing up in Italian-speaking households, to mainstream American life. A talented teacher of literature and elocution, a basketball coach, a musician and bandmaster, Fusco devoted himself to the upward mobility of his charges: their mastery of Dante and Shakespeare, their performance at Sacred Heart or St. Ignatius high schools, their skills on the basketball court, wearing the Winged-S on their jerseys. Joseph Lawrence Alioto of the Fisherman's Wharf family acquired from Fusco (and later from Brother Leo of St. Mary's College) a range of reading and forensic skills that would win him innumerable jury trials and serve him equally well in his time as mayor of San Francisco. Joe DiMaggio, the Yankee Clipper, played for the Salesian Boys' Club as a teenager and returned to Sts. Peter and Paul on 19 November 1939 to marry Dorothy Arnold in a nationally covered ceremony.

As the Italian National Church in San Francisco, Sts. Peter and Paul was a mandatory stop for visiting Italian dignitaries: Piero Parini, director of Italian Schools in Foreign Countries, for example, who came in 1934; tenor Tito Schipa, who came and sang in 1935; Eugenio Cardinal Pacelli, Vatican special delegate, later Pope Pius XII, who arrived in 1936; New York Mayor Fiorello La Guardia, who visited in 1939. If the truth be told, the mood around Sts. Peter and Paul and the Salesian Boys' Club in the 1930s, indeed around all of North Beach, was pro-Mussolini in a subdued sort of a way. Smartly attired in their paramilitary uniforms, teenagers of the Gruppo Giovanile Italo-Americani marched in cadence to drums, banners flying, or sat proudly for their portrait in Washington Square, alongside pastor Joseph Galli and the Consul General of Italy.

The scavenger community constituted a world of its own. Close, insular, encouraged by their calling to live almost exclusively among themselves, rising for work while the rest of the city slept, finishing their day at noon, the scavengers created for themselves a prosperous, highly autonomous life. They were peasants, most of them, Genovesi and Sicilians, with some Calabresi. In 1920, when ninety-two scavengers formed the Sunset Cooperative Agreement, a number of them signed their names with an X. Nine out of ten major American cities had publicly owned and operated garbage companies; but San Francisco preferred to run its scavenger system as a public utility, privately owned and operated, publicly regulated. The 1930s witnessed the coalescence of thirty-six scavenger companies into, by 1935, two organizations, the Scavengers Protective Association (later renamed the Golden Gate Disposal Company) and the Sunset Scavenger Company, which bought out its last competitor, Mission Scavengers, in 1939. The scavengers owned their own companies and managed them cooperatively. Those designated to management received the same salary as those hauling garbage cans. No scavenger could be promoted into management unless he had served time on the trucks. By the early 1940s the two surviving scavenger companies rivaled the internationally famed fire department in excellence. Taking the dirtiest, least prestigious job in the city, the Italian scavengers of San Francisco had, by owning and operating their own company, by working together in an atmosphere of equity and participatory management, turned their vulnerability to advantage. Scavengers worked together, socialized together, married their sons and daughters to each other. They were Catholic in culture but, in the true style of Mediterranean skepticism, lacked the overt piety of their Irish counterparts, the men at least. The women attended church regularly and gave more authority to the priests. By the 1940s many scavengers were living in handsome homes in the Marina district and were investing in apartment houses and other rental property.

The ethnic diversity of San Francisco was its most salient characteristic. The city abounded in Irish, Italian, German, Scandinavian, French, Russian, Mexican, African-American, and Chinese neighborhoods. As in the case of New York and Chicago, however, white Anglo-Saxon Protestants more than held their own. Symbolically, the social bastion of Episcopalian San Francisco, the Pacific Union Club on Nob Hill, stood adjacent to Grace Cathedral, with only Huntington Park between them. Administered by its dean, the Very Reverend J. Wilmer Gresham, Grace Cathedral had been under construction since the late teens, slowly filling out its square block atop Nob Hill, donated to the diocese early in the century by the Crocker family. Its architect, the Beaux Arts–trained Louis Hobart, envisioned Grace Cathedral as a Notre Dame of the West, equal in ambition and beauty to the Cathedral of St. John the Divine in New York or the National Cathedral in Washington, D.C. Thinking in these terms, Hobart and his clients—Dean Gresham, the cathedral trustees, and two succeeding bishops, Edward Parsons and Karl Morgan Block—adjusted themselves to a half century of construction. Sitting over a martini in the early evening in the Pacific Union Club, Hobart would discuss with his young assistant Paul Ryan, also a graduate of the Beaux Arts, the long, patient process of cathedral building. Grace Cathedral, Hobart told his assistant, might take a century or more to complete. In May 1937 construction commenced on the North Tower, which was to be surmounted by a carillon of forty-four bells on temporary loan to the Golden Gate International Exposition, all this the gift of physician Nathaniel Coulson.

Spreading below Grace Cathedral (appropriately, to the east) was Chinatown. The Chinese had a difficult time of it in the teens and twenties. In 1913 a measure was introduced into the state senate making ineligible to vote the son or daughter of any man in California not eligible to vote, whether born in the United States or not. Astonishingly, this measure proposed to disenfranchise every Chinese-American and Japanese-American citizen in the state. Although the measure eventually died in committee, the very fact that it was introduced into the state senate and seriously debated testified to the anti-Asian animus of the era. To counteract the virulent attacks of organizations such as the Native Sons of the Golden West, the Chinese of San Francisco organized the Native Sons of the Golden State in 1912 and fought the disenfranchisement. In 1915 the Native Sons of the Golden State changed its name to the Chinese-American Citizens Alliance and continued its lobbying efforts.

With their resident status, even their citizenship, under such assault, the Chinese of San Francisco lived in fear of not being able to return to the United States if they ever went to China for a visit. In October 1915 the Department of Labor adopted a regulation that denied citizens of Chinese ancestry the right to verify their citizenship prior to leaving the country. The alliance fought this measure on constitutional grounds, and it was rescinded. In 1924 Congress passed the National Origins Law, which in effect barred any further Asian immigration to the United States. Even the Chinese wives of American citizens were denied entry. Once again, the Chinese-American Citizens Alliance went into action, but it took until August 1936 for non-citizen Chinese wives to regain fully the right to join their citizen husbands in the United States.

The breakup of Chinese families effected by the National Origins Law was a special affront to the Chinese, for whom family was the beginning, middle, and end of social organization and loyalty. Standing on Grant Avenue on the morning of 10 January 1937, San Franciscans had proof positive of the strong family ties of the Chinese as the funeral cortege of Mrs. Yick Jung Shee, the recently departed matriarch of the Yick family, passed by. Arriving in the United States from Canton when she was eighteen, Mrs. Yick had died at seventy-six, leaving behind a family of two hundred. The procession wound its way slowly down the entire length of Grant Avenue, led by a herald holding aloft a green and silver banner proclaiming in Chinese characters the loss of Mrs. Yick. The hearse followed the banner. As the hearse slowly wended its way, a family member from within threw good luck coins wrapped in white strips of paper to bystanders. Behind the hearse came the Yick sons—Frank, Charles, and Yun—each accompanied by a close friend, according to Chinese custom. Then followed the sons-in-law, carrying a great red banner on a fifteen-foot pole. The banner proclaimed in Chinese: "These are the devoted sons-in-law." Then came the daughters, followed by the granddaughters, followed last by the grandsons. Everyone was attired in an appropriate costume. The sons wore black robes and black headbands. The sons-in-law wore the same, but with a red dot in the center of each headband. The women wore black robes and hoods. The grandchildren wore blue robes if descended from a son, black if descended from a daughter. Buddhist priests in full regalia accompanied the procession and later officiated at graveside services in the Happy Valley Cemetery south of San Francisco. Also in the procession were two floats. One bore a life-sized photograph of the departed, this being the Buddhist float;

and the other, the Yick family float, bore a similar photograph surmounted by a stuffed pigeon symbolizing peace. Inscribed across the side of the Yick family float, again in Chinese characters, were the words "Though her face and voice are gone, her teachings to her children are everlasting." When the procession ended, the participants entered a line of automobiles for the drive south to the Happy Valley Cemetery. Each car had a sticker on the windshield denoting the precise relationship of the occupants to the departed matriarch.

Family loyalties saw the Chinese through the dark times. By the late 1930s, they were experiencing an increasing level of assimilation. For its weekend dances, the Chinese-American Citizens Alliance building on Stockton Street was filled with prosperous couples, resembling their Caucasian counterparts in everything save race. Chinatown had its own telephone exchange, its own branches of Wells Fargo Bank, the Anglo-French Bank, and the Bank of America, its own Boy Scout troop, its own YMCA, its own Catholic, Congregational, Methodist, and Baptist churches, and its own Salvation Army depot, together with the Yoke Choy Club, which sponsored after-school games and athletic teams, and the Square and Circle Club, a women's social and philanthropic organization. There was a Chinese-language newspaper, the *Chinese Times*, and an English-language newspaper, the *Chinese Digest*, co-published by Chingwah Lee and Thomas Chinn. A Chinese radio program, the *Golden Star Chinese Hour*, made its debut on radio station KSAN in 1939. There were also a Chinese hospital, a Chinese playground, a Cathay Post of the American Legion, even a special program for Chinese in the WPA. It was a complete world, prosperous and conservative (not until 1948 were contestants in the annual Miss Chinatown pageant allowed to parade in their bathing suits), reflective in its structures and institutions of the larger society, fixed forever by one of its members, Chin-Yang Li, in her novel *Flower Drum Song* (1957), which later became a Broadway and film musical.

Although some might see in this Flower Drum Song world an enclave born of discrimination, others might see it as a perfect solution to the challenge of urban living, a way of preserving values, language, and cultural heritage while enjoying the good life, American style. The Chinese were systematically excluded from clubs and from law, brokerage, and CPA firms. They were not appointed to the bench or elected to the Board of Supervisors, nor could they buy homes in many neighborhoods. Such enfranchisements would take another forty years. On the other hand, while Chinatown might be a ghetto, it was simultaneously—in its YMCA, its Boy Scout troops, its basketball games, its dances at the Chinese-American Citizens Alliance—an aspiring American place. Next to the enduring loyalty to family, this generation of Chinese-American San Franciscans wanted nothing more deeply in its heart of hearts, as a matter of social agenda, than to become Americans while remaining Chinese. Fortunately, Chinatown, despite its claustrophobic aspects, was also a thriving business and a national tourist attraction, through which hundreds of thousands of visitors poured each year, spending their dollars in the Chinese community, and where non-Chinese San Franciscans were wont to repair, at least once a month, for the Chinese cuisine that had by the 1930s become a fixed element of local life.

Certainly, neither Chingwah Lee nor Charlie Low, two very contrasting but totally representative types, had any trouble moving back and forth between Chinatown and the larger city. Both had grown up in Chinatown and, despite the different paths each had taken and for all their assimilation, remained close to it. While in his mid-twenties in the 1920s, Charlie Low persuaded a downtown brokerage firm, Russell Colvin and Company, to open a Chinatown office with Low in charge. When Prohibition was repealed, Low got into the bar business, opening the Chinese Village on Grant. Two years later, he hit upon an even more impressive idea: an all-Chinese nightclub, with an orchestra, dancing, and a floor show. ("One chorus girl," Charlie Low would later say, "is worth ten thousand egg foo yung.")[2] Leasing premises at 363 Sutter, just a block and a half away from the official entrance to Chinatown at Bush and Grant, Low opened the Forbidden City on 22 December 1938. It was an instant success, not just in Chinatown, or in the Bay Area for that matter. With its exotic decor, its Chinese chorus girls and comics, its featured performers Li Tei Ming, whom Charlie married, and the incomparable, the one and only Jessie Tai Sing, with Charlie himself acting as master of ceremonies, Forbidden City became a nightspot known throughout the Far East as the place to go when in San Francisco.

Elevated to celebrity status, Charlie Low devoted himself to his wives, his wardrobe (in his heyday Low was widely acknowledged as the best-dressed man in San Francisco), his convertible, his ranch, his golf game, and his polo ponies. Married four times (Minnie Louie from Fresno who died of meningitis in 1931, after only a year of married life; singing star Li Tei Ming; Betty Wong of New York; Ivy Tam of Hong Kong), Charlie Low loved night life and the ladies as a matter of vocation and avocation. Buying a luxurious seventy-two-acre ranch outside Pleasanton in the East Bay, Charlie named it Forbidden Acres and built two large barns, one for his polo ponies and another for his Arabian show and race horses. There were also a deer paddock and an enclosed grove for pheasants and peacocks. On weekends, Charlie would entertain thirty to forty of his closest friends, holding forth at the side of his over-large swimming pool or demonstrating his equestrian skills in the riding ring. The first Asian to crack the upper strata of San Francisco social life, Charlie played four-goal polo alongside the best players in San Francisco, Will Tevis and William Gilmore, and was elected president of the San Francisco Polo Association.

Chingwah Lee, on the other hand, divided his time between Hollywood, where he starred in films, and Chinatown, where he dealt in Chinese objets d'art and antiques, having become an internationally ranked expert in this field. The son of a Chinatown herbalist, Chingwah Lee had as a thirteen-year-old in 1914 helped organize Boy Scout Troop 3, the first all-Chinese Boy Scout troop in the United States. He later became active in the Chinese YMCA. Graduating from

UC Berkeley, where he studied anthropology, psychology, and art, Chingwah Lee opened an art and antique business. Film studios would contact him to serve as technical advisor for the dressing and decoration of Chinese sets. When Irving Thalberg decided to produce Pearl Buck's *The Good Earth* (1937), he decreed that at least half the cast be Chinese, which led to film actor Paul Muni suggesting to Chingwah Lee that he try out for a part. Successfully cast in *The Good Earth*, Chingwah Lee rapidly became one of the most dependable Chinese supporting actors in Hollywood. Meanwhile, he continued in the antiques business and co-founded with Thomas Chinn the *Chinese Digest*, Chinatown's first English-language newspaper.

Each in different ways, Charlie Low and Chingwah Lee escaped many of the restrictions of ethnicity while remaining close to its essential strength. Just a few blocks outside of Chinatown, at the Church of the Fellowship of All Peoples on Larkin Street, Pastor Howard Thurman, en route to becoming one of the most influential African-American ministers in the twentieth century, would soon be preaching an innovative philosophy and theology of multi-cultural reconciliation. A graduate of Morehouse College and the Rochester Theological Seminary, Thurman served as a pastor in Oberlin, Ohio, before joining the School of Religion at Howard University. In 1935, he visited India and met Gandhi, who had a powerful effect on Thurman, as did numerous conversations with Hindu, Buddhist, and Moslem clerics. These transforming experiences dovetailed with Thurman's earlier studies in comparative religion, which included a strong interest in Meister Eckhart and medieval mysticism. The result: while remaining a Baptist proud of his African-American heritage, Thurman began in his sermons and books to speculate that certain great truths were characteristic of all religions, not because they were dogmas or insights of any particular creed, but because they were true in the first place. As a legitimate mode of human inquiry, religion had the capacity of discerning common truths as well as arriving at differing doctrines and symbols.

But could such inclusive ideas be put into practice? In October 1944 Thurman launched the interdenominational Church for the Fellowship of All Peoples in San Francisco. "Here at last," he later wrote, "I could put to the test once more the major concern of my life: Is the worship of God the central and most significant act of the human spirit? Is it really true that in the presence of God there is neither male nor female, child nor adult, rich nor poor, nor any classification by which mankind defines itself in categories, however meaningful?"[3] Under Thurman's guidance, the Church for the Fellowship of All Peoples crossed racial barriers, not just between black and white, but among Asian, black, and white and, with a program of guest sermons by local rabbis, between Gentile and Jew.

Thurman came into a city whose pre–World War II African-American population had always been small, hovering around five thousand. Yet it had always had its own press, beginning in 1855 with the *Mirror of the Times*, founded by Mifflin Gibbs, later American consul general to Madagascar, a newspaper that became

The Pacific Appeal in 1862 and the *Elevator* in 1865, edited by Philip Bell, later described as the Napoleon of the African-American press. While small in comparison to the African-American community across the Bay in Oakland, which even before World War II was en route to becoming a significantly black city in which the all-powerful Pullman porters' union would exercise significant influence, African-American San Francisco nevertheless possessed a level of coherence and leadership that came from its newspaper, from its flourishing church life, strongly Baptist and African Methodist Episcopal, and from a tradition of employment on the waterfront, in the hotel industry, and in drayage and freight. During World War II, thousands of African-Americans migrated to the Bay Area, from Louisiana and Texas especially, to work in the defense industry. In 1953 Thurman accepted a call to the graduate school of theology at Boston University, where he exercised a decisive influence on a young student from Atlanta, Martin Luther King Jr., who in turn put Thurman's message of peaceful non-violent reconciliation at the core of his civil rights program.

As Charlie Low and so many others knew full well, San Francisco was a fun town, with plenty of great restaurants and night life. Surprisingly, many restaurants—Maye's Oyster House on Polk, Sam's on Bush, Jack's on Sacramento, the Fior d'Italia in North Beach, Schroeder's on Front Street, Tadich's on California—had their origins in the Gold Rush and were to flourish through the entire twentieth century. Others—the Cliff House at Ocean Beach, Julius's Castle and the Shadows atop Telegraph Hill, John's Grill on Ellis (Dashiell Hammett's favorite restaurant), Des Alpes on Stockton, Ernie's on Montgomery—had later origins but would last into the 1990s. Still others—Bernstein's Fish Grotto on Powell, Solari's on Geary, Gino's at Front and Clay in the heart of the produce district, Lucca's at Powell and Francisco, the Hoffman House on Market, the Tortola Tamale Café on Polk, Veneto's on Bay, the Sinaloa Mexican Cantina and Restaurant on Powell near Broadway, Vanessi's on Broadway in North Beach, Omar Khayyam's on O'Farrell at Powell in the theater district, DiMaggio's on Fisherman's Wharf, the Poodle Dog on Post—would not survive the century but did manage to flourish through the 1930s, the war, and the post-war period.

When it came to bars and nightclubs, San Francisco was equally endowed. Aside from Low's Forbidden City, the Bal Tabarin on Columbus Avenue at Chestnut, an Art Deco cabaret designed by Timothy Pflueger, featured two nightly floor shows. Izzy Gomez's upstairs joint at 848 Pacific Avenue set new standards for informality (Izzy encouraged patrons to dance on the linoleum table tops) with the gargantuan Izzy, dressed ever in suit, vest, and black hat, a cigarette dangling from his lips, inviting guests to come back into the kitchen and help him fry a steak. Upscale rendezvous in the better hotels included the Circus Lounge in the Fairmont Hotel, the Top of the Mark atop the Mark Hopkins, the Orchid Room (later the Patent Leather Lounge) at the St. Francis, and the Happy Valley

Bar at the Palace Hotel. On the other end of the spectrum was Mona's at 440 Broadway on the old Barbary Coast, a lesbian hangout, with naked ladies painted on the walls and an all-girl orchestra. At Mona's waitresses and singers dressed like boys, and the predominantly female clientele featured either dressy feminine or butch. Nearby, the Black Cat at 710 Montgomery Street was equally *outré* with a raffish bohemian clientele lesbian, homosexual, or bisexual in inclination. (During the Second World War, the Black Cat went immediately on the Off Limits list of the Military Police and Shore Patrol.) The press did its drinking at Breen's at 71 3rd Street, just down from the *Examiner*. Cops, criminal defense lawyers, bail bondsmen, and reporters on the crime beat preferred the Star Café on Kearny near the Hall of Justice. Around lunch time, scavengers unwound at the end of their work day at the Yosemite out on 3rd Street. Union leaders, civil servants, and small businessmen preferred Dago Mary's in Bay View–Hunter's Point, Bruno's in the Mission, or Original Joe's and the Polo in the Tenderloin. Sports fans and the betting crowd hung out at Shanty Malone's near the Produce Mart or the Kezar Club on Stanyan at the entrance to Golden Gate Park.

Was San Francisco, it might be asked, a truly sinful town or merely a city pretending to be sinful? District Attorney Matthew Brady and private detective Edwin Atherton claimed that San Francisco was rotten to the core. In 1935 DA Brady hired Atherton, a retired FBI agent based in Los Angeles, to do an in-depth investigation of prostitution and police payoffs in San Francisco. Issued in March 1937, the Atherton Report revealed a vast network of gambling, prostitution, and abortions orchestrated by the McDonough brothers, Peter and Tom, bail bondsmen by profession. San Francisco, Atherton reported, had resisted the attempts of East Coast– or Midwest-controlled organized crime to take over the city because the city itself, in its totality, was one big racket. The Atherton Report slowed San Francisco down somewhat. The Police Commission allowed sixteen officers to resign; five were indicted, but there were no convictions. If the truth be told, San Franciscans preferred their home-grown, home-operated system of organized vice to either organized crime or a closed—and very dull!—town.

Ever since the Gold Rush, prostitution had flourished in San Francisco, and while the anthropological necessity for such an institution, the extreme shortage of women, had long since vanished, prostitution persisted as a social and cultural pattern, kept alive, in part, by the temporary sojourning in San Francisco of thousands of single men, laborers in from the wheat ranches, sailors in from the sea, especially in winter. For more upscale clients, many so-called French restaurants offered opportunities for sexual adventure. In the posthumously published *Vandover and the Brute* (1914), Frank Norris told the story of an upper-class San Franciscan who contracts venereal disease from a waitress at the Imperial Café and goes into serious mental and physical decline. The Mann Act of 1910 and the Red Light Abatement Act of 1914 had a chilling effect on the wide-open prostitution culture of San Francisco, which nevertheless managed to survive on a more discreet basis. Jessie Hayman ran a successful bordello at 130 Eddy Street in the early part of the century. Her successor, Tessie Wall, was perhaps the most successful San Francisco madam of the century.

Born in May 1869 to an Irish Catholic working family living south of Market (her real name, Teresa Susan Donohue), Wall was widowed in the early 1890s with the death of her fireman husband. Desperately, she tried to support herself and small son as a domestic servant in the household of Judah Boas, a respected banker and capitalist who had risen from simple beginnings as a peddler. Boas maintained an elegant home on outer O'Farrell Street in the Western Addition, and from the Boas family Tessie acquired a taste for the finer things, together with the realization that such things were totally beyond the reach of a domestic servant. By the late 1890s, Mrs. Wall had gone into another business, ostensibly a lodging house at 137 O'Farrell. The establishment prospered, and she moved it to larger quarters at 337 O'Farrell Street. In her own way, Tessie Wall became a prominent San Franciscan. In the 1920s it became her custom to lead the grand march at the annual Policeman's Ball in the Civic Auditorium. In one such promenade, Mayor Sunny Jim Rolph served as her escort.

Tessie Wall died in April 1932, just a few years before her successor, Mable Spagnoli, professionally known as Sally Stanford, entered the business. Born Mabel Janice Busby in Baker City, Oregon, in May 1903, Sally Stanford had married young, at sixteen, and at the age of seventeen had been sent to the Oregon State Penitentiary by a very harsh judge for obtaining goods under false pretenses, to wit, an electric iron valued at $9.80. (She was later pardoned by the governor of Oregon for this draconian conviction.) Separating from her husband, a criminal defense attorney in San Francisco, in the early 1930s, Mrs. Spagnoli went into the business, rather splendidly, using her divorce settlement to purchase a small hotel at 793 O'Farrell. She chose her professional name, Sally Stanford, because Stanford beat Cal in the Big Game that year. (Otherwise, she later noted, she might have gone through life as Sally California.) By 1937 Sally Stanford was operating an even more lavish establishment at 450 Geary, which she then moved to 750 Taylor, then 1526 Franklin, before settling in May 1939 into an elaborate establishment at 1001 Vallejo on the eastern slope of Russian Hill.

Sally Stanford and others in the demimonde frequently required the assistance of attorneys at law, and San Francisco had a number of rising figures—Jake Ehrlich, James Martin MacInnis, George Davis, Vincent Hallinan, Melvin Belli—in this flamboyant branch of legal practice. George Davis played a key role in securing a pardon for the most famous client of them all, Tom Mooney, and was at Mooney's side in January 1939 when the newly pardoned, newly released Mooney led a triumphant parade up Market Street past a quarter of a million spectators. Vincent Hallinan, on the other hand, had not been so lucky in 1932 when defending San Francisco public defender Frank Eagan on murder charges resulting from a quarrel over a bad debt. The Eagan case brought together some of the most theatrical figures from both sides of the aisle, prosecution and defense: captain of inspectors Charles Dullea, later the police chief of San Francisco; Hallinan, the rising star in the criminal defense bar; Public Defender Eagan, who now required defense against his counterpart District Attorney Matthew Brady, a brilliant prosecutor. Adroitly, Hallinan, an agnostic in matters religious yet showing all the forensic skill instilled in him by the Jesuits at St. Ignatius High School, fought a virtually impossible case. Eagan was convicted, but Hallinan saved him from the gas chamber.

Melvin Belli was not so lucky with his first courtroom appearance, the defense of two San Quentin convicts, Joe Kristy and Alexander MacKay, who on 16 January 1935, having secured pistols, had in the company of two other convict colleagues the *chutzpah* to break in on the parole board itself as its members were dining at warden James Holohan's residence. Piling a number of hostages into a commandeered automobile, the four convicts forced their way out of San Quentin. Inevitably, the police surrounded them in a rural barn. There was a shootout, and one of the convicts was killed. The other turned state's evidence in exchange for life imprisonment, which led McKay and Kristy to contact, via San Quentin chaplain Father George O'Meara, a recent graduate of the Stanford Law School by the name of Melvin Belli. Belli lost the case, as everyone knew he would. He also formed a close relationship with McKay and Kristy, spending time with each of them on the night before their execution. In his final hours, Kristy played "Clair de Lune" on his phonograph. The next day, Belli served Father O'Meara's morning mass, and the two went over to the gymnasium to witness the hangings.

The press loved such figures as Davis, Ehrlich, Hallinan, MacInnis, and Belli: Davis with his brilliant legal maneuvering on the part of a client who could pay him nothing; Ehrlich's flashing French cuffs, the way his attractive female clients crossed their legs as if coached (which was probably the case) when giving crucial testimony; Hallinan's feisty willingness to test the parameters of court etiquette, a trait that earned him a number of sojourns in jail for contempt of court; the erudition of MacInnis, who would later defend Edmund Wilson when *Memoirs of Hecate County* (1946) was charged with obscenity; the showmanship of Belli, the self-described King of Torts, combined with his gargantuan appetite for life, which would take him through a succession of wives and keep his flat atop Telegraph Hill the scene of a seemingly non-stop party. Still caught in the era of *The Front Page*, enthralled with the romantic myth of newspapering, San Francisco did not differ from New York, Boston, Chicago, Los Angeles, or any comparable city in the diversity, colorfulness, flamboyance, often sheer self-destructive exuberance of its hard-drinking, hard-smoking, poker-playing press corps, pounding their typewriters at the *News* and *Chronicle* on Mission, the *Call-Bulletin* on Annie, the *Examiner* at 3rd and Market.

Yet in one trait, the importance of feature writers and columnists, San Francisco showed a distinctive tendency. A city so colorful, yet so insecure—an insecurity born of its early isolation from the metropolitan centers of the East and its continuing fear that it was not big enough to warrant full metropolitan status—required constant celebration and interpretive commentary. While San Francisco did not exactly invent the talk-of-the-town, first-person column, it learned to depend upon this journalistic genre and later, after World War II, to be dominated by it in a manner different from any other city, save for those years when Walter Winchell prowled the streets of New York. Early in the century, Fremont Older charged columnist John Barry to go out and get the mood and feel of San Francisco, the talk of the town, the gossip: a genre carried through the 1920s by Edward O'Day, a graceful writer versed in the classics and English literature, who ended his career as editor of the *Recorder*, the daily legal newspaper and in many ways, given the importance of the law business in San Francisco, the fifth newspaper of the city. In 1936 whiz-kid editor Paul Smith at the *Chronicle* assigned an equally twenty-something journalist from Sacramento by the name of Herb Caen to this beat, posting him to a radio column, which soon evolved into a general interest format. Caen showed a genius for columnizing. With the exception of his service as an Army Air Force officer in the European theater during the war, Caen would meet six deadlines a week for something approaching sixty years. No other American columnist, again with the exception of Walter Winchell, would ever sustain such a dominating presence in an American city. Years later, California Court of Appeal justice William Newsom, writing in a decision regarding the *Chronicle*, would cite Herb Caen as the journalistic equivalent, in Bay Area terms, of the Golden Gate Bridge.

Two other *Chronicle* writers, meanwhile, Lucius Beebe and Idwal Jones, were pioneering in another distinctive area of San Francisco journalism, the coverage of wine and food. A Bostonian, educated at Harvard and Yale, omnivorous in his appetites for rare books, fine wines, good cuisine, and antique railroad cars, Lucius Beebe revered the legend of high living on the frontier as experienced in San Francisco and Virginia City in the 1860s and 1870s when the Comstock Lode was pouring millions of dollars into the local economy. Brought to San Francisco and later to Virginia City by this myth, Beebe did his best to write about and act out the Lucullan lifestyle of the Gilded Age. With his collaborator and life partner Charles Clegg, Beebe purchased and reconditioned a Victorian parlor car, in which he and Clegg toured the Far West in the company of their martini-drinking St. Bernard, T-Bone Towser.

Idwal Jones, by contrast, a Welsh immigrant, was enthralled by San Francisco as the capital of the wine industry—and Chinese food. Prior to the 1930s, Chinese cuisine, perceived as the daily diet of the Asian working class, was of only marginal interest to food critics in San Francisco. Jones, however, was a close friend of San Francisco chef Tao Yuen, who had been trained before the Revolution at the Imperial School of Cookery in Peking where the textbook was the 753-volume, three-million-page *Imperial Encyclopedia of National Cookery*. From Tao Yuen, Jones absorbed an appreciation of Chinese food, which he wrote about extensively; and this appreciation was in and of itself a cultural bridge and statement, alerting San Franciscans, Californians, then the East Coast, as Jones's work became syndicated, to the exquisite levels of culinary and historical experience, even philosophical statement, contained in the cuisine of China. Jones was also the first wine writer to come to prominence in the Bay Area after Prohibition. Not only had the vineyards of California remained fallow for thirteen years, Jones argued, California, indeed the rest of the country, had lost its nose and palate. As a working journalist, Jones sought to reintroduce Californians to their restored vineyards and the fine wines that were once again coming from California wineries, sketches later gathered into a book, *Vines in the Sun* (1949), an early classic of post-war wine criticism.

The concerns of Herb Caen, Lucius Beebe, and Idwal Jones in the late 1930s— talk of the town, wine and food, historical myth and legend—might seem trivial in comparison to the stories on the front page chronicling a world rushing headlong toward cataclysm. Yet these Bay Area journalists were anticipating a preoccupation with lifestyle that was to become increasingly characteristic of American journalism after 1960. Herb Caen was especially prophetic of the celebrity-oriented *People* journalism that would come into vogue toward the end of the century; indeed, even as Caen was getting his start in the late thirties, many of the San Franciscans who would later fill his paragraphs were getting their start as well. San Franciscans Kathleen Norris, Imogen Cunningham, Yehudi Menuhin, Isaac Stern, Janet Gaynor, Mervin LeRoy, and Gracie Allen were already well-known figures in entertainment and the arts. Others—Tillie Olson, Ansel Adams, Lana Turner, Merv Griffin, Tony Martin, Art Linkletter, Mel Blanc, Peter Lind Hayes, Lew Christiansen—were in the process of starting their careers, as was Norton Simon, who was only beginning to acquire companies in Southern California. Still others—Phyllis Diller, Carol Channing, Richard Egan—were in grammar or high school. Natalie Wood was just being born, in 1940, to Russian émigré parents in the Richmond district; and longshoreman Eric Hoffer was still putting in long days on the docks, reading in his room in the evening or at the public library in the Civic Center on weekends, thinking about what he read, keeping a journal, taking notes.

In 1927 Kenneth Rexroth and his wife Andree arrived in San Francisco by automobile from Chicago. They found a civilized if provincial city still, in literary terms, in the grip of the memory of Jack London, Frank Norris, and George Sterling. "Everybody we met considered George Sterling the greatest poet since Dante," Rexroth later remembered. "We had never heard of him, so it took us a little time to catch up on our manners. . . . I don't want to give the impression that we were, young as we were, snobs about all this. One provincial culture is much like another, and San Francisco, in those days, was rather better than most."[4] Remote from the intellectual and literary markets of New York, San Francisco still had much to offer the aspiring poet and critic. There was something encompassing about the city, evident in its many ethnic restaurants, and something friendly, evident in the way sculptor Ralph Stackpole took Rexroth and his wife around town, showing them the ropes. But something else as well: San Francisco was an urban village in the Mediterranean style, as Rexroth encountered it, "yet it had none of the horrors of poverty that still make Marseille, let alone Genoa, Barcelona, or Naples, impossible for a sensitive person to work in very long. On the other hand, it had none of the cheapjack tourism which makes the Riviera unliveable. It was like an untouched Mediterranean village, like St. Tropez or the Cinque Terre in those days—and yet it was a great city, and in its own way not a provincial one, but the capital of its own somewhat dated culture."[5]

Two figures, Gertrude Atherton and Charles Caldwell Dobie, embodied and continued through the 1930s the provincial autonomy and dated culture described by Rexroth. As if to confirm that life begins at seventy, Gertrude Atherton, born in San Francisco in October 1857 and publishing continuously since 1883, wrote her best book, *Adventures of a Novelist* (1932), when she was seventy-five. Returning to San Francisco from a long European sojourn when the Great War broke out, Atherton spent her late fifties and sixties in an indefatigable production of novels, including the best-selling *Black Oxen* (1923), a story of sexual rejuvenation in middle age. She also spent much of the twenties as a co-hostess, along with Blanche (Mrs. Downey) Harvey, for the constant entertainments sponsored by former United States Senator James Duval Phelan at Villa Montalvo in Saratoga. Atherton was very much on the scene throughout the 1930s, a figure from the post-frontier era of San Francisco letters who in the 1880s had walked the streets of San Francisco with her friend Sybil Sanderson, later of the Paris Opera, dreaming of shaking the dust of this ramshackle frontier city from their feet. San Francisco, as she later recalled, was in those days "a jumping-off place to nowhere"; but she had been plenty happy to find refuge there as war broke out in Europe in 1914, and middle age advanced, and she became officially old. In her home town, she could carry on in the grand manner of an earlier era: long gowns that revealed her shoulders, cigarettes smoked in an over-long holder, her hair still corn-colored, her eyes remaining bright blue. Atherton lived on Green Street with her daughter Muriel Russell, waited on by her grandson George, who seemed to have no other role in life but to chauffeur his grandmother to and from her various appointments: lunch on Mondays at the St. Francis Hotel, the opera, the symphony, dinner meetings of the San Francisco chapter of PEN, the international writers' organization which she locally organized in conjunction with Charles Caldwell Dobie, the two of them bringing together such figures as the novelists Stewart Edward White, Peter B. Kyne, Ruth Comfort Mitchell, Kathleen and Cigi Norris, and such local men of letters as Oscar Lewis, the novelist and historian, and literary critic Albert Guerard, who taught at Stanford. It was a safe group, mainstream and high provincial, unbothered by the likes of Robinson Jeffers or Dashiell Hammett.

In 1931 Atherton commenced a trilogy set in contemporary San Francisco. It began with *The Sophisticates* (1931) and continued through *The Fog Horn* (1934) and *The House of Lee* (1940). In one sense, it was remarkable how much she was still capable of observing through her seventies and early eighties—student life at Berkeley, social life among the young and the privileged, even a Communist or two—although the basic focus of these novels was on women at home together without men, reflecting her own life, a sharp contrast to the overwhelming presence of virile males (Hamiltonian Men she called them) in her earlier fictions. Mayor Angelo Rossi appointed her to the Art Commission in January 1932, and in 1935 and 1937 Mills College and UC Berkeley awarded her honorary doctorates; 21 February 1939 was declared Gertrude Atherton Day at the Golden Gate International Exposition. She deserved this, if only for *Adventures of a Novelist*, which has been rediscovered today as a notable document in the search for identity, role, and work among American women in the late nineteenth and early twentieth centuries. Astonishingly, Atherton was not through yet, publishing two more books, *Golden Gate County* (1945) and *My San Francisco, a Wayward Biography* (1946), before her death in 1946.

In 1933 D. Appleton-Century issued Charles Caldwell Dobie's *San Francisco: A Pageant*. In 1939 a second edition was released to reflect the completion of the San Francisco–Oakland and Golden Gate bridges and to capture the market for a comprehensive book on San Francisco, which visitors to the Golden Gate International Exposition could be expected to purchase. Exquisitely illustrated with drawings by E. H. Suydam, Dobie's *San Francisco Pageant* remains a high-water mark of interpretive celebration of a city that has attracted more than its share of self-praise. A native San Franciscan, born in 1882 of Gold Rush stock, Dobie developed and exercised his talent in a San Francisco that, like the whaling ship to Ishmael, provided him with his Harvard and his Yale. At the age of fourteen, with the sudden death of his father, he had been forced to leave school and go to work as an office clerk for a fire and marine insurance company. As man and legend, the late Frank Norris shaped and inspired Dobie's autodidactic development. From Norris, Dobie absorbed a conviction that one could write about San Francisco and live there as well without growing bored or running out of material. Under Norris's influence, Dobie made a specialty of Chinatown and the Chinese, together with the other ethnic groups—the Italians of North Beach, the Russians of the Western Addition, the Latinos of Broadway hill—of the city. By the 1920s Dobie was appearing regularly as a short story writer in Mencken's *Smart Set*, and New York publishers were beginning to issue a regular series of his short stories, which continued to the time of his death from a heart attack at age sixty-one in 1943.

Depicting San Francisco as a symbol of achieved urbanism, Dobie established an archetype that became San Francisco's identity for the next half century. Dobie could do this so well because, in part, he had no other origins, no other influences—no college, no coteries, no frame of reference—other than San Francisco itself. He knew what an artist was, in part, because Isadora Duncan had taught at his dancing school and Frank Norris had urged him to write. He knew and loved the Chinese, it must be said, because the resident Chinese cook had become, as was often the case in those days, a virtual member of the family. He had grown up with an instinctive regard for the stylish, for cutting a graceful figure under pressure, because it was a special legacy of the earthquake and fire of April 1906. For the rest of his life, Dobie remembered with admiration the panache with which his mother had taken the time to don her most elegant dress, together with long black gloves and a hat with a dotted veil that swept across her face majestically, to accompany her two sons—she carrying a canary cage in one hand and a Wedgewood pitcher in the other—out of their burning quarter of the city. (Dobie himself carried off a collection of rare German beer mugs and a copy of Edith Wharton's *Italian Villas and Their Gardens* [1904], with illustrations by Maxfield Parrish.) While he remained local, provincial, and relatively untraveled, San Francisco presented to him a pageant of picturesque diversity that went a long way to substitute for the constricted struggles and somewhat narrow circumstances in which he remained until H. L. Mencken discovered him in the 1920s. By the 1930s, as he entered the last decade of his life, Dobie had become—with his excellent if well-worn suits, his pencil mustache, his slicked-back gray hair parted in the center of his forehead, his modest but persistent record of publication, his bachelor's flat atop Russian Hill—a quintessentially San Franciscan figure, provincial but in a distinctively non-provincial San Francisco sort of way.

Like Charles Caldwell Dobie, Oscar Lewis sustained, as a matter of lifestyle and subject matter, a type of direct contact with the nineteenth-century frontier about which he wrote. In an age of increasing specialization, Lewis supported himself as a literary jack of all trades (the designation "man of letters" would have embarrassed him) equally at home in the novel and history. As a freshman at Berkeley, Lewis received some unorthodox advice from his English instructor, B. H. Lehman. The best way to become a writer, Lehman told Lewis, was to start writing. Taking Lehman's advice literally, Lewis quit Berkeley before his freshman year was out, rented an office, and set himself up as a freelance. That was in 1912, and with the exception of time spent in the Ambulance Service in France during the war and some wandering about Europe and North Africa after his discharge, Lewis had been supporting himself by his typewriter ever since. In the mid-1930s Lewis was discovered by New York publisher Alfred A. Knopf, traveling through the West in search of writers. Two immediate results of this discovery—*The Big Four* (1938), a history of the transcontinental railroad, and *Bonanza Inn* (1939), written in conjunction with newsman Carroll Hall, a history of the Palace Hotel—remained active sellers for more than half a century. Knopf also published Lewis's novel *I Remember Christine* (1942), which UCLA librarian and literary critic Lawrence Clark Powell ranks as one of the two best novels ever written about San Francisco, alongside Frank Norris's *McTeague* (1899).

Lewis was also solidly based in the fine print community of San Francisco. Not until these best-sellers from Knopf, in fact, was he able to detach himself from his part-time position with the Book Club of California, an association of bibliophiles that maintained an active publishing program from its offices on Sutter Street. Nearby, at 47 Kearny near Market, on the fifth floor, above the Orange Blossom Candy Store (and later on Pine, and finally on Commercial) was the Grabhorn Press. Founded in 1920 by Edwin and Robert Grabhorn, the press was producing through the 1930s some of the most beautifully designed books in America in addition to surviving as a job-printing establishment. The Grabhorn style—eighteenth-century typefaces, rubricated initial letters, an Asian employment of empty space—carried on a graphic tradition first established in San Francisco in the 1870s by Edward Bosqui, the most noted fine printer in the United States of that era.

In 1934 two San Franciscans of differing literary inclinations—Irving Stone and William Saroyan—burst onto the best-seller list. Born on Washington Square in North Beach on 14 July 1903 (his real name, Irving Tenenbaum), Stone followed the well-worn path of Jewish San Francisco to Lowell and UC Berkeley, where he took a degree in economics in 1923, followed by a master's at USC. Returning to Berkeley for his Ph.D., Irving Tenenbaum experienced a change of heart. In 1926, along with so many other Americans, he headed off to Paris with dreams of becoming a writer. His first novel, *Pageant of Youth* (1933), a college novel set in Berkeley, was rejected nineteen times before it was published. Stone, meanwhile, had become obsessed with the life, art, and letters of Vincent Van Gogh, then relatively unknown in the United States. He began to research Van Gogh's life meticulously, to the point of sleeping in the beds in which Van Gogh had slept. In 1930 Stone returned to the United States. Settling in New York, he wrote *Lust for Life* in six months; yet it took him four more years to get it published. Appearing in 1934, *Lust for Life* became one of the best-selling novels in the history of American publishing. Somehow, in the depths of the Depression, a time of overwhelming personal and social confusion, the straightforward story of a high-minded, deeply religious artist tormented by poverty and emotional despair struck a chord among readers who were themselves wrestling with their own personal and economic demons.

So too were readers drawn to William Saroyan's *The Daring Young Man on the Flying Trapeze and Other Stories* (1934), with its Depression-defying message of anarcho-individualism, supreme and triumphant, contemptuous of politics and economics as the measuring rod of worth. Born in Fresno on 31 August 1908, Saroyan was raised in an Oakland orphanage when his father died of peritonitis and his mother was unable to support her children. Reunited with his mother in Fresno at the age of eight, Saroyan quit school when he was fifteen and went to work as a telegraph messenger. In 1927, at the age of nineteen, he moved to San Francisco, where he got a job as a counter clerk for the postal telegraph office in the Palace Hotel building. His mother and brother eventually joined him in San Francisco, with the family moving into a flat on Carl Street in the Haight Ashbury, where Saroyan divided his time among his telegraph job, playing the ponies at the Tanforan Race Track, drinking in North Beach dives, losing money in card games, and writing, writing, writing on his upright Royal in his Carl Street flat short stories by and about himself, written in a headlong, free-associational manner and concerned (in the midst of every kind of aside, anecdote, and shaggy dog story) with the perennial theme of the human condition: the existential drama of a prismatic Saroyan-Self through whom, in a manner that mingled Montaigne and the Marx Brothers, the young Armenian-American was exploring questions of love, life, creativity, death, the universe, the whole catastrophe, as Zorba the Greek would later put it. Like Montaigne, Saroyan believed that if he knew himself, he would know everything.

His Armenianism—or at least his interpretation of what it meant to be an Armenian—tilted Saroyan in favor of an archetypal Little Guy, preferably colorful, encountering an absurd world with courage and a zany ability to out-absurdize the absurd itself: to up the ante, that is, as in one of Saroyan's interminable poker games. If life chose to be so nutty, by turns comic and tragic and tragi-comical, then the best defense was the defense of a performing self. From this perspective, Saroyan's short stories were more in the nature of stream-of-consciousness monologues with some narrative content. "I am a story-teller," he exulted with near-incoherent bravado, "and I have but a single story—man. I want to tell this simple story in my own way, forgetting the rules of rhetoric, the tricks of composition. I have something to say and I do not wish to speak like Balzac. I am not an artist; I do not really believe in civilization."[6]

Saroyan's skill as an extemporaneous performer—posing, attitudinizing, filling the void with words—made him an effective playwright as well. At the end of the decade, in 1939, he won the Pulitzer Prize for his Broadway play *The Time of Your Life*, set in a bar on the Embarcadero, which he also directed. Saroyan turned down the thousand-dollar honorarium as an affront to his artistic integrity. As usual, he was posing. When broke from losses incurred at the poker table or on the track, which was frequently, Saroyan was capable of cadging a thousand or two from friends, or anyone else for that matter, without any sense of artistic compromise whatsoever.

William Saroyan belonged to a world wider than San Francisco. He belonged to Hollywood and New York, to London, where he spent the war years as an Army writer, and most especially to Paris, where he lived for much of the time after the war. Yet San Francisco, like his home town of Fresno in the San Joaquin Valley, held him in a special way, and the city returned the compliment. In 1938 Carey McWilliams was noting in his "Tides West" column in *Westways* that the literary culture of San Francisco now seemed to consist almost exclusively of William Saroyan, so rapidly had Saroyan achieved fame and so strongly was he identified with the city. With his Broadway earnings, Saroyan built a house for his mother in the Sunset district where he maintained a pied-à-terre writing studio. He returned to San Francisco at regular intervals in 1939, 1940, and 1941 to hang out at the Black Cat or at Breen's, or to meet Herb Caen or John Fante for dinner at Omar Khayam's, or to play the ponies at Tanforan. San Francisco had been good to William Saroyan in the early years, from 1927 to 1934, when he awoke to find himself famous, and he never forgot this. He always came home.

Artists of stature had special status in pre-war San Francisco. The Bohemian Club twice elected sculptor Haig Patigian, a popular local artist, to its presidency and extended a subsidized membership to such respected figures as Theodore Wores, Charles Dickman, Arthur Mathews, Jules Pages (living in Paris since the Earthquake), Robert Aitken, Xavier Martinez, William Ritschel, Percy Gray, Maurice Logan, and the Russian émigrés Gleb and Peter Ilyin. A young artist such as Antonio Sotomayor could arrive, as he did, from La Paz, Bolivia, in 1934, the scion of a Spanish colonial family, fluent in Spanish, French, and English, intending to study architecture at UC Berkeley, and spend the rest of his life, as Sotomayor did, busy with innumerable commissions, beginning with the historical murals general manager Archie Price commissioned for the newly planned Happy Valley Room in the Palace Hotel, followed by a series of caricatures, opposite the famous mural by Maxfield Parrish, in the Pied Piper Room.

If William Saroyan stood at the center of literary life in San Francisco by 1938, sculptor Ralph Stockpole stood at the center of artistic circles. "He knew everybody in town from top to bottom," Kenneth Rexroth remembered of Stackpole in 1929, "and he took us everywhere."[7] This was Ralph Stackpole's fourth sojourn in the city. A ranch boy from Williams, Oregon, Stackpole had gone to work as an unskilled worker while still a minor to support himself and his mother after his father, a rancher and millwright, was killed when he fell into a circular saw. From his teenage years onward, the diminutive Stackpole had a sinewy strength and the physical presence of a manual laborer, explosive with energy, which supported so well the demands of the direct-cut style of sculpturing he practiced. At sixteen he came down to San Francisco to study at the Mark Hopkins Institute under Arthur Putnam, sculptor, and Gottardo Piazzoni, muralist, supporting himself as a handyman in a local dance hall and a stock boy at the Emporium department store. When earthquake and fire destroyed San Francisco in April 1906, the New York art world created a burse for dislocated San Francisco artists. Stackpole used his $200 to follow Putnam and Piazonni to Paris, where he served as Putnam's apprentice while taking courses at the Ecole des Beaux Arts and living in Putnam's garret. He returned to San Francisco in 1908 but left again in 1911 to study for a year under Robert Henri in New York. From Henri, Stackpole absorbed a vividness, an immediacy, which built upon the Putnam legacy.

In 1928 Timothy Pflueger commissioned from Stackpole two heroic pieces, *Mother Earth* and *Man and His Invention*, for the front of the new Stock Exchange at Pine and Sansome. Carved between 1928 and 1931, the sculptures were the two most ambitious granite sculptures undertaken in the United States in those years. Then came the commission for a frame and stucco version of the eighty-foot-high *Pacifica*, scheduled after the closing of the Golden Gate International Exposition in 1941 to be recast in steel, stone, and concrete for placement on Alcatraz Island, Angel Island, or some other prominent point near the Golden Gate: a plan that, if achieved, would have made Stackpole the Frédéric Bartholdi of the Pacific. Was it bitterness over the dynamiting of *Pacifica* by the Navy in 1942 that led Stackpole to return to France in 1949, where he spent the rest of his life in the village of Chaurit Puy-de-Dôme in the center of the garlic country? Or merely his recognition that the golden age of figurative public sculpture was in temporary eclipse?

Stackpole's colleague, in any event, Beniamino Bufano—fully Stackpole's equal in talent and creative output—productively sojourned in San Francisco until his death in 1970. Even more diminutive than Stackpole and equally explosive in his physical energy, the Italian-born Bufano moved to San Francisco from New York after World War I. A pacifist, he had cut off his trigger finger and was alleged to have mailed it to President Wilson. He remained in San Francisco for the next half century, with time out for visits to Europe, India, and the Far East. For all his dedication to his art, Ralph Stackpole was bourgeois in his attitudes and life-style. Bufano, by contrast, was thoroughly bohemian, shaped as he was by the mood of Greenwich Village in the early 1900s: an anarcho-pacifist Roman Catholic with a strong attachment to St. Francis of Assisi and to Sun Yat-sen and Gandhi, whom he had met in China and India. In the 1920s Bufano produced an extraordinary series of pieces in the style of the Italian Renaissance, including a *Crucifixion* (1924) in which Bufano cast himself as the Christ, including the amputated trigger finger. In the 1930s he undertook a series of animal sculptures—frogs, rabbits, cats, penguins, seals, snails, hedgehogs, parrots, rams, elephants, camels, ducks, mice, owls, a great mother bear nursing two cubs, a California bear surmounting an emblem of peace—which he steadily continued for the rest of his long career. Bufano's animal sculptures remain, so many of them, masterpieces of their genre, elegantly and simply shaped, dynamic with the essential innocence, the unconscious joy, of the animal world as perceived by a disciple of St. Francis.

Also in the 1930s Bufano began a series of statues of St. Francis himself, including a St. Francis on horseback. In February 1937 the Art Commission of San Francisco, in a narrow vote, "disapproved without prejudice" a proposal by the WPA to erect a monumental statue of St. Francis by Beniamino Bufano, 180 feet high and constructed of stainless steel, atop Twin Peaks. A local Franciscan priest was denouncing the statue as a monstrosity, although Archbishop Hanna had praised the work in its model stage. In 1939 Bufano completed what is perhaps the greatest of his St. Francis series. It later stood in front of the Church of St. Francis of Assisi in North Beach until yet another priest had it removed to the Longshoremen's Hall on Fisherman's Wharf. However hostile these two clerics, San Franciscans in general adored Bufano, making of the elfin sculptor a permanent artist-in-residence to the city. Eventually, local patrons established the Bufano Society of the Arts, which handled the affairs of the master, selling his works, paying the expenses of his South of Market studio, meeting Bufano's simple needs with a monthly retainer. Thanks to the society, statues by Bufano eventually embellished the entire Bay Area: at Aquatic Park, the Steinhart Aquarium, the Stonestown and Hillsdale shopping centers, San Francisco State University, the Golden Gateway Center in downtown San Francisco, the College of Notre Dame in Belmont. Bufano lived rent free at the Press Club and took his meals at no cost at a Powell Street cafeteria where three of his most ambitious murals were on display. In time, he became a figure very much resembling St. Francis himself: seraphic, detached, living on tea, fruit, and brown bread, his mere presence constituting an invocation of place, a form of civic blessing.

As the art and musical programs of the Golden Gate International Exposition were proving by 1939, and as the continuing success of the symphony and opera had already proven, San Francisco enjoyed an active community of music and art patrons. It took only one patron, however, Alma de Bretteville Spreckels, to get the city into the museum business. Then in her fifties, Alma de Bretteville Spreckels deserves a novel, an opera even, capable of reflecting the will, the self-determination, the self-invention of a displaced aristocrat, an artist's model, lush and Rubenesque in the style of the *fin de siècle*, who used her sexual magnetism to parlay her way back into the upper class, if not quite to the complete respectability that ever eluded her.

An adventuress in the grand style, Alma de Bretteville—christened Alma Emma Charlotte Corday le Normand de Bretteville—was born and raised in San Francisco in marginal circumstances. Throughout his life, Alma's father used the fact that he was directly descended from Franco-Danish nobility to avoid employment. Her mother, the sole support of the family, ran a combination bakery and French laundry on Francisco Street. As a girl, Alma helped her mother bake, and wash and deliver the clean clothes back to the big houses. By the time she was fifteen, she stood nearly six feet in height and was exquisitely proportioned in the ample style of the era. Ambitious, she trained as a stenographer, found work in the downtown, and enrolled in night classes at the Mark Hopkins Institute atop Nob Hill. To earn extra money, she worked as an artist's model, posing in the nude for individual artists and for classes at the institute. Sketches of Alma in the nude became well-known items, an early version of the pinup, in the bars of the Cocktail Route up and down Kearny Street. In 1899 sculptor Robert Aitken immortalized a near-nude Alma as the Republic atop the Dewey monument in Union Square.

Robust in her physical and imaginative appetites, Alma de Bretteville read widely, dreamed of a better life, plugged away at her stenographer's job, continued to pose, attended artists' parties and balls, and worked as an extra at the Opera House, where she met Ashton Potter, an aspiring theatrical critic who, on a secluded knoll in the Presidio, claimed from Alma that which hundreds of other young men had also dreamt of claiming. While Alma enjoyed the experience and frequently repeated it with Potter, she quickly came to realize that her beauty and sexual magnetism were at once a vulnerability and an opportunity. It was, after all, rather inappropriate for the direct descendant of one of Napoleon's generals to be lavishing her favors *gratis* in an outdoor setting on a charming but impoverished newspaperman. There had to be a better way. In 1902, at the age of twenty-one, Alma most likely became the mistress of Charles Anderson, a Klondike millionaire. When Anderson refused to marry her, Alma sued him for breach of promise. She sought a $50,000 judgment, but the jury awarded her a mere $1,250. Shortly thereafter, she met sugar and shipping millionaire Adolph Spreckels, a man twice her age, for an intimate dinner in an upper room in the Poodle Dog restaurant on Post Street: a private elevator, a private room, a dining table and couch, a door that locked from inside. Their knees touched and they dined no more.

It took Alma de Bretteville five years to get Adolph Spreckels to marry her, but even as his mistress she began to display the grand style: elegant clothes, great ostrich-feathered hats, box seats at the opera, dinners in fine restaurants, a voyage to Europe, where Alma visited her cousins in Copenhagen. When she became pregnant with the first of their three children, an overjoyed Spreckels (who feared that an earlier venereal complaint had left him sterile) tore the pre-nuptial agreement into shreds. In 1913 he built her one of the most elaborate private homes in the nation, the Spreckels mansion on Washington Street across from Lafayette Park, a gleaming white Beaux Arts extravaganza designed by George Applegarth, currently the home of novelist Danielle Steel.

Being French, Alma de Bretteville Spreckels, as she now was, adored French culture. Before the war broke out in August 1914, she spent long periods of time in Paris, where she formed an intense friendship (many claimed that it was more) with the celebrated Illinois-born dancer Loie Fuller, formerly of the Folies Bergères. Loie introduced Alma to Auguste Rodin, a meeting that would have great consequences for San Francisco. Showing Rodin photographs of her mansion in San Francisco, Alma described it as a museum as well as a residence, which she would like to fill with the works of the Master. It took Alma another ten years to realize her dream. She returned to San Francisco, busied herself in relief work, and continued to collect Rodin, Arthur Putnam, and other sculptors; and when the war was over, she began to plan nothing less than the creation of a new museum *a novo*, the California Palace of the Legion of Honor, sited on Land's End in Lincoln Park overlooking the Golden Gate, an exact replica of the Legion of Honor in Paris. Adolph agreed to foot the bill, despite opposition from other members of the Spreckels family; and on Armistice Day, 11 November 1924, Alma presented to the city a stunning nineteen-gallery museum, dedicated as a memorial to Californians who had lost their lives in the Great War.

Mrs. Leonora Wood Armsby, by contrast, sole support of the San Francisco Symphony during the Depression, was a model of propriety. In its brief existence thus far, the San Francisco Symphony had enjoyed the services of two impressive maestros, Alfred Hertz in the 1920s, followed by Pierre Monteux in the 1930s.

There could be no greater contrast than that between Hertz, the imperious Teuton, schoolmasterish, almost military in his *pince-nez* and bushy beard, and the jovial Monteux, Clemenceau-like in mustache and hair style, the epitome of Gallic *joie de vivre* as he strolled along the sunny streets of the city in the company of Madame Monteux and the family poodle. Hertz was a drillmaster and a scholar; Monteux, an impresario of new music and a delightful performer; yet each conductor possessed a high sense of musical purpose and was devoted to the orchestra and city he served. Under Hertz the San Francisco Symphony, founded in 1911, began to record for Victor, performances still astonishing for their technical polish. Monteux brought the orchestra into dialogue with living composers and edged it, occasionally, into the avant-garde.

Opera, meanwhile, flourished even more grandly, now that San Francisco was enjoying, since October 1932, a first-rate opera house. Sydney, Buenos Aires, Rio de Janeiro, Chicago, San Francisco: frontier capitals have a special affinity for opera. The highest and most complex art form speaks in a special way to cities in emergent circumstances, evoking for them the culture they have temporarily left behind. From the Gold Rush forward, San Francisco was an opera-loving city. When Beniamino Gigli arrived at the Ferry Building in 1923 to sing with the newly organized San Francisco Opera Company directed by Gaetano Merola, he was met by the chief of police and escorted to his hotel through a cheering crowd under police escort. When San Francisco determined upon its official War Memorial in the early 1920s, the complex included an art museum and an opera house. (At the time, the San Francisco Opera was performing at the Civic Auditorium.) Dissenting veterans, charging that the arts establishment had hijacked their memorial, delayed the project for nearly a decade; but when an exasperated Mayor Rolph put Charles Kendrick in charge, the project began to move forward. Actual construction began in the spring of 1929, with Kendrick functioning as a voluntary project manager on behalf of the city. Architects Arthur Brown Jr. and John Bakewell, assisted by Gustave Albert Lansburgh, designed a Beaux Arts classical building in the grand European style, seating more than three thousand. Its orchestra pit could seat up to seventy-five musicians. A gigantic chandelier, worthy of the Phantom of the Opera himself, loomed overhead. On a warm Indian summer evening, 15 October 1932, San Francisco defied the Depression with a grand opening of its new structure. Gaetano Merola conducted *Tosca* with Alfredo Gandolfi singing Scarpia and Claudia Muzio singing Tosca. The most expensive ticket in the house cost five dollars. Thousands listened on radio station KPO and hundreds of thousands over the Red Network of NBC. *Lucia di Lammermoor, Die Meistersinger, Rigoletto,* and *Hansel and Gretel* completed the 1932 season.

In 1933 the San Francisco Opera spun off a secondary institution, the San Francisco Opera Ballet, under the direction of Adolph Bolm. Reorganized in 1938 as an autonomous entity under the direction of William Christensen, the San Francisco Ballet went on tour of the Far West, bringing its complex art form to many cities for the first time. A talented dancer, the Utah-born Christensen in

1937 danced the lead in the American premiere of George Balanchine's *Apollo*. The next year, in New York, Lew Christensen, an equally talented performer, soon to join his brother in San Francisco, danced the lead role of Mac in the premiere of *Filling Station*, an innovative ballet that sought to bring American settings and themes to this almost exclusively European art form. Over the next four years, *Filling Station* enjoyed three hundred performances. In 1939 the San Francisco Opera Ballet mounted its first full-length production, *Coppelia*, staged by William Christensen, which toured the Northwest. As fragile as were these beginnings, they represented an almost unique entree of an American city outside New York into the world of ballet. It would take another forty years for this fragile repotting to take firm root; yet the audacity of it all—the building of a world-class opera house, the launching of a ballet company—said something about the mind-set and aspirations of San Francisco as the city struggled through the Depression years.

San Francisco entered the 1940s an achieved and achieving American city, its past structured and useful, its myth more flourishing than ever. For the next twenty years, San Francisco would remain the financial and political capital, not just of California, but of the entire Far West as well. A beautiful city, San Francisco had resisted succumbing to its beauty. It had remained, rather, a dynamic and engaged urban center, on the forefront of banking, manufacturing, and foreign trade, as well as arts and culture, on the Pacific Coast. Yet its most important achievement—the sense of well-being it conferred on its citizens—was perhaps the most subtle of its characteristics. Despite the anti-urban bias that remained so deeply in the American psyche through the 1930s, no novel, no personal testimony, no witness of any sort seems to have appeared in this period indicating that San Francisco, the city itself, was a source of darkness. Even the ferocious maritime strike of 1934 yielded no such attacks. On the contrary, San Francisco seemed uniquely possessed of the ability to communicate the message, however illusory, that in San Francisco everyone had a stake in the city. Living day by day in San Francisco, encountering problems great and small within the context of a supportive urban environment, the Barbours of Sea Cliff represented One Man's Family living in a city that had achieved its own brand of inclusiveness.

6

Pershing Square

Los Angeles Through the 1930s

*L*OS Angeles, the City of Angels, was a city of palm trees and flowering plants and shrubs of every kind. At the turn of the century, the citizens of the city had planted all types of trees—eucalyptus from Australia, cypress from Italy and Monterey, the pepper tree from Peru, acacia in fourteen species, jacaranda and camphor, even rubber trees—but it was the towering palm tree that was most frequently used to define the streets of the emerging city. Throughout the 1890s and early 1900s, palm trees were planted by the hundreds, by the thousands—the California fan palm, the Mexican fan palm, the Canary Island palm, the Guadalupe palm, the blue palm, the windmill palm, the Senegal date palm— in an energetic effort to create a sense of space through horticulture, to define the city centered on the Los Angeles plain. And now, by the 1930s, the palms had grown to great height. They stood against the skyline, their rich green fronds in flight or at rest atop soaring slender trunks. When the wind blew, it was as if thousands of magical beings, floral giraffes, were nodding approvingly over the city.

Architecturally, it was an eclectic, even a hodgepodge city. Visitors such as Edmund Wilson, even longtime residents such as Aldous Huxley, loved to satirize the sometimes phantasmagoric variety of streetscapes. "A wee wonderful Swiss shilly-shally snuggles up beneath a bountiful bougainvillea which is by no means artificially colored," noted Edmund Wilson in 1932. "And there a hot little hacienda, a regular enchilada con queso with a roof made of rich red tomato sauce, barely lifts her long-lashed lavender shades on the soul of old Spanish days."[1] One critic compared the region to an aggregation of movie sets, with retail outlets of various kinds in the shape of frogs, hats, oranges, sphinxes, and windmills. European émigrés could never make up their minds whether Los Angeles was one of the most hideous or most beautiful cities in the world, or a strange combination of both. Vicki Baum saw Los Angeles as an idyllic panorama of creamy white stucco walls, red-tiled roofs, and palm trees. Carl Zuckmayer, by contrast, found it "one of the ugliest and most brutal metropolises in the world."[2]

Aldous Huxley began his novel *After Many a Summer Dies the Swan* (1939) with the most sweeping, comprehensive, and still, for all its datedness, the most successful description of Los Angeles as idiosyncratic cityscape. Running for fifteen pages and including architectural description, screaming billboards and neon signs (CLASSY EATS, MILE HIGH CONES, JESUS SAVES, HAMBURGERS, FINE LIQUORS, TURKEY SANDWICHES, GO TO CHURCH AND FEEL BETTER ALL WEEK), a catalog of movie star homes, and descriptions of people on the street, played off against a luxuriant listing of palms, shrubs, and flowering plants, Huxley's evocation announced to the English-reading world the palpable presence of a new metropolis on the planet, in which distinctions between fantasy and reality, eccentricity and the norm, dissolved in the tense complexity of a new and vivid genre of urban theater.

Yet there was some pattern, some orderly sequence, in the array of architectural styles that so amused, or even outraged, visitors. Los Angeles had begun in Mexican adobe, then made the transition to Victorian wood, granite, and brick, followed by an era of wood-built Craftsman lasting through the 1910s. Then came stucco-dependent Spanish Revival in all its variants, so powerful a force through the 1920s; finally, in the 1930s architects were turning with great success to the International Style, Art Deco, and Streamline Moderne. Throughout the decade, the Austrian-born Richard Neutra and Rudolph Schindler practiced a Southern California version of the International Style, with roots in Viennese Seccessionism, for clients of cultivation and taste who tended to live on the western side of the city. Austere, geometric, appealing more to a Platonic sense of architecture than to the senses, the work of Neutra and Schindler bespoke Los Angeles as Vienna on the Pacific, a notion rendered increasingly realistic with the wholesale arrival of refugees from Nazi oppression.

A client such as Philip Lovell, however, a physician, an intellectual, an internationalist—for whom Schindler designed a beach house in Newport Beach in 1926 and for whom Neutra created a home off the remote and bare Commonwealth Canyon in West Los Angeles in 1929, which remains a primary icon of modernism—represented one sector in Los Angeles, but not its dominant part. It was in the more popularly based Art Deco that Los Angeles, a populist city, most directly expressed its sense of itself in these years. The Zig-Zag styling of Bullock's on Wilshire (1929); the chevron and floral motifs of the Sunset Tower Apartments (1929) on Sunset; the glazed black and gold terra cotta tiling covering the Richfield Oil Building (1929) in the downtown; and the glazed aquamarine and gold terra cotta tiling and recessed copper spandrils of the Eastern Columbia Building (1930) on South Broadway: in expressive, even excessive Art Deco concoctions such as these, Los Angeles most directly revealed itself as Oz on the Pacific, Emerald City on the plain; as Hollywood, as imagined place, eclectic, eccentric, of and by and for the Folks in all their rage for amusement and escape. As the decade progressed, which is to say, as the Depression continued, Art Deco yielded to Streamline Moderne: the Los Angeles Times Building (1935) on 1st, the Pan Pacific Auditorium (1935) on Beverly Boulevard, the Coca-Cola Bottling Plant (1936) on South Central Avenue in the industrial district—as if to suggest that the eclectic comforts of Art Deco, its release into fantasy, were inappropriate in a city battling a Depression that only a renewed industrialism, symbolized by Streamline Moderne, could conquer.

Los Angeles was an enormous city: 441.7 square miles in extent in 1930, with a population of 1,238,048, which made it the fifth largest city in the nation. By 1940 the City of Angels had gained another nine square miles of territory and more than a quarter million more people. The sheer expanse of Los Angeles—a region that would encompass all five boroughs of New York, together with Boston and San Francisco—made it as much of a city-state as it was a freestanding metropolis. Los Angeles even had its own agricultural region, the vast and largely agricultural San Fernando Valley, annexed in 1915. "The map of the city," noted one observer, "resembles nothing so much as an amoeba gone berserk."[3]

Conventional wisdom holds that the automobile was largely responsible for the horizontality of Los Angeles; yet even in the pioneer era there was something in the Southern California formula—the vast spaces of the Spanish and Mexican land grants, the bold and continuous progress of the Los Angeles plain between mountains and the sea—that might have foretold, were the signs read correctly, the distinctive shape Los Angeles would later take. Long before the automobile, the citizens of the region had embraced horizontality as an ideal: embraced the horizontal, that is, as the fundamental orientation of the urban settlements filling the coastal plain between mountain and sea. The acquisition of water from the Owens River in 1913, together with the interurban electric system created by Henry Huntington, reinforced this early tendency on the part of the residents of the Los Angeles plain to envision their settlement as one continuum, one vast horizontal city, even if that imagined city, gridded and subdivided seven times larger than was necessary, would take more than a half century to settle. For Los Angeles to make the transition from town to city, as it did between 1890 and 1900, was to begin a process of expansion—29.21 square miles in 1890, 43.26 square miles in 1900—that would continue through the century. Between 1900 and 1910, Los Angeles doubled its land mass. Then in the 1910s, after water came, it quadrupled its size through the willful, sometimes enforced annexation of townships seeking a connection to the aqueduct. Horizontality was at the core of the Los Angeles identity. Expansion was its DNA code.

The 1910s represented the first decade of the automobile in any meaningful way; hence the quadrupling of the city after 1913 was the mixed result of water, the interurban electric, and the automobile building upon the horizontality of the Spanish and Mexican rancho land forms and the equally horizontal orientation of the nineteenth-century American city. By the 1930s, however, the automobile

had become the primary symbol, the signature icon, of the emergent metropolis.
By the late 1930s, there were 124 cars to every hundred families in the city. "The
distances are so vast," noted novelist James M. Cain, "the waste of time so cruel
if you go by bus or street car, that you must have your own transportation. . . .
Everybody has some kind of second- or third- or ninth-hand flivver; even the cook
comes to work in her car."[4] Arriving at the Los Angeles train depot, H. L.
Mencken—as a matter of course, as if he were in an Eastern city—piled into a
cab and asked the driver to take him to his host's house on San Vicente Boulevard.
Forty miles and sixteen dollars later, Mencken knew he was in a different kind of
city.

For geographical reasons—the barrier formed by the San Gabriel and Santa
Monica mountains on the north and the Pacific Ocean on the west—the City of
Los Angeles was forced to accommodate the entire north-south traffic of Southern
California, including the distribution of automobiles to the forty-three cities and
towns in Los Angeles County. Not surprisingly, the City of Angels pioneered the
one-way street, the traffic island, the rigid restriction of the left turn into oncoming
traffic, and, with the opening of the Arroyo Seco Parkway in 1940, the interurban
freeway. By the late 1930s, Los Angelenos were enjoying drive-in restaurants and
automobile-friendly motels and bungalow courts and were discussing the possibility of the drive-in bank. Shops and department stores, churches and synagogues,
even high schools and junior colleges sustained large rear surface parking lots; and
the model pioneered by the Richfield Building, an underground garage in an
office building, was becoming increasingly commonplace in new construction.
For Los Angeles, the automobile represented not merely a technology for negotiating the city. The automobile and the road structure created to support it had
become a permanent urban form. The automobile was a way of being in Los
Angeles, a way of relating to the city in social and psychological terms. Even more:
the sound of traffic had become the music of the city, like a Max Steiner score
in a Hollywood film. A group of musicologists, so Carey McWilliams reported in
late 1937, measured the wave frequency of traffic noises in various pitches throughout the city and discovered that the tonal pitch of Los Angeles was F natural, the
fourth interval of the diatonic scale.

Despite its dispersion across 450 square miles, Los Angeles still enjoyed a downtown in the classic sense of that term, revolving around the Plaza where the city
had been founded on 4 September 1781. Daily mass was still being celebrated at
the Church of Our Lady the Queen of the Angels, established in 1784, rebuilt in
1822, and improved in 1875, 1881, 1912, and 1923, which remained an active
parish of the archdiocese. Beginning in the late 1920s, new life had come to the
nearby Olvera Street with the restoration of its historic adobes and the redevel-
opment of El Paseo as a cluster of shops, restaurants, and outdoor markets stressing
the Spanish and Mexican origins of the city. Flanking the Plaza was a distinguished survivor from the past, the Pico House at 430 North Main, the first three-

story building in the city, completed in 1869 as one of the most luxurious hotels in the Far West. With powerful symbolism, directly in sight of the Plaza, was rising in the last years of the 1930s the last great Spanish-style building to be constructed in the city, the Union Passenger Terminal at 800 North Alameda, completed in 1939. Designed by John and Donald Parkinson in a combination of Spanish Colonial and Streamline Moderne, the Union Passenger Terminal ranked with City Hall (1928) and Bertram Goodhue and Carlton Winslow's Central Library (1926) as one of the signature buildings of the city. At once restrained, even minimalist, and—in the intricate tile patterns of its floor and walls, its oversized leather seating, its metal lighting fixtures, its exposed beams soaring overhead—luxuriant, the Union Passenger Terminal was by 1940 greeting arriving and departing passengers with a complex, highly satisfying evocation of Los Angeles as an up-to-date American place with a romantic regard for its reimagined Hispanic past.

In September 1931 El Pueblo de Nuestra Señora la Reina de Los Angeles de Porciuncula, more commonly known as Los Angeles, or less frequently as the City of Angels, and even more frequently as just plain L.A., celebrated the 150th anniversary of its founding by the Spanish with a ten-day fiesta. (During the celebration, telephone operators at City Hall were instructed to answer calls with a cheery *buenos dias!*) On 4 September 1931, the Honorable John Porter, mayor of the city, an Iowa-born dealer in new and wrecked auto parts and an evangelical Protestant and avid prohibitionist by religious conviction, Babbitt personified, costumed himself as a Spanish Catholic *ranchero* of the early nineteenth century for ceremonies on the Plaza attended by ten thousand spectators. Governor Rolph was also on hand in *caballero* attire, a colorful sash around his ample waist, as were actors Douglas Fairbanks and Leo Carrillo. The *California Eagle*, voice of the African-American community, took umbrage at the fact that all the couples and children chosen to represent the *pobladores* of the city were white, ignoring the fact that the majority of the founders of 1781 were African, Indian, or *mestizo* in their ethnic identity. "Those who saw the parade," thundered the *California Eagle*, "must have a sense of the utter childishness of a race so saturated with prejudice that it attempts to change the color of its founders' skins."[5]

Nearby, Chinatown and Little Tokyo offered visual evidence of the important role the Chinese and Japanese had played in the emergence of the city. With Chinese immigration severely curtailed in the 1880s, and a new wave of immigration not to begin until the 1960s, Chinatown had a small population, no more than three thousand, and blended into an African-American neighborhood. Quaint, picturesque, more than a little ramshackle, Ferguson Alley in Chinatown perfectly expressed the Chinese-American presence in Los Angeles: something more a matter of the past than the present. In July 1937 more than 850 Chinese graves were opened in Chinatown under the supervision of the Ning Yung, Yin Hoi, and Kwong Chow benevolent societies. Piously disinterred, each set of remains was placed in a small tin container for shipment to Hong Kong and reburial on the Chinese mainland. There could be no better testimony to the interrupted arc of Chinese Los Angeles than the sending back to China of the remains of 850 Chinese men who had died alone in an alien land, wishing only that their bones and dust might someday be returned home for burial.

Little Tokyo, by contrast, with its flourishing restaurants and shops, its open-air market, its Japanese newspaper, its Shinto temple on Jackson Street, its imposing Hompa Hongwanji Buddhist temple near 1st Street and Central Avenue a few blocks from City Hall, testified to the fact that Los Angeles was the capital of the largest overseas Japanese population outside Hawaii: 41,382 by 1935, with 32,714 living in Los Angeles County and 13,000 living within city limits. A baby boom had been underway in the Japanese community since the mid-1920s when Japanese women, the so-called Picture Brides, were allowed to emigrate to California by the thousands and marry Japanese men living in California according to arrangements finalized in Japan. Despite prejudice and the legal harassment of two state laws prohibiting Japanese immigrants from holding property in their own names, Japanese Los Angeles, the capital of an even more impressive Japanese Southern California, was evolving into a flourishing society of Japan-born *Issei* and American-born *Nisei*. Los Angeles depended upon Japanese farmers in its hinterlands for fresh fruits and vegetables. In the Wholesale Terminal Market in the Downtown, Japanese jobbers handled $10 million of an annual $70 million in trade. More than five hundred Japanese fishermen worked out of San Pedro Harbor.

Civic Center anchored this portion of the Downtown, a cluster of public buildings dominated by the thirty-two-story City Hall topped by a replica of the tomb of Mausolus in Halicarnassus, one of the Seven Wonders of the Ancient World. Only this structure, completed in 1928, was allowed to exceed the 150-foot height limit; and so the great shaft of the City Hall, topped by a ziggurat, floated above the skyline with a moody, evocative replica of an ancient shrine to power and wealth at its apex: a Cecil B. DeMille set soaring above the city. Diagonally across from City Hall, as if to suggest the power of its newspaper as a governing element in the city, stood the new Los Angeles Times Building, completed in 1935. Designed by Gordon Kaufmann, the architect of Hoover Dam, this polished granite edifice, a fortress in Art Deco Moderne, housed both editorial offices and printing plant and in its assertive architecture boldly expressed the predominate power of the *Times* in the region. The sheer proximity of City Hall and the Times Building signaled to one and all that in terms of ownership and influence the *Times* was more than a mere newspaper and its chief executive Harry Chandler was more than a mere publisher. In an age unbothered by later niceties regarding conflict of interest, the *Times* was, like the granite monolith that housed it, a concentration of publishing, real estate, and political power, triunely exercised, without apology or embarrassment.

At the *Times*, Iowa-born, Los Angeles-raised Harry Carr had begun his career as a cub reporter in the 1890s and had been writing a daily column since 1899.

In 1935 Carr published *Los Angeles: City of Dreams*, with illustrations by E. S. Suydam, a parallel volume to Charles Caldwell Dobie's *San Francisco: A Pageant* (1933) in the D. Appleton-Century series profiling the cities of the United States. Carr's rubric and thesis—that Los Angeles was an imagined city, a dreamed city, self-invented and more than a little illusory—established a pathway of interpretation that many other observers of Los Angeles have since pursued. A devoted publicist of the Los Angeles way of life, Carr intended the dreaminess in the city of dreams to be taken as a compliment. Others were not so sure. At what point, they asked, did dreams become delusions?

Nowhere were the dreams of Los Angeles more centrally located than on Bunker Hill, which divided the Civic Center and the Plaza from the newer portions of the Downtown. Served by Angel's Flight, a funicular railroad with a terminal on South Hill Street near the Grand Central Market, Bunker Hill was a forgotten island in time: a cluster of Victorian mansions, ramshackle hotels, rooming houses, and once grand residences subdivided into apartments. Colonel J. W. Eddy, an engineer, built Angel's Flight in 1901, putting into service two cable cars, the Sinai and the Olivet, sacred mountains of the Old and New Testaments. At the top of Bunker Hill the Colonel built a hundred-foot steel observation tower, which provided uninterrupted views of the city. If Los Angeles had a bohemia, a Montmarte, a Soho, a Greenwich Village or North Beach, Bunker Hill was it. Here lived the dreamers of the city, with their fugitive ambitions of life and art, as testified to by dozens of novels set on or near Bunker Hill in this period, beginning with Don Ryan's *Angel's Flight* (1927), and a smaller but equally impressive number of paintings, beginning with Millard Sheets's *Angel's Flight* (1931), the painterly masterpiece of the decade.

Hungry for nourishing fare, bohemians and others—up to thirty-five thousand a day—might do their shopping at the Grand Central Market at the base of Bunker Hill. If Los Angeles needed any testimony to the notion that, despite its vast distances, its dependence upon the automobile, its growing obsession with private life, the City of Angels remained a centralized urban place, this gigantic retail market, covering an entire square block and renting stalls to more than a hundred businesses, the Les Halles of L.A., continued the tradition of the marketplaces of Europe and the *mercados* of Latin America vividly into the American present. A synesthesia of piled-high fruits and produce, breadstuffs and grains in great burlap sacks, meat counters, delicatessens, floral shops, and lunch counters, the Grand Central Market assembled the diverse population of the city under one roof, day by day, in a flood of humanity—mulling over produce, discussing a cut of meat with a butcher, seated over coffee and donuts at a marble counter—that would reach fifty thousand a day by the late 1940s.

The Grand Central Market opened onto Broadway, the most dynamic street in the Downtown. Two of the most architecturally intriguing buildings in the city anchored the northern and southern extensions of Broadway: the futurist Bradbury Building (1893) at 304 South Broadway at 3rd, designed by neophyte George

Wyman under the inspiration of Edward Bellamy's utopian novel *Looking Back-ward* (1888); and the Los Angeles Examiner Building, a Mission Revival extrava-ganza at 1111 South Broadway, between 11th and 12th, designed by Julia Morgan in 1915. Broadway was also Movie Palace Row, with the last of the palaces, the Los Angeles Theater at 615 South Broadway, opening on 30 January 1931 with a showing of Charles Chaplin's *City Lights* and a stage show featuring Carlton Kelsey and his Orchestra. Theater magnate E. L. Gumbiner wanted the Los Angeles Theater to rival the Fox Theater in San Francisco, and architect S. Charles Lee did everything to accommodate his client's wish. Moviegoers stepped off Broadway into a rotunda supported by stately Corinthian columns worthy of Versailles. In the theater itself, there were 2,190 seats on three levels. Patrons guided themselves through the darkness by tubes of pale blue neon on either side of the aisles. Downstairs, beneath the theater, were a restaurant, a ballroom, a smoking room, and restroom facilities in different shades of marble. For those waiting for the next movie in the main lounge, a periscope system of mirrors projected the film being shown within onto a television-like screen. Ominously, opening night guests, including Charles Chaplin and Albert Einstein, visiting at Cal Tech, were met with hoots and boos from a line of shabby men in a breadline across the street. Since the Los Angeles Theater was not affiliated with a studio, however, it could not book first-run films, and Gumbiner was soon reduced to filling his fantastic palace with double bills of B pictures and old releases.

Across the street, at 648 South Broadway, Clifton's Brookdale Cafeteria, the largest public cafeteria in the world, opened in 1935. Owned by cafeteria magnate Clifford Clinton, the son of two Salvation Army captains, Clifton's Brookdale Cafeteria, like Frank Miller's Mission Inn in Riverside in an earlier generation, offered unembarrassed testimony to the tastes of the Folks. The main dining room replicated a redwood forest, complete with running water and real redwood trees. There were also a bookstore selling inspirational literature, a bulletin board pro-viding a Friendship Exchange for strangers to the city, and a full-time hostess whose main task was to help Clifton patrons with personal or administrative prob-lems. Clifford Clinton also operated Clifton's Pacific Seas Cafeteria at 618 South Olive Street, the second of his Cafeterias of the Golden Rule, serving some twenty-five thousand meals daily. Pacific Seas featured waterfalls, fountains, arti-ficial palms, tropical murals, a controlled rainfall every twenty minutes, and a Garden for Meditation containing a statue of Christ in the Garden of Gethsem-ane. An organ was played over the lunch hour, followed by instrumental ensem-bles in the late afternoon and inspirational floor shows in the evening. Both cafe-terias served a nutritious meal for pennies a serving; credit was extended to the respectable, and the respectably impoverished were allowed to dine free.

The Clifton Cafeterias, Schaber's Cafeteria at 626 South Broadway, and the Boos Brothers Cafeteria at 530 South Hill catered to the Folks. Hearty fare appeal-ing to working men and women as well as the white-collar crowd was available at three restaurants that never closed: Philippe's Sandwich Shop on Aliso, where the

French dip sandwich was invented; the Original Pantry Cafe at the corner of Figueroa and 9th; and the Pacific Dining Car, located in a reconverted railroad car at 6th and Witmer. The Hollywood crowd (Louella Parsons, George Raft, Mae West) favored the Pacific Dining Car, as did the gamblers and the demi-monde. Cops, journalists, and working folk favored Philippe's and the Pantry. Higher on the culinary ladder were such establishments as Taix at 321 Commercial Street, where the full table d'hôte—soup, salad, entree, fruit, French bread—cost fifty cents; Bee Carson's at 523 South Spring, where bench and bar and the financial crowd dined around a circular bar called the Roman Well; Bernstein's Fish Grotto at 424 West 6th (minimum charge, twenty-five cents), which boasted that each fish served on any one day was alive and well that very morning; and the Paris Inn at 210 East Market, where the French and Italian cooking was served by singing waiters and an operatic floor show was presented at one-thirty in the afternoon and nine and eleven in the evening. Constructed in the early 1920s as the premier hotel and rendezvous for the city, the Biltmore on Pershing Square maintained its position through the 1930s. Its five restaurants—the Coffee Shop, the Grill, the Renaissance, the Rendezvous, the Bowl—were persistently busy, despite the hard times, with the Bowl rivaling the Cocoanut Grove as the premier dance-oriented nightclub of greater Los Angeles.

Despite the black-tie crowd at the Bowl and the buzzing to and fro of lemon-colored taxicabs at the Biltmore entrance on South Olive, downtown Los Angeles was where the Depression became most visible and where relief efforts were concentrated. In contrast to San Francisco, Los Angeles was hit harder and more openly by the bad times. Already, by 1930, Southern California had the highest bankruptcy rate in the country. Seventy-nine despairing investors plunged to their deaths from the Arroyo Seco Bridge in Pasadena in the first four years of the decade, forcing the construction of anti-suicide barriers. The unemployment problem came up as an agenda item before the Los Angeles City Council on 297 separate occasions in 1931. By 1933 Los Angeles had become one of the most depressed cities in the country. Downtown teamed with shabby men selling pencils and apples, panhandling, or washing automobile windshields at stoplights, hoping for tips. In the mid-1930s the relief load in Los Angeles County was multiplied by ten in three years, a combination of locals going broke and the influx of impoverished transients.

Despite Mayor Porter's boasts in the course of the September 1931 Plaza celebration that Los Angeles had no need of soup kitchens, there were soup kitchens aplenty by the mid-1930s. Cafeteria owner Clifford Clinton was offering meals at five cents. For a penny, customers could have a bowl of brown rice over which was ladled vegetable soup. Lines began forming up to three hours before the cafeteria opened. Clinton was forced to establish a second cafeteria for this penny-a-meal plan so as not to inconvenience paying customers. He later estimated that he served a million such meals through the 1930s, in addition to extending credit to many of his paying customers. Established in August 1931 by Mary Covell, director of the Midnight Mission, in a former Southern Pacific warehouse, the Los Angeles Food Conservation Warehouse helped feed up to twenty-five hundred families a week with food donated by regional farmers, the Bean Growers Association, even bootleggers, whose sugar, seized by federal authorities, was sent over to Mrs. Covell. The Jewish Social Service Bureau distributed milk to some four hundred families with children in Boyle Heights. The Catholic Welfare Bureau experienced a tripling of its caseload in 1930–31 as more than nine thousand families turned to it for assistance, and the Family Welfare Agency and Aimee Semple Macpherson's Angelus Temple saw another tripling of needs in the Evangelical Protestant community.

A new problem, meanwhile, had surfaced on the streets of Los Angeles: indigent transients, even then known as the homeless. In 1928 the city established a Municipal Service for Homeless Men as part of the social service department. By the spring of 1932 the bureau was offering seven days of meals and lodgings to homeless indigents, followed by a cash grant for a ticket out of town and a warning that Los Angeles had strict vagrancy rules. In 1931 the bureau processed close to forty thousand indigents, a fivefold leap from 1929. Located in the San Fernando Building near Bunker Hill, the bureau offered cursory medical examinations to detect venereal or other communicable diseases and determine ability to work. Initially, the bureau occupied offices on an upper floor, but when patrons of the San Fernando Building began to complain about having to ride with bums in the elevator, the bureau was moved to the poorly ventilated basement, which soon became a stifling Hogarthian scene of human misery. The Midnight Mission, meanwhile, which was supported by the city and the county and by the Community Chest, offered up to three hundred beds in its dormitories, together with two meals a day, in return for four hours of work for the able-bodied. The healthy were allowed to stay for a week; the aged and infirm were allowed as much as two weeks. As in the case of the city-operated facility, transients were expected to leave Los Angeles upon their release. In the years 1931 and 1932 the Midnight Mission served more than eight hundred thousand meals and made available 330,000 nights of lodging.

As one obvious result of the Depression, Los Angeles changed from a Republican to a Democratic city. There were a number of causes for this change: the influx of migrants from Democratic strongholds in the Midwest and Southwest; the radicalization of older voters through the EPIC, Townsend, and Ham and Egg campaigns; the sheer charisma of Franklin Delano Roosevelt. In any event, Democrats, who accounted for 29 percent of the Los Angeles vote in 1928, represented 58 percent of the vote by 1940. The most obvious sign of this switch was the defeat in the spring of 1933 of Mayor John Porter in his bid for a second term and the election of Frank Shaw, a county supervisor, by a thirty-thousand-vote majority. Stupidly, Porter, a Republican, had refused to greet Roosevelt when FDR was making a campaign swing through the city. Shaw, by contrast, a Democrat, idolized the President and made endless trips to Washington in search of federal programs. When Roosevelt swung through Los Angeles in mid-July 1938, Shaw squeezed himself into a little jumper seat in the President's car just to be seen in his company.

Genial, outgoing, the Jimmy Walker of Los Angeles, Frank Shaw presided over a city slipping precipitously into corruption. In the first half of the decade, Los Angeles proved especially vulnerable to fraud on the micro and macro scale. The state commissioner of corporations estimated that in just 1931 and 1932 alone the citizens of Los Angeles had been the victims of fraud cases amounting to $200 million. Los Angeles abounded in hustlers of every sort: from boxing promoter John Browne, who committed suicide in his room in the Ambassador Hotel in June 1931 when a deal went bust, to the three top executives of Richfield Oil who went on trial in April 1932 for bilking their company of $213,267, spending the money on starlets and parties, to attorney E. E. Wiley, indicted by the grand jury in 1934 for selling stolen and forged bonds. Los Angeles liked to think of itself as mob-free, meaning Mafia-free, which was generally true (although Benjamin Siegel had other ideas); yet the home-grown syndicates were perfectly capable of controlling the flourishing prostitution and gambling business. One report estimated that by 1937 eighteen hundred bookies were openly doing business in the city and twenty-three thousand illegal slot machines were in operation. Bribery seemed a way of life. Mayor Shaw appointed his brother Joe as his personal secretary, and Joe Shaw ran all patronage, bypassing the civil service process with impunity—for a consideration.

Cafeteriateur Clifford Clinton, meanwhile, had more than food service on his mind. Throughout the 1930s Clinton was bent upon nothing less than the political reform of Los Angeles. Among other things, Clinton had his eye on the police department. In 1931 criminologist Ernest Hopkins, writing in *Our Lawless Police*, claimed that the Los Angeles Police Department seemed to have a distinctive disregard for the Constitution—or for law of any sort, for that matter. Hopkins described how the LAPD as a matter of course used rubber hoses to beat suspects under interrogation. Throughout the 1930s an atmosphere of runaway authority, even lawlessness, a sense of being a kingdom, a conspiracy, unto itself, characterized the LAPD. Police Chief James Davis, a commanding military figure in his pressed uniform and shiny Sam Browne belt, openly boasted of the department's policy of shooting first and asking questions later. Davis made a specialty of holding a cigarette in his mouth and allowing one of his top marksmen to shoot it from his lips, just to show how dangerous it was to mess with the LAPD. In 1933 alone, Davis bragged to an interviewer, forty-three offenders had been killed in gun battles with L.A. police. So much for street criminals. Whether the LAPD was equally tough on its own when they strayed was a more ambiguous issue.

Corruption ran through the system. While Mayor Frank Shaw was never indicted, the same could not be said for District Attorney Buron Fitts. In 1934 the criminal grand jury looked into the case of one John Mills, a millionaire playboy brought up on charges of statutory rape. Responsible for presenting evidence to the grand jury, District Attorney Fitts persuaded, indeed prevented, the victim from testifying by keeping her in seclusion in a downtown hotel. The district attorney, it seems, was Mills's partner in a complicated land deal out in Claremont. Questioned about the relationship by the grand jury, the DA denied the connection and was later indicted on charges of perjury. Fitts won an acquittal in February 1936, but for more than a year and a half the chief prosecuting officer of Los Angeles was himself under felony indictment.

In May 1937 Frank Shaw defeated challenger John Anson Ford, a county supervisor, and was reelected to a second term. Already, however, Shaw's days were numbered, thanks to a reform group calling itself the Minute Men, spearheaded by Clifford Clinton. Winning a seat on the 1937 grand jury, Clinton uncovered evidence from both testimony and his own personal investigations and those of private detectives Clinton hired with his own money and funds made available by the Minute Men. Los Angeles, Clinton discovered, was supporting an intricate network of brothels, gambling houses, and clip joints, all of it run by well-organized syndicates headed by gambler Guy McAfee and Bob Gans, chief concessionaire of slot machines throughout the city, with attorneys Kent Parrot and Charles Kradick serving as mouthpieces. Obviously, a number of police were on the take for so many operations—an estimated six hundred brothels, three hundred gambling houses, eighteen hundred bookie joints, twenty-three thousand slot machines—to be flourishing. Clinton also found evidence of corruption in Mayor Shaw's office, specifically the way the mayor's brother peddled civil service appointments and fueled the Shaw political machine with cash payments from gambling interests. District Attorney Fitts, Clinton discovered, was using the grand jury system to settle old scores and to protect old and new friends. Clinton's charges seemed only confirmed in April 1938 when the former city attorney of Los Angeles, Erwin (Pete) Werner, and his wife Helen (more commonly known as Queen Helen of Los Angeles) were convicted of soliciting a $50,000 bribe from the Italo Oil Corporation and were sent to the slammer. A few months later, in July, a Long Beach court convicted Eloi Amar, president of the Los Angeles Harbor Board, of renting a warehouse he owned in Long Beach as a gambling den. Police Commissioner Charles Ostrom, an attorney, soon surfaced as the legal representative of two of the most prominent gambling chieftains in the city.

Far from becoming a hero for his investigations, the stern-faced Clinton, righteous in rimless glasses, found himself the object of scathing denunciations in the Los Angeles *Times*, which backed Mayor Shaw and DA Fitts and wanted no interference from a self-appointed Savonarola. John Bauer, meanwhile, the foreman of the grand jury, a crony of both Shaw and Fitts, was doing his best to turn the other grand jurors against Clinton, calling him an egomaniac, a showboater, the Cafeteria Kid. Suddenly, Clinton's cafeterias were being cited for unsanitary conditions, and he found himself facing nuisance suits from patrons claiming to have been poisoned.

At this point, things began to get violent. When notary Frank Angelillo testified before the grand jury that grand jury foreman John Bauer had a monopoly on city paint contracts, a squad of detectives from DA Fitts's office led personally by Fitts and Bauer paid an evening visit to Angelillo. The detectives beat the hapless notary so badly he had to be hospitalized. Even for Los Angeles, the event was shocking: the district attorney, the chief law enforcement officer of the county, and the foreman of the grand jury, the highest judicial panel in the county, standing by as detectives from the district attorney's office, sworn police officers, worked over a grand jury witness. Even Raymond Chandler, soon to make his debut as a crime novelist, would not have had the nerve to fabricate such an event. Other witnesses found themselves arrested on fake charges or had bullets fired through their houses. On the night of 28 October 1937, Clinton's home at 5470 Los Feliz Boulevard at the western entrance to Griffith Park was bombed by unknown assailants. Miraculously, Clinton, his wife, and their three children were sleeping on the other side of the house and escaped with their lives. Incredibly, the police suggested that Clinton might have engineered the explosion himself as a publicity stunt.

Little more than two months later, on the morning of 14 January 1938, Harry Raymond, a private detective working for Clinton and other reformers, stepped into his automobile in the garage of his home at 955 Orme Street. Raymond pressed the starter, and the car exploded, destroying the car and the garage but somehow leaving Raymond alive, although he was bleeding from more than fifty head and body wounds. Evidence soon pointed to none other than Police Captain Earl Kynette, head of police intelligence, who for some months had been eavesdropping on Raymond from a house next door. Kynette may or may not have been working with others in authority. It is highly probable, however, that Kynette was working for Chief Davis in surveillance of enemies of the Shaw administration. Compromised in so many instances, District Attorney Fitts was not in on this particular caper, and so on 25 January 1938 Fitts ordered the arrest of Captain Kynette, Detective Lieutenant Roy Allen, and Detective Lieutenant Fred Browne on charges of attempted murder. The grand jury handed up indictments on 23 February 1938, and the three police officers were convicted on 16 June 1938 and sent to San Quentin.

That summer, Clinton and his associates persuaded Superior Court Judge Fletcher Bowron to step down from the bench and run for mayor against Shaw in a recall election scheduled for September. Despite constant harassment from the police, Clinton and his associates had managed to gather 120,000 signatures for the recall from Los Angeles voters shocked by the bombings. They had already turned to the diminutive, cherubic judge in their efforts to get control of the grand jury. Under petition from Clinton and his colleagues, Bowron had instructed the grand jury to investigate graft in municipal government. Very soon, members of the grand jury were calling for an investigation of the district attorney himself. In September, Shaw went down in defeat with 122,692 votes to Bowron's 233,427.

The following year, Joe Shaw, the mayor's brother and private secretary, was indicted and later convicted on sixty-three counts of selling civil service appointments and promotions. Joe Shaw served no time. In 1940 District Attorney Fitts was defeated for reelection. Clifford Clinton went back to the cafeteria business.

On the western side of Bunker Hill, centered on Pershing Square, was the business and financial district that had been migrating west from Broadway since the 1920s. Lined with banks, insurance companies, law offices, and business buildings in those variations of Italian Renaissance so beloved by corporate America through the 1920s, Spring Street and the cross streets of 4th, 5th, and 6th comprised the financial district, the Wall Street of Los Angeles. A lunching oligarchy was served by the California Club on Flower at 6th, the Jonathan Club on Figueroa at 6th, the University Club on South Hope, and the Los Angeles Athletic Club on 7th and Olive. Elegantly appointed and graced with collections of local art that would increase geometrically in value over the next half century, these four clubs served a cohesive downtown establishment predominantly Anglo-American in composition.

A club of another sort was Pershing Square itself, flanked by the Biltmore Hotel and the Philharmonic Auditorium. Set aside by the City Council in 1866 for public use and designated a public park in 1872, Pershing Square, like St. Vibiana's Roman Catholic Cathedral (1876) on South Main, was a surviving legacy of the 1870s when Los Angeles made the transition from cattle town to city. Convenient to the Central Library, Pershing Square had become by the 1930s the Hyde Park of Los Angeles, although the City Council, with a contempt for the Constitution that seemed so characteristic of official L.A. in this period, passed an ordinance forbidding inflammatory speeches. "The benches are littered with literary material for a de Maupassant," noted Harry Carr of Pershing Square, "— discouraged, ragged, jobless, sick people, bums—lonely tourists who want some one to talk to—Reds breathing Communism."[6] The proximity of Pershing Square to the Central Library sustained its Hyde Park atmosphere as a multitude of autodidacts divided their time between reading in the library and discussion and debate in the square.

Like Los Angeles itself, the Central Library bore a special relationship to Everyman and Everywoman, especially in the Depression era. "Here in these halls," City Librarian Everett Robbins Perry had said at the dedication ceremony in July 1926, "the petty distractions of the earthly pilgrimage may be laid aside and their place taken by the inspiration and serenity that come from communion with the poet, the prophet, the philosopher, the artist, the scientist."[7] Throughout the Depression, Perry's successor Althea Warren, a Phi Beta Kappa of the University of Chicago with a library degree from Wisconsin, saw the democratic importance of a public library at once corroborated and put sorely to the test by the hard times. Its budget slashed, the Central Library nevertheless opened its doors each morning to long lines of readers, many of them out of work, looking for a place to be, an hour or two of release from the terror of unemployment.

The writers of Los Angeles, not the eventually great names earning a living in Hollywood, but the workaday writers of the city—Rupert Hughes, Edgar Rice Burroughs, Zane Grey, Harold Bell Wright—tended to be popular entertainers. Hamlin Garland, who lived in the Hollywood Hills near Cecil B. DeMille and Jack Dempsey, was long past his best work. Then there was the curious case of Nathaniel Hawthorne's son Julian, also a writer, the author of over thirty books, who was ending his days in the early 1930s in Newport Beach. "My father was buried in Sleepy Hollow, Concord, in 1864," Hawthorne told *Westways* in June 1934; "my mother in Kensal Green, London, seven years after; my elder sister beside her in 1879. My younger sister joined them in 1926, and her grave is in New York. I alone delay to complete the family circle, but my chance will come in due season."[8] Many an old man sitting in the sun in Pershing Square had similar memories—and similar expectations.

Equally eclectic and populist as Pershing Square was the Trinity Auditorium at 851 South Grand, a few blocks south of the Central Library. Constructed in 1914, the elaborate Beaux Arts auditorium and hotel complex belonged to the Methodist Church. Trinity Auditorium had once housed the Los Angeles Symphony Orchestra and its successor the Los Angeles Philharmonic, and Aimee Semple McPherson had preached there upon her arrival in 1918. Throughout the 1930s Trinity Auditorium—an acoustically perfect structure surmounted by a soaring stained-glass dome—served as the venue of choice for militant unions and other organizations on the left, such as EPIC and the Townsend Plan. On 13 October 1933, in the opening stages of a city-wide strike by the International Ladies Garment Workers Union, fifteen hundred women dressmakers, the majority of them Mexican-Americans, crowded Trinity Auditorium and voted to break with their male counterparts in the Cloakmakers Union, who had refused to go out on strike. Led by ILGWU organizer Rose Pesotta, the striking dressmakers won an increase in wages and official recognition of their separate union. The strike astonished labor and management alike with the unexpected ability of Mexican-American women to mount and successfully conduct a city-wide strike in a city famous for its anti-union attitudes and its willingness forcibly to repatriate to Mexico undocumented workers proving troublesome.

Throughout the 1930s, the early 1930s especially, the repatriation of Mexican nationals remained an ongoing Los Angeles County program. Its alleged justification: the removal of Mexican nationals from county relief rolls. In February 1931 Carey McWilliams watched the first shipment of repatriated Mexicans leave from the Los Angeles train terminal. "The loading process began at six o'clock in the morning," McWilliams remembered. "*Repatridados* arrived by the truckload— men, women, and children—with dogs, cats, and goats; half-open suitcases, rolls of bedding, and lunch baskets."[9] When the shipment was complete, county officials estimated that while it had cost $77,249 to repatriate this one trainload, the savings in relief payments would amount to $347,468 on this one shipment alone. In 1932, McWilliams estimates, more than eleven thousand Mexicans were shipped from the city. And so it continued, intermittently, down the decade. Each so-called repatriation—with its overt program of ethnic cleansing, its poignant scenes of grieving farewell at the train platform between family members who had papers and could stay and those who had no papers and must go—chillingly reflected comparable scenes in Europe in relocation programs that would soon be seeking a final solution.

The Mexican *colonía* in Los Angeles County was centered in four major *barrios*—Dogtown, Alpine, the Flats, Happy Valley in East Los Angeles—together with a number of smaller *barrios* in unincorporated areas of the county. For most of the twentieth century, the Mexicans of greater Los Angeles, Mexican nationals and Mexican-American citizens alike, had been living on the margins of white society. Although white California, Southern California especially, was willing to sentimentalize Old California, as in the 1931 Plaza celebration, neither white California nor the Mexican population of the Southland (with the exception of a few surviving Old California families) saw any continuity between the Spanish and Mexican founders of California and the present population of the state. Even the Roman Catholic Church, to which most Mexicans adhered, had become Anglicized, hence psychologically part of the Anglo-California that existed on the other side of a great cultural and ethnic divide. Had Southern California been heavily industrialized, which it was not, Mexican immigrants might have been forced to accommodate themselves to—and be accommodated by!—the dominant Anglo culture. But Southern California lacked an integrative industrial system and so remained an assemblage of ethnic enclaves, each of them self-contained, each of them excluding and being excluded, up and down the social scale.

Along with African-Americans and Asians, the Mexicans of Los Angeles were restricted to certain districts by custom and real estate covenants, were assigned to a separate second-tier, even third-tier, school system ("Why teach them to read and write and spell?" the principal of a Mexican school in the San Fernando Valley asked social worker Beatrice Griffith. "Why worry about it? . . . They'll only pick beets anyway"), and, along with African-Americans, were excluded from many public swimming pools on all but the day before the pool was to be drained.[10] Mexicans were frequently turned away at the door of numerous theaters and dance halls and saw the sign SE SIRVE SOLAMENTE A RAZA BLANCA (WHITE RACE ONLY SERVED) in numerous restaurants. Seeing a primarily Mexican group of passengers gathered on a corner, streetcar drivers were known to whiz by rather than stop.

Throughout the 1930s the LAPD and the sheriff's deputies made war on young Mexican men in the continuing belief that such young men were by definition criminal in fact and intent. The sheer presence of young Mexicans on the street-corners in the *barrio*—an expression of a time-honored preference for street life tracing itself to the social customs of Mexican villages—was seen by patrolling police or deputies as virtual proof of a crime in progress or about to happen. Again and again, young Mexican men found themselves hauled into jail for seventy-two hours on mere suspicion, then released. Beatings were frequent, as were frame-ups of young Mexican men who talked back or otherwise resisted arrest. A number of young Mexican men were shot dead in the street by trigger-happy officers. Not even Mexican celebrities were safe, as radio singer Pedro Gonzalez discovered in 1934. Having angered the police and other members of the Anglo community on his popular radio program on station KMPC, Gonzalez found himself framed on rape charges and sent to San Quentin for six years until the alleged victim recanted in 1940. Within a few years, in the famous Sleepy Lagoon murder trial of late 1942 and early 1943, an equally oppressive Anglo establishment would be sending nine young Mexican-Americans to San Quentin on even more flimsy evidence.

Anti-Mexican sentiment gave an irony to the Spanish names that dotted the streets and landforms of Los Angeles: names such as Figueroa, the great boulevard that proceeded south from the Downtown, following the path of the *zanja* that once took water from the Los Angeles River to this part of the city and remained in operation until 1904. Broad, stately, lined with such important structures from the 1920s boom as Patriotic Hall (1926), St. John's Episcopal (1923), the grand headquarters of the Automobile Club of Southern California (1923), St. Vincent de Paul Roman Catholic Church (1925), the Shrine Civic Auditorium (1926), and the Spanish Romanesque structures of the University of Southern California, Figueroa swept south toward Exposition Park. Since the 1890s the southern sweep of Figueroa had been taking fashionable Los Angeles along with it, as evidenced by the mansions of Chester Place, an enclave between 23rd Street and West Adams, just off Figueroa, which had been laid out as a residential park in 1895 and contained thirteen stately mansions from the turn of the century.

As it had been doing since the 1880s, the nearby University of Southern California, a private institution, Methodist in origin, continued to educate the professionals of the region and a significant percentage of the undergraduates. Like Los Angeles itself, USC had grown too fast and with uneven quality. Personally uninterested in research (although he did authorize the establishment of a School of Research in 1933), USC president Rufus B. von KleinSmid—an imperious Teuton, who ran USC like a *Junker* administering his estates—burdened his faculty with high school–level teaching loads in an effort to contain costs. To obtain further revenues, von KleinSmid established an open admissions University Junior College, which put further strain on the faculty. It was in its professional schools that USC came closest to its best sense of itself. Here teaching, and even research, were carried on at a high level. Not until 1927 did the University of California have a full-fledged campus in Southern California, UCLA in Westwood; and so it befell the privately funded USC to take on the role of a land grant university. During the 1930s, USC continued to produce the doctors, dentists, pharmacists, engineers, architects, and lawyers of the region. Its campus crowded with the automobiles of commuting students, who also arrived by the hundreds each morning by streetcar, USC only obliquely served the disinterested pursuit of learning for its own sake (if such a pursuit is at all possible in the American temperament!); USC served, rather, the desire for professional training and upward mobility in an emergent region. In doing this effectively, USC evolved an institutional identity— serious-minded professional schools and a rah-rah undergraduate culture, fraternity and sorority oriented—that would remain with it for the next four decades.

It was on the football field that USC connected with its most powerful energy, its poetry even, as an institution. In alternate years, USC played Notre Dame, its Roman Catholic counterpart, another private university using football as its primary means of development. The entire City of Los Angeles shared in the pre- and post-game frenzy, for USC was in a very fundamental way a key prism through which Los Angeles glimpsed its identity, just as USC itself was dramatically the product of Anglo-American Los Angeles. When Howard Jones's Thundering Herd made the Rose Bowl, as it did in 1932, 1933, 1939, and 1940, winning victories over Tulane, Pittsburgh, Duke, and Tennessee, the frenzy continued through New Year's Day, now connected to one of the most powerful rituals of the region, the annual Tournament of Roses Parade and Rose Bowl football game.

First laid out as a fairgrounds and racecourse by the Southern District Agricultural Society, Exposition Park, where USC played its home games in the Coliseum, had been under development since the 1890s as the museum and cultural center of the city. In 1932, however, its name was changed to Olympic Park when the defining event of the 1930s came to the city: between 30 July and 14 August, Los Angeles hosted the Tenth Olympiad, the first American city to do so since the Games had been revived in Athens in 1896.

In 1919, urged by the daily newspapers of the city, the oligarchs of Los Angeles formed the California Fiestas Association, with the purpose of promoting tourism in Los Angeles with a series of public celebrations stressing the Spanish and Mexican heritage of the city. The very next year, the oligarchs set their sights even higher: on securing the Olympics. Dissolving the California Fiestas Association, the oligarchs—among them, *Times* publisher Harry Chandler, *Evening Express* publisher and UC regent Edward Dickson, former United States senator Frank Flint, real estate developer William May Garland, Pasadena investor Henry Robinson, agriculturalist G. Harold Powell, Robert Millikan of Cal Tech, and gadfly Manchester Boddy—formed an even more ambitious Community Development Association, which had as its goal the upgrading of Los Angeles into a city that stood a chance of winning an Olympiad. The first step: the financing and construction of an Olympic Stadium in Exposition Park. More commonly known as the Los Angeles Coliseum, the seventy-five-thousand seat structure was ready for use by 1923. The rapid completion of the Coliseum helped William May Garland, now one of the two United States representatives on the International Olympic Committee, secure the Tenth Olympiad for Los Angeles nine years hence when the committee met in Rome, a triumph for the aspiring city. Los Angeles soon became the first city fully to discern and maximize the developmental possibilities of an Olympiad.

Throughout the 1920s, Los Angeles, then in the process of absorbing a million newcomers, knew that it would soon find itself being showcased on the international level as had few other American cities. The prospect of the Tenth Olympiad framed and oriented an entire decade of boosterism. In 1927 the legislature passed the California Olympiad Bond Act, making a million-dollar loan available to Los Angeles for the development of sites for the Olympic Games. Fortunately, the financing of the Tenth Olympiad occurred before the Crash of October 1929, which might have conditioned the generosity of the legislature. On the other hand, as Los Angeles entered the Depression, preparations for the Olympics provided a ready-made public works employment program under the auspices of the private sector. By the time athletes began arriving in mid-July 1932, natty in their blazers and flannels, Los Angeles stood ready, with hundreds of national flags and Olympic banners decorating the streets of the city.

The Coliseum, for one thing, had been expanded to 105,000 reserved seats, making it the largest sports arena in the world. A 180-foot-long enclosed press and broadcast box, the absolute state of the art, soared across the south tier, and on the eastern entrance stood an Art Deco arched peristyle flanked by double arcades and surmounted by the Olympic torch, all this prepared by the original architects of the structure, John and Donald Parkinson. Nearby stood the Los Angeles Swimming Stadium, its great concrete grandstands seating five thousand. An Olympic Auditorium on Grand for indoor competition had been in use since 1924. Track and field events were also scheduled for the Rose Bowl in Pasadena and the newly developed UCLA campus in Westwood. Crew and sculling competition took place in the newly developed Marine Stadium at Long Beach; sailing events were organized from Los Angeles Harbor. The Los Angeles Police Department made available its shooting range in Elysian Park for pistol and carbine competition and the shooting sequences of the Pentathlon. Equestrian events were assigned to the Riviera Country Club off Sunset Boulevard in the Santa Monica Mountains in West Los Angeles.

Most spectacular of all Olympic facilities, with the exception of the Coliseum itself, was Olympic Village, a cluster of 550 two-bedroom Spanish cottages on five miles of circular streets atop Angelus Mesa on the Baldwin Hills west of Exposition Park, with clear sightlines to the Pacific, the Coliseum, and downtown Los Angeles. Planted with palm trees and lawns, Olympic Village represented a triumph of planning and development. It was a reverse coda, a Potemkin village shielding athletes and the international press from the more somber realities of the Depression-ridden city. Each cottage housed four male athletes with a wash bowl in each room and a shower. A total of fifty kitchens and dining rooms of various sizes, each staffed by a specially selected chef, served a variety of national cuisines. Each evening, motion pictures of the day's competition were shown in an open-air amphitheater, followed by a first-run film and guest appearances by

Hollywood actors. Steam, sauna, massage, and rubbing rooms were in constant use. Olympic Village also featured a hospital, a post office, a bank, a telegraph and cable office, a fire station, and a commissary. Women athletes lived in equal style in the Chapman Park Hotel in the Wilshire district, with equally selective meals, a daily tea each afternoon, and a squad of motor buses to transport them from the hotel to competition sites. All this at the subsidized rate of $2 per day per athlete!

The Games opened on 30 July 1932, preceded the previous evening by a black-tie dinner for the Organizing Committee in the Biltmore Hotel. Vice President of the United States Charles Curtis sat as guest of honor. Douglas Fairbanks and Mary Pickford entertained the International Olympic Committee and the Organizing Committee at dinner at Pickfair in Beverly Hills on 9 August. The Games closed on Sunday afternoon, 14 August, with the traditional parade of athletes, the retiring of the official flag, and the extinguishing of the Olympic torch. When it was over, what had Los Angeles accomplished on its own behalf? A profit of $1.5 million, for one thing, which was immediately used to retire the million-dollar debt to the state and to pay off the Coliseum, which was now turned over to a joint city-county-state commission. Working with the Southern California Telephone Company, the Los Angeles Olympics had pioneered an intricate telephone and teletypewriting system that represented a quantum leap in communications technology, linked via direct feeds to international print and broadcast media. For perhaps the first time in human history, significant parts of the developed world were in direct communication with events occurring almost simultaneously at dozens of separate sites. Then there was the temporary employment for hundreds of Los Angelenos before and during the Games and the hundreds of other jobs in hotels and restaurants stabilized by visitor spending. Of most importance, the City of Angels had showcased itself to the world. To one and all, Los Angeles announced that the United States, indeed the world, had a new metropolis that was its own kind of place, yet for all its differences a recognizable civic commonwealth, a city boosting itself by its bootstraps into international recognition. The era of media saturation and live broadcast had begun.

South of Olympic Park extended the blue-collar and lower-middle-class districts of Los Angeles, its Bronx and Queens, together with its Harlem. Immediately adjacent to Olympic Park, South Central remained largely working- and lower-middle-class white in the 1930s, although in the mid-1920s Los Angeles had annexed the heavily African-American township of Watts to the southeast. White as well was the Crenshaw district, formerly known as Angeles Mesa, bounded by Van Ness Avenue on the east, Exposition Boulevard on the north, La Brea to the west, and Florence Avenue and the independent City of Inglewood on the south. Down through the center of these two white districts ran Central Avenue, the north-south axis of African-American L.A., passing the forty thousand mark by the mid-1930s. As in the case of white Los Angeles, the 1920s had been the boom decade for black L.A. The African-American population more than doubled itself.

The bulk of the 1920s migration tended to come from Texas, Louisiana, and Georgia, with Texas far in the lead.

African-Americans migrated to Los Angeles for the same reasons as did their white counterparts: the chance for home ownership in a salubrious climate in a new city where things might be better. At first, at the turn of the century and in the first decade of the 1900s, it seemed, momentarily, that they might have their wish. Biddy Mason, after all, brought to Los Angeles as a slave in 1856 and freed by a court order, had died in January 1881 as a wealthy property owner. The mood of African-American Los Angeles in the 1890–1910 era exuded a hope, an innocence even, regarding prospects for a better life in the City of Angels. Issues of the *Liberator*, a local African-American newspaper, from March 1904 describe the opening of a small African-American hotel and two African-American real estate companies. A black attorney opened a law office, and a black doctor from Memphis was relocating. By 1909 Los Angeles had five African-American doctors, two dentists, a pharmacist, a veterinarian, and five lawyers. A young black woman, Bessie Bruington, was enrolled at the State Normal School en route to becoming the first certified African-American schoolteacher in the city. Another young woman, Ruth Temple, was heading for medical school and would eventually become the first African-American female physician on the West Coast. Working African-Americans had jobs as shopkeepers, blacksmiths, household movers, and construction workers. Many Santa Fe Railway porters, cooks, and waiters, who could live in any number of locations, chose to live in Los Angeles. Visitors noted a high rate of African-American home ownership. An avid abolitionist who had fought in the Union Army in the Civil War, Harrison Gray Otis, publisher of the Los Angeles *Times*, took a special interest in African-American affairs. On 12 February 1909 the *Times* ran eight pages devoted to the African-American community in honor of the one hundredth anniversary of Lincoln's birth. A decade later, the *Times* published Delilah Beaseley's *The Negro Trailblazers of California* (1919), a pioneering history that remains of value to this day.

In these years, there emerged more than twenty-nine lodges, auxiliaries, or other voluntary associations in the African-American community: organizations such as the Sojourner Truth Industrial Club, formed in 1904, to promote the guidance and development of young African-American women, or the Women's Day Nursery of Los Angeles, formed in 1907 to provide day care for working African-American mothers. The black community supported three newspapers: the Los Angeles *Liberator*, the Los Angeles *Sentinel*, and the *California Eagle*. Later on, the locally owned Golden State Mutual Life Insurance Company emerged as one of the most prosperous African-American-owned businesses in the country. Ever since 1903, the Forum, a weekly town hall meeting, eventually located in a public hall on South Central Avenue, afforded the African-American community the opportunity to address the issues of the day and to learn, via digests from the *Amsterdam News* in New York and other African-American newspapers, of developments in other black communities across the country.

Things began to change around the time of the First World War, with race riots in Midwestern and Eastern cities, lynchings in the South, and the rise of an urban Ku Klux Klan as millions of African-Americans migrated into northern cities. The Tulsa race riot of 1921 brought several hundred African-Americans to Los Angeles. Already, in 1914, the blacks of Los Angeles had been especially offended by the depiction of African-Americans as sadistic rapists in D. W. Griffith's *The Birth of a Nation*. Compounding the insult, it had been filmed in their city. Los Angeles became an increasingly Jim Crow town throughout the 1920s and 1930s, due in part to an influx of white Southerners into the city. African-Americans found themselves banished from streetcar and construction jobs, snubbed at white department stores and restaurants, kept in segregated schools. Not until a court order of June 1931 were they allowed to swim in municipal swimming pools at the same time as whites.

African-Americans also found themselves excluded from many of the jobs they had held since the turn of the century. Unions, already suspicious from the time blacks were used in 1916 to break a strike at the Llewellen Iron Works, became almost universally hostile. The Los Angeles County civil service system practiced *de facto* segregation, with African-Americans relegated almost exclusively to janitorial positions. L. G. Robinson, head janitor for the county, emerged as one of the most politically influential African-Americans in the city. By 1931, black women held 30 percent of the domestic service jobs in the city. Despite these restrictions, an African-American, Frederick Madison Roberts, a Republican, was elected by the Central Avenue district to the California assembly in 1917, the first African-American to serve in that body. Politically influential as well was the all-black post of the American Legion meeting in the Armory at Exposition and Figueroa, which maintained paradoxical links to white American Legion posts in the region, which were generally to the far right on any social issue.

While interracial marriages were rare, sexual contact continued in subterranean channels, as it had from day one of the American experience. A 1931 USC sociology thesis offers evidence of African-American prostitutes catering to the white trade and even more impressive numbers, possibly more than 250, of white prostitutes serving an African-American clientele. At places such as Frank Sebastian's Cotton Club in Culver City and the Apex Night Club on Central, whites partied alongside blacks, danced on the same dance floor to the music of all-black orchestras, and enjoyed black cabaret. The Central Avenue scene resembled that of Harlem in the same period, albeit on a lesser scale, with such local celebrities as Stepin Fetchit, Bill (Bojangles) Robinson, Ethel Waters, Hattie McDaniel, and Eddie (Rochester) Anderson on hand and such Harlemites as Duke Ellington, Count Basie, and Billie Holiday making the scene on tour. African-American musicians maintained a steady employment through the Depression, at the Cotton and Apex clubs, in other places around town, and in the taxi-dance halls and the burlesque houses along Main Street.

With the hardening of racial attitudes during World War I, the ghetto made its appearance, in Los Angeles as in other cities. In the early part of the century, the

African-American community had been multi-sited: along Weller, 1st, and 2nd Streets in the Downtown, along West Temple in the northwest portion of the city, in Boyle Heights in the northeast, in the Furlong Tract in the southeast, and along Jefferson Boulevard between Normandie and Western. But as more African-Americans arrived in the 1920s, their community—prevented from multi-sited expansion by increasingly restrictive covenants in the decade of a revived Ku Klux Klan—tended to advance south along Central Avenue. In 1934 Leon Washington, publisher of the Los Angeles *Sentinel*, led a boycott of white-owned businesses along Central Avenue that refused to employ black workers.

At the same time, the presence of middle-class African-Americans in the city enabled the African-American community to establish a flourishing communal life centered on the First African Methodist Episcopal Church, the First Baptist Church, the People's Independent Church, the YMCA, and the lively *California Eagle* newspaper. In 1928 African-American investors built the Hotel Somerville to host the NAACP convention. As the most popular church in the African-American community, the People's Independent Church, founded in 1915 as a progressive alternative to the more conservative AME and Baptist churches, was fielding by the mid-1930s a wide array of social programs, among them a home for boys, a dental screening program, an employment service, and a civil rights office. Its minister, Clayton Russell, became the first black clergyman to preach on Los Angeles radio.

Two figures, architect Paul Williams, the most prominent African-American in the city, and housemaid Crenner Hawkins Bradley, expressed the sequences and polarities of African-American Los Angeles in the 1930s. Educated at the Los Angeles School of Art and USC, Williams began his career in the offices of another master of taste, Reginald Johnson, then went on for a second apprenticeship with John Austin, who designed many of the most prominent public buildings of the early 1920s. Licensed to practice in 1921, Williams established his own firm the next year and a year later, 1923, became the first African-American elected to the American Institute of Architects. As a designer, Paul Williams was scholarly, elegant, impeccably tasteful—and correct. In the 1920s he performed exquisitely in the Mediterranean and Tudor styles of the period. In the 1930s he turned to the resurgent Colonial American–Palladian and, toward the end of the decade, to Streamline Moderne with equal facility. Williams was a master at working with his clients, interpreting their needs and upgrading their tastes, coaxing them to the best possible decisions. At a time when racial prejudice was corrosive in America, Williams managed to secure commission after commission—in Flintridge, Pasadena, Beverly Hills, Hollywood, the Hancock Park and Los Feliz districts of Los Angeles, Westwood, Brentwood, Bel Air, and Pacific Palisades in the newly developing western edge of the city—many of them from celebrities such as Lon Chaney, John Charles Thomas, ZaSu Pitts, Barbara Stanwyck, Tyrone Power, and the African-American stars William (Bojangles) Robinson and Eddie (Rochester) Anderson. Ironically, Williams designed a ten-thousand-square-foot mansion in Beverly Hills for Charles Correll, the white actor who played an African-American in the *Amos 'n' Andy* radio series, while Williams himself was still living in an unpretentious bungalow in South Central. Such was the paradox of Williams's life: an architect who chose to inspect sites with his hands clasped behind his back so as to avoid the embarrassment of having whites refuse to shake his extended hand, who made it a practice never to socialize with white clients, especially if white women were present, being asked to materialize the dreams of a largely white clientele.

Crenner Hawkins came from Beaumont, Texas. Already, even as a young woman, hers had been a hard life in a cotton sharecropping family in which the children were expected to work side by side with their parents from the time they were six or seven. In the early 1900s Crenner Hawkins married another cotton sharecropper, Lee Bradley, who had worked in the cotton fields since boyhood. The couple leased some acres near Calvert in Central Texas and began to repeat the cycle of endless labor under a blazing sun in the flat, hot, hard, cotton country. Expectations were minimal for the Bradleys: the chance perhaps to mortgage next year's cotton crop and pay off this year's debt in a cycle of serfdom that would never end. Lee and Crenner Bradley had eight children in these Texas years. Five of them died in infancy. Lawrence, born in 1911, Tom, born in 1917, and Willa Mae, born in 1921, survived.

That might have been the story, all of it, except the Bradleys moved off the land, to Dallas initially, where Lee worked as a handyman and Crenner as a maid, then two years later to Arizona, the whole family piling into a decrepit jalopy packed with their belongings and heading west in the flivver migration of 1924. Reaching Arizona, Crenner and the children stayed with relatives in Somerton, while Lee continued on to Los Angeles to scout the prospects. Lee found work in Los Angeles and eventually got a position as a porter on the Santa Fe, and in late 1924 Crenner and the children joined him in Los Angeles, where Crenner entered domestic service. The family settled in Boyle Heights, where two more children were eventually born, Ellis, who was afflicted with cerebral palsy, in 1929, and Howard in 1933.

With her husband away for long periods of time on the Santa Fe or working a coast passenger ship, Crenner Bradley bore much of the responsibility for raising the five children, an obligation greatly complicated by the fact that Crenner herself worked five, sometimes six, days a week as a maid and cleaning lady, traveling to work early each morning by streetcar, returning home in the late afternoon to fix dinner for her children and discuss their day at school. (Years later, her son Tom remembered Crenner's sweet potato pie and the way she could make the most inexpensive meats—tongue, ham hocks, neck bones—into tasty dishes.) In the evening, before the children went to bed, Crenner Hawkins Bradley read to them from the Bible, which she read daily in search of consolation and a guide to life. On Sundays, the family worshipped in the New Hope Baptist Church, where Tom sang in the choir. By then, the early 1930s, the Bradleys had moved with so many other African-Americans to South Central. When they first arrived, Tom was sent to school in overalls and was chagrined when the other kids made fun of him as a hick. He was also baffled, then hurt, when at the age of ten a white friend, with whom he loved to play kick the can, told him that his parents did not want him to play with colored children.

Tall, serious, an avid reader, Tom Bradley helped his mother look after the family in the times when Lee Bradley was away. Tom was especially solicitous of the handicapped Ellis. He had a paper route for the Los Angeles *Record*, and already, in games at the Central Recreation Center, he was showing marked athletic abilities. At the Lafayette Junior High School in South Central, counselors tended to steer African-American students toward vocational programs, but Tom Bradley, who had read *Moby Dick* and the *Iliad* and the *Odyssey*, wanted to take the academic course at Polytechnic High School, not the vocational course at Jefferson High in his district. Crenner Bradley was working as a maid for a family who lived in the Polytechnic district. Since Tom did chores for the family as well, the employers allowed him to claim their address for school registration. Tom Bradley enrolled in Polytechnic High School in 1934, one of 113 blacks among thirteen hundred students. He took the regular academic course and lettered in football and track. His hero was Jesse Owens, who had so enraged Hitler that summer in Berlin by outperforming German runners. In 1936 Tom Bradley set a new record for the 440-yard dash in Los Angeles and made All City tackle. In 1937, his senior year, he made All City tackle again and won the All Southern California quarter-mile championship.

UCLA offered Tom Bradley an athletic scholarship. He commuted to the Westwood campus from 27th Street near Main in the Watts district, where the family now lived, in a 1931 Model A Ford, along with five other students whom he charged ten cents a day for a ride. The six young men were among one hundred African-American students at UCLA out of a student body of seven thousand. Along with his studies and sports, Bradley was devoted to the all-black Kappa Alpha Psi fraternity. A skilled photographer, he worked for comedian Jimmy Durante, preparing publicity stills. (Bradley had been introduced to Durante through his girlfriend Ethel Arnold's sister, who worked for Mrs. Durante as a maid.) In the late spring of 1940, Tom Bradley placed near the top in the Los Angeles Police Department exam, with an overall grade of 97 percent. He and Ethel were married on 4 May 1941 and set up housekeeping on 57th Street in the Central Avenue district, next door to Ethel's parents. Tom Bradley went on to become a police lieutenant, a lawyer, a city councilman, and a longtime mayor of Los Angeles.

When African-American professionals such as Paul Williams returned home from work in the 1930s, it was not to the newly developing affluent Westside, but to South Central Los Angeles, the Harlem and the Bronx of Los Angeles, where working people like Lee and Crenner Bradley lived. Running south toward Long

Beach, the Los Angeles River divided East Los Angeles, the Queens of L.A., from the rest of the city. Lined by railroad tracks, the river also demarcated the industrial and shipping zones of the city. Eastern observers such as James M. Cain and Lillian Symes criticized Los Angeles for its lack of industrial grittiness. Los Angeles, Cain chided, would have to learn to sell something other than its climate. What picture-perfect Los Angeles needed, Symes noted, was a New Jersey factory town dropped in its midst. Cain and Symes were tipping their hand. These temporary sojourners from the East, writing for an upscale market, were spending too much time on the Westside; for Los Angeles had grit aplenty along its river: a region of railroad tracks, warehouses, manufacturing plants, truck terminals, lumber and construction years, even a stockyard.

At the J. A Bauer Pottery Plant on West Avenue, thirty-three kilns fired away. The Los Angeles Brewery on North Main, the Capitol Milling Company Flour Mill on North Spring, the Cudahy Packing Plant on East Macy Street (the largest meat-packing plant in the Far West), and the Los Angeles Soap Company Plant on East 1st Street were hardly in the business of selling climate. Food processing was represented by the Ben Hur Products Plant on Traction Avenue, where coffee was roasted and tea and spices packaged, or the National Biscuit Company Bakery on Mateo Street, or the California Walnut Growers Association shelling plant on East 7th, where 650 workers processed more than twenty million pounds of walnuts each year. Also indicative of the vitality of Los Angeles as a food-processing center was the packing house of the Calavo Growers of California on Everett Avenue, which packed and shipped 85 percent of the avocados moving to market from Southern California. Incongruously, given the much-too-pretty-to-be-serious canard of Cain and Symes, the Los Angeles Union Stockyards on Downey Road was the largest stockyard in the eleven Western states. Admittedly, the business of slaughtering and meat packing was administered from a picturesque Spanish Revival headquarters; but the business at hand was as realistic as anything going on in Chicago.

The General Cable factory on East Olympic Boulevard provided the electrical hardware for the region. Nearby, on East Olympic, the O'Keefe & Merritt factory, covering several acres, rolled and stamped sheet metal parts, molded iron, and produced gas ranges, water heaters, refrigerators, and stoves. The Studebaker plant on Loma Vista Avenue served as a branch assembly plant for the Studebaker Corporation of South Bend. Here Studebakers were assembled from manufactured parts for sale to the Western market. Chrysler also maintained a regional assembly plant, at the corner of Slauson and Eastern avenues, where cars and trucks for California, Nevada, Arizona, and Hawaii were assembled. Goodyear Tire and Rubber on South Central supplied the eleven Western states, Alaska, and Hawaii and helped make Los Angeles the second largest center of tire manufacturing in the United States after Akron, Ohio. Near the Chrysler plant, Consolidated Steel covered almost fifty acres. Here were fabricated 2,422 steel towers for the Hoover Dam transmission lines and much of the hydro-electrical hardware of the Far West.

All in all, more than a hundred thousand wage earners were producing more than half a billion dollars worth of manufactured goods and products out of greater Los Angeles by 1939. Oil refineries at El Segundo, Wilmington, and Long Beach made Los Angeles County the number one refinery center in the nation. The Port of Los Angeles, twenty-five miles from the Downtown, soon to be the third busiest port in the United States, shipped a hundred million barrels of petroleum every year and seventy-seven thousand tons of citrus fruit. The port also served the shipping needs of the aircraft assembly plants, now on the verge of their wartime productivity, and was port of call to 115 separate shipping lines. Approximately 350,000 passengers passed through the port each year.

Here, then, was no picture-perfect city but a real-life working town that was rapidly unionizing, despite the ferocious and effective anti-unionism of the region. In 1933 Los Angeles had approximately thirty-three thousand union members; by 1940 union membership was pushing the quarter-million mark, which meant that approximately half of the working people in Los Angeles held union memberships. Eastern companies opening Los Angeles branches, for one thing—Chrysler, Dow Chemical, General Foods, Armour Meats, General Motors, Studebaker— were accustomed to dealing with unions in their home plants and did not share the near-fanatical anti-unionism of the Los Angeles establishment. The passage of the National Labor Relations Act in 1935, guaranteeing the right of workers to organize and hold elections, further empowered unionism in L.A., as did the rise of the CIO, with its philosophy of the horizontal enrollment of entire industries. By 1939 more than fifty thousand Los Angeles workers belonged to the CIO.

Everything and everybody seemed to be moving west in the Los Angeles of the 1930s, following Sunset and Wilshire boulevards to Pacific Palisades and Santa Monica on the shores of the sundown sea. The shift of Los Angeles from its nineteenth-century north-south axis along the river to an east-west axis paralleling Sunset and Wilshire boulevards was a matter of inevitability and invention. In ancient times, the Native Americans of Yang-na in the vicinity of downtown Los Angeles and the Chumash of Malibu had each moved along this east-west axis to reach the centrally located tar pits of La Brea in search of tar to caulk their baskets and feathers to affix to their arrows. The east-west trail they padded in their bare feet over the centuries became a cattle trail in the Spanish and Mexican era and a farmers' road in the first phases of American settlement. In 1895 H. Gaylord Wilshire, a Fabian socialist with a flair for real estate, glimpsing the possibilities for development along this ancient roadway (El Camino Viejo, it was called, the Old Road), purchased and subdivided the first western tracts along the dusty trail that, with characteristic reticence, Wilshire named in his own honor.

Taking up Wilshire's dream in the 1920s, developer A. W. Ross set about the creation of a shopping district on eighteen acres he owned on Wilshire Boulevard between La Brea and Fairfax. At the suggestion of another developer, Foster Stewart, Ross in 1928 renamed his tract the Miracle Mile. Already, in 1924, Wilshire had been widened to create a major traffic artery to the ocean. In 1934 a cut was made through Westlake Park, bringing Wilshire to Grand Avenue in the Down-town. A sixteen-mile boulevard, which Ross envisioned as an automobile-friendly Champs-Elysées, now connected downtown Los Angeles with Santa Monica on the sea. Like a great river released into its destined channel, Los Angeles reversed its north-south axis and began to flow westward to the Pacific.

After 1929 Los Angeles had a new institution, the University of California at Los Angeles, to serve as terminus and catalyst of this westward advance. In 1924 the UC Board of Regents, having decided to upgrade its Southern Branch on Vermont Avenue to a full-fledged campus, located a 347-acre site near Westwood Village on the former Rancho San Jose de Buenos Ayres between Beverly Hills and the ocean. Seeing the developmental possibilities of a UC campus on the western edge of Los Angeles, four adjacent cities—Los Angeles, Venice (which became a part of Los Angeles the next year), Beverly Hills, and Santa Monica—voluntarily taxed themselves to the tune of a million dollars, which they donated to the regents for the purchase of the site. Alphonzo Bell, then developing the adjacent Bel Air, donated further property valued at $3.5 million. The legislature granted $3 million toward construction, which began in 1927. On 20 December 1929 UCLA welcomed its first students to its campus at Sunset Boulevard and Hilgard, a quadrangle of Romanesque and Italian Renaissance buildings, with a library designed by George Kelham of San Francisco and a two-thousand-seat Royce Hall designed by the Los Angeles firm of Allison and Allison.

Throughout the 1930s UCLA, under the guidance of its provost Ernest Moore, developed a distinctive culture. The new university was, in that era, primarily a commuter school, drawing heavily upon the Jewish community of the Westside; and it took on a different character from USC across town. While USC was Anglo-American and conservative, UCLA was Jewish and liberal, to the point of being accused by Harry Carr, as early as 1933, of being the Little Red School House. For the time being, USC dominated the city and would continue to do so through the 1940s; but UCLA, a Mediterranean quadrangle rising from near-bare hills, contained within itself the formula, the DNA code—a scholarly faculty, an intellectually eager student body, an attractive campus in what was already by the 1930s the best part of town, a tradition of dynamic leadership (Chancellor Franklin Murphy and university librarian Lawrence Clark Powell come to mind), and the generosity of the California taxpayer—that would propel it by the 1960s into the forefront of American universities. Through the prism of USC, Los Angeles might see itself as Anglo, Protestant, locally rooted, upwardly mobile, networked, loving the good life. Through the prism of UCLA, Los Angeles looked over its shoulder to Berkeley, Harvard, Yale, and, in the early years, the City of College of New York, where, as in the case of UCLA, an entire generation of intellectuals was commuting to school by streetcar.

The Jewish kids coming to UCLA lived in mid-Wilshire along Fairfax Avenue. Their parents had grown up in Boyle Heights across the river, where the very street names (Hester, Brooklyn), the shops and delicatessens, the kosher slaughterhouses and butchers, the kosher restaurants, the synagogues (ten for a population still numbering sixty thousand in the early 1930s), the Old People's Home, the marriage brokers and circumcision surgeons, the dark clothes, the heavy accents, the sounds of Yiddish, recalled the textured, flavorful Jewish life of New York and the cities of the Pale in the old country. Mid-Wilshire Judaism, by contrast, tended to be more assimilated, including the motion picture industry and European refugees as well as prosperous American-Jewish professionals moving to Los Angeles and the upwardly mobile moving out of Boyle Heights. While Boyle Heights was Orthodox and Conservative, Mid-Wilshire was Reform, as expressed most gloriously in the stunning B'nai B'rith Temple on the corner of Wilshire and Hobart (1929), presided over by the dynamic Rabbi Edgar Magnin, Rabbi to the Stars, as attested to by the many Hollywood marriages, bar mitzvahs, bas mitzvahs, and funerals over which he officiated. A scion of the I. Magnin department store family, Rabbi Magnin arbitrated Mid-Wilshire and Westside Jewish life with a mixture of scholarship, *noblesse oblige*, civic-mindedness, and wit. (Asked to say something nice about the unlikable Jack Warner, now that he was gone, Magnin replied: "He's dead.") In Rabbi Magnin, downtown Los Angeles, with its residential extensions into Pasadena and San Marino, encountered a Jewish leader fully equal, if not superior, in lineage and resources. Here was no bearded rabbi from Boyle Heights, ringlets cascading from beneath a black homburg. Here was the well-tailored and passionately civic paradigm of Los Angeles as world center of Jewish civilization.

Financed in great part by movie money, Wilshire Temple was designed by architect Abraham Adelman (Allison and Allison consulting) with the theatricality of a Hollywood stage set. An immense mosaic-inlaid dome surmounted a triple entrance in Italian marble under a rose window, graced with doors of East Indian teak and Byzantine columns of black Belgian marble. Within, eight cast-bronze chandeliers designed to resemble ancient prayer spice boxes soared over an altar, ark, and choir screen of inlaid mahogany and walnut, richly carved and framed in black marble and mosaic. No wonder people from the Business loved to worship there. As a stage set, the Wilshire Temple matched Hollywood itself.

If Wilshire Boulevard anchored the emergent Jewish Los Angeles, it sustained the Protestant community as well in such structures as Immanuel Presbyterian Church (1929), a Gothic extravaganza at Berendo Street intersection, the Wilshire Boulevard Christian Church (1922) at Normandie Avenue, modeled on the Cathedral of Rheims, Wilshire Methodist at Plymouth (1924), replicating the Church of St. Francis at Brescia, Italy—and the twenty-three-acre residential section of Hancock Park on the north side of Wilshire between Bronson and Highland avenues, where so many of the upscale people who worshipped at these churches lived. Here in stately mansions along equally stately streets resided the Old Money of Los Angeles that had not migrated to Pasadena or San Marino. When not at church, the residents of Hancock Park might be found further west at the Los Angeles Country Club between Beverly Hills and UCLA. Lined with palm trees and mansions, Hancock Park was as much a point of view and a state of mind as it was a district of the city. Here reposed the deepest establishment values of Los Angeles and its most formalized folkways. To experience Hancock Park in this era—its succession of parties and benefits, its engagements, marriages, and anniversaries, its ritualized celebrations of Thanksgiving and Christmas, its connections to club life in the Downtown and beach clubs in Santa Monica— was to realize that the stately patterns of upper-class Anglo-America on the Atlantic shore had found a happy translation to Southern California.

Hancock Park did its shopping at Bullock's Wilshire (1929) at 3050, a masterpiece of Art Deco by John and Donald Parkinson; I. Magnin (1939) at the corner of Wilshire and New Hampshire, black granite without, soothing apricot within, designed by Myron Hunt; the May Company (1939) at the northeast corner of Wilshire and Fairfax, a tribute by architect Albert Martin to Streamline Moderne. A. W. Ross had done an excellent job in persuading the big downtown department stores to move west along Wilshire along with the rest of the city. In 1936, for example, the Phelps-Terkel men's store, long a tradition at the USC campus, moved to the Miracle Mile: in and of itself a symbol of the shift from the south-seeking impulse that had created Exposition Park and USC to the new westering impulse that was creating the Miracle Mile and UCLA. Opened in 1933, the Farmers Market at the corner of Fairfax and 3rd in the Mid-Wilshire offered a direct retail outlet to the agriculturalists of the region in an environment resembling the Grand Central Market in the Downtown.

Increasingly, in the 1920s and 1930s, Los Angeles was doing its eating, drinking, and nightclubbing along Wilshire as well. Night life, after all, in the modern sense of the term (meals, a live orchestra, dancing, entertainment) had first come to Los Angeles in the mid-1920s on Wilshire through the Cocoanut Grove in the Ambassador Hotel, an Arabian Nights fantasy decorated with artificial palm trees from the set of *The Sheik*, thanks to the generosity of Rudolph Valentino, who loved to dance the tango there. The Cocoanut Grove was perhaps the only place where Hancock Park and the film colony broke the icy silence between them and ate, drank, and danced in each other's company. Across the street, at the Brown Derby, in a building shaped like a hat, restaurateur Herbert Somborn and his partner Robert Cobb, inventor of the Cobb salad (ham, turkey, bacon, avocado, hard-boiled eggs, black olives over a bed of lettuce, a creamy dressing: a local favorite, like cracked crab and sourdough bread in San Francisco), likewise catered to a mixed Hollywood-Downtown crowd in a clubby atmosphere of leather booths, celebrity caricatures crowding the walls, telephones brought to the table, and an American Standard menu emphasizing steaks, chops, hamburgers, turkey, and lobster thermidor. Somborn and Cobb met with such success that they opened a second Brown Derby on Vine just south of Hollywood Boulevard, followed by a third on Wilshire in Beverly Hills, and a fourth on the road to Glendale. Lawry's on La Cienega off Wilshire specialized in prime rib served from a gleaming sidecart inspired by Simpson's-in-the-Strand in London. More delicate appetites might be satisfied in the Tea Room at Bullock's Wilshire, the rendezvous of choice for shopping matrons. Further west, Perino's, a Paul Williams building, Streamline Moderne without, continental elegance within, offered an extremely formal atmosphere—no music, no dancing, an almost reverential silence as tuxedoed waiters glided about their duties—and an ambitious French and Northern Italian cuisine (pheasant, quail, and crab legs bordelaise were specialties of the house), with prices rising as high as $2.50 a person in 1939 for the table d'hôte.

Created by and for the automobile, Wilshire supported fourteen drive-in restaurants by the late 1930s: places such as Simon's Drive-In at the corner of Wilshire and Fairfax, an Art Deco mirage of glass and neon served by car-hops, a new variation of the American Girl, a cross between a waitress, an usherette, and a starlet, who emerged as a protagonist in the new relationship between the restaurant and the automobile. Car-hops were young and pretty. They wore uniforms: a paramilitary cap and jacket, a cowgirl, a bonnie lass in kilts, the tight-fitting jacket and slacks of an usherette, a Mexican blouse and sash; but they were more than a pretty face. They were entrepreneurs. Most car-hops acted as self-employed brokers between passengers and the restaurant. Although a few drive-ins preferred to employ car-hops on the basis of a minimum wage plus tips, the majority of Los Angeles car-hops earned their livelihood from tips and the differential between menu prices and the lower price the car-hop paid the drive-in for the meal she had just sold. When a bill was introduced in the state legislature to force restaurateurs to pay salaries to car-hops and end the revenue-sharing system, some fifteen hundred car-hops signed a petition asking the legislators to leave the system as it stood, which they did.

In its brief florescence in the 1930s, car-hop culture evolved its standards and rituals. Car-hops were to wait on line in front of the restaurant and to step off the curb in orderly succession only after a customer had pulled into the lot, stopped the engine, and pulled the emergency brake. Once a car-hop stepped off a curb and approached a specific car, the business was hers. The majority of car-hop drive-in business was male. Sailors were the best tippers, followed by middle-aged men. Flirtation by male customers was commonplace; but car-hops were dissuaded from dating customers. "How to side-step advances from customers without offending them and losing their patronage," noted *Westways* in March 1940, "is a delicate problem, but car-hops solve it effectively and tactfully." [11] It was a measure of the sexual competition involved in car-hopping, however subliminal or controlled, to note as *Westways* did that most car-hops refused to work alongside platinum blondes, who were judged to have an unfair advantage in sex appeal.

Bypassed by the westward turn of the Los Angeles axis, the Arroyo districts north of the Downtown en route to Pasadena, Silver Lake and Mt. Washington, could only be described as urban chaparral. Residents lived in semi-rustic isolation but had a clear view to the Downtown. By night, the Lindbergh Beacon atop City

Hall shimmered in the distance, while just outside, on semi-improved streets, packs of coyotes loped in search of their evening meal or howled to the moon within hearing distance of the city.

Other hillside districts, most noticeably the Los Feliz area adjacent to Griffith Park, continued their drive to density and urbanism, propelled by the development of Hollywood. In the 1920s and 1930s, Los Feliz evolved into a wonderland of Spanish Revival homes, forever fixed as an image of L.A. in the film version of James M. Cain's *Double Indemnity* (1936). Atop the nearby Mount Hollywood, between 1933 and 1935, the Park Commission was constructing the Griffith Observatory and Planetarium in Griffith Park. Like the nearby HOLLYWOODLAND sign erected in 1923 (shortened to HOLLYWOOD in 1949), Griffith Observatory, a Deco-Classical domed temple of science, at once demarcated the east-west run of the Hollywood Hills and offered a stunning view of the city, especially by night, when not surprisingly it became a favorite lovers' lane.

As in the case of the coyotes howling in Silver Lake or on the slopes of Mount Washington, wild nature had its primal presence in Griffith Park as well. Only the lower regions of the park were developed in any traditional sense of the term. Above a certain height, the park became woodland and chaparral, with all the possibilities for firestorm that such a wilderness implied. On 4 October 1933, as more than three thousand men were busy building roads in the wilderness-park as part of a work-relief program, a brush fire broke out in Mineral Wells Canyon. A line of men, picks and shovels in hand, marched upwards along a narrow cow path from the San Fernando Valley side of the park with the intention of creating a firebreak. En route, a fire warden warned them that there could be a sudden shift in the wind. As the firefighters approached the blaze, the pathway entered a very narrow canyon. The wind shifted, and a firestorm raged down the narrow declivity. Desperately, the men struggled to claw their way up the hillside. Thirty-six charred bodies were recovered from the steep slope, most of them with arms outstretched and hands grasping the earth.

All this horror a few short miles away from Hollywood, dream capital of the City of Dreams! Fortunately, no such fires afflicted another important Hollywood site, the Hollywood Bowl near the intersection of Highland Avenue and Cahuenga Boulevard. A fifty-acre natural amphitheater owned by Los Angeles County, the Hollywood Bowl seated more than twenty thousand and had standing room for half that number. (A sudden firestorm in such an environment during a concert would represent an apocalypse from the darkest visions of Nathanael West.) No institution more perfectly expressed the ethos of Los Angeles, its formula as a city, than the Hollywood Bowl. Here were brought into dynamic synergy nearly all the elements of the Los Angeles formula: a Protestant regard for choral music and religious pageantry, the growing influence of Jewish intelligence and taste, a celebration of good weather, the shaping presence of the movie industry and radio broadcasting, and an increasing desire for recognition of the region as a performing arts capital.

Ever since the first of the Symphonies under the Stars debuted in 1922, the summer performances of the Hollywood Bowl Orchestra, conducted by the German-born Alfred Hertz, maestro of the San Francisco Symphony, followed in turn by Otto Klemperer, Bruno Walter, Leopold Stokowski, Sir Thomas Beecham, and a host of guest conductors, had grown steadily in popularity. In 1925 the Board of Supervisors of Los Angeles County, which owned the property, asked the Allied Architects collaborative to draw up plans for permanent seating and a performance shell. A temporary music shell was ready for use in July 1926. Lloyd Wright, the brilliant architect son of Frank Lloyd Wright and a Los Angeles resident, designed two further temporary structures: a pyramidal shaped shell in Zig-Zag Moderne, ready for the 1927 season, and for 1928 an acoustically brilliant half-trumpet shell, which recalled the proscenium arch designed by Louis Sullivan for the Auditorium Theater of Chicago in 1889, at a time when Lloyd Wright's father was working in Sullivan's office. The next year, 1929, Wright's shell was rebuilt in permanent materials, with modifications by the Allied Architects. Lloyd Wright had done a brief stint as a set designer at Paramount. As a stage set, his Hollywood Bowl music shell worked perfectly. Sleek, curvilinear, in the forefront of the Moderne movement, Wright's shell, like the music of George Gershwin, so popular at Hollywood Bowl concerts, spoke to the mood of the 1930s, not just in Los Angeles or even in Hollywood, where the shell had a strong influence on stage set designs for Busby Berkeley musicals, but in New York as well, where Wright's designs were echoed in the proscenium arch of Radio City Music Hall.

George Gershwin himself, whose music spoke so evocatively to the mood of New York, was now, in 1936 and 1937, living with his brother Ira at 1019 North Roxbury Drive in Beverly Hills, working on songs for the *Goldwyn Follies* (1937). On 10 and 11 February 1937, in concerts organized by Los Angeles impresario Merle Armitage, Gershwin performed his *Rhapsody in Blue* (1924) and *Concerto in F* (1925) in the Philharmonic Auditorium. Gershwin also conducted his *Cuban Overture* (1932), and the African-American baritone Todd Duncan, backed by a local black chorus, sang excepts from *Porgy and Bess* (1935). There was talk of an all-Gershwin evening in the Hollywood Bowl. While playing the *Concerto in F* on the night of the 11th, however, Gershwin's mind went momentarily blank, and somewhere in the blackness that overcame him, so he later said, he smelled something resembling burning rubber.

In the months to come, Gershwin suffered increasingly from headaches and listlessness, and the rubber smell frequently returned, although repeated examinations by Dr. Gabriel Segall, Greta Garbo's doctor, showed him to be in good condition. Gershwin, however, refused to undergo an excruciatingly painful spinal test; and so the real cause of his malaise, a cystic tumor on the right temporal lobe of the brain, never surfaced until late on the day—Friday, 9 July 1937— Gershwin fell into a coma and was rushed to the Cedars of Lebanon Hospital and X-rayed. Operated on at three the next morning by Los Angeles surgeon Carl

Rand, one of the foremost brain specialists in the nation, Gershwin died without regaining consciousness. So terrible was the tumor, it would have left him disabled or blind, or both, had he recovered. And so the crown prince of American music, the creator of a hundred melodies and the center of a thousand memorable New York and Hollywood nights, slipped away at the age of thirty-eight and was memorialized in joint ceremonies in the two cities he knew so well: at Temple Emanu-El on Fifth Avenue in New York and Temple B'nai B'rith on Wilshire Boulevard, with Rabbi Edgar Magnin officiating.

That fall, on 8 September 1937, there was the George Gershwin evening at the Hollywood Bowl that had been talked about earlier that year, only it was now a memorial concert before a capacity crowd and an international audience listening in through a shortwave transmission by the Columbia Broadcasting System. Otto Klemperer and José Iturbi conducted. Oscar Levant, Gershwin's nightclubbing pal, played the *Rhapsody in Blue*. Todd Duncan sang from *Porgy and Bess*. Edward G. Robinson and George Jessel read tributes. Lily Pons and Fred Astaire also sang. The last word Gershwin was heard to utter as he was rushed to the hospital had been "Astaire."

They had palled around together, Gershwin, Astaire, Levant, George S. Kaufman, and the rest of the New York/Hollywood crowd—standing around the piano at the Garden of Allah or at one or another night spot as George played the songs he was writing for the *Goldwyn Follies*, including two, "Love Walked In" and "Our Love Is Here to Stay," that remain high points of American popular music. It was easy to be out on the town in Hollywood in the 1930s. The New York crowd, and their counterparts from Vienna and Berlin, increasingly a force in the city, relished night-life, cabaret, and nightclubs; and so Hollywood, still a sleepy town in the 1920s, began in the 1930s to develop its late-night scene. In addition to the Hollywood Brown Derby, there were Sardi's on Hollywood Boulevard (designed by no less than Rudolph Schindler), and the Embassy Club, another ultramodern chrome and glass establishment, and the It Café on North Vine, and the nearby Hollywood Tropics, where the bar specialized in rum drinks, not to mention the Trocadero on Sunset, opened in 1934 by Billy Wilkerson, owner and editor of the *Hollywood Reporter*, the gossipy newspaper of the film colony. The Knickerbocker Hotel on Ivar featured the Parisian Cocktail Terrace and Nightclub, and the Hotel Roosevelt on Hollywood Boulevard had its Blossom Room. Further west, Paul Williams created the Polo Lounge in the Beverly Hills Hotel. Serious nightclubbers might drive a bit south to Sebastian's Cotton Club in Culver City, a neon-lit gin joint, hazy blue in smoke, with dancing and a black floor show for which Frank Sebastian claimed a direct linkage to the Cotton Club in Harlem.

Sebastian's Cotton Club was risky but respectable, which could not be said for the Clover Club on Sunset Boulevard in unincorporated West Hollywood, a place where the syndicate, petty crookdom, and Hollywood met and where, in October 1937, gambler Les Bruneman had his professional career terminated in a hail of gunfire. Bruneman had already survived an earlier assassination attempt as he walked arm in arm with his girlfriend down the promenade at Redondo Beach, a bullet missing his heart by an inch. This time, he would not be so lucky. Bruneman had an inkling that his time was up. He bought drinks for the house and listened to repeated performances of "Smoke Gets in Your Eyes" on the jukebox before two torpedoes walked in, carrying automatics. Unfortunately, a young man who tried to get the license number of the triggermen as they drove off was also gunned down. Insisting that it was a contract job from outside California, the police made only a lackadaisical investigation.

If hoods preferred the Clover Club, screenwriters preferred the leather and mahogany clubbiness, generous drinks, and New York–style food of the Musso & Frank Grill at 6667 Hollywood Boulevard, especially on Saturday afternoons after the completion of the work week when the back room was filled with the likes of Nathanael West, F. Scott Fitzgerald, Budd Schulberg, S. N. Behrman, Dashiell Hammett, Lillian Hellman, Horace McCoy, John Fante, A. I. Bezzerides, Frederick Faust (Max Brand), William Faulkner, and other literary folk in various stages of engagement with or disengagement from the studios.

"Bill sat drinking with me," Twentieth Century–Fox script girl Meta Carpenter later reminisced of those Saturday afternoons, "smoking his pipe, laughing freely. He did not mingle much with his colleagues, yet he was happy to be among writing men." [12] Carpenter was living at the Studio Club when she met Faulkner, a hard-drinking writer with a wife and daughter in Oxford, Mississippi. Faulkner took Carpenter to the usual spots: Sardi's, the Brown Derby, the Knickerbocker Hotel, the Cocoanut Grove, Sebastian's Cotton Club; but the couple preferred the Musso & Frank Grill for its honest ambience and reasonable prices. It was after dinner there one night that Faulkner, instead of escorting Carpenter back to her residence club on Ivar as was his wont, steered her instead to the Knickerbocker Hotel, through the brilliant light of the lobby, past the scrutinizing glance of the night clerk, up the elevator, and down the long hallway leading to his room.

Benjamin (Bugsy) Siegel first visited Southern California in 1933 and came to stay in 1936, leasing opera star Lawrence Tibbett's home at 326 McCarthy Drive in Beverly Hills, before building his own $150,000 showcase in the late 1930s— swimming pool, library, oversized dining room, bar and lounge, projection room, beds and bathrooms innumerable—at 250 Delfern Avenue in the Hombly Hills district off Sunset Boulevard. Siegel's goals were straightforward. He wanted to do what Al Capone had thought of doing in 1927 but decided was beyond his immediate powers: organize Los Angeles and the Southland, all of it, especially bookmaking. Whatever else he was involved in (including a few nasty jobs for his friends in Murder, Inc.), Siegel was first and foremost a gambler.

A handsome man, vain of his good looks, Siegel spent his afternoons in the steam room of the Hollywood YMCA or working out in the gym and went to bed at night with skin cream plastered on his face and an elastic chin strap slung under his jaw to ward off wattles. His good looks, his money, his $175 suits, his monogrammed handkerchiefs and shirts, his friendship with George Raft: there was much to Siegel that made him acceptable to Hollywood, especially since Hollywood had already embraced the gangster as a mythic type. Siegel was the real thing. Friendly with Raft and comedian Joe E. Lewis from the old days in New York, Siegel met Countess Dorothy Taylor DiFrasso at the Santa Anita Race Track. The Countess, a leather-business heiress from Watertown, New York, derived her title from her Italian husband, a marriage that did not preclude other interests. At the time she met Siegel, the Countess had just ended a relationship with Gary Cooper and there, in his sharp suit and Warren Beatty good looks, was Bugsy. Siegel soon became Dorothy DiFrasso's great and good friend and a frequent guest at the Countess's thirty-room home at 913 North Bedford Drive in Beverly Hills, where he met the likes of Marlene Dietrich, Loretta Young, Charles Boyer, Jean Harlow, Bruce Cabot, Clark Gable, Cary Grant, George Jessel, Jimmy Durante, Fred Astaire, Dolores Del Rio, and Frederic March.

For all his pretty-boy demeanor and his Hollywood acquaintances, however, Bugsy Siegel was primarily a hood, packing a .45 in his shoulder holster at all times, capable of personally assisting, as he did, in the execution of Harry (Big Greenie) Greenberg in Hollywood, for which he was indicted and jailed in the fall of 1940. The indictment cost Siegel his membership in the Hillcrest Country Club, but little else. While in jail, Siegel was treated like a celebrity. A bribed prison doctor gave him leave to visit his dentist and to dine out, a privilege only revoked when the *Examiner* ran photos of Siegel in a restaurant. In December Siegel's case was dismissed for lack of evidence, and he returned to his pursuits. Later, Siegel would admit to Del Webb, the contractor who built the Flamingo Hotel for him in Las Vegas, to killing twelve men. Seeing the look on Webb's face, Siegel laughed. "There's no chance that you'll get killed," he told Webb. "We only kill each other." [13]

Further west, in the seaside city of Santa Monica, another gambling man, Tony Cornero, had a brilliant idea of how to avoid Los Angeles altogether, now that the reform administration of Fletcher Bowron was in office. Raymond Chandler would soon be chronicling Santa Monica as Bay City, the most corrupt town in Los Angeles County, despite its pristine location along the beach where Wilshire Boulevard ran into the Pacific. Like Long Beach further south, Santa Monica was a popular resort. Its Ocean Park amusement district—roller coasters, skating rinks, carousels, shoot-the-shoots, carnival booths—boasted itself the Coney Island of the West. Like Long Beach as well, Santa Monica had an impressive Municipal Auditorium, seating more than twelve hundred, and an amusement pier extending into the sea, which on weekends might attract more than a hundred thousand visitors. Here, Tony Cornero realized, in both Santa Monica and Long Beach, were good places to go into the gambling business. Refurbishing four ships as gambling casinos—the *Rex, Texas, Tango*, and *Showboat*—Cornero anchored them beyond the three-mile limit off Santa Monica and Long Beach. Claiming that his offshore operation was legal, Cornero had the temerity to advertise in local newspapers, comparing his ships, the *Rex* especially, anchored off Santa Monica, to the best gambling establishments of Biarritz, the Riviera, Monte Carlo, and Cannes. Open twenty-four hours a day and served from shore by high-speed boats, the *Rex*, flagship of Cornero's gambling fleet, hosted between one and three thousand customers on the hour for gambling, cocktails, dining, and cabaret. White-jacketed waiters served the clientele. Dealers and croupiers wore black tie. Cornero's gambling fleet represented a flamboyant defiance of state and local law, but no one seemed to want to take jurisdiction in the matter until Alameda County district attorney Earl Warren became California's attorney general in 1938.

It was the most flamboyant raid of Warren's already flamboyant career. Working with the Coast Guard, Warren organized a flotilla of ships and a contingent of three hundred state and local police officers, whom he launched against the *Texas* and the *Rex* on the afternoon of 2 August 1939. Establishing his headquarters at a beach club in Santa Monica, Warren monitored the raid through binoculars in the style of the commanding officer of a military force. Aboard the *Rex*, Cornero resisted the officers with fire hoses. Not until three the next morning did the *Rex* capitulate. Finally, Warren sailed out to the *Rex* on a Fish and Game patrol boat to take Cornero's surrender, one commodore to another. Warren had the *Texas* and the *Rex* towed to shore, then seized and sold for back taxes. In the course of being booked at the Santa Monica police station, Cornero was asked to give his occupation. "Mariner," he replied. [14] Mouthpiece Jerry Giesler got Cornero off with a stiff fine.

Since Los Angeles was such a hospitable city for criminals, amateur and professional, it most definitely generated excellent business for lawyers such as Jerry Giesler, who devoted themselves to criminal defense. Acquiring his training in the offices of the legendary Earl Rogers, whom even Clarence Darrow had for a lawyer, Giesler came into prominence in 1931 when he won a new trial and an acquittal in the rape conviction of theater magnate Alexander Pantages. Giesler spent the next two decades, or so it seemed, getting his clients, many of them celebrities, acquitted. On 8 September 1935, for example, a thoroughly boozed Busby Berkeley, speeding south on the Pacific Coast Highway toward Santa Monica Canyon, got into a three-car accident near Malibu. Three people lost their lives. It took Giesler three trials to win Berkeley's acquittal.

In 1937 Giesler won the famous White Flame case, as the press dubbed it. On 9 November 1937 aviation enthusiast Paul Wright took his wife and his best friend John Kimmel, an airline pilot, to a dinner given by the Quiet Birdmen, an aviation fraternity, at the Hollywood Athletic Club. After dinner, the Wrights and Kimmel repaired to the Wright home at 1830 Verdugo Vista in Glendale for a nightcap. After a few drinks, Paul Wright excused himself for the evening. At three that morning, he was awakened by the irregular tinkling of the parlor piano. Creeping downstairs, Wright looked into his living room and saw his wife having sex with her guest Kimmel, who was sitting on the piano bench, leaning against the keys. A white flame exploded in his head, Wright later testified. Although he had no memory of the event, so he claimed, he secured the family pistol from its drawer and fired nine shots into the otherwise busy couple. Giesler pleaded Wright "not guilty and not guilty by reason of insanity" to the two murder charges. It was a brilliant strategy, allowing the jury to condemn the murders but not the murderer. As he expected, Giesler lost the not guilty plea—but, this being Los Angeles, won the second half of his plea, not guilty by reason of insanity, after sixteen hours and seven ballots of deliberation. Paul Wright left the courtroom a free man.

As the White Flame case proved, Jerry Giesler was a master of the unusual plea. He was also an expert in pre-trial motions and appeals. He temporarily lost his case, for example, in December 1938 when his client Moe (the Gimp) Snyder was convicted on charges of the attempted murder of his former wife, singer Ruth Etting's, accompanist Myrl Aldermann. No matter, Giesler won an acquittal on appeal. In November 1940, in a pre-trial motion, Giesler won the dismissal of the indictment against Bugsy Siegel for the alleged murder of Harry (Big Greenie) Greenberg on the grounds that there were no witnesses (no stupid witnesses, that is) to the alleged event.

Criminal defense attorneys such as Jerry Geisler had no lack of business in L.A., not just from professional crooks falling afoul of the law, but from the Folks as well, who showed a tendency every now and then—as when Paul Wright discovered his wife and his best friend in the downstairs parlor—to commit mayhem. Crime reporter Veronica King noted this aspect of Los Angeles, the ability of the Folks to indulge in bizarre crimes, as far back as 1924 in her pioneering study *Problems of Modern American Crime*. Taking up a number of recent Los Angeles murder cases, King analyzed them as distinctive Los Angeles phenomena. The murderers, first of all, tended not to be career criminals but the Folks of the city, white, Protestant, middle-class, temporarily incited to murder. Clara Phillips, for example, hammered her husband's lover, Alberta Meadows, a respectable young widow, to death. Madalynn Obenchain drove happily with her lover Belton Kennedy into remote Beverly Glen, at the time rural countryside, then just as happily pumped him full of lead. In each instance, Veronica King noted, newspapers reported the crimes as serial melodrama, giving each case or each murderer a specific designation to heighten theatrical interest. Phillips, for example, was dubbed the Tiger Woman because she had used the claws of the hammer to eviscerate her victim, prompting the cop who discovered the body to say that it looked as if a tiger had attacked the deceased. The Los Angeles public, moreover, and this included the Los Angeles public sitting as juries, tended to view such crimes as part and parcel of everyday life. For white people at least, especially the Folks, acquittals were frequent, and just as frequent were verdicts on lesser charges, and even more frequent were comparatively light sentences. In Los Angeles, murders seemed a way of life. Forty were reported in the first five months of 1922, this in a city of six hundred thousand, "living," as King noted, "in a perfect climate, under almost unique conditions of expansion, progress, and opportunity." [15]

The late 1920s, 1930s, and 1940s continued this saga of the Folks in the throes of colorfully portrayed mayhem. In August 1935, for example, Los Angeles thrilled to the Rattlesnake Murder, in the course of which one Robert S. James, aged thirty-eight, a barber, tried to kill his wife Mary Busch James, aged thirty-five, by holding her leg against a wire mesh cage of rattlesnakes purchased for him by an accomplice, Charles Hope, aged thirty-eight, a short-order cook. When execution by rattlesnake venom proved too cumbersome, James drowned his wife in a bathtub. Sometimes the Folks could explode into mass mayhem, as in the case of Verlin Spencer, principal of the South Pasadena Junior High School, who, fearing a plot to oust him from his job, ran amuck with a rifle on 6 May 1940, killing five school employees.

The Los Angeles press, which favored various shades of yellow, had a field day with each and every incident. Through the 1920s and 1930s, indeed through the 1940s, Los Angeles was a *Front Page* kind of a town, and no one knew this better than ace crime reporter Agness (Aggie) Underwood, whose career went into high gear in January 1935 when, age thirty-two, a married woman raising two children, she joined Hearst's *Herald-Express*. Ever since the early 1900s, Hearst newspapers had had at least one saving grace: they were willing to give women a chance on the news desk. Underwood shared the Los Angeles beat with a number of prominent women reporters who had got their start as, or who remained, Hearstlings: reporters such as Hollywood correspondent Adela Rogers St. Johns, also of the *Herald-Express*, daughter of Los Angeles attorney Earl Rogers, the greatest trial lawyer in the city through the first three decades of the century; Marjorie Driscoll of the *Examiner*, who began with Hearst in San Francisco, then migrated south to become one of the best reporters in Los Angeles history; Florabel Muir, who covered Los Angeles and Hollywood for the New York *Daily News*; and Louella Parsons and Hedda Hopper, each of them proving that pluck and ruthlessness were every bit as good as literacy when it came to covering the film colony.

Agness Underwood lived in an unpretentious house at 112th and Figueroa near Florence Avenue in South Central, where her husband managed an automobile agency. For all her skills as a reporter, she remained one of the Folks: the white middle class who had poured into Los Angeles in such great numbers (like Underwood herself, who had arrived at the age of seventeen, an orphan) in the first three decades of the twentieth century and would form the majority of the city through the 1950s. Walking in the Downtown in the late 1930s, one visitor remarked that she had never seen so many people wearing suspenders. "The first impression I got," she noted, "was of a vast procession of suspenders over crumpled shirts holding up pair after pair of unpressed pants."[16] The face of Los Angeles, noted journalist Garet Garrett at the opening of the 1930s, was the representative American face, "the truest conceivable representation of the whole American face, urban, big town, little town, all together."[17] Los Angeles, Frank Lloyd Wright told the *Times* on 20 January 1940, was "as if you tipped the United States up so all the commonplace people slid down here into Southern California."[18] "Mentally and morally," noted another observer, "and—to lug in an often misused word—culturally, Los Angeles is a glorified Middle-Western town."[19] Morrow Mayo was not so kind. "Here," he noted, "is an artificial city which has been pumped up under forced draught, inflated like a balloon, stuffed with rural humanity like a goose with corn." The City of Angels, Mayo snorted, "has retained the manners, culture, and general outlook of a huge country village."[20]

Whether or not that country village had long-range possibilities remained a matter of doubt. James M. Cain, on the one hand, liked the fact that Los Angeles had no regional accent. Its natives or longtime residents, he believed, spoke with the enunciation of a radio announcer, which was to the good. On the other hand, Cain continued, rural immigrants to the city, so much in the majority, were not prepared for the subtle tasks of urban life. Restaurants lacked trained waiters; bookstores showed a scarcity of knowledgeable clerks. The hotel operator would call your room to tell you that you had a telephone call but neglect to give you the name and number of your caller. All this, Cain argued, suggested that it would take the Folks a generation or two fully to urbanize. As usual, Morrow Mayo was more outspoken. Los Angeles, Mayo noted dismissively, lacked even a fifth-rate music, drama, art, or literary critic on any one of its newspapers. With the exception of Carey McWilliams, its literary culture was on a par with that of Scranton, Pennsylvania. Los Angeles might very well be the Big Orange, but "when the sweet, watery juice is squeezed out," Mayo chided, "there remains little but a pretty, unnutritious pulp."[21]

Los Angeles, noted Lillian Symes, was beautiful but dumb, an Attica minus the intellect. The people of Los Angeles, noted Oswald Garrison Villard in the *Nation*, lacked ambition and generosity of spirit. All anyone seemed to aspire to was a bungalow with palm trees. The city had deliberately turned its back on the rest of the nation in a gesture of reactionary selfishness. Los Angeles, noted another observer, seemed preoccupied with itself, bored with the rest of the nation. It had, said another, "all the crudities, vulgarisms, and mediocrity of nineteenth-century America with none of its saving graces."[22]

Many distrusted the easy life of the region, its orientation toward golf, the outdoor life, the beach. In certain cases, Los Angeles provided visitors a Rorschach test, often with surprising results. Aubrey Burns and Denis Ireland saw Los Angeles in terms of sexual desire. "Los Angeles," noted the otherwise staid Burns, "is a loose-limbed giant girl sprawled carelessly in the sunshine by the seashore. Blond, wanton, throbbing with the sun's heat, she stretches voluptuously with the sensations of growth. She has none of the restraint and brooding repose of her northern sister. Her desires are of the flesh; she thinks only of pleasures to which she may abandon herself."[23] British visitor Denis Ireland was even more obsessed. "If I lived long in this damnably monotonous sunlight," confessed Ireland with polymorphous candor in the English magazine *Life and Letters*, "I should become either a sexual maniac or a drug fiend. All the young women in Los Angeles seem to be beautiful, and all the young men tall and handsome."[24]

Pervading all these opinions was the question of eccentricity, the screwy factor. Los Angeles, Bertrand Russell opined in 1931, represented the ultimate segregation of the unfit. Covering the Ham and Eggs pension campaign in Los Angeles in November 1938, syndicated columnist Westbrook Pegler had an even more radical assessment. "It is hereby earnestly proposed," wrote Pegler on 22 November 1938, "that the USA would be better off if that big, sprawling, incoherent, shapeless, slobbering civic idiot in the family of American communities, the City of Los Angeles, could be declared incompetent and placed in charge of a guardian like an individual mental defective."[25]

Had Pegler been covering the religious cults of Los Angeles as well as Ham and Eggs, he might have been even more splenetic. At its moderate center, Los Angeles was an actively evangelical town. By 1910 it had 225 churches, mostly Protestant, for a population of 319,198. Even now, in the late 1930s, the great neon JESUS SAVES sign atop the Bible Institute at 558 South Hope Street in the Downtown proclaimed the continuing evangelical allegiance of the city. Yet with so much uprootedness, so much detachment from Midwestern anchorages in solid religion, it is not surprising that the instinctive, persistent religiosity of the city, indeed of all Southern California, showed a strong eccentric edge. Like the Greeks described by St. Paul, the citizens of Los Angeles seemed to have ears itching for new doctrines. For some observers, such as Michael Williams, writing in the *Catholic World* for April 1919, all California had a natural affinity for pagan cults. The great god Pan, piping his hedonistic tune, was alive and well on the coast. If this were true, then Los Angeles had more than its share of religious eccentricity, beginning with Scotsman William Money, who arrived in the early 1840s and declared himself a bishop of the Reformed New Testament Church of the Faith of Jesus Christ. Aimee Semple MacPherson was carrying on in this tradition of folk evangelism at the Four Square Gospel Church in Echo Park, although her scandalous disappearance (a faked kidnapping, a sojourn in Carmel with her lover) in 1926 somewhat stalled her momentum. The syncretic Asian-oriented Vedanta movement flourished in Hollywood, with Christopher Isherwood arriving at the Vedanta Center in late 1939 from Germany via London and New York to enter the community as a novice.

All this, even the Vedanta Society, represented mainline religion, in that it was related in one way or another to the great religious traditions of the world. More eccentrically, Los Angeles witnessed the founding of the Krotona community in Hollywood in 1911 by Albert Powell Warrington, a lawyer from Norfolk, Virginia. Krotona ("the place of promise," according to Warrington) featured a temple, a lotus pond, a vegetarian cafeteria, a Greek theater for outdoor pageants, and several tabernacles for worship. The Los Angeles–based Asian affairs writer Will Levington Comfort, who had covered the Russo-Japanese War with such distinction, had his life changed by contact with the Krotona movement, as he related in *The Story of a Quest* (1920), which chronicled his travels in China and India and his contact with the mystical traditions of the Far East.

Why did so many Los Angelenos come under the spell of various forms of Asian or Middle Eastern mysticism? Carey McWilliams was asking by March 1937. Did it come to Southern California with Hindu immigrants? Was it indigenous, arising from the very nature of life and society in Southern California? Even at this late date, McWilliams noted, Theosophical terminology and its variations were very much part of the discourse of many otherwise mainstream Los Angeles households. "In Los Angeles," noted McWilliams, "I have attended the services of the Agabeg Occult Church, where the woman pastor had violet hair and green-painted eyelids; of the Great White Brotherhood, whose yellow-robed followers celebrate the full moon of May with a special ritual; of the Ancient Mystical Order of Melchizedek; of the Temple of the Jeweled Cross . . . of the Self-Realization Fellowship of America, which proposes to construct a $400,000 Golden Lotus Yoga Dream Hermitage."[26]

The screwiest of these cults, McWilliams noted, was the I AM movement, headquartered in Los Angeles. At one point, in the mid-1930s, I AM enrolled more than 350,000 members across the nation. Its founder, Guy Ballard, had fled to Los Angeles in 1929 after being indicted in Illinois for stock fraud. Under the pen name of Godfrey Ray King, Ballard self-published *Unveiled Mysteries* in 1934, in which he related how on a hiking trip near Mount Shasta he was offered a cup of "pure electronic essence" and a wafer of "concentrated energy" by the Ascended Master Saint Germain, who took him on a voyage to ancient Karnak, Luxor, and the cities of the Inca. Arthur Bell, the founder of another Los Angeles cult, Mankind United, established in 1934, promised its adherents a four-hour day, a four-day week, and an eight-month work year at a salary of $300 a month, plus a $25,000 home, with radio and television and professional gardening service. Both the I AM and the Mankind United movements, McWilliams noted, emphasized energy and power and material well-being in a decade when so many Americans, including the citizens of Los Angeles, felt so powerless, so poverty-stricken, so hopeless. Bizarre and grotesque as they were, these cults nevertheless offered valuable probes into the collective psyche of Los Angeles, hence Southern California, at its most destabilized and distressed.

Even at its best, noted one observer, Los Angeles remained a utopia touched by sadness. So much, after all, had been invested by each migrant when he or she moved to the City of Angels in hopes of a better life. The native-born had their psychological investment as well, hearing of how parents and grandparents had made the same journey in the same hope. And when it was over, as the eighteenth-century English poet Thomas Gray so evocatively suggested in "Elegy

Written in a Country Churchyard" (1751), all paths, whether glorious or obscure, fulfilled or frustrated, led but to the grave.

On the other hand, surmised real estate salesman Hubert Eaton on New Year's Day 1917, standing atop a hill above the San Fernando Road in Tropico just outside Los Angeles and surveying the small Forest Lawn Cemetery he represented, the Southern California departed should have every opportunity, even across the great divide, to take some of Southern California with them. Why did cemeteries have to be gloomy and ugly, Eaton asked himself, so crowded with clumsy tombstones and repulsive statuary? Why should not cemeteries be beautiful and ennobling? Hubert Eaton, in other words, was projecting onto Forest Lawn the Southern California experience as it pertained to the search for a better life by the Folks. Why should the Folks abandon their quest for beauty, for a better existence in the sunshine, merely because they were dead? On the back of an old envelope (so he later tells us), Eaton scribbled the first draft of his "Builders' Creed." Forest Lawn, he vowed, would fulfill each promise of the Southern California dream: beauty, serenity, redemption, and peace. It would be a theme park for the departed, a true City of Angels, a Los Angeles beyond disappointment or compromise.

Twenty years later, by the late 1930s, Hubert Eaton had created a utopia of death, Forest Lawn Memorial Park, "a first step up towards Heaven," as a local publicist described it.[27] Forest Lawn was a Protestant Vatican for the Folks: more than three hundred acres of lawns and gardens, courts, churches, monuments, and statuary, which, taken cumulatively, offered a folkloric probe into the imaginative life of the region where even Congregationalist and Presbyterian churches were designed in churrigueresque. The three freestanding chapels at Forest Lawn were especially expressive of Anglo-Protestant value. The Little Church of the Flowers was inspired by the English church at Stoke Poges whose adjacent graveyard inspired Thomas Gray's elegy. The Wee Kirk o' the Heather replicated the church at Glencairn, Scotland, associated with the romantic Scots heroine Annie Laurie. The Church of the Recessional, named in honor of Rudyard Kipling's 1897 poem, faithfully reproduced the parish church of St. Margaret in Rottingdean, England, where Rudyard Kipling and his family worshipped. The great Mausoleum and Columbarium, by contrast, a Vatican-like assembly of cathedral, chapels, galleries, and courtyards, was filled with replicas from the Italian Renaissance, most notably Michelangelo's *Pietá* and the Madonna of Bruges and an oversized stained-glass version of Da Vinci's *Last Supper*, together with a twenty-two-figure setpiece entitled *The Mystery of Life* by the contemporary Italian sculptor Ernesto Gazzeri. The Court of David featured a ten-ton replica of Michelangelo's statue (with the addition of a fig leaf), and a replica of Michelangelo's *Moses* stood at the entrance to the Cathedral Corridor in Memorial Terrace.

Every other year, beginning in 1923, Eaton would travel to Europe in search of art and statuary to purchase or replicate. His favorite haunt was Rome, the Vatican especially. Mortician to the Folks, Eaton cultivated excellent relations with the Vatican. He once boasted that it had taken quite a few dinners, much wine, and many transatlantic cables to persuade church officials to close the Church of Saint Peter in Chains for a day so that Eaton and his staff could make clay masks of Michelangelo's *Moses*. For the twenty-two members of the Council of Regents at Forest Lawn (the group included Charles Dawes, former vice president of the United States, later ambassador to Great Britain, Rufus B. von KleinSmid of USC, and John Craven, president of Southern California Edison) Eaton provided red hats and robes, worn with gold shoulder chain and a Maltese cross, which made the formal sessions of the council seem a Folks version of the College of Cardinals.

A shrewd businessman, Eaton in 1933 organized Forest Lawn around the concept of the single telephone call by the family of the bereaved. Everything, including embalming, occurred on the premises, although Eaton had to fight the undertakers' association when it complained to the grand jury that a mortuary on the Forest Lawn premises constituted restraint of trade. Eaton spurred his salesmen, nearly fifty by the late 1930s, to sell plots in advance. The Before Need Plan, as it was called, became a thriving part of the Forest Lawn business. So too did weddings at the Little Church of the Flowers and the Wee Kirk o' the Heather. After the marriage ceremony, bride and groom pledged their love before the Ring of Aldyth, a replica of a Saxon betrothing site. Southern Californians, it seemed, refused to consider Forest Lawn as merely a burial ground. It was a theme park as well: a place to stroll on Sundays, to admire original and replicated art, to attend concerts, to read the Builder's Creed carved in stone. Forest Lawn had become a counterpart to Pershing Square, one of the great gathering places of the city.

To Forest Lawn, for twenty and more years, had been coming the people of the city, great and small alike, provided, of course, that they were of the white race. Even in death, Los Angeles maintained its recently embraced Jim Crow status. In the Court of Honor, which Eaton envisioned as an American version of Westminster Abbey, were interred Gutzum Borglum, creator of Mount Rushmore, and Carrie Jacobs Bond, whose song "The End of the Day" was such a favorite with the Folks. From the business world came (or were soon to come) King Gillette, inventor of the safety razor; William Peet, founder of Colgate-Palmolive-Peet; Charles Webber Buck, founder of Pet Milk; John Luther Maddux, founder of Maddux Airlines. Here were Charles Nash, who manufactured the Nash automobile, and William Mulholland, who brought water to the city from the Owens Valley, and E. F. Scattergood, who brought hydro-electricity. Here were Joseph Strauss, catalyst behind the Golden Gate Bridge, and John Hix, cartoonist and creator of *Strange as It Seems*. Comedian Joe Penner, now silent, no longer amused one and all with the query "Want to buy a duck?" Aimee Semple Macpherson no longer preached. Irving Thalberg, crown prince of Hollywood, lay in a splendid mausoleum as befitted his rank. (Eaton would later open Mount Sinai in the Hollywood Hills for his Jewish clientele, if they preferred a separate interment.) Elsewhere throughout Forest Lawn were (or were soon to be) many of those—Jean Harlow, Marie Dressler, W. C. Fields, Warner Baxter, Flo Ziegfeld, Alexander Pantages, Earl Carroll, Jean Hersholt—who had shared Thalberg's Hollywood. In 1945 Theodore Dreiser arrived, another Midwesterner dying in Los Angeles, author of sprawling novels of aspiration and defeat in the great cities of mid-America, in whose ranks Los Angeles, by 1940, believed itself to have arrived.

Over at Pershing Square, by contrast, the atmosphere was decidedly less somber; for here the people of the city, the Folks, yet remained on the earthly side of the Forest Lawn experience. For Carey McWilliams the crowds in Pershing Square epitomized the eclectic, democratic, thoroughly eccentric nature of the City of Angels. For the rest of his life McWilliams would remember the first time he truly considered himself a Los Angeleno. It was like St. Paul being struck on the road to Damascus.

> My feeling about this weirdly inflated village in which I had come to make my home (haunted by memories of a boyhood spent in the beautiful mountain parks, the timber-line country, of northwestern Colorado), suddenly changed after I had lived in Los Angeles for seven long years of exile. I have never been able to discover any apparent reason for this swift and startling conversion, but I do associate it with a particular occasion. I had spent an extremely active evening in Hollywood and had been deposited toward morning, by some kind soul, in a room at the Biltmore Hotel. Emerging next day from the hotel into the painfully bright sunlight, I started the rocky pilgrimage through Pershing Square to my office in a state of miserable decrepitude. In front of the hotel newsboys were shouting the headlines of the hour: an awful trunk-murder had just been committed; the district attorney had been indicted for bribery; Aimee Semple McPherson had once again stood the town on its ear by some spectacular caper; a University of Southern California football star had been caught robbing a bank; a love-mart had been discovered in the Los Feliz Hills; a motion-picture producer had just wired the Egyptian government a fancy offer for permission to illuminate the pyramids to advertise a forthcoming production; and, in the intervals between these revelations, there was news about another prophet, fresh from the desert, who had predicted the doom of the city, a prediction for which I was morbidly grateful. In the center of the park I stopped to watch, a little self-conscious of my evening clothes, a typical Pershing Square divertissement: an aged and frowsy blonde, skirts held high above her knees, cheered by a crowd of grimacing and leering old goats, was singing a gospel hymn as she danced gaily around the fountain. Then it suddenly occurred to me that, in all the world, there neither was nor would there ever be another place like this City of the Angels. Here the American people were erupting, like lava from a volcano; here, indeed, was the place for me—a ringside seat at the circus.[28]

Carey McWilliams's testimony is today set in concrete on a half wall running through Pershing Square. The volcano that is Los Angeles is still erupting.

III

REFRACTIONS

7

An All-Seeing Eye

Edward Weston, Ansel Adams, and the Landscape of California

*I*N the fall of 1932, a coterie of Bay Area photographers were intermittently gathering for wine and conversation at the Berkeley home of Willard Van Dyke. The circle included photographers in various stages of development. Henry Swift, Sonya Noskowiak, Preston Holder, John Paul Edwards, and Ansel Adams were at the beginning of their careers. Imogen Cunningham, by contrast, nearing fifty, enjoyed an established reputation. Under the influence of the best-known member of the group, Edward Weston, then in his mid-forties, Cunningham was making the transition from Pictorialism to a sharper, more realistic style. Cunningham's transition emphasized what had brought the entire group together in the first place: a determination to practice photography as autonomous art form. Up to now, the group agreed, photography had not fully liberated itself from the intellectual and aesthetic dominance of painting and literature: a control quite evident in the soft-focus, narrative-dominated Pictorialist style. Even the Photo-Secessionism practiced by Alfred Stieglitz, Edward Steichen, and the other photographers gathered around An American Place Gallery in New York, so the Berkeley gathering argued, had not completely established photography as an art form ontologically distinct from the other arts. As a matter of theory as well as practice, photography yet awaited its liberation.

Whether or not the Berkeley group was totally accurate in its assessment, the photographers meeting at Van Dyke's home had a point. Mathew Brady and Timothy O'Sullivan, for example, had documented the Civil War in such a way as to show the powers of the new medium; yet even Brady and O'Sullivan took many of their photographs with literary and painting references in mind and were known, on occasion, to stage their shots. The Photo-Secessionism led by Stieglitz and Steichen was a step in the right direction, but it had not gone far enough. Photography, it was felt, should not be in the business of posing or rearranging reality to fit formalist criteria of pattern and design, much less shape itself according to the aesthetic standards and intellectual content of other art forms. As technology and as art, photography should be a pure moment of existence, a pure act of sight, spontaneous and unstaged. Photography should place no big metaphor, no grand idea, between the seer and the seen.

Like all such groups, the Berkeley circle needed a name, a manifesto, and an exhibition. Preston Holder suggested that the group call itself US 256 in honor of the small lens aperture many were using to achieve greater sharpness and depth. Ansel Adams liked the idea but said that US 256 sounded too much like a highway. Grabbing a pencil, Adams sketched f/64, the designation that was replacing US 256 in the new terminology. Adams elongated the f and gave it a generous curve. The group now had a name, Group f/64, chosen in honor of the lens opening that provides the greatest depth and precision of line and detail.

Hearing of Group f/64, Lloyd Rollins, director of the M. H. de Young Memorial Museum in San Francisco, offered an exhibition, which ran from 15 November to 31 December 1932. Eighty photographs were displayed, most of them selling for $10, with Weston charging $15 per print. By the opening of the show, Group f/64 had polished and printed its manifesto. The group, thundered the manifesto (all manifestos have a way of thundering), believed "that photography, as an art form, must develop along lines defined by the actualities and limitations of the photographic medium, and must always remain independent of ideological conventions of art and aesthetics that are reminiscent of a period and culture antedating the growth of the medium itself."[1]

As a formal organization, Group f/64 lasted only a year or so. Yet the idea it introduced into photography—that photography should have no idea except the idea of itself—has earned for the group perpetual mention in histories of the medium. Was it a California idea? Yes and no. On the one hand, Group f/64 was linked to photographic trends in Europe and elsewhere in the United States. In his studio in Taos, New Mexico, for example, Paul Strand was producing lean and modernist prints, documentary in impulse, closely allied to the theory and practice of Group f/64; indeed, it was the personal influence of Strand that persuaded Ansel Adams to devote himself to photography rather than to the concert piano. On the other hand, California was not irrelevant to Group f/64 either as an artistic environment or as subject matter. From the nineteenth century, photography, as represented by Eadweard Muybridge and Carleton Watkins most notably, had remained the preeminent art form of the state. From the beginning, seeing California, truly seeing it, as natural and man-made environment, had been the special prerogative of the photographer. Such photography as Group f/64 called for, moreover, swift and spontaneous, implied a relationship to an environment in which there was much to photograph: a relationship that by the 1930s, after eighty years of photography, had become a flourishing regional tradition.

The English-born, San Francisco–based Eadweard Muybridge was the most technically inventive of the pioneer photographers; indeed, photographic experiments by Muybridge on the Palo Alto farm of Leland Stanford, subsequently published in *The Horse in Motion* (1882), assisted in the evolution of the motion picture camera. But it was Carleton Watkins, a New Yorker based in San Francisco since the 1850s, who forged the most direct and immediate relationship between California and the camera. Arriving in San Francisco in 1851, Watkins moved to Sacramento and clerked in a store owned by Collis P. Huntington, subsequently one of the Big Four. Around 1854, Watkins, who possessed no special educational or technical background, became interested in photography, seeing in the medium the possibilities of a more profitable livelihood than clerking. Returning to San Francisco, Watkins opened the Yosemite Art Gallery and began a photographic career that would produce by the early 1900s, in both the Old and New Series, an epic of documentation that continues to astonish photo-historians with the diversity and power of its images. An indifferent businessman, Watkins lost control of the Yosemite Art Gallery and most of his negatives to I. W. Taber in 1876. Taber printed many of Watkins's negatives as his own. Photographs taken by Watkins before he lost the Yosemite Gallery constitute the Old Series of his work; those taken after 1876 constitute the New Series. Up to 1883, Watkins employed a wet-plate process. After 1883, he used factory-prepared dry-plate negatives, although he occasionally returned to wet plates.

Although Carleton Watkins practiced photography as a fine art, he did not regard himself as an artist, which is to say, a man apart. Watkins saw himself, rather, as an artisan, a mechanic, as the nineteenth century described men who worked with their hands. Like Walt Whitman, whom he came to resemble in his person, Watkins saw value and beauty everywhere. A market-driven commercial photographer, he took his subjects as they came to him. His clients, hence his photographs, reflected California in every aspect of its existence, natural and man-made. Watkins did a bread-and-butter business as a portrait photographer, for instance, and in the course of such work became the most accomplished portrait photographer in the state. Even his passport photographs were works of art. When dignitaries passed through San Francisco—a nobleman from Korea, Professor Louis Agassiz of Harvard—it became almost a matter of protocol for them to stop by the Yosemite Gallery and be photographed.

Watkins's first big commission came in 1858: the photographing of the Guadalupe Quicksilver Mine in New Almaden for evidence in one of the most protracted court cases of mid-nineteenth-century California. Other commissions afforded Watson the opportunity of documenting for the first time the factories and industrial machinery of California, Nevada, and the Far West: the lumber mills of the North Coast, with their raft-palisades of logs, their fierce cutting machinery; the hydraulic mines at Malakoff Diggings in Nevada County, with gigantic hoses washing away entire mountainsides. And the workers as well: standing before the camera, sweat-stained faces and drooping mustaches, as only Walt Whitman might imagine them. Allied to this industrial photography was Watkins's growing portfolio in the documentation of public works: a flume in Nevada County, photographed sometime between 1869 and 1871, soaring across a wilderness declivity with Gothic elegance; Golden Gate Dam on the Feather River in Butte County, photographed in 1891, solid and workmanlike, the perfect image of a society creating itself through irrigation and agriculture. As agriculture replaced mining as the lead element in the California economy, Watkins documented that process as well: the Pasadena Citrus Fair of March 1880, the nearby Sunny Slope Winery that same year; haying time in the sweeping fields of Buena Vista Farm, Kern County, in 1887 or 1888. Some of the photographs done by Watkins in 1888 for the Kern County Land Company—rows of cheeses drying in their racks, a close-up of a box of cling peaches—show a formalism, a regard for pattern, verging on the abstract.

Wilderness and the man-made environment provided Watkins a means of making a living, which in his case nearly always resulted in important work. Watkins pioneered the photographing of the Yosemite and remains its master. He photographed the wild rivers of the north. He captured the clusters of sea lions clinging to the edge of Sugar Loaf Island in the Farallones, this in 1868, and the great waves breaking, this in 1883, against the Santa Cruz shore. As a photographer of nature, Watkins seems to us today to have been seeing California for the first time, hence pioneering the emergence of fixed reference points in the landscape. In April 1885, for example, he photographed a solitary Monterey cypress on Cypress Point in present-day Pebble Beach. This image, a cypress tree poised against the sea and the horizon, was destined to become one of the most repeated icons in the visual vocabulary of California.

More than any other photographer, Watkins documented the rise of nineteenth-century San Francisco. In 1858 he photographed Washerwoman's Bay, subsequently filled for the Panama-Pacific International Exposition of 1915, and today the seismically volatile Marina district. Catching the juxtaposition of bay, lagoons, wetlands, dry lands, and scratchy settlements, Watkins created a stunning evocation of the beginnings of urbanism in this part of the San Francisco peninsula. By 1864 the overnight city was complete, and Watkins created a five-part panorama of the city: its church spires and brick warehouses, its elegant private homes, the straight streets of Jasper O'Farrell's 1847 grid marching up and down the hills, the mass of ships in the Bay. Watkins could do urban action scenes as well: a pro-Union gathering at the corner of Post and Market streets in 1861; the firing of cannons in the Presidio by blue-coated artillerymen in 1876. When the Viscata washed ashore on Baker Beach in 1868, Watkins photographed it for insurance purposes, and the resulting albumen silver print remains his masterpiece.

In 1864 Watkins photographed the new First Unitarian Church in San Francisco, built under the leadership of its pastor Thomas Starr King, a photograph that inaugurated architectural photography on the West Coast. Merely by being so powerfully and directly present, the Gothic Revival structure bespeaks the hunger for urbanism at the core of the San Francisco identity. In the years that followed, when newly rich plutocrats wished their estates recorded for reasons of insurance and for more subliminal purposes, they turned to Watkins. The resulting images—ornate reception halls, book-lined studies, dining rooms, and gardens—established Watkins as a pioneer of the interior photograph. He photographed the interior of his own studio at 427 Montgomery Street. His children Collis and Julia stand in the doorway. Julia's doll sits by the door, as if posing for the camera: this in 1884, a rare instance of a candid interior domestic photograph from nineteenth-century San Francisco. It was Watkins, moreover, who pioneered photographing the surviving missions, beginning this in 1880 with views of Mission San Carlos de Carmelo and San Juan Capistrano, each of them in ruins, awaiting the renovations and restorations that would come fifteen to twenty years in the future.

More subtly, Watkins documented the social fabric of California, unobtrusively, indirectly, by suggestion. Capturing the managing owner, the superintendent, the engineer, the tenant, the clerk, and the Chinese cook together on the porch of the Poso Ranch in Kern County in 1888, he managed to suggest the social structure of ranch life in late nineteenth-century California. Twenty years before Arnold Genthe, Watkins photographed the Chinese in a spirit of respect and dignity. A Chinese family poses for Watkins in Monterey in 1883, not as strangers or exotics, but as Californians of a slightly different sort, as a family, as human beings. There is an ambition, an inclusiveness, in Watkins that contrasts dramatically with the California painters of the period, riveted as they were to landscape. Without Watkins, there would have been little visual testimony to the panorama of frontier and provincial California, its people and buildings, its machinery and interiors, as well as its landscape.

As extraordinary as his achievement is known to be, however, it was most likely even more impressive in actual fact. We can only guess. In April 1906 the fire following the earthquake destroyed Watkins's studio. Thousands of negatives were lost. An old man, Watkins had to be led, dazed, from his burning studio. A newspaper photographer captured this tragic moment. By this time, Watkins had already lost most of his eyesight. He retired to a small ranch given to him by Collis P. Huntington. In 1910 Watkins's family had him committed to the Napa State Hospital for the Insane, where he lived out the remaining six years of his life.

A lowly but popular medium, the tinted photographic postcard, was in the early 1900s humbly but effectively carrying on the task of seeing California first begun by Carleton Watkins. Not that tinted photographic postcards achieved the artistic levels of Watkins's work. They did not. But they did carry on the visual documentation of California and its rapidly developing social environment. There is virtually no place in California, no city or town, no institution or industry, from 1900 to 1930 that did not receive postcard documentation. Taken cumulatively, these thousands of images, carefully preserved in research libraries, constitute an informal but encompassing photo-inventory. Only recently have these postcards been analyzed, not just in terms of their commercial intent—the resort hotel to be publicized, the subdivision to be sold—but in terms of the social values, myths even, that structured the manner in which Americans perceived California on the national level. These postcards, it must be remembered, were primarily intended to be sent outside the state; hence they functioned as a form of advertisement and definition, describing to non-Californians in the most attractive imagery possible the idealized realities and possibilities of the emergent American commonwealth.

The primary intent and concern of postcards was tourism and leisure, so evident in the multiple images of yachting, beach life, fishing, skiing, tennis, golf, polo, and other outdoor activities. Tourism, after all, remained the second industry in Southern California, after agriculture, through the 1920s. Agriculture itself—orange groves in blossom, date palms, orchards of plum and pear, oversized fruits and vegetables on display at county fairs—follows a close second to tourism as a theme, followed in turn, as might be expected, by real estate development, perceived in terms of bungalows and gardens, garden suburbs, and emergent towns in the interior, all of them inviting non-Californians to consider a move to the Golden State. Even industrial development received its postcard testimony, with the great oil derricks of the Southland receiving their fair share of attention. The entertainment industry—studios, broadcast centers, theaters, the homes of the stars—pushed forward to dominance after 1929. As war approached in the late 1930s, postcards began to emphasize scenes of military life and the defense industry, especially in San Diego: a PBY in flight over the city, recruits standing inspection at the Naval Training Station, ships of the Pacific Fleet.

Year by year the rise of Los Angeles was chronicled, until a full and complete inventory was available by 1940: Union Station, Angel's Flight, the Central Library, Angelus Temple, Bullock's Wilshire, the Coliseum, the Hollywood Bowl, Santa Anita Race Track, Forest Lawn, the Huntington Library, the Bel Air Country Club, the new UCLA campus, Mulholland Drive curving its way atop the Santa Monica Mountains. Nor are such scenes and places statically presented. It is surprising, in fact, how much social history found its way into postcard presentation: innumerable scenes of Californians at the beach (the beach, in fact, was the leading theme of all postcards), Californians strolling at the seaside, Californians seated in restaurants, Californians dancing in pavilions, gardening in their backyards, streaming toward the Rose Bowl on New Year's Day, touring the state in shiny new automobiles. All this was intended as promotion, of course, but it also chronicled an idealized reality that became a fixed part of the cumulative California image. Through the tinted postcard photographs, millions of Americans saw California for the first time and liked what they saw.

Seeing California was far from the mind of Edward Weston as he built his photographic practice in Tropico (later Glendale) between 1914 and 1917. Born in Highland Park, Illinois, in 1886, Weston had been taking photographs since 1902, when his father presented him with a Kodak Bull's Eye #2. The Westons were Maine people, the first generation not to be living Down East in more than two centuries. With a certain dour Maine practicality, Weston left high school at sixteen and went to work as an errand boy for Marshall Field and Company. In 1906 he visited his married sister Mary, whom he adored, in Tropico and fell in love, simultaneously, with this orange grove–carpeted suburb and Mary's good friend Flora May Chandler, a schoolteacher, whom he married in 1909.

On his first visit to Tropico, Weston started an informal door-to-door photography business—babies, pets, family groups, weddings, funerals—which he formally established after his marriage. The father of four sons by 1919, Weston followed the conventional career of a portrait photographer: flattering his clients via a soft-focus Verito lens, so adept at eliminating wrinkles, arranging a chiffon this way or that, turning his subject ever so cunningly at an angle to conceal portliness or a double chin. The outdoor photographs he did for his own satisfaction were Whistlerian in inspiration: hazy, dreamy, Pictorial, drenched in *japonisme*. Weston did a thriving business for his non-portrait photographs, still lifes and garden scenes among the Japanese of Little Tokyo. In 1917 he was invited to membership in the London Salon of Photography, the most prestigious peer group in Pictorial circles.

Viewing the work of contemporary painters at the Panama-Pacific International Exposition, Weston began to have doubts about himself as a photographer. He was successful, to be sure; but his work lacked the boldness, the directness, of contemporary European and American art in the avant-garde now on exhibition in San Francisco. Ceasing to exhibit with commercial and Pictorial associations, Weston began to experiment with a more abstract mode of photography, with unusual angles and lightings, with nudes and faces perceived as fragments. Straying from the domestic hearth, he moved in bohemian circles and acquired a lover, the Italian actress Tina Modotti, who brought some of Weston's experimental images to Mexico City, where they were appreciated by Diego Rivera and David Alfaro Siqueiros.

In July 1923 Weston, aged thirty-seven, made the big break—from Glendale, from Pictorialism, from his wife—and sailed from Los Angeles to Mexico with Modotti and his oldest son, Chandler. Established first in Tacubaya, then in Mexico City, Weston spent the next three years, with the exception of a six-month stay in San Francisco in 1925, at the vital center of the Mexican Renaissance, whose artists and intellectuals considered Weston their *gringo compadre*. As a place, a community, an occasion for photographic practice, Mexico grounded Edward Weston in the simple, the direct, the elemental. He continued to do portraits to support himself, only now they were taken rapidly, with no posing, since Weston could barely communicate with his subjects in his halting Spanish. In the countryside, he photographed peasants with equal spontaneity. He photographed the towns and marketplaces. He turned his camera to cacti, trees, and rocks, to the awesome landscapes in the distance, the great sky overhead. During his second sojourn he traveled with Tina and his son Brett, even then developing as his father's apprentice and artistic near-equal, photographing the remote regions and archeological sites for a book on pre-Columbian Mexico.

In November 1926, having broken with Modotti, Weston returned to Glendale, partially by default. Having abandoned his prosperous practice, he was reduced to photographing high school graduation classes and Mexican laborers in their coffins. Yet Mexico had changed him forever. He was now an artist, obsessed, as Rivera said of him, with a new way of seeing. What to see became the question. Nudes, shells, vegetables, rocks, trees, and, finally, California emerged as the answer.

A wit among photography critics once wrote that Edward Weston wanted his nudes to look like bell peppers and his bell peppers to look like nudes. Certainly, in each instance, and in the case of his equally well known sea shells, Weston was searching for interconnected patterns in differing life forms. Such similarities of line and form afforded Weston the opportunity to establish cross-references in the organic world that asserted the interconnectedness and interdependence, the web, of organic life. From this perspective, nudes and bell peppers have much in common. Yet Weston insisted that his nudes were not intentionally erotic, despite the fact that he was sexually involved with the subjects of his most successful nudes: his student and business partner Margarethe Mather, the actress Tina Modotti, and Charis Wilson of Carmel. For Weston, a sexual encounter functioned as an almost inevitable part of the photographic process. On the other hand, there is much to justify Weston's assertions. So many of his nudes approach a coolness, a formalism, that belies Kenneth Clark's assertion that all successful nudes must contain within themselves some element of erotic feeling. Weston's bell peppers, on the other hand, which could very well have remained serene studies of volume, organic form, and texture, have frequently been seen by critics as Freudian eruptions from Weston's over-charged libido: fifty studies, it has been claimed, of male and female parts masquerading as bell peppers.

Completing his bell pepper and sea shell series by the late 1920s, Weston returned to outdoor subjects in 1928. He photographed the Mojave Desert, followed by close-up encounters with the rocks and trees of Southern California. Not until Weston moved to Carmel in 1929, however, did his effort to see California move into high gear. For so many poseurs of the period, Carmel offered a way of dropping out, of avoiding the issue, of living an artistic lifestyle whether or not one produced art. For Weston, Carmel soon became, as it had for his friend Robinson Jeffers, more than a place to live or even more than a place to live and work. Carmel—Point Lobos, the rocky beaches awash in kelp edging south to Big Sur, the cypress trees, the fog and the sunlight—became one unified force field of being and seeing, one amalgam of existence and sight. In Carmel, Edward Weston achieved by the late 1930s a lifestyle and an art that linked California to the Zen Buddhist cultures of Japan, China, and Tibet: a linkage that would have profound influence on the aesthetics of Northern California in the second half of the twentieth century.

Rediscovering the desert, Americans rediscovered a new connection to California as resort. Palm Springs, late afternoon, winter, the mid-1930s: guests of the Desert Inn take their ease on the patio, awaiting a purple twilight. *Security Pacific Collection, Los Angeles Public Library; Harry Wissig, photographer.*

Events of the day might have included a morning horseback or stagecoach ride, followed by luncheon served from a chuck wagon. The admixture of Western- and Eastern-style riding clothes bespeaks Palm Springs as a national resort. *Security Pacific Collection, Los Angeles Public Library.*

(Above) Or perhaps there was a midday round of golf at the Desert Golf Course. By the mid-1930s, the game of golf, like so much else in California, was evolving from an elite to a more democratic pastime. *Security Pacific Collection, Los Angeles Public Library.*

(Below) Swimming and competitive diving, also Palm Springs favorites, enjoyed here at the El Mirador Hotel, were also increasingly characteristic of popular California life. A lifestyle was taking shape that, following World War II, would be exported to the rest of the nation. *Whittington Collection, University of Southern California Library.*

(*Above*) Even the sun tan was being democratized, although this guest, availing herself of the solarium services at El Mirador, was experiencing a more pampered style of defying the winter. Once the sign of outdoor work, hence low status, the sun tan now bespoke the glamour of California, increasingly available to everyone. *Whittington Collection, University of Southern California Library.*

(*Right*) Take barbecuing as an example. In an earlier era, outdoor barbecuing bespoke the ranch elite, successors to the dons of Old California. Now *Sunset*, the magazine of western living, was urging the middle classes to build barbecues in their backyards as centers for socializing and signs of suburban identity. *California State Library.*

Key to this expanded lifestyle was the automobile. By the late 1930s, in the City of Los Angeles, there were 124 cars to every 100 families. On Sundays, many of these automobiles could be found in Palm Springs. *Whittington Collection, University of Southern California Library.*

To service the automobilization of California, an entire subculture soon arose whose central institution was the gas station. Here at the concrete and tile California Petroleum service station in Los Angeles, uniformed attendants in para-military attire await their customers. *California State Library.*

Equally attentive are the car-hops at the McDonnell's Ever Eat drive-in restaurant in Los Angeles. Self-employed entrepreneurs, car-hops, a new variety of the Southern California girl, made their living on tips and the price differential between what the customers paid them and what they paid the drive-in. *California State Library.*

Because so many of its citizens were moving by so swiftly in automobiles, Southern California buildings were required to identify themselves unambiguously at a distance. No passing driver, for example, would misread the services of the Ben-Hur Coffee Shop. *California State Library.*

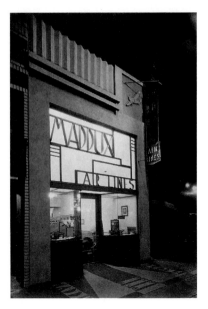

(Left) Likewise did the Villa Riviera at Long Beach announce a bold and clear message. The New York- and Chicago-style apartment building had arrived in the Southland. *California State Library. (Right)* The Los Angeles-based Maddux Air Lines was by the early 1930s offering service to a number of West Coast cities. By the end of the decade, thanks to air travel, a bi-coastal lifestyle had become available to the favored few, most of them in show business. *California State Library.*

At the opening of the 1935 Bohemian Grove Encampment were, among others, architects Timothy Pflueger (*fourth from left*) and Bernard Maybeck (*eleventh from left, in knicker-bockers*), the diminutive gentleman of leisure J. Downey Harvey (*center, in flowing cravat*), and, next to Harvey, sculptor Haig Patigian (*in dark suit*), twice president of the Club. Illustrated by the cartoon above the bar, the Grove Play that year was a medieval allegory, *The Quest. California State Library; Gabriel Moulin, photographer.*

(*Left*) By the late 1920s astronomer George Ellery Hale (*left*), chemist Arthur Noyes (*center*), and Nobel physicist Robert Millikan were presiding over an important new American research institution, the California Institute of Technology in Pasadena. Thanks to Cal Tech, Pasadena had become a regional capital of the national scientific establishment. *The Archives, California Institute of Technology.*

(*Below*) Challenged by the observations and theories of Cal Tech scientists Edward Hubble and Richard Chase Tolman, Albert Einstein, a Visiting Fellow at Cal Tech during the winter of 1931, modified his notions regarding the expanding universe. Einstein also avoided the winter cold of Oxford in favor of the Southern California sunshine. *The Archives, California Institute of Technology.*

On 31 January 1931, Einstein and Charles Chaplin attended the premiere of Chaplin's new film, *City Lights*, which also marked the opening of the spectacular new Los Angeles Theater at 615 South Broadway. A line of shabby men stood across the street, hooting at and booing the celebrities in black tie as they entered the theater. *The Archives, California Institute of Technology.*

When sailors were quartered during the Great War in the neo-Spanish Colonial quadrangles of the Panama-California International Exposition in Balboa Park, three civic ambitions coalesced: San Diego as American capital of the Southwest, as first Pacific port of call north of the newly opened Panama Canal, and as Gibraltar of the Pacific. *California State Library.*

The arrival of the Pacific Fleet in San Diego in June 1935–the single largest assembly of warships in American history–confirmed San Diego's new identity as the naval capital of the nation. Backed by his aides and a delegation of officers and men from the fleet, Admiral Joseph Reeves welcomed San Diego into the Navy. *San Diego Historical Society.*

Sailors of the Pacific Fleet soon discovered that San Diego was a good liberty town. The show girls at the Le Moulin Rouge cabaret review in Balboa Park, for example, were quite generous in posing for photographs after the show. *San Diego Historical Society.*

(*Above, left*) *Angel's Flight* (1931) by Millard Sheets brought the sensibilities and purposes of the American Scene art movement to Bunker Hill, Los Angeles. Here was Social Realism without the squalor. Here was a newly recognized American city and the people who made it work. *Los Angeles County Museum of Art; gift of Mrs. L. M. Maitland.*

(*Above, right*) As far as work was concerned, Bunker Hill resident John Fante, an aspiring novelist, squeaked through 1933 working as a bus boy. Like Arturo Bandini, Fante's fictional protagonist and alter ego, the twenty-two-year-old would-be novelist was hungry for life and the city. *Hearst Newspaper Collection, University of Southern California Library.*

Some of the glamour and good times Bandini sought might be found at Frank Sebastian's Cotton Club in Culver City, where Don Herriford and his orchestra and other African-American entertainers played to a mixed black and white audience. An increasingly Jim Crow town, after all, needed some relief from apartheid. *Security Pacific Collection, Los Angeles Public Library.*

(*Above, left*) Los Angeles was corrupt to the core and required reformation, thundered Clifford Clinton, cafeteria magnate turned Savonarola of the Southland. On the night of 28 October 1937, Clinton's home at 5470 Los Feliz Boulevard was bombed by unknown assailants. *Herald Examiner Collection, Los Angeles Public Library.*

(*Above, right*) Bombs, cops, gambling joints, politicians on the take: the revelations of Clifford Clinton read like a novel by Raymond Chandler, prose-poet laureate of LA *noir*. Chandler's Los Angeles was a city of imagination as well as fact, the one reinforcing the other. *Hearst Newspaper Collection, University of Southern California Library.*

(*Left*) Photographing Charis Wilson at Lake Ediza in the Sierra Nevada in July 1937, Edward Weston achieved a portrait which, like his similarly unrehearsed portrait of Robinson Jeffers, was destined to survive as an enduring icon of California identity. Flesh against stone, beauty pervaded by forceful strength, female triumphant, Charis emanates the mysterious power of California itself. *Charis, Lake Ediza 1937, photograph by Edward Weston;* © *1981 Center for Creative Photography, Arizona Board of Regents.*

(Above, left) Tor House, Carmel, the late 1930s: patron of the arts Albert (Mickey) Bender pays a call on poet Robinson Jeffers. Progressively disturbed by events in Europe, Jeffers is meditating a series of isolationist jeremiads, brooding and prophetic, which would endanger his reputation after Pearl Harbor. *California State Library*.

(Above, right) A veteran of the first Old Left, still traumatized by the carnage of the Great War, Charles Erskine Scott Wood shared Robinson Jeffers's apprehensions. Once again, violence was threatening to engulf the planet. Best to retreat to The Cats, a thirty-acre hillside estate in Los Gatos; and there, in the company of one's wife and circle of friends, await a better day. *California State Library*.

The French Riviera, sometime in the late 1930s: Heinrich Mann and his soon-to-be-wife Nelly enjoy the good life at the seaside resort of Sanary-sur-Mer, where many members of the anti-Nazi intelligentsia have taken refuge. If one has to be in exile, Sanary-sur-mer is not such a bad place. It is, in fact, a sort of training ground for Southern California. *Feuchtwanger Memorial Library, University of Southern California Library*.

With the establishment of Vichy France, however, Sanary-sur-Mer proved as dangerous as any place in the Third Reich for dissidents such as the exiled German Jewish novelist Lion Feuchtwanger. After seeing this photograph, Eleanor Roosevelt helped arrange Feuchtwanger's escape to Southern California. Millions of others were not so fortunate. *Feuchtwanger Memorial Library, University of Southern California Library.*

Back in San Francisco, on 5 December 1940, muralist Diego Rivera and painter Frida Kahlo, having decided to give their dissolved marriage one more try, applied for a second marriage license. In the face of the impending world conflict, Rivera was creating for the Golden Gate International Exposition on Treasure Island a mural extolling Pan-American unity. *San Francisco Public Library.*

Like Lion Feuchtwanger (*left*), playwright Bertolt Brecht also made it to the safety of Southern California. All German letters had migrated to the Southland, claimed Thomas Mann. Throughout the winter of 1942–1943, Brecht and Feuchtwanger collaborated on a play centered on a Joan of Arc-like heroine in the French Resistance. *Feuchtwanger Memorial Library, University of Southern California Library.*

The Brecht-Feuchtwanger collaboration collapsed because the authors could not agree on the exact identity of the Joan of Arc figure. It remained for another émigré, Franz Werfel, successfully to evoke the visionary heroine representing a better Europe. Sitting in his sunny Los Angeles garden, Werfel meditated a novel set in the heart of a Catholic Europe now betraying itself. *Library, University of California at Los Angeles.*

(Above, left) Lecturing at Harvard when war broke out, Igor Stravinsky settled in Hollywood. For Stravinsky, the exile of the war years would witness an astonishing burst of creativity and audience appreciation. Between 1940 and 1945, Stravinsky completed two symphonies, a concerto, a mass, an opera, film scores and other incidental music, and a circus ballet for elephants. *Hearst Newspaper Collection, University of Southern California Library.*

(Above, right) Arnold Schoenberg, by contrast, professor of music at UCLA, found it more difficult than Stravinsky to adjust himself to Southern Californian circumstances. Except for tennis! Schoenberg played the game with total dedication and some skill. *Archives of the Arnold Schoenberg Institute, Los Angeles.*

Very soon, émigrés such as Katia and Thomas Mann of Pacific Palisades found themselves even further linked to Southern California by their American-born or Americanized children and grandchildren. Seated on their lawn beneath the palm trees, the Manns point their American-born grandsons Anthony (Toni) and Fridolin (Frido) towards the camera. *Feuchtwanger Memorial Library, University of Southern California Library.*

(*Above, left*) San Francisco, 14 January 1942: dancer-singer Jessie Tai Sing, singer Tony Martin, on active duty as a chief petty officer, and Charlie Low, owner of the Forbidden City nightclub, announce a $10 per plate champagne dinner to benefit the Red Cross. Throughout the war, Low's Forbidden City served as the crossroads and rendezvous in San Francisco for old and new Asia hands. *San Francisco Public Library.*

(*Above, right*) Entertaining the troops in North Africa and the war zones of western Europe, Marlene Dietrich, traveling with the honorary rank of colonel, brought the spirit of a better Berlin, via Hollywood, to American troops and her homeland. For the past two decades, the best of Berlin had been migrating to Southern California. With Dietrich on tour, pre-Nazi Berlin made a triumphant return. *Hearst Newspaper Collection, University of Southern California Library.*

Emerging from hiding just outside Oroville, a mining town on the Feather River in Butte County, in August 1911, Ishi, last of the Yahi, offers in retrospect a chilling paradigm of the extermination of peoples that would preoccupy so much of the twentieth century. Ishi survived genocide and prevailed in body and spirit. Mastering his culture, knowing who he was, Ishi became an avatar of enduring human value. *California State Library.*

In 1903 Arnold Genthe became the first notable photographer to move to Carmel. Genthe built a redwood bungalow and experimented in color. Weston's San Francisco partner Johan Hagemeyer spent the year 1924 in Carmel, then subsequently divided his time between Carmel and San Francisco. Toward the end of 1928, Hagemeyer persuaded Weston that Carmel would be the best place for him to live and work. Hagemeyer agreed to rent to Weston his studio cottage there until Weston could get established. Also living in Carmel was photographer Roger Sturtevant, who like Weston was searching for a more simple and direct style of photography. Moving to Carmel, Weston placed a sign reading UNRETOUCHED PORTRAITS outside his studio.

The simplicity and uncrowdedness of Carmel immediately appealed to Weston, speaking as they did to his Down East heritage. Comparisons between Carmel and Maine were easy to come by for someone only one generation removed from a two-hundred-year legacy of life on the Maine coast. For years, Weston had been keeping a daybook, writing early each morning an hour before dawn in his large clear handwriting. The entries for March, April, May, and June of 1929 testify to the satisfactions of his new life. He spent the previous day at Big Sur, Weston noted on 2 March 1929, a day he should write in color and capitals, it was so exhilarating and productive. Weston spent a number of hours on Wednesday, 15 May 1929, photographing Robinson Jeffers in front of Tor House. It was a dull, overcast day, with flat light, and Jeffers was a little uneasy in front of the camera; yet when Weston later examined his negatives, he realized that gray days were better for photographing the Carmel poet. The resulting portrait—Jeffers in flannel jacket and open-necked shirt against the stones of Tor House, a steady gray light suffusing everything—is the most well known portrait Weston ever photographed. It also remains an enduring icon of California. Like all his photographs since Mexico, the Jeffers portrait was unretouched.

By early 1932 a psychological coherence arising from clarity of purpose and peace of mind, a sense of mission wedded to place, has entered Weston's daybooks. "Peace again!" he writes on 21 February 1931. "The exquisite hour before dawn, here at my old desk—seldom have I realized so keenly, appreciated so fully, these still, dark hours."[2] His hour of contemplation complete, Weston would be up and about two tasks, photography or the development of negatives. If at home, he would work steadily through the day, with time off for breakfast (cereal with honey, wheat germ, and milk), a mid-day meal (salad and cold vegetables), a nap, more work, then dinner (another salad accompanied by split pea, lentil, or lima bean soup, nuts and dates for dessert). A physical fitness advocate, Weston kept his five-foot-five frame lean and spare on a quasi-vegetarian diet and burned what calories he did consume on rugged photographic treks. With the exception of sexual activity, it was a life of monastic simplicity, albeit with no intention to convert anyone or serve in any way as a role model. "I am not a reformer, a missionary, a propagandist," he wrote in March 1931. "I have one clear way to give, to justify myself as part of the whole—through my work. Here in Carmel I can work, and from here I send out the best of my life, focused onto a few sheets of silvered paper."[3]

From the beginning, Weston kept a certain distance from the rest of Group f/64. He was older, for one thing, and as a photographer already more than half-way to the point they were only now beginning to seek. The images he had been photographing and printing in Carmel since 1929—the storm-twisted cypress trees atop Point Lobos, the tangled kelp on the shore, the scarred and eroded rocks, the salt pools, the skeleton of a pelican, gnarled and lined driftwood, coastal fog, the unretouched portraits of Jeffers and Mexican muralist José Clemente Orozco, who was passing through Carmel in 1930—more than met the criteria set forth in the Group f/64 manifesto. Yet Weston welcomed the companionship of the younger artists. "We are all friends," he noted in his daybook, "free from politics; and I have no desire to be the founder of a cult!"[4]

Among those younger artists was Ansel Adams, just turning thirty and destined to share with Weston high honors in the photographic Hall of Fame. Far from regarding Weston as a guru, or even a leader, Adams was already well launched into the creation of images that would equal Weston's work and, in the minds of some, surpass it in sweep and grandeur and ambition. Adams first met Weston in 1928 at a dinner at Albert Bender's studio apartment in San Francisco. Being shown some of Weston's prints after dinner at Bender's request, the twenty-six-year-old photographer and concert pianist was impressed by their seriousness of purpose but found them "hard and mannered." Later in the evening, Bender, an early patron of Adams, showed Weston some of Adams's prints from his collection. Examining them, Weston remained silent. After an embarrassing period of silence, Bender asked Adams to play the piano.[5]

In the ensuing three years, Ansel Adams struggled to appreciate the work of his older colleague. When Weston had a one-man show at the de Young Museum in 1931, Adams reviewed it for the *Fortnightly*, a San Francisco–based journal of the arts. Describing Weston as "a genius in his perception of simple, essential form," Adams went on to praise Weston's close-ups of rocks, trees, driftwood, household utensils, bell peppers, and female torsos. Yet the very precision of Weston's images, together with their extreme formalism, stood in contrast to the path upon which Adams himself had already embarked. By the time Group f/64 organized itself in 1932, Weston and Adams had formed the beginnings of a lifelong friendship. "We had both come to be sympathetic to each other's work," Adams later remembered, "though we were never on an identical wavelength."[6] How could they be? Edward Weston was small, tight, precise, skeptical, Carmel-based, increasingly reclusive in lifestyle, with photography and eroticism constituting his sole concerns. Ansel Adams, by contrast, was bear-like and gregarious, a lover of food and drink, a boon companion in a wide circle of friends, a faithful husband, a busy, busy man with multiple involvements in commercial and fine art photography, the museum world, the conservation movement, San Francisco and New York. Yet become friends they did. Despite their differences, they shared a common goal, the seeing of California.

Whereas Edward Weston had been forced to struggle to find himself, forced like Paul Gauguin to repudiate his bourgeois life and flee to a more primitive region, Ansel Adams emerged almost naturally from a supportive city, San Francisco, which had been profoundly shaped by the nature-mysticism of Swedenborgianism, by environmentalism, by science, and by photography. Born there in February 1902, Adams was raised in a Craftsman bungalow overlooking the Golden Gate, set amidst the sand dunes in what would soon be developed as the West Clay Park and Sea Cliff districts. The Adamses were affluent New Englanders, educated, Progressive, with a self-conscious relationship to Northern California as Outdoors, expressed most directly by their energetic membership in the Sierra Club. Largely tutored at home, Ansel Adams grew up in an atmosphere of books and music, sensitized to beauty by the daily drama of sunlight and fog, the ebbing and flowing of the Golden Gate strait, the hills of Marin in the distance, all this visible from his second-floor bedroom. On Baker Beach near his home, the seashore would glisten in the sunlight from the iron particles in the sand, and driftwood of every shape and size washed ashore. C. H. Adams, Ansel's father, was himself an excellent photographer and presented his son with a Kodak when Ansel was still a boy. By the time Ansel was fifteen, he had become an accomplished photographer, as early studies of the sand dunes at Baker Beach clearly show. There was a naturalness, a steady unfolding, to Ansel Adams's development, although he would remain through his twenties equally committed to photography and the concert piano. "I never went to war," he would later write, "too young for the First and too old for the Second. The great events of the world have been tragic pageants, not personal involvements. My world has been a world too few people are lucky enough to live in—one of peace and beauty. I believe in beauty. I believe in stones and water, air and soil, people and their future and their fate."[7]

Quite early, at age fourteen, on his first visit to Yosemite Valley, Ansel Adams found his special place. He photographed the Yosemite that first visit with his Box Brownie and upon his return to San Francisco apprenticed himself to a photofinisher so as to master the printing aspects of his craft. In 1919 the Sierra Club appointed Adams summer custodian of the LeConte Memorial in Yosemite, a position he held until 1927. He later became assistant manager for the annual Sierra Club treks, which in those days meant some two hundred people and a pack train of fifty or more mules spending a month in the wilderness, hiking and packing by day and gathering by night around great campfires for gourmet meals and organized entertainment: Bach's Double Violin Concerto, perhaps, played by Adams's friend Cedric Wright, another photographer-musician, and Wright's best violin pupil, Dorothy Minty; or a lecture on astronomy, with a sky full of stars overhead; or a performance, complete with impromptu costumes, of a mock Greek drama (*Exhaustos, The Trudjin' Women*) Adams had helped write.

In the summer of 1923, on a pack trip into the regions south of Mount Lyell, Adams took his first famous photograph, *Banner Peak and Thousand Island Lake*. Significantly, the experience was unrehearsed. Everything, Adams later remembered—rock, cloud, mountain, exposure—fell together in a most agreeable way. Four years later, hiking in Yosemite in the spring of 1927 with his fiancée Virginia Best and a few other friends, Adams coaxed to consciousness the process he was subconsciously mastering. Adams and Virginia climbed to the Diving Board, a slab of granite jutting from the west shoulder of Half Dome. Adams had only four plates left. He wasted the first plate by forgetting to shield his lens from the direct sun. He used the second plate to photograph Virginia standing on one of the thrusts of the Diving Board, surveying Mirror Lake below. After lunch, the couple waited for two hours for the sun to come into proper position. Here he was, face to face with Half Dome, waiting for the proper sunlight—and only two plates in his possession! At approximately two-thirty Adams set up his camera and began to compose in his mind the image he wanted: Half Dome, half in sunlight, half in shadow. Over his 8 ½-inch Zeiss Tessar lens, he placed a K2 yellow filter so as to darken the sky ever so slightly. He waited for the shadowing of Half Dome to reach the proper moment, then made his exposure. Even as he placed his fourth and final plate into the camera, Adams continued to visualize in his mind not the Half Dome before him, but the Half Dome he wished to photograph and print. In his mind's eye, he saw the brooding face of Half Dome, the dark sky, and Tenaya Peak, showy and sharp in the distance. Only a deep red filter, Adams decided, would bring him to the emotional effect he desired. Attaching his other filter, a Wratten #29(F), to the lens and increasing the exposure by a factor of sixteen as such a filter required, Adams released the shutter.

Even as he descended to the valley floor, he later remembered, "I felt I had accomplished something, but did not realize its significance until I developed the plate that evening. I had achieved my first true visualization! I had been able to realize a desired image: not the way the subject appeared in reality but how it *felt* to me and how it must appear in the finished print."[8] Visualization, as Adams later defined the term, involved the full and complete integration of the photographer, the object photographed, environmental conditions, and the photographer's visualization of a print he wished to see, together with his emotional response to that print. Guided by this visualization, judging conditions of light and shadow, the photographer chose the appropriate technology of lens and filter, sometimes almost simultaneously with the other judgments, waited—seconds, minutes, hours—then pulled the shutter.

Adams's stunning photographs of the High Sierra brought him to the attention of San Francisco patron Albert Bender, who purchased Adams's work and sponsored its publication in the portfolio *Parmelian Prints of the High Sierra* (1927), the first of Ansel Adams's many books. Bender also widened Adams' horizons, introducing him to Robinson and Una Jeffers in Carmel, taking him down to the art colony in Santa Fe, and bringing him into contact with the Mabel Dodge

Luhan circle in Taos. While in Taos, Adams photographed the images published in *Taos Pueblo* (1930), with text by Mary Austin. There he met photographer Paul Strand, and this meeting, over dinner with the Strands and Georgia O'Keeffe, followed by an afternoon examining Strand's negatives in his studio, turned him finally in the direction of photography over the concert stage. "I returned to San Francisco," Adams noted of this visit, "resolved that the camera, not the piano, would shape my destiny."[9]

Despite his mere thirty years, then, it was no aspiring amateur who joined Edward Weston in the Group f/64 circle in the fall of 1932. Already in Ansel Adams's portfolio were the best photographs of the High Sierra to be taken since Carleton Watkins, together with equally outstanding photographs from New Mexico. By then Adams was on retainer ($10 a day plus expenses, reduced to $5 in the worst of the Depression) to the Yosemite Park and Curry Company, which ran the Ahwahnee Hotel, Camp Curry, the Yosemite Lodge, and other tourist concessions in the Park. For the YPCC Adams produced a classic series of images promoting the Yosemite in season and out, images that made the distinction between fine and commercial art irrelevant. Shown to President Lincoln and members of the Congress in 1864, Carleton Watkins's photographs had helped get the Yosemite set aside as a federal preserve. Forty years later, John Muir had promoted knowledge of the Yosemite in his prose. Now, and for the next fifty years, Ansel Adams would send forth into the world thousands of images, many of them among the finest photographs ever taken, documenting the natural wonders of the valley and its hinterlands.

No wonder Ansel Adams became the chief spokesman for Group f/64! Among other things, he was the best-known photographer in the group and the most financially secure. At this point, 1933, the depth of the Depression, Ansel Adams forged a connection with New York that would soon make him one of the most respected photographers in the United States. Calling on Alfred Stieglitz at An American Place, Adams was welcomed into the charmed circle of Stieglitz-approved photographers. Already, Adams was writing for the national photographic press, for *Camera Craft* and *Modern Photography*. In 1935 he published *Making a Photograph* to enthusiastic reviews. In the fall of 1936, Steiglitz gave Adams a one-man exhibition, forty-five photographs, at An American Place. The show and its critical response made Adams a national figure at age thirty-four. In 1937 Virginia Adams inherited the lucrative Best Studio concession in the Yosemite, and the Adamses moved there permanently, with continuing trips to San Francisco, Carmel, New Mexico, and New York, where his reputation continued to grow. Beaumont Newhall, librarian and historian of photography at the Museum of Modern Art in New York, took note of Adams's work, as did his wife Nancy Parker Newhall, a photographic critic. The Newhalls and the Adamses became close friends, and Nancy Newhall eventually became Ansel Adams's leading editor and interpreter, as well as the editor of Edward Weston's daybooks, which were published in two volumes in 1961.

In 1940 Beaumont Newhall invited Adams to serve as co-curator for the first exhibit of the newly established Department of Photography at the Museum of Modern Art. Entitled "Sixty Photographs," the exhibition sought to display the finest American photography from the 1840s to 1938. As co-curator, Ansel Adams personally called on Arnold Genthe, then an elderly man living in the New York area, to arrange for a printing of Genthe's *The Street of the Gamblers* (1904), a classic view of San Francisco's Chinatown, and *View Down Clay Street, San Francisco* (1906), the single greatest image of the Earthquake and Fire. "Sixty Photographs" opened in December and remains a watershed in the history of photography. Ansel Adams had the double satisfaction of being listed as co-curator and having his work, along with that of Edward Weston, included in the ranks of the greatest American photography. His reputation still obscure, Carleton Watkins was not represented in the New York show.

In the winter of 1936, Ansel Adams introduced Edward Weston to Yosemite. Accompanying Weston was the strikingly tall and beautiful Charis Wilson, twenty-eight years Weston's junior. It was the first time Weston had been in Yosemite. Weston, Ansel Adams noted, was always suspicious of "postcard scenery."[10] The conjunction of Ansel Adams, master photographer of the High Sierra, Charis Wilson, a young woman who had brought new meaning to Weston's life, and the Yosemite, with its attendant tradition of landscape photography going back to Carleton Watkins, offered a symbolic *tableau vivant* against a backdrop of snowy scenery of the fact that Edward Weston's life and work were moving in new directions.

Twenty-eight years earlier, Arnold Genthe had photographed Charis Wilson's mother in a poppy field outside Carmel. The resulting photograph, *Helen Cooke, Monterey Poppy Field* (1908), is a masterpiece of posed Pictorialism, albeit with Genthe's realistic touch, rendered even more compelling by the fact that it is an Autochrome, an early mode of color. Dressed in something Pre-Raphaelite, an astonishingly beautiful young woman, her neck swan-like in its extension and arch, a crown of braided hair framing her classic profile, half-kneels before a bed of golden poppies gathering the beginnings of a bouquet. Not surprisingly, Genthe was in love with Helen Cooke at the time, as was another Carmelite, the young writer Sinclair Lewis. Cooke eventually married screenwriter Harry Leon Wilson, who divided his time between Carmel and Hollywood.

Born in 1914, Charis inherited her mother's beauty and her father's gift for language. A precocious girl, with a taste for bohemia, Charis attended Hollywood High and took after-school training as a secretary-stenographer. Her command of French, together with her good looks, resulted in a brief period of employment as a bit player in the French Theater in San Francisco. At the time she met Weston at a concert at the Denny Watrous Gallery in Carmel, Charis was running a dress shop that one of her mother's tenants had abandoned. She had just turned twenty. Weston was forty-eight. He invited her to his studio to see his prints the following

Sunday. It was Sonya Noskowiak, however, Weston's current live-in model, lover, and housekeeper, and not Weston, who greeted Wilson that Sunday. Weston had been called to Los Angeles for work on a Federal Art Project. Noskowiak showed Wilson Weston's prints: the trees and rocks of Point Lobos, the twisted piles of kelp, the weathered barns, the dead birds, the eroded planks, the seashells, the bell peppers—and the nudes. Charis Wilson was fascinated by the nudes, and when Sonya Noskowiak, subconsciously selecting her own replacement (or was something even more intricate involved?), suggested to Charis that she pose for Weston, Charis readily agreed.

"Why this tide of women?" Weston had recently asked in his Daybook, reviewing in his mind his ceaseless womanizing.[11] Ansel Adams believed that Weston equated sexual freedom with creativity because he was fleeing the equation of monogamy and artistic frustration at the center of his life in Glendale. In any event, on Sunday afternoon, 22 April 1934, Charis Wilson joined the well-staffed ranks of Weston's model-mistresses. This relationship, however, was destined to last longer than Weston's previous liaisons and would have a profound effect on the direction of his photographic career. In early 1935 Charis moved in with Weston: not in Carmel, but in a sprawling house in Santa Monica Canyon in Los Angeles County, where impresario Merle Armitage had found Weston employment with the Public Works of Art Project photographing museum holdings. Weston brought along his sons as well. Two of them, Chandler and Brett, were older than Charis, and Neil was just her age; yet Charis instantly established her authority in the household. She later remembered these years, 1935 and 1936, as an idyll of canyon and seaside life: of scouting the beaches for driftwood for the fireplace, of rollicking parties at Gavin Arthur's place in nearby Oceano, where the grandson of President Chester Arthur, a devotee of astrology and mysticism, presided over an ever-shifting community of artists, eccentrics, beach people, and passers-through.

In the midst of this idyll, in the winter of 1936, Edward and Charis visited Ansel and Virginia Adams in Yosemite. Already, a new vitality and spontaneity had come into the nudes taken by Weston of Charis on the sand dunes at Oceano. No longer was Weston concerned with the arrangement of anatomical parts into High Modernist modes of hyper-formalism. His interest had turned, rather, toward capturing the complete body of a recognizable human being in tune with her physical self and the sand, sea, and sky framing her body. Now, in Yosemite, being driven about with Charis by Ansel Adams (Weston never learned to drive an automobile), Weston photographed the incomparable beauties of the Yosemite in winter. Ansel Adams was doing more than driving a car. Generously and with good humor (as was always the case with Adams), he was helping Weston, a near-obsessive modernist, with his bell peppers and shells, his driftwood and dead birds, evolve for himself a new way of seeing his surroundings. Adams was bringing Weston to the outdoors, to a return forward to landscape interests on hold since Mexico.

Charis Wilson, Ansel Adams, and the Yosemite did not abruptly change the direction of Weston's interests. Already, his interest in the larger aspects of landscape had been in a process of revival. Yet the images produced by the Yosemite sojourn (magnificent, Ansel Adams had called them, payment enough for the fact that he, Adams, had been able to do so little of his own work while serving as Weston's chauffeur) pointed in a more expansive direction. The restricted aestheticism of High Modernism might suffice for the 1920s, but the 1930s, with its broad and ongoing documentarian impulse in the service of social crisis, called for a larger engagement and a more ambitious way of seeing. Returning to Santa Monica Canyon, Weston completed an application to the John Simon Guggenheim Memorial Foundation proposing that he be supported for one year, renewable to two, so as to complete a portfolio of photographs of California and the West he had been working on, Weston claimed, since 1929. In 1937 Weston was awarded the first Guggenheim fellowship in photography.

Critics have traditionally divided Weston's career into five phases: pre-Mexican (1918–23), Mexican (1923–27), pre-Guggenheim (1927–37), Guggenheim (1937–39), and post-Guggenheim (1939–48). There are continuities from phase to phase. Yet Weston's Guggenheim years, part of the high tide of creativity in California in the late 1930s, show him most focused on California as an ecological and man-made environment. Dramatically, the horizon now enters his photographs, along with complex interactions between natural and constructed images. Even such urban scenes as the San Francisco Embarcadero and that classic reference point of the Hollywood novel, the back lot of MGM, attract his attention. Financed by a $2,000 grant from the Guggenheim and a $50 a month retainer from *Westways*, Edward and Charis criss-crossed California in a brand new Ford V-8 sedan into which Weston had packed his equipment: one camera (an 8″ x 10″ Century Universal), two lenses (a triple convertible Turner Reich 12″21″28″), three filters (K2, G, A), one lens shade, a tripod, a focusing cloth, two camera cases, film sheets and twelve film holders, one insulated wooden box to hold exposed films, a canvas tarpaulin to throw over the car to create a dark room, food supplies for up to three weeks of outdoor cooking and sleeping bags. Charis did the driving, twenty-three thousand miles in the first year alone, and kept a detailed diary.

On one of their Guggenheim excursions, in late July 1937, Edward and Charis joined Ansel Adams in Yosemite for a trip in Adams's Oldsmobile over Tioga Road to Tenaya Lake, then on to Mammoth and the Minaret mountain range. Weston, Adams later remembered, seemed almost unsettled by the spectacular scenery, as if there was too much before him demanding to be photographed, and used up forty-eight sheets of film before the trip was over. Adams photographed Weston photographing Tenaya Lake. In another exposure, Adams photographed Weston in a pith helmet photographing Charis at Lake Ediza.

The resulting photograph of Charis Wilson by Edward Weston is among his finest portraits. It is also an enduring icon, along with the Jeffers portrait, of

California identity. Charis sits against a background of granite, facing the camera. She is wearing khaki pants and a flannel shirt. Her hiking boots, caught in precise detail (twenty-eight shoe eyes surmounted by four rows of thirty-two gleaming rivets), rising to mid-calf, accentuate her long legs drawn symmetrically to her body, her equally long hands draped between her legs in an attitude equally stylized and erotic. Charis has wrapped her head artfully in a towel as protection against mosquitoes, and the cloth frames her handsome face as if she were a Bedouin princess in the desert. No other woman in Weston's life had ever or would ever receive the tribute of a portrait remotely approaching Weston's unretouched photograph of Charis against the granite. Whatever their relationship was, or was to be, it was now receiving the grandest possible testimony in an image that is, simultaneously, private and personal: yet an image underscoring as well in its depiction of Charis as female triumphant (eros and the environment, flesh against stone, beauty pervaded by forceful strength) some mysterious power felt by so many in California itself.

A few days later, a fire at Best's Studio in Yosemite destroyed one-third of Ansel Adams's life's work. Edward and Charis stayed up all night rewashing and drying whatever smoke-damaged negatives could be saved.

Weston exposed more than a thousand negatives in 1937 and another five hundred or so in 1938. When his divorce came through that year, he and Charis were married on 24 April 1938, and in celebration of the marriage Neil Weston built for his father and young stepmother an eight-hundred-square-foot one-room studio cabin on Wildcat Hill in the Carmel Highlands overlooking Point Lobos, with a clear view of the Pacific, on land that had belonged to Charis's father. Craftsman-comfortable, with a fireplace, a corner kitchen, a bedroom alcove, a bathroom with a shower, and an attached darkroom, sunlight streaming through a skylight and three glass-paneled doors, the studio cost a mere $1,000 and revealed Carmel as a site for the simple life lived for art. The Westons furnished the studio sparsely—a desk, a couch in front of the fireplace, a large table for work and dining, a few captain's chairs, a bed behind a screen—and Charis, an inveterate gardener, planted flowers and laid out stone pathways and retaining walls against the steep slope. Here, especially on long foggy days when they were not out picnicking or photographing, Weston developed the Guggenheim negatives, and Charis edited her diaries.

Two publications—*Seeing California with Edward Weston* (1939) and *California and the West* (1940)—resulted from these Guggenheim treks. Issued by *Westways*, the magazine of the Automobile Club of Southern California, *Seeing California with Edward Weston* is album-like in nature and marred by banal commentary. It does, however, show Weston in dialogue with the entire state, from the North Coast and Modoc Plateau to Death Valley and the Colorado Desert, from Monterey to Tahoe. Not since Carleton Watkins had a photographer of such talent traveled the state in search of representative images.

For all its faults, especially its trite commentary, *Seeing California with Edward Weston* reconfirms what philosopher Josiah Royce had theorized and Carleton Watkins had proven in the nineteenth century: that there was an abstract, bold, even heroic simplicity to the landscape of California. Mountains, valleys, plains, desert, and seacoast: each element remains clear in itself and in an equally clear relationship to adjacent forms. There is little mystery, little of the intimacy of New England, or the intricacy of the mid-Atlantic Coast, or the moist luxuriance of the South. "Everything in the West," noted Weston in his daybook for 19 March 1937 in the course of selecting photographs for *Westways*, "is on a grander scale, more intense, vital, dramatic. Forms are here which never occur in the East,—in fruits, flowers, vegetables, in mountains, rocks, trees. . . . All these forms,—trees, rocks, natural manifestations of Western vitality are my neighbors, my friends—I understand and love them. I do not lie about them." [12] Was Weston being sensitive in this early morning mediation to the High Modernist formalism of so many of his nature studies in the pre-Guggenheim period? Were formalist studies of seashells, driftwood, and bell peppers paling in comparison to the California he was photographing for *Westways* on his Guggenheim? Departing from his usual close-ups, Weston was now lifting his camera to the horizon and seeing land and sky forms, vistas of orchards, sequences of seacoast in their entirety.

Yet even these larger vistas, seemingly so spontaneous, so unaware of themselves, are structured by formal, abstract relationships, as all art must be. In *Tomato Ranch, Monterey Coast* (1937) Weston delights in depicting the well-ordered rows of tomato plants as they march over an undulating landscape toward the Pacific. *Borego Desert* (1938) shows dry landforms breaking from each other like waves rolling toward the shore. *Embarcadero, San Francisco* (1937) brings order to a bustling urban-industrial cityscape, as lines of boxcars come into diagonal dialogue with the waterfront.

Publishing only ninety-six of the more than fifteen hundred prints Weston accomplished, *California and the West* was not an album like the *Westways* book, but a highly selective portfolio that might have served as the catalog for the museum exhibition Weston's Guggenheim series deserved but never received because of the war. Framed by Charis's narrative, *California and the West* is as much her book as it is her husband's, filled with Charis's lively descriptions of the California of 1937 and 1938. Charis had long since been serving as Weston's ghostwriter and editor as well as his model, housekeeper, mistress, and wife. She is the human presence in *California and the West*. She provides the descriptive language and the metaphor. She is the source of observation and anecdote.

When the Guggenheim images first began to appear in *Westways*, Weston was asked why there were no people in his photographs. "For nearly thirty-five years," Weston replied, "I have been a professional portrait photographer. People were my bread and butter, and when I had the opportunity I was only too glad to have a vacation from them." [13] Recognizing the austerity of Weston's photographs, the editors at Duell, Sloan and Pearce were only too eager to combine it with Charis's narrative so as to turn a photographic portfolio into a more encompassing exploration. With a blend of warmth, wit, and documentary ambition Charis Wilson Weston gives us the people: the truck drivers and truck-stop waitresses, the bartenders and rummies, the gas station attendants and hitchhikers, the ranchers and studio technicians. Thanks to Charis, we hear ordinary Californians of 1937–38 talking off camera in their own voices, while Weston gives us the images of the California from which they are so curiously absent. Once again, Weston became defensive. "I have actually done people, in my own way," he claimed of his Guggenheim images. (Did Charis write these words for him?) "Wrecked automobiles and abandoned service stations on the desert, deserted cabins in the high Sierras, the ruins of Rhyolite, ghost lumber towns on the bleak north coast, a pair of high-buttoned shoes in an abandoned soda works, the San Francisco embarcadero, the statue of a leering bellhop advertising a Los Angeles hotel—all of these are pictures of people as well as of life." [14]

Ever in search of ambiguity, critics have been quick to point to the many images of death and decay in so many of the photographs taken by Weston during the Guggenheim treks. On the one hand, Weston insisted both in his Guggenheim application and in an article published in *Camera Craft* for February 1939 that his ambition as a photographer was nothing less than the documentation of Life itself, which Weston spelled with a capital L. To Weston's way of thinking, his camera had an obligation to transcend the mere documentation of geography, history, or sociology in the effort to depict Life itself, pure and simple. "I have come to realize Life as a coherent whole," Weston had written in his Daybook on the morning of 24 April 1930, "and myself as a part, with rocks, trees, bones, cabbages, smokestacks, torsos, all interrelated, interdependent—each a symbol of the whole." [15] In this ambition, Weston is linked to another creative Californian of the late 1930s, John Steinbeck, who had similar ambitions for his fiction. A good biologist, Weston argued, must show ruin and decay and death as part of the natural process, hence the steer skulls, the abandoned desert towns, the charred remnants of a forest destroyed by fire, the gravestones in the Mother Lode, the bleached bark of trees, the burnt-out automobile, the wrecked car, the abandoned industrial site, and the other images of decay and decline in the Guggenheim series.

There are only two portraits in *California and the West*: the Charis portrait, so vital with Life as Weston was in search of it, and that of a dead man lying in the desert. While on the road in southeastern California, Weston and Charis had come across a sign attached to a stake in the middle of the road in the Colorado desert on a hundred-plus-degree day. "Please Help Sick Man at Carrizo Station," it read. They found his body under a tree on the creek bank: not an old man, but middle-aged, much too young to die this way, so abandoned, so alone. Near him was a tin cup of water, a half bottle of milk, and a bandanna bundle holding his scant and pitiable possessions. As the sun set behind the Laguna Mountains, Weston made two exposures, one of the full body and its attendant belongings, a second of the man's head. Shaken by what he had found, Weston made a rare technical error, which he discovered just in time to take one last exposure before the light was lost. Back in Los Angeles, developing his negatives, Weston discovered that the full-length portrait had been double-exposed with an image of cow bones photographed earlier that day. Yet the third image was there, the partial portrait, which Charis augmented in *California and the West* with as complete a biography of the dead man, an Okie Everyman, as could be assembled from the items in his bandanna bundle, one old letter, and the subsequent coroner's report. Protest as he might, Edward Weston is more than half in love with easeful death in this startling and unexpected image. California could very well signify little more than the end of the trail. The image of Charis against the granite at Lake Ediza barely holds its own against this bleak depiction of a lonely desert death.

Shortly after *California and the West* appeared, the Limited Editions Club commissioned Weston to do a series of photographs illustrating a deluxe edition of Walt Whitman's *Leaves of Grass*. While no specific directives were given, the photographs were expected to be in the mood and style of the American Scene movement of the early 1940s. With the nation emerging from the Depression, yet heading toward war, photographers such as Russell Lee and others working under the direction of Roy Emerson Stryker in the historical section of the Farm Security Administration were explicitly instructed to work in the American Scene mode: to capture, that is, images of a nation and a people in the process of recovery. A half decade earlier, working for the Resettlement Administration, Dorothea Lange had ventured into the strike-struck fields of California and returned with images of a people under terrible stress. Russell Lee, by contrast, traveling these same roads in 1940 and 1941, returned with images asserting that the New Deal was taking hold. A scruffy, dirty-faced little girl, holding her equally scruffy doll, photographed by Lange at a migrant camp on the American River near Sacramento, yields to the image of a well-nourished little girl in a clean puffed-sleeved velvet dress, proudly held by her father John Frost in equally clean overalls, the two of them photographed by Russell Lee for the Farm Security Administration in November 1940. John Frost, we are told, is the part owner of 135 acres of semi-marginal land in Tehama County, where he raises turkeys, hogs, and dairy cattle.

This American Scene attitude dovetailed perfectly with the lyrical and affirming energies, the triumphant vision of America according to Walt Whitman, which Weston was now commissioned to illustrate. Once again, Weston and Charis took to the road in their Ford V-8, logging twenty thousand miles as they traveled through twenty-four states. While funereal themes were not entirely absent from the forty-nine photographs Weston selected for the edition (a crumbling Southern plantation, one graveyard), the images in the Limited Edition *Leaves of Grass* show Edward Weston reaching out as he had never reached out before, reaching out in the spirit of Walt Whitman and under the influence of the American

Scene: seeing ordinary people; seeing rural and small-town America, main streets and country courthouses; seeing urban industrial America; seeing steel bridges, skyscrapers, and railroad yards. Having learned to see California as a totality, as a web of Life, the part in the whole and the whole in the part, Edward Weston, the recluse, the formalist, was now trying, even as bombs fell on Pearl Harbor, to see America as Walt Whitman had seen it, energetic, multitudinous, whole and entire. Seeing California, Edward Weston found America itself.

8

Angel's Flight

Social Realism Comes to California Art

*I*N the late nineteenth and early twentieth centuries, the artists of California created, cumulatively, a painterly map of the state. From Mount Shasta in the north to San Diego Bay near the Mexican border, a visual atlas of California was achieved by 1929, materialized in thousands of paintings that would only begin to find their way into comprehensive collections in the mid-twentieth century. Structuring this multi-canvas gazetteer were four geographical and cultural reference points: the Spanish Southwest, Mediterranean Europe, Japan, and the South Pacific. Like the *New Yorker* cover depicting the view of America from Manhattan, these four regions, so favored by California artists, offered imaginative affinities to California that became part of the definition of California itself.

Throughout the 1890–1920 era, Californians had been wont to perceive their region through the Mediterranean metaphor: as a second Italy, a new Greece, an echo of Spain on the Pacific. The influential nineteenth-century painter Virgil Williams, for example, received his training in Rome in the 1850s in the studio of William Page, and in such a painting as *View South from Sonoma Hills Toward San Pablo Bay and Mount Tamalpais* (1864) was more than capable of making this portion of California seem very much Italy redux, with its own *contadini* and mellow landscape. Not only did the Spanish Southwest provide California artists an imaginative linkage to Spain and Mexico, which had brought European civilization to California, the region also offered California painters flourishing examples of Native American cultures, Hopi, Navajo, and other pueblo peoples, dramatic survivors from the pre-Columbian past.

From the start, California was Japan-oriented as well. The acquisition of California made the United States a Pacific power and helped motivate the entrance of Commodore Perry into Tokyo Bay in July 1853. James McNeill Whistler made *japonisme* and *japonaiserie* all the rage in Europe in the 1870s; but it took the

San Franciscan–born artist Theodore Wores, urged by no less than Whistler himself (this in London in 1881), to live in Japan for two long sojourns between 1885 and 1894, where he created a pioneering series of canvases. So taken was the Japanese government with Wores's paintings, it arranged an official exhibition of his work in 1887. As in the case of the Mediterranean metaphor, Japan helped Wores perceive California more aesthetically: as a magical, transformed place, that is, with the flowering apricot trees of the Santa Clara Valley replacing the cherry blossoms of Japan when Wores returned to California to live and work.

Regions of art build upon regions and lifelines of travel and commerce. Like Japan, San Francisco maintained a commercial relationship and direct steamship service with Hawaii and the South Pacific from the late 1860s onwards. In the late 1870s, San Francisco poet and essayist Charles Warren Stoddard introduced the Paris-born artist Jules Tavernier to Hawaii and the South Pacific. (Stoddard also introduced a temporary San Franciscan, Robert Louis Stevenson, to the same region.) Fleeing his creditors to Honolulu in 1884, Tavernier became court painter to the king before Tavernier's untimely death from drugs and alcohol in 1889. By the early 1900s, the South Pacific oeuvre of Paul Gauguin, with its bold palette and woodcut blocking, was exercising a strong influence on the artists of California. Had they not similar intensities of color to communicate, they challenged themselves, especially in the maritime environments around Monterey Bay? The long-standing connection between California and Hawaii, together with the influence of Gauguin, encouraged a number of artists to visit the South Pacific, paint it, and, more important, to reperceive coastal California—Monterey Bay especially, but also Laguna Bay to the south—as a Polynesia of its own.

Even such a bourgeois painter as Theodore Wores fell under the Hawaiian/Polynesian spell, directed there, once again, by Stoddard. Wores visited Hawaii in 1892 and returned in 1901 for a second stay, which included a long sojourn in Samoa. Wores's Hawaiian and Samoan canvases, showing a new boldness in color, took their place alongside his Japanese paintings and were augmented in 1903 by a series of paintings of Granada, Spain—an ancient Moorish mill, the gates and walls and corridors and gardens of the Alhambra—which showed the strong influence of Velázquez. Between 1915 and 1918 Wores spent long periods of time in Arizona and New Mexico, painting the scenery and Hopi, Zuni, and Navajo life. In and of themselves, then, the settings of Wores's work—California, Japan, Polynesia, Mediterranean Spain, and the Spanish Southwest—offered a paradigm of the fixed non-Californian reference points in the imaginative map of California that its artists were creating.

By and large, the artists of California remained committed through the 1920s to landscapes, *en plein air* or studio in production, which they perceived through the dreamy astigmatic lens of Post-Impressionism. The New York Armory Show of 1913, which introduced avant-garde art to the United States, had little effect on the Coast. What did have effect, however, was the ambitious exhibition of

French Impressionists presented in San Francisco in 1915 in the Palace of Fine Arts during the Panama-Pacific International Exposition, followed in 1924 by an equally impressive exhibition of French Impressionism at the newly constructed California Palace of the Legion of Honor. With its preference for landscape and romantic architecture over people, its dreamy mysticism, its mood of art as spiritual encounter, Post-Impressionism spoke powerfully to the genteel painters of California, so many of them so securely ensconced in the upper middle class. With the exception of the work of the German-born genre painter William Hahn and the San Francisco Chinatown scenes of Theodore Wores, the painterly map of California as it emerged in the nineteenth century was noticeably scarce in city scenes, urban interiors, industrial settings, or even close-ups of ranch life. Such subjects were left to photographers.

The persistence of Post-Impressionism through the 1920s was not unique to California, but it did say something important about the genteel tradition on the Coast. As an upper-middle-class enterprise, art in California came under the tutelage of the dean of upper-middle-class painters, William Merritt Chase, the presiding prelate of American Post-Impressionism, who maintained constant contact with California and its artists. Numerous Californians, even such an established figure as Theodore Wores, studied with Chase either in New York or in the summer schools Chase conducted in California, such as the one he offered in Carmel in the summer of 1914 in conjunction with Childe Hassam. In both his life and his art, Chase embodied the style, taste, and preferences of the *haute bourgeoisie*, the same audience for whom Henry James and William Dean Howells wrote their novels.

Then there was the crypto-religious dimension to Post-Impressionism, its affinity for landscape as spiritual text. For deeply historical reasons—the general tendency of Protestant America to read the continent as a direct revelation of Divinity; the importance of Swedenborgianism in Northern California painting circles, with its apprehension of the co-existence of matter and spirit; the persistence of the nineteenth-century tradition of regarding landscape art as a form of religious meditation—American painters in California, Northern California especially, were intensely drawn to the spiritual implication of landscape. Asked what his religion might be, the Bay Area painter Gottardo Piazzoni replied: "I think it is California."[1]

A member of the Theosophical Society at Point Loma, the Hungarian-born Maurice Braun, who had studied for a year in New York with William Merritt Chase, made this religious connection even more explicit. For Braun, the countryside around San Diego—its rolling hills carpeted in brown grass, its blue mountains, its multi-hued rock formations—represented a revelation of spiritual power, even Divinity itself. A leader in the so-called Eucalyptus School of Southern California, Braun and his contemporaries—among them, Benjamin Brown, Roi Clarkson, Edgar Payne, Guy Rose, Hanson Smith, Marion Wachtell—their output peaking in the 1920s, created with the same loving attention paid by the

Impressionists and Post-Impressionists to the landscapes of France innumerable compositions in which the stately eucalypti, rolling hills, flowering fields and plants, and a suggestion or two of architecture evoked California as the South of France, a Giverny on the Pacific. (Seventy-plus years later, the leading art dealer of California, John Garzoli, would see in this Frenchification, in Guy Rose especially, an enervating evasion of the true and primal power of the landscape of the Southland. Pasadena was not Giverny. It did not have to be. It was already Pasadena.) In the north, Percy Gray, another student of William Merritt Chase, carried on a similar celebration of the yet undeveloped landscapes of Marin, Alameda, and San Mateo counties. Like Braun and the other Southern California painters, Gray had a fondness for eucalyptus trees and for dreamy, mystical landscapes. The fact that both Braun and Gray were studio painters, as opposed to working *en plein air*, is important. Each artist worked deliberately in his studio from field sketches to create landscapes rich in otherworldly suggestion.

Like coastal Southern California, the Bay Area offered the immediate presence of undeveloped landscape adjacent to settled communities. Marin County remained virtually empty; the East Bay, sparsely settled; the San Francisco Peninsula, undeveloped save for a few small towns; and San Jose was a small marketing town. So compelling was this wilderness next door, it easily became a lifetime obsession for Marin painters such as Thad Welch, Welch's successor Percy Gray, and Gray's successor George Demont Otis. Ensconcing himself in a rustic cabin in Kentfield in Marin in 1934, Otis spent the next twenty-six years painting the North Bay. A leader in what eventually came to be called the Western Impressionist School, Otis demonstrated the continuing vitality of Impressionism and Post-Impressionism through the upheavals of the 1930s, the war years, and the post-war boom. What gives great appeal to Otis's work, aside from the ever-present eucalyptus, are the glimpses of the built environment: the Palace of Fine Arts seen from the Presidio highlands with Alcatraz in the distance, the suburban villas of the Belvedere peninsula, San Francisco seen from Tiburon Point like Atlantis rising from the sea. What is totally absent from Otis's work, however, and from virtually all Impressionist and Post-Impressionist landscapes, whether produced in a studio or *en plein air*, are people, cities, towns, social realities. The Impressionists and Post-Impressionists preferred a California that remained in so many ways a garden landscape. They felt next to no obligation to suggest who had brought this garden into being. The Pacific Grove canvases of Lillie May Nicholson, dominated by Impressionist-Pointillist portraits of fishermen working on the docks, represent a significant exception to this Post-Impressionist preference for place over people; but Nicholson was out of the mainstream: a native-born ranch girl, locally educated, a self-supporting teacher who never managed fully to believe in her talent. In the 1930s Nicholson abandoned her art altogether in favor of social work. In 1947, nearing the end of her life, she ordered her relatives to destroy all her paintings stored on the family ranch. Knowing better, they refused.

Hence the power, the stunning, unexpected power, of the Society of Six, a loose fraternity of East Bay painters—Selden Gile, William Clapp, August Gay, Maurice Logan, Louis Siegriest, and Bernard von Eichman—who through the 1920s brought art in California into new realms of color and figurative verve. At a time when art in California was continuing along a professional and competent (if provincial) path of Post-Impressionist tonalism, these bohemian painters were pursuing weekends of tramping and painting and riotous color in the Contra Costa hills and North Bay countryside, followed by drinking sessions—bootleg red wine and San Jose Cheer (a prune whiskey)—and abundant meals prepared by Selden Gile, a more-than-competent chef, in the Chow House, Gile's home on Chabot Road in Oakland.

Masculine, bohemian, honestly working- and lower-middle class, the Six defied an otherwise proper and genteel Impressionist/Post-Impressionist ethos, not only in their frank appetites and robust lifestyle, but in Fauvist-inspired canvases exploding in color and depicting California not from an aesthetic distance but from close up: its cabins and docks, its farms and towns, even its people. Of the Six, only William Clapp, a Canadian who had attended the Academie Julian, was upper middle class in background and had studied in Europe. The rest of the Six were educated locally if at all, with Logan studying under Theodore Wores at the San Francisco Institute of Art and Siegriest and von Eichman studying with Frank Van Sloun at the California School of Fine Arts. Self-educated as a painter, Gile was a close friend of Jack London, whom he revered as the paradigm of the self-taught working-class artist. Von Eichman had survived a decidedly harsh childhood. His mother and brother were abandoned by his father, who fled to Mexico when von Eichman was twelve. At times the family survived from food young Bernard scrounged from garbage cans in the backyards of San Francisco. Not surprisingly, this gifted boy from the streets, no stranger to ash cans, was the favorite student of the only prominent representative of the Ash Can School in California, Frank Van Sloun, who taught at the California School of Fine Arts, which von Eichman intermittently attended.

All this—their working- and lower-middle-class origins, their spotty educations, their quasi-amateur weekend status (Clapp managed an art gallery, Logan did commercial art, Gile managed a ceramic tile company, von Eichman shipped out with the merchant marine)—was a long way from the affluent and leisurely art circles of Pebble Beach, Carmel, Santa Barbara, Pasadena, and San Diego. On the other hand, the Six took as their point of departure the same event that had inspired the Post-Impressionists: the exhibition of French and American Impressionists—more than eleven thousand paintings, seen by ten million visitors—at the Panama-Pacific International Exhibition of 1915, especially the works of such venturesome American artists as Maurice Prendergast, John Sloan, John Marin, William Glackens, George Luks, Ernest Lawson, and Robert Henri. Van Gogh was represented by only one painting, however, and Gauguin by two, and the Fauves were entirely absent. Yet the physical presence of great French Impressionist canvases was enough to inspire these provincial young Californians to launch themselves in bold new directions. As art historian Nancy Boas points out, the Society of Six may have been the last group of American painters to be inspired directly by the Impressionists.

In any event, the Six plunged themselves into new realms of figurative color. Their impasto canvases represent a Bay Area Fauvism achieved by artists who, with the exception of Clapp, had never seen a Fauvist painting. (During his student days Clapp had attended the 1905 inaugural exhibition of the Fauves at the Salon d'Automne.) With characteristic bravado, the Six cultivated a style of rapid painting, finishing their canvases within a few hours in the outdoors, rarely bringing them back to a studio to be fussed over. Paintings by the Six have their vitality in their powerful primary colors, their bold brush strokes, their figurativism, so assertive in black line against the color, their blocking into arrangements verging on the abstract. When von Eichman found himself stranded for two years in China when the shipping line he worked for went bankrupt, he supported himself by painting and selling a series of Chinese scenes strongly influenced by Hans Hofmann that enter the borderlands between the representational and the abstract. In later years Siegriest would move totally into abstraction.

Between 1923 and 1926 the Six exhibited their paintings in annual exhibitions organized by Clapp and his colleague Florence Wieben Lehre at the Oakland Art Gallery. Local critics praised their work: which in itself is interesting, showing an early receptivity in the Bay Area for something more than Post-Impressionist propriety. Their fourth show, in 1926, dramatized the group at its boldest and most successful. Also at the Oakland Art Gallery in 1926 occurred the first museum exhibition in the United States of the Blue Four—the Russian painters Alexej Jawlensky and Wassily Kandinsky, the Swiss painter Paul Klee, and the American-born Lyonel Feininger—whose canvases had been brought to Oakland by their American representative Emmy (Galka) Scheyer. Clapp retained Scheyer to represent the Oakland Art Galley in Europe, which she did between 1925 and 1938. Thanks to Clapp and Lehre, a publicly supported art gallery in a provincial California city achieved a direct connection with the most avant-garde of avant-garde art in Europe and in turn through Scheyer was introducing Europeans to the equally innovative work being done by the Six in far-off Northern California. Galvanized by Impressionism, reconfirmed and reinspired by the Fauves, the Six now found themselves even further corroborated and stimulated by the Blue Four and the other avant-garde artists whose canvases Galka Scheyer was sending from Europe to Oakland for exhibition.

By 1929 the Six had done their work. Theirs was not a society in the formal sense of the term and only minimally a school. Theirs was a moment, brilliant and fugitive, in which Jack London–like artists had reestablished art in California on a new basis of color, even if it would take another half century for their work to be recognized. In their manifestos of 1923 and 1925, the Six expressly renounced any ambition to portray California or tell its story; yet a representational world of astonishing vitality is present in their work. The Six mapped their special portion of California through line and color: the hills of Tiburon on San Francisco Bay in Selden Gile's *Boat and Yellow Hills* (n.d.), exploding in yellow, with trees presented in blue-green with a rose-red under-painting; or Gile's *The Soil* (1927), with its sunburst-orange mountain, its ocher paths, its aquamarine sky; or Maurice Logan's *The Old Milk Ranch* (1925), with its bleedings and interplays of orange and yellow. Here were colors that Californians knew instinctively to be their own: colors that were seen in mind long before they were seen in the landscape. Here was a palette of color, at once primal and subtle, worthy of the red, orange, and yellow sunlight streaming down upon the California coast.

Before the Depression and the sudden rush of realism into California art, Frank Van Sloun stood as a lonely exponent of Social Realism on the coast. Having studied under Robert Henri in the early 1900s at the Art Students League alongside George Bellows, John Sloan, Edward Hopper, and Rockwell Kent, Van Sloun worked in monotypes and etchings as well as oils. He preferred people and cities over landscapes. Van Sloun once went on a trek into the Southwestern desert with artists Maynard Dixon and Jimmy Swinnerton but could find very little to paint. It can be argued that an artist with Van Sloun's Ash Can instincts made a big mistake in removing himself from New York in 1911 for genteel and provincial San Francisco, where taste ran to Impressionist and Post-Impressionist landscapes. In 1920, in any event, Van Sloun painted a work without precedent in California: *Flossie*, a life-size oil portrait of a young lady of the streets, powerful, real, with touches of the ironic in Flossie's grand manner—very much an exception to local tastes and arguably, despite its remoteness from New York, one of the best portraits of the Ash Can School. *Flossie* remained, however, only a suggestion of what might have been, had the genteel tradition not held such sway in California, or had Frank Van Sloun chosen to live and work in nitty-gritty New York.

The Depression brought Social Realism to the coast. The slump found Maynard Dixon in his mid-fifties and flat broke. He and Dorothea Lange were forced to board their two sons in Carmel while they moved into Dixon's studio on Montgomery Street to cut down on living costs. There Dixon brooded to the point of upsetting his mental health, depressed by the sense of impending doom that was gripping the Republic. His Native American portraits of the 1920s, as represented in *Pony Boy* (1920) and *Earth Knower* (1931), so serene, philosophical, and triumphant, were replaced by such portraits as *Shapes of Fear* (1933), a grouping of blankets draped over invisible figures emerging ominously from the darkness, the very embodiment of Roosevelt's evocation in his first inaugural address of "fear itself—nameless, unreasoning, unjustified terror which paralyzes needed efforts to convert retreat into advance." (Ironically, it was this very canvas, purchased by the National Academy of Design for $1,500, which got Dixon through the worst of the Depression.)

Leaving behind the colorful certainties of the Spanish Southwest, Dixon created in 1934 a series of Social Realist works in subdued documentarian tones. *Law and Disorder*: striking workers assault a policeman. *Destination Unknown*: an unemployed older man, his hat and well-tailored overcoat showing signs of a former prosperity, hikes the railroad tracks. *Free Speech*: angry workers mill around a speaker, a policeman lurking threateningly in the obscure background. *Keep Moving*: a line of unemployed files aimlessly down a city street. *Forgotten Man*: a job seeker squats down on a curb in despair as the rest of the city walks heedlessly by. *No Place to Go*: a bindle stiff, a blanket roll slung over his shoulder, stares blankly at the Pacific. *Destination Nowhere*: two men hit the road, with nothingness in the distance.

Like so many other artists in this era, Dixon got through the second half of the 1930s thanks to an alphabet soup of federal programs that would altogether support more than a hundred thousand art projects throughout the nation. First came the Public Works of Art Project (PWAP), set up in December 1933 with a grant by the Civil Works Administration to the Treasury Department. Also established that year: the art program at the Public Works Administration (PWA). In 1934 the Treasury Department authorized its Section of Painting and Sculpture (SPS) as part of its Treasury Relief Art Project (TRAP). In 1935 came the Federal Art Project (FAP) of the Works Progress Administration (WPA), which lasted until 1943. In 1938 the Treasury Department established its Treasury Section of Fine Arts (SECTION), renamed the next year the Public Buildings Administration (PBA). The first report of the Public Works of Art Project, encompassing the period 8 December 1933 to 30 June 1934, lists five closely printed pages of California artists receiving support. More than sixty years later, it is a true indication of the widespread economic dislocation of the Depression to discover in this list a Who's Who of California art.

The preeminent art form favored by these agencies was the mural. In December 1933 George Biddle, an admirer of Diego Rivera, persuaded his Harvard classmate FDR to see the pioneering Public Works of Art Project as an opportunity for creating across the nation murals that would celebrate local history and life, together with more generic themes that would reinforce public values. While the President was attracted to the project, he had political misgivings about supporting art for the sake of art in the midst of the Depression. Relief czar Harry Hopkins soothed FDR's anxiety with a reminder that artists "have got to eat just like other people!"[2] With Hopkins's encouragement the PWAP began its mural program, followed by the mural programs of the Treasury Department and the WPA.

Roosevelt's second misgiving—the fact that he did not want "a lot of young enthusiasts painting Lenin's head on the Justice Building"—was a little more difficult to deal with, especially when in one of the first PWAP projects, Coit Tower in San Francisco, Bernard Zakeim painted *Das Kapital* and other controversial books on the shelves of the San Francisco Public Library, Victor Arnautoff portrayed the *Daily Worker* and *The Masses* on sale at a Powell Street newsstand, and

Clifford Wright placed a hammer and sickle near the Blue Eagle of the NRA. A furor arose, and the Park Commission closed the doors of Coit Tower for a number of weeks while a compromise was worked out. Wright's hammer and sickle disappeared, but *Das Kapital*, the *Daily Worker*, and *The Masses* remained.

All things considered, it was a much more civilized response than the controversy surrounding Diego Rivera's mural *Man at the Crossroads* (1933) for the RCA Building at Rockefeller Center in New York. When Rivera refused to paint out a portrait of Lenin, he was paid off, and the mural, two thirds complete, was destroyed. Subsequently, the WPA explicitly forbade revolutionary or controversial manifestos or themes in any work it sponsored, together with gratuitous nudity or, interestingly enough, excessively abstract art. In Los Angeles, Leo Katz would later have his mural removed from the Frank Wiggins Trade School because it depicted a bare-breasted woman in one section and, in another, a man and woman embracing. When Victor Anautoff, forgiven his Coit Tower escapade, was later given the commission for *Lovers' Point* (1940), a mural in the Pacific Grove post office, he had to submit preliminary cartoons of his figures so as to preclude the possibilities of overtly erotic behavior.

The late 1920s and 1930s was a golden age for Mexican muralists. Four of them—José Clemente Orozco, David Alfaro Siqueiros, Alfredo Raymos Martinez, and Diego Rivera—worked in California and exercised decisive regional influence. Orozco arrived in Los Angeles in 1930, commissioned by Pomona College and Claremont to paint the mural *Prometheus* (1930), a bold instance of assertive expressionism rendered in black and red, depicting the struggle of the masses toward a higher ideal. Siqueiros and Martinez spent most of the 1930s in Southern California. Siqueiros taught at the Chouinard School of Art, and Martinez was at work on an ambitious series of murals for the Margaret Fowler Memorial Garden at Scripps College. As a teacher at Chouinard, Siqueiros urged his students (they included such leading protagonists of the developing California School as Paul Sample, Lee Blair, Barse Miller, Phil Paradise, and Millard Sheets) to get out on the street, see what was around them, and take a spontaneous, engaged attitude toward the creation of art. Innovatively, Siqueiros used industrial materials in his murals. Even more boldly, he applied paint with a spray gun. A committed Marxist like Rivera, Siqueiros caused a Rivera-like controversy with his mural *American Tropicale* (1932) for the Olvera Street restoration project. Incensed by the suppression of Mexican workers in Imperial Valley and the deportation of Mexican nationals from Southern California, Siqueiros placed an eagle atop the figure of a crucified Mexican peasant. The mural caused such a furor that the offending image was painted over, and shortly thereafter the entire wall was whitewashed.

To San Francisco, a city of murals, came (thrice!) the greatest muralist of them all, Diego Rivera. There he produced three ambitious works: *Allegory of California* (1931) at the Pacific Stock Exchange Club; *The Making of a Fresco, Showing the Building of a City* (1931) at the San Francisco Art Institute; and *Pan-American*

Unity (1940), created for the Golden Gate International Exposition and later relocated to the City College. Ralph Stackpole, himself an accomplished muralist, had known Rivera in Paris in 1921 and had traveled to Mexico City in 1926 to view the 124 frescoes Rivera was creating for the courtyard of the Ministry of Public Education. Acting in his role as the informal impresario of the arts in San Francisco, Stackpole persuaded William Gerstle, president of the San Francisco Art Commission, to hire Rivera to paint a mural in the California School of Fine Arts on Chestnut Street. Stackpole also suggested to Timothy Pflueger, architect of the Stock Exchange and the adjacent Stock Exchange Club, that Rivera was the perfect artist to paint the mural planned for a staircase wall in the club.

Exhilarated by a $2,500 offer from Pflueger and a $1,500 offer from Gerstle, the largest single commission he had yet received, Rivera and his long-suffering wife Frida Kahlo, an artist in her own right, after some difficulty in obtaining a visa because of Rivera's pro-Communist sympathies, arrived in San Francisco on 10 November 1930 and ensconced themselves in Stackpole's studio at 716 Montgomery Street, where they were to live and work over the next few months. The bringing of Rivera to San Francisco caused a strain between Stackpole and another denizen of the 700 block of Montgomery Street, Maynard Dixon, who, along with Frank Van Sloun, organized a protest over the awarding of two such significant commissions to a foreign artist who was also a Communist. Not wishing to seem too peevish, Dixon admitted that Rivera "is the greatest living artist in the world," but his professed Communism and previous caricatures of American financial institutions, Dixon insisted, made Rivera an inappropriate candidate for a commission connected with the Stock Exchange.[3]

The controversy died almost as soon as Diego and Frida arrived and took the city by storm. Dixon and Van Sloun knew that the oligarchy who had commissioned Rivera and was now feting him and his wife with a round of luncheons, dinner parties, fifty-yard-line seats at the Big Game (Diego wore an oversized sombrero to protect himself from the sun; Frida wore a colorful peasant costume), who were offering him a one-man exhibition at the California Palace of the Legion of Honor and a summer lectureship at the University of California at the hefty fee of $3,000, was the same oligarchy to whom Dixon and Van Sloun must turn for support. Three years later, Van Sloun, himself an accomplished muralist, responsible for more than forty murals throughout the state, was commissioned to execute a mural in the Grove Room of the Bohemian Club on Taylor Street. Assisted by Louis Siegriest of the Society of Six and a handful of unemployed young artists, Van Sloun produced an ambitious Pointillist-Impressionist portrayal of the Bohemian Grove. It remains one of the most impressive privately commissioned indoor murals of the 1930s, in California or anywhere else.

For the Stock Exchange Club, Rivera executed his famous portrait of Helen Wills Moody as California. Exhausted from his effort, Diego spent six weeks of rustication at the Atherton summer home of San Francisco patron Mrs. Sigmund Stern. The almond and apricot orchards were in bloom and, leisurely, to pass the time and repay his hostess, who was in Europe, Rivera created a lyrical fresco on one wall of the dining room depicting a Santa Clara County almond orchard at harvest time.

Dissatisfied with the smallness of the 120-square-foot wall offered him at the California School of Fine Arts, Rivera chose another wall ten times that size and augmented his depiction of the design and construction of a modern building with a second mural framing the first, showing Rivera and his assistants at work. With sly humor, Rivera depicted himself from the rear, his huge back and the ample buttocks of his three-hundred-pound frame drooping over his scaffold seat, boldly presented to one and all. The anti-Rivera claque interpreted this gesture as an insult to San Francisco. Rivera's supporters preferred to see humor in Rivera's posterior self-portrait. By then, Diego Rivera and Frida Kahlo had become honorary San Franciscans, with Rivera's work flowing into the permanent collection of the San Francisco Museum of Art, thanks to patrons William Gerstle and Albert Bender. Not only was he a great artist, Diego Rivera also possessed an instinctive genius for celebritydom. A gargantuan aficionado of the good life, Rivera was almost child-like in his appreciation of the color and spectacle of Bay Area ways. The card routines of the rooting sections at the Cal-Stanford game made him ecstatic. He considered these stunts living murals and praised them to the press, which seemed to follow him about during his entire sojourn in search of the *obiter dicta* of this most unusual figure, a Communist artist who loved the United States and was being so lionized by San Francisco.

In 1939 Timothy Pflueger, supervising architect of the World's Fair, flew to Mexico City to invite Rivera to paint a mural at the Golden Gate International Exposition in full view of the public as part of the Art in Action program. After the exhibition, the mural would be installed in the new campus Pflueger was designing for the City College of San Francisco. Not only did Rivera relish the commission, he saw the trip as a perfect opportunity to remarry Frida Kahlo, who had divorced him for his infidelities but had been rewooed. Frida loved San Francisco, seeing in it, as she told the press, the perfect City of the World, a city belonging to one and all. Once again, Rivera and Kahlo were lionized (by everyone, that is, except for the elevator operator at the Mark Hopkins Hotel who refused to take the artist to the Top of the Mark because Rivera was not wearing a necktie). Ensconced in a studio apartment on Russian Hill, Rivera journeyed daily to Treasure Island, where he created yet another masterpiece, this one depicting the confluence of the Americas, North and South, in terms of landscape, flora and fauna, arts and industries, and diverse peoples.

The Mexican muralists encouraged their American counterparts, Californians included, to engage contemporary and historical themes with an eye toward their social significance: which is to say, to link art, history, and public identity in the mural format. From this perspective, Mexico liberated California from the genteel, although the restraints, indeed the *de facto* censorship, of the federal programs remained in force. The new American mural made its California debut in San Francisco in 1933 with the Coit Tower project, which brought together such established figures as Ralph Stackpole, Lucien Labaudt, Bernard Zakhein, Mallette Dean, and Victor Arnautoff, and younger figures such as Edith Hamlin, Frede Vidar, George Harris, and Fred Olmsted Jr., for the creation of a series of murals depicting San Francisco in the 1930s. For sweep, for detail, for sociological complexity, for overall artistic excellence, the Coit Tower murals remain among the most successful murals in the nation.

The Coit Tower artists sought nothing less than the depiction of San Francisco in its exuberant range and diversity as an American city in that most public of eras, the 1930s. Here it was, then, the city, all of it: the agricultural hinterlands, the port and industrial infrastructure, the railroad and shipping; the cops, the capitalists, the factory workers, the dames and society matrons; the newspaper offices, the screaming headlines (B. BUFANO'S ST. FRANCIS JUST AROUND THE CORNER; ART COMMISSION AWAKENS FROM ITS DEEP SLEEP); the Public Library in Civic Center, Powell Street on a busy afternoon, crowds heading toward the Ferry Building; the law firms, the Stock Exchange, the department stores; the secretaries snatching a quick lunch at the lunch counter, the children in the playground. Although scenes of group-man, as John Steinbeck described them—factory workers, longshoremen, railroad men, meat packers, white-collar workers—predominated, the Coit Tower murals also depicted golf, tennis, and polo players, baseball games and archery contests, the Big Game between Cal and Stanford, and such bourgeois amusements as bridge, a tea dance, and a family evening by the great mahogany radio in the living room.

The most controversial, even angry, murals belonged to the first years of the 1930s. By the late 1930s, federally supported (and monitored) muralists were contenting themselves with non-controversial contemporary topics, with allegory, and with California history, in contrast to the sociological engagement and political controversy evident at Coit Tower. Domesticated by comforting myth, California history offered muralists a variety of topics from the Native American, Spanish, Mexican, and American frontier that lent themselves to depictions of social experience unbothered by controversy. While Siqueiros's Mexican peasant might be crucified on a cross surmounted by an American eagle, the Native Americans depicted by Boris Deutsch for the Terminal Annex Post Office in Los Angeles were envisioned as figures from a positive past. A similar mood of well-being pervades such Spanish and Mexican era murals as Milford Zornes's panels in the post office at Claremont and Belle Baranceanu's *The Departure of Portola* (1937) and *Building Padre Dam* (1938) for the Roosevelt Junior High School in San Diego. Only the Russian-born Anton Refregier broke through the comfort barrier in a twenty-seven-panel, twenty-four-hundred-square-foot series depicting the history of San Francisco, which he began for the Rincon Annex Post Office in 1941 and did not complete until 1948. Depicting scenes of frontier violence and injustice and the waterfront strike of 1934, the Refregier murals caused controversy aplenty in the post-war era, and Refregier returned to the Soviet Union.

California history did wonders for Maynard Dixon, who had begun his career as a muralist in 1912 with a series of Native American panels in Anita Baldwin's mansion in Sierra Madre near Pasadena. In 1921 and 1923 Dixon had completed landscape and Native American murals for the SS *Sierra* and the SS *Silver State*, and in 1926, with the help of Frank Van Sloun, he produced a stunning panorama of early California history for the Room of the Dons in the Mark Hopkins Hotel atop Nob Hill in San Francisco. In 1927 Dixon completed a masterful mural of the arrival of pioneers (strangely, he ignored the Chinese) for the reference room of the California State Library in Sacramento. Like these previous efforts, Dixon's federally supported murals—*The Arrival of Frémont in California* (1933) for Frémont High School in Los Angeles, *The Road to El Dorado* (1937) for the post office in Martinez, *The Indian Yesterday* (1940) and *The Indian Today* (1940) for the Department of the Interior building in Washington, and *Palomino Ponies* (1943) for the Canoga Park post office—represent high points in the art of the mural as practiced in this period. An accomplished creator of magazine covers for *Sunset* and, earlier, of billboards for Foster and Kleiser, Dixon fully understood the requirements of public art: color, line, and accessible narrative. In Dixon's murals, fully realized figures, bold in color, billboard-like in their flat and commanding presence, stand against a near-empty but subtly suggested background.

Maynard Dixon's continuing preoccupation with the Native American and Spanish-Mexican California had its sculptural counterpart in the work of Donal Hord of San Diego. In the late 1920s, Hord studied in Mexico City, met Rivera and Siqueiros, and visited the pre-Columbian ruins of Teotihuacán and Monte Albán. Hord returned to San Diego with the dream of fusing the energies of pre-Columbian art and contemporary Southern California. For most of the thirties, Hord worked in small figurative sculptures in polished wood and stone, but in July 1937 he at last got his big chance: commission to create from a twelve-foot-tall, twenty-two-ton block of granite a sculpture for the fountain in front of the City-County Administration Building in San Diego. Completed in the spring of 1939, Hord's *Guardian of Water*, a Mexican peasant woman holding aloft a water jar, offered dramatic testimony, at once pre-Columbian and Art Deco in inspiration, to the Mexico of the mind ever haunting the Anglo-California imagination.

It would not be granite, however, nor even the solid materials of the mural, that would most passionately and directly connect with California in the 1930s. It would be the watercolor, an unpretentious medium favored by amateurs, but capable as well, when in the hands of a master, of a vividness, an immediacy of engagement, comparable to photography in its ability to capture the contemporary scene. Inexpensive, portable, rapidly applied and drying fast, watercolors, like the box camera, welcomed amateur involvement. By the 1920s an impressive number of accomplished watercolorists were at work throughout California. Nowhere was this more true than in Los Angeles. In September 1921 the California Water Color Society, an association of amateurs and professionals organized around artists Dana Bartlett and Hanson Puthuff, held its first exhibition in the Museum of History, Science, and Art in Exposition Park in Los Angeles. Also that year art educator Nelbert Chouinard founded the influential Chouinard Art School in Los Angeles, renamed the Chouinard Art Institute in 1935. Phil Dike enrolled at Chouinard in 1924, Millard Sheets in 1925, Phil Paradise in 1927, Hardie Gramatky in 1928. By the early 1930s Los Angeles was supporting a strong art community, centered around Westlake Park, where many artists lived, and the Chouinard School, the Art Center School, the Otis Art Institute, and the art departments of USC and Pomona College, where they taught or took classes. Los Angeles had three important galleries—Stendahl Galleries, Dalzell Hatfield Galleries, and the gallery attached to Jake Zeitlin's Bookshop—and such exhibiting organizations as the Los Angeles Art Association, the Foundation of Western Art, and the Federal Art Project Center. Also of crucial importance was the film industry, most noticeably the Disney Studios on Hyperion Avenue. The studios provided artists livelihoods as set and costume designers or commercial illustrators (the Hollywood film poster achieved an art form of its own) and, in the case of Hardie Gramatky, Charles Payzant, and Phil Dike, even more challenging work in the production of such Disney epics as *Snow White and the Seven Dwarfs* (1937), *Pinocchio* (1940), and *Fantasia* (1940).

An art community centered in the newly emergent, risk-taking city of Los Angeles; a dominant medium, watercolors, equally flexible and capable of risk; the popular orientation of artists active in film work: forces were converging for the emergence of a distinctive movement emphasizing vivid, democratic, and eclectic values. From the Mexican muralists teaching and painting in Southern California, the Los Angeles–based watercolorists absorbed a love of vibrant color, together with a preference for landscapes and scenes that were simultaneously representational and symbolic. Many of the watercolors they produced, in fact, would resemble miniature murals with a Mexican accent. In *Apparition over Los Angeles* (1932), as an example, Barse Miller presented Aimee Semple McPherson soaring over the Echo Park temple alongside a winged cherub in top hat and tails attending to the money bags. In its blatant allegory, the painting was thoroughly Mexican in inspiration (with deeper origins in the Baroque) and caused the expected controversy. From the Mexican muralists as well, the California watercolorists absorbed a style of artistic engagement. From the Midwest, specifically the American Scene movement being led by Thomas Hart Benton, also called Regionalism or Social Realism, the Southern Californian watercolorists and their counterparts in the Bay Area absorbed a preference for scenes from everyday life:

for people, cities, suburbs, towns, industries, as opposed to pastoral landscapes, which dovetailed with the Mexican influence. Even their landscapes, in fact, were vivid with implied sociology.

From their film and animation work or from the sheer presence of moviemaking in the region, the artists of Southern California absorbed an instinct for unusual angles of vision, such as that in Millard Sheets's *Angel's Flight* (1931), the masterpiece of the decade, and for depth as a result of angle and perspective. Influenced by the entertainment industry that surrounded them—films, live and animated, radio, even records—the artists of the California School sought to be entertaining, to tell dramatic stories, to present situations that seized attention immediately, like the opening scene of a good movie. From the cartoons of Walt Disney, they absorbed an avoidance of pedantic detail, a preference for well-defined outlines, a mastery of depicting action or movement, a rapid employment of representational clichés and compositional schemes. They also absorbed from Disney a sense of the animate implications of non-animate reality. Lee Blair, for example, director of color and animation at the Walt Disney Studios, depicted for *San Francisco Cable Car Celebration* (c. 1938) a cable car that is almost a living being, smiling through its single headlight as it surmounts the Hyde Street hill.

And so emerged the California Group, as it was sometimes called, or the California Regionalists, or the California Water Colorists, or the White Paper Painters. In reviewing the eleventh annual exhibition of the California Water Color Society in the fall of 1931, Los Angeles *Times* art critic Arthur Millier coined the term California School, and it stuck. It must be emphasized that while watercolors pervaded the movement, giving it its vividness and flexibility, many of the artists worked in oils as well, carrying the same values into that medium. Sheets's *Angel's Flight*, for example, is an oil on canvas. Watercolors paced and set the tone of, but did not exclusively dominate, the movement.

What did the California School depict? Quite simply, the entire range of daily life, which had been previously so absent in the Post-Impressionist preference for landscape. Even the landscapes of the California School, such as Phil Paradise's *Ranch near San Luis Obispo, Evening Light* (c. 1935), an oil on canvas with linkages to Grant Wood and Thomas Hart Benton, so filled with animals, houses, fences, and barns, exulted in signs of human settlement. On the other hand, many of the California School painters had studied with Hans Hofmann at UC Berkeley and the Chouinard School in the early 1930s, and from Hofmann they had learned—as is so evident in Milford Zornes's *Nipomo Hills* (1936)—to render landscape in terms of its abstract patterns, realized through line and color.

California School painters moved with gusto into the urban scene, Los Angeles especially. Long neglected, Los Angeles was now thoroughly mapped in its bungalows and ever-present palm trees, its juxtapositions, such as that so evident in Phil Dike's *Elysian Park, Los Angeles* (1934), of the Los Angeles River, adjacent industrial zone, and freight trains, all this alongside parks and picnickers; or, elsewhere, the side-by-side emplacements of Victorians, water tanks, and scratchy rural neighborhoods nestling against wild chaparral. Ben Messick's *Chavez Ravine* (c. 1940), depicting a ramshackle Mexican village just minutes from the Downtown, transmits the same message: Los Angeles had grown so fast and so far that it had left behind rural pockets. In *Echo Park* (1934) Phil Dike achieved a watercolor dynamic with urban vitality. Picnickers of all races and genders lounge beneath the palm trees. A sailor walks with his girl. Lovers embrace on the grass. A nanny takes her charges for a walk in the park. Boaters and anglers enjoy themselves on the lake. In the distance is the slightest suggestion of the Downtown, which becomes fully evident in Milford Zornes's *Downtown L. A.* (1939), a crowded streetscape at the foot of Angel's Flight. Tom Craig's *Plaza Los Angeles* (1935), by contrast, depicts the plaza where Los Angeles began its existence in 1781 as an Edward Hopper–like center of stillness at twilight, save for a restaurant and storefront ablaze with electric light. A long Los Angeles sunset fills the sky with carmine color, and above it all, half seen in the twilight haze, the ziggurat summit of the Los Angeles City Hall soars on the skyline.

Phil Paradise's *Flophouse, Taxi, Whore* (n.d.) is Ash Can in inspiration, as is Fletcher Martin's boxing scene *Lad from the Fleet* (1938), with its suggestion of George Bellows (not to mention macho Martin's own memories as a boxing contender in the Pacific Fleet). In *Saturday Night* (1931) Hardie Gramatky takes a watercolor snapshot of African-American life on Central Avenue. In Charles Payzant's *Wilshire Boulevard* (n.d.) we enter the high-rent district and the Miracle Mile, at whose entrance stands the Bullock's Wilshire department store, its Ozlike tower rising dark green against a sky created with a wonderfully subtle green, yellow, and blue wash. Nor is suburban life ignored. Suburbia accounts for one of the most enjoyable paintings of the California School, Phil Paradise's *Suburban Supper* (1939), a watercolor on paper that in its depiction of eighteen suburbanites dining by candlelight in their backyard offers proof positive that the Folks had truly found homes and happiness in the Golden State. In Phil Dike's *California Holiday* (1933), a watercolor on paper, the Folks take a holiday at the beach— swimmers, picnickers, sunbathers, boaters—the whole panoply of Southern California beach culture as it had consolidated itself by the late 1930s.

If there is one discernible difference between the painters of the California School in the South and those in the North (the group sometimes known as the Berkeley School), it is the attraction of the Northern Californian painters to an Asian approach to sky and land, even to cityscapes, as lightened washes of color: what might be described as an Asian-Disney ambience, a world not quite real but not quite unreal either. The Asian-Disney style is most discernible, as might be expected, in the work of the one Asian-American in their midst, the Oakland-born, Hong Kong–trained Dong Kingman, whose San Francisco paintings caught (for perhaps the first time) San Francisco as a city in which Asian-Pacific and Euro-American imagery coalesced.

Berkeley painter John Langley Howard, however, had something other than ethereal cityscapes in mind. The son of the prominent architect John Galen How-

ard, he shifted to art from engineering in the 1920s. In the early 1930s he turned
to the John Reed Society and fellow traveling on the Far Left. The artistic result
of this involvement was a series of powerful canvases (Howard worked in oil)
depicting fishing fleet and dock life, and the Social Realist *Embarcadero and Clay*
(c. 1936), a celebration of the longshoremen who had pulled off the 1934 general
strike. Fletcher Martin's *Trouble in Frisco* (1938), an oil on canvas, defines the
outer limits of Social Realism in the California School: a fight on the docks between two longshoremen, framed through an open portal. Paul Sample's *Speech
near Brewery* (1932), an oil on canvas, suggests a strike either in the beginning
stages or fizzling out. Sample's *Unemployment* (1931), by contrast, a crowded
streetscape of the idle unemployed, suggests the dangers to society of an economy
brought to a standstill.

   If one were to single out one artist to represent the California School, Millard
Sheets presents the most likely candidate. Born in Pomona in June 1907 and
trained at the Chouinard School in the late 1920s, Sheets had his first one-man
show reviewed glowingly by Arthur Millier in the Los Angeles *Times* before he
turned twenty-two. By the time he was twenty-three, Sheets had a painting accepted by the International Exhibition of Painting at the Carnegie Institute in
Pittsburgh, an unprecedented honor for such a young artist and the only award of
its kind that year to an artist west of the Mississippi. Secure in a teaching job at
Scripps College, represented by the Milch Galleries in New York, where he was
favorably reviewed, elected after the war (in which he served as an artist correspondent for *Life*) to the National Academy of Design, Millard Sheets proved, as did
so many of his colleagues in the California School, that young artists could get
their start in Los Angeles during the Depression, thanks to good galleries, an
abundance of local art schools, and the film industry. In his teaching at Chouinard and Scripps, his directorship of the Public Works of Art Program in Southern
California from 1933 to 1935, but most of all in his own work as an artist, Millard
Sheets set the pace for the California School.

   Sheets's *Angel's Flight* (1931), oil on canvas, today in the collection of the Los
Angeles County Museum of Art, is one of the finest American paintings of the
decade and certainly the single finest work of art to be produced by the California
School. Painted when Sheets was twenty four, *Angel's Flight*, a crowded cityscape
set atop Bunker Hill, is energized by nearly every ambition of Depression-era art.
Critics have remarked on its extraordinary depth, realized through its cinematic
angle of vision. Others have seen in it a triumph of restrained Social Realism: the
inexpensive dress of the women, the wash on the fire escape, the billboard advertising, the mounting progression of boarding and rooming houses up Bunker Hill,
the people taking the air on fire escape and porch. All this is seen from above,
from the vantage point of the two young women, as in the best possible shot from
a crane-mounted camera on a Hollywood lot. Others have seen a link in its color
to the work of Siqueiros, with whom Sheets collaborated on a mural for Chouinard. Here, in any event, is the triumph of the American Scene in its Los Angeles

dimension: Angel's Flight on Bunker Hill, ground zero of the Los Angeles experience, the setting of John Fante's *Ask the Dust* (1939) and a dozen other minimalist-realist Los Angeles novels from the decade. What George Bellows's *Cliff Dwellers* (1913) was to New York, Sheets's *Angel's Flight* is to Los Angeles: an unabashed, unapologizing evocation of urbanism in all its density and human drama.

Who are these young women whose robust bodies are so vividly present under thin dresses in the heat of a Los Angeles summer? Secretaries or waitresses? Artists' models? Whoever they are, they are women of the people, strong of limb and confident, as is so evident in the angle of their legs and arms and hips: confident of being in this city at this time of economic struggle, women unafraid to work and fend for themselves. They are not the straw-hatted princesses of Post-Impressionism, serene in their garden of roses, but young women who, like most Americans in this era, must struggle to survive and manage to sustain in the process the essential power of their physical and psychological selves. Looking down Angel's Flight, the two young women see Los Angeles, see life, see the Depression, see it all rising toward them. They are ready. They can take it. They will make it through.

9

Dreaming Through the Disaster

Hollywood Battles the Depression

SCREENWRITERS in Hollywood kvetched in the 1930s that they had fallen among philistines. Their talents, they claimed, were being sorely misused by studios run by idiots. Indeed, their plight—creative artists reduced to assembly-line production—represented an affront to literature itself. Just one of the many anti-Hollywood novels of the period, *For the Sake of Shadows* (1936) by Max Miller, can be taken as an example of a continuing chorus of lament. In the novel, a well-paid screenwriter, modeled on Miller himself, spends his days in his studio office writing to formula, tortured by the better possibilities of his material, which the front office would never buy. Because of their subsequent reputations (the group included, after all, William Faulkner, F. Scott Fitzgerald, Nathanael West, Budd Schulberg, Raymond Chandler, Dashiell Hammett, Maxwell Anderson, Robert Benchley, Stephen Vincent Benét, Moss Hart, Ben Hecht, Aldous Huxley, Christopher Isherwood, George S. Kaufman, Frederick Lonsdale, Dorothy Parker, and S. J. Perelman, among others), critics and historians have by and large accepted this scenario. The setting and the situation—a talented writer being misused by Hollywood, personified by a brash, semi-literate producer, unmistakably Jewish—have become cultural folklore.

At the same time, the brilliant achievement of Hollywood in the 1930s has also been recognized. Never have so many great films been produced in such rapid order, critics readily acknowledge; and never, as historian Arthur Schlesinger Jr. has pointed out, did Hollywood sustain such a powerful and direct contact with its audience or play such a significant role in the subliminal and public life of the nation.

How can both things be true? How could the Hollywood that allegedly so brutalized its literary talent achieve so much filmic art that helped the nation cope with unprecedented suffering? Could it be, as some suggest, that many talented screenwriters were exaggerating their plight as a way of coping with their guilt? They, after all, so many of them left-liberal in politics, were making big bucks ($500 to $1,000 a week was a standard salary) for a reasonable amount of work while the rest of the nation, including so many of its artists, languished in poverty. Very rarely, if ever, does an anti-Hollywood diatribe from the period by a distressed writer end with an account of him (women screenwriters seemed not to complain) quitting his job at the studio and devoting himself purely to literature.

While guilt might have been a factor, prompting so many Hollywood writers to flirt with or even join the Communist Party toward the end of the decade, mere guilt does not go far enough as an explanation. The fact is: film and literature were competing, some would claim irreconcilable, modes of expression; and in the 1930s, film—by which is meant the assembly-line product of the industrialized studio system—outperformed literature as both an art form and a social necessity. Some of the reasons for this are self-apparent. By its very nature literature is an elite mode of expression, even at the most literate of times. The Depression, by contrast, was a mass experience, and it required a mass medium, film, through which to address the issues, assuage the fears, and release the anxieties of a nation under mass stress.

From this perspective, Hollywood represented industrial America correcting itself through the industrial techniques of its industry of dreams, just as (to use a later association) a diagnostic and corrective computer program can search out and destroy a computer virus. Literature, by contrast, while it could address the subliminal needs of the Depression, was not fully compatible to the industrial system. Even best-selling novels and the short stories of the *Saturday Evening Post*, while products of the publishing industry, hence mass-produced, scored lower on the scale of collective communication than did the film.

As early as September 1912, William Dean Howells was describing the cinematographic show, as he called it, "the most universally accepted of all modern amusements." The moving picture show, Howells noted, "prevails everywhere, in Europe as well as America, and doubtless Asia, Africa, South America, and Oceanic."[1] The art of the photoplay, observed the *Nation* a year later, was "created for the masses and largely by them."[2] Film audiences, commented a *Harper's* critic that same year, fell into a dream-like state as if the flickering images on the screen had induced in them a form of collective trance. In his pioneering *The Photoplay: A Psychological Study* (1916), psychologist Hugo Munsterberg described the power of film as coming from its ability to allow the individual to recreate an inner reality structured by what Munsterberg considered the four forms of the interior life: attention, memory, imagination, and emotion. Universal in its technology and mode of presentation, Munsterberg argued, demanding a minimum of patterned preparation, hence formal culture, the film induced in each viewer a new and exhilarating mastery over the previously hard and fast conditions of external experience. Hence the early and vocal advocacy of the photoplay by populist poet Vachel Lindsay. In *The Art of the Moving Picture* (1915) Lindsay exulted that at long last the masses had their own art form.

Film historians have long since noted dozens of genre-cycles or genre-cycles within genre-cycles during the 1930s: pacifism, Ruritania, the fallen woman, quickly followed by the sexually liberated woman, the gangster, the convict or the ex-convict, the shyster, horror films, the costume epic, the backstage musical, the G-man, the reforming populist, the lynch film, right-wing films, left-wing films, a Chinese cycle, a Dead End Kid cycle, a western cycle, films of utopian escape, the films of *annus mirabilis* 1939 in which just about every genre-cycle was recapitulated and fulfilled. No consensus exists as to the fixed and precise taxonomy of these genre-cycles. Some peak within a year. Most overlap. Each film in each genre-cycle, moreover, is at once like and subtly different from the other. Enough genre-cycles have been identified and plotted, however, to suggest the workings of an industrial mechanism keyed to external event and the shifting subliminal needs of an industrialized mass audience conditioned to the consumption of a mass-produced and -distributed product. The confusion and anger of the early 1930s, as an example, was met with the parallel revolt of the gangster and the sexually liberated woman. The coming of the New Deal prompted a G-man cycle in which government restored order. When the Depression turned out to be longer than anyone initially expected, a genre-cycle of costume dramas came to the rescue.

To suggest this process of systematic compensation and adjustment is not to deny chance, serendipity, or individual preference, taste, and will. Such contingencies are always in the marketplace. Operating as a corrective market, Hollywood might still have produced a spate of costume dramas in the mid-1930s even if Irving Thalberg had remained in Brooklyn. On the other hand, because Irving Thalberg was very much on the scene at MGM in those years, the necessities of the costume requirement were met with panache. Economists, in other words, can discern the functioning of a market, even describe it mathematically, without making any reference to individual choice and chance, while at the same time subsuming the play of choice and chance into their analysis. From Adam Smith onwards, the invisible hand of the marketplace has included dream and desire, together with the eventual market solutions offered by King Kong, Mae West, or W. C. Fields.

Industrially structured by mass production and consumption, film might have developed differently in America, although its swift bypassing of formal culture seemed to have destined it to become a mass medium. Film might have divided into two distinct camps: an artist-dominated sector, diversified and personally controlled, and a more commercialized sector geared toward mass production. The visual arts developed this way, into distinctive sectors of fine and commercial production, with many talented artists (three generations of Wyeths come to mind)

DREAMING THROUGH THE DISASTER

spending time in each sector. With the rise of mass circulation magazines, literature also became, simultaneously, an industrialized and a cottage industry.

With the exception of United Artists, however, founded in 1919 by D. W.
Griffith, Charlie Chaplin, Douglas Fairbanks, and Mary Pickford as an artist-
controlled enterprise, film in the United States developed as a front office–controlled, studio-centered business, en route to becoming a vertically integrated industrial monopoly. The organizational and financial history of Hollywood has
been overshadowed by the analysis of its product and a chronicling of the celebrities created by its star system. Not for nothing, however, is film production to this
day referred to as the Business. The underlying history, the enduring reality, of
motion pictures is to be found in the story of its financial and organizational
dynamics, its business, as film production became increasingly industrialized
through the studio system.

Like many other commercial enterprises in the industrializing economy of the
early twentieth century, the pioneering studios of the 1910s—Fine Arts, Fox,
Lubin, Laird, Universal, DeMille, Goldwyn, Famous Players, Jesse Lasky's Feature Play Company, Metro, Reliance, Majestic, Vitagraph—underwent a process
of consolidation in the 1920s and 1930s. Metro-Goldwyn-Mayer led the consolidation process in 1924. RKO was organized in 1928. In 1929 Warner Brothers
absorbed Vitagraph and consolidated itself in Burbank. Founded in 1933 by Darryl Zanuck and Joseph Schenck, Twentieth Century Pictures merged with Fox in
1935, the same year Paramount was consolidated into its final form. Trailing such
giants as MGM, RKO, Warner Brothers, Twentieth Century–Fox, and Paramount were the smaller studios: Universal, founded in 1915; United Artists, organized in 1919; and Columbia, formed in 1922. Lower down the feeding chain,
on Poverty Row, were such smaller studios as Monogram, founded in 1931, Republic, founded in 1935, and a number of other seat-of-the-pants operations.
Producers Charles Chaplin, Hal Roach, Samuel Goldwyn, David O. Selznick,
Walt Disney, and Walter Wanger, meanwhile, maintained freestanding operations, at once survivors of the earlier multi-studio era and suggestions of another
path Hollywood might have taken in the direction of smaller studios dominated
by independent producers.

As in the case of all corporations, each studio resembled the other—and was
different. Located in Culver City in twenty-two sound stages with a hundred-
acre back lot, Metro-Goldwyn-Mayer dominated the industry, with an average
production of forty-two feature films a year. Its chief, Louis B. Mayer, was a
former ragpicker and nickelodeon owner who had become the highest-paid executive ($1.3 million in 1937 alone) in the United States. Mayer epitomized studio
power in all its arriviste splendor. Under Mayer's direction, and that of his production chief Irving Thalberg, MGM made movies that were bright, glittery, and
mid-American in orientation. Paramount Studios, by contrast, underscored Hollywood as a multi-national corporation. Financially linked with UFA-EFA in Ger-

many, Paramount employed a large number of German directors and technicians who gave to the films of Paramount a polished Europeanism in contrast to the mid-American appeal of MGM. Warner Brothers, by even further contrast, made films quick and fast in its Burbank studios, with a single director producing as many as five features a year. Founded and operated by two no-nonsense brothers, Harry and Jack Warner, apprentice butchers in their youth, Warner Brothers might be said to resemble a meat-packing factory. Because it operated on such a quick schedule, Warner Brothers also stayed close to daily experience, like a newspaper on deadline. Warner Brothers films were topical, overtly political even, given to an upfront portrayal of social stress and class conflict.

Two factors, sound and money, enabled Hollywood to meet the Depression head on with an appropriate product. Each was controlled by Wall Street, which acquired the film industry in the late 1920s as one of the last and most significant additions to its portfolio. In the mid-1930s, with the most recent reorganization of Paramount, Hollywood became permanently structured as the entertainment wing of an urban-industrial economy dominated by a handful of banks and investors who had every reason to wish the economy to recover and, most important, wanted the American people to remain orderly and well-behaved during the recovery process.

While sound pre-dated the Depression, Hollywood was forced to master the new technique amidst the chaos of a collapsed economy. It took a half decade and more for film to absorb this new medium. Initially, because of the necessity of encasing the noisy camera in a soundproof booth, films lost the mobility they had acquired in the previous decade. "Give us back our beauty," William DeMille remembers D. W. Griffith pleading at a meeting of the Academy of Motion Picture Arts and Science in 1928. "What use are pictures unless they are beautiful? These chattering horrors will destroy all we have achieved in twenty years of hard work."[3] Significantly enough, DeMille remembered that Griffith sat down to thundering applause.

In time, directors learned to employ the new medium in such a way as to align it with Munsterberg's notion that it was the essence of film to take objective reality and detach it from the strict confines of time, space, and causality. In *Hallelujah!* (1929), his first talking picture, King Vidor achieved an intricate web of synesthetic sound—African-American spirituals, swamp noises, the barking of a dog in the distance, the screeching of birds, the heavy breathing and sucking footsteps of a black man escaping through the swamp—that was in and of itself a paradigm of what the new medium could accomplish. The next year, Rouben Mamoulian employed a two-microphone technique in *Applause* (1930) to record simultaneously a mother singing a lullaby to her daughter and the daughter whispering a prayer in her bed. Mamoulian also took his camera out of its soundproof box, mounted it on wheels, located microphones throughout the set, and, most important, rigged a microphone to follow the camera. In an instant, film regained its fluidity. Just as it had broken down and rearranged the visual world, so too could film now separate, combine, and re-combine the sound environment. With the production of *The Thin Man* (1934), directed by W. W. Van Dyke, the microphone—in this instance moving through a crowded cocktail party, catching snatches of conversation, intermixing laughter, the tinkle of ice, a half-heard wise-crack—had become, in counterpoint to visual imagery, an active protagonist in its own right.

All this cost money. Making the transition to sound, in fact, brought Hollywood under the control of Wall Street by 1935, specifically the Morgan and the Rockefeller investment groups. The enormous expense of refitting the studios for sound could not have come at a worse time. By late 1930 Hollywood understood that it would not be exempt from the hard times. Throughout 1931 the industry went into financial free-fall. Fox made $9.2 million in 1930 and lost $5.5 million in 1931. RKO made $3.3 million in 1930 and lost $5.6 million in 1931. Warner Brothers went into an even steeper decline, falling from a $17.2 million profit in 1929 to a $7 million profit in 1930 to a $7.9 million loss in 1931. Paramount-Publix (Publix being the theater chain) survived 1931 with $6 million in profit. The next year, Paramount-Publix lost a staggering $21 million and went into receivership, with Yellow Cab magnate John Hertz of Chicago becoming chairman of the finance committee in the reconstituted board. Adolph Zukor survived the reorganization, but another Hollywood founder connected with Paramount, Jesse Lasky, was forced out and went to work as an independent producer ($3,000 a week, a percentage of the profits) on a three-year contract at Fox.

Hollywood haters were ready to dance on its grave. "Recent rumors," exulted Sidney Howard in the *New Republic*, "report that Hollywood, so long bankrupt in all other respects, is now financially bankrupt as well and that the industry which has spent so many years in its infancy may die even before the age of puberty."[4] Three big studios, Howard reported, were on the verge of collapse. In the imminent collapse of Hollywood, Howard exulted, could be seen the larger vulnerability of capitalism itself.

Howard was correct in his facts—the studios were in trouble—but wrong in the outcome he predicted. Warner Brothers, for example, which had acquired the First National distributing company just before the crash, should have collapsed between 1930 and 1933, as it racked up a staggering $113 million loss, had it not been for the driving will, the sonofabitchness, of Harry and Jack Warner, Jack especially, who pushed employees to the limit. Directors were assigned five to seven films a year. Films went into production before scripts were complete. Actors and actresses were cast in simultaneous productions and required to commute from one sound stage to another by bicycle. Sets were darkly lit and kept to a minimum. Along with the fast-paced direction, this *noir* approach resulted in the smoky *verismo* of Warner films from this era. By late 1933 Warner Brothers was showing a meager profit of $105,752, but it had turned the corner.

With sound and finance as its battering rams, Wall Street spent the first half of the 1930s breaching and occupying the citadel. A year before the crash, in 1928,

Wall Street was already positioning itself for the campaign. That year, the Rockefeller-dominated Radio Corporation of America (RCA), American Pathé, and the Keith-Albee Theater Circuit combined to found the Radio-Keith-Orpheum Corporation (RKO). For the first time in film history, RKO was showing the possibilities of Hollywood becoming a vertically and horizontally integrated industrial trust. The Rockefellers, operating through the Chase National Bank, had the money. RCA, operating through its subsidiary Photophone, had the sound technology. American Pathé had the production capacity. Keith-Albee had the theaters. Western Electric, meanwhile, a Morgan-dominated manufacturing subsidiary of the American Telephone and Telegraph Company, also entered the sound technology business, marketing its system through Electrical Research Products, Inc. Warner Brothers and Fox had their own systems, Vitaphone and Movietone, soon to be absorbed by the giants. By 1935 RCA and Western Electric, which is to say, the radio-oriented Rockefeller Group and the telephone-oriented Morgan Group, after a number of bruising court battles, thoroughly dominated Hollywood through their patented technology and investments.

As a further integration of the system, the Morgan Group and the Rockefeller Group cross-invested in each other's enterprises. Because of the structure of the motion picture industry, moreover, in which theater chains were either owned by the studios, or themselves owned the studios, or were the captive markets of the studios, the dominance of the Morgan Group and the Rockefeller Group via sound technology and investment became in effect a hegemony over the entire industry. Production, distribution, screening, the collection of box office receipts: all was now one business. Eight gigantic companies — Paramount, MGM, Twentieth Century–Fox, Warner Brothers, RKO, Universal, Columbia, United Artists — were now producing nine-tenths of all features. These vertically and horizontally integrated monopolies would remain in force through the 1940s when the anti-trust division of the Justice Department after a long struggle leveraged a partial breakup of the system.

While Wall Street consolidated its hold on the film industry, the industry itself spent the mid-1930s regaining its momentum at the box office. The low point came in midsummer 1933 when nearly one-third of the sixteen thousand regularly operated theaters in the United States closed their doors. Theater owners gave away chinaware to lure Americans back to pictures. One promotion technique, Bank Night, a form of lottery, was so successful that the man who patented and franchised it, Charles Yeagar, formerly with Fox Theaters of the West, became an overnight multi-millionaire. By 1937 the crisis had passed. Motion pictures were now the fourth largest industry in the United States, representing an overall capital investment of $2 billion. Each week more than 150 million people across the planet viewed the productions of the Hollywood studios, then in the beginnings of an ambitious $12 million expansion program. Twentieth Century–Fox, for example, was spending $4 million to improve its ninety-six-acre site in west

Los Angeles. While not commonplace, the million-dollar film budget made its first appearance.

In its first phase of response, Hollywood countered the Depression with dark, problematic genre-cycles dealing with gangsters, prisons, horror, revolution, and rebellious sex. Indeed, the 1930s witnessed a fusion of mob and Hollywood interests in the evolution of the gangster movie and the rise to stardom of an actor, George Raft, who bridged the cultures of Hollywood and the hoods. Although he pleaded guilty to one count of income tax evasion in later life, George Raft was not a gangster. He was, rather, a gangster-manqué who as an actor traded on his early gangster connections and whose successful on-screen depiction of gangsters helped determine the way gangsters behaved in real life. The vehicle in which Raft, gangster-manqué, achieved fame — the gangster film and its sub-genre, the prison film — continues to intrigue cultural historians. More than two hundred identifiable gangster or gangster-prison films were released in the 1930s, a figure falling by more than half in the next decade.

Gangster films were allegories of the Depression, most obviously, with the gangster standing in as capitalist hero or anti-hero, depending. The inspiration of Al Capone got the genre off to a lively start in *Little Caesar* (1930), directed by Mervyn LeRoy and starring Edward G. Robinson as Caesar Enrico Bandello. The career of Capone was also in the background of *Scarface* (1932), tautly directed by Howard Hawks, with Paul Muni as Tony Camonte. In terms of cinematic excellence, *Little Caesar* and *Scarface*, together with *Public Enemy* (1931), directed by William Wellman and starring James Cagney and Jean Harlow, dominate the more than ninety gangster films released between 1930 and 1932. The real-life references in these films were obvious. *Doorway to Hell* (1930), for example, clearly told the story of Legs Diamond, and *Little Caesar* and *Scarface* were obviously based on the career of Al Capone, who was more or less flattered by all the attention and entertained a number of Hollywood celebrities when they passed through Chicago. Even John Dillinger was watching a gangster film at the Biograph in Chicago — *Manhattan Melodrama* (1934), starring Clark Gable — the day he was gunned down by the cops.

Each of these gangsters — Robinson as Rico, Muni as Tony, Cagney as Tom Powers — is an ethnic Roman Catholic up from big-city streets at a time when Protestant America was reestablishing itself in the suburbs and voting, in 1927, for Herbert Hoover of proper Palo Alto over Al Smith of the Lower East Side. Film gangsters are definitely not from the suburbs. They dress sharp, like George Raft, with dark shirts, white ties, double-breasted suits, and hats with rakishly styled bands and brims. They roar around the city by night in large automobiles. They spend a lot of time on the telephone. Indeed, the city — especially the city by night, *mise-en-scène* for violence, a long black car careening out of the darkness, tommy guns chattering from the open windows — is the negative anti-environment, fearsome and repelling, of the gangster film. *Scarface* was banned in a number of states for being too violent, and Nazi Germany refused the film an import license.

Then there is the question of sexual ambiguity. In *Little Caesar,* Rico displays an almost openly homosexual attraction toward Joe, a professional dancer, played by Douglas Fairbanks Jr., and is ultimately destroyed by his refusal to let Joe leave his influence. In *Scarface*, Tony Camonte has an incestuous attraction to his sister Cesca, played by Ann Dvorak, and the brother and the sister are reconciled in the final scene, like lovers, shooting it out with the cops. In *Public Enemy*, Cagney's Tom Powers, in one of the most misogynist gestures in film history, rubs his girlfriend Kitty's face (Mae Clarke) with a breakfast grapefruit. (The real-life gangster did it with an omelette.) All three gangsters, however, Rico, Tom, and Tony, love their mothers (as did George Raft), who represent not only maternal love but the straight path they might have taken.

Early gangster films, in other words, spoke to an America deeply disturbed about capitalism, the ethnic and minority dominance of cities, the pros and cons of sexual liberation, and the breakup of the traditional extended family as younger and early-middle-aged couples migrated to the rapidly expanding suburbs. In its critique of capitalism, however, a critique made at the very moment capitalism was reeling on the ropes, the gangster genre-cycle most dramatically (and paradoxically) stabilized the capitalist status quo by establishing the gangster as a capitalist run amuck. On the one hand, the gangster represented the entrepreneurial capitalist *par excellence*, with organized crime functioning as a displaced anti-type of industrial capitalism under stress. By putting capitalism, temporarily, outside the law in framing it in the gangster cycle, Hollywood allowed capitalism to be simultaneously critiqued and reaffirmed. Gangsters, after all, met a violent end. Capitalism run amuck—whether through organized crime or through the rigged stock market that most Americans believed had caused the Depression—demanded correction. When the gangsters fell, when Little Caesar died exclaiming, "Mother of Mercy, is this the end of Rico?," disordered capitalism was corrected, at least subliminally, and, if only by indirection, legitimate capitalism, meaning the system, was reaffirmed.

Running parallel to the gangster cycle and dependent upon it (gangsters, after all, were caught and sent to jail) was the prison film, beginning with *The Big House* (1930), starring Wallace Beery. The prison film was even more schematic than the gangster movie. Here were no distracting themes of social class and urban sociology. Instead, society was collapsed back into its basics, prisoners and guards, the powerless and the all-powerful, for a drama that awaited the probes of Michel Foucault for its full construal: the prison, in short, as prime paradigm of power and control in society. If society is a prison, and a prison is society, then Wallace Beery, the convict boss who foments a prison riot, represents the system, which is to say, industrial capitalism, run amuck. As boss of the Big House, Beery plays outside the rules with the tacit cooperation of the warden, just as capitalism played beyond the rules prior to October 1929. There are few if any redemptive possibilities in *The Big House*. The Depression has only begun. The American economy, like Wallace Beery, has been sent to solitary. His response is to lead a prison revolt. Would industrial capitalism, comparably compromised and comparably paranoid, lead to comparable disorder? *The Big House* has no answers, yet in merely allowing a scenario of prison revolt to play itself out, the film provided subliminal release to parallel tensions in a Big House otherwise known as the urban industrial United States.

The psychological horror of prison films dovetailed with the mental torment of the early 1930s horror films, many of them coming from Universal. The horror genre-cycle began in 1931 with film versions of two literary classics, *Frankenstein*, directed by James Whale, and *Dracula*, directed by Tod Browning. Like Weimar in the 1920s, the American film industry was turning to the horror film as objective correlative for social and psychological stress. As the Depression worsened, Hollywood met the deepening anxieties of America with even more excruciating contributions to the horror genre-cycle. With the release of *Freaks, Doctor X, The Mask of Fu Manchu*, and *Doctor Jekyll and Mister Hyde*, 1932 represented a banner year for grotesquerie, cruelty, and terror. Tod Browning's *Freaks*, in which only two performers are normally proportioned, still holds the record for grotesquerie in American cinema. In the conclusion of the film, one of these normal circus performers, a strong man, is emasculated by his deformed colleagues, and the other, his girlfriend, is crushed by them so badly that she goes on exhibition as the Chicken Woman, squatting in a bran pit. *Doctor X* is concerned with necrophilia, cannibalism, dismemberment, and rape. In *The Mask of Fu Manchu*, Boris Karloff, back from his performance in *Frankenstein* the previous year, perfects various modes of torture. He attaches one victim to a huge bell, injects another with the venom of reptiles, starves another to death with food held inches away from parched lips. In *Doctor Jekyll and Mister Hyde*, Rouben Mamoulian coaxed from Fredric March a higher level of psychic torment, a more grotesque evocation of physical deformity as emblem of moral evil, than was even present in Robert Louis Stevenson's novel.

Torture and revenge are the key motifs of *Kongo*, another 1932 release, directed by William Cowan. Played by Walter Huston, the dictator of an African kingdom, confined to a wheelchair, tortures his mistress, played by Lupe Velez, by twisting her tongue with a loop of wire. Luring the daughter of the man who broke his back from her convent boarding school, he confines her to a brothel in Zanzibar, where she becomes an alcoholic whore. In *The Black Cat* (1934), which had little to do with Poe's masterpiece, Austrian director Edgar Ulmer provided American audiences with ninety minutes of pure psychic torment, totally Weimar in inspiration, albeit in clean-lined sets inspired by Le Corbusier. The subliminal release offered the American people by such horror films is self-evident. Tormented, so many of them, in their personal lives, American audiences required objectifications of their psychic states, just as Germans of the Weimar Republic had responded to *The Cabinet of Dr. Caligari* (1919) in the previous decade.

Despite its ostensible theme of Beauty and the Beast stated by Bruce Cabot over the body of the dead ape fallen from the Empire State Building, *King Kong* (1932) derived its fundamental and continuing power from something deeper than even the love of the Beast for Fay Wray: something suggested by Max Steiner's relentless score, brooding and ominous, played throughout the film by an eighty-piece orchestra. In some obscure way, Kong was standing in for the American people. Like the giant ape, Americans had been kidnapped from the certainties of a prelapsarian economy, antebellum in its simplicities of exchange and tribute, and had been thrust, like Kong, into the fearsome complexities of the urban industrialism symbolized by New York where Kong is put on display as the eighth wonder of the world. Betrayed by his capitalist captors, Kong escapes and inadvertently terrorizes the city in his search for Fay Wray, his lost innocence, his Daisy Buchanan. When Kong is besieged atop the Empire State Building by attacking aircraft, the parable is complete. Urban industrialism destroys natural innocence. Will the Depression do the same to the American people?

Provocative in her clinging slip, platinum blonde Fay Wray upstages the great ape himself. Until the enactment of a new Production Code in 1934, Hollywood, after a brief flirtation with the fallen woman theme, countered the Depression with a lush outpouring of female-centered, female-dominated sexuality that asserted the resistance, the effrontery, the sheer desire on the part of women threatened with marginality to defy the odds and seize life and by so doing to hold off the possibilities of defeat and collapse. Frank, female-oriented, and rebellious, screen sexuality between 1931 and 1934 compensated audiences through vicarious eroticism for the growing sense of fear and hopelessness in personal lives.

Initially, Hollywood tried to adhere to the Protestant ethic through a short-lived genre-cycle of fallen woman films, as if to suggest that America somehow deserved the Depression or at least was responsible for it. In *Applause* (1929), a former burlesque queen, fifty and alcoholic, played by Helen Morgan, commits suicide when her daughter takes to the stage as a striptease artist. In *The Divorcée* (1930), Norma Shearer discovers that she must pay with the loss of her marriage for a retaliatory affair initiated when she learned that her husband had been unfaithful. Tit for tat cannot work for a woman. In Clarence Brown's *Anna Christie* (1930), Greta Garbo's sound debut (GARBO TALKS! ran the billboards), and George Cukor's *A Bill of Divorcement* (1932), Katharine Hepburn's screen debut, young women are held from happiness by the mistakes of their fathers. Anna Christie's father, a merchant seaman, leaves her as a child in the care of predatory cousins, who rape her, which leads to a life of prostitution, which prevents her marriage to Charles Bickford. In *A Bill of Divorcement*, Katharine Hepburn's mentally ill father, John Barrymore, escapes from his asylum and drives Hepburn to break off her engagement to care for him. In each of these films, to be female is to be wounded and vulnerable. Women must pay for their sins or bury their lives in the service of others. The Depression is everybody's fault and must be accepted by everyone as part of an inevitable and tragic destiny.

But what about rebellion? What about a contrary message, as in: the Depression is a disaster beyond anyone's personal responsibility and must be met, as Weimar Germany met the equally depressed 1920s, with defiant bravado, sexually expressed? Already, Hollywood had achieved a dynamic equation of money, self-determination, and female sexuality in the figure of Lorelei Lee, the diamond-loving flapper heroine of screenwriter Anita Loos's best-seller *Gentlemen Prefer Blondes* (1926), which was quickly brought to the screen. So cunning was Loos's conjunction of money, female independence, and female sexuality, George Santayana half-seriously declared *Gentlemen Prefer Blondes* to be the finest philosophical work ever written by an American. Traveling to Vienna, Lorelei Lee is analyzed by Sigmund Freud, who, astonished by her sexuality, advises her to cultivate some inhibitions. Freud might have given the same advice to Lorelei Lee's real-life contemporary Clara Bow, the It Girl, star of *Mantrap* (1926), *It* (1927), and *The Wild Party* (1929). A working-class girl who spoke in a Brooklyn accent, Bow had no trouble playing a telephone operator, a lingerie salesgirl, or a barbershop manicurist unintimidated by big shots, taking life and love as she found them. Bow's off-screen persona was equally confident and concupiscent. While untrue, the legend that Bow entertained the entire USC football team only reinforced the larger-than-life sexuality she pursued and projected. As the Depression worsened, sexual defiance became increasingly characteristic of the Hollywood film as Clara Bow's rebellion on screen and off became Hollywood's rebellion as well.

The 1930s opened with Erich von Stroheim, playing a butler in an English mansion, unpacking Constance Bennett's lingerie, piece by piece, with loving admiration. In 1931 Norma Shearer countered her sadder but wiser role in *The Divorcée* with the unashamed female sexuality of *A Free Soul* (1931). Then came the sex comedies *Her Majesty, Love* (1931), *Three on a Match* (1932), and *Trouble in Paradise* (1932), which brought the *ménage à trois* to the level of high art— until, that is, the release of Noel Coward's *Design for Living* (1933). *Scarlet Dawn* (1932), a story of the Russian Revolution, set new standards for openly suggested sex and offered an orgy scene more Weimar than American in its inspiration. In *The Sign of the Cross* (1933), Cecil B. DeMille perfected the genre of sex pageant masquerading as religious epic. Allowed to tap into his own secret homosexual life, Charles Laughton played Nero as a raging queen. DeMille also provided an explicit subplot of lesbian seduction. The orgy scenes in *The Sign of the Cross* equaled those of *Scarlet Dawn*. In one instance—a near-naked woman chained to a statue of Priapus being admired by an amorous gorilla—DeMille out-Freudianized King Kong himself. The next year, in *Cleopatra* (1934), arguably the best film of his career, DeMille achieved a shimmering Roman/Art Deco pageant of costumed sexuality. Cleopatra's seduction of Mark Antony (Claudette

Colbert and Henry Wilcoxon) on her royal barge to the rhythmic pounding of a drum setting the pace for the oarsmen achieves a sensuality operatic in scale and intensity.

A new breed of female star, meanwhile—Marlene Dietrich, Jean Harlow, Bette Davis, Carole Lombard, and the improbable Mae West—was busy breaking barriers. Arriving from Germany in 1930, Marlene Dietrich brought the sexuality of Weimar, including its bisexuality, to the American screen in such films as *Morocco* (1930), *Dishonored* (1931), *Shanghai Express* (1932), *Blonde Venus* (1932), *Song of Songs* (1933), and *The Scarlet Empress* (1934), in which Dietrich played with great success the sexually voracious Catherine the Great. If Dietrich represented the liberated woman as bisexual Weimarite, Jean Harlow, in such films as *Red Dust* (1932), *Bombshell* (1933), and *Dinner at Eight* (1933), brought to perfection the persona Clara Bow had pioneered, a woman of the people in sexual rebellion. Her hair peroxided to a platinum sheen, her eyebrows plucked to razor sharpness, her silken dresses clinging like skin to a voluptuous body devoid of undergarments, Harlow was every working woman as she knew herself or wanted herself to be: intelligent, ironic, redeemed from prudery by a touch of the tart. To these formidable attributes, Harlow added the demeanor of the wisecracking, sometimes tough-talking dame with the gift for comedy she displayed in *Libeled Lady* (1936), playing a lady capable of taking both men and the Depression as they came, a mixed bag, while silently keeping her options open. Seducing Richard Barthelmess in *Cabin in the Cotton* (1932), Bette Davis, a young contract player at Warner's, brought a Southern sultriness, with more than a touch of Erskine Caldwell, to the screen. If Marlene Dietrich suggested Berlin and Jean Harlow suggested New York or Chicago, Bette Davis came across as a basically well-bred Jezebel from Dixie with country club connections. Madeleine Carroll, by contrast, was urban like Harlow, but with a thinner, even more tense sexuality: a sorority girl from Delaware or Connecticut who just might go bad. Another peroxide blonde, Carole Lombard, split the difference between Harlow's demotic sexuality and Carroll's suggestion of the wayward debutante. Lombard, like Clark Gable, could be bad and good at the same time. On her best behavior, she might wind up a doctor's wife in Evanston.

As frankly sexual as each of these actresses was, it was the most improbable figure of them all, Mae West, aging, overweight, big-hipped, and ungainly, who pushed the genre of the openly sexual peroxide blonde to its outer limits and brought down upon herself and Hollywood the wrath of the Roman Catholic Church. West's first film, *She Done Him Wrong* (1933), made $2 million in three months and most likely saved Paramount from bankruptcy. Because Mae West had the gift of irony, comedy, and self-parody, her screen persona continues to intrigue critics with its multiple layers of meaning. Recent research suggests that West derived her style, so self-mocking, so self-aware, from the equally self-conscious parody of Broadway drag queens, who were themselves sending up the flashy *demimondaines* they so admired, who were in turn imitating Lillian Russell and other music hall vamps of the *fin de siècle*. (Today, drag queens imitate Mae West, which brings the cycle full circle.) Recognizing that she was too improbable to be a true vamp, West presented her sexuality through a comic prism. The songs she sang in *She Done Him Wrong*—"I Wonder Where My Easy Rider's Gone," "I Like a Man Who Takes His Time"—were breathtaking with double entendre. The one-liners of this film and its successors—*I'm No Angel* (1933), *Belle of the Nineties* (1934), *Klondike Annie* (1936), and *My Little Chickadee* (1940), in which West played opposite another comic genius, W. C. Fields— have, like the malapropisms of Samuel Goldwyn, entered American folklore. (To a gangster: "Is that a pistol in your pocket, or are you just glad to see me?" To an admirer: "Between two evils, I always pick the one I never tried before.") Through self-parody, West advanced into increasingly frank expressions of female sexual appetite by dissipating and deflecting their shock value without destroying their underlying force.

The Roman Catholic hierarchy was not amused. A decade earlier, in 1922, Protestant America, showing a similar reaction to sexual explicitness in films, had forced the formation of the Motion Picture Producers and Distributors of America. Under the presidency of Will H. Hays, formerly Postmaster General of the United States, this organization served as the *de facto* censoring board of Hollywood. Catholics, meanwhile, also began to organize, beginning in 1923 in Los Angeles with the formation of the Catholic Motion Picture Actors Guild headquartered in Blessed Sacrament Church in Hollywood. The guild issued an increasingly influential monthly journal, the *Motion Picture Guild News*, later the *Motion Picture Herald*, edited by Catholic newsman Martin Quigley. Work- ing with Quigley and the American hierarchy, Jesuit priest Daniel Lord drew up a Production Code, which the Hays Office formally accepted in 1930. Hays, however, had very few sanctions or resources with which to enforce the 1930 ordi- nance.

In the sexual sensationalism of its early 1930s films, Hollywood was defying both the Protestant and the Catholic forces, which had unified behind the Code of 1930. (In his autobiography, Cecil B. DeMille boasted how Will Hays called him on the telephone, with Martin Quigley at his side, and begged him to take out a particularly explicit dance scene from *The Sign of the Cross*. DeMille re- fused.) Meeting in November 1933 at the Catholic University of America in Washington, the American hierarchy appointed a special subcommittee to deal with the motion picture industry. Fully a quarter of the films made in Hollywood, claimed Bishop John Cantwell of Los Angeles, a member of the subcommittee, writing in the *Ecclesiastical Review*, the professional journal of the Catholic clergy in the United States, were either repugnant or offensive. Recent releases, he noted, dealt with adultery, seduction, concubinage, rape, prostitution, and aphro- disiacal drugs. (Bishop Cantwell was especially outraged by the dance scene in *The Sign of the Cross* that DeMille had refused to delete.) "Jewish executives are the responsible men in ninety percent of all the Hollywood studios," the bishop

continued, "and it is these Jewish executives who have the final word on all scenarios before production is actually launched. Certain it is that if these Jewish
executives had any desire to keep the screen free from offensiveness they could
do so."[5]

As if shocked by the implications of what he had just stated—with its implicit
call for a *Kulturkampf* against Jews, a crusade that Father Charles Coughlin
would soon take up—Cantwell quickly dropped the issue of Jewish producers and
shifted the blame to the ethnically undifferentiated writers of Hollywood for what
was going on. Seventy-five percent of the screenwriters of Hollywood, the bishop
claimed, were pagans, "men and women who care nothing for decency, good
taste, or refinement. Most of them are living lives of infidelity and worse, wherein
there is to be found not a suggestion of respect for religion or for spiritual values.
. . . Our writers for the screen spend much of their talents in glorifying the
female libertine and the public prostitute."[6] The federal government, Bishop Cantwell concluded ominously, acting through the newly created National Recovery
Administration, should be expected to do something regarding the deplorable output of Hollywood. In the meanwhile, Catholics must act.

Meeting in June 1934 in Cincinnati, the American Bishops Committee on
Motion Pictures established a clearing house and lobbying organization called the
Legion of Decency. Councils of the legion were formed in each Roman Catholic
diocese throughout the United States and were asked to organize boycotts of offensive films. The American bishops also opened a Hollywood office headed by Joseph Breen, a former newspaperman who had previously served as the chief of
Production Code enforcement in the Hays Office. Breen represented a confluence
of both the Protestant-dominated Hays forces and the Catholic bishops operating
through the Legion of Decency.

Soon, very soon, Mae West was replaced by Shirley Temple, a five-year-old moppet from Santa Monica, dimpled, curly-haired, two inches over a yard in height,
and preternaturally talented as an actress and dancer, to whom Hollywood turned
in the crucial year 1934 as Christian America, in its Roman Catholic wing, was
launching its attack. Temple had begun her career two years earlier in the Baby
Burlesk series produced by Educational Studios, a small operation specializing in
films for children. In the Baby Burlesk series, children played adults, including
celebrities. Temple herself had played Marlene Dietrich and Louella Parsons.
Make-pretend Hollywood swiftly yielded to the real thing, however, as the film
industry, threatened with censorship, even the direct supervision of the National
Recovery Administration, turned to the ferociously intelligent child actress for a
way of checkmating the censors and forging a fresh connection with the American
people. In 1934, her first year under contract to Twentieth Century–Fox, Temple
made six films for Fox and one for Paramount. By the end of 1934, she was in
eighth place at the box office, sharing honors, among others, with Mae West. By
the end of 1935, she placed first, a position she held in 1936, 1937, and 1938, a

year in which, having earned $307,014, she became the seventh highest paid person in the United States.

The money expressed the gratitude of Hollywood, as did the special Oscar it gave her in 1934. According to press releases, she placed it on her shelf next to the rest of her dolls. Temple enabled Hollywood to put its Weimar period behind itself within one dazzling year, 1934, with a moppet mega-star who embodied both personally and in the roles she played the triumph of innocence. In just about every film, Temple played the healer, the reconciler, the interventionist. In *Little Miss Marker* (1934), she played an orphan who reforms her temporary guardian, gambler Sorrowful Jones, played by an upstaged Adolphe Menjou. In *Now and Forever* (1934), she inspired Gary Cooper and Carole Lombard into forming a wholesome family relationship. In *The Little Colonel* (1935), she reconciled her mother with her estranged grandfather, played by Lionel Barrymore. In *The Littlest Rebel* (1935), she saved her father from a Union firing squad. Sitting atop Abraham Lincoln's desk, she convinces the Great Emancipator that her father had crossed the Northern lines not to spy but to visit his sick wife. Lincoln was obviously an FDR stand-in, and a few years later, at the height of the New Deal, Temple spent an afternoon in the White House with the President discussing, among other things, the cross-country trip she was taking with her parents (a journey covered extensively by *Life*) and a recently lost tooth.

What accounted for Shirley Temple's popularity? Why did such figures as Eleanor Roosevelt, Noel Coward, J. Edgar Hoover, Henry Morgenthau, and Thomas Mann consider it an honor and an obligation to visit her on the set? Why did the American Legion make her an honorary colonel, the Texas Rangers appoint her an honorary captain, the Treasury Department name her an honorary G-woman? Why was her entry in *Who's Who* half as long as the President's and only two lines short of Eleanor Roosevelt's? Why did *Life* and dozens of American and English newspapers chronicle her 1937 cross-country tour as if it were a momentous event, fraught with implications for the recovery of America itself?

Because it was. Like the New Deal itself, Shirley Temple embodied the nation in the mid-1930s when it was most dramatically struggling for healing, reconciliation, recovery. Between 1930 and 1933, eroticism had expressed the rage and confusion, the rebellion against a threatening void, that had come with the first shock of economic collapse. And now the system was offering subliminal release with the new image of a child who was somehow, curiously, a stand-in for adults. As a child, Shirley Temple could keep alive the take-charge femininity of the early 1930s that remained so necessary to the psychic life of the nation, but without the explosive sexuality that had precipitated the censorship crisis of 1933. Of all prominent observers, only the English writer Graham Greene dared suggest that there was something ambiguous in the Shirley Temple fixation, which Greene insisted had erotic overtones. For the rest of the nation, Shirley Temple was fixing it, making it whole, when such fixing was sorely necessary. In her antebellum Southern films, which anticipated the central message of *Gone with the Wind* (1939) by four years, she reconciled North and South. Dancing up and down the stair-case with Bill Robinson in *The Little Colonel*, Temple accomplished not only a prodigious feat of dancing, she also managed to suggest that black and white had nothing to fear from each other. It was a stereotype, of course, the kindly black Uncle figure, the winsome white child; but it was better than a race riot.

"What are we pretending today?" Temple would ask her mother each morning in the early days of her film career.[7] Mrs. Temple might very well have told her daughter that today Shirley would be pretending the recovery of America itself. With the assistance of Mickey Rooney, Judy Garland, Deanna Durbin, and other juveniles, Shirley Temple was pretending a 1930s replay of what Huck and Jim found as they lay side by side on a raft in the middle of the Mississippi: an escape from fear, a renewal of hope, the illusion of innocence.

Comedy and musical comedy showed the same progression from cynicism to in-nocence, from Mae West to Shirley Temple. It is of the essence of comedy to reconcile opposites, to pull the world apart and then put it back together again. Offering a necessary escape valve, comedy is essential to the stability of any soci-ety. Political systems that seek to control comedy or banish it completely inevita-bly collapse; for comedy can always go underground, as it did in the former Soviet Union, and continue to undermine a repressive social order with a subversive humor devoid of that very reconciliation which comedy invariably shows when it functions freely and in the open.

In contrast to other genres, comedy, screwball comedy especially, remained a screenwriters' show. Uncertain of the wacky outer limits of *goyische* humor, the front office tended to give the largely WASP cadre of screwball comedy writers more of a free rein. With the exception of the Marx Brothers (and they were another matter), screwball comedy belonged to the *goyim*, like the Rose Bowl or the drag line at a Hasty Pudding production. For the duration of screwball com-edy, Hollywood replaced the Broadway stage as the comedy capital of the country. In comedy at least, all that was bright, witty, collegiate, and urban in the sensibil-ity of the literary exiles in the Writers' Building triumphed. To borrow from the famous *Variety* headline, while hicks might have nixed sticks pix, they and city-folk alike loved screwball comedy.

In its musical comedy genre-cycles, as in so much else, Hollywood began the thirties in a Weimar mode with a return to Ruritania as Erich von Stroheim had recently left it in the unfinished and unreleased *Queen Kelly* (1928). Producer Joseph Kennedy had canceled *Queen Kelly* in the final days of silent film at the insistence of his mistress Gloria Swanson because of the disgusting things director von Stroheim was asking Miss Swanson to do before the camera. A French Jew masquerading as a Prussian, von Stroheim had brought Ruritania to Hollywood in the 1920s with such costume epics of kitsch and kinkiness as *Foolish Wives* (1922), *The Merry-Go-Round* (1923), *The Merry Widow* (1925), and *The Wedding March* (1928). In the latter film, costumed officers from *Mitteleuropa* party in a brothel whose details—black male attendants in chastity belts sealed with heart-shaped padlocks, courtesans blindfolded so as not to recognize their famous clients, a pair of Siamese twins—set new standards for on-screen depravity. The collapse of *Queen Kelly* sent von Stroheim to Coventry, meaning life as a supporting actor, usually a monocled *Junker* ("the man you love to hate") and an occasional novelist whose *Paprika* (1935) carried on his obsession with Ruritania as sexual underground.

Von Stroheim's colleague and survivor in Ruritania, the German-born Ernst Lubitsch, was equally enamored of eros and the costumes and uniforms of *fin-de-siècle* Central Europe. Lubitsch, however, avoided von Stroheim's excess in favor of a more slyly rendered eroticism, titillating yet sustainable in mid-America, a trademark soon known as the Lubitsch Touch. Working at Paramount, with its connections to Vienna and Berlin, Lubitsch greeted the Depression with *The Love Parade* (1930), his first sound film; *Monte Carlo* (1930); and *The Smiling Lieutenant* (1931). *The Love Parade* and *Monte Carlo* featured Jeanette MacDonald, whom Lubitsch brought to stardom in *The Merry Widow* (1934). Playful and sly, even cynical, in their sexual themes, Lubitsch's musical comedies, together with such parallel efforts as Rouben Mamoulian's *Love Me Tonight* (1932), another Maurice Chevalier–Jeanette MacDonald costume vehicle, were very much part of the early 1930s in mood and tone, which is to say, subversive and rebellious in a Weimar sort of way.

In the crucial Depression year of 1933, a more aggressively American genre of musical comedy, energized by an explicit economic critique, replaced Ruritania. In a rush, from Warner Brothers, where everything was rushed, came in one hectic year *42nd Street* (1933), *Gold Diggers of 1933* (1933), and *Footlight Parade* (1933). The sudden appearance of these films from Warner's was all the more unexpected in that Hollywood had commenced its sound era just a few years earlier with an excessive production of musical reviews designed to demonstrate the capacities of the new medium, and these poorly made films had driven the genre to the ground by 1932. At Warner's, however, executive producer Darryl Zanuck had something in mind other than the static, plotless musical reviews of the first years of sound. Zanuck wanted musicals strong on plot and contemporary themes, as was the style at Warner's, fast-paced, another Warner's trademark, and sassy, with wisecracking chorines, stage door johnnies, chorus boys with over-busy hands, and equally amorous producers in polo coats. With director Lloyd Bacon at the helm, Zanuck got what he wanted: three breathtaking musicals whose themes—breezy sexuality ("She makes forty-five dollars a week and sends her mother a hundred of it"), stories of chorus girls surviving on Broadway, disquisitions on the brutal economics of a Broadway show, sermons on the necessity of dedication and hard work as a condition of economic success ("You're gonna work nights," the choreographer tells the chorus girls in *42nd Street*. "You're gonna work until your feet fall off!")—directly spoke to the anxieties and urgencies of 1933.

Each of these three musicals had a backstage and an on-stage component. The backstage story was explicitly economic. A Broadway show is organized, funded, rehearsed, and produced. Directed by Busby Berkeley, the stage components offered intricately choreographed dance reviews filmed at dramatic angles. While ends in themselves, the Berkeley routines also made economic critiques ranging from fantasy to a surprisingly high level of social commentary. In *Gold Diggers of 1933*, for example, in the famous "We're in the Money" sequence, near-nude chorus girls dance with great gold coins in their arms, insisting that the Depression is over. In the same film, on the other hand, Joan Blondell sings "Remember My Forgotten Man" accompanied by a marching chorus of the unemployed and Army doughboys in uniform, memorably suggesting the veterans of World War I whose sacrifices were being betrayed by the Depression but who still knew how to march, perhaps on Washington. In *Footlight Parade* a line of sailors, in a more hopeful mode, count cadence behind the NRA eagle and a gigantic portrait of Roosevelt. Breezy, wisecracking, good-humoredly sexual, open in their gold-digging ways, the chorus girls of these films — Joan Blondell, Ruby Keeler, Ginger Rogers, Una Merkel — advance their central notion: both a girl and America have got to get by by doing whatever it takes. Hard work and luck are always welcome (Bebe Daniels sprains her ankle, Ruby Keeler takes her place and becomes a star) but sometimes a girl has got to break the rules and do what she has to do.

As in the case of other genre-cycles, Hollywood moved from the economically and sexually explicit critique of the Warner Brothers musicals of 1933 to the more escapist mid-decade modes of RKO. The transition began just as the 1933 Warner Brothers cycle spent itself. On 29 December 1933 RKO released *Flying Down to Rio*, in which Fred Astaire and Ginger Rogers steal the show from the top-billed Dolores Del Rio. For the rest of the mid-decade, no year passed without an Astaire-Rogers vehicle, beginning with *The Gay Divorcée* (1934) and continuing through *Roberta* (1935), *Top Hat* (1935), *Follow the Fleet* (1936), *Swing Time* (1936), and *Shall We Dance* (1937). Flushed by this string of successes, which RKO sorely needed for both its finances and reputation, producer Pandro Berman provided Rogers and Astaire the best that Hollywood could offer: the best music to dance to, first of all (Cole Porter, Con Conrad, Oscar Hammerstein II, Irving Berlin, Jerome Kern, George and Ira Gershwin); the best musical directors (Max Steiner, Nathaniel Shilkret); the best supporting actors (Edward Everett Horton, Betty Grable, Irene Dunne, Lucille Ball, Randolph Scott); the best choreographers and dance directors (Dave Gould, Hermes Pan, Harry Losee, Astaire himself); skilled directors (Thornton Freeland, Mark Sandrich, George Stevens); elaborate costumes and elegant sets: all of it orchestrated toward those enchanting minutes in which Astaire and Rogers dance with a joyous partnership whose intensity transcends the perfect symbiosis of maleness and femaleness they are so precisely achieving. In these dances, Astaire and Rogers offered an experience of release and affirmation to millions of Americans whose lives were otherwise so terribly bound to the earth. Thin, balding, pushing forty, Astaire dancing is transformed into an American Everyman, debonair and adept; and Ginger Rogers becomes an equally insouciant American Everywoman, her life released of all burden in sequences of dance exquisitely reinforcing the mood of the mid- to late thirties when the New Deal, after the stumbling start of the NRA, was getting into high gear.

When not dancing, Rogers and Astaire were equally adept at comedy, a genre-cycle remaining vital throughout the rest of the decade. For the first four years of the 1930s, however, Depression America had had trouble laughing. Hence the power and significance of the Marx Brothers in *Animal Crackers* (1930), followed by *Duck Soup* (1933) and *A Night at the Opera* (1935), each film co-starring Margaret Dumont, a solitary figure of beleaguered and long-suffering sanity in the symbolist-absurdist, anarchistic universe created by the madcap brothers. The humor of Groucho, Chico, Harpo, and Zeppo had European origins in the subversive humor of the Pale, where suppressed Jews had fine-tuned the ability to mock the establishment for nearly a thousand years. From this perspective, America accentuated and refined this defensive subversion, allowing it a freedom it never enjoyed in Europe. Now the establishment—its colleges, its government, its opera, its social protocols as epitomized by the WASP-matronly Margaret Dumont—could be openly satirized by three zany brothers (Zeppo soon faded from the scene) whose Jewishness, the Pale polished by Broadway, was speaking for an entire nation wishing to tweak (if not worse) the establishment that had caused the hard times.

Likewise, in these first years, before the more indigenously American screwball comedy got its start, did another imported tradition, the English music hall comedy of Stan Laurel and Oliver Hardy, help the nation through the first terrible years of the collapse. A Cockney veteran of English vaudeville, Stan Laurel arrived in the United States as part of the Fred Karno Music Hall Company on the same boat as Charlie Chaplin, another member of the troupe, with whom Laurel briefly roomed in New York. Chaplin never mentions this fact in his *Autobiography* (1964), however, nor did he ever mention Stan Laurel, seeing in him a comparably talented comic who, from Chaplin's paranoid perspective, posed a threat.

In 1929 Hal Roach teamed Stan Laurel with a rotund comic from Georgia named Oliver Hardy and began the production of a series of two-reel (occasionally three-reel) comedies—eight in 1930, ten in 1931, nine in 1932, eight in 1933, six in 1934, four in 1935, three in 1936, and two a year thereafter—which became the staple comic fare, especially in the early 1930s, of millions of ordinary Americans. While Laurel and Hardy had much in common with the Marx Brothers—slapstick, the pacing and progression of an increasing level of misbehavior—the Englishman and his American partner lacked the anarchistic edge of Groucho and his brothers. The Marx Brothers challenged all authority. Oliver Hardy remained pointedly polite to policemen. The Marx Brothers dressed in outlandish getups, Harpo especially. Laurel and Hardy dressed in bowler hats, cutaway coats, bow ties and Hamilton collars, and other elements of bourgeois attire. The Marx Brothers, Groucho especially, were knowledgeable, fiercely intelligent, totally in control. Groucho provoked, then orchestrated, each and every absurd situation. Laurel and Hardy, by contrast, were innocents, almost child-like. They stumbled into each absurdity. The duo deliberately destroy a piano in the Academy Award–winning *The Music Box* (1932). Laurel and Hardy dutifully make every effort to move their piano up a flight of stairs, only to have it disintegrate despite their best efforts. Like children, Laurel and Hardy could sleep side by side in the same bed without the slightest hint of homoeroticism. They achieved their finest moment as children manqué in *Babes in Toyland* (1934). Through the comedy of Laurel and Hardy, Americans, given the satisfactions of rebellion by the Marx Brothers, experienced an opposing message of resignation and acceptance, of child-like simplicity in the face of an absurd universe. The message of the Marx Brothers, rebellion, and the message of Laurel and Hardy, acceptance, were each necessary. The system knew this and presented the American people with complementary alternatives.

To cite the European origins of Marx Brothers comedy and the English music hall origins of Laurel and Hardy is not to suggest the absence of an American element in early 1930s film comedy. Jimmy Durante, for example, translated to film the broad humor of the late-night New York saloon scene. Wide-mouthed Joe E. Brown, introduced in *You Said a Mouthful* (1932), represented another indigenous style, the well-meaning hayseed, as expressed in Brown's role as a baseball player in *Fireman, Save My Child* (1932). Totally American in his comic style, silent screen star comic Harold Lloyd made the transition to sound in *Professor, Beware* (1932); and no one could be more traditionally American, even tediously so, than Will Rogers in *A Connecticut Yankee* (1931). Yet the comedies of the early 1930s had something shaky and uncertain about them: a confusion of value and point of view that reflected their generally incoherent socio-economic critique. Comedy demands clarity of perspective and ideas, and such was lacking in the first years of the Depression, so much better suited to the anarchy of the Marx Brothers, the minor apocalypses of Laurel and Hardy, the raspberry given his boss by Charles Laughton in *If I Had a Million* (1932).

In 1934, however, screwball comedy was formally launched with the release of Frank Capra's *It Happened One Night*. Capra had spent the previous three years discerning the dynamics of screwball and trying them out. In *Platinum Blonde* (1931), for example, a Jean Harlow vehicle, he satirized the rich, rather savagely. In *American Madness* (1932) he softened his touch, portraying Walter Huston as an inept but not reprehensible banker. Yet in both vehicles the rich, which is to say, the capitalist class who might be accused of bringing the Depression to ordinary America, are out of harmony with the American people. The story of a runaway heiress, played by Claudette Colbert, and the wise-guy newsman who befriends her, played by Clark Gable, *It Happened One Night* swept America off its feet. It was funny, for one thing. It also reconciled the classes by leaving the heiress in the arms of a brash and unpretentious all-American guy. Among the other sub-genres contained in its mix, this Opus One of screwball comedy was a road show: a traveling across America by bus; an evocation of highways and motels (the famous overnight scene in which Colbert and Gable sleep chastely in their single beds); an inventory of ordinary Americans, cops, bus drivers, newsmen, all willing to help out the runaway heiress when she goes on the road. She in turn sheds her snobbery. No wonder the film won five Oscars! It showed the capacity of screwball comedy to reintegrate the fragments, to reconcile the disparities, of an embattled socio-economic order. At the end of the laughing, everyone felt so much better about the country.

Introduced as well that year, in a movie titled *The Old-Fashioned Way* (1934), was the improbable W. C. Fields, who out-scrooged Scrooge in his dislike of children, animals, policemen, motorists and mothers-in-law. Among other things (all comedy is multi-faceted) W. C. Fields—in his parodic costume of frock coat, spats, and top hat, his bulbous nose a monument to drink, his mumbling asides, his admixture of levity and lubricity—represented a send-up of the upper-class clubman as hard-drinking sociopath: beyond work, beyond family, almost beyond society, brilliant but frustrated by the world of action, ruined by excess, the kind of figure propping up the bar of any number of men's clubs across America in the year 1934, surveying the plight of the masses through the prism of a glass. Fields's equally alcoholic counterpart, William Powell as detective Nick Charles in *The Thin Man*, yet another 1934 release, showed the upper classes in a more favorable light. The fact that both Fields and Powell, together with John Barrymore in *Twentieth Century* (1934), another screwball comedy from this screwball-founding year, should make so much of drinking is easily attributable to the recent end of Prohibition; yet being drunk also blunts their upper-class persona, vitiating its meanness, its capacity for counter-revolution, in a miasma of booze. Addled by drink, the ownership class could be left to its own devices.

At this point, the mid-1930s, having barely escaped the wrath of the righteous, Hollywood decided upon the strategy of promoting an image of itself as a whole-some, even winsome sort of place: as mid-America, only more so. Hollywood, ran the new argument, was a workaday district of Los Angeles, a factory town, as well as a state of mind. It had a Chamber of Commerce and a Bank of Hollywood as well as a mythic dimension. It had a fine public high school and library, a flourishing YMCA and YWCA, a private athletic club, elegant Spanish Revival homes on palm-lined streets, and homes in more innovative styles by Frank Lloyd Wright, Lloyd Wright, Gregory Ain, and Rudolph Schindler. It had beautiful apartment buildings, including Richard Neutra's Garden Apartments (1927) and the Garden of Allah complex, some of the best bungalow courts in the city, an American Legion post, a number of churches, two fine hotels, the Roosevelt and the Hollywood, a business district lined with stately buildings in the American Renaissance style, a cemetery, Schwab's Drug Store, Grauman's Egyptian and

Chinese theaters, the Pantages Theater, the Crossroads of the World shopping complex, the Western headquarters of NBC, as well as the studios of Columbia, RKO, United Artists, and Paramount. By the end of the decade, this newly conceptualized and repackaged mid-sized mid-American town—Akron, Ohio, only producing films, not tires, an ordinary American place—would be fixed in the minds of the rest of the country as a recognizable, hence acceptable, mid-American community.

It was not always that way. In the 1920s Hollywood presented itself to itself and the world as something fantastic, exotic, lavish to the point of excess. The stars of the 1920s, for whom Rudolph Valentino and Gloria Swanson might stand as archetypes, were chauffeured about the city in exotic automobiles, lived on great estates, spent fortunes on their couture. With her exotic Spanish Revival mansion in the Hollywood Hills, a great pipe organ in its public room, a gold-plated bathtub in its inner sanctum of a black marble bathroom, with $100,000 a year spent on lingerie, fur coats, headdresses, perfume, with her stately Lancia upholstered in leopard skin waiting grandly in the garage and a uniformed chauffeur on call, Gloria Swanson had only to play herself when she accepted the role of Norma Desmond in *Sunset Boulevard* (1950). The actresses of the 1920s (in this instance, Pola Negri might stand as a type) were prized for their aura of foreignness, for being defiantly non-American in their accent and lifestyle. Theodosia Goodman, a Jewish girl from Cincinnati, was transformed by the studios into the French-Arab vamp Theda Bara, born, it was claimed, in the shadow of the Great Pyramid. Gloria Swanson acquired a title, becoming the Marquise de la Falaise de la Coudray through marriage. On camera, actresses appeared in costumes blending Aubrey Beardsley and Art Nouveau, such as the elaborate gown Pola Negri wore in *The Cheat* (1923)—floor length, decorated in an arabesque of seed pearls in rose patterns, her hair bedecked in ropes of pearl, a black bird-of-paradise in her hand—when she was ostensibly playing a mid-American Long Island housewife giving a dinner party to help her husband win a promotion. Throughout the decade, costume designers such as Natacha Rambova created even more opulent effects in their efforts to de-Americanize the American film actress and hence make her, paradoxically, even more saleable to the American public. Rambova herself began life as Winnifred Shaughnessy of Salt Lake. In 1922 she married Rudolph Valentino, and a photograph of the two of them entraining from Los Angeles—Rambova in turban and cape, Valentino in a rakish hat, white flannel slacks, brown-and-white shoes, a herringbone blazer—epitomized the 1920s Hollywood style in all its Euro-centric chic.

Valentino had arrived as a penniless immigrant in 1913, the graduate of an agricultural college in southern Italy, and had hung around New York for a number of years getting by as a café dancer and gigolo. At the time of his death in 1926, he was living in luxury in Falcon Lair, a walled Spanish Revival palace atop Bella Drive above Benedict Canyon in Beverly Hills, playing out the role of the Anglicized Italian nobleman Hollywood purported him to be. The library of

Falcon Lair held shelves of leather-bound classics. Above the fireplace was arrayed a collection of medieval weapons; on another wall hung a portrait of Valentino as a Saracen warrior. The stable held four Arabians. Valentino rode each morning, splendidly attired in English-tailored riding togs. Twenty purebred dogs in the kennel awaited their master's call for a ride or a walk, and there were four cars in the garage, including a majestic Isotta Fraschini limousine, in which Valentino was chauffeured to the studio each working morning like a sovereign prince.

Even such quintessentially non-European figures as Mary Pickford, Douglas Fairbanks, John Barrymore, Harold Lloyd, and Marion Davies built for themselves elaborate European-style estates: Pickfair belonging to Pickford and Fairbanks, flagship estate for 1920s Hollywood; Harold Lloyd's Greenacres, a forty-room mansion on twenty-two acres off Benedict Canyon Drive in Beverly Hills, with a four-room playhouse for the children, complete with its own plumbing and electricity; Barrymore's Belle Vista, also in Beverly Hills, with its skeet range and private zoo; and Marion Davies's Spanish-style mansion on Lexington Road in Beverly Hills, ground zero of Hollywood party life in this era. In 1928 Davies's mentor and companion, mega-publisher William Randolph Hearst, built for his protégée a hundred-plus-room beachfront mansion in Santa Monica, capable of accommodating up to two thousand guests. In this seaside palazzo, Davies carried into the 1930s the large-scale star-style of the previous era. Hearst, a Hasty Pudding man at Harvard, loved costume parties, and Muggins, as Hearst called Davies, was ever willing to accommodate W.R., as she called him, to the point of maintaining a costume press on site, which she stocked with costumes rented from the studios. Mid-decade Davies gave her famous Baby Party, which brought the likes of Norma Shearer, Irving Thalberg, Constance Bennett, Clark Gable, Joan Crawford, and the Talmadge sisters (Natalie, Constance, and Norma) in a variety of Little Lord Fauntleroy, Boy Scout, and sailor outfits, with most of the women featuring baby-doll dresses and oversized bows in their hair. Lavish parties of this sort continued into the early 1930s and were noted in the popular press. Carole Lombard gave a party in 1933, Elsa Maxwell reported, in which everyone came as a hospital patient. Guests were brought in on stretchers. Food was served on surgical trays, X-ray pictures were hung on the walls, and the odor of iodoform pervaded the house.

Yet an element of caution, even self-doubt, was surfacing. George Cukor's *What Price Hollywood?* (1932), from a script by native daughter Adela Rogers St. Johns, chronicled the bittersweet rise of a waitress played by Constance Bennett to stardom. *What Price Hollywood?* survives in only a few copies. Was it suppressed—this sudden rush of self-awareness, this admission, made by Hollywood itself, and not by novelists from the East Coast, that Hollywood had its *noir* side? Hollywood likewise showed its insecurity in this period by its fawning relationship to Broadway, as in another Cukor vehicle, *The Royal Family of Broadway* (1930), co-directed with Cyril Gardner, a thinly disguised depiction of the Barrymore family written by Edna Ferber and George Kaufman. Ostensibly intended to satirize the Barrymores, hence Broadway and the legitimate stage, *The Royal Family of Broadway* also provided Ina Claire, playing an Ethel Barrymore–like figure, lines dismissing sound-studio Hollywood as "all action, all talking, all terrible." In *The Guardsman* (1931), Sidney Franklin, directing under the tight control of MGM's Irving Thalberg, fawned over Alfred Lunt and Lynn Fontanne, giving Broadway's leading couple a stagy Ferenc Molnár story, with copious excerpts from Shakespeare, as if to showcase some class, real class, on the silver screen.

Only recently has it become acceptable to note, without incurring suspicions of anti-Semitism, the root cause of so much of Hollywood's insecurity: the origins of so many of its founders in the ghettos of Central and Eastern Europe. (Significantly, Jewish scholars have led in the assessment.) As late as 1936, fifty-three of Hollywood's eighty-five best-known producers were Jews, many of them born in Europe. Far from turning Hollywood into a Zionist conspiracy, as some were charging, the Jewish elite, so insecure in its own lowly origins, was doing its best to purge Hollywood of anything that smacked of the Pale. In the films they produced, they celebrated every ethnic group but their own. With the conspicuous exception of *The Jazz Singer*, one searches in vain for a Jewish-oriented movie or even a discernibly Jewish character, other than a psychiatrist or two, in the productions of the period. While most Jews voted Democrat, the studio chiefs remained staunch Republicans. They loathed Roosevelt, whom most Jews adored. Later in the decade, the moguls showed a curious reluctance to acknowledge what was going on in Europe, despite the fact that their studios were filling with Jewish refugees. Occasionally, they might assert their Jewishness, however obliquely. Was the lion roaring at the opening of each MGM film, one might ask, the fearsome Lion of Judah, warning the *goyim* in thousands of theaters across the land not to take for granted the ancient and proud race providing them with entertainment?

Ever since its founding, Hollywood, which is to say, Jewish Hollywood, had been an object of scorn for proper, which is to say, WASP, Los Angeles. Hollywood people were excluded from the better clubs from the double vulnerability of being both Jewish and Hollywood. Even Cecil B. DeMille, an Episcopalian, was blackballed from the California Club. When Hollywood tried to establish its own club, Harry Carr reported in the early 1930s, it was a disaster. Fistfights broke out on the ballroom floor. One club member destroyed a painting of a star from a rival studio. What else could one expect, asked Carr, from a club whose admissions committee included a former junk dealer, a former glove salesman, a one-time minstrel, and an ex-jobber in secondhand clothes? Carr was showing the dismissiveness edging into anti-Semitism that was a strong local characteristic. Internal evaluations could be equally critical. "Hollywood," thundered director Sidney Howard in the *New Republic* for 9 November 1932, "is a part of that five-and-ten metropolis called Los Angeles. . . . From its stucco bungalows to its stucco boosting, it is self-dedicated to the mean, the reactionary, and the phoney."[8]

Yet even as these critiques were being made, another opinion was forming. Eastern observers such as Vincent Sheehan and Lillian Symes were fascinated by the ability of one district of Los Angeles, little more than a small town, to become, in Sheehan's terms, "the aesthetic capital, and in some ways the emotional capital, of the country."[9] For Symes, Hollywood, and by extension Los Angeles itself—an amalgam of New England, the South, and the Midwest, which in and of itself constituted a powerful American statement, a reconciliation of sections in the creation of a new movie-oriented culture—had become, "whether we like it or not, a dominant element in contemporary American life."[10] The movies, both Sheehan and Symes observed, had the ability to confer magic on what was otherwise, as the 1930 census revealed, a town of 153,000 people, thirty-seven banks, one daily newspaper, and nineteen motion picture palaces.

In the mid-1930s, as part of its strategy of re-earning respectability and acceptance in mid-America so as to continue its even more important task of reconciling the nation to itself, and hence saving nothing less than the established social order, Hollywood began to promote itself to the nation as not just the capital of the American film industry, a company town, but the alternative capital of America itself, the one city everyone had in common. In the 1920s Hollywood and its stars had done their best to be or to seem exotic, European. Now Hollywood advanced itself to the nation as a Midwestern American town with palm trees, organized, like other American towns, around the effort to fight the Depression while maintaining the openness, the good humor, that was so characteristic of the American temperament.

After all, publicists pointed out, for all the talk of its wealth, Hollywood itself was battling the Depression. In 1932 alone the Motion Picture Relief Fund, headquartered in the Bank of America building at Western Avenue and Santa Monica Boulevard, dispensed $190,000 to needy film workers. Anyone earning more than $200 a week was expected by the studios to earmark one-half of 1 percent of his or her earnings to the fund. In 1939 the fund acquired its own radio program, *The Screen Guild Show*, which premiered in January 1939 over sixty-one CBS stations. Top stars donated their talents to *The Screen Guild Show*, allowing more than $10,000 a week to be raised for local relief efforts. By late 1939 some 642 Hollywood families, representing nearly sixteen thousand individuals, were receiving help from the Motion Picture Relief Fund, which was expending $279,000 a year under the presidency of the Danish-born actor Jean Hersholt and five full-time social workers. Certain cases were typically Hollywood. An impoverished and aging actor was provided money for a toupee so he could find work as a bit player. An alcoholic screenwriter was allowed to dry out at a local sanitarium. An extra was given money to get his tuxedo out of hock. An aspiring actress was sent to the dentist to have her teeth capped.

The success of *The Screen Guild Show* underscored the rising importance of national radio to Hollywood. In 1932 NBC originated a mere twelve hours a year of national broadcast time from California. By 1937 NBC was broadcasting more than seven hundred hours of national radio from San Francisco and Los Angeles. By 1938 NBC was constructing a five-acre, two-city-block studio on Melrose; and CBS was building an equally impressive facility on Sunset to serve a wide array of Hollywood-oriented programs featuring such stars as Nelson Eddy, Don Ameche, Edgar Bergen and Charlie McCarthy, Dorothy Lamour, George Burns and Gracie Allen, and Bing Crosby. Through national broadcasting such programs as *The Kraft Music Hall, The Camel Caravan, Hollywood Hotel, Hollywood Playhouse, Hollywood Mardi Gras, Your Hollywood Parade, Thirty Minutes in Hollywood, Hollywood in Person, Hollywood Screen Scoops, Lux Radio Theater,* and *The Jell-O Program with Jack Benny,* Hollywood communicated with the rest of the nation with the vivid intimacy that is the special gift of radio. Millions of listeners soon came to believe that in some personal way they were also part of the Hollywood community, part of its mood and style, aware of its locales and special places, in on its jokes.

Jack Benny, who moved his show from New York to Hollywood in 1935, was especially adept at creating among his thirty million listeners each Sunday evening a close personal connection with Beverly Hills, the residential suburb of Hollywood where Jack lived, kept his money in an underground vault, and garaged his vintage Maxwell touring car. Each Christmas season, Benny shopped for his entourage—girlfriend Mary Livingston, portly announcer Don Wilson ("Jell-O, six delicious flavors"), butler Rochester (played by the gifted comic and song-and-dance man Eddie Anderson), the tippling bandleader Phil Harris, the kid singer Kenny Baker (later replaced by Dennis Day), and Benny's arch-nemesis Fred Allen, with whom Benny carried on a twenty-five-year mock feud. These annual shopping expeditions, heard by millions, helped make Hollywood seem a quintessentially American town over the Christmas season, complete with the lights and decorations strung over Hollywood Boulevard. By 1940 comedian Bob Hope, sponsored by Pepsodent toothpaste, was mounting a similar Hollywood-centered show rivaling the Jack Benny program, with an equally stable entourage and array of local references. As host of *The Lux Radio Theater,* Cecil B. DeMille, among others, became a nationally known figure, with his signing on ("Greetings from Hollywood, ladies and gentlemen") and his signing off ("This is Cecil B. DeMille saying good night to you from Hollywood") heard on Monday evenings by some forty million listeners. "I like big numbers," DeMille later remarked of these broadcasts, "but what the Lux program meant to me cannot be measured by any numbers. It meant families in Maine and Kansas and Idaho finishing the dishes or the school work or the evening chores in time to gather around their radios. It meant the shut-ins, the invalid, the blind, the very young, and the very old who had no other taste of the theater. It meant people, not in the mass, but individuals, who did me the honor of inviting me into their homes."[11]

Through the radio broadcasts and nationally syndicated columns of humorist Will Rogers, the adjacent community of Beverly Hills became equally known and nationally accepted. It is impossible, in fact, to distinguish between Hollywood and Beverly Hills in this era, with Beverly Hills serving as the residence of choice for most successful Hollywood stars. Like Hollywood, Beverly Hills prided itself on being, for all its glitz, an ordinary American town, with a first-rate public high school (adjacent to the back lot of the Fox Studios); an elegant Spanish Revival civic center, completed in 1932; the famed Beverly Hills Hotel, where the polo crowd, led by Darryl Zanuck, Walter Wanger, and Will Rogers, persuaded the management to transform the former children's dining room into the Polo Lounge; and an equally active Chamber of Commerce whose annual banquets featured a noted celebrity as guest of honor. Like Hollywood, Beverly Hills, a noticeably Jewish community, featured a gigantic Christmas tree each year in parkland fronting Santa Monica Boulevard. In 1926 Beverly Hills elected Will Rogers its honorary mayor, and the conjunction of Rogers and his town—the rangy Oklahoman, quintessentially Anglo-American Protestant in appearance, frontier folksy in humor, and the lush Mediterranean Revival estates of a largely Jewish city—in and of itself bespoke the movie industry reaching out towards the heartland.

By 1937, with the release of William Wellman's A *Star Is Born*, starring Fredric March and Janet Gaynor, Hollywood had recaptured not only its self-esteem and acceptability to the American people, but the moral high ground as well. A remake of George Cukor's *What Price Hollywood?* (1932), A *Star Is Born* takes the plot, setting, and characters of the first film—an aspiring actress, the alcoholic actor whom she marries, and the studio system—and reverses all the *noir* implications of the previous effort. In the 1932 film, Hollywood is at fault. Hollywood devours. Hollywood destroys. In the 1937 remake, it is actress Vicki Lester's alcoholic husband Norman Maine, not Hollywood, who causes the trouble. Pauline Kael has branded the 1937 A *Star Is Born* as masochistic in its depiction of the Main-Lester relationship and oozingly self-congratulatory in its depiction of the studio system. In any event, the transformation of attitude in five short years is significant, as is the fact that Hollywood would return to the A *Star Is Born* vehicle in 1954 and once again in 1976 in an ongoing effort to recast and rejustify itself.

Two years later sociologist Leo Rosten, after two years of research, published *Hollywood: The Movie Colony, the Movie Makers* (1939). Assisted by a team of statisticians and data gatherers, Rosten probed every aspect of the film industry, front office and back lot, stars and directors, technicians, producers, distributors, the entire business. The result: a pioneering social science survey that, together with Hortense Powdermaker's *Hollywood: The Dream Factory* (1950), remains a classic in its field. The evidence, Rosten argued, debunked the myth that Hollywood represented an exception, a place apart, in the American economic scheme. Hollywood, Rosten advanced, citing table upon table of statistics to prove his point, participated in the overall corporate and industrial culture of the United States and was structured accordingly. With the exception of the self-made moguls at the top, who resembled the self-made leaders at the helm of comparable enterprises, Hollywood was administered by college-trained managers who practiced the same techniques as their peers in other businesses. While film stars had a higher divorce rate than the rest of the nation, Hollywood was in Rosten's opinion refreshingly ordinary in its sexual and family life. Most important, Rosten claimed, the era of excess in Hollywood was long past; and besides, even when excess was at full tilt, the conspicuous consumption of Hollywood—the homes, the parties, the sexual escapdes—in no way surpassed those of the robber barons of the Gilded Age at a time of comparable exuberance and consolidation in American economic history. The robber barons, after all, as well as the first generation of buccaneering movie moguls, tended to be succeeded by golf-playing executives.

The ability of Hollywood to alter its image so dramatically between 1933 and 1940 underscores the multi-faceted affinity between the film industry and the press. Press people filled Hollywood as correspondents, publicists, and screenwriters. While suggestions of ambivalence entered such early 1930s newspaper films as *Scandal Sheet* (1931) and *Five Star Final* (1931), which implied that not every newspaper story was gospel truth, the more telling paradigm came from *The Front Page* (1931), a film version of the 1928 Broadway play by Ben Hecht and Charles MacArthur, in which newsmen and newspapers, however compromised, are finally to be counted on the side of truth, justice, decency, and the American way. Many, if not most, screenwriters had spent stints in newsrooms. Daily journalism had given them a sense of writing as a collaborative effort, together with a taste for brevity, crisp dialogue, and jump cuts that helped them bat out scripts in similar circumstances. Both newspapers and Hollywood were industries. (Ex-journalists were especially adept at writing screwball comedies. Wacky stories were a dime a dozen around the newsroom.) While the ex-newsie turned screenwriter had no urge to return to daily deadlines, battered Remingtons, and rotten newspaper pay, he or she also tended to depict newspapers at their best, even glamorize them, down through the 1930s and beyond. From this perspective, Orson Welles's *Citizen Kane* (1941), however multi-faceted, is the greatest celebration of newspaperdom of them all.

Columnists such as Louella Parsons and Hedda Hopper, meanwhile, joined by Sidney Skolsky, Sheilah Graham, Jimmy Starr, Walter Winchell, Jimmy Fidler, and more than five hundred correspondents directly or indirectly covering the film industry by the late 1930s, filled newspapers and radio airways with an avalanche of commentary that soon made Hollywood—already the aesthetic and emotional capital of America, as Vincent Sheehan claimed—even further known to millions as well as they knew their own town. William Randolph Hearst first and most clearly grasped the value of Hollywood gossip as an important American industry. Enamored of Ziegfeld Follies star Marion Davies, Hearst entered Hollywood in the early 1920s with a full-scale assault, including the formation of Cosmopolitan Pictures, intended to make Davies a star. By the 1930s Hearst had become the grand old man of Hollywood. An invitation to San Simeon represented the Hollywood equivalent of election to the Social Register. A powerful affinity developed between Hearst and the film colony, especially actors and actresses. In a world uncertain of its status and taste, Hearst functioned as a reference point of stabilized identity. Here, in vivid personal terms—a Hollywood mistress ensconced in a hundred-room, antique-filled beach house in Santa Monica, his own studio and newsreel service, his newspaper empire and chain of radio stations, Hearst Castle up the coast—were coalesced all the power and clout of the developing communications industry.

At just about the same time that Hollywood was being founded, moreover, Hearst was perceiving in newspaper terms what the founders of Hollywood were glimpsing in the new medium of film: the coalescence of information and entertainment. With his screaming headlines, dramatic photographs, publicity stunts, bylined columnists, Sunday supplements, and comic strips, Hearst made newspapers appeal to the same broad masses being discovered and developed by Jesse Lasky, Samuel Goldwyn, Adolph Zukor, Cecil B. DeMille, and the other founders of the film industry. Both Hearst and Hollywood achieved a new and direct power with their audience. Each masterfully fused information, interpretation, and entertainment. From this perspective, Hearst occupied a role in Hollywood more powerful than that of the great studio heads. Physically present, giving party after party alongside his actress-mistress, entertaining at San Simeon like a sovereign prince, Hearst embodied Hollywood as embryonically connected to something awesome and powerful, if as yet without a name: the communications industry: print, radio, film, later television vertically and horizontally integrated, synthesized as entertainment, enriching itself at an unprecedented rate—and within the century destined to become the primary medium of politics and culture.

With Heart's encouragement, Los Angeles *Examiner* reporter Louella Parsons—a matronly woman, twice married and divorced (once secretly, to a riverboat captain) before she found happiness as the wife of a Los Angeles physician specializing in venereal diseases—pioneered the genre of syndicated Hollywood gossip columnist, beginning in the late 1920s. Some whispered that Hearst conferred such power on the hard-drinking Parsons, who by her own admission was only quasi-literate, because Louella had been privy to the greatest Hollywood scandal of them all: the mysterious death of producer-director Thomas Ince on 19 November 1924 following a cruise on Hearst's yacht *Oneida*. Louella, it was claimed, had seen things she should have not seen but knew how to keep her mouth shut. (No inquest was ever held into Ince's death, ostensibly from acute indigestion. Ince's body was immediately cremated. The Hearst newspapers initially published conflicting accounts of the affair. Hearst himself was conspicuously absent from Ince's funeral.) The rumor that Louella had something on the Old Man remained current through the 1930s and added to her mystique.

In 1937 Parsons acquired a rival in the business of Hollywood gossip, Hedda Hopper, syndicated out of the Los Angeles *Times*, a former actress given to oversized flowered hats and equally baffled by the English language. At the height of their popularity, Louella Parsons and Hedda Hopper reached a worldwide audience of seventy-five million readers. Each turned to radio with equal success. "Only Hollywood could have spawned such a couple," David Niven would later write, "and only Hollywood, headline-hunting, self-inflating, riddled with fear and insecurity, could have allowed itself to be dominated by them for so long."[12]

True, as Niven suggests, Parsons and Hopper were scandalmongers and bullies, dispensers and destroyers of reputation; but they also kept the Hollywood community in line in matters sexual and political. Monitoring Hollywood's behavior, Parsons and Hopper helped keep at bay the witch hunt that had almost materialized in 1933. In that year, in fact, the last of the great sexual scandals of the period had erupted, the affair between actress Mary Astor and Broadway playwright George Kaufman, which Astor chronicled in a sexually explicit diary unfortunately discovered by her husband. In the divorce proceedings, Los Angeles Superior Court Judge Goodwin Knight ordered Astor's diary destroyed as pornography ("it all worked perfectly, and we shared our fourth climax at dawn. . . . Ah, desert night—with George's body plunging into mine, naked under the stars"), which most likely deprived the literature of erotica of a minor classic.[13]

Significantly, both Louella and Hedda were politically to the right, which suggests yet another role they played: keeping Hollywood from getting a reputation for being even the slightest shade of pink when, by the late 1930s, it was showing deep streaks of red, especially among its screenwriters. Charlie Chaplin made the mistake of being both sexually unconventional and on the far left, which earned him the special wrath of each columnist. Any star who might deviate from a mid-American norm—Greta Garbo, Katharine Hepburn, Laurence Olivier, Vivien Leigh, Ingrid Bergman—was equally castigated. Orson Welles's *Citizen Kane* (1940), a thinly disguised biography of William Randolph Hearst, earned Parsons's lifelong enmity. Along with his spendthrift ways, Parsons's hostility helped make Welles *persona non grata* in Hollywood for most of his career. Clark Gable, by contrast, was promoted by Parsons, Hopper, Adela Rogers St. Johns, and other columnists as, in St. Johns' terms, "the Great Common Denominator of this village": the Hollywood star as self-respecting American, devoid of even the slightest suggestion of 1920s decadence. Gable's earlier ambiguity in matters sexual, as well as the active homosexuality of Tyrone Power, remained a matter of private knowledge.

Magazine articles from the late 1930s describing Hollywood homes made every effort to stress the taste, the restraint, of the new Hollywood lifestyle. Writing in the *Lutheran* for March 1936, Dr. J. George Dorn, pastor of the Hollywood Lutheran Church, went out of his way to underscore the religious vitality of the Hollywood community. Eddie Cantor, Al Jolson, and Norma Shearer, Dorn reported, attended temple. Greta Garbo and Lew Ayres were Lutherans. Mary Pickford and Douglas Fairbanks practiced Christian Science. Bette Davis, Leslie Howard, and George Arliss remained active Episcopalians, with Arliss serving as president of the Association of Episcopal Actors. Marlene Dietrich and Marion Davies, Dorn reported, together with Mae West, were practicing Catholics.

Such protestations of respectability came at a time when the Far Left and the Communist Party were most active in the screen community. Throughout the decade, Hollywood bobbed and weaved, year by year, sometimes month by month, in an effort to keep in corrective relationship with political life—more precisely, with the subliminal aspects of political life—in a nation beset by a Depression it could not shake. Doing this, Hollywood assisted the American people in entertaining for themselves political alternatives without the necessity of following them through. Thanks in part to Hollywood, there was neither revolution nor *coup d'état*.

Nor was the enduring problem of race neglected. While innovative in its theme (an African-American preacher in the rural South betrayed into murder by the infidelity of his wife), King Vidor's *Hallelujah!* (1929), played by an all-African-American cast and released less than three months before the Crash, cannot be classified as strictly a Depression film. *Hallelujah!* had its origins, rather, in the intense interest on the part of whites in African art and African-American culture that was very much part of the elite urban scene of the 1920s, most notably in New York City. Transitional in nature, poised between the Harlem Renaissance and the more militant African-American consciousness of the late 1930s, *Hallelujah!* nevertheless contained within itself an idea—African-Americans as citizens of the Republic, as protagonists in American life—that remained a revolutionary notion in the Jim Crow 1930s. The fact that an important director, Vidor, and an important studio, MGM, were willing to mount an all-African-American film was not lost on the African-American press of the period. *Hallelujah!*, noted Floyd Covington in *Opportunity* for April 1929, released African-Americans from the bit parts—butlers, mammies, song-and-dance men—to which they had been confined. Casting agencies, Covington pointed out, listed nearly four thousand black actors, actresses, and extras as of 1927. Some of them—James Lowe, Lincoln Peary (better known as Stepin Fetchit), Zack Williams—had already achieved reputations. "In the wake of this new experiment in all-Negro pictures," Covington concluded, "comes the Negro's chance to be articulate in his own behalf. Greater still, the success of these pictures shall erect the foundation of the Negro's permanent place in the cinematographic industry in California."[14]

It would take a half century and more for Covington's hope—African-American actors in films dealing directly with African-American life outside the perspective of white stereotype—to begin the struggle toward realization. In the late thirties, Hollywood began to film a number of all-African-American productions—*Dark Manhattan* (1937) comes to mind, an all-black gangster film suggestive of the later *Shaft* series—intended for African-American audiences and bringing to bear the talents of African-American screenwriters and producers as well as actors and actresses. That year as well, 1937, Million Dollar Productions, a company in which African-Americans were important but not exclusive investors, began work on *Spirit of Youth* (1938), starring heavyweight champion Joe Louis.

In the meanwhile, such African-American actors and actresses as Hattie Mc-Daniel, Butterfly McQueen, George Reed, Rex Ingram, Myrtle Anderson, James Fuller, Edna Mae Harris, Frank Wilson, Eddie (Rochester) Anderson, Bill (Bojangles) Robinson, Ernest Whitman, and Ethel Waters performed brilliantly in the parts they were assigned, waiting for a better day. For all its shortcomings, *The Green Pastures* (1936), an adaptation of Marc Connelly's successful Broadway play depicting heaven as perceived and peopled by Louisiana blacks, showcased the broad range of black acting talent available in the United States and introduced millions to the emotional power of African-American spirituals. Then came Hattie McDaniel's Academy Award–winning performance as Mammy in *Gone with the Wind* (1939), the one person in the world unafraid of Scarlett O'Hara. Subsequent criticism of *GWTW* has dwelt increasingly upon the Scarlett-Mammy relationship as a probe into the complexity of America's enduring dilemma, race. Already, in previous films—*Blonde Venus* (1932), *I'm No Angel* (1933), *The Little Colonel* (1935), *Show Boat* (1936), *Saratoga* (1937), among others—McDaniel had proven that even in her accustomed role as maid ("I'd rather play a maid than be one," she once remarked) the larger-than-life black actress was more than a match for the likes of Jean Harlow, Mae West, Shirley Temple, and now, Vivien Leigh. In the case of Jean Harlow, in fact, a certain hostility between maid and employer adds to the complexity of the film. In no film, in any event, did Mc-Daniel communicate the slightest sense of intimidation or inferiority. In *GWTW*, McDaniel's Mammy, legally a slave, deals with Leigh's Scarlett on terms of honesty and genuine concern for each other on both their parts. Awarding Hattie McDaniel the Oscar for Best Supporting Actress in 1939 (she was the first African-American to receive this honor), Hollywood acknowledged not only McDaniel's superior performance but the deeper complexities of the Scarlett-Mammy relationship, which in turn reflected the racial complexities of America itself.

Equally challenging was the spate of pacifist films—Lewis Milestone's *All Quiet on the Western Front* (1930), Howard Hawks's *The Dawn Patrol* (1930), Ernst Lubitsch's *Broken Lullaby* (1932), Mitchell Leisen's *The Eagle and the Hawk* (1933), and the last and in many ways the best of the series, Hawks's *The Road to Glory* (1936)—with which Hollywood opened the thirties. Compelling in their indictment of World War I, each of these films contained within itself, if only by association, a powerful critique of the current situation. The established order, based in industrial capitalism, implied these films, had sent Lew Ayres and his classmates to death in the trenches, had made Neil Hamilton sacrifice an entire fighter squadron, had destroyed the family of Lionel Barrymore by killing its only son, had forced Fredric March to commit suicide rather than send any more young men into battle. Was the established order not now up to its old tricks as it squeezed and manipulated the economy? Was this Depression inevitable—or was it contrived, just as the politicians and munitions manufacturers had contrived the First World War? The mood of these pacifist films, so cynical and despairing, equaled Weimar in anger and bleakness. For this critique alone, made in the early 1930s when the film industry was still locally controlled, Hollywood became an inevitable candidate for takeover by Wall Street. No such subversive presence could be allowed to maintain its independent hold over millions of Americans. On the other hand, these pacifist films also allowed the American public to vent its anger against the system that had given the people World War I and was now giving them a Depression that betrayed the better life after the Armistice that had been promised the doughboys in the trenches.

The notion that something was very wrong with the system also pervades Mervyn LeRoy's *I Am a Fugitive from a Chain Gang* (1932) and the spate of cynical topical films appearing in the early 1930s such as *The Phantom President* (1932), which depicted politics as a racket; *The Mouthpiece* (1932) and *Night Court* (1932), which saw lawyers and judges as shysters; and *American Madness* (1932), which portrayed banking as a con game in which the little guy was left holding the bag. Realistically directed by LeRoy, brilliantly acted by Paul Muni, who played an American Everyman beaten by the system (the film was based on a true story), *I Am a Fugitive from a Chain Gang* offered a cynical parable of American life. A veteran of World War I returns to a dead-end job, gets implicated in a holdup in a small Southern town, and is sentenced to ten years on a chain gang. Escaping, he assumes a new identity and works his way into senior management. Promised a pardon, he returns to the chain gang pending his immediate release but is betrayed by corrupt politicians. Escaping for the second time, he returns to the underground, twice betrayed by the system.

As the American Depression continued, the beaten-by-the-system genre-cycle showed remarkable endurance. It continued into the mid-1930s with such cynical commentaries as *Wild Boys of the Road* (1933), which depicted officials of the system, great and small, as being on the take, and such other America-is-being-betrayed films as *Massacre* (1934), *Black Legion* (1936), and *They Won't Forget* (1937). Also part of this cycle was an early genre-cycle of urban films, speaking to the persistent American distrust of cities—*Min and Bill* (1930), *Street Scene* (1931), *Taxi* (1932), *The Strange Love of Molly Louvain* (1932), *Two Seconds* (1932)—which saw in the city the very essence of a system that debilitated, corrupted, and finally destroyed the little guy.

In the pivotal year of 1933, as Roosevelt was telling the American people that they had nothing to fear but fear itself, Hollywood presented Americans with a fascist alternative. In Gregory LaCava's *Gabriel over the White House* (1933), the Archangel Gabriel, disguised as Judd Hammond, an inconspicuous party hack played by Walter Huston, is elected President of the United States through political machinations, then astonishes everyone by becoming a benevolent dictator. Among other things, President Hammond dismisses Congress, suspends the Constitution, and sends death squads to eliminate the criminal and the recalcitrant. He also inaugurates a nationwide program of public works and ends Prohibition by opening government-run liquor stores. When angry gangsters, disturbed by the threat to their bootlegging profits, attempt a drive-by shooting at the White House and are apprehended, President Hammond has them lined up against the wall and tommy-gunned, thus reconciling the New Deal with the St. Valentine's Day massacre. *Gabriel over the White House* was produced by Hearst's Cosmopolitan Pictures and, distributed by MGM, was released in the same month that Roosevelt was inaugurated. Could it be that Hollywood, or at least William Randolph Hearst, was making some rather blatant suggestions to the new President? That same year, in Cecil B. DeMille's *This Day and Age* (1933), a group of boys kidnap a corrupt tycoon and dangle him over a pit of hungry rats so as to extract from him a confession of murder.

On the other side of 1933, in Howard Hawks's and Jack Conway's *Viva Villa!* (1934) and King Vidor's *Our Daily Bread* (1934), Hollywood veered sharply to the left. As Pancho Villa—simple, idealistic, betrayed, and very angry—Wallace Beery personalized the forces that could lead to revolution. Vidor's more irenic *Our Daily Bread*, by contrast, independently produced and released through United Artists, was revolutionary only by implication in its depiction of unemployed workers successfully starting a cooperative farm despite the opposition of local bankers. The next year, in *Mutiny on the Bounty* (1935), even the upper classes, as represented by Clark Gable's Fletcher Christian (more an affronted American gentleman, as Gable plays him, than a British aristocrat), decide to throw in their lot with the oppressed common folk. Yet *Mutiny on the Bounty* also offered a subtle reconciliation of folks and patricians to the American public. The established order needs no revolution, the rebellion of Fletcher Christian suggests, only better people at the helm. Despite his command of the *Bounty*, Captain Bligh is not the real McCoy, not a true oligarch at all, but a lower-middle-class straw boss drunk with power, whom the admirals snub in a final scene.

Political revolution is the last thing on the mind of Longfellow Deeds in Frank Capra's *Mr. Deeds Goes to Town* (1936), although Deeds, masterfully played by Gary Cooper, has some very sharp things to say about the rich folk in New York. ("They created a lot of grand palaces here, but they forgot to create the noblemen to go in them.") Both Deeds and Jimmy Stewart's Smith in Capra's *Mr. Smith Goes to Washington* (1939), a reprise of an earlier film, have some sharp things to say about the establishment—the idle rich of New York, dishonest politicians in Washington—but the perspective is not that of revolutionary anger but rather that of small-town America setting the big city straight. Affirmation of the American experience begins dramatically with Mr. Deeds's visit to Grant's Tomb ("I see a small-town farm boy becoming a great general") and continues for the rest of the decade in a cycle of westerns and historical melodramas—*San Francisco* (1936), *The Plainsman* (1937), *The Buccaneer* (1938), *Of Human Hearts* (1938), *Alexander's Ragtime Band* (1938), *Stagecoach* (1939), *Young Mr. Lincoln* (1939), *Drums Along the Mohawk* (1939), *Union Pacific* (1939)—which for all their vari-

ety of plots and directorial styles contain an essential message expressed in historical terms: America is a good place; its people have true grit and will make it
through the slump as they have made it through past crises.

From this perspective, David O. Selznick's *Gone with the Wind* (1939) was the
greatest reconciling film of them all. By 1939 it had long since become clear that
there would be no revolution: that, in fact, there would be national healing and
reconciliation in the face of the conflicts in Asia and Europe into which the
nation might soon be drawn. The United States had already had its Rebellion,
suggested *Gone with the Wind*, Atlanta had already been burned and rebuilt, and
each side had in its own way already prevailed, the North in victory, the South
in code and courage. America, North and South, was an enduring experiment
that even a great Civil War could only strengthen. The option of violence as a
solution to American social and economic problems was gone with the wind.

Cities, however, continued to be regarded with ambivalence as evidenced in
The Devil Is a Sissy (1936), *Kid Galahad* (1937), *Dead End* (1937), *The Great
O'Malley* (1937), and the ultra-bleak *You Only Live Once* (1937). In W. S. Van
Dyke's *The Devil Is a Sissy*, Mickey Rooney, a tough but likeable street kid, must
live through the electrocution of his father in Sing Sing. ("It took three jolts to
kill him," he brags through his tears.) In *Kid Galahad*, director Michael Curtiz
depicted the brutal world of city-centered boxing, the brain-numbing thud of
gloved fists on heads, as it had never been depicted before. In Howard Hawks's
Dead End, gangster Baby Face Martin, played by Humphrey Bogart, is shot
down, and the Dead End Kids who admire him seem destined for continuing
delinquency. In William Dieterle's *The Great O'Malley*, Pat O'Brien plays an
Irish cop who bullies everyone on his beat. Fining Humphrey Bogart for a noisy
muffler, O'Malley prevents him from making an appointment and getting a job.
Bogart then turns to crime to support his wife and lame daughter, and O'Malley
arrests the man he drove to crime in the first place. In *You Only Live Once*,
German director Fritz Lang, having just fled the Nazis, presented a scenario equal
to *I Am a Fugitive from a Chain Gang* in its bleakness. In the final scene,
Fonda—an escaped convict, falsely accused of murder—and his pregnant wife are
caught in the cross-hairs of a sheriff's rifle.

And all this in the year 1937, in which such escapist ventures as *Lost Horizon*,
The Goldwyn Follies, *The Prisoner of Zenda*, and *Snow White and the Seven
Dwarfs* were more characteristic. Hollywood had economically recovered itself by
1937 and was expanding its facilities. In addition to such overtly utopian films,
two new genre-cycles, also profoundly escapist, were also underway: inspirational
biographies—*Cardinal Richelieu* (1935), *The Story of Louis Pasteur* (1936), *The
Life of Emile Zola* (1937)—and costume classics—*A Midsummer Night's Dream*
(1935), *David Copperfield* (1935), *Becky Sharp* (1935), *A Tale of Two Cities*
(1935), *Anna Karenina* (1935), *Little Lord Fauntleroy* (1936), *Mary of Scotland*
(1936), *Romeo and Juliet* (1936), *Anthony Adverse* (1936), *Camille* (1937), so
many of them coming from Irving Thalberg's MGM. Despite such efforts at an

up mood, however, Hollywood could not completely banish the deep and terrify-
ing strains of *noir* that pervaded the Republic: the continuing sense of betrayal
and doom that Fritz Lang detected in the United States as well as in pre-Reich
Germany and expressed in his first American film, *Fury* (1936), based on the
November 1933 lynchings in San Jose. Lynching—as horrible social fact and
symbol of a disordered America—returned as a theme in Mervyn LeRoy's *They
Won't Forget* (1937), a film which even in the officially get-happy year of 1937
suggested an America deeply divided by class and sectional conflict and, even
more chillingly, by the continuing corruption of political power embodied in prosecutor Claude Rains's determination to become governor by sending an innocent
man to the gallows.

Much has been made, deservedly, of *annus mirabilis* 1939—with the release
that year of *Gunga Din, Stagecoach, Wuthering Heights, Goodbye, Mr. Chips,
The Wizard of Oz, Gone with the Wind, Each Dawn I Die, The Hunchback of
Notre Dame, The Private Lives of Elizabeth and Essex*, and other film classics—
yet 1937 was in its own way a remarkable year, even more so given the social
complexity, the admixture of light and dark, of the films released that year. Rarely
has American society been so cynically, so hopelessly, depicted as in Lang's *You
Only Live Once* or LeRoy's *They Won't Forget*. On the other hand, *Lost Horizon,
Snow White and the Seven Dwarfs*, and *The Goldwyn Follies* present remarkably
hopeful, if somewhat open-ended, parables. In its vivid depiction of Shangri-La,
an Art Deco–Moderne utopia in the Himalayas, Frank Capra's *Lost Horizon*,
based on the novel by James Hilton, mesmerized millions, including Franklin
Delano Roosevelt, who had the film shown repeatedly in the White House, referred to Shangri-La in his speeches, and selected the name Shangri-La for a
proposed aircraft carrier. Like millions of others, Roosevelt saw in Shangri-La—
its Art Deco and Moderne pavilions, its tasteful interiors adorned with the art of
the world, the rationality of its governance, its essential civility, the contentment
and good order of its people, all this buoyed by the sustaining sweetness of Dmitri
Tiomkin's score—a fairy-tale paradigm of an America that had been lost but was
now being recovered. Likewise in *Snow White and the Seven Dwarfs* did Americans encounter in the busy industry of the seven dwarfs and the rescue and redemption of a fairy princess a paradigm of renewal as the result, simultaneously,
of social cooperation and hard labor—and the redeeming power of love coming
as an unexpected gift.

"Love walked right in and stole the shadows away," ran the lyrics of the theme
song to *The Goldwyn Follies*, another 1937 parable of renewal: of the corner being
turned, realized this time in the lyrical last songs of George and Ira Gershwin and
the choreography of George Balanchine. George Gershwin first introduced the
Russian choreographer to Goldwyn. Each man required an interpreter despite the
fact that they were both speaking English. At one point, Goldwyn rejected Balanchine's suggestion for a ballet, saying that the miners in Harrisburg would not like
it. Balanchine retorted that there were no miners in Harrisburg. He knew, he had

been there, and besides, he was not President Roosevelt and so he did not have to worry about the miners in Harrisburg, even if there were any. Balanchine was right: there were no miners in Harrisburg. But he had missed the point. Goldwyn was referring not to the real Harrisburg but to a mythic America somewhere out there, for which he had been providing stories and dreams for the past two decades. Better than almost anyone else, Samuel Goldwyn represented the paradox of Hollywood, the saga of Jewish immigrants providing stories and dreams for their adopted nation. His malapropisms were legendary, and yet in many of his reported utterances ("Include me out . . . A verbal contract isn't worth the paper it's written on . . . Our comedies are no laughing matter . . . He treats me like the dirt beneath my feet . . . That's the way with these directors, they're always biting the hand that lays the golden egg . . . I had a monumental idea this morning, but I didn't like it . . . We shoot tomorrow, whether it rains, whether it shines, whether it stinks . . . I have been laid up with intentional flu . . . Didn't you hear me keeping still?") is revealed not so much the malapropisms on the verbal surface as the underlying presence of a cunning intelligence, gnomic, folkloric, hovering between Yiddish and English, America and the Pale. Through the prism of Goldwyn's intelligence had been refracted many of the best films of the 1930s, the best directors, the best actors, the best songs. From this perspective, he represented the type, Jewish Hollywood: the front office, the bottom line, keyed in a paradox of vulgarity and taste, delicacy and cunning, to the dreams and subliminal releases needed by Americans to make it through the slump.

Goldwyn was also an inveterate Anglophile, proud of his Savile Row suits and the English stars such as Ronald Colman and David Niven whom he held under tight contract. In Goldwyn's Anglophilia and the growing Anglophilia of his colleagues lies the turning point for Hollywood in the final years of the 1930s. Since the nineteenth century, the British had favored Southern California and settled there, and the Hollywood Raj represented the latest phase of an ongoing love affair. Even as Hollywood was getting its start in the late 1910s, Sir Gilbert Parker, a former Conservative MP out of office and looking for work, showed up in the Southland and found steady employment in the studios. In the 1930s Charles Aubrey Smith (Sir Charles after 1944) replaced Sir Gilbert as honorary consul general of the Hollywood Raj, sharing these honors with Ronald Colman, who had fought in the trenches in the Great War. Tall, craggy faced, beetle-browed, a cricketer who had attended Charterhouse and Cambridge, Smith enjoyed countless walk-on parts and a number of significant roles as well, most notably as the prime minister in The Prisoner of Zenda, co-starring Ronald Colman, David Niven, and the Anglo-Canadian actor Raymond Massey, the four of them brought together in celebration par excellence of Ruritania and the Raj. Smith, it was noted, looked as if he had just returned from a tour of the Empire. He flew the Union Jack in the garden of his Beverly Hills home and took his news exclusively from the Times, two weeks late from London.

Nattily attired in white flannels, striped blazer, and cricket cap, Aubrey Smith came into his own as president of the Hollywood Cricket Club, on which a number of Public School men—David Niven (Stowe), Clive Brook (Dulwich), Basil Rathbone (Repton), and others, including Boris Karloff, a Londoner (real name: William Henry Pratt), the only Anglo-Transylvanian in Hollywood captivity— wielded a bat. At the annual dance of the Cricket Club, held in the Roosevelt Hotel, C. Aubrey Smith, otherwise known as California's Greatest Living Englishman, presided regally over a company that included his cricketers, augmented by Ronald Colman, Cedric Hardwicke, P. G. Wodehouse, Douglas Fairbanks Jr., Laurence Olivier, Stan Laurel, and other august Britishers living permanently in or passing through California. Among the other guests at the Cricket Club dance could be spotted in various years directors James Whale, Alfred Hitchcock, and David Butler; actors Charles Chaplin, Clive Brook, Charles Laughton, Cary Grant, and George Arliss; actresses Merle Oberon, Vivien Leigh, Maureen O'Hara, Deborah Kerr, and Ida Lupino; writers Hugh Walpole, J. B. Priestley, and W. Somerset Maugham, together with such occasional sojourners and permanent residents as Christopher Isherwood, Aldous and Maria Huxley, and journalist Sheilah Graham. Even Bob Hope and child star Elizabeth Taylor were English-born.

Hollywood adored the British for a variety of reasons, including their ability to speak the English language with grace and clarity—and to act. Charles Laughton was undoubtedly the most brilliant actor working in Hollywood in the decade, capable of bringing to his parts—the subliminally incestuous Edward Barrett, the raging queen Nero, the sado-masochistic Captain Bligh, a uxorious Rembrandt, a frustrated Quasimodo—all the powerful suggestions of his own fierce and complex emotional life seething within a prison of ungainly flesh. Hollywood also wanted something even more important from its Raj: an evocation of things British— Aubrey Smith's Union Jack and two-week-old editions of the *Times*, the crisp white uniforms of the Cricket Club, the bookish anecdotes of Hugh Walpole, the brilliant wit of Somerset Maugham—reminding one and all that there would always be an England, a higher standard of taste, and that some of its cachet had rubbed off on the film colony. The Hollywood Raj, indeed, was at once a true outpost of empire and something that Hollywood kept in being as its own continuing fantasy of British life. Hollywood could hence nurture the genuine genius of Charles Laughton, but it could also bring into being, almost overnight, the equally symptomatic career of David Niven, an upper-class Sandhurst graduate, late of His Majesty's Highland Light Infantry, who, tiring of the army, presented himself as an extra to Central Casting in 1934 and, after some delay in obtaining a work permit, was hired and caught Irving Thalberg's attention, then that of Sam Goldwyn, who put him under long-term contract. Niven's starring roles in *The Charge of the Light Brigade* (1936), *The Dawn Patrol* (1938)—each of these alongside an honorary member of the Raj, the Australian-born Errol Flynn—*Wuthering Heights* (1939), and the quintessentially Anglophilic *Raffles* (1939) signaled the new course Hollywood had set for itself: pro-British and, by strong implication, interventionist.

So many of the films released in *annus mirabilis* 1939 — *The Story of Vernon and Irene Castle, Gunga Din, Goodbye, Mr. Chips, The Adventures of Sherlock Holmes, The Hound of the Baskervilles, Nurse Edith Cavell, The Private Lives of Elizabeth and Essex, The Rains Came, Wuthering Heights, Raffles* — were explicitly intended to shore up a sense of identification with Great Britain and the English tradition among American people. Each of Errol Flynn's swashbucklers — *Captain Blood* (1935), *The Charge of the Light Brigade* (1936), *The Adventures of Robin Hood* (1938), *The Private Lives of Elizabeth and Essex* (1939), and *The Sea Hawk* (1940) — contained explicit parables of British resistance to tyranny and aggression. *The Sea Hawk* opened with a voice-over narration illustrated by an animated map depicting the Spanish hegemony over Western Europe in the sixteenth century and its invasion plans for England, which hardly required much intelligence for Americans to link with the fall of Dunkirk and the ongoing Battle of Britain.

Dropping the pretense of allegory altogether, Warner's issued *Confessions of a Nazi Spy* (1939), which chronicled in near-documentary fashion a largely factual story of Nazi espionage in the United States. Screenwriter John Preston Buschlen's novel *Heil! Hollywood* (1939), meanwhile, suggested that even Hollywood was not immune to Nazi infiltration. Continuing its agitation on behalf of Spanish Loyalists, the Hollywood Anti-Nazi League filled the Shrine Auditorium in 1937 for a rally addressed by Loyalist aviator and French man of letters André Malraux in which hundreds of fur-coated and tuxedo-clad Hollywoodites extended the clenched fist.

The Left was stunned to silence when Hitler and Stalin signed a non-aggression pact in August 1939. The Left should not have been so scandalized. A look at the ledgers would have shown that Hollywood had already signed its own non-aggression pact. Nazi Germany remained a profitable market through the end of the decade, and it does not take too far a stretch of imagination to see in such films as *My Lucky Star* (1938), *Happy Landing* (1938), and *Second Fiddle* (1939), each starring Norwegian ice queen Sonja Henie, a personal favorite of Adolf Hitler's, a gesture in the direction of Aryan audiences on the Continent and elsewhere.

Troubled by Hollywood's regard for its continental markets, even in wartime, and by the strong isolationist movement in the United States, British Intelligence arranged the pseudo-defection of Alexander Korda to Hollywood in 1940, where the Hungarian-born producer, a Jew, directed a pro-interventionist network on behalf of the Crown. Korda's overt work in Hollywood, the completion of *That Hamilton Woman* (1941), starring Laurence Olivier as Admiral Nelson and Vivien Leigh as Lady Hamilton, was in and of itself ("England expects each man to do his duty") the most open invitation to the American people of any of the British or British-oriented films of the period to join Great Britain in its struggle. *That*

Hamilton Woman was Winston Churchill's favorite film. Churchill, in fact, most likely wrote large portions of the script. He played it innumerable times for his guests and would recite the dialogue along with the players. In 1940 the House Un-American Activities Committee began investigations of what it called "premature anti-fascism in Hollywood," which is to say, anti-fascist propaganda HUAC suspected was inspired by either the Soviet Union operating through the American Communist Party or by the British ring reporting to Korda. Korda was on the verge of receiving a subpoena when Pearl Harbor temporarily ended the HUAC enquiry.

Korda remained in Hollywood to help facilitate the MGM production of *Mrs. Miniver* (1942), the most successful pro-British Hollywood film ever. Among other things, Korda supplied the talents of composer Arthur Wimperis. It took two tries for Wimperis to reach Hollywood. His first ship was torpedoed in mid-Atlantic. For Wimperis, Korda, and the others, it was all in the line of duty. *Mrs. Miniver* was an astonishing success. Only now, since the United States was in the war, *Mrs. Miniver* was intended not so much to persuade Americans to get into the conflict as it was to convince them that England was worth dying for. Korda returned to London in 1942 and was given a knighthood, despite the fact that he had been an English resident for a mere six years. Critics of Korda's knighthood (and there were many) complained that Sir Alexander could only recognize "God Save the King" because people stood up when the orchestra started to play. Winston Churchill knew better.

Even Walt Disney went internationalist in 1940 with *Fantasia*, which deliberately brought the high-brow musical arts of Europe—the music of Schubert, Mussorgsky, and Stravinsky, the conducting of Leopold Stokowski—to middle-brow and even to lower-middle-brow American audiences, as if to convince them, by making high culture palatable, that they too were part of the cultural heritage of Europe, to whose defense they must now rally. By this time, 1940, Hollywood was dropping all pretense, all strategies of indirection, and was replaying World War I as a prelude to American involvement in World War II, with Gary Cooper assuming the role of Sergeant York and James Cagney rallying the Fighting Sixty-ninth in the trenches of France. A few short years earlier, at the opening of the Depression, pacifism had been all the rage. Now the requirements of the industrial system had shifted. Sitting in the theaters of America, watching films exquisitely keyed to the psychological needs of the moment, Americans were able to respond to the complexities of a Depression decade. Now, once again, it was time for war. Hollywood prepared the American people for the conflict, and after Pearl Harbor Hollywood moved them through the war years, year by year, genre-cyle by genre-cycle, just as it had led them through the shifting complexities of the Great Depression.

10

The Boys and Girls in the Back Room

Minimalism and the California Novel

B Y the 1930s Californians interested in fiction were anticipating a golden age for the novel on the Coast. The talent pool was there, it was argued, and society was reaching the point of complexity that would generate better and better fiction. What most critics had in mind, invariably, were novels of sociological sweep and grandeur: big novels, with diverse casts of characters and complexity of theme, conceived and written in the style of the European masters. Working under the influence of Emile Zola, Frank Norris had begun to bring into being such a genre at the turn of the century, an effort peaking with *The Octopus* (1901), perhaps the greatest California novel of them all. Among his fifty-plus books, Jack London had also contributed to the inclusive mode with his sociologically ambitious *Martin Eden* (1909). But London and Norris died young, Norris in 1902, London in 1916, and seminal careers that should have continued into the 1930s ended abruptly. The California novel never recovered from the premature loss of these two commanding talents, despite the efforts of Norris's younger brother Charles to continue the attempt to chronicle California life in the naturalist mode and format.

But now, things were different. The sheer sweep and intensity of California as a civilization, Farnsworth Crowder argued in *Westways* in February 1936—the cities of San Francisco and Los Angeles, Hollywood, the oil derricks of Signal Hill, the public works projects either in the planning stages or already under construction, the saga of landowning families, the influx of migrants and immigrants—bespoke the need, if not the inevitability, of novelists willing to take on a vast and challenging setting and subject matter. Nobel Prize winner Sinclair Lewis agreed. Everywhere around him in Los Angeles, Lewis noted in *Newsweek* for 21 February 1938—in miles and miles of tract houses, in the palm trees and neon lights, in trailer parks and oversized grocery stores, at the Santa Anita Race Track, at hundreds of tennis courts, in illegal roadhouse gambling dens, in the scandals at the Los Angeles Police Department, among the scholars at the Huntington Library—were people and scenes calling for a Balzac, a Dickens, a Turgenev, a second Frank Norris.

Sinclair Lewis, who knew California quite well, made no effort to write such a novel himself; nor did Theodore Dreiser, master of the naturalist saga, then living in Los Angeles. In two long sojourns spanning the late 1910s and early 1920s and the late 1930s and early 1940s, Dreiser spent most of his time trying to sell his novels to the studios. It took him more than twenty years to find a studio, RKO, courageous enough to purchase the film rights to *Sister Carrie* (1900). This $40,000 payment in the fall of 1940 saved Dreiser from the poorhouse. Although Dreiser twice lived in the heart of Los Angeles, had many Los Angeles contacts, and got about the city rather extensively, he showed no interest in writing a novel set in the City of Angels. From the early nineteenth century, Americans had been equating the power of their landscape and the noble experiment of their society with what they believed would be an equally impressive and inevitable literary result. From this perspective, the call for the encompassing California novel, as inclusive and diverse as the state itself, represented the repetition of this tendency.

By the end of the decade, Edmund Wilson, surveying in 1940 the work of the California novelists whom he considered most interesting—James M. Cain, Horace McCoy, Richard Hallas (Eric Knight), John O'Hara, William Saroyan, John Steinbeck, and Hans Otto Storm—was suggesting that California had at long last found its fictive voice. Far from being diverse and encompassing, however, Wilson wrote in an essay entitled "The Boys in the Back Room," the best fiction in California tended to be sparse, minimalist, hard-boiled, as in the well-known admonition "Set 'em up for the boys in the back room," from which Wilson took his title. Surveying the broad field of fiction in California, together with more precise notes on selected authors, Wilson described a California school that was radical, minimalist, concerned with the performing self as opposed to society, reductively environmental to the point of biologism, and, last, centered on the literal and symbolic void represented by the Pacific.

Wilson found the best and most characteristic fiction in California in the 1930s to be instinctively dissenting, radical even, not just because of the Depression but because of the long Pacific Coast tradition of intellectual radicalism, whose founding fathers were single tax theorist Henry George and Socialist Jack London. The persistent minimalism of California fiction, Wilson noted, derived, as did most minimalism in America, from Ernest Hemingway; but it also possessed a special valence on the Coast: a paring down of fiction to the sparsest possible presentation of reality in an environment lacking social complexity and traditionally recognizable material for description and analysis. The best writers of fiction in California, Wilson suggested, wrote minimally because in California there was so little to talk about. Hence California writers avoided grand themes and literary structure in favor of an intense presentation of fragments of experience, with an emphasis not on the drama of society but upon the experiencing self.

Wilson did not use the term *existential*, which had not yet entered the American critical vocabulary, but that is what he meant. Even as Wilson was writing, Jean-Paul Sartre was encountering in Horace McCoy's *They Shoot Horses, Don't They?* (1935) what he would later describe as the first important existential novel. The biologism of California fiction, so noticeable in Steinbeck, and before him in Jack London, was linked to this lack of social complexity. In an undeveloped environment, human beings were easily perceived and presented by writers of fiction as natural figures in a landscape, conditioned and impelled not by social complexity or by psychology and the superego but by the dynamics and motivations of their biological selves. Characters in California fiction came most alive not when they thought or talked, but when they ate, drank, copulated, struggled for survival or dominance, or otherwise expressed human life as irreducible biological fact.

Above all else, Wilson concluded, there was a strange lack of density, of weight, in California fiction, even in the best of it as represented by John Steinbeck. Why was this? Because California could never lose its essential unreality. To prove his point, Wilson quoted the protagonist of Eric Knight's *You Play the Black and the Red Comes Up* (1938) as he leaves California: "It was like all I had done in California was just a dream. And at first it felt good, and then it felt worse, because Sheila was only a dream with everything else. And that was bad. I could remember everything about California, but I couldn't feel it. I tried to get my mind to remember something that it could feel, too, but it was no use. It was all gone. All of it. The pink stucco houses and the palm trees and the stores built like cats and dogs and frogs and ice-cream freezers and the neon lights round everything."[1]

The key fact and symbol of this unreality, Wilson argued, was California itself as a place: its empty sun, its dry mountains, its uniform weather, its distance from the East Coast and Europe, and, most important, "the vast void of Pacific space" that fronted its shoreline and gave definition to its culture. The Atlantic Ocean, Wilson argued, at once faced and suggested Europe. The Atlantic Ocean implied a continuity of culture and identification with Western civilization. California, by contrast, "looks away from Europe, and out upon a wider ocean and an Orient with which, for white Americans, the cultural communication is slight."[2] Vast in extent, ceaseless in its rolling surf, unassimilated by American myth and symbol, the Pacific negated what little there was of culture and social development in California. The Pacific represented, indeed the Pacific enforced and reinforced, in Wilson's view, California as abyss, as negation, as void.

Although he was not cited by Wilson, San Diego writer Max Miller fits vividly into this context with his persistent theme of San Diego and La Jolla as places where one might secede from American culture and, edged up against the Pacific, drop out of time and history. In the highly autobiographical *The Man on the Barge* (1935), Miller managed to write a novel with virtually no action and no plot: just a middle-aged man living on a barge in San Diego Harbor, day in and day out, his world reduced to sky and sea. "Out here on the barge at night," wrote Miller in an observation strongly reinforcing Edmund Wilson's view of the Pacific, "he felt off the world somehow. He was not of it. He felt as though he never would die, or else had died already. He was not quite sure, nor did it matter. The water between him and the mainland formed a separation more mysterious than merely two miles of sea. The water could as well have been a void, a nothingness, and he was suspended beyond it."[3] In *A Stranger Came to Port* (1938), Miller has slightly more plot, albeit the same setting. An overworked businessman drops out of his company, his marriage, and other involvements in favor of life on a San Diego houseboat devoid of telephone, clock, or calendar. He spends each day in ceaseless rumination. Facing the emptiness of California, Edmund Wilson suggested, writers tended to defy the abyss with a torrent of language, as in the case of William Saroyan, or to present experience in its most bleak and minimalist terms, as in the case of Horace McCoy and James M. Cain. The void could be countered by words, as Saroyan did, talking like a frightened child in the dark; or it could be checkmated by a sparse tough-mindedness, an avoidance of as many words as possible, that wiseguyed the bleak emptiness tit for tat. In either case— Saroyan talking, talking, talking; the hard-boiled minimalists hardly talking at all—it was the void, the Pacific void, the California void, that drove the process.

A half century after Wilson's observations, it is difficult, indeed impossible, for any Californian, or any American for that matter, to perceive the Pacific Ocean as the fact and symbol of the void or of California as meaningless space. Far from it: a sense of Pacific Rim culture, of California as Asia, dominates the demographics and consciousness of the late twentieth century. Yet for all his myopia, Wilson correctly fixed on a sense of unreality in California and the fiction it produced, which cannot be dismissed as merely the cultural chauvinism of a New York–based literary critic. It was difficult, as Wilson noted, for the novelists of California to engage in social diagnosis and write accordingly. California seemed so uncertain, so new, so unreal, especially to Eastern expatriate writers hacking it out in the studios and, so many of them, not wanting to be there in the first place. Native-born writers, by contrast, or those with a longtime California residence found it easier to write fiction centered on ranching, agriculture and farm labor, small-town life, the unions, the strikes, the public works projects, the universities, the elites and ethnic minorities. And even among the minimalist masters, there is sociology aplenty as well as powerful social themes, if only by indirection.

Charles Gilman Norris, the younger brother of Frank, kept the California-based naturalist novel alive through the 1940s. Norris devoted his career to three pursuits: the editing and publication of his brother's oeuvre, the management of his wife Kathleen's writing career (by the mid-1930s, she was the highest-paid writer in the United States, the Danielle Steel of her day), and the steady composition of a series of naturalist novels—*The Amateur* (1916), *Salt* (1918), *Brass* (1921), *Bread* (1923), *Pig Iron* (1925), *Zelda Marsh* (1927), *Seed* (1930), *Zest* (1933), *Hands* (1935), *Bricks Without Straw* (1938), and *Flint* (1944)—dealing in a broadly sociological manner with such topics as the art world, university life, marriage and divorce, working women in the downtown, the steel industry, the stage, birth control, sexual incompatibility, agriculture, and the San Francisco strike of 1934. Detailed, plodding, frequently elephantine in their descriptions and overly topical conversations, Norris's novels are nevertheless capable of moments of valuable social observation. A younger brother's tribute, Charles Norris's novels are shadow versions of what Frank Norris might have accomplished had he lived. The last of them, *Flint*, published a year before Charles Norris's death, is the most relevant to the 1930s in its story of class consciousness and warfare, the union movement, and the general strike. In the figure of Rory O'Brien, loosely modeled on Harry Bridges, Norris presents a complex and sardonic longshoreman leader who in his his total commitment to the cause makes plausible the eventual victory of labor in the class struggle.

Living and writing as they did in a city that possessed a social complexity akin to the cities of the East, San Francisco novelists such as Charles Norris, George Albee, and Lawrence Rising were especially attuned to the drama of class conflict. In *Proud Flesh* (1924), Rising vividly depicts the removal of the ownership class from San Francisco to the polo-playing haunts of the Burlingame Country Club and the newly created enclave of Hillsborough, the rise of a new middle class in the city itself, and the growing presence of self-respecting, independent-minded working people who represent a new class entirely. Rising's hero, labor leader Patrick O'Malley, makes no apology for his class, not even to the upper-class woman who finds herself irresistibly drawn to him. An equally compelling drama of social class in San Francisco is Albee's *Young Robert* (1937), whose working-class hero wins a scholarship to Stanford but renounces the bourgeoisie in favor of life as an itinerant strike leader.

While the male novelists of San Francisco exulted in the intrinsic triumphalism in their virile working-class heroes, two women novelists of the city, Kathleen Norris and Gertrude Atherton, had a more subtle insight into the corrosive damage that can come from class consciousness and snobbery. In *Little Ships* (1929), Norris deftly depicts how upward mobility and a resulting class distinction can do damage to a large Irish Catholic family. Gertrude Atherton's *The Sophisticates* (1931), by contrast, showed that even life at the top could be slippery in uncertain economic times. In Atherton's *The House of Lee* (1940), the daughter of an established family, attending Berkeley, undergoes a mild form of radicalization in which, as part of her attraction to a radical student leader, she comes to realize that upper-middle-class San Francisco represents a distorted view of the world. Rhoda Townsend, heroine of Adriana Spadoni's *Not All Rivers* (1937), goes much further, leaving her Berkeley professor husband and the comforts of their upper-

middle-class existence for the uncertainties of life with her lover David, an organizer of agricultural unions. San Francisco newspaperwoman Gladys Johnson,
meanwhile, produced *Desire* (1929) and *Late September* (1932), novels of marriage and adultery in the upper crust, notable for the telling detail and the social
observation one might expect from a working reporter.

The conclusion of Spadoni's *Not All Rivers* finds Rhoda and David on the road
in search of social justice, which suggests another flourishing sub-genre of California fiction in the 1930s, the road novel. The road novel accounted for two parallel
but dissimilar efforts, Albert Isaac Bezzerides's *Long Haul* (1938) and Darwin
Teilhet's *Journey to the West* (1938). A Hollywood screenwriter from Fresno, half-
Greek, half-Armenian in descent (another source says half-Greek, half-Turk, an
even more volatile combination!) and a master of minimalist narrative, Bezzerides
had worked as a wildcat trucker before trying his luck in Tinsel Town. Bezzerides's
knowledge of the road pervades his gripping story of wildcat truckers hauling between Los Angeles and San Francisco, fighting fatigue with endless doses of black
coffee, dodging repossession suits, constantly in danger of being cheated by clients, and always and ever facing the dangers of the road: the collapsed portions
of Highway One, the washed-out bridges, the sudden fogs, which finally catch
up with Bezzerides's hero Nick Benay, no matter how skillfully he drives. Fast-
paced, hard-boiled, sparse and lean, *Long Haul* reads like the screen treatment it
also was for *They Drive by Night* (1940), starring George Raft and Humphrey
Bogart.

Darwin Teilhet's *Journey to the West*, by contrast, runs to more than six hundred thousand words as it chronicles a journey down the coast to Southern California via Yuba City and Sacramento, over to San Francisco, then down El Camino Real from San Francisco to San Diego, via San Jose, Salinas, Carmel, San
Luis Obispo, Santa Barbara, Long Beach, Los Angeles, and Hollywood, taken by
one Rufus Cobb, a New York copywriter fired from his job for publishing a freelance article in a lefty magazine. Each locality affords Teilhet the opportunity for
sub-plot and local description that manages to confer intervals of energy on a
picaresque narrative constantly threatening to collapse under its own weight. From
Journey to the West, in fact, can be extracted a separate and freestanding travel-
ogue describing California in the mid-1930s: from the Filipino, Mexican, and
Dust Bowl workers in the field to the civility of San Francisco, the beauty of the
coastal towns between Monterey and Santa Barbara, the Folks in Long Beach, the
writing crowd hanging out in the Musso & Frank Grill on Hollywood Boulevard.

The journey of Rufus Cobb down the California coast takes him to place after
place that novelists were doing their best to use for fiction throughout the decade.
Janet Lewis, for example, the wife of Stanford professor Ivor Winters, spent the
second half of the 1930s transmuting into fiction the San Jose lynchings of 1934,
which, after some delay, she succeeded in doing with the publication of *Against
a Darkening Sky* (1943), a skillfully wrought evocation of Santa Clara County
life, including its underside. Depicting the construction of the gigantic hangar at

Moffett Field in Sunnyvale for the Navy dirigibles *Macon* and *Akron*, Lewis linked her novel to the drama of engineering and public works with which so many critics were saying the California novel should concern itself.

George R. Stewart, meanwhile, a professor of English at Berkeley, was writing *Storm* (1941), a novel concerned with the titanic forces of weather that had driven the *Macon* and the *Akron* from the sky and, together with the fiery destruction of the *Hindenberg*, ended forever hopes for lighter-than-air flight on a mass scale. Concerned with a twelve-day storm sweeping across California, *Storm* represents an intricate docudrama, a disaster film before its time, involving a cast of thousands from the Highway Patrol, Pacific Gas & Electric, Pacific Telephone & Telegraph Company, Southern Pacific, Western and United airlines, the Coast Guard, the California Division of Highways, and other agencies struggling to cope with adverse conditions. Vast and compelling, giving equal weight to natural processes and human beings, *Storm* manages to suggest the social complexity of California, not as a dropout zone or wackos' paradise, but as a large-scale Western state peopled by recognizable Americans, publicly and privately managed by scores of mega-agencies and devoted professionals brought to their best as they confront the violent weather.

Stewart also contributed to the academic novel set in California, a genre pioneered by Berkeley resident Clarkson Crane in his realist Lost Generation saga *The Western Shore* (1925). Concerned with the Ph.D. examinations of Joe Grantland, an over-age-in-grade graduate student who has gotten his girlfriend pregnant, *Doctor's Oral* (1939) is also Lost Generational in feeling: not because of World War I this time, but because the Depression is sending Berkeley Ph.D.'s in the humanities into a non-existent market or dooming them to the relief rolls of the WPA.

In his journey down the coast, Rufus Cobb, hero of Teilhet's *Journey to the West*, spends time on the Monterey Peninsula, where the art colony of Carmel-by-the-Sea was proving itself so compatible to another sub-genre of California fiction: the *South Wind* novel, inspired by Norman Douglas's 1917 story of life on Capri among the aesthetes. Writing under the name Mary Cavendish Gore, Mrs. H. H. Hopkins, a local resident, did her best in the *South Wind* genre, with an equal dash of Noel Coward, in *Mad Hatter's Village* (1934), a tale of sex, literature, and literary posturing among Carmel writers who spend their days lying on the beach, or ambling to the local post office for their rejection slips, or dallying with each other in bed during long dreamy afternoons. Also set in Carmel is John Evans's perplexing *Shadows Flying* (1936), a claustrophobic tale in which the sex, one guesses, is of an incestuous sort. The use of the pseudonym John Evans by the writer suggests that something of an actual Carmel story is being retold in this inconclusive and rather morbid novel dedicated to Una and Robinson Jeffers.

Los Angeles novelist Myron Brinig took the *South Wind* genre even further south, to Laguna Beach, with *The Flutter of an Eyelid* (1933), a venomous satire of the Jake Zeitlin circle. So vicious was Brinig's first version of the novel, built around the character Ike Lazarus, a Los Angeles poet and bookseller very much resembling Zeitlin, Jake went to court and forced the publishers to withdraw the book. In the revised version Ike Lazarus becomes Sol Mosier, a dealer in antiques, still very much a Zeitlin figure. (Years later, still smarting, Zeitlin described Brinig as "a baby elephant with the heart of an adder.") The vitality of Brinig's satire comes from its depiction of the Los Angeles–Laguna Beach bohemia of the early 1930s, with the usual—and deliciously scandalous—depictions of boozing and coupling, dinner parties and talk of art, in the Silver Lake district of Los Angeles and on the shores of Laguna Beach. There is even an Aimee Semple MacPherson figure, Angela Flower. Like everyone else she meets a watery end when Brinig employs the most apocalyptic *deus ex machina* of them all, an earthquake that sends Southern California sliding into the sea.

Teilhet's *Journey to the West* also touches upon agriculture, the leading element in the California economy and the inspiration for another flourishing sub-genre, the ranch novel, whose high point had been achieved by Frank Norris in *The Octopus*. Without Norris's talent, yet with an energy that must be recognized, three decades of California novelists devoted themselves to the theme of life on the land. In *The Pride of Palomar* (1921), a sprawling, frequently engaging, but ultimately mean-spirited anti-Japanese diatribe, Peter B. Kyne attempted to carry on the work of the ranch novel as social tract so strongly realized by *The Octopus* with a multi-generational saga of the half-Irish, half-Spanish Farrel family whose south coastal ranch comes under threat not from Norris's Southern Pacific but from Japanese farmers nibbling away at the land, so Kyne suggests, like so many insects. Thankfully, the more characteristic California ranch novels of the 1920s were not so racially vicious. They were concerned, rather, with variations on one recurring theme: redemption on the land. In Robert Welles Ritchie's *Deep Furrows* (1927), a dissipated New York reporter rebuilds himself morally, psychologically, and physically as a ranch hand in the Sacramento Valley. In Florence Bingham Livingston's *This Man and This Woman* (1928), a troubled couple regain their marriage while ranching in the San Joaquin.

With the Depression, a new realism and a notable minimalism of style enter the ranch novel, temporarily pushing aside the sprawling saga: with the exception, that is, of May Merrill Miller's *First the Blade* (1938), an ambitious reworking of the epic clash between San Joaquin Valley ranchers and the Southern Pacific culminating in the shootout at Mussel Slough. Howard Baker's *Orange Valley* (1931) inaugurated the minimalist ranch novel genre. Written by a former San Joaquin Valley ranch hand who later studied at the Sorbonne, *Orange Valley* chronicles pitilessly, remorselessly, the efforts of fruit growers to establish citrus, olive, and fruit orchards in the dry harsh plains of the San Joaquin. Arnold Armstrong's *Parched Earth* (1934) and Francine Findley's *Treeless Eden* (1934) are similarly minimalist, although Findley's novel is also a multi-generational saga of a Southern family in the Sacramento Valley. Even the Napa Valley, otherwise so idyllic, is endowed with *noir* tones in Frances Marion's *Valley People* (1935), a *My Antonia* (1918) in reverse, with young hope crushed early on in the game.

From this cadre of ranching minimalists arose in the late 1930s and early 1940s two notable talents, Judy van der Veer and Robert Easton. A single woman, fragile and slight, van der Veer went into the arduous business of cattle and dairy ranching on her own in the early 1930s in the rugged backcountry of San Diego County. "A yellow and brown world," she described it, "with sparse touches of green." Having broken her leg and forced to spend time in bed, she began to write, with an elegantly controlled pointillist-minimalism, of the pains and pleasures and final meanings of her ranch life: the local Native Americans and Mexicans whom time had forgotten; the cycles of birth, growth, mating, and death in men and animals; her own blasted hopes when a possible husband is crippled in a terrible accident; the smell of coffee and bacon in the morning; the "mystical time" of late afternoon when the canyons grew quiet beneath the sun; the flowering in springtime of the hill country in a riot of yellow and green. Two themes dominate van der Veer's slender but compelling output—*The River Pasture* (1936), the classic *November Grass* (1940), *A Few Happy Ones* (1943), and the late memoir *My Valley in the Sky* (1959)—the search for personal peace on the part of a single woman living on the land and the inter-relatedness of the environment. Like Robinson Jeffers and John Steinbeck in other terrains, van der Veer found release in accepting the otherness of nature, the web of life—cattle, birds, insects, people—that existed in and of itself, and for itself, and included her in its symbiotic embrace.

In 1940 Viking published *The Happy Man: A Novel of California Ranch Life* by Robert Easton, who managed to produce this minimalist tour de force while undergoing Army training at Camp Roberts near San Miguel in San Luis Obispo County, squeezing time on weekends—Sunday afternoons, usually—and late at night, or on off hours during the day. Writing the novel, among other things, enabled Easton to keep alive his hopes for after the war by celebrating the life he had so recently led as a ranch hand with A. B. Miller's B. B. Cattle Company in the Sacramento Delta, the biggest feedlot operation in the West, followed by a stint at the McCreery Ranch in the Coast Range near Hollister. Lyrical, episodic, written with minimalist grace, *The Happy Man* evokes a ranch very much like the B. B. Cattle Company as seen through the eyes of a protagonist very much resembling Robert Easton. Like van der Veer, Easton is concerned with presenting as directly and vividly as possible, without commentary, the essential livingness, the existential clarity, of men and women living and working alongside the animals in the big ranch country of California.

Van der Veer and Easton each possessed a special regard for minority ranch workers, Filipinos and Mexicans especially, which suggests another characteristic of the California minimalist novel in this period, whether set on the ranch or in the big city: a sympathetic presentation of racial minorities that ran counter to the pervasively racist, or at the least stereotypical, attitudes of the period. Few white writers of the era have depicted African-Americans with the clarity, even-handedness, and sympathy so evident in Dorothy Baker's *Young Man with a Horn* (1938), a jazz novel based on the life of Leon (Bix) Beiderbecke, the renowned jazz cornetist who died in his late twenties in 1931. *Young Man with a Horn* is naturally concerned with the interaction between blacks, who invented jazz, and whites like Beiderbecke who wished to learn it, in this instance in the Cotton Club in Culver City where Edward Richard Martin, a young white Los Angeles High School student, learns jazz from an assortment of black musicians. Baker's novel appeared at a time when African-Americans in fiction by whites were either exotics or stereotyped characters speaking in dialect; yet Baker's African-Americans are vital and fully realized personalities, beyond stereotype, as are the Chinese and Japanese characters in Idwal Jones's *Chinaboy* (1936). John Fante immersed himself in the Filipino community of Long Beach in the hopes of writing a novel dealing with this minority group, in its own way an object of prejudice compara-ble to that leveled against blacks, Mexicans, and the Japanese. Fante never com-pleted the novel, but the excerpt that appeared in the *Saturday Evening Post* early in 1941 under the title "Helen, Thy Beauty Is to Me" showed the strong possibili-ties of sympathetic treatment that the novel might have had.

Edwin Corle, a Los Angeles–based radio writer, based *Fig Tree John* (1935) on the true story of a Cahuilla Indian who lived on the fringes of white society in the Colorado Desert near the Salton Sea. After extensive travel and research through-out the Southwest, Corle, who had studied ethnology at UCLA and Yale, got to work on his novel on 3 September 1934 and finished it in four months. Fortu-nately, the minimalism of Corle's style (he was, after all, very much in the current California mode) prevents *Fig Tree John* from becoming a polemical or ethno-graphical tract. *Fig Tree John* is, instead, a sparse and tragic story, almost classical in its structure and restraint. Agocho, a White River Apache from Arizona, mi-grates west to Imperial Valley and sets up his camp near a grove of fig trees by the Salton Sea. Two white tramps kill his wife, and Agocho becomes a hater of white men. How tragic, then, for Agocho to see his son Johnny Mack, who has named himself after a nearby fig rancher whom he admired, drift closer and closer to white ways. Working on local ranches, Johnny Mack buys a green Ford roadster and marries a Mexican girl named Maria. In the time-honored tradition of the Apache, Agocho rapes Maria to demonstrate to his son that she is a foreigner, chattel, belonging to all men of the tribe. His son, wanting to be a good Apache, tries to accept the rape but eventually kills his father in a fight and rejoins his wife and seeks employment in town. Agocho, as Edwin Corle presents him, is a far from sympathetic figure. The power of *Fig Tree John* comes from its minimalist presentation of Agocho's bleak life, the would-be Apache warrior living on the fringes of a white world that he hates.

As might be expected, the novelists of California were fascinated with Mexicans. What is not so expected, however, given the prejudice of the time, is a Mexican-American novel as sympathetic as Dan Totheroh's *Wild Orchard* (1927), the story of the Marchios, a Mexican family from Los Angeles who follow the crops during harvest time. Carey McWilliams considered *Wild Orchard* to be the best novel written about California in the 1920s, and there is much to back this assertion, especially the highly realized descriptions of life in the Los Angeles *barrio* and camp life, the organization and conduct of the harvest, and, with gentle irony on Totheroh's part, the delight the Mexican migrants feel playing themselves in the annual outdoor Ramona Pageant at Hemet.

The heroine of *Wild Orchard*, Trina Marchio, meets a violent end, which underscores the *noir* dimension of Mexican women in California fiction written by Anglo males in the 1930s. So many such figures—Trina herself; Juana Montes, the Mexican whore turned Joan of Arc in James M. Cain's *Serenade* (1937); Sheila, the fey, possibly disturbed and secretly Mexican socialite in Eric Knight's *You Play the Black and the Red Comes Up* (1938); Camilla Lopez, the marijuana-smoking Mexican waitress in John Fante's *Ask the Dust* (1939); Frances, the Mexican-American dance hall singer in Frank Fenton's *A Place in the Sun* (1942)—are doomed to violent fates or, like Camilla Lopez, merely drop off the ends of the earth. All this, of course, must be taken within the larger context of the Doomed Dame as a persistent figure in so much of the fiction written by Californians in the 1930s: all the hard-boiled dames or spoiled heiresses who meet a bad end in the detective stories of Raymond Chandler; the doomed Cora Papadakis (a Mexican passing for Anglo) in Cain's *The Postman Always Rings Twice* (1934); Anne Minton in Myron Brinig's *Anne Minton's Life* (1939), a young woman who spends the entire novel standing on a hotel ledge gathering the courage to commit suicide. San Francisco *Call-Bulletin* reporter Gertrude Crum's *Strumpet Wind* (1938) is among the best of these Doomed Dame novels. A Texas girl, betrayed at sixteen, runs away from home, works as a small-town waitress in Texas, answers a mail-order advertisement to marry an older farmer in the foothills of the Mother Lode, comes to Sonora, where she is miserable, poisons her husband, confesses, gets life in prison: all this in an ultra-minimalist style, with the Okie waitress having been doomed from the get-go.

Why so many of these Doomed Dames should be Mexican women remains an intriguing question. In its volatile alembic of Indian and European blood and culture, Mexico, indeed Latin America in general, communicated high levels of pessimistic fatalism to Anglo California writers, as it did to white writers in the rest of the country. The Mexico of Cain's *Serenade*, for example, is dark, sinister, violent, replete with destructive sexuality, and politically corrupt, as are the Panama and Peru of Hans Otto Storm's *Pity the Tyrant* (1937) and *Count Ten* (1940), two partially California novels that Edmund Wilson found Conradian in their depiction of tyranny and lurking menace in a setting of Latin American dictatorship. In the formula of Anglo fascination with Mexico, Mexico functioned as the Other, the unconscious, the libido in all its glory and frequent cruelty. Mexico evoked a remorseless sense of fate as strange, sinister, and impenetrable as the basilisk stare of the iguana that John Howard Sharp boils alive and devours in *Serenade* as if to feed on Mexico itself. Then came the Anglo male perception of the Mexican female as instinctively sexual, hot in her Indian blood, giving and taking without considering the cost. The Mexican women are of course doomed for their sexuality, but while they are alive, they burn with a fury that mesmerizes Anglo males by its self-destructive brilliance. Such women seem to come from another place. They embody another state of consciousness. Then, last in this fictive California brew, lurked the memory that California was Mexican long before it was Anglo and would eventually be Mexican again. A tragic race, passionate and enduring, would one day return.

Where would they go? To Los Angeles, of course, which by the 1930s was emerging, in fact and fiction, as the metropolitan prism through which California was first glimpsing its polyglot future. In this process of sortage and prophecy, the Los Angeles novel played its part. As early as 1924, the Argentinean novelist Vincente Blasco Ibañez paid Los Angeles the tribute of a rather ambitious novel, *Queen Califia*, which shifted its action back and forth between Los Angeles, Paris, and Madrid, which was itself a form of flattery to the emergent City of Angels; but then again, Blasco Ibañez was in a good mood, having made a bundle in 1921 when Hollywood filmed his novel *The Four Horsemen of the Apocalypse* (1916), directed by Rex Ingram and starring Rudolph Valentino. In *Angel's Flight* (1927), Don Ryan got the Los Angeles novel off to its true start, with a more inclusive, indeed flamboyant, depiction of Los Angeles people and places as encountered by a newspaperman covering the cops and the courts and living atop Bunker Hill. Dillwyn Parrish carried on the genre in *Praise the Lord!* (1932), a novel of the Folks who attached themselves to Aimee Semple MacPherson's Angelus Temple in Echo Park. "It was just as though the power of God lifted us out of the corn fields of Iowa and carried us straight to the foot of His throne!" testifies one character of his migration to Los Angeles. Prays yet another before going to bed: "We thank Thee, dear God, for leading us into the beautiful city of Los Angeles."[4] Parrish was intending to be satirical, yet there is much that is truly touching in the gratitude of these Folks for their new home.

The end of the decade witnessed a veritable explosion of Los Angeles novels. An *annus mirabilis* for films, 1939 also saw the publication of Myron Brinig's *Anne Minton's Life*, Aldous Huxley's *After Many a Summer*, and John Fante's *Ask the Dust*. While appearing in the early 1940s, such strong Los Angeles novels as Rupert Hughes's *City of Angels* (1941), Frank Fenton's *A Place in the Sun* (1942), Jo Pagano's *Golden Wedding* (1943), and Nellise Child's *If I Come Home* (1943), as well as a collection of short stories by Timothy Turner, *Turn Off the Sunshine: Tales of Los Angeles on the Wrong Side of the Tracks* (1942), remain connected to the pre-war era in terms of their time frame and general inspiration.

Two other novels, meanwhile, Hans Otto Storm's *Count Ten* (1940) and Peter Viertel's *The Canyon* (1940), set in Santa Ana and the Santa Monica Mountains respectively, remained in the Los Angeles orbit.

In their own ways and with differing levels of talent, Brinig in *Anne Minton's Life* and Huxley in *After Many a Summer* each sought to bring off the great big Los Angeles novel, panoramic, inclusive, sociological. The central event of Brinig's novel—a young woman stands on the ledge of a hotel window on Wilshire Boulevard for half a day, deciding whether to jump; a crowd gathers; radio stations and newspapers conduct an hour-by-hour death watch—was taken from real life. Brinig uses this crisis to gather a number of stories, including Ann Minton's, into one countdown. A socialite in her late thirties finds herself divorced and flat broke (fifty-six cents in her purse) and flirts with the idea of becoming a call girl. A young Catholic woman, single, pregnant, is tempted to an abortion. A Jewish refugee from Nazi Germany wonders whether he has the strength to start all over again. In Huxley's *After Many a Summer* a figure very much resembling William Randolph Hearst, living in a place very much resembling San Simeon, seeks rejuvenation through medical science. But the true vitality of the novel, saving it in many cases from collapsing under the weight of Huxley's erudition and constant referencings and comparisons, is its vivid descriptions. Few writers of fiction, before or since, have caught the distinctive, eccentric look of L.A.— its boulevards and gas stations, its eclectic architecture so straining to make Los Angeles seem real through narrative historicism, its funeral parlors and drive-in restaurants, its palm trees and billboards, its astonishingly beautiful young women wearing shorts and chewing gum—than this English savant turned Hollywood screenwriter, even then settling into Los Angeles for the rest of his highly productive life.

The themes of the Los Angeles novel include, most obviously, the city itself, so vast in form, so eccentric in its various lifestyles. On the other hand, the better the novel, the more Los Angeles is used as a *mise-en-scène* for more important matters—birth and death, love and work, the search for identity—rather than the mere evocation of place. Although its setting in a Santa Monica canyon is superbly realized, the more fundamental purpose of Peter Viertel's *The Canyon* is its autobiographical portrait of a boy growing into adolescence and young adulthood in this still-wild backcountry as remembered by the son of German émigré director Berthold Viertel and his screenwriter wife Salka, hostess extraordinary to the émigré community. A fire sweeps through the canyon at the conclusion of the novel, as if to clear it for the asphalt and bungalows that make their appearance in the final scene. The sketches by *Los Angeles Times* newsman Timothy Turner collected in *Turn Off the Sunshine* are near-journalistic in their evocations of the specific settings and peoples of the city. Frank Fenton's *A Place in the Sun* splits the difference between theme and place. Fenton's protagonist, a young Midwesterner semi-crippled by polio, settles in the San Fernando Valley expressly in the hope that the climate will restore his weakened legs. Seeing a young man and woman playing tennis, he has the perfect image of what he is seeking: the restoration of his physical health, the finding for himself of his own special place in the Southern California sun.

An argument can be made that the pre-war and early war Los Angeles novel, as represented most strongly in the work of John Fante, but also in novels by Nellise Child and Jo Pagano, belongs most dramatically to Italian-Americans. As a sub-genre, the Italian-American Los Angeles novel is most often set with great precision on Bunker Hill and Lincoln Heights, the Little Italy of Los Angeles, and revolves around the drama of social class. Los Angeles, these novels suggest, is either a WASP or a Jewish city, and everybody else is marginal. This theme of a young man on the outside and looking in, of having an excess of heart in a cold-hearted town, of wanting into the magic circle—wanting the nice homes, the tennis courts, the lush backyards and pools, the good restaurants, the beautiful women—characterizes the novels of Pagano, Child, and Fante. Pagano's *The Golden Wedding* is the least alienated, for the Italian family involved, based on Pagano's own, migrating from Salt Lake, has secured a flourishing produce business in the Grand Central Market on Broadway and a home on the top of a palm-lined street in Lincoln Heights, with fig, pomegranate, and lemon trees in the backyard. Still, the Depression makes it tough for the second generation to capture the full promise of Los Angeles life, which is to say, for members of the generation in its twenties to achieve social and educational parity with their WASP and Jewish peers. Child's *If I Come Home* is overtly bitter in its story of Tony Casino, an Italian Catholic working man, who fails to provide for his wife, a middle-class Protestant, and their child in the last years of the Depression, losing them when she, tired of poverty, returns to her parents, divorces Tony, and remarries. When Tony at last gets a decent job and shows some sign of winning her back from her second husband, he is drafted into the Army.

Like everything else John Fante wrote, with the exception of his screenplays, the central situation (plot is too strong a word) of *Ask the Dust* (1939)—young Arturo Bandini lives in a hotel room on Bunker Hill and writes and dreams of making it big as a writer—is directly autobiographical. In his twenties in the 1930s, John Fante belonged to a rising generation of Los Angeles writers under the spell of H. L. Mencken. The circle included Louis Adamic, Carey McWilliams, Frank Fenton, and Jo Pagano, all personal friends of Fante's in an informal coterie revolving around McWilliams. Born in Denver, raised in Boulder, educated by the Jesuits at Regis College, Fante moved to Los Angeles with his mother, sister, and two brothers (Fante Senior had temporarily deserted the family for another woman) after a brief stint at the University of Colorado. Fante spent the 1930s supporting his mother and brothers as a day laborer, hotel clerk, stevedore, and cannery worker on the San Pedro docks while intermittently attending Long Beach City College. From age twenty-one, he carried on a self-initiated correspondence with H. L. Mencken, who offered encouragement and eventually published some of his short stories. Fante was an inveterate letter writer, and these accumulated effusions—to Mencken, to McWilliams, to his mother—document the sprawling range of Fante's assimilated experiences, which he was even then transmuting into autobiographical fiction.

Fante had in mind a saga centered on his alter ego Arturo Bandini that would begin in Colorado and move west to Los Angeles across a number of volumes. At some point in 1932 he began *Pater Doloroso*, the first novel in the sequence, largely set in Colorado, which Alfred A. Knopf optioned, then rejected. Fante then began a second installment entitled *The Road to Los Angeles* while simultaneously working on the third installment, *Dreams from Bunker Hill*. Beginning in 1935, he supported himself as a screenwriter at Warner Brothers, RKO, Republic, and other studios. Then came the fourth installment, *Wait Until Spring, Bandini*, finished in 1938 and published by Stackpole Sons, who published *Ask the Dust* the next year. In the midst of all this, Fante wrote short stories for the *Atlantic Monthly*, the *American Mercury*, *Story*, and *Harper's Bazaar*, gathered by Viking in 1940 as *Dago Red*. Not until the 1980s would the entire "Saga of Arturo Bandini" be published, by the Black Sparrow Press of Santa Rosa, publisher of Fante's leading fan, Charles Bukowski, and the best-known publisher of alternative fiction and poetry in the United States.

It is too easy to say that John Fante was the William Saroyan of Los Angeles, although the comparisons between *Ask the Dust* and *The Daring Young Man on the Flying Trapeze* are obvious. Each young writer, facing the void, counters it with words and becomes the performing self. Fante, however, possesses a compression, an existential intensity, together with a sense of the world as a real place, out there, solid and objective, which Saroyan lacks. Among other things, *Ask the Dust* presents a map of Los Angeles, Bunker Hill and the Downtown especially, which is at once a real and an imagined city. Living in a cheap hotel room on Bunker Hill, Bandini survives on a crate of oranges tucked under his bed. When not writing, he wanders down Angel's Flight to Hill Street, then over to the Plaza, then back along Broadway to the Downtown, then down Olive Street to the Philharmonic Auditorium on Pershing Square, past the Biltmore Hotel, then back to his hotel past the burlesque houses and the taxi-dance halls. A fierce hunger rages in his heart all the while for all that Los Angeles was promising, for a big bite of the Big Orange. "Los Angeles, give me some of you!" Bandini cries. "Los Angeles, come to me the way I came to you, my feet over your streets, you pretty town I loved you so much, you sad flower in the sand, you pretty town."[5] And yet, Bandini is more than half aware that Los Angeles has a way of promising people and things—the gorgeous girls on the street, the golf clubs in the window at Spalding's on 6th, the cool lawns and green swimming pools of Bel Air—that it will never deliver. "You'll eat hamburgers year after year," he tells himself, "and live in dusty, vermin-infested apartments and hotels, but every morning you'll see the mighty sun, the eternal blue of the sky, and the streets will be full of sleek women you never will possess, and the hot semi-tropical nights will reek of romance you'll never have, but you'll still be in paradise, boys, in the land of sun-shine."[6]

For most Hollywood writers—and Fante can also be grouped in this category—Los Angeles was at best an abstraction, an infrastructure to support the studios, and at worst a zoo, a sideshow, an experiment gone wrong. For the New York gang living at the Garden of Allah apartment complex on Sunset Boulevard, Los Angeles beyond the studios hardly existed at all; and even if it did, they regarded it from their enclave as the British Raj might regard the teeming masses outside the compound. Established in 1927 as a hotel-apartment complex by the Crimean-born émigré actress Alla Nazimova, the Garden of Allah—Nazimova's house converted into a hotel, and twenty-five bungalows arranged around a swimming pool shaped in the form of the Black Sea—brought to its portion of Sunset Boulevard the wit and spirit, together with the drinking, of the Algonquin Circle of New York. Master of the revels was the New York raconteur turned Hollywood actor Robert Benchley and his aides-de-camp screenwriters Charlie Butterworth, Donald Ogden Stewart, and Johnny McClain: a group that seemed (so Garden resident Lucius Beebe remembered) to be at the center of a party seven nights a week. (Asked if he had gotten the DTs while staying at the Garden of Allah, W. C. Fields replied: "How would I know?") It was Butterworth who, looking out the window of Benchley's living room one evening, uttered the classic line: "H'mmm, looks like it's going to get drunk out tonight"; and it was Benchley, on another occasion, coming in from a rainstorm, who said: "I've got to get out of these wet clothes and into a dry martini."[7]

As an archetype as well as a hostelry, the Garden of Allah symbolized the growing presence of New York–affiliated writers in Hollywood, and, in the case of Dorothy Parker, Alexander Woollcott, and Benchley, of writers who epitomized the spirit of Manhattan as embodied in the Algonquin Circle. The Musso & Frank Grill on Hollywood Boulevard, just up from Vine, balanced the Garden of Allah with a more localized polarity, yet it was still touched by the mood and ambience of New York. Established in 1919, Musso & Frank was a New York–style bar and restaurant: two great dining rooms, and a back room for writers, booths and leather banquettes, a sweeping bar, ample drinks, unintimidated waiters, steaks and chops at reasonable prices. Here ate the screenwriters of the 1930s, sometimes on credit when out of work, and here on Saturday afternoons, after a half day at the studio, would gather for drinks and a long lunch many of the subsequently revered names in American literature: Fitzgerald, Cain, McCoy, O'Hara, Saroyan, Faulkner, Hammett, Hellman, Chandler, Bezzerides, a roll call resembling the list of required reading for a sophomore survey of the mid-twentieth-century American novel.

All these writers, whether hanging out at the Garden of Allah or at Musso & Frank, had already stumbled into a previously existing genre, the Hollywood novel, which got its start in the 1920s with such novels as the comic *Merton of the Movies* (1922) by Harry Leon Wilson, the more somber *Souls for Sale* (1922) by Rupert Hughes, Edgar Rice Burroughs's exposé *The Girl from Hollywood* (1923), *Maiden Effort* (1927) by Samuel Hopkins Adams, a novel that managed to bring Howellsean realism to Hollywood, and Carl Van Vechten's brittle-brilliant *Spider Boy* (1928). As a sub-genre of the American novel, the Hollywood novel participated in a number of fundamental American modes: the Horatio Alger success story most frequently turned against itself; the muckraking investigative tract, with the studios functioning as a parallel to the Chicago stockyards in Upton Sinclair's *The Jungle* (1906); the jeremiad, lamenting lost opportunities; and the Indian captivity narrative, in this case, the captivity of a sensitive artist-intellectual by the crass studio system.

On a more subliminal level—since it was a more incoherent, even underground genre—the Hollywood writers also came indirectly into contact with the novel of Los Angeles apocalypse. The 1920s witnessed an outpouring in Los Angeles of locally written, locally published novels, many of them Theosophical in inspiration, many of them millenarian, some of them apocalyptic, all of them a little wacky. In Louis Molnar's *Deka Parsec* (1921), a shell-shocked veteran turns to mysticism and social prophecy. In Michal Reepmaker's *Tuned Higher than the Race* (1923), Christ returns to Los Angeles; in its sequel, *The Birth of Humanity* (1923), a world teacher uses modern technology, including supersonic flight, to promote a higher California-centered state of consciousness throughout the planet. Ada White Taylor's *The Mystic Spell: A Metaphysical Romance* (1923), Evelyn Whitehill's *A California Poppy* (1925), and Thomas Sawyer Spivey's *The Last of the Gnostic Masters* (1926) each told Theosophical stories with Los Angeles or Southern California settings. To read these novels is not to encounter literature—far from it!—but it is to touch base with the eccentric dream life of the evangelical-Theosophical Southland that would soon make Los Angeles ground zero of science fiction, Scientology, and other prophetic movements and cults, most of them animated by a sense of impending doom, of apocalypse, should certain steps not be taken. Even such a staid writer as the Englishman J. B. Priestly succumbed to these apocalyptic suggestions in *The Doomsday Men* (1938), in which three brothers, a physicist, a mystic, and a millionaire, threaten to blow up the world from their stronghold in the Mojave Desert unless the world reforms itself. William Tom Pilkington's *My Blood's Country* (1939) concludes with the destruction of L.A. In Albert Nelson's *America Betrayed* (1940), the apocalyptic genre edges into wartime consciousness as Los Angeles is invaded by an offshore power with the assistance of a Fifth Column.

Enter yet another element in the emergent literary landscape of Hollywood in the 1930s, the hard-boiled detective story. Although there were some precursors, *Black Mask* writer Dashiell Hammett of San Francisco can be said to have invented the genre in *Red Harvest* (1929), *The Dain Curse* (1929), *The Maltese Falcon* (1930), and *The Glass Key* (1931). Sometimes, a genre begins its existence at its high point, which is true of the hard-boiled detective story as fashioned by

Hammett. Only Raymond Chandler of Los Angeles equals Hammett in perfection of plot and character, intensity, minimalism—and bleakness. With his buried romanticism, however (detective Philip Marlowe is envisioned as a knight errant), Chandler can seem an Edwardian recidivist keeping to a Public School code in comparison to the remorselessly amoral world, unrelieved by ethics or sentiment, created by Hammett.

Like Steinbeck's *Grapes of Wrath*, Hammett's most famous novel, *The Maltese Falcon*, had both the fortune and the misfortune to have inspired a film of equal achievement. Hammett's Sam Spade, however, and Humphrey Bogart's Sam Spade are two different characters. Their differences underscore the austerity, the willingness to look the gorgon in the face, of Hammett and the fiction he wrought in one brief burst of creativity. For all his tough-guy stance, his trenchcoat and slanted fedora, Bogart's Sam Spade is essentially a man with a code in residual contact with classical Western values. Like Rick, whom he would soon be playing in *Casablanca* (1942), Bogart's Spade conceals a highly developed sense of code behind a facade of cynicism. Hammett's Spade, by contrast, would intimidate even Thomas Hobbes in his willingness to see life as something nasty, brutish, and short, untouched by code or finer feeling. Bogart's Spade wishes to avenge his partner Miles Archer's death. Hammett's Spade is screwing his partner's wife and is only reluctantly drawn into the effort to solve his murder. Hammett's Spade is alone and devoid of consolation—if, indeed, the merest thought of consolation ever crossed his mind. Beyond code, beyond emotion, beyond ideology or metaphor, Sam Spade encounters life unflinchingly as a calculus of self-interest and deceit, which perfectly reflects, as far as it can be determined, the interior life of Hammett himself: a sometime private detective for Pinkerton, cynical, steely-eyed, pharaonic.

American letters is replete with bleak lives, but few lives were as bleak, or as subversive of bourgeois value, as Dashiell Hammett's. Peering into the darkness, Dashiell Hammett wrote as well as anyone—then threw it all away along with wife and children to spend the next thirty years in alcoholic inactivity, an occasional Hollywood hack, a sporadic and inconclusive political activist, a semi-kept man and a poster boy for the Left. Yet in a few swift years, in less than a decade of effort, Hammett invented the hard-boiled detective story and set its standards for all time to come.

Writing under the name Paul Cain, screenwriter George Sims brought the genre to Los Angeles with *Fast One* (1933), which built on such earlier efforts as Jesse Allen McManus's *The Hood Asp* (1928). A half decade and more before Philip Marlowe, private detective Gerry Kells encounters a Los Angeles of gambling syndicates, crooked cops, prizefighters, and reporters on the take, with scenes set in the Biltmore, the Ambassador, the Brown Derby, Musso & Frank, offshore gambling ships, and cars chasing through the Santa Monica Mountains: all of it worthy of the kind of B-grade movies Sims wrote for a living but also true to the headlines and the hidden history of the Los Angeles that is at once the setting and lead element of the novel. Like Hammett, Sims had honed his hard-boiled skills under the tutelage of *Black Mask* mystery magazine editor Joseph T. Shaw, an exacting Harvard-trained perfectionist obsessed with minimalism as a literary style. Blue pencil in hand, Shaw taught Hammett, Sims, McCoy, Chandler, and others how to present experience as minimally as possible, with a detachment and a restraint, a hard-boiledness, totally appropriate to swift-paced stories of crime and betrayal. Screenwriters George Sims and Horace McCoy, each of them *Black Mask* veterans, took easily to the hard-boiled genre because the swiftly paced, minimally presented short stories and novels in this style—rapid, staccato, quick-cutting from scene to scene—were constructed and written like screenplays. For the same reason, Raymond Chandler, who began as a *Black Mask* writer, was able to make the transition from short story writer to novelist to Hollywood screenwriter.

Written under the pen name Richard Hallas, Eric Knight's *You Play the Black and the Red Comes Up* (1938) is the most sociologically explicit of the hard-boiled California novels. It is astonishing how many social references Knight manages to pack into this fast-paced first-person narrative, as if Knight, a screenwriter, were consciously trying to pack it all into one novel while staying within the near-novella length paralleling the screenplay. The story of an Oklahoman in Southern California in search of his estranged wife and son, *You Play the Black and the Red Comes Up* inventories virtually all the working elements of the Southern California scenario. The novel begins in Texas, then proceeds across the Southwest via the freights, with a vivid description of hobo culture, moves south to San Diego, then centers itself on San Pedro, with detailed excursions to Long Beach, Palos Verdes, Hollywood, and Malibu, lovingly described in terms of local road conditions and automobile performance. There is almost enough Hollywood material—especially the party scenes in the home of a bisexual Hollywood director—to qualify it as a para-Hollywood novel. Yet there is also a crackpot utopian subplot, with the narrator's girlfriend getting involved in an evangelical-economic reform movement, Ecanaanomics, which combines elements of Aimee Semple Macpherson's Four Square Gospel, Sinclair's EPIC, Utopianism, Technocracy, and Ham and Eggs. Movie stars, Palos Verdes socialites, Long Beach amusement park workers, cops, Mexicans, Japanese, Hawaiians, and assorted Folks flit on and off a stage centered on the oceanside amusement park at Long Beach. Knight creates this diversity of social reference, however, only to have his narrator repudiate it all at the end in a longish paean to Southern California that simultaneously inventories the region while asserting its fundamental lack of reality.

To penetrate the bleakness, the instability, of Raymond Chandler's life, both before and after a measure of fame came to him, is to voyage into a heart of darkness, an existential void—the edge of nothingness, as Chandler described it—which Edmund Wilson saw as the first premise of the best writing in California during this period. To meet Raymond Chandler in 1931, vice president of the

South Basin Oil Company, was to encounter just another fifty-something Southland Babbitt driving a Hupmobile and following USC football. Closer examina-
tion, however, would reveal that the downtown executive, anonymous in his business suit, puffing contentedly on his pipe, was a volcanically tortured snob,
Chicago born but London reared, a proud graduate of Dulwich College (hence
a Public School man), a failed poet, the sole survivor of his unit in the trenches
of the First World War, a skirt-chaser married to a much older woman, a boozer
of heroic proportions, obsessed with crime and violence. Chandler had been living
in Los Angeles since 1912, with time out for the war, in which he served in the
Gordon Highlanders of Canada, but he remained at heart an English expatriate:
a marginal member, eventually, of the Hollywood Raj, drinking gin with lime
juice, cultivating his Public School accent, reading English books and magazines.
Later, when England treated him as a serious writer, he was thrilled. "In England,"
he remarked, "I am an author. In the USA, just a mystery writer." [8]

In a city of restless people living on the edge of the void, Raymond and Cissy
Chandler set new standards for instability. Even Chandler's exacting biographer
Frank MacShane seems to despair of chronicling the innumerable moves, up to
two or three a year, and the numerous places in which the Chandlers lived
through the 1930s. Silver Lake, the Downtown, Hancock Park, Fairfax, Hollywood
Hills, Santa Monica, Brentwood Heights, Monrovia and Arcadia in the San Gabriel Valley, Cathedral City near Palm Springs, then into the hills in Idyllwild,
then back to Cathedral City—the Chandlers moved from place to place, the bulk
of their possessions in storage, urban gypsies drawing from their storage lockers
what they needed for a specific rental, which they frequently abandoned after a
few months. In all these years of move after move, the Chandlers seemed to see
no one, rarely go out, have few friends. They lived alone, claustrophobically, and
they wanted it that way. (Even in Chandler's fiction there are rarely more than
two people in the room.) Out of a job at South Basin Oil, Chandler secured a
small stipend, $100 a month, for assistance in a suit against his former company,
then launched himself into his literary career with a series of short stories published in Black Mask. He listed himself as a writer in the Los Angeles directory.
He was not exaggerating. Raymond Chandler was a writer: wielder of a tough-
minded, minimalist prose, born in part from his admiration of Hemingway and
Shaw's blue pencil but also of the Greek and Latin classics he had mastered at
Dulwich, with their laconic presentation of complex action and their restraint in
description and commentary.

From his Black Mask stories, Chandler mined his first full-length novel, The
Big Sleep (1939), and portions of the other seven major novels to be published in
his lifetime. Chandler was essentially a 1940s and 1950s writer. His Black Mask
stories from the 1930s are important, but they came most alive as sections of the
later novels. More important, Chandler's point of view, his style, his tone, his
obsessions were 1940s: 1940s Los Angeles, more precisely, the city of Bugsy Siegel
and George Raft; LAPD Detective Lieutenant Harry Fremont, capable, it was

alleged, of shooting a suspect down in cold blood, and all the other LAPD cops not reluctant to administer a beating to Philip Marlowe or anyone else who got in their way; the city of five daily newspapers and sixteen hours of headlines; the city of the Black Dahlia murder and the dives on Beacon Street down by the port and the homosexual action in Santa Monica. Working in a sub-literary genre ("He, as much as anyone else," notes Matthew J. Bruccoli, "took a sub-literary genre and made it into literature. Hammett did it first, but Chandler did it better"), Raymond Chandler became the prose-poet laureate of film *noir* Los Angeles.[9] Not accidentally, Chandler's brief career as a writer coincided with the film *noir* years of Hollywood, in which Chandler himself played an important part as screenwriter and story source. Six of Chandler's novels were made into movies in his lifetime, and Chandler himself was nominated for Academy Awards for his work on *Double Indemnity* (1944) and *The Blue Dahlia* (1946). Chandler might complain about Hollywood (everyone did), but in the 1930s he was living on $2,000 to $3,000 a year, and in 1945 he was paying $50,000 in income tax.

As a writer, Chandler created a world as coherent as Faulkner's Yoknapatawpha County. Chandler's peripatetic life as a householder had soaked him in the ambience and details of metropolitan Los Angeles. Standing one night alongside Chandler on a terrace in the Hollywood Hills overlooking the nighttime sea of light that is the Los Angeles basin, producer John Houseman experienced a powerful sense of imaginative appropriateness, a feeling almost of interactive power, flowing between Chandler and the city. Since he had not enjoyed much of a life (or so he believed), Chandler re-created himself in Philip Marlowe—not directly, not autobiographically, but with sufficient clues and connections—and through Marlowe, Chandler was able to reappropriate on the level of moral imagination the City of the Angels and its attendant suburbia, which he had otherwise failed to master. Aficionados have located and catalogued every site, every building, every home, every bar and seedy hotel presented in Chandler's fiction, and cumulatively it offers an inventory, a *catalogue raisonné* of place, which, because it is embedded in enduring art, becomes something like James Joyce's Dublin or Dashiell Hammett's San Francisco, a city of imagination as well as fact, the one reinforcing the other. With evident pride, Chandler once took Christopher Isherwood on a tour of Los Angeles sites he used in his fiction. Only the English-born artist David Hockney, Billy Wilder later suggested, equaled Chandler in his ability to fix Los Angeles as an imagined place.

Like all such places—the Paris of Honoré de Balzac, the London of Charles Dickens, the Alexandria of Constantine Cavafy, the Chicago of James T. Farrell—Chandler's Los Angeles yields an inventory of places that, when extracted, form a factual and symbolic map of the city: City Hall, Union Station, Bunker Hill and Angel's Flight, the Oviatt and Bradbury buildings and the Hotel Cecil in the Downtown; the black bars and jazz joints along Central Avenue; Baldwin Hills to the south; Bullock's Wilshire and the 1920s apartment buildings scattered throughout the Inner Wilshire and up along Rossmore into Hollywood; Hollywood itself—the Guaranty Building at Hollywood and Ivar where Philip Marlowe has his office, the Musso & Frank Grill, Stanley Rose's bookstore next door (Rose was busted for pornography, and his store becomes Bennett's Bookshop, a front for pornography in *The Big Sleep*); Greystone Mansion in Beverly Hills, Laurel Canyon, Malibu, and Santa Monica (Bay City, Chandler's second favorite place) with its Municipal Pier and Bel Air Bay Club; Pasadena, where Marlowe makes his debut at the Sternwood mansion in *The Big Sleep*, an establishment combining elements of the Doheny Senior mansion in Chester Place and Greystone, the Doheny Junior mansion in Beverly Hills, where the most famous murder-suicide in Los Angeles history occurred, a scandal fictionalized by Chandler in *The High Window* (1942), together with the home of Joseph Dabney, president of the Dabney Oil Syndicate at 420 South Lafayette near Hancock Park. Thanks to Chandler, pre- and post-war Los Angeles, beautiful and sinister in the sunshine, became permanent by becoming literature.

Private detective Philip Marlowe lives and works in this *mise-en-scène*, in part an idealized version of what Chandler might have wished for himself, in part an unconscious expression of some of Chandler's more submerged traits. Critics have noted Marlowe's repressed sexuality. He couples but once, possibly twice, in the entire Chandler oeuvre and in *The Big Sleep* is driven to raging disgust when he finds the nymphomaniacal Carmen Sternwood in his bed. He practically delivers himself up as a willing victim for beatings by dominant men, gangsters or cops, beatings he seems to relish in ways best left to the insights of psychiatry. Pansies (Chandler's term) are everywhere in Marlowe's world, as metaphor and villain. Like Chandler, Marlowe frequently gets his courage from the bottle. More profoundly, despite the fact that he was born in Santa Rosa and went to the University of Oregon, Marlowe is an honorary Public School man, an urban knight errant (the comparison is explicit in *The Big Sleep*): "an English gentleman transplanted to one of the bizarre colonies," Matthew Bruccoli describes him, "setting an example for the natives."[10] Philip Marlowe, in short, is, like Chandler, a sexually repressed boozer, living in isolation (no wife or girlfriend, no family, few if any friends), keeping to his chivalric code despite the venality of the natives, caught forever between "the romance of sordidness" and the unattainable blonde with cornflower blue eyes who comes and goes in various guises.

It was a complex relationship among writer, fictional detective, and city. Chandler despised Los Angeles. To a certain extent, it had eaten up his life, kept him on the edge of nothing, as he put it. Yet without Los Angeles he, and Marlowe, were less than nothing; they were disembodied ghosts; for the city had energized Chandler's imagination, and he in turn had energized the city through his art. Without the crime, the gangsters, the corrupt cops, the shakedowns, the payoffs, the seedy hotels of Los Angeles, what would Chandler have to write about? Or how would Philip Marlowe make his living? Like Chandler, Marlowe knows the nasty underside of the town, knows how it could eat up little people by giving them impossible hopes. Yet where is Marlowe to go? The pain and misbehavior of Los Angeles are not only his craft and profession, they are his obsession as well. It is too late to leave, too late to learn another place. And besides: Marlowe himself, like so many of his clients, is a victim of the siren call of L.A. What betrayed dreams, one might ask, brought him down from Santa Rosa and set him to the task of walking and driving these mean streets? "I used to like this town," Marlowe says in *The Little Sister* (1949), Chandler's most explicitly sociological novel. "A long time ago. There were trees along Wilshire Boulevard. Beverly Hills was a country town. Westwood was bare hills and lots offering at eleven hundred dollars and no takers. Hollywood was a bunch of frame houses on the interurban line. Los Angeles was just a big dry sunny place with ugly homes and no style, but goodhearted and peaceful. It had the climate they just yap about now. People used to sleep out on porches. Little groups who thought they were intellectual used to call it the Athens of America. It wasn't that, but it wasn't a neon-lighted slum either." [11]

By the mid-1930s, all the literary elements available to the Hollywood writer— the Hollywood novel, minimalism, the hard-boiled detective story, the subtle but persistent sense of impending doom that seemed to attach itself to Los Angeles— converged in the inspirational matrix of two screenwriters, Horace McCoy and Nathanael West, with dramatic results: *They Shoot Horses, Don't They?* (1935) and *The Day of the Locust* (1939). In terms of its subject matter (a dance marathon on the Santa Monica pier), its effective structure (the passing of a death sentence on Robert Syverten for the murder of Gloria Beatty, the words of the judge's sentence being flashed onto the pages of the novel like dialogue in a silent film, all this framing a reminiscence by Syverten of what led up to the murder), and its sociological sweep (Gloria Beatty's West Texas origins, Robert Sylverten's Arkansas background, the fringe world of Hollywood extras, the dance marathon itself, which only the desperation of the Depression could produce), *They Shoot Horses, Don't They?* is worthy, among other accolades, of being called by Sartre the first great existential novel. Written with the vividness and quick cuts of a screenplay, *They Shoot Horses, Don't They?* manages as much as any other novel of the period to express in distinctively Hollywood terms the desperation of the Depression as a national event.

Gloria Beatty and Robert Syverten are for all practical purposes displaced Folks, Crackers, Okies, as desperate as any in the novels of John Steinbeck; only in their case, because they are young, there is the illusion of making it in Hollywood. Gloria gets work as an extra in four films but cannot get registered in Central Casting because Hollywood has little need of Cracker types: half-pretty girls, capable of exciting the lust of small-town lotharios in West Texas, but not good enough for the silver screen. Syverten's hopes of getting on as even an errand boy for a director are equally doomed, and so the two enter a dance marathon on the amusement pier at Santa Monica: scenes vividly realized by McCoy; scenes, in fact, that seem to be filming themselves page by page. With one suicide attempt already behind her, Gloria hates life and wants to die, and says this frequently. When the marathon is canceled after a stray bullet fired by a minor hood kills both its intended victim and Mrs. Layden, the elderly woman who watches the dancers each evening and finds Robert and Gloria a sponsor, Gloria, walking with Robert to the end of the pier, no prospects in sight beyond the fifty bucks each has been given as a payoff, hands him a small pistol and begs him to put her out of her misery. Robert shoots her instinctively, remembering how his grandfather back in Arkansas had once been forced to shoot a favorite horse with a broken leg. Only certain novels by James M. Cain equal *They Shoot Horses, Don't They?* in construction, pace, intensity, and social amplitude; and while McCoy's two subsequent novels—*No Pockets in a Shroud* (1937) and *I Should Have Stayed Home* (1938)—are good (especially *I Should Have Stayed Home*, in which McCoy revisits the fringe world of Hollywood extras), neither has the Aristotelian inevitability of character, action, and plot of his first effort.

Nathanael West's *The Day of the Locust*, by contrast, never finally becomes a unified act of fiction, despite the compellingness of individual characters and the vividness of individual scenes. For all the brilliance of his social observation, West cannot make character, action, and plot function together in real time. From the start, Horace McCoy worked in the mode of minimalist realism, with its strict economy of language and reference. West, by contrast, began his career with the talky-talky and allegorical *The Dream Life of Balzo Snell* (1931), which is the kind of novel thousands of bookish undergraduates have written, their heads crammed with literary references, before going on to newspapering, a Ph.D., or law school.

For all its surface realism, *The Day of the Locust* is also very allegorical. Each character embodies a vivid social and psychological state, which is also, for West and for the reader, an analytical notion, an intellectualized critique in the time-honored manner of satire, which always runs to type. How else but as allegorical types can one explain such characters as Harry Greener, a broken-down vaudevillian and burlesque comic turned salesman of silver polish; Earle Shoop, a cowboy actor from Arizona; Mama and Papa Gingo, Eskimos stranded in Hollywood after working on a film about polar expeditions; Chief Kiss-My-Towkus, a Native American who speak Yiddish; Maybelle Loomis, a mother trying to get her eight-year-old son Adore into the movies; Adore himself, grotesquely capable of singing in a style totally suggestive of adult sexuality; Abe Kusich, a dwarf bit player; Mrs. Jennings, the janitress in a Hollywood apartment house filled with studio extras—each of them stylized figures from the comic stage? They are instantly recognizable as types verging on allegory, which is how the central protagonist of the novel, Todd Hackett, a set and costume designer planning a panoramic canvas entitled *The Burning of Los Angeles*, sees each of them, down to the point of knowing how he would depict them when he painted the final conflagration of the city. Recognizable as types as well are Faye Greener, Harry's daughter, a studio extra doing now-and-then gigs as a call girl, and Miguel, a Mexican running illegal cockfights. From the perspective of West's cultural parable, it is no accident that Faye and Miguel wind up in bed. Miguel the Mexican is the primordial spirit of place, a figure from the rancho era. Blonde, sexual, a figure of unconscious strength, Faye Greener is Anglo-California, a nature goddess equal in presence and intensity to Queen Califia herself, the mythic Amazonian who once ruled this kingdom. No matter what else happens, Miguel and Faye, Aztec and Cracker, are destined to couple, just as they are conjoined, Mexican and Anglo, in the creation of Southern California.

Homer Simpson, by contrast, an Iowan lost in Hollywood, embodies the hundreds of thousands of Midwestern people who have come to Los Angeles seeking redemption but have been cheated, who mill about the streets of the city in their outlandish sports clothes, waiting for something to happen. (West originally intended to call his novel *The Cheated*.) Something does happen, finally, at a Hollywood premiere. Homer breaks into the violence he has long suppressed and bashes Adore to death, which precipitates an arsonous riot among the crowd outside the theater. Carried off from the conflagration in an ambulance, Todd Hackett has now experienced a real-life enactment of the burning of Los Angeles he has so long planned to paint. The terror of it all leaves him screaming to the wail of the ambulance siren as smoke rises above the city.

The contrast between *They Shoot Horses, Don't They?* and *The Day of the Locust* reflects the contrast between McCoy and West. Horace McCoy was a matter-of-fact Anglo-Texan, trained in the *Black Mask* school, grateful for his work in the studios, not a hack exactly but willing and unashamed to grind out B scripts; and West was a Jew who would eventually change his name from Nathan Weinstein and renounce his Jewish identity, a high school dropout who forged transcripts to get into Tufts, then transferred to Brown by using the Tufts transcripts of another Nathan Weinstein, a litterateur who dressed from Brooks Brothers and went to Paris in the twenties to become a writer, winding up a hotel clerk in New York, then going on to Hollywood in 1933 after selling *Miss Lonelyhearts* to Twentieth Century–Fox. Practical, workmanlike, hard-boiled, Horace McCoy belonged to Los Angeles/Hollywood in a way that Nathanael West, ever dreaming of Literature with a capital *L*, never could. McCoy never faked anything. West faked his entire identity. McCoy took the doom of Hollywood in a straightforward, hard-boiled way. West perceived and presented it through allegory. Each wrote novels that will be long remembered.

Significantly, Nathanael West and another exile from the East and from Literature, F. Scott Fitzgerald, were good friends in Hollywood. West revered Fitzgerald as the one figure embodying above anyone else the spirit of Paris in the twenties. In *The Day of the Locust*, West echoed Fitzgerald's phrasing and tone; but the influence went the other way as well, with Fitzgerald most likely learning from West, or developing it alongside him in discussion, the power of a Hollywood lot, with its jumbled scenery from every historic period, as an allegory of timelessness and rootlessness and, paradoxically, all history made present in an artificial but compelling way: which accounts for strong scenes in both *The Day of the Locust* and Fitzgerald's unfinished *The Last Tycoon* (1941).

On the evening of Friday, 13 December 1940, Fitzgerald and Sheilah Graham came over from Fitzgerald's house in Encino to the Wests' home at 12706 Magnolia Boulevard in North Hollywood, a *faux* farmhouse in a grove of walnut and pear trees, where West had moved with his new bride, Eileen McKenney, the leading character in Ruth McKenney's novel-memoir *My Sister Eileen* (1938). It was a great evening, with talk of Paris and Hollywood and novels planned or underway. Eight days later Fitzgerald died of a heart attack in Graham's Hollywood apartment, and the next day Nathanael and Eileen West, returning in their station wagon from a hunting trip in Mexico, met death on Route 111 between Calexico and El Centro.

The Hollywood sojourn of F. Scott Fitzgerald, his last years, has inspired a library shelf of biography and criticism even longer than that inspired by West. F. Scott Fitzgerald in Hollywood! A dozen images come instantly to the screen. Fitzgerald outside his $400-a-month studio apartment in the Garden of Allah, an Andalusian fairy cottage, one floor up a tiled staircase. Fitzgerald at the Beverly Hills Tennis Club, dressed in Brooks Brothers, defiant of the sunshine, as if it were a Saturday football game at Princeton, followed by cocktails at Tiger Inn. Fitzgerald and Sheilah Graham, meeting at a party at Robert Benchley's bungalow at the Garden of Allah on 14 July 1937, a soiree celebrating Bastille Day and Graham's engagement to a titled Englishman, whom she soon threw over (so she tells us) for the forty-something flamed-out paragon of Flaming Youth, trying for a comeback as a screenwriter at MGM, with hopes of a Hollywood novel. Fitzgerald and Graham: holding hands at the Hollywood Bowl, bending over chocolate malts at Schwab's, browsing at the Pickwick bookshop, lunching at the Beverly Hills Brown Derby, nightclubbing at the Clover Club on Sunset Strip, driving there in Fitzgerald's Buick, with Humphrey Bogart saying hello as they moved through the bar. Fitzgerald and Graham at Malibu, where she found him a house where it might be easier for Scott to fight the booze than at the Garden of Allah, followed by a move to the even more remote Encino in the San Fernando Valley.

By 1939, dispirited by the way the studios were treating his scripts, Fitzgerald returned to fiction with one last outburst of creativity. The duality of Fitzgerald's Hollywood fiction—the minimalist and frequently cynical Pat Hobby stories, the six chapters of the unfinished *The Last Tycoon*—manages to put Fitzgerald, however obliquely, within the context of California fiction as formulated by his friend and Princeton classmate Edmund Wilson, who edited *The Last Tycoon* for posthumous publication. Between September 1939 and his death, Fitzgerald wrote seventeen Pat Hobby stories for *Esquire*. Editor Arnold Gingrich paid Fitzgerald $250, later $350, per story. Conventional wisdom considers the Pat Hobby stories hack work, ground out by Fitzgerald in the last year of his life to keep body and soul together after his screenwriting career collapsed. This is true as far as it goes.

Yet for all their casualness, the Pat Hobby stories are not to be dismissed either in terms of their minimalism, their contribution to Hollywood fiction, or the function writing them played in Fitzgerald's mind as he raced the clock on *The Last Tycoon.*

In *Hope of Heaven* (1938), John O'Hara, another disciple of F. Scott Fitzgerald, had already shown the possibilities of a minimalist novel with a screenwriter as anti-hero. O'Hara was also a Garden of Allah resident, which is where the two first met. Defiantly Eastern in dress like Fitzgerald and equally obsessed with the drama of social class, a snob as only the college dropout son of Pottsville, Pennsylvania's leading doctor could be, O'Hara, like Nathanael West, worshipped Fitzgerald as the embodiment of all that he wanted to be as a writer. Fitzgerald's dreams became O'Hara's dreams, although there was something harsh and hardboiled in O'Hara, nine years Fitzgerald's junior, which contrasted itself to the essential romanticism of Fitzgerald's temperament. The two of them, side by side in the Garden of Allah (O'Hara briefly dated Sheilah Graham), emanated the contrasting moods of the 1920s: of Princeton and Paris in Fitzgerald's case and the more gritty texture of O'Hara's life as a newspaper reporter in Pottsville covering crime and local sports. Like Fitzgerald with the publication of *This Side of Paradise* (1920), O'Hara awoke one morning and found himself famous with the overnight success of *Appointment in Samarra* (1934), and like Fitzgerald, O'Hara headed to Hollywood to cash in on his fame. Like Fitzgerald, O'Hara revered New York City, the 21 scene especially, aromatic of scotch and cigarettes, and the more raffish Broadway sporting crowd whom he memorialized in *Pal Joey* (1940). Like Fitzgerald, O'Hara drank too much and could occasionally become unruly. Dave Chasen banned O'Hara from his restaurant when O'Hara accused him of padding the bill.

Like so much of O'Hara's work, *Hope of Heaven* is the loosely structured, offhanded story of screenwriter James Malloy, very much a John O'Hara alter ego, who narrates in the first person with a minimalism verging on the hard-boiled. From one perspective, *Hope of Heaven* is a detective story; from another, a Hollywood novel; yet like everything O'Hara ever wrote, it has its fundamental vitality as a narrative attitude and a novel of manners. Casually yet with cumulative detail, O'Hara gives us the studios, the night life on Melrose and Sunset, the taste of corned beef hash at the Beverly Hills Brown Derby, the feel of a Buick convertible cruising down Wilshire on a sunny Sunday morning, the big houses for rent in Beverly Hills, the price of every item necessary to keep a screenwriter living in style, including his shoes and socks. Through Malloy, O'Hara holds Hollywood at a distance by itemizing it in its most minimal terms. Hollywood is a crap shoot. In the course of the novel, Malloy is hired and fired at least twice, but no matter, there is always New York, where Malloy has a play very much resembling *Pal Joey* in production, and the scene at 21. New York is real; Hollywood, an interlude. New York is full; Hollywood, empty. Facing the emptiness, the phoniness,

of Hollywood with no show of superiority or self-pity, Malloy/O'Hara can take it
or leave it with a wisecrack or dismissive nod of the head. The boys in the back
room had a way of telling the void to get lost.

No one needed to defy the void more notably by late 1939 than O'Hara's pal
F. Scott Fitzgerald, the number one case study of a literary figure (in his case, a
past tense literary figure) brought to Hollywood from the East and paid $1,000 a
week to have his ideas rejected. All things considered, the legend aside, the studios
did okay by Fitzgerald. MGM paid him a total of $68,000 in 1938. Fitzgerald
worked on such projects as A Yank at Oxford (1938), The Women (1939), and
Madame Curie (1943) and did some last-minute work on Gone with the Wind
(1939); but no producer ever allowed him any kind of controlling presence on a
film. Joe Mankiewicz, for example, told Fitzgerald that the script he had done for
Three Comrades (1938) was the best he had ever read, whereupon Mankiewicz,
himself a former screenwriter, rewrote Fitzgerald's draft beyond recognition.
Heartbroken, Fitzgerald wrote Mankiewicz a pleading letter ("Oh Joe, can't producers ever be wrong? I'm a good writer—honest. I thought you were going to
play fair"), then went on a class-A bender, despite the fact that the studio had just
upped his salary to $1,250 per week.

Like his alter ego Pat Hobby, Fitzgerald was nipping frequently from a flask of
gin in his desk drawer to keep himself going, and like so many in that fast-paced
town, he was resorting to pharmaceutical encouragement. "I was going to sleep
every night," he confessed of his time at MGM, "with a gradually increasing dose
of chloral—three teaspoonsful—and two pills of Nembutal every night and forty-
five drops of Digitalin to keep the heart working to the next day. Eventually one
begins to feel like a character out of the 'Wizard of Oz.' "[12] Hired by Walter
Wanger to work with Budd Schulberg on Winter Carnival (1939), a Dartmouth
film, Fitzgerald began a spree on the plane heading East. At Dartmouth he passed
out in the snow and showed up drunk at a faculty reception, where he told off
some professors who had criticized the script. Wanger fired Fitzgerald from the
project. Schulberg delivered Fitzgerald to Graham in New York, where he was
hospitalized for two weeks. Novelized by Schulberg in The Disenchanted (1950)
and by Graham in Beloved Infidel (1958), Fitzgerald's Dartmouth drunk has become one of the most noted sprees in American literary history, second only to
the last fatal bender of Edgar Allan Poe.

Deeply in debt from the effort to pay Zelda's sanitarium bills, hence barely able
to make his daughter's $615 tuition at Vassar, his copybook blotted at the studios,
vulnerable to intermittent sprees, heading toward his first heart attack, Fitzgerald
defied the abyss through his alter ego Pat Hobby. To use a well-worn phrase, Pat
Hobby is a survivor. Like Fitzgerald, Hobby had been big in the twenties, writing
scenarios for the silents; but these days, the late 1930s, age forty-nine, Hobby is
scraping by at $350 a week, the lowest possible salary for a screenwriter, a hack of
all work, fueling his flagging self-esteem from bottles stashed in his desk, playing
the horses at Santa Anita, trying to get lucky with one or another of the young

extras impressed when Ronald Colman acknowledges Pat in the commissary. Like Fitzgerald, Hobby, even in decline, maintains a bit of 1920s elegance: a hounds-tooth check sport coat, knit tie, button-down shirt, and saddle shoes, a snappy convertible. Hobby will do anything to get by: lie, steal a script, con an ex-wife, anything, to hang on to his desk in the Writers' Building. Thus Fitzgerald was exorcising his fears as to what he might himself become, should he descend to the $350 rung. Satirizing himself as a washed-up, hard-drinking hack, he managed to forestall or at least to stabilize the disaster. For all his faults, Pat Hobby is indomi-table. He survives each story, each disaster, and goes on to the next reel. He does this, moreover, in a short story format that is brisk, witty, minimalist, and totally lacking in self-pity.

Even as Fitzgerald was producing these semi-hard-boiled stories, hence helping himself to control a chaotic experience by fixing it with controlled language and a calm eye, he was also busy at work on a lavish, anti-minimalist novel, *The Last Tycoon* (1941), lush and elegiac, soaked through with commentary, symbol, and myth, centered on producer Monroe E. Stahr, a self-made romanticist modeled on Irving Thalberg, the Great Gatsby of American film. Like *The Great Gatsby* (1925), *The Last Tycoon* presents its hero through the first-person observations of an outside observer, Cecilia Brady, a convent-educated junior at Bennington and the daughter of Stahr's crass and racketeering partner. The completed six chapters of *The Last Tycoon* convinced Edmund Wilson that Fitzgerald was heading in the direction of his best novel ever. *The Last Tycoon* is about democracy and its myths, about the old order of silent film, sweeping and heroic, and the need Stahr feels to provide the American people with comparable myths and dreams in the midst of a great Depression. What stories should he tell? How best to serve the American public over whose nation he flies in the opening scene of the novel, making a necessary but highly symbolic stopover at Nashville, Tennessee, where he visits the home of that quintessential self-made American democrat, Andrew Jackson? In terms of its characterization, its evocative descriptions of the studios (a studio set by moonlight; the back lot of MGM struck by earthquake, thrown into a phantasmagoria of historical periods) its encompassing social detail (parties, story conferences, lunch hour at the commissary), and a realistic plot centered on Stahr's fight against the infiltration of the studio unions by mobsters and Commu-nist unions, *The Last Tycoon* promises and partially delivers that panoramic Los Angeles/Hollywood novel critics had been calling for, lo, these many years.

A year later, Random House published perhaps the best Hollywood novel to date, *What Makes Sammy Run?* (1941), by Budd Schulberg, Fitzgerald's partner and caretaker in the Dartmouth debacle. Interestingly enough, Hollywood's best novel was written by a longtime resident of Hollywood, the son of producer B. P. Schulberg, an early partner of Louis B. Mayer and, later, executive producer at Paramount Studios. As Budd Schulberg described himself, he was a Hollywood Prince, for whom palm trees and Spanish Revival bungalows were as real as pine trees and Cape Cod cottages. Schulberg's childhood friends, his honorary aunts and uncles (including Uncle Louis B. Mayer), and his friends at Los Angeles High School, where he excelled in tennis before going on to Deerfield and Dartmouth, were drawn from the studio elite. Returning to Hollywood after graduation from Dartmouth, Schulberg supplemented his Hollywood Prince's knowledge of life at the top with the more complete picture of Hollywood types he encountered as a screenwriter for David Selznick, Walter Wanger, and Sam Goldwyn.

Bennett Cerf accepted *What Makes Sammy Run?*, Schulberg's first novel, for Random House, believing it to be the most brilliant Hollywood novel he had ever come across. At the same time, Cerf warned Schulberg, Hollywood novels tended not to sell that well. *The Day of the Locust*, for example, had not even earned back its $500 advance, much less free Nathanael West from grinding out B westerns at Republic. Disappointed in the sales of *Hope of Heaven*, Schulberg's friend John O'Hara made the same caution. Both Cerf and O'Hara were wrong. *What Makes Sammy Run?* remains one of the all-time best-sellers in American publishing history and has not been out of print since 1941.

Schulberg insisted that Sammy Glick was not based on any one individual. Suggestions of Sammy were everywhere in Hollywood, Schulberg argued, although one incident had galvanized the character in his mind. Fresh from college, Schulberg was working on his first project. At a cocktail party, a casual acquaintance, another screenwriter, asked him what he was working on, managing to convey a sense of sympathy for the young writer. Schulberg told him. A few days later, he read in the *Hollywood Reporter* that the writer had sold Schulberg's idea to a studio. The rip-off had taken but a few minutes. Complaining to other writers, Schulberg was told: it happens all over town, you should hear what happened to me!

Over the years Sammy Glick has been studied by psychiatrists, psychologists, sociologists, economists, and moral philosophers as well as by literary critics as a powerful probe into the American national character. More than any other figure in modern American fiction, Schulberg's repellent but fascinating anti-hero, Hollywood hustler Sammy Glick, embodies that ruthless rage for success, that capacity for self-invention, self-deceit, and deceit of others, that egotism verging on the narcissistic, that lurks in the darker underside of laissez-faire capitalism. A Jew writing about a Jewish heel in a Jewish-dominated industry, Schulberg initially attracted charges of anti-Semitism, which have never really stuck: not because Schulberg himself is Jewish, but because the entire New York immigrant world from which Sammy Glick is running so hard by clawing his way through the studios is portrayed by Schulberg with all its variety of characters and social types, good and bad and in between. *What Makes Sammy Run?* was no more anti-Semitic, Schulberg insisted, than Richard Wright's *Native Son* (1940) was anti-black.

Hollywood, on the other hand, was insulted. Louis B. Mayer told Schulberg's father that his son should be deported. "For Christ's sake, Louie," B.P. replied, "he's the only novelist who ever came *from* Hollywood. Where the hell are you going to deport him, Catalina Island?"[13] Privately, however, B.P. warned his son that he might never find work in his home town. John Wayne considered the novel a Communist plot and threatened to settle the matter personally. For years following its publication, Wayne accosted Schulberg at Hollywood parties, at Chasen's, Ciro's, and Romanoff's, encounters Schulberg compared to the face-off in Fred Zinnemann's *High Noon* (1952). In the mid-1960s, meeting Schulberg at a hotel in Puerto Vallarta, the Duke, still sore, challenged the writer of Hollywood's best novel to a fistfight. Schulberg later described the match, which his wife broke up, as a draw.

In terms of sales, national reputation, and enduring impact, John Steinbeck's *The Grapes of Wrath* (1939) remains the fictive high point of the decade. Yet James M. Cain's *Mildred Pierce* (1941), linked to the 1930s in terms of its composition and the time span of its plot, set new standards of sociology and reportage. Of all the writers of the era, Cain took most to heart—and answered—Sinclair Lewis's challenge to transmute the materials of ordinary life in Southern California into a fiction of engaged realism.

From the first, James M. Cain was hard-boiled. Even at his most minimalist, by contrast, John Steinbeck sustained a lyricism and a regard for the mytho-poetic that were totally foreign to Cain's classic realism, which is Aristotelian in its empiricism and structured economy. Cain's provenance was the Southern California to which he had come as a screenwriter in the early 1930s and which he described in March 1933 for his Baltimore friend H. L. Mencken's *American Mercury* in "Paradise, the Civilization of Southern California," an essay that is the best nonfiction analysis of the Southland from the decade. Few novelists or short story writers of the 1930s present a more encompassing atlas of Southern California than Cain: roadside Los Angeles and Ventura counties in *The Postman Always Rings Twice* (1934); downtown Los Angeles and the Los Feliz district in *Double Indemnity* (1936); Hollywood, the Hollywood Bowl, and the Mexico *noir* that remained appended to the imaginative landscape of Southern California in *Serenade* (1937); Glendale, Burbank, Pasadena, and Lake Arrowhead in *Mildred Pierce* (1941).

Steinbeck's California is centered on the Central Coast, on Monterey and the Salinas Valley where he had grown up. Although he lived in suburban Los Gatos and had many friends in San Francisco, Steinbeck shunned cities and suburbs as settings for his fiction, preferring rural scenes and people. Steinbeck's fiction from the 1930s—*The Pastures of Heaven* (1932), *To a God Unknown* (1933), *Tortilla Flat* (1935), *In Dubious Battle* (1936), *Of Mice and Men* (1937), *The Red Pony* (1937), *The Long Valley* (1938)—rarely strays from an area bounded by Watsonville, Gilroy, and Hollister to the north, Soledad to the south, Salinas in the center, and Monterey, Carmel, and Big Sur on the Pacific. Free from the influence and coloration of either metropolitan Los Angeles or metropolitan San Francisco, Steinbeck country is neither Northern nor Southern California. It is, rather, its own distinctive place, the Salinas Valley on the Central Coast, a world of ranches and small towns. Even Monterey, capital of the Central Coastlands, despite its origins as the capital of Spanish and Mexican California, remained little more than a ramshackle fishing village through the 1930s, centered on wharfs and canneries.

The comparative narrowness of Steinbeck country precluded a fiction of manners and society, which was not Steinbeck's intent in any event, being as he was in search of a larger and more prototypically Californian drama: that of human beings and the environment, or rather, human beings *in* the environment as biological creatures. Steinbeck, Edmund Wilson noted, tended to see human beings as biological creatures acting in groups; indeed, although Wilson does not cite this, Steinbeck's own analogy for what he was seeking to do in his fiction was a tide pool in which a complex biological community flourished. Like the biologist, Steinbeck believed, the writer of fiction could never focus on an individual without seeing that individual in the tide pool of his or her natural environment. Wilson argued that this preoccupation with biology and group process kept Steinbeck from the higher reaches of literature. On the other hand, whatever social reference is present in Steinbeck's fiction from the 1930s is thoroughly mastered and skillfully presented, and even Wilson, begrudgingly, makes a comparison of Steinbeck's preoccupation with the Salinas Valley to that of William Faulkner with Oxford, Mississippi.

Steinbeck was native to the state, rooted in his region. Even in post-war years, living in Sag Harbor or a townhouse on the Upper East Side, he could never purge himself of Monterey and the Salinas Valley. James M. Cain, by contrast, was from Annapolis, Maryland, a transplant, writing brilliantly of Southern California, but never, absolutely never, giving himself to the place in any emotional way, and leaving the region permanently for the East after the war. Steinbeck had an almost naive devotion to literature. His mother, a schoolteacher, read the English classics to him as a child. For all his posturing as a proletarian writer, Steinbeck remained bookishly obsessed with biblical themes and the Arthurian cycle, and much of his fiction shows the controlling presence of these two literary sources. Cain, by contrast, spent most of the 1920s as an editorial writer for the New York *World*, working alongside Walter Lippmann, before moving to Hollywood. Steinbeck made his debut with the over-written *Cup of Gold* (1929), a florid novel based on the life of Henry Morgan, the seventeenth-century Caribbean buccaneer, which Steinbeck wrote painfully, agonizingly through a long winter spent in a fire-watch station in the Sierra Nevada. Cain, by contrast, was from the school of H. L. Mencken, whom Cain adored: a journalist, that is, capable of batting out copy on deadline, prizing clarity and pungency of phrase, accustomed to an atmosphere of booze, cigars, late nights, newspaper talk. Like Mencken, Cain revered erudition, yet his novels are devoid of literary reference. Their essential power comes from their perfect structure, their Aristotelian unities of time, place, character, and event, and their intense economy (next to Cain, noted one critic, Hemingway reads like a lexicographer), which can only be compared to the laconic literary ideals of classical Greece.

In purely formalist terms of plot, structure, character, event, and dialogue, Cain's first novel, *The Postman Always Rings Twice*, published when he was forty-two, comes as close to perfection as any American novel of the period. Its opening paragraph, establishing themes of rootlessness and lust (the rapid reference to being tired after three weeks in Tijuana) has been justly ranked as one of the best opening paragraphs in American fiction. By the second page, in little more than a thousand words, Cain has established an engine of character, situation, and plot that will run remorselessly for the next one hundred pages. Frank Chambers, drifter, goes to work for Nick Papadakis at the Twin Oaks Tavern, a lunchroom–gas station outside Los Angeles. He is drawn to Nick's young wife Cora, an ex–Hollywood extra with a touch of Mexican in her ancestry, by a lust instantaneous and compelling, and the two are coupling by page ten and planning Nick's murder by page fourteen. Cain's second novel, *Double Indemnity*, has the same remorseless power, the same rapid movement energized by lust. Insurance salesman Walter Huff sits down with a client, Phyllis Nirdlinger, in the cool recesses of her Spanish-style home in Los Angeles. Within three days they are lovers plotting an insurance scam involving the murder of Phyllis's husband.

Set in Mexico, Los Angeles, and New York, *Serenade* is a more diffuse performance. *Serenade* brings the Mexico *noir* sub-genre to perfection, in fact, with depictions of cantina and bordello life, a sacrilegious rape in an empty church, and the equally ritualized cooking and eating of an iguana, as if to consume Mexico itself. Cain's anti-hero John Howard Sharp, a down-and-out opera singer who is fighting a streak of bisexuality, regains his career as a last-minute substitute at the Hollywood Bowl, which leads to a movie career. The Hollywood portions of *Serenade* make it, in part, a Hollywood novel, with all the standardized indictments of the studio system common to a literary genre in which abused screenwriters got their chance at revenge.

Then, at the end of one decade and the beginning of another, James M. Cain came as close as anyone would in the pre-war period to taking up Sinclair Lewis's challenge to write about the everyday life of ordinary people in greater Los Angeles in the spirit of Turgenev. Setting *Mildred Pierce* in the Los Angeles suburb of Glendale between 1931 and 1940, Cain pays Southern California the compliment of writing his longest and most sociologically ambitious novel with hardly any reference whatsoever to Hollywood, presenting instead an epic of middle-class aspiration that depicts the social and psychological dynamics of that broad class of Americans who were most influential in the shaping of the culture and society of Southern California, without the faintest suggestion of patronage or resort to the grotesque. *Mildred Pierce* is in the tradition of realism as practiced and expounded by Turgenev and by William Dean Howells, albeit updated in matters of marriage, divorce, sexuality, and alcohol.

Throwing her husband out of the house for his philandering, Mildred Pierce of

Glendale is forced to support herself in the early lean years of the Depression. She bakes pies and sells them to neighbors, then to a bakery. She gets a job as a waitress and learns the restaurant business, then opens one, two, three restaurants of her own. Strictly as a parable of economic recovery through small business carried on by a single mother with a gift for entrepreneurialism, *Mildred Pierce* offers a story directly connected to the anxieties and aspirations of the Depression, with Cain having mastered and made interesting the details of restaurant operations and management, property acquisition and development, and retail marketing and distribution. If Mildred Pierce can make it back, Cain suggests, so can the United States.

As long as Mildred Pierce stays in her social class, she flourishes. When she acquires a playboy lover from upper-class Pasadena whom she marries, her fortunes go into decline, especially as Monty, her husband, seduces his stepdaughter Veda, on whom Mildred Pierce is already obsessionally fixated in what must be one of the most complicated mother-daughter relationships in American fiction.

Through it all—Mildred's initial divorce, the death of one of her two daughters, her affair with Monty, the rise and fall of her business, her unrequited love for Veda, her second divorce and remarriage to her first husband—Cain presents greater Los Angeles, its people and places, with a realism that only the most skilled Hollywood cameraman might match. Here are the waitresses and caterers, real estate agents and funeral parlor directors, doctors and nurses, ministers and music teachers, restaurant customers and next-door neighbors of a white middle-class suburbia only then coming into its own. Although their passions are intense, Cain feels no need to render his characters as eccentric or grotesque in the patronizing style of Nathanael West. Neither are they exalted or vilified. *Mildred Pierce* presents suburban Southern California as a recognizable mid-American landscape, with palm instead of pine trees, Spanish Revival instead of Cape Cod. The characters in *Mildred Pierce* make no reference to being in Southern California as if it were anything other than a comprehensibly mid-American place. Here is yet one more instance of America, Cain suggests, one more place to get on with the business of living.

In doing this—in resisting the exotic and the grotesque in favor of suburban verisimilitude—*Mildred Pierce* stabilizes Southern California by anchoring it in ordinary American experience. More than any other novel of the period, *Mildred Pierce* manages to suggest the coherence and stability of Southern California as a regional American civilization. For a decade, James M. Cain had been grappling with the meaning of Southern California. In *Mildred Pierce* he suggested a possible solution. Along with the apocalyptic and the eccentric, Southern California contained the commonplace. Nut cases might be easy to find, but ordinary Americans remained in the majority. Their lives, like Mildred Pierce's, ran to type, to the ordinary: an ordinariness that had driven Henry James, F. Marion Crawford, and others to renounce American scenes and lives entirely. But not James M. Cain. In the surfaces and recesses of everyday Southern California,

Cain found the setting, materials, and inspiration for ambitious fiction. Edmund Wilson wrote "The Boys in the Back Room" before the publication of *Mildred Pierce*. Hence Wilson did not know, as he passed judgment on the hard-boiled minimalist school on the Coast, that James M. Cain, facing the alleged emptiness of the Pacific, found not the void but a recognizable American place.

IV

WAR AND RUMORS
OF WAR

11

War and Peace and the Survival
of the Species

Californians Contemplate a World on the Verge
of Self-Destruction

*I*NCREASINGLY, through the 1930s, Carmel poet Robinson Jeffers, like millions of others, beheld a world in decline, marching to the drumbeats of war. Once again, as in 1917, the United States, in decline as well, or so Jeffers believed, was being seduced into violence on foreign shores. "Powerful and armed, neutral in the midst of madness," Jeffers had recently written, "we might have held/ the whole world's balance and stood/ Like a mountain in a wind. We were misled and took sides. We have/ chosen to share the crime and the punishment."[1] Motoring east in February 1941 in the company of his wife Una and his patron Noel Sullivan, Jeffers lectured at the Library of Congress and at Harvard. His pessimism and outspoken isolationism had long since made him a controversial figure, yet Jeffers was still respected (and respectable) enough to be introduced in Washington by Librarian of Congress Archibald MacLeish and at Harvard by poet-novelist Theodore Morrison. Lecturing from typewritten notes, the reclusive Jeffers, living in isolation since the First World War in a stone tower on the Carmel coast, explicated the dominant themes of his poetry. Never before or after would he be so willing to reflect so openly and so publicly on his work.

There are cycles in every age and culture, Jeffers told his audience. Civilizations rise and fall in periodic rhythms. The ancient Etruscans believed this. The Italian philosopher Giovanni Battista Vico reintroduced the idea in 1725 with the publication of *New Science*; and most recently, in *The Decline of the West* (1918–22), German historian Oswald Spengler had alerted an entire generation regarding the impending and inevitable decline of European civilization that was now in process. How, Jeffers asked, does one transcend one's own cycle, especially if it is a cycle of decline? Was there a vision to be glimpsed beyond the phenomena of a declining social order? Was there an Archimedean point from which one might move oneself to safety?

The answer, Jeffers argued, was the effort to make direct contact with the universe as Other: as an Entity complete to itself, known and understood, accepted and loved, for itself, on its own terms, beyond anthropomorphic projection. The fundamental barrier to such knowledge and acceptance—from such Inhumanism, as Jeffers called his philosophy—was a turning away from the universe as Other, austere and complete, beautiful and transcendent, in favor of that self-preoccupation with the drama of one's own soul, that solipsism, morbid and all-consuming, that was the bane of modern existence. "The whole human race spends too much emotion on itself," Jeffers noted. "The happiest and freest man is the scientist investigating nature, or the artist admiring it; the person who is interested in things that are not human. Or if he is interested in human things, let him regard them objectively, as a small part of the great music."[2]

What, then, did one encounter in making contact with the universe as transcendent Other? Jeffers admitted to a certain pantheism, a belief "that the world, the universe is one being, a single organism, one great life that includes all life and all things; and is so beautiful that it must be loved and reverenced; and in moments of mystical vision we identify ourselves with it."[3] And yet this universe, this Other, this God if you will, was not, to Jeffers's way of thinking, the serene and transcendent One of neo-Platonic mysticism, much less the anthropomorphic father figure of Judaism or the equiposed deity of trinitarian Christianity. The universe, God, Jeffers believed, was self-torturing. "This divine outer universe is after all not at peace with itself," Jeffers asserted, "but full of violent strains and conflicts. The physical world is ruled by opposing tensions. The world of living things is formed by a perpetual struggle and irreconcilable desires; and pain is an essential part of life."[4]

Greek mythology responded to this truth, Jeffers argued, with the figure of Prometheus crucified on Caucasus; Christianity with Jesus, the Son of God, assenting to his own crucifixion; Scandinavian paganism with the figure of Odin, chief of the gods, hanging himself and suffering through nine days of strangulation so as to learn the runes of wisdom, or, in another version of the story, hanging himself because as chief of the gods he demanded the greatest victim for sacrifice, who could only be himself. "There is a tortured God in every mythology," Jeffers claimed, "and this seemed to me the fittest symbol to express something that is most beautiful, and painful, and true."[5]

Jeffers ended his Washington and Harvard lectures with a reading of the single poem, "Rock and Hawk," that best expressed his view of the universe. It was a poem, Jeffers pointed out, that drew directly upon the environment and imagery of the Monterey coast. A hawk alights atop a rock on the headlands facing the Pacific.

> I think, here is your emblem
> To hang in the future sky;
> Not the cross, not the hive,

But this; bright power, dark peace;
Fierce consciousness joined with final
Disinterestedness.[6]

Had this been all—the philosophy of Inhumanism, the rock and the hawk—Jeffers
might have remained in reputation what he was in the deepest dimension of his
being: a philosophical poet drawing upon the imagery of the Carmel–Big Sur
coast and the leading representative of that naturism verging on pantheism so
characteristic of California aesthetics. But Jeffers wished to be a social philosopher
as well as a philosophical poet. The lectures at Harvard and the Library of Congress, so concerned with religious and philosophical themes, were followed by the
fiercely isolationist poems of *Be Angry at the Sun* (1941). In one poem Jeffers
wrote: "It is war, and no man can see an end of it. We must put freedom away
and/ stiffen into bitter empire./ All Europe was hardly worth the precarious freedom of one of our states:/ what will her ashes fetch?"[7] In the terminology of the
1990s, Robinson Jeffers—like Charles Lindbergh, like the whole America First
movement—became suddenly, overwhelmingly, Politically Incorrect on the
morning of Sunday, 7 December 1941. Like Lindbergh, Jeffers, having been
caught by Pearl Harbor in isolationist mid-sentence, would never fully recover
his respectability.

Yet the central tenets of Jeffers's philosophical vision—nature as All and Other,
together with the desire to forge a healing connection with nature through understanding and acceptance—were among the prime imperatives of intellectual and
imaginative life in California. If there were any one California formula, any one
philosophical or imaginative preoccupation, it was this: to seek and find a healing
connection with the universe. Again and again, high-minded Californians, be
they painters, poets, or naturalists, astronomers, anthropologists, or photographers, had sought to find in nature the source and imagery of a great prophetic
power that could lift them beyond the ordinary while keeping them connected to
simple things. Ishi came the closest to achieving such a communion because he
possessed two great gifts, culture, and identity; yet as distinctive as he was (the last
Native American to come to maturity in completely aboriginal circumstances),
Ishi was not a solitary figure in the California context. What Ishi represented—
the harmonization of nature, culture, and identity—constituted the most powerful
subliminal ideal in California as a regional civilization.

Robinson Jeffers sought to juxtapose, hence oppose, this California ideal, which
he believed should be the ideal of the entire nation, against American involvement in European and Asian wars. Such a repudiation of the bright promise of
America as a new beginning, a full and complete break with Europe, Jeffers believed, constituted a failure of nerve, a refusal to embrace the American destiny,
a lusting after the fleshpots of Egypt. In his isolationism, Jeffers shared this concern regarding the effect of war on the United States with another Californian,
former president Herbert Hoover, now devoting himself to the creation of an
institution in Palo Alto devoted to the study of war, revolution, and peace. As

Californians at the peak of their creativity in the 1930s, Robinson Jeffers, the University of California anthropologist Alfred Kroeber, who kept alive the memory and message of Ishi in the pre-war and post-war eras, and Herbert Hoover were each concerned with the violence once again spreading itself across the planet.

In September 1911 two very different Californians, a professor of anthropology at Berkeley and the last surviving Yahi on Planet Earth, came into contact with each other. The anthropologist, Alfred Kroeber, thirty-five, had his origins in the privileged center of Euro-American civilization. Born to a prosperous upper-middle-class German Protestant family, Kroeber grew up in Manhattan, privately tutored in Latin and Greek and speaking English and German to his parents. Several maids saw to the needs of the household. Educated at the Ethical Culture School, Kroeber spent a preparatory year at the Gunnery Academy in Connecticut prior to entering Columbia College in 1892 at the age of sixteen. As an undergraduate, Kroeber majored in English literature, taking an A.B. in this subject in 1896 and an M.A. in 1897. By then, his interests had turned to anthropology, a subject only then entering the American university as a field of teaching and research. Switching programs, Kroeber took his Ph.D. in anthropology under Franz Boas, the founder of the discipline in North America. Kroeber was Boas's first Ph.D. and held the second Ph.D. in anthropology granted in the United States. In 1900, at the age of twenty-four, Kroeber accepted a position with the California Academy of Sciences in San Francisco. A year later, he transferred to the University of California, becoming the founding faculty member of the department of anthropology on the Berkeley campus and director of the anthropology museum attached to the Affiliated Colleges medical campus in San Francisco. Phoebe Apperson Hearst sponsored the department and the museum and paid a portion of Kroeber's salary. After extensive field work in the Philippines, Kroeber turned his attention to the Native American cultures of California.

One such Native American, meanwhile (he would later be called Ishi), born most likely in 1862, had spent most of his life in what his people called the Long Concealment, seeking in vain to avoid the murderous whites. From time immemorial the Yana people, of whom the Yahi were a sub-tribelet, had lived in peace amidst the forests and streams of the foothills of Mount Lassen. In 1850, approximately eight years before Ishi was born, between two and three thousand Yana flourished across some twenty-four hundred 2400 square miles. By 1872, when Ishi was ten, perhaps as few as twenty Yana remained alive. As for surviving Yahi, including Ishi himself, there were only five or six. The rest had been slaughtered by the whites or had died of old age and disease.

On 9 November 1908 a group of engineers from the Oroville Light and Power Company encountered Ishi fishing with a harpoon in the junction of Deer and Sulphur creeks. Brandishing his harpoon, Ishi waved them away. Back in camp, the engineers told their story. The next day, a group of whites returned to the scene and found Wowunupo, the last Yahi encampment. An old woman, Ishi's mother, was there, and an old man, Ishi's uncle. They also caught a glimpse of Ishi and his sister as they fled. The men gathered everything in the encampment to take as souvenirs. It was a terrible, violent looting. Upon these Stone Age bows and arrows, harpoons, baskets and a few other implements, the last four Yahi in the world depended for their survival. Ishi's sister most likely drowned in Deer Creek as she fled. Ishi's aged mother and uncle died shortly thereafter. This was the end of the Yahi as a people. Ishi was alone, the last of his tribe, with only his culture, shared by no one else on the planet, to guide his survival.

He remained in the forest, terribly alone, for two and a half years before the loneliness drove him to creep tentatively to the corral of a slaughterhouse just outside Oroville, a mining town on the Feather River in Butte County. Dogs barked as he stumbled into the clearing, emaciated and exhausted. Awakened by the barking, the butchers found Ishi and telephoned Sheriff J. B. Webber in Oroville. Arriving by wagon, Webber took Ishi into custody, as kindly as possible, and drove him to the Oroville jail in handcuffs. Not knowing what else to do, Webber locked Ishi in a cell reserved for the insane. Given food, Ishi ate ravenously and began to regain his strength. After what he had been through, so he later noted, he was finding jail a pleasant place.

Reading an account of Ishi's capture in the San Francisco *Call*, Professors Thomas Talbot Waterman and Alfred Kroeber of the anthropology department at UC telegraphed Sheriff Webber, asking him to hold Ishi until they arrived. While Waterman went north to Oroville and made contact with Ishi via the Yana language, which he knew, Kroeber arranged with the Indian Bureau in Washington (as a Native American, Ishi was automatically a ward of the government) for Ishi to be released into his and Waterman's custody. On Labor Day 1911, Ishi left Oroville by train with Waterman and arrived in San Francisco just before midnight. In one day he stepped ten thousand years into the future, from the age of stone to the age of industrial democracy. He took up residence in the anthropology museum atop Parnassus Heights adjacent to Sutro Forest in the montane center of San Francisco a few blocks from Golden Gate Park. This would be his home for the remaining four years and seven months of his life.

At the museum, where he was employed as an assistant janitor and where he also functioned (if the truth be told) as a living exhibit, fashioning arrows for the public on weekends, Ishi displayed a remarkable adaptation to modern civilization while preserving his Yahi culture and identity. When he first stepped aboard the train in Oroville, Ishi believed the hissing engine to be the Great Demon itself; yet within a year of his arrival in San Francisco, he was capable of going on his own to Berkeley and returning, a trip that involved taking the streetcar to the Ferry Building, transferring to a ferry, crossing the Bay, then taking another streetcar to the Berkeley campus. He memorized the configuration of numbers on the various streetcars, knew what these numbers meant in terms of destination, and never got lost. Taken to the Berkeley home of Professor Waterman for dinner, he soon mastered the use of fork, spoon, and napkin by watching the Waterman family as they ate. At the museum, Ishi liked to dress in serviceable suits or lapel jacket and work pants and favored brightly colored neckties. He devoted himself steadily to his job as janitor and learned to trace out his name so as to endorse his check from the university. He had an instinctive understanding of how money worked as a medium of exchange. He also understood how saved money could structure the future. Scrupulously, he set aside part of his $25 salary each month, keeping a growing supply of fifty-cent pieces neatly stacked in a safe. He did his own shopping and prepared his own food on a gas burner. Ishi knew the individual shopkeepers in the neighborhood and would greet them on his shopping expeditions. At stores, Ishi would ask the price of things: "How-muchee?" If the item was too expensive, he would reply, "Too-muchee!" He died leaving an estate of more than $250 in half-dollar coins.

Ishi loved certain aspects of the white man's civilization. He was intrigued, for example, with the sweeping capacity of the white man's broom. He prized the white man's glue, which made it so easy to feather arrows, and kept a pot of glue on hand at all times. He sustained a near-reverence for the white man's tools: hammer and nails, saws and pliers, files, and clasps. He loved to see them neatly arranged in a tool box. Above everything else, Ishi prized matches. He never lost his delight in his ability to strike a match and have fire, as opposed to the necessity of rubbing two sticks together in the forest. Ishi loved chewing tobacco, talcum powder, and ice cream sodas. He read the funny papers and caught the humor of some of the more obvious panels and laughed. In San Francisco, Ishi kept to the orderly habits of his earlier life. He kept his gear neatly arranged in his room. He folded his clothes, wrapped them in paper, and arranged them neatly in a bureau drawer. Ice cream sodas were the one exception he made to his general dislike of creamy sauces, puddings, and dairy products in general. He preferred vegetables and meat, slightly underdone, with no spice or sauce. He did not drink, equating whiskey with death after tasting it only once.

As a Yahi, Ishi prized the skills of the forest. As early as the first Oroville interviews, he had had conversations with Professor Waterman about deer hunting and the making of acorn soup and arrowheads, which he demonstrated. Ishi was an expert arrow maker and never lost his relish for this task. He also made elegant bows of hickory, ash, and yew. (Ironically, many of the items plundered from Wowunupo would eventually find their way to the museum where Ishi was spending his final years.) He maintained his dignity as he worked, living as he did in a time and a place within himself that was not fully equatable to San Francisco in the 1910s. Visitors to the museum, for example, were fond of shaking his hand. As a Yahi, Ishi had an aversion to handshaking, but he endured the custom as a matter of courtesy, although he never initiated the gesture.

Yahi-like, Ishi bonded with his friends, and they became his new family, his tribe. Ishi considered Professor Alfred Kroeber his *majaupa*, his headman or chief, and addressed him in the most formal of terms. He approved of Kroeber's beard as a sign of his authority and felt it presumptuous when another Native American, part Yana, raised in the white man's civilization, also allowed whiskers to grow on his face. Since the Yahi reserve their name as a personal secret, Kroeber had been forced to name Ishi *ishi*, the Yana word for man, when reporters in San Francisco demanded that the "wild Indian" be given a name. (When the newspapers carried a story in November 1911 that Ishi was in search of a wife, he received a number of proposals in the mail.) Ranked almost as high as Kroeber was Professor Thomas Talbot Waterman, the first white man with whom he had spoken and in whose Berkeley home he lived in the summer of 1915.

Ishi also became a close friend of Doctor Saxton Pope, a professor of medicine in the Affiliated Colleges. He taught Pope the art of the bow, and the two of them would enjoy target practice in the nearby Sutro Forest. Ishi called Pope "Popey," and the two of them evolved a language of their own, a mixture of pidgin Yana and pidgin English. If Kroeber was his chief and Waterman his teacher and guide, Saxton Pope was Ishi's friend of the heart, his companion in the forest. And so too was another Native American living intermittently at the museum, Juan Dolores, a Papago from Arizona and a graduate of the Hampton Institute. On weekends and holidays, Ishi and Juan palled around San Francisco together, with Juan Dolores guiding Ishi through Golden Gate Park and taking him to restaurants and movies. (It was most likely Juan Dolores who persuaded Ishi to wear shoes.)

At the museum, Ishi befriended the Englishman John Warburton, who prepared the exhibits, and Llewellyn Loud, the Welsh-born jack of all trades and security guard, whom Ishi called Loudy. Warburton had held a rating in the British navy and knew how to handle tools, which was something Ishi respected. Ishi loved to look into Warburton's tool chest and see the various instruments arrayed in orderly pattern. Loud taught Ishi how to cook for himself on the little gas stove in the museum. Having survived in the wild, Ishi admired Loud's frugality and learned from him that day-old bread was less expensive. Ishi also became friendly with Edward Gifford, the assistant curator. Putting aside the restrictions of Yahi culture that called for a separation of the sexes, Ishi became friends with Mrs. Gifford as well. On weekends when he would visit the Giffords, he would walk with Mrs. Gifford in the Berkeley hills, reciting the Yana names for the various flowers and wild plants they encountered in their stroll.

Encouraged by Pope, Ishi would make regular rounds through the university hospital, greeting the staff in the kitchen and the laundry, even calling on some of Pope's patients in their hospital rooms. When informed of what treatment was being offered this or that patient for one or another ailment, Ishi would reply with descriptions of more effective Yahi remedies. At other times, he would sit quietly with a patient for some mysteriously set interval of time, then take his leave with a word or two in Yahi of encouragement. The doctors, nurses, and staff of the UC hospital accepted Ishi's presence in the wards as something calming and soothing, healing even, in a subtle but indescribable way. When the Bureau of Indian Affairs offered Ishi the opportunity to live on a reservation or even to return to Deer Creek and live on his own, he refused. Informed of these proposals, Ishi replied in Yahi: "I will live like the white man for the remainder of my days. I wish to stay here where I now am. I will grow old in this house, and it is here I will die."[8]

In May 1914 Ishi returned to his homeland for a month-long visit in the company of Kroeber, Waterman, Pope, and Pope's eleven-year-old son Saxton Junior. It was a lyrical and idyllic homecoming, with many of its most beautiful and touching moments captured in still photography and motion pictures. Doffing his San Francisco clothes, Ishi reverted to his Yahi breechclout. Along with his friends, he swam and fished in Deer Creek, hunted deer with bow and arrow (special out-of-season permission had been secured from the Fish and Game Commission), and cooked food over an open fire. Ishi showed himself an especially strong swimmer, piloting young Saxton through the water by having the boy cling to his long hair. Ishi took his guests to the site of Wowunupo and showed them all the places he had known throughout his life: the place, for example, where they had once killed a bear and feasted on its haunch. Ishi knew exactly where to dig up the claw, which had been ceremonially buried decades earlier. By the time they left, the anthropologists had a complete map of Yahi territory, thanks to Ishi's memory.

The trip was more than an idyllic return to the Yahi homeland. It was a farewell to life itself. Shortly before they left San Francisco, Pope did a medical history of Ishi. At approximately fifty-four years of age, Pope reported, Ishi looked no more than forty-five, despite the hardness of his life. There was no evidence of serious illness or disease. Ishi's teeth were good, his muscles were well formed, and his feet were so perfect Pope had them cast in plaster, so taken was he by their anatomical elegance. From the start, however, Kroeber and Pope had worried over Ishi's vulnerability to the white man's diseases. Already, Ishi had shown a tendency to colds and mild pneumonia. Tuberculosis was especially feared, and Pope gave Ishi tuberculin vaccinations, then in the experimental stage.

Shortly after his return from Deer Creek, Ishi contracted tuberculosis. Even as he lay in his hospital bed, he did not lose his sense of humor. Watching the steel workers construct the new hospital outside his window, he wryly observed to Pope: "All a same monkey-tee," Ishi's way of saying, "Just like a monkey." Kroeber was on sabbatical in Germany as the end drew near, then in England and New York. He wrote Ishi three times a week. He sent him a purse, in which Ishi kept his sacred tobacco. Growing weaker, Ishi asked to be brought back to his room in the museum next door. He died there on 25 March 1916, at noon, with Dr. Saxton Pope, Popey, Ishi's *kuwie* (medicine man), at his side. Just before dying, Ishi said to Pope: "You stay. I go."[9]

Ishi was cremated according to Yahi burial practices at the Mount Olivet Cemetery in Colma. Waterman, Pope, Warburton, Gifford, and Loud were in attendance. Placed in Ishi's coffin prior to cremation were one of his bows, five arrows, a basket of acorn meal, some shell bead money, a purse full of tobacco, obsidian flakes for arrowheads, three rings, and ten pieces of dentalium tooth shells. The inscription sealing the urn read ISHI, THE LAST YANA INDIAN, 1916. Half of Ishi's estate went to the UC Medical School. Dean Moffitt used it to establish a fund in Ishi's memory.

In the spring and summer of 1913, following the death of his wife from tuberculosis, Alfred Kroeber experienced something approaching a nervous breakdown, or at the least, a period of anguish and deep confusion. Kroeber had married Henriette Rothschild, a German-Jewish San Franciscan, in 1906, shortly after the Earthquake. He adored his wife and found in his mother-in-law Fanny an equally beloved second mother. With Henriette gone at the tragically young age of thirty-six, Kroeber could not recover. Two people, his mother-in-law Fanny Rothschild and Ishi, helped him through the pain and disorientation of the next three years. When Kroeber's sabbatical came due in 1915, he was reluctant to take it because he did not wish to leave Fanny and Ishi. Saxton Pope insisted that Kroeber go, for the sake of both his scholarship and his recovery. It was Kroeber who adamantly insisted that Ishi be buried according to Yahi custom. Writing from New York the day before Ishi's death, Kroeber forbade an investigative autopsy for purposes of anthropology. "If there is any talk about the interest of science," he insisted, "say for me that science can go to hell. We propose to stand by our friends." [10]

At the time of Ishi's death, Kroeber was afflicted in both mind and body. Sometime in 1915 he had contracted Meniere's disease, which remained undiagnosed until 1922. The affliction gave him excruciating pain in one ear, together with vertigo and headaches. He once passed out on the street and fell to the gutter outside a saloon. The saloon keeper brought him to consciousness with a cup of coffee, and a policeman sent him home in a cab, hardly a dignified experience for a distinguished academic. The disease made Kroeber walk with an eccentric gait as he tried to keep his balance. Not until the Meniere's disease had destroyed the hearing in one ear did it abate. Throughout the ordeal, Kroeber feared that he might have a brain tumor, or worse, that he was going insane.

While in New York in 1915, Kroeber went through psychoanalysis with an analyst trained by Freud. Upon his return to San Francisco, Kroeber studied psychoanalysis and qualified as a lay analyst. Between 1918 and 1920, in addition to directing the anthropology museum and department at UC, Kroeber practiced psychoanalysis at the Stanford Clinic in San Francisco, working under the supervision of two M.D. psychiatrists. For a time, he seriously considered leaving academic anthropology and going into full-time practice. From Freudian theory, Kroeber obtained deep and healing insights into the conflicts and repressions that were bedeviling him in addition to his bereavement and the afflictions brought on by Meniere's disease. But of what use are such insights without a pattern of life, without love and work and identity? From Freud, Kroeber learned the structure and functioning of his unconscious. From Ishi he learned pattern and the Way of his life. Ishi, Kroeber realized, had never forgotten who he was, a Yahi. Despite incredible suffering and the time warp of ten thousand years, Ishi had kept to his pattern, to his culture and identity, to his Way. Ishi had transcended suffering by achieving that very connection to the cosmos that Robinson Jeffers could only glimpse as a matter of metaphor. Ishi knew nature, but he also knew culture as a mediating force between himself and the cosmos. Through pattern, through being a Yahi and remaining true to that identity, Ishi had transcended tragedy and terrible pain.

If Kroeber was suffering, physically and psychologically, what was this, he asked himself, in comparison to what Ishi and his people had endured? Even before their genocide, they were succumbing to measles, chicken pox, smallpox, malaria, typhoid, dysentery, influenza, pneumonia, tuberculosis, and virulent strains of venereal disease. Their mass murder had begun in 1853 when twenty-five Yahi were killed in retaliation for the stealing of one, or possibly several, cows. Contemporary documents and later recollections and interviews of early settlers in the area reveal a horrendous story of Yana and Yahi being exterminated—men, women, children—like rodents and reptiles. Women and babies were slaughtered. Worse, babies were slaughtered in front of their mothers before the mothers themselves were killed. One particularly vicious Indian hunter, Robert Anderson, kept forty Yana and Yahi scalps hanging from a poplar tree near his house. Between August and December 1864, the United States Army all but finished the work of extermination as two fully armed companies of the Second Cavalry California Volunteers from Camp Bidwell in Chico under the command of Captain A. W. Starr ravaged Yana territory.

There may have been as many as three thousand Yana in their homeland at the start of 1864. A few scattered bands were left alive by 1865. Even then, at the beginning of the Long Concealment, the few surviving Yana and Yahi were discovered and destroyed, such as the band ferreted out by Robert Anderson in 1867 or 1868. (Accounts differ.) Driven into a cave north of Mill Creek, the entire party, thirty-three in all, including children and babies, were massacred. Somehow, other Yahi—a young Ishi among them—returned to the cave and gave each victim proper cremation and burial. When Ishi stumbled into civilization, he was wearing his hair burned short, the Yahi sign for mourning. He was mourning his mother, his sister, his uncle. He was mourning his entire people.

Both before and after Ishi's death, Kroeber marveled at how Ishi's strength of character, patterned and reinforced by his ancient culture, had seen him through this unimaginable ordeal. The last one to have lived there, Ishi never forgot where he came from. Kroeber would later describe Ishi's origins according to the white man's scheme of classification. The Yana belonged to the Hokan, one of the six super-families of North America. The Yahi, a tribelet of the Yana, lived in the southern tier of Yana territory along Mill Creek, which flowed into the Sacramento River. Running in the same direction, Antelope Creek delineated the northern border of Yahi land, and Deer Creek the southern limit. To the northeast, the Yahi could see Mount Lassen rising in splendor. The Yahi were few, but over the centuries they had achieved a viable culture at once localized and cosmic in its focus. Yahi culture had been transmitted to Ishi intact by the half dozen or so adults who had survived the slaughter. Yet it had been transmitted in a complete and powerful way. As in times past, the last surviving village of Wowu-nupo Mu Tetna off Deer Creek had a living house, a smokehouse, a storehouse, a communal latrine.

Ishi knew the many songs and stories of his people: cosmological songs and stories about the creation of the universe and a very long and droll tale about Wood Duck in search of a wife. When Ishi spoke, it was with full confidence in the range and resources of his language. Wax cylinder recordings of Ishi's singing, chanting, and talking were made at the museum. Restored in 1957, they make it possible across three-quarters of a century (across ten thousand years!) to hear Ishi speak the Yahi names for the animals and birds, the trees and plants and flowers, of the Northern Californian forest. Initially, Ishi had refused to count beyond ten. Kroeber judged that Ishi had no need to count beyond ten in his previous environment. Later, Kroeber learned that Ishi's arithmetic was based upon intricate combinations of four, the sacred Yahi number of balance and beauty. Ishi could count plenty but according to a different system.

With their number reduced to six, Ishi had nevertheless learned the codes and protocols of his people. The Yahi were a peaceful folk. They took no scalps. Even when forced to become marauders during the Long Concealment, they kept to their codes. In April 1885, for example, Yahi were caught stealing clothes from a cabin. Catching the Yahi in the act, the owner of the cabin waved them off, allowing them to keep their pathetic loot. A few months later, the owner discovered that the Yahi had returned to the cabin, entered it, and left behind two baskets as gifts in exchange for the clothes they had taken. Run to the ground by the whites, the Yahi had refused to become thieves.

Ishi knew how to make bows and arrows and how to weave beautiful baskets. He knew the distinctive dialects for men and women and the many prohibitions and taboos between the sexes. (It was bad taste, for example, to talk at length with one's mother-in-law.) Sexuality was linked to procreation and a stable family life. The aged were revered, and children were cherished, girls and boys alike. Sadly, there was no one left alive with whom Ishi might mate. He was forced to spend his life in involuntary celibacy, with no wife to share his time on the planet, no children to instruct in the Yahi way.

Ishi might have been expected to go into culture shock upon emerging from the forest. The fact that he did not—more than this, the fact that he became in his own way a Yahi anthropologist studying the white man—testified to a sense of well-being, of psychic wholeness born of culture. From 1911 onwards, Ishi serenely interpreted his new circumstances from the Yahi perspective. The jail in Oroville was a good place, a big house where he was treated kindly and fed like a chief. Even before he was taken to the Pacific Ocean through Golden Gate Park via motorcar, he was already aware of the ocean. Yahi tradition knew of the great water. He seemed, moreover, to take the white man's culture with a grain of salt and believed that he had as much to tell the white men as they had to tell him. Shown an airplane in flight, he admitted that it flew well, but an eagle or a hawk flew better. He maintained his sense of class and status. A mounted policeman, for example, had to be a chief.

Kroeber marveled at Ishi's understanding of the racial alliance between Asians and Native Americans. The Chinese of San Francisco, Ishi observed, were *yana*, the people. Whites were *saltu*, another order of being, not better than *yana*, or worse, merely different. And there were so many of them! Ishi was constantly impressed by the sheer number of *saltu* in San Francisco. Crowds simultaneously fascinated and repelled him. Taken to the theater and seated in a box, Ishi pre-ferred to watch the audience instead of the vaudeville act on stage. "*Hansi saltu, hansi saltu!*" he exclaimed. "So many white people, so many white people!" [11]

The one thing that disturbed Ishi at the museum was the presence there of Egyptian and Peruvian mummies and Native American skulls and skeletons. At night, he locked the door of his room against these spirits. The white man, Ishi believed, had become a special victim of an evil spirit, the Coyote Doctor. The Coyote Doctor kept white people cooped up in cars, offices, and houses. The *saltu* should spend more time outdoors. The Coyote Doctor could make people mean and crazy. The one object he held under a taboo, never to touch or use in any way, was the white man's gun, which had exterminated his people.

Kroeber had spent time outdoors with Ishi, escaping Care, the Coyote Doctor, in the May 1914 return to Yahi-land. A photograph taken during the visit shows Kroeber smiling and robust in his field clothes, visibly happy, perhaps for the first time since Henriette's death. Ishi had known Henriette and had taken dinner in the Kroeber household. He knew of her illness and her death and of Kroeber's grief, but according to Yana custom he could never speak directly to Kroeber of his loss. The healing came in a different way, both before and after Ishi's death. The healing came from a friendship that was also a form of cross-cultural therapy: came in the month-long idyll in the land of the Yahi; came from the soothing presence of Ishi, sitting on a canvas tarpaulin, chipping arrowheads from obsidian, telling his stories, singing his songs, whole and complete. The healing came from the example of Ishi's devotion to his janitorial chores, to his self-appointed rounds through the kitchen, the laundry, the hospital wards. Most of all, the healing came from something in Ishi that was more than a matter of culture: a fundamen-tal goodness in the man himself.

Ishi's goodness, Kroeber decided (this sophisticated anthropologist who was also the product of an Ethical Cultural education), was realized in and through Yahi culture; but it was also a force emanating from Ishi as an individual. Ishi was no Noble Savage to be covered in sentiment. Here was a human being possessed of a capacity for choice, a human being who had been led to the good life, to pattern and identity, by the Yahi way and had remained faithful through personal choice to the path destiny had set before him. All successful cultures, Kroeber believed, contained some overlapping vision of the good. In his connection to what was universal in Yahi culture, Ishi had become a teacher, a healer of Kroeber's troubled spirit, a moral paradigm, a Californian for others to follow.

Thanks in part to Ishi (and to Sigmund Freud), Alfred Kroeber recovered his way, his path, his pattern. In 1926 he married Theodora Krakaw Brown, a widow with two young sons, Clifton and Theodore. The couple had two of their own children, Carl and Ursula. The Kroebers purchased a redwood-shingled Craftsman home designed by Bernard Maybeck and landscaped by John McLaren on Arch Street in Berkeley. It had a stunning view of the Bay and the Golden Gate. The couple also acquired a forty-acre hillside estate on the western edge of Napa Valley, watered by a creek and graced with a redwood house and barn built a generation earlier by a French vintner. Kishamish, they called it, the Wappo word for rest, relaxation, retreat. Thirty-plus years of productive life followed in Berkeley and Napa, in houses filled with books and growing children (including the future novelist Ursula Kroeber Le Guin), around the world on field trips and conferences. For all the *Sturm und Drang* he had experienced in the matter of identity, Kroeber became the paradigm of a German or German-American professor, particularly German in the regularity of his work, writing book after book in longhand, and his devotion to the academic life as a near-ministerial vocation.

Ishi remained a moral presence in the Kroeber household. Alfred would often speak to his wife of the things he had learned from Ishi. Inspired by these conversations, Theodora Kroeber researched and wrote a biography, *Ishi in Two Worlds* (1961). Published a year after her husband's death, it grew into a classic of anthropology and biography. *Ishi in Two Worlds*, in fact, represents a high plateau in the search for identity and value in California that has since earned Theodora Kroeber an equal place alongside her husband in the ranks of those who have profoundly shaped and interpreted the California experience.

In 1925 Alfred Kroeber brought to triumphant conclusion seventeen years of field research with the publication of the *Handbook of Indians of California*, a thousand-page pointillist-realist epic of ethnographic description that was in its own way a tribute to Ishi. The *Handbook* was followed by the equally impressive *Cultural and Natural Areas of Native North America*, researched in the 1920s and completed in 1931 but delayed in publication until 1939 due to a shortage of funds. Kroeber was finding himself increasingly intrigued in the 1930s with the inter-activity of culture, personality, social experience, and history. For some time now, he had been finding himself more and more drawn to a historical and comparative perspective: to the diachronic aspects of culture across time and history as opposed to the more trans-historical structural perspective of his mentor Franz Boas. Even the *Handbook of Indians of California*, a monument of structural analysis, was soaked through, Kroeber insisted in the preface, with a historical appreciation of each Native American culture in its distinctive time and place and its precise chronology of development.

Widely read, trained in literature as well as psychoanalysis, respectful of social transformations across time, Kroeber was more and more practicing anthropology as cultural history as well as social science. He began to think of himself as "a humanistically-tinged natural historian."[12] Far from limiting his perspective to the structural, anthropology had made Kroeber a better cultural theorist and historian. Because he had so profoundly absorbed the spirit of anthropology, Kroeber could hold in comparative perspective, balancing them against each other, the Yahi and the most urbanized segment of modern society, or, more tellingly, link the extermination of the Yahi with the rising tide of aggression and anti-Semitism in fascist Europe. Indian hunter Robert Anderson and Adolf Hitler belonged to the same tribe.

Like Robinson Jeffers, like so many Californians, Kroeber was worried by the mid-1930s about the direction of Europe and the possibilities of American involvement in a renewed global conflict. Since he was an anthropologist and a historian and theorist of culture, however, and not a poet, Kroeber confronted the question by probing the nature of culture itself. With so many clouds looming on the horizon—the Depression, the Civil War in Spain, the Italian aggression in Abyssinia, the Seig Heil! madness of Nazi Germany, the Japanese invasion of Manchuria—Kroeber began to reconsider the question of how Ishi had survived a catastrophe comparable to the one looming on the world horizon. Was there a mechanism in human life, Kroeber asked himself, that, when functioning properly, represented a force for survival equal to biology in effectiveness?

Yes, Kroeber concluded, there was such a mechanism. It was culture linked to ethics: culture, that is, based on universally discernible premises and patterns of goodness that could be found in nature by human beings of all sorts, living in differing conditions across time, place, and history. Culture was no mere contrivance, Kroeber insisted. Culture linked to a broadly defined concept of the good represented a force equal to biology as a wellspring of psychic survival amidst catastrophe. Ethical culture, by which Kroeber meant everything he had learned as a boy and relearned through Freud and Ishi, anthropology and history, extended a footbridge across chaos: even that chaos that came most terribly—to Ishi, to Europe, to Asia, soon to the rest of the world—through war and the handmaidens of war: hatred, rage, murder, mass destruction, genocide. Such a footbridge would soon, Kroeber feared, be more needed than ever.

Down the San Francisco Peninsula in Palo Alto, in another academic setting, Herbert Hoover, former president of the United States and a lifetime trustee of Stanford University, was likewise probing in his mind resurgent questions of war and peace. Like Robinson Jeffers, like Alfred Kroeber, Hoover—so representatively Californian in his background and point of view—was preparing to meet the impending catastrophe with a response at once universal and distinctively Californian. From 1914 onwards Hoover had been sponsoring the creation of an archive documenting the First World War and its aftermath, including the rise of fascism. In the 1930s, after leaving the White House, Hoover began to shape this archive into its final institutional format. He would found a library and research institute, the former president resolved, devoted to the study of war, revolution, and peace in the twentieth century. Only by studying the origins and dynamics of mass violence in the recent era could there be any chance of avoiding similar catastrophes in the future.

As a public servant, Herbert Clark Hoover was the most distinguished Californian of his era: a mining engineer with a passion for reading and books, independently wealthy by the outbreak of the First World War and having absorbed at Stanford in the 1890s the internationalist outlook promoted by the founding president, David Starr Jordan, as a prized component of the Stanford style and identity. When it seemed probable, in the fall and winter of 1914, that the people of Belgium might face mass starvation, Hoover, a private citizen, organized the Committee for the Relief of Belgium, which soon mushroomed into a virtual state within a state, with its own fleet, flag, and diplomatic corps. Crossing the North Sea in 1914, Hoover read a comment by Andrew White, the historian president of Cornell, that most of the contemporaneous literature and documentation of the French Revolution had been lost. White's observation galvanized Hoover's already strong collector's instinct. He vowed to see to it, among his many other duties, that the documentation of this great conflict now overshadowing Europe would not be lost. From 1914 to 1917, Hoover directed the CRB, which kept alive some eleven million people in Belgium and northern France, expending more than a billion dollars. In 1917 President Wilson called Hoover back to the United States to serve as wartime Food Administrator. Following the Armistice, Wilson sent Hoover to Europe to organize relief for the starving millions of Germany, Eastern Europe, and Russia. Hoover next served as director of the American Relief Administration, which soon became the major source of food for three hundred million people in twenty-one countries in Europe and the Middle East. In 1919 President Wilson requested Hoover's presence as a member of the American delegation at the Paris Peace Conference. Hoover next went on to found the European Children's Fund, which assisted in the feeding of millions of children through the summer of 1921.

Through it all, Hoover collected, collected, and collected. Bales and bales of documentation, soon boxcars and boxcars, found their way to warehouses on the East Coast for eventual shipment to Palo Alto. Hoover hired collectors and did his own collecting. (When he attended the Paris Peace Conference as an aide to President Wilson, Hoover made a systematic collection of all pamphlets and brochures slipped under his door at the Crillon Hotel.) After the Armistice, he worked out an arrangement with General Pershing to have Stanford academics in uniform—faculty members Edgar Eugene Robinson and Ephraim Douglass Adams, together with recent Ph.Ds and graduate students such as Robert Brinkley and Ralph Lutz—released directly to the archival project, and in April 1919 Hoover put up $50,000 of his own money toward their support. Like characters in a novel by Somerset Maugham, the Stanford academics fanned out over Europe,

Russia, and the Middle East, bent upon their task: to acquire the archives and documentation of the war and its aftermath, all of it—the newspapers, the minutes and proceedings of ministries and high commands, the diaries of diplomats, the posters and broadsides, the private papers and correspondence, the files of secret police. Among the most active and successful of the collectors, Ralph Lutz criss-crossed Europe negotiating with officials of collapsed governments, interviewing officers of armies that no longer existed, making deals with bureaucrats shipwrecked on uncertain political shores. In Vienna Lutz attended a gala performance of *La Bohème* as a guest of the president and chancellor of the new republic. In Milan he ran into a machine gun battle, and a bullet nicked his belt. When the British government deaccessioned its collection of wartime propaganda in Wellington House, Hoover collectors purchased the material, packed it on the spot, and hastily conveyed the collection in a fleet of hired taxicabs to a shipping agent.

In 1921, while feeding millions of children in famine-stricken Russia, Hoover secured the services of the Russian-born Stanford historian Frank Golder, who began collecting materials relating to Imperial Russia, the Russian Revolution, and the first years of the Soviet regime. Traveling throughout the country in 1921 and 1922, Golder collected the priceless documentation of a history only then in the making. He also persuaded the Soviet government to provide him a copy of every document for publication it was producing in its effort to establish itself. Thanks to the assistance of Senator Vittorio Ricci, Italian ambassador to the United States, Italian materials began to flow into the Hoover collection in the fateful year of 1922. A thousand pounds of papers and ephemera reached Stanford that year alone, documenting Italian public life on the verge of Mussolini. In 1926 Hoover agents acquired the archives of the Paris office of the Okhrana, the czarist secret police, 225,000 documents in all, with dossiers on Lenin, Trotsky, and Stalin.

In 1919 Hoover organized his collection as a semi-autonomous library connected to Stanford University. Very soon, he added $100,000 to the first $50,000 grant. He also provided Stanford with $150,000 to house the material, which had begun to arrive by the ton in the academic year 1919–20. Throughout the 1920s and 1930s, Hoover supported further collecting, staffing, and archival organization out of his own pocket. During the 1930s the former president turned his attention to assembling materials on the political movements engendered by the Great War: Soviet Communism, Italian Fascism, the National Socialism of Germany. Once again, Ralph Lutz, by then professor of history at Stanford and chairman of the library, resumed his underground collecting. In early 1939, thanks to a grant from the American Children's Fund, another foundation Hoover controlled, Lutz made a last-possible tour of Germany and Italy to collect Nazi and Fascist materials. In Germany, at great personal risk, Lutz dealt secretly with Communists and other dissidents and with leaders of the persecuted Jewish community. Among other collections, he acquired the papers of the assassinated German Communist leader Rosa Luxemburg from her former secretary for shipment back to Nina Almond, the skilled archivist, librarian, and administrator personally selected by Hoover. Initially called the War Library, the Hoover collection went through a number of changes of nomenclature until it became in 1938 the Hoover Library on War, Revolution, and Peace. Hoover envisioned the library as an active center of thought and scholarship regarding these three great preoccupations of the twentieth century, staffed by permanent and visiting research scholars and expert archivists and librarians.

Stanford University begrudged the project, despite the presence on the board of directors of the Hoover Library by 1941 of Stanford president Ray Lyman Wilbur, the university librarian, and six Stanford professors. In the 1920s university librarian George Clark wanted the Hoover collection under his jurisdiction. Clark allowed much of the material to remain in packing crates. Throughout the 1920s and 1930s, Hoover fought a constant battle with Stanford authorities wishing to subordinate his collection to the university library rather than see it develop as a semi-autonomous research institution. When Leon Trotsky offered his archives to Hoover on the condition that he be given an academic appointment and a position in the library, it could not be arranged because of faculty resistance; Trotsky stayed in Mexico City, where he was soon assassinated, and his papers went to Harvard.

By 1939, however, Hoover had raised funds for a building, thanks in part to major grants from the American Relief Administration, the Committee for the Relief of Belgium Educational Foundation, and the John D. Rockefeller Foundation. All in all, five-sixths of the cost of the new Hoover Library and its half-million-dollar endowment came from organizations in which Hoover exercised great influence and from personal friends of the former president. Stanford University contributed a mere $100,000 of the total cost. For the new Hoover Library, architect Arthur Brown Jr. of San Francisco designed a 285-foot-high Art Deco–Moderne tower with twenty-three levels, seventeen of them devoted to library stacks. Atop the tower was a thirty-five-bell carillon, a gift to Hoover from the Belgium American Educational Foundation. Hoover Tower was very much the last great building to be constructed in California in the 1930s. Its bold and unrelieved surfaces, its upper rotunda of arched windows, and its stylized cupola suggested futurity in dialogue with the predominant Spanish Romanesque Revival of the Quadrangle and other Stanford buildings.

The dedication of the new Hoover Library of War, Revolution, and Peace on 20 June 1941 was broadcast nationally on the Blue Network of NBC. In the dedicatory speeches, Professor Sidney Fay of Harvard compared the Hoover to the Widener Memorial Library of his own institution and to such privately sponsored libraries dealing with the Great War as the Weltkriegsbucherei at Schloss Rosenstein near Stuttgart, founded by the Swabian industrialist Richard Franck in August 1915, and the Bibliotheque et Musée de la Guerre at Vincennes, founded by M. and Mme. Henri Leblanc in the first days of the Great War. Charles

Seymour, president of Yale, who had worked with Hoover more than twenty years earlier at the Paris Peace Conference, evoked the current Nazi occupation of so much of Europe. When it came Hoover's turn to speak, he gave equal weight to the search for peace and to the study of war and revolution. "Here can be found," noted the former president, "the record of the ideas and forces which made for failure of the last peace and the ideas and forces which might have made its success. Out of these files the world can get great warning of what not to do and what to do when it next assembles around the peace table."[13]

Meanwhile, it was time for millions and millions of human beings, military and civilian alike, to die violent deaths or to have their lives and bodies permanently broken. The peace to which Herbert Hoover referred would be a long time in coming, if it ever came at all. As bad as it was, the Depression was being followed by something worse. To their credit, Californians such as Robinson Jeffers, Alfred Kroeber, and Herbert Hoover—the three of them linked by a common California-inspired worldview—sought to warn against the conflict, to preclude it through a better understanding of culture, to study its causes and effects, to map the ways human beings might see beyond the impending tragedy. Poet, president, anthropologist—each had glimpsed the apocalypse. A special synergy of meaning existed between Kroeber, carrying within him the memory and lessons of Ishi, and Hoover, who had documented the systematic violence of the twentieth century in the hopes that it might not be repeated.

From this perspective, Ishi had emerged from the forest in 1911 as a representative of all those who had known or were about to experience the ravages of war and genocide in the twentieth century. The murderous rage that drove the white settlers of Lassen County to exterminate the Yahi like so much vermin, to destroy whole villages, to stab and shoot women and children to death as if they were clearing a field of rabbits, had its parallels in the massacre of the Armenians prior to World War I, the Great War itself, which raised the slaughter to new levels of efficiency, and, by the 1930s, the first stages of the Holocaust. Prophetically, the photograph of Ishi taken in Oroville resembles the photographs of survivors of the death camps taken in late 1945.

For all his involvement in the deterministic natural and social sciences, Alfred Kroeber sustained a paradoxical belief in the ability of individuals profoundly to affect the future. Such creativity, Kroeber believed, usually appeared in the penultimate phases of a culture, just before it ended. Of no one could this be more true than of Ishi, the last Native American to live in a condition that the whites of the early twentieth century could only describe as "wild." A later and more sympathetic era would describe Ishi as the last Native American to receive his culture completely from Native American sources. As the final figure in more than thirty thousand years of pre-contact Native American experience, Ishi was surely positioned to exercise that form of individual creativity that Kroeber, in the humanistic side of his imagination, believed could always make a difference, could always affect the future. As Theodora Kroeber so skillfully documented, moreover, Ishi exercised his creativity in two worlds. Like a number of great figures before him—Pocahontas, Squanto, Sacajawea, Chief Logan, Chief Sequoia, Chief Seattle—Ishi belonged to that genre of Native Americans who sought to teach the white people, to bring them to better ways, to heal the sickness at the center of their souls.

It would take many years for the white man finally to hear, much less assimilate, Ishi's message; but no matter: it was waiting at the core of what was best about California. In the 1930s, through Kroeber, Ishi's message regarding the ability of the human being to transcend moral and physical catastrophe by remaining true to an inner identity structured by culture around true and good beliefs and patterns was more valuable than ever. Sadly, just when Ishi's message, subsumed and interpreted by Kroeber, was being published, just as Herbert Hoover was dedicating his library to the cause of peace, war and destruction enveloped two-thirds of the planet.

"The history of Ishi and his people is, inexorably, part of our own history," wrote Theodora Kroeber in her epigraph to *Ishi in Two Worlds*. "We have absorbed their lands into our holdings. Just so must we be the responsible custodians of their tragedy, absorbing it into our tradition and morality." By tragic violence Yahi-land had been absorbed into California; but on a more hopeful note, so had the message and meaning of Yahi-land as well. Ishi and his people embodied, and continued to embody in memory, a persistent point of reference in the California identity. Was Ishi the last of the First Californians—or an avatar of a better California to be? Peace, dignity, a harmonious relationship to nature, appropriate technology, culture and identity, all of it joyously rooted in place: bringing such a message, Ishi became a Founder, an enduring representative of an inner and better California landscape.

As seen in Jeffers, Kroeber, and Hoover, a heightened consciousness emerged from this California and broadcast its message—respect for nature on its own terms, the need for culture and identity, the avoidance of war, the struggle for peace and harmonious patterns of life—to a world that could no longer receive such simple lessons. It was difficult, in fact, for California itself to hear such a message now that it was being swiftly transformed into a garrison state in support of global war. Yet the message could not be suppressed. Whatever else it might be as environmental and social engineering, California had also become by 7 December 1941 a place where Americans had glimpsed and were pursuing what they believed to be a better way of life. Whether it was or not, only time could tell.

In the meanwhile, bombs were falling on Pearl Harbor, and hundreds of young men were being entombed in the sea with the near-crippling destruction of the Pacific Fleet. The message of Ishi awaited a better day.

12

Ich Bin ein Sudkalifornier

Life and Art Among the Emigrés

THE notion of Los Angeles/Hollywood as Berlin or Vienna in exile is not far-fetched. In the late 1910s immigrants from Central Europe helped found the film industry. German-speaking producers, directors, actors, and actresses shaped Hollywood in the crucial decade of the 1920s. In the 1930s, following the proclamation of the Third Reich, artists and intellectuals of every sort poured into Southern California and found employment in the studios. Indeed, the argument can be made that Hollywood, from the 1920s through 1930s, was more Berliner and Viennese than Yankee-American in style and feeling, or, more subtly, it can be argued that Hollywood contained within itself in these years, just beneath the surface, a Vienna/Berlin paradigm: a community of sentiment, lifestyle, and symbol having more in common with *Mitteleuropa* than mid-America. Carl Laemmle from Germany, William Fox and Adolph Zukor from Hungary, Samuel Goldwyn from Poland, Louis B. Mayer and Louis J. Selznick from Russia: European-born Jews founded Hollywood. From this perspective, Jesse Lasky, an American Jew born in San Jose, and Cecil B. DeMille, an Episcopalian Anglo-Dutchman from New York, and David Wark Griffith, an Anglo-American from Kentucky, stand in contrast to the other founders.

Only recently has the American Jewish community felt at ease in acknowledging the founding role played by European-born Jews in the creation of Hollywood. After all, a hostile awareness of the prominence of Jews in Hollywood led in the early and mid-1920s and again in the mid-1930s to a war on Hollywood by mid-America that was strongly possessed of anti-Semitic overtones. The Jewish moguls of Hollywood dealt with this hostility by becoming, at least in the products they produced, more mid-American than Uncle Sam. Sadly, they also banished Jewish life, with a few exceptions, from the films they produced.

In the 1920s Hollywood began to turn its attention to the German film industry. Having lost World War I on the battlefield and in the Treaty of Versailles, Germany proceeded to win the peace through its films. As both an industry and an art appropriate to the expression of German culture, Germans took filmmaking seriously—and made of it a public enterprise. The German government was a key investor in the Berlin-based conglomerate Universum Film AG (UFA). Whatever was surrendered on the battlefield was regained in the UFA studios in Berlin, which were run along military lines with the director as commanding officer bringing to his role the full authority of the *Junker* caste. At UFA, the director, attired in paramilitary uniform of jodhpurs and field boots, a swagger stick in hand (DeMille brought this uniform to the United States), presided over his actors, cameramen, and technicians like a general on campaign. The results were some of the greatest films ever made, and by the mid-1920s the moguls of Hollywood were taking serious notice. Over the next fifteen years, they formed a connection that brought Berlin and to a lesser extent Vienna (Vienna being more concerned with music and the performing arts than film) to Los Angeles.

Ernst Lubitsch was among the first to arrive, coming in 1922 to direct *Rosita* (1923) and remaining in Hollywood until his death in 1947. Not only was Lubitsch the first Berliner to arrive, he was the most successful, exercising important influence on American film tastes as head of production at Paramount. Lubitsch's films of the 1920s—among them *The Marriage Circle* (1924), *Kiss Me Again* (1925), *So This Is Paris* (1926), *The Student Prince* (1927), and *Eternal Love* (1929), the last of Lubitsch's silent films—first showed what film historians now call the Lubitsch Touch, which is to say, a blend of costumed Ruritania and Berliner sexuality toned down for American tastes. A son of Berlin, Lubitsch delighted in sexual comedy, but he also knew that the whole question of sexuality, marital or otherwise, had to be handled more discreetly in the United States than in Europe. With the coming of sound, Lubitsch continued his string of successes through *The Love Parade* (1930), *Trouble in Paradise* (1932), *Design for Living* (1933), *The Merry Widow* (1936), *Angel* (1937), and *Ninotchka* (1939), each of which perpetuated the Lubitsch Touch of lavish costumes, whether historical or contemporary, and a subtle byplay of sexual innuendo and drollery within American limits. *Ninotchka* starred Greta Garbo as a Soviet commissar in Paris succumbing to Western romantic sexuality and *haute couture*. "Garbo laughs," proclaimed the billboard publicity for *Ninotchka*; indeed, in every Lubitsch film there persisted a suggestion of a smile—not a smirk, which Berliners were also capable of, but a smile at the ever-revolving merry-go-round of men and women in amorous pursuit.

Outside the studio, Lubitsch reigned as the acknowledged leader of émigré Hollywood, *Mitteleuropa* branch, up to the year of his death. Lubitsch's parties in the 1930s and early 1940s, at which practically only German was spoken, were legendary for the range of émigrés in attendance—screenwriters Vicki Baum of *Grand Hotel* fame and Billy Wilder, one of the screenwriters for *Ninotchka*; stars Peter Lorre, Oscar Homolka, and Hedy Lamarr; directors Max Reinhardt, William Wyler, Robert Siodmak, and Otto Preminger; maestro Otto Klemperer, the German conductor of the Los Angeles Philharmonic—and the spirit of Berlin and Vienna animating each gathering.

While not as clearly successful as Lubitsch, the Vienna-born Erich von Stroheim and Friedrich Wilhelm Murnau exercised in their brief careers as directors a powerful influence on American film. A Silesian Jew by birth, the son of an impoverished Vienna tailor, Erich von Stroheim ennobled himself with a *von* and devised a persona more Prussian than even the most shaved-headed, duelling-scarred, and monocled *Junker* might ever aspire to be. In the late 1930s, von Stroheim attained brilliance as an actor in such vehicles as *Grand Illusion* (1937), in which he played the most Teutonic of any Prussian ever depicted on the screen, *Five Graves to Cairo* (1943), in which he played Field Marshal Rommel with equal Teutonicism (British-born James Mason would later soften von Stroheim's interpretation of the German general), and *Sunset Boulevard* (1950), in which von Stroheim played himself, a director fallen upon evil days, once married to an aging film star whom he now serves as uniformed chauffeur.

In the 1920s, however, von Stroheim made his mark as a director, most notably in *Greed* (1923), a four-hour saga (it originally ran to eight hours) based on Frank Norris's novel *McTeague* (1899), the story of a brutish dentist and his miserly wife. With Middle European gusto, von Stroheim delighted in bringing sexuality, including its bizarre displacements, to the screen. In *Greed* McTeague's wife Trina sleeps naked on a pile of hoarded gold coins. In *Queen Kelly* (1928) von Stroheim went too far in a scene in which Gloria Swanson, playing a convent girl, looses the elastic in her panties, which drop to her feet, and von Stroheim, playing a cavalry officer, lifts them from the ground with his saber, holds them delicately to his nose, inhales their fragrance, then returns them to a blushing Gloria. This scene, so audacious for the United States in 1928, was too much, much too much, for Stroheim's producer Joseph Kennedy. Even worse, Kennedy's mistress Gloria Swanson was bitterly complaining to Kennedy regarding the kinky suggestions von Stroheim insisted on putting into the love scenes. The irate Irishman canceled the rest of the film, and only snippets of this masterpiece, including the panties-and-sword sequence, ever reached the public.

In his brief sojourn in Hollywood, F. W. Murnau created *Sunrise* (1927), loosely based on Theodore Dreiser's novel *An American Tragedy* (1925). Many critics consider *Sunrise* the greatest silent, perhaps the greatest film, ever made and point especially to its brilliantly mobile camera and the almost mystical Swedish ambience (Murnau was born in Sweden of German parents) of the outdoor scenes. A graduate in literature and art history from Heidelberg, with post-graduate studies at Oxford, Murnau served as an infantry officer in the war before transferring to aviation. Fortunately, he mistakenly landed in Switzerland in a thick fog, was interned, and survived the conflict. Even before the war, Murnau had begun to act in student productions at Heidelberg, which is where the great Max Reinhardt discovered him and brought him to the Deutsches Theater in

Berlin. Following the war, Murnau formed his own film company and created such classics as *Nosferatu* (1922), loosely adapted from Bram Stoker's *Dracula* (1897), *Phantom* (1923), and *The Last Laugh* (1924), which many film critics rank alongside *Sunrise*.

In *The Last Laugh* Emil Jannings plays an aging hotel doorman demoted to lavatory attendant who is suddenly enriched when he becomes the sole heir of an American guest who dies in his arms. Murnau was anticipating his own fate, for two years later William Fox brought Murnau to Hollywood with a $650,000 contract (in 1926 dollars, mind you!), spaced over four films. The first of these, *Sunrise*, provided Murnau with his enduring American reputation. Tall, aristocratic, aesthetic and homosexual, Murnau chafed under the studio system and found Hollywood in general a distressingly low-brow community. In 1930 he formed an independent partnership with Robert Flaherty to film *Tabu* (1931) in the South Seas. The success of *Tabu*—its depictions of a South Sea paradise, its pastoral eroticism, the powerful Polynesian music and singing of its pioneering soundtrack—brought Murnau back to Hollywood in triumph to another lucrative contract. Unfortunately, motoring north to Santa Barbara in a rented Packard, his handsome Filipino valet at the wheel, Murnau fractured his skull against a wooden post when the Packard careened off the road. He died a few hours later, and his body was returned to his mother in Germany.

In 1934 Murnau's mentor, Berliner Max Reinhardt, brought his opulent production of Shakespeare's *A Midsummer Night's Dream* to the Hollywood Bowl. Warner Brothers proceeded to film the spectacle at the cost of $1.3 million, at the time a record in the industry. Featuring Olivia de Havilland as Hermia, Victor Jory as Oberon, Anita Louise as Titania, Dick Powell as Lysander, James Cagney as Bottom, and a teenaged Mickey Rooney making his film debut as Puck, Reinhardt's spectacle was lavishly mounted, brilliantly acted, and backed by Erich Korngold's scoring of Mendelssohn's music. At both the Hollywood Bowl and in motion picture theaters, Reinhardt introduced to an American audience the pageantry and spectacle of the Deutsches Theater of Berlin. In 1936 Reinhardt staged Hugo von Hofmannsthal's *Everyman* and *Faust* at the outdoor Pilgrimage Play Theater in Los Angeles, directed by his pupil Johannes Poulson of the Royal Opera in Copenhagen.

As impressive as these outdoor pageants were, however, they represented a genre that had already passed its peak in the United States. Such spectacles were easier to mount in Europe, where there was a tradition of state-subsidized theater; but Hollywood would prove more cautious, especially after *Midsummer Night's Dream* bombed at the box office. At home in Hollywood (the consequences of the failure of *Midsummer Night's Dream* would not make themselves fully felt for another year or two), Reinhardt reigned supreme in his rented mansion overlooking the Pacific, to which he shipped his furniture and *objets d'art* from Berlin. To step into Reinhardt's mansion was to step into Berlin itself. Adapting to local custom, Reinhart even became a booster, albeit of a more exotic metropolis than the Los Angeles Chamber of Commerce had in mind. "You simply must stay here," Reinhardt told Klaus and Erika Mann in 1939. (Reinhardt had trained these two children of Thomas and Katia Mann at the Deutsches Theater.) "It's going to be a new center of culture. America is going to take over the cultural heritage of Europe, and there is no more hospitable landscape, none lies under happier stars, than the Californian. Here is a youthful country. European and American scientists and artists will meet to prepare a home for our old culture and for the new one that is coming into being here."[1]

The importation of the Berliner sensibility to American film also involved actors, actresses, and screenwriters. In 1926 two of Germany's greatest film actors, Conrad Veidt, star of *The Cabinet of Dr. Caligari*, and Emil Jannings, star of Murnau's *The Last Laugh*, arrived in Hollywood. When Jannings detrained in Pasadena, he was met by a crowd carrying a banner that proclaimed him the greatest actor in the world. Veidt and Jannings each brought along his Berliner sexual appetites as well as his acting talent, in Veidt's case a homosexual orientation and in Jannings's case an exuberant pursuit of women, food, and drink that ballooned his already massive frame to more than three hundred pounds by 1930.

Other German-speaking émigrés of the 1920s included the novelist William Wyler, a Berliner born in Alsace-Lorraine who quickly established a reputation as a screenwriter and director; novelist Vicki Baum, whom Lubitsch brought over to Paramount at $2,500 a week; and screenwriter, later director, Billy Wilder from Vienna via New York. The success of Marlene Dietrich in *The Blue Angel* (1930), directed by Josef von Sternberg from Heinrich Mann's novel *Professor Unrat* (1905), brought both Dietrich and von Sternberg to Paramount. Dietrich's equally successful American debut in *Morocco* (1930) intensified the rage for bringing European *femmes fatales* to the United States that had begun with the arrival of Greta Garbo in 1924. Like Erich von Stroheim, von Sternberg had added the *von* on his own account, letting it be known that he was of noble Austrian descent. In the first phases of his American career, von Sternberg moved easily between Berlin and Los Angeles.

The 1932 Olympics intensified an already vital connection between these two cities. UFA produced a Los Angeles–based film, directed by E. A. Dupont, with a plot revolving around the Olympics. All exterior shots were filmed on location. As if to emphasize the Berlin–Los Angeles connection even further, German planner Anton Wagner published *Los Angeles . . . Zweimillionstadt in Suedkalifornien* (1935), an exhaustive inventory of the city completed before, during, and after the Olympic year. Urban theorists Reyner Banham and Mike Davis, among others, have praised Wagner's exhaustive inquiry as the founding text of Los Angeles as a world city in the making. Long before Eastern observers (and even San Franciscans!) had ceased dismissing Los Angeles as an eccentric, formless sprawl, the Berlin-based Wagner was seeing in the two million-plus city an innovative polynucleated metropolis that constituted a new version of the urban form.

After Hitler came to power in 1933, the Berlin-Hollywood connection began to tilt even further in favor of the City of the Angels. Born in Vienna in 1890, the son of a successful architect, Fritz Lang studied painting in Munich before joining the Imperial Army of the Austro-Hungarian Empire. Furloughed from the front to recover from his wounds, the young lieutenant was sitting in a Viennese café, resplendent in his uniform, when a local director, spotting him at his table, walked over and offered him a part in a new play. After the war, Lang continued his acting, then went into directing. By 1933 Fritz Lang stood at the top of the German film industry, having produced such classics as *Dr. Mabuse* (1922), *The Nibelungen* (1924), *Metropolis* (1926), and *M* (1931), his first sound film. Lang had also become highly Prussianized in his personal style, including an ever-present monocle. He was, in short, the very model of the UFA director. Seeking an overlord for the film industry in the Third Reich, propaganda minister Joseph Goebbels summoned Lang to his office in Berlin and offered him the position. Goebbels was willing to overlook the fact that Lang was half Jewish; for the other half—the half that had filmed the German national epic *The Nibelungen*, one of Hitler's favorite films, and had in his person brought the Prussian *Junker*-director genre to perfection—was certainly German enough. That night, Lang slipped quietly out of Berlin and headed for Hollywood via Paris and New York. Within eight years of his arrival, one of the two or three most respected directors in Berlin had achieved the same status in Hollywood with such efforts as *Fury* (1936), *You Only Live Once* (1937), and *Manhunt* (1941).

The German singer Lotte Lehmann had a similar experience when she refused Herman Goering's invitation to take a state-sponsored role in opera. Lehmann fled to Santa Barbara, leaving behind a house, which the Nazis sacked, and a horse and dog, which they shot. Peter Lorre, the Berlin actor who had played the child murderer in Fritz Lang's *M* (and thereby done the impossible, turning the sympathy of the viewer in his direction) followed Lang and Lehmann to Hollywood in 1935: a bug-eyed, slightly bizarre troll of a man soon to reestablish himself as one of the greatest character actors in the United States. Also arriving: Otto Preminger, the son of a prominent Viennese lawyer who had served a term as Attorney General of the Austro-Hungarian Empire. The holder of a law degree from the University of Vienna, Preminger had gone on the stage as an actor before turning to theater and film direction.

Thanks to this influx of Berliners and their Viennese allies into Hollywood and the translation there of the best of the Berlin film industry, Los Angeles/Hollywood was in the position—once Berlin was shut down by the heavy hand of Nazism, or later, lay prostrate under Allied bombing—to keep the best, and some of the worst, of the Berliner spirit alive through 1945. During the 1930s and the first half of the 1940s, many a citizen of Hollywood might continue to say with little interruption *Ich bin ein Berliner*, which like *civis Romanus sum* announced a point of view, an attitude, an empire of mind and imagination transcending the limits of one physical city. Berlin, as it flourished before 1933 and as it came to

Hollywood, prized wit, sociability, café and bohemian life, opera and theater, together with the posters, songs, slang, and wisecracks of the street. Each city was
the product of self-invention. Each city had been set down in a plain near a river
as the deliberate, indeed artificial, heart of an expanding empire.

Los Angeles succumbed, alas, to a dreary at-homeness after its takeover at the
turn of the century by the Folks from the Midwest. Even Pickfair, capital of pre-
Berlin Hollywood, emanated a dreary, defensive domesticity crying out for the
festive sociability of *Mitteleuropa*. Arriving at Pickfair for dinner in the mid-1930s,
the English actor Cedric Hardwicke was astonished to encounter little talk, much
less gossip, no pre-dinner cocktails or wine, Jell-O salads with mayonnaise from a
jar as dressing, and a movie right after dinner: a far cry from the 1920s when
Hollywood people, according to director Raoul Walsh, went to dinner parties to
get drunk and have sex.

The private nature of Los Angeles, its obsession with being at home, did not
dovetail with the Berliners and the Viennese. They were used to the public life
of their cities. Hence before Pearl Harbor, when resident aliens were free to move
about the city, or by 1943, when the curfew on resident aliens was lifted, Berliners
and Viennese could be found in great numbers at such watering holes as the
Brown Derby, the Cocoanut Grove, Chasen's, and Romanoff's. These places, after
all, represented something akin to the restaurant and cabaret life of Middle Europe. Thanks to the arrival of Berlin and Vienna in Hollywood, a golden age of
Hollywood restaurants and nightclubs ensued, which lasted through the 1950s.
Berlin was also the morphine and cocaine capital of Europe, and, while it is
difficult to document drug usage, it must be noted that Klaus Mann brought with
him to Southern California a drug habit that eventually helped precipitate his
suicide.

To cite the presence of so many Berliners or Viennese with strong Berlin connections in Hollywood is not to slight such Russian émigrés as Lewis Milestone,
director of such classics as *All Quiet on the Western Front* (1932), *Rain* (1932), *The
General Died at Dawn* (1936), and *Of Mice and Men* (1939); or Armenian émigré
Rouben Mamoulian, director of such classics as *Applause* (1929), *Love Me Tonight*
(1932), *Queen Christina* (1933), and *The Mark of Zorro* (1940). Nor is it to overlook
such resourceful Hungarians as the woefully under-estimated Michael Curtiz, director of *Casablanca* (1943). While he has never attracted a cult following, Curtiz
must be considered in the top ranks of Hollywood directors in terms of the range,
versatility, and overall excellence of his oeuvre, one hundred films in all, forty-six
of them A-budget, including at least three masterpieces, *The Sea Wolf* (1941),
Casablanca (1943), and *Mildred Pierce* (1945), and such other near-masterpieces
as *The Adventures of Robin Hood* (1938), *Dodge City* (1939), *The Charge of the
Light Brigade* (1936), and *The Sea Hawk* (1940).

Born in Hungary in 1888, Mihaly Kertesz got his start as a film actor in his
native country before moving to Vienna in 1919, where he became active in the
Austrian film industry. Kertesz's most important breakthrough occurred when he

collaborated with his fellow Hungarian Alexander Korda in the costume drama *The Slave Queen* (1924), one of the most ambitious spectaculars of the European silent cinema and a film that shaped the career of Cecil B. DeMille. *The Slave Queen* brought Kertesz to the attention of the Warner brothers, Harry and Jack, who brought him to Hollywood to direct their own spectacular, *Noah's Ark* (1928), which Warner's hoped would out-DeMille DeMille himself in production values. Anglicizing his name to Michael Curtiz, the émigré director slogged through a series of lesser-budget efforts, acquiring a reputation as a thorough professional, capable of turning to any type of film vehicle and getting the job done on time and on budget. Curtiz's American breakthrough came with *Captain Blood* (1935) in which he directed the second debut of Errol Flynn, who had previously played the non-speaking part of a corpse in Curtiz's *The Case of the Curious Bride* (1934). Despite Flynn's tendency to blow his lines or otherwise misbehave on the set, the Tasmanian ocker with English mannerisms and the minimally Anglicized Hungarian were made for each other; and through such vehicles as *Captain Blood, The Adventures of Robin Hood, The Charge of the Light Brigade*, and *The Sea Hawk*—productions that continue to this day to define the costume adventure— Curtiz took Flynn to stardom.

Volatile and demanding, Curtiz was famous for his outbursts on the set. When Errol Flynn fluffed his lines in *Captain Blood*, Curtiz screamed: "I picked you up from a corpse and made you a hero. And now from a hero I'll put you back to a corpse and you'll be a bum again!" For the rest of the film and for the others they made together, Curtiz insisted on referring to Flynn as Earl Flynt.[2] When Flynn and David Niven were cutting up on the set of *The Charge of the Light Brigade*, Curtiz yelled: "You men think I know fuck nothing, whereas in fact I know fuck all!"[3]

Throughout his Hollywood career, which tapered off in 1954 with two very diverse efforts, *White Christmas* and *The Egyptian*, Michael Curtiz communicated in an idiosyncratic pidgin patois that blended Hungarian, German, and English. It was rumored that only one person, a British grip nicknamed Limey, fully understood Curtiz and moved with the director from film to film as his translator. Many of the malapropisms attributed to Samuel Goldwyn, in fact, may have actually originated with Curtiz. Angrily, to Jack Warner: "Don't call me back until you're not ready." At a story conference: "This scene vill make your blood curl." On the set of *The Charge of the Light Brigade*, calling for a stampede of one hundred riderless horses: "Bring on the empty horses!"—a phrase that co-star David Niven memorialized as the title of a best-selling autobiography. To some extras gathered in dense groups: "Stop standing around in bundles." To an underling at a story conference: "No, I don't vant yes men. If you don't agree, say so even though I vill fire you." When questioned by Jack Warner regarding the accuracy of the background of *Casablanca:* "Vell, Jock, the scenario isn't the exact truth, but vee haff the facts to prove it."[4]

Jack Warner's selection of Curtiz to direct *Casablanca* was as accidentally brilliant as everything else connected with this film. Warner knew and trusted Curtiz, and Curtiz had just worked with screenwriters Philip and Julius Epstein on revamping the initial script for the Academy Award–winning *Yankee Doodle Dandy* (1942). Curtiz had also recently directed Edward G. Robinson in a film adaptation of Jack London's novel *The Sea Wolf* (1904), a film giving major evidence that Michael Curtiz was capable of the highest levels of filmic art as well as his usual on-time, on-budget professionalism. Thus Michael Curtiz, émigré director, speaking in a frequently indecipherable tongue, was on hand to pull together *Casablanca*, a film that continues to this day to offer insights into American character and identity. In its émigré director and its largely émigré cast—Ingrid Bergman from Sweden; Paul Henreid, S. Z. Sakall, and Ludwig Stossel from Austria; Claude Rains from England; Conrad Veidt and Peter Lorre from Germany; Madeleine Le Beau and Marcel Dalio from France, together with a dozen other European émigrés in supporting roles—*Casablanca* recapitulated and expressed for decades to come the intrinsic internationalism of Hollywood and the acceptability of this internationalism to American audiences, provided that it was anchored in someone as recognizably American as Humphrey Bogart.

Berliners were connoisseurs of sexuality in all its forms and manifestations. More important, sexuality in Berlin possessed a public, even defiant, presence that was part of the strong anti-establishment streak running through Berliner psyches. Marlene Dietrich played an important role in bringing Berliner sexuality to Hollywood, where it dovetailed with an already thriving obsession with physical beauty. Josef von Sternberg had initially considered other actresses to play Lola-Lola in *The Blue Angel*, but when he met Dietrich he knew that he had found just the right person to communicate the devil-may-care sexuality, sometimes harsh, frequently obsessive, of Berlin. Under von Sternberg's direction, Dietrich created a role that for the rest of the century set standards for portrayals of sex, power, vulnerability, and obsession.

Dietrich stole the film from Emil Jannings, who resented his co-star so strongly that he physically attacked her under cover of a scene in which Professor Unrat tries to strangle Lola-Lola. Jannings had to be pulled from Dietrich by von Sternberg, who slapped Jannings across the face to bring him to his senses. There was talk of turning Jannings over to the police. But then again: Jannings might have pleaded an actor's vulnerability to role. Dietrich had vanquished him just as Lola-Lola had reduced the gymnasium professor to a comic figure in a rooster's suit crying "Cock-a-doodle-do! Cock-a-doodle-do!" on stage before his former students. With Unrat dead from disgrace and shame, Lola-Lola sings triumphantly in the final scene: an image that seared itself into the Berliner imagination as the very embodiment of Berliner defiance and joy of life at a time of once and future doom.

At the premiere of *The Blue Angel* in the Gloriapalast Theater, the audience stood in a cheering ovation at the completion of the film, and an equally noisy crowd milled outside, waiting for Dietrich to appear. Thronged by the press of people, she was barely able to make her escape in an open truck. Dietrich left Berlin that night for Hollywood, an overnight international star, under contract to Paramount. Even James Joyce was impressed when he ran into Dietrich at Fouquet's restaurant in Paris in 1938. "I saw you in *L'Ange bleu*," Joyce told Dietrich. She replied: "You saw the best of me."[5]

Prior to her departure for Hollywood, Marlene Dietrich had been a fixed figure in the café life of Berlin. Despite marriage and motherhood, and her own proper upbringing as the daughter of a war hero and police official, Dietrich liked to hang out with a raffish crowd, which included Billy Wilder, then a journalist in Berlin; the novelist Erich Maria Remarque, with whom she conducted a longtime affair; Ernst Udet, the German air ace; novelists Leonhard Frank and Heinrich Mann; cabaret singer Fritzi Massari; and the celebrated comedian Max Pallenberg. In addition to these friends from High Bohemia, Dietrich could also be found at the various transvestite clubs of Berlin, where she frequently wore male dress; or the Ring Club, a scandal-ridden rendezvous favored by ex-convicts; or the bar at the Hotel Eden; or such vibrant cafés as the Silhouette, the White Rose, and the Always Faithful. Everywhere she went, Dietrich exuded a comradely demeanor toward one and all, gay or straight, high or low in the social hierarchy. "She was like a free and easy boy," film director Geza von Sziffra later remembered, "and with her buddy-like comradeship she stifled every possible emotion of her would-be dates."[6]

In Hollywood Dietrich resumed her café and cabaret crawling, as much as she could in a city devoid of Berlin's night life. She shifted the scene of her socializing to private parties and premieres in addition to hotel bars and restaurants. As in Berlin, Dietrich preferred to hang out with men, as one of the boys. In 1932 she electrified Hollywood when she appeared with Maurice Chevalier and Gary Cooper at the premiere of *The Sign of the Cross* wearing a man's fedora hat and tuxedo. Dietrich loved to cross-dress. She played one of her Berlin films, *The Ship of Lost Men* (1929), almost exclusively in male attire. In Hollywood, aside from her tuxedo, she pioneered the wearing of slacks, attending parties around town in various pants outfits. After some confusion, the public relations team at Paramount got the point. The PR office issued publicity stills of Dietrich in slacks and other forms of male attire, which it packaged with the slogan "The woman even women can adore!"[7] In her first American film, *Morocco* (1930), Dietrich did the closest thing to a lesbian love scene that American censors would allow or American audiences tolerate.

Émigrés such as Dietrich enlarged the vocabulary of sexual expression and gesture in American film. When Paul Henreid, playing opposite Bette Davis in *Now, Voyager* (1942), placed two cigarettes in his mouth, lit them both, then handed one to Davis, he created one of the most electric moments in film. The act was rather commonplace in Europe, Henreid later remembered. He used to do for it for his wife Lisl when the two of them were motoring. In the United States, however, Henreid's dual cigarettes constituted a sophisticated declaration of sexual intent worthy of being placed alongside Greta Garbo's drinking from the same communion chalice as her lover John Gilbert in *Flesh and the Devil* (1927).

Along with its capacity for symbolic gesture, émigré sexuality also fostered a high degree of self-awareness through Freudian theory and psychoanalysis, which also came to Los Angeles in a major way through the arrival of a generation of émigré psychiatrists and psychoanalysts who put Hollywood on the couch. Hedy Lamarr, for example, formerly Hedwig Kiesler of Vienna, spent a good deal of her time and some of her fortune on psychoanalysis. A dark Dietrich, Lamarr could have come only from one place, German-speaking *Mitteleuropa*. Her Americanization, like that of Dietrich, brought a new resonance to Hollywood's depiction of sexuality on the screen. Like Dietrich, Hedwig Kiesler came from respectable bourgeois stock, being born in Vienna on 9 November 1913 to a proper Catholic family. Educated in a convent school in Vienna and a boarding school in Lucerne, where she experienced her first lesbian interlude, Hedwig Kiesler was gifted (or cursed) with an extraordinary beauty and an urgent libido that would propel her, by her own admission, to the borderlands of nymphomania.

Kiesler had the confidence to present herself at the age of fourteen to the Austrian director Alexis Granowsky and successfully petition him for a part. Shortly thereafter, she persuaded her parents to allow her to enroll as an acting student with Max Reinhardt at the Deutsches Theater in Berlin. Yet it would not be the legitimate stage that would propel Hedwig Kiesler into international notoriety at age sixteen, but her starring role in *Extase* (1933), an erotic idyll released by Elektra Films, directed by the famed Czech director Gustav Machaty. In August 1933 Hedwig Kiesler married into the very center of the new world order, becoming the bride in an elaborate Roman Catholic ceremony in Vienna of munitions manufacturer Fritz Mandl, leader of the industrial clique supporting National Socialism and Adolf Hitler. (Mandl began almost immediately to buy as many copies of *Extase* as he could and have them destroyed.) The couple maintained a ten-room apartment in Vienna and a palace in Salzburg. At one reception, Adolph Hitler bent to kiss Hedwig Mandl's hand. At another event, Mussolini held her chair as she sat to dinner.

As Nazism descended over Germany and Austria, Hedwig Kiesler Mandl found herself a prisoner of the Third Reich. It was as if the German world itself, acting through her husband, were holding her closer and closer in erotic obsession: a fixation for her personalized in the image of her husband in a remote part of the palace, viewing yet another confiscated reel of *Extase*. By 1936 Hedwig Kiesler Mandl was plotting her escape—from Austria, from Fritz Mandl, from *Extase*, from the whole mordant mess. She fled secretly in the dead of night, carrying a few jewels. Safely arrived in Paris, she sued for divorce in the French courts, waiving all rights to alimony and community property.

There also she was introduced to Louis B. Mayer by film agent Robert Ritchie, and after some sparring over salary (Mayer offered her $125 a week; Mrs. Mandl laughed in scorn and demanded, and got, $500), Mayer offered her a contract and Hedwig Kiesler Mandl moved to Hollywood. Arriving at the Los Angeles train station in 1937, stylishly European in her well-tailored, slightly mannish pin-striped suit, Mrs. Mandl brought to the United States a dangerously high level of notoriety. (Not until 1940 would American censors allow a severely edited version of *Extase* to be shown to American audiences.) Louis B. Mayer set about to change Hedwig Kiesler Mandl's image. First of all, he gave her a new name, Hedy Lamarr, in honor of Barbara Lamarr, the late Hollywood actress (she had died in 1926 at the age of twenty-seven, following a nervous breakdown) whom Mayer felt had been the most beautiful woman ever to act in Hollywood. Second and more important, Mayer sought what might initially seem the impossible: the glacialization of Hedy Lamarr's sexuality. Sensing the elements of obsession, bisexuality, and near-nymphomania in his Austrian import, Mayer sought to transform her into an Ice Queen à la Greta Garbo and a recent Swedish import, Ingrid Bergman.

The tension between who she was, a near-nymphomaniac by her own confession, and the role she played on screen, the controlling Ice Queen, gave Lamarr an unusually forceful on-screen presence, as omnivorous instincts and a fierce, highly stylized element of control confronted each other in dynamic tension. That Hollywood so perfectly controlled the duality, subsuming the woman whose hand had been kissed by Adolph Hitler into the tireless seller of American war bonds, testified to the degree and the intensity with which the American film industry had comparably subsumed Vienna and Berlin.

Occasionally lesbian by her own admission, a trait she shared with a number of other émigré actresses, Hedy Lamarr skirted, discreetly, the gay dimension of Hollywood as Vienna or Berlin. While certainly not finding open acceptance in the film industry, men and women of homosexual and lesbian inclination at least encountered some degree of acceptance—within limits, of course; one cannot push the Berlin comparison too far. In director George Cukor, for example, a gay artist reached the top of the slippery Hollywood ladder and took a generation of American women to a higher plateau as well. Cukor was not an émigré, but the next thing to it, a Hungarian Jew born and raised in a trilingual household in New York City, where the languages were equally English, Hungarian, and German. Despite his American birth, much of *Mitteleuropa* remained in Cukor's style and accent. More important, Cukor sustained a fundamental and creative insight into the interaction of gender, role, and identity as they pertained to female sexuality that connected him to the rich inner world of Middle Europe in the age of Sigmund Freud. Not that Cukor's depictions of women were clinical or that he sought power over women through male authority. (One senses, by contrast, Claudette Colbert fighting constantly in *Cleopatra* against the off-screen domination of Cecil B. DeMille.) Far from it. A homosexual well before gay liberation, Cukor had the greatest respect for discretion, subtlety, and taste in matters of sexual identity and behavior.

In film after film, Cukor liberated his actresses into roles that expanded what it meant to be female at this time in these United States. Even in such outrageously romantic vehicles as *Camille* (1936), Cukor guided Greta Garbo to an exquisite depiction of how the most vulnerable female of all, a courtesan with tuberculosis, was the conscious protagonist and in part the master of her destiny. Cukor began his career, significantly, with taking on the matter of divorce in *A Bill of Divorcement* (1932), in which it is the woman, not the man, who initiates the proceedings. In another divorce vehicle, *The Women* (1939), screenplay by Anita Loos and Jane Murfin from the play by Clare Boothe, Cukor even more brilliantly explored the female side of the divorce equation. In *A Woman's Face* (1941), starring Joan Crawford, Cukor tackled what is perhaps the most egregious form of male control of females, physical beauty as the prime determinant of self-esteem and social success.

But it was through actress Katharine Hepburn that Cukor made his most subtle and effective statements. First of all was the matter of intelligence, which Cukor liberated so exuberantly in his direction of Hepburn as Jo in *Little Women* (1933). Whatever else it was, Louisa May Alcott's 1868–69 two-part novel announced, triumphantly, the intelligence of American women, even when that intelligence was confined to domestic issues. Katharine Hepburn incorporated tensions that connected powerfully with Cukor's own situation. Her femininity, for one thing, played off against an assertiveness usually reserved for the male. In *Sylvia Scarlett* (1935), which Hepburn played almost completely in disguise as a young man, Cukor exploited Hepburn's androgyny in a film electric with sexual ambiguity. A later creation, Judy Garland, was likewise androgynized by Cukor in *A Star Is Born* (1954).

Not accidentally did George Cukor help develop the persona of two actresses beloved by gay America, Katharine Hepburn and Judy Garland. In so many respects, George Cukor represented one of Hollywood's best-kept secrets, homosexuality as a source of creative action. In part because of his own sexual orientation and life situation, George Cukor was able to transcend the technicality of his maleness and project himself into the existential place occupied by women. Cukor directed women not as objects of desire but as objects of the mind: as nearly Platonic ideals of various modes of perfected femaleness. It is of course theoretically possible for a heterosexual director to do this, but few of them bothered before George Cukor, and he in turn was bothering because a new sensibility had translated itself from *Mitteleuropa* to Hollywood.

Like the rest of the nation, however, pre-war Hollywood kept homosexuality in the closet, despite the prominence of such homosexual directors as F. W. Murnau, James Whale, and George Cukor. Among actors, William Haines and Conrad Veidt belonged to the world of Twilight Men, as homosexuals were then known in Hollywood, as did Charles Laughton, one of the most brilliant actors in Hollywood through the 1950s. Living in an open marriage with the English actress Elsa Lanchester, who accepted his homosexuality, Laughton maintained a high level of discretion, having learned the dangers of his double life a few years earlier in London when a young man he had picked up reported him to the police. An understanding judge dismissed Laughton with a warning, and the matter stayed out of the press, but the trauma of it all—Laughton appearing on the London stage by night and spending his days in court—kept him discreet for a lifetime. In 1932, however, Laughton came obliquely out of the closet in his performance of Emperor Nero in Cecil B. DeMille's *The Sign of the Cross*. Supervising his own makeup—plucked eyebrows, rouged cheeks, a touch of lipstick—Laughton played Nero as a raging queen, surrounded in some scenes by near-naked young men who fed him bunches of grapes. How this got by the censors is anyone's guess. And yet, in so many of Laughton's masterful performances in the 1930s— as Captain Bligh, as the emperors Nero and Claudius, as Inspector Javert—the brilliant British actor managed to convey an oblique homosexuality channeled into malevolence. Ironically, Laughton would end his career playing Dixiecrat Senator Cooley in *Advise and Consent* (1962).

Allegations of bisexuality clung, at one time or another, to Greta Garbo, Tallulah Bankhead, Hedy Lamarr, Cary Grant and Randolph Scott, who lived together in the 1930s, and Clark Gable, who was alleged to have done some bisexual hustling in his early career. As far as homosexual Hollywood was concerned, the eleventh commandment, Thou Shalt Not Get Caught, represented the price of continuing stardom. Tyrone Power, for example, the top draw at Twentieth Century–Fox in the late 1930s, pursued a vigorous homosexual life throughout his entire career without ever edging into scandal. Married to the French actress Annabella (Suzanne Georgette Charpentier), Power enlisted in the Marine Corps in August 1942, went through basic training at Camp Elliott in San Diego, qualified for OCS at Quantico, Virginia, followed by flight training at Corpus Christi, Texas, won his wings, and logged eleven hundred hours of flight time, a considerable part of it under enemy fire, as an R5C pilot in the Aerial Transport Service in the South Pacific—maintaining all the while, at various intervals, his bisexual life.

Intensifying and destabilizing all sexuality, World War II brought homosexuality almost into the open in Los Angeles/Hollywood. For officers and the otherwise affluent, the homosexual scene centered in the Biltmore Hotel. For enlisted men and the otherwise less privileged, the adjacent Pershing Square served as a favored meeting place, with couples repairing to the nearby YMCA. Stretches of Sunset Boulevard in Hollywood were also favored pickup points. Even more furtive was the men's room in the downtown station of the Pacific Electric red car trolley system, although this assignation site was constantly monitored by the LAPD. Out in Santa Monica, the park in the palisades above the city, totally unlit in the blackout darkness, became a favored rendezvous for cruising gay servicemen: a sex jungle, Christopher Isherwood described it, filled with servicemen and their hunters. Working in the summer of 1943 as a screenwriter at MGM for $250 a week, Tennessee Williams went into the thrilling darkness of the Santa Monica palisades evening after evening or made pickups as he cruised along on his secondhand motor scooter or met other servicemen on the bus between Santa Monica and Hollywood, having spent the day at work on *The Glass Menagerie*, which his light schedule at MGM gave him time to complete.

Beneath the palisades was a long stretch of public beach running down to Muscle Beach south of the Santa Monica Pier. Famous for its displays of body culture, Muscle Beach had its homosexual dimension, and it was there, a few yards offshore, that Tennessee Williams's friend Christopher Isherwood failed in the effort he was making to remain celibate as a religious novice in the Vedanta Center in Hollywood. Arriving in Hollywood in late 1939 from Germany via London and New York, the preternaturally handsome—blond hair, piercing blue eyes, the demeanor of a cavalry major in a guards regiment—novelist Isherwood was destined to become, along with George Cukor and a later arrival, the English artist David Hockney, the high priest of Los Angeles/Hollywood as homosexual utopia. Initially, Isherwood attempted to remain celibate as part of his religious commitment, but by late 1943, after much tension and struggle, which he would later write about with total candor, Isherwood found himself a habitué of the Santa Monica beach scene—"the Pits," as the homosexual section of the beach north of Santa Monica was called. On a more refined level, Isherwood was delighted to discover that something of his beloved Berlin homosexual-oriented night life had survived translation to Los Angeles. On 3 February 1943, for instance, a friend brought him to the Club Gala for a nightcap. "I haven't been to a place of this sort in ages," Isherwood noted in his diary, "and it was so nostalgically reminiscent of all the other times—the baroque decorations and the cozy red velvet corners, the sharp-faced peroxide pianist with tender memories and a tongue like an adder, the grizzled tomcat tenor, the lame celebrity, the bar mimosa, the public lovers, the amazed millionaire tourist and the daydream sailor."[8]

Along with Tennessee Williams and others, Isherwood befriended the legendary hustler Denham (Denny) Fouts, the celebrated Best Kept Boy in the World, as Truman Capote would later describe him. In and of himself, Denny Fouts embodied the international homosexual underground that was now relocating, along with the other émigrés, in Los Angeles/Hollywood. At the age of sixteen Fouts had run away from his Florida home with a cosmetics tycoon, whom he abandoned in Capri. Fouts spent the pre-war years as a homosexual Holly Golightly in England and on the Continent, the Best Kept Boy of a number of prominent millionaires and assorted celebrities. Fleeing to Hollywood at the outbreak of the war, Fouts roomed with Isherwood for a while in 1941, the two of them making every effort to devote themselves to prayer and celibacy. Despite his lack of formal education (together with his addiction to hard drugs), Fouts wanted to qualify for medical school and become a psychiatrist. He eventually gained admission to Santa Monica Junior College, which was perhaps the wrong place to be, given the frenzied activities on the beach. In any event, Denny Fouts—a handsome hustler with impeccable connections, poignantly seeking to understand himself and others as an M.D. psychiatrist—survives in history and in legend, chronicled by Isherwood, Truman Capote, and Gore Vidal, among others, as being in the vanguard of hundreds of thousands of homosexual young men who would deliberately choose California, north and south, in the post-war period.

By the end of the war, Isherwood stood at the center, strictly because of his class and charm and dazzling talent as a writer, of a loosely organized British homosexual Hollywood circle that included, at various times, such longtime residents as James Whale and Charles Laughton, W. Somerset Maugham (in and out of Hollywood throughout the period and a good friend of George Cukor, who held honorary membership in the circle), W. H. Auden (in town to collaborate with Stravinsky on *The Rake's Progress*), composer Benjamin Britten, and photographer Cecil Beaton, who arrived in late 1946 in passionate pursuit of Greta Garbo, for whom Beaton had temporarily laid aside his homosexuality. Isherwood and Laughton became especially close. At one time they seriously discussed collaborating on a dramatized version of certain Platonic dialogues. In 1960 the Laughtons bought a house next door to Isherwood's on Adelaide Drive in Santa Monica, with a pool big enough for Laughton's young friends to swim in, and when Laughton died of cancer in December 1962, Isherwood gave the eulogy.

Aldous Huxley, a heterosexual, was decidedly not part of the group, and Isherwood believed that Huxley's disapproval of his homosexuality put a barrier between them, despite their mutual attraction to the teachings of Swami Prabhavananda of the Vedanta Center in the Hollywood Hills. On the other hand, some sort of homoerotic feeling bonded Isherwood to Thomas Mann, who called Isherwood "the starry-eyed one." Isherwood was a constant visitor to the Mann household and a regular at Salka Viertel's Sunday salons in Santa Monica, which the Manns also attended. Isherwood was also a close friend of Mann's homosexual son Klaus. Humorously, Mann once described Isherwood to a visiting journalist as "the family pimp."[9] Comments such as this cannot be taken lightly. Isherwood fascinated "the Kaiser." As Mann's published diaries would later reveal, the Kaiser had a strong homoerotic dimension to his nature, perhaps even a bisexual past. Mann was fixated on physical beauty whether in men or women, and Isherwood more than met that need.

Not for Isherwood, however, would homosexuality lead to self-destruction as it did with Klaus Mann, although Isherwood was pushing the envelope through 1945, 1946, and 1947, when he was living with his rough-trade lover William Caskey in an apartment over Salka Viertel's garage and drinking heavily. Escaping Los Angeles, Isherwood and Caskey spent a year and a half traveling through Latin America. When they returned, they moved to South Laguna, sixty miles south of Santa Monica, so as to be free from the temptations of Hollywood and Santa Monica. Isherwood devoted himself to serious work, beginning with a narrative of his South American travels, *The Condor and the Cows* (1949). Caskey eventually left, and in the winter of 1953 Isherwood met Don Bachardy, an eighteen-year-old college student from Florida. Their age difference, thirty years, scandalized many of Isherwood's friends. It would have been too much, some of them claimed, for even the ancient Greeks. Isherwood's landlord asked him to leave when Bachardy moved in. In any event, Isherwood and Bachardy established a home in Santa Monica that set the standard, along with the home of George Cukor, for homosexual lifestyle and taste in the Southland: a world of bright colors, canyon-side homes, and, always and everywhere, swimming pools, blue and expansive as in a David Hockney painting: pools for gathering in the late afternoon, pools for Laughton's friend Bruce Ash to swim in, or for Isherwood and Don Bachardy to sit beside in flowing Moroccan tunics, as Hockney depicted them in 1976, barefoot in their robes in their Santa Monica home, the king and crown prince of the Los Angeles celebrated so vividly in Hockney's vivid paintings, in which the eternal blue of the swimming pool bespeaks the achievement of a momentary utopia.

Paris, as well as Vienna and Berlin, arrived in Hollywood/Los Angeles in these years; and the French adjustment, while not as inevitable, pervasive, and intense as the German-speaking relationship, was successful enough to create a Franco-Southern Californian community whose style, values, and creativity were likewise subsumed into the metropolis. From France in 1940 came director Jean Renoir, son of the Impressionist painter, and the poet-aviator Antoine de Saint-Exupéry, sharing a cabin on the voyage from Lisbon to New York. Even as they sailed, Saint-Exupéry was busy on *Flight to Arras* (1942), which he continued to write in Hollywood while living as a house guest of the Renoirs, dictating all night into a dictaphone for transcription the next morning. In Hollywood Renoir joined his fellow French émigré director René Clair, a 1939 arrival, who had recently completed *Flame of New Orleans* (1941), starring Marlene Dietrich. Renoir secured permission from Darryl Zanuck to film *Swamp Water* (1941) on location in Georgia. Living and working with the swamp people, Renoir knew for certain that he was no longer in Paris. In one remote cabin he encountered a closed bedroom door. A woman told Renoir that her brother had been in that bedroom for thirty years. In 1911 the man's girlfriend had run off to Atlanta and become a prostitute. In grief, the man had taken to his bed and stayed there. Renoir loved the swamp-country blend of Grand Guignol and American Gothic. Here was a nation with stories to tell!

Charles Boyer, who had gotten his start in French-language films produced by UFA of Berlin, stood at the center of the French émigré community, which included directors René Clair and Julien Duvivier and actors Jean Gabin (Marlene Dietrich's lover), Jean-Pierre Aumont, and Louis Jourdan. Maurice Chevalier had returned to Paris and would earn a great deal of post-war enmity for entertaining there during the German occupation. Jean Renoir, on the other hand, was contemptuous of the French émigrés hanging out at The Players, a restaurant-café owned by Francophile director Preston Sturges. Renoir called this group the Hollywood Resistance Movement. "Wonderfully victorious attacks on Vichy were launched from that Sunset Strip café," Renoir later observed. "It is not hard to be a hero when the enemy is 10,000 kilometers away."[10]

Dazzled by his salary at Fox, Renoir rented a house large enough for himself and his wife, Saint-Exupéry, and an African-American couple in their employ. Émigrés seemed to have come in two categories: those who succeeded in Hollywood and those who failed miserably. If an émigré was able to achieve regular employment in the studios, he or she must be ranked among the successful; for Hollywood salaries, impressive enough to Americans, dazzled the émigrés. English émigré Aldous Huxley suffered morbid pangs of guilt when he was making $1,500 a week at MGM as a screenwriter for *Pride and Prejudice* (1940) while England was at war. Only when Anita Loos advised Huxley to send part of his salary home each month was he able to adjust to the money he was making.

Man Ray, by contrast, felt absolutely no guilt whatsoever over his Los Angeles success; but then again, Ray was an American of Russian descent returning after nineteen years in Paris, and Los Angeles, while distinctive, was an American city. In spite of his American origins, however, Man Ray's rapid adjustment to Southern California can stand as a model for all those émigrés who modestly or conspicuously put it together in the Southland. Having fled the Nazis across France into Spain and Portugal before sailing from Lisbon to the United States, Ray drove cross country with a male friend to Los Angeles via Route 66. Their first night in town, Ray and his friend dined in a drive-in off trays attached to their car doors. The next morning Ray's pal phoned a girl whom he knew in New York and arranged a date for himself and for Ray that evening. Ray was delighted with his escort, Juliet Browner, a Martha Graham dancer with fawn-like features and slanted eyes. After dinner the foursome went off to a nightclub where they listened and danced to some of the best music Ray had ever heard in his life. Juliet was like a feather in his arms.

The next day, Juliet and Ray met for lunch, followed by a long talk in a rowboat on Echo Park Lake. Ray literally invited Juliet back to his hotel to see his etchings, in this case the portfolio of drawings, watercolors, and Rayographs (direct contact photographs) that he had smuggled out of Europe. Ray suggested that Juliet move into her own room in the hotel so the that they would not have to travel across town to see each other. Juliet agreed instantly. Shortly thereafter, the couple set up housekeeping at the Château des Fleurs, a Hollywood apartment house. They later found a combination studio-living quarters in a four-story brick building on Vine Street, conveniently located opposite the Film Art Theatre, which frequently showed French films, thereby providing Man Ray with a weekly dosage of idiomatic French. In a used car lot downtown on Flower Street, Ray purchased a four-seater metallic blue sedan, whose interior upholstery thoroughly complemented, Ray noted with delight, his favorite blue tweed jacket. "Well, now

I had everything again," Man Ray noted with delight, "a woman, a studio, a car. The renewal of my existence every ten years, as predicted by an astrologer, was running true to form. Having provided for my immediate material needs, I could now concentrate on the long-range project of re-establishing myself as a painter." [11]

Man Ray loved Los Angeles as a surreal city: the eccentricity, the multiplicity of shapes, the incongruous juxtapositions of imagery from all places and times, the glitter, the hard edge, the bright sunshine, the outrageous colors, the palm trees, the beaches. Suggested in such paintings as the highly autobiographical *Night Sun—Abandoned Playground* (1943), Man Ray's Los Angeles, like that of Christopher Isherwood, anticipated the pop-surreal paradise of the 1960s David Hockney era. If the homosexuals had their golden boys at poolside, Man Ray had Ava Gardner, whom he photographed lovingly in his studio in 1950. He later remembered her as the perfect emblem, the distilled essence, of all the astonishingly beautiful women he was seeing everywhere in L.A.

Although his lifestyle differed from the bohemianism of Man Ray, another Russo-Parisian, Igor Stravinsky, was doing equally well in exile. Born in Russia of Polish descent in 1882, Stravinsky emigrated to Switzerland in 1914 before settling in France, where he lived from 1920 to 1939, becoming a French citizen in 1929. In September 1939, when the war broke out, Stravinsky was at Harvard delivering the Charles Eliot Norton Lectures, which were later published in English as *The Poetics of Music* (1947). Moving on to Chicago, Stravinsky finished his *Symphony in C*, which the Chicago Symphony premiered on 7 December 1940 with Stravinsky conducting. The war in Europe, together with the warm reception Stravinsky received at Harvard and Chicago, convinced him, if convincing were necessary, to remain in the United States. But where to settle? *Fantasia* and the climate of Southern California answered the question.

Like so many other émigrés, Stravinsky chose Southern California in part for his health. He had already suffered a bout of tuberculosis, the dreaded disease that had carried off his first wife and their daughter. Just before Christmas 1939, Stravinsky traveled west to visit the Disney Studio, where the music from his *Le Sacre du printemps* (1912) was being scored to a story line suggesting the evolution of the galaxies, solar system, and Planet Earth through the era of the dinosaurs. As far back as 1935, Walt Disney had been excited by the prospect of visualizing *Rite of Spring* in an epic film that would break new ground for animation as an art form. The Disney Studio first contacted Stravinsky in Paris in April 1938 and requested film rights to *Rite of Spring*. Cagily, Disney's representatives informed Stravinsky that if he did not accept their offer, the *Rite of Spring* could be used anyway since it was not copyrighted in the United States. Wisely, Stravinsky signed a contract for $6,000 in January 1939. Visiting the Disney Studio in the company of choreographer George Balanchine in December 1939, Stravinsky was delighted by the storyboards and models for the *Rite of Spring* sequence and the soundtrack recorded by the Philadelphia Orchestra under the direction of Leopold

Stokowski. When *Fantasia* premiered at the Broadway Theater in New York on 13 November 1940, Stravinsky felt, for the first time perhaps, the possibility of connecting with popular culture in the United States as represented by Hollywood.

Settled briefly from March to April 1941 in Beverly Hills, followed by a permanent move to North Wetherly Drive in Hollywood, Stravinsky began his Los Angeles life. Like most successful émigrés, Stravinsky worked by the clock: calisthenics in the morning, followed by an uninterrupted sequence of composition, followed by lunch at two, followed by a game of Chinese checkers, followed by a nap, followed by a walk and more work before the evening meal. Writers Franz Werfel, Lion Feuchtwanger, and Thomas Mann followed similar schedules, day in, day out, six days a week, working in exile as if they were yet in the heart of Europe in a time of prosperity and peace. In general, the émigrés avoided—the successful ones, at least—the irregular, frenetic work pace of Hollywood in favor of the slow, steady, cumulative commitment of the artist who is capable of living by his work. To the *Symphony in C* completed in 1940, Stravinsky added a *Symphony in Three Movements* (1942/1945), a *Mass* (1944/1947), the *Concerto in D* (1946), and the *Rake's Progress* (1948/1951), for which W. H. Auden did the libretto, based on the series of illustrations by William Hogarth, which Stravinsky first saw in 1947 at the Art Institute in Chicago.

While Stravinsky did not experience the success he had hoped for as a film composer, he was able to salvage unused film scores for his serious music. Music he wrote for Columbia in 1942, for example, for a film dealing with the Norwegian Resistance, *The Commandos Strike at Dawn* (1943), was salvaged for the concert piece *Four Norwegian Moods* (1942). Music he wrote for the "Apparition of the Virgin" sequence for the film version of *The Song of Bernadette* (Franz Werfel and Stravinsky were close friends), while rejected for the film, was later recycled as part of the *Symphony in Three Movements*. Stravinsky's continuing interest in popular music is evident in *Tango* (1940), composed for the Werner Janssen Orchestra of Los Angeles, the *Scherzo à la Russe* (1944), composed at the request of Paul Whiteman, and the *Ebony Concerto* (1945), composed for Woody Herman. When toward the end of 1941 the Ringling Brothers and Barnum & Bailey Circus approached Stravinsky to write music for an elephant dance to be choreographed by Balanchine, Stravinsky threw himself enthusiastically into the composition of the *Circus Polka* (1942). Premiering in Madison Square Garden on 9 April 1942, this delightful contribution to circus music and choreography (the dancing of the elephants Modoc and Zorina was especially pleasing, and Balanchine gave them bows to the applause) by two important European émigrés said something special—as had *Fantasia*—about the possibilities of émigré creativity connecting with American popular culture.

Stravinsky, of course, was building upon an entire decade of Euro-American musical connections, in film scores especially, as represented in the work of the Russian-born Dimitri Tiomkin, the Polish-born Franz Waxman, and the

Austrian-born Max Steiner and Erich Wolfgang Korngold. In Berlin Waxman had orchestrated and conducted the score for *The Blue Angel*. Arriving from Vienna in 1929, Max Steiner wrote more than three hundred film scores, including the spectacularly successful music for *King Kong* (1933), *The Informer* (1935), and *Gone with the Wind* (1939), whose Tara theme is one of the best known pieces of American music. Korngold first came to Hollywood in 1934 to score the background music for *Midsummer Night's Dream* (1934). Commuting between Hollywood and Vienna, Korngold saw the Nazi handwriting on the wall early enough to smuggle his family and his furniture out of Austria before the *Anschluss* and to settle permanently in Hollywood. The music Korngold wrote for such films as *Green Pastures* (1936), *Anthony Adverse* (1936), *Robin Hood* (1938), and *The Sea Hawk* (1940) set even higher standards for film music. A man of some means, Korngold could pick and choose his projects and could coax studio heads to higher levels of taste than could normally be expected. Korngold continued writing for concert performance as well as for films during these years, transferring some of his film music into a violin concerto and a symphony.

The Hungarian-born composer Miklos Rozsa likewise continued parallel careers as film and concert performance composer. Arriving in Hollywood in 1940, Rozsa composed the scores for Alexander Korda's productions of *The Thief of Baghdad* (1940), *That Hamilton Woman* (1941), and *The Jungle Book* (1942). Meanwhile, he continued to compose for the concert stage. In November 1943 a very young Leonard Bernstein conducted Rozsa's *Theme, Variations, and Finale* in a concert broadcast live from Carnegie Hall. Although Miklos Rozsa did not drink, he provided an absolutely nerve-wracking score depicting the physical and psychological devastations of alcoholism in *The Lost Weekend* (1945), which won him an Academy Award. That year as well, Rozsa joined a fellow émigré, director Alfred Hitchcock, and scored the music for *Spellbound* (1945), another film *noir* thriller.

Settled in as professor of music at Mills College in Oakland on the east side of San Francisco Bay, French émigré composer Darius Milhaud looked forward with relish to his annual working visits to Hollywood, where he earned extra money in film work and enjoyed socializing with Stravinsky, René Clair, Jean Renoir, and other members of the French community. Despite the stresses of the war—exile, worry about friends and relatives, so many of them fated to perish in the Holocaust—the war years were extraordinarily fruitful for Milhaud. Not only did he complete an astonishing array of music while teaching at Mills and writing for the studios, his music—which must be considered challenging for the tastes of America at the time—received premiere performances from the St. Louis Symphony Orchestra, the San Francisco Symphony Orchestra, the United States Marine Corps Orchestra in Washington, and the New York Philharmonic.

The fact is: émigré composers did well in Hollywood and the rest of the country. Writing impressive film scores for their support and, secondarily, their aesthetic satisfaction, the Hollywood composers, paychecks in hand, could also turn to more high-brow efforts supported by, among other groups, the Los Angeles chapter of Pro Musica, which sponsored performances of their more challenging music. They could also hang out with each other at the monthly dinners of the Crescendo Club, where in addition to running into composers and musicians from the studios they might schmooze with the likes of Sergei Rachmaninoff, Artur Rubinstein, and Jascha Heifetz.Everyone, that is, except atonalist Arnold Schoenberg, teaching at UCLA, who tended to keep his distance.

So did Bertolt Brecht. Some German émigrés, in fact, could never adjust to Southern California. Arnold Schoenberg and the novelists Heinrich Mann and Alfred Doblin come immediately to mind. Yet no single émigré better embodied the outer limits of alienation than the German Marxist playwright Bertolt Brecht, who from 1941 to 1947 lived on 25th Street in Santa Monica, struggling on the margins of the film industry. In terms of speech, dress, demeanor, and attitude, Brecht made no effort whatsoever to accommodate himself to capitalist California. Eschewing Southern California sport clothes as well as the business suits of his bourgeois colleagues, Brecht—a gnome of a man with thin lips, close-cropped hair, owlish rimmed glasses, the eyes of a Stalinist inquisitor—dressed defiantly as if he were living in a workers' commune: flannel jacket, shirt open at the collar, jeans or canvas pants, industrial boots. When Brecht recited his poems at a Jewish club in Los Angeles, a tailor in the audience offered to make him a new suit, and an optician volunteered to grind him a new pair of glasses. Brecht accepted the suit but preferred to keep his owlish hornrims. When he wore the suit, he ceased to look like a worker and was transformed instead into an out-of-favor commissar, recently sentenced to the gulag.

Brecht had extremely bad teeth, which he rarely brushed, and he smoked very cheap and terrible-smelling cigars, whose stench, combined with body odor (Brecht rarely bathed) and a malodorous foot fungus, rendered Brecht a party of one in the making. (Elsa Lanchester, Charles Laughton's wife, claimed that her house smelled of cigar smoke and other odors for days after Brecht had been there.) At home in Santa Monica, Brecht lived in Marxist-monastic severity: a few books, a typewriter, some copies of *Freies Deutschland*, a Communist magazine published in Mexico. His one indulgence seems to have been women: his wife the actress Helene Weigel, his mistress the actress Ruth Berlau, who lived nearby, and other women of the Marxist-Stalinist persuasion willing to put aside Brecht's failings so as to bed down with the next best thing to Stalin himself.

Some of Brecht's poverty was a pose, especially after the war. On the other hand, Brecht was truly broke in the early years of his Santa Monica sojourn, getting by on a $125 monthly stipend from the studios until Fritz Lang hired him to collaborate with veteran screenwriter John Wexley on *Hangmen Also Die* (1943), for which Brecht was paid $150 a week. Wexley received $1,500 a week, by contrast, and the Screenwriters Guild awarded him full credit for the script after a bitter dispute. But then again: Brecht earned $20,000 for rights to a screenplay about the French Resistance, which he co-authored with Lion Feuchtwanger. Throughout his time in Southern California, Brecht lived adequately if austerely, and he does not seem to warrant the image, partly of his own devising, of being the neglected genius in capitalist Hollywood, which his admirers continue to perpetuate.

If Brecht seemed so at odds with Southern California, with Los Angeles and Hollywood, it was because he wanted it that way. Brecht brought to the Coast a high level of Marxist alienation, and this in turn determined what he saw and how he felt. He refused to sightsee, for example, and considered picturesque Westside Los Angeles, with its beaches and palm trees, a "metropolitan Tahiti," superficial in the sunshine, incongruous in the mind when one contrasted it to the war raging on the other side of the planet. The only local landscapes to which he could relate with any degree of affinity were the industrialized areas of southern Los Angeles County and the San Pedro waterfront. (Brecht's disaffinity was shared by many émigrés who could not adjust to the unreality of sunshine and beaches and beautiful boys and girls, all of it in such contrast to the horror they had fled.) Brecht brought a vision of America with him: the vision of the United States as capitalist-gangster nightmare that pervades his play *St. Joan of the Stockyards* (1932). In one sense, Brecht had already been to Los Angeles before he arrived. It was the City of Mahagonny as depicted in his play *The Rise and Fall of the City of Mahagonny*, a city in which the lack of money was the only capital crime and greed and self-indulgence the only civic duties. On stage in Leipzig in March 1930, Brecht had previewed his play, with music by Kurt Weill, and now in Los Angeles he found in perfection the laissez-faire dystopia his imagined Mahagonny had embodied.

In and behind the ferocious hate poems Brecht wrote to Los Angeles in his exile, one senses a perfect congruence between prior need and encountered city. As a Marxist, Brecht needed Mahagonny, needed Los Angeles, needed Hollywood to confirm his convictions of capitalist debacle. In his six-part "Hollywood Elegies," Brecht distilled an indictment against the film industry—its worship of money, its devaluation of art, its commercialization of sex, the distraction it offers a consumerist society—which has remained so persistent, before, during, and after Brecht, as to become a strategy of survival, an inoculation, for Hollywood itself. Nevertheless, Brecht—who, as recent research has shown, stole the work of his mistresses and passed it off as his own, thus out-Hollywooding Hollywood itself—was honest enough to see himself as part of the problem.

Brecht had a way of infuriating people in the Hollywood community who might have been of use to him, such as Orson Welles, who loathed Brecht: the Byronic, self-indulgent Welles, his face and frame already showing signs of filling out with good living, affronted by the wry, lean, foul-smelling, crew-cut commissar with comparable pretensions to genius. Such an instinctive disaffinity, however, was not extended to Charles Laughton, despite Laughton's comparable portliness, self-indulgent romanticism, and distaste for politics or ideologies of any sort. Polar opposites, Brecht and Laughton met at Salka Viertel's in 1943 and fell into a kind of love with each other that remained platonic, Brecht being a committed heterosexual, but brought to Brecht nevertheless the one close friendship of his Southern California sojourn. In his poetry Brecht humorously chided Laughton for his weight and praised Laughton's garden overlooking Santa Monica Bay.

Laughton spoke no German, and Brecht little English, but intermittently through 1943, 1944, 1945, and 1946 the two of them collaborated in the library of Laughton's home in Pacific Palisades or outdoors in the garden on a recasting into English of Brecht's play *Galileo*, first drafted in 1938. Despite all the complaining and bitterness of Brecht's Los Angeles years, the *Galileo* he co-authored with Laughton may very well be his masterpiece. Certainly, under Laughton's influence—and perhaps under the influence of Southern California, a metropolitan Tahiti divorced from European obsession—Brecht laid aside the aggressive Marxist argument of *Galileo* so evident in the 1938 draft and achieved instead a more human, a more open, a more Charles Laughton–like hero. *Galileo* premiered at the Coronet Theatre in Hollywood on 30 July 1947 with Laughton in the lead. The cream of émigré Los Angeles, led off by the Thomas Manns, and the best of Hollywood—Charles Chaplin, Charles Boyer, Ingrid Bergman, Van Heflin—were in the audience. At long last, Brecht had his Hollywood triumph. Less than three months later, Brecht multiply perjured himself in Washington before the House Commitee on Un-American Activities, then fled the country.

By this time, Brecht's fellow Berliner Marlene Dietrich had become a national heroine for her work at the front during World War II. Dietrich left the United States for her first USO tour in February 1944 in the company of the young Lebanese-American comedian Danny Thomas, who acted as her master of ceremonies, singer Milton Frome, and pianist Jack Schneider, who also played the accordion. She traveled with fifty-five pounds of baggage, which included four wrinkle-resistent sequinned evening dresses and her musical saw, which she had learned to play in Berlin. Traveling from base to base in North Africa, Dietrich opened her act with a rendition of "See What the Boys in the Back Room Will Have," followed with a performance (as if to emphasize the point of the song) on the musical saw, which she held between her legs. The troops inevitably went bananas, filling the tent or the outdoor amphitheater with a whining, high-pitched noise suggestive of an entire species in heat.

It was the cry of eros over thanatos, life over death, which Freud had declared in the opening days of the war in *Civilization and Its Discontents* (1940) to be the real issue behind the conflict: the battle as to whether the destructive forces of darkness and death would in their ancient enmity rise up once again and extinguish life. Throughout the war, Dietrich was worried about her mother and sister in Berlin. She later learned that her sister had been arrested and taken as a hostage. In the hospitals of North Africa and Italy, she saw the burned and broken boys, American and German; and later, on her second tour, moving into Germany itself, Dietrich went to the concentration camp at Belsen and examined body after body after body in search of her sister, whom Goebbels had ordered arrested in an effort to dissuade Dietrich from touring the front. Miraculously, both Dietrich's mother and sister survived the conflict. But so many of the young men who cried out for her when she was on stage did not survive, including many of those who were there to greet her for her first show in February 1944 at the Opera House in Algiers. A bomb fell during the performance and knocked out all power. But the men yelled, "On with the show!" and thousands of Army-issue flashlights were turned on the stage, and Marlene Dietrich stepped into this light and sang, and for one glorious moment Hollywood as Berlin was receiving from the American people an even better tribute than it could ever possibly give itself.

13

From Catastrophe to Covenant

Jews and Christians in Exile Together

AN estimated two hundred thousand refugees from Germany and Austria fled to the United States between 1933 and 1941. Ten thousand settled in greater Los Angeles. Half of these were Jews. Jews and Christians alike, they represented the most complete migration of artists and intellectuals in European history. In Southern California, they remained what they had been: Jews, Christians, Europeans; but they also came into a new relationship to each other, this remnant of a better Europe, yet bearing within itself the many tensions and contradictions, the subeval antipathies, that in Europe had erupted into war and genocidal rage. Here they were, together beneath the sunny blue skies and palm trees, common victims of a horror that was feeding itself on a hatred that was bad enough at the best of times but had by now become a monstrous, hideous thing that could barely be named and would only reveal its final evil when the camps were liberated.

Naturally, in their life and art, they turned to their own traditions, to the mindsets and protocols of Jewish and Christian Europe. But because they were together, comparable victims—learning the same new language and an even more strange new country, observing the same alien curfew, working at the same studios, meeting together on the same Sundays at Salka Viertel's home in Santa Monica, bearing the same shame of a shared German civilization gone berserk—they also faced each other with a special intensity and a very urgent need for continuing dialogue, lest their mutual flight lose its mutual meaning, or worse, lest what happened in Europe happen to them as well, if only on a petty scale. They were the remnant, Jews and Christians together. What did they have to say to each other? What did they have to say to themselves? What was the salvageable meaning of their Europe in the context of the Southern California that had welcomed them?

Persecution began as soon as Hitler attained power. Not only was novelist Lion Feuchtwanger Jewish, he had had the temerity to satirize Hitler in *Success* (1929), a novel based on the failed putsch of 1923. Portraying Hitler as Rudolf Kutzner, a thoroughly vulgar fellow, Feuchtwanger added insult to injury when he dismissed the prose of *Mein Kampf* as clumsy, ungrammatical, filled with solecisms. Not surprisingly, given Hitler's concept of himself as an artist, Feuchtwanger had the distinction of appearing on the first list of Germans deprived of citizenship, issued on 23 August 1933. Feuchtwanger's home on Mahlerstrasse in Berlin was confiscated, together with his ten-thousand-volume library. Lecturing in the United States at the time, Feuchtwanger was being honored in Washington at a banquet attended by Herbert Hoover and the German ambassador at the very moment the revocation of his citizenship and his University of Munich doctorate was being announced in Germany. A few days later, a sympathetic German consul general in New York warned Feuchtwanger that to return to Germany would be to invite death.

Novelist Franz Werfel likewise decided not to return to Vienna in May of 1933 when the Nazis placed his books on their proscribed list, along with those of Erich Maria Remarque, whose *All Quiet on the Western Front* (1929) ranked alongside Martin Luther's translation of the Bible and Hitler's *Mein Kampf* as one of three all-time best-sellers in the German language. (Hitler despised Remarque's pacifism.) Composer Arnold Schoenberg lost his German citizenship at this time as well. Fleeing to Paris, Schoenberg formally reentered the Judaism of his ancestors. Among non-Jews, Heinrich Mann, president of the Prussian Academy of Literature, had signed a manifesto just before Hitler had come to power calling on socialists and Communists to form a united front against the Nazis. Deprived of citizenship, Heinrich Mann secured a Czech passport. His fellow non-Jewish leftist playwright Bertolt Brecht was stripped of his citizenship in June 1935. Heinrich Mann's brother Thomas kept silent for three more years. He later claimed that it was out of loyalty to his German publisher, but in 1936 Thomas Mann followed his brother to Czechoslovakia.

Many refugees eventually reconvened in Sanary-sur-Mer on the French Riviera, a resort town destined to function as a way station between Berlin/Vienna and Los Angeles/Hollywood. In climate and seaside setting, Sanary-sur-Mer anticipated the lifestyle of Southern California. With its sunshine and beaches, its creamy-walled, red-tile-roofed villas, and its profusion of fruits and flowers, Sanary-sur-Mer accustomed such émigrés as Thomas and Katia Mann, Franz and Alma Werfel, Ludwig Marcuse, and Lion and Marta Feuchtwanger to an outdoor, beach-oriented lifestyle—swimming in the morning, lunch on the terrace, walks in the late afternoon—which they would find to perfection in Southern California. At Sanary-sur-Mer, Feuchtwanger acquired Villa Valmer, his second grand home, and began to assemble yet another library of reference books.

Then came the invasion of France in June 1940, and the idyll of Sanary-sur-

Mer crumbled as well. Thomas Mann described the flight of the émigré artists and intellectuals as "a civilian Dunkirk—a retreat that was so difficult and successful as to merit the name of victory."[1] If so, it was a victory for the privileged few. The Emergency Rescue Committee established by Roosevelt was interested in refugees of prominence and achievement, and before the United States entered the war such refugees, provided they had the means, could easily enter the United States. On their behalf, the American journalist Varian Fry set up an underground railroad in France and Spain, which rescued thousands. The rest went behind barbed wire and, eventually, into the gas chambers. Others—the Thomas Manns, the Franz Werfels, the Lion Feuchtwangers—had the help of the Emergency Rescue Committee to get them out of France and across the Pyrenees to Spain, from where they could travel to Lisbon, then on to New York.

Caught in Lourdes on 27 June 1940, a distraught Franz Werfel, a Jew with strong Roman Catholic sympathies, drank of the spring at the religious shrine there and vowed that he would write the story of the teenaged peasant Bernadette Soubirous, to whom a mysterious Lady was said to have appeared in 1858, if and when he reached safety. Despite his corpulence and shortness of breath, Werfel made it across the Pyrenees on the night of 12 September 1940 along with his much older wife Alma (who seemed to take the hike with ease), the seventy-year-old Heinrich Mann, and Mann's nephew Golo. Starting their hike at noon, the Werfels and the Manns followed a network of steep goat paths across the mountains until they came to a small customs station where the Spanish guard let them through. Reaching Barcelona, the refugees caught a night train to Madrid, where they transferred to a Lisbon train. In Lisbon they secured passage to New York on the Greek steamship *Nea Hellas*.

Lion Feuchtwanger was not so lucky. Soon after the invasion, Feuchtwanger found himself in a Vichy concentration camp in Les Mille. A photograph of Feuchtwanger standing behind barbed wire went out on the wires and appeared in a number of American newspapers. Seeing the photograph, First Lady Eleanor Roosevelt interested herself in Feuchtwanger's rescue. Under the infamous Clause Nineteen of the agreement between Vichy and the Nazis, Feuchtwanger was scheduled to be turned over to the Germans, which would have meant his eventual but certain death. Working with the American consul general Miles Standish, Marta Feuchtwanger arranged her husband's escape from Les Mille. Feuchtwanger was allowed a daily swim just outside the camp. The day before the escape, Marta had a note smuggled in to her husband that said in German: "Ask nothing. Don't talk to anyone about this. Leave all belongings behind."[2] The next day, Feuchtwanger was swimming in the pond when Standish's chauffeured limousine drove up bearing the license plates of the United States consular corps. Standish pushed the door open and told Feuchtwanger to get in. Feuchtwanger leapt into the limousine in his bathing suit. Following Standish's directions, he hastily put on a woman's coat, scarf, and dark glasses. Standish spirited Feuchtwanger from the camp, telling guards that the lady in his car was his mother-in-law. From there, the American Unitarian minister Hastings Waitstill Sharp assisted the Feuchtwangers across the Pyrenees.

Even aboard ship, a refugee's life was not safe. Sailing on the *City of Benares*, Monica Mann, Thomas Mann's daughter, and her husband, the art historian Jeno Lanyi, were torpedoed by a German submarine. Pulled into a lifeboat, Monica Mann watched her husband drown before her eyes.

Once in the United States, the three German-language authors with the strongest European reputations—Franz Werfel, Lion Feuchtwanger, and Thomas Mann—each did exceedingly well in their new circumstances. Two others, Heinrich Mann and Alfred Doblin, failed completely to connect. Werfel, Feuchtwanger, and Thomas Mann seemed hardly to miss a literary or financial beat despite all they had been through. All three had been prosperous for a number of years in Europe and continued to prosper in Southern California, even though the European market had collapsed, from new work completed or from American royalties on translations of previous publications. Franz Werfel's *The Forty Days of Musadagh* (1934), for example, a novel dealing with the Armenian resistance to their genocide by the Turks, not only made Werfel a revered figure in the international Armenian community—as he would soon become among Roman Catholics with the publication of *The Song of Bernadette* (1942)—*Forty Days* kept steadily selling through the 1930s and continued to pay royalties through the 1940s from its many translations. No sooner had Werfel walked down the gangplank in Hoboken, temporarily broke (with the exception of the jewels Alma Mahler Werfel had secreted in her handbag), than *Harper's Bazaar* commissioned him to do an article. A week later, the Book-of-the-Month Club published Werfel's *Embezzled Heaven* (1940), and it sold 150,000 copies. Six months before publication, *The Song of Bernadette*, Werfel's novel of Lourdes, was selected as the main choice of the Book-of-the-Month Club—a surprising selection, given the Roman Catholic focus of the material. Viking issued a first printing of two hundred thousand, which it augmented with another hundred thousand copies three weeks later. By Christmas 1943 *The Song of Bernadette* had sold more than a million copies, with the Armed Forces purchasing fifty thousand copies in a special edition. By Werfel's death in 1945, *The Song of Bernadette* had become one of the top best-sellers in American publishing history. Twentieth Century–Fox paid Werfel $125,000 for film rights, an extraordinarily high fee for the time. Even Thomas Mann, usually so Olympian in his detachment, found himself disconcerted by the scale of Werfel's royalties.

In the fall of 1942, Franz and Alma Werfel moved into a spacious Spanish Revival home at 610 North Bedford Drive, Beverly Hills, at the corner of Santa Monica Boulevard, diagonally across from the Church of the Good Shepherd. August Hess, a forty-year-old operetta tenor who had defected from Germany with his troupe, served the Werfels as chef, butler, all-round handyman, and chauffeur of the Werfels' sleek new Oldsmobile. Werfel engaged a German-speaking private secretary, Albrecht Joseph, succeeded in 1945 by William Melnitz, to do research and take dictation. To replace the wardrobe left behind in Sanary-sur-Mer, Werfel had recourse to the London Shop on Rodeo Drive, where he purchased a rack of expensive English-cut suits. Despite the efforts of his tailors, Werfel soon reduced each suit to a rumple, flecked with cigar ash and food stains from elaborate meals at Chasen's and Romanoff's. On 17 April 1943 the Werfels enjoyed a duck dinner at Romanoff's with their guests Thomas and Katia Mann and the Manns' daughter Erika. (The next day, Mann noted in his diary that the duck was not up to Romanoff's best standards.) In April and May 1942, the émigré community went into crisis when their Japanese gardeners, housemaids, cooks, and chauffeurs were sent to the internment camps.

Lion Feuchtwanger was only slightly behind Werfel in financial success, helped by the fact that Feuchtwanger's European royalties were banked, hence available, in Switzerland and that his historical novels were continuing to sell throughout the world in numerous translations, including English editions in the United States. Ever since his best-seller *Judd Suss*, released in the United States under the title *Power* (1918), Lion Feuchtwanger had been having no trouble making money by his pen. He had, indeed, written a novel, *Erflog* (1930), published in English as *Success*, that celebrated with Dreiserian gusto and ambivalence the rewards of money and power. Feuchtwanger resembled Dreiser, in point of fact, in his obsession with status and wealth, his love of luxury, his womanizing, and his far left political sympathies. Like Werfel, who was born in Prague to prosperous glove manufacturers, Feuchtwanger came from wealth as well, in his case a Munich banking and legal dynasty.

An epicure, oenophile, and ardent bibliophile, an avid amorist and gambler, Feuchtwanger required—and earned!—steady streams of money to afford the excellence and variety in food, wine, books, and adventures in bed and at the gaming table his insistent sensuality constantly craved. When barely off the boat in Hoboken, Feuchtwanger was receiving royalty checks. His first address in New York was a suite in the Hotel St. Moritz overlooking Central Park. Having lost homes and libraries in Berlin and Sanary-sur-Mer, Feuchtwanger established himself for a third time in Pacific Palisades at 520 Paseo Miramar, a Spanish Revival twenty-room villa on a bluff, with a breathtaking view of Santa Monica Bay. Surrounded by extensive lawns, fruit trees, and flowers, Feuchtwanger's Villa Aurora, as he named it, soon housed yet a third library of reference and rare books, one of the finest of its kind in the country, which Feuchtwanger bought from catalogs and from Los Angeles book dealers, who were in turn buying their German-language books from less fortunate émigrés forced to peddle them to survive.

No wonder a note of ambivalence toward Feuchtwanger creeps into émigré accounts of his prosperity. "Yesterday we were at the Feuchtwangers' for tea," wrote émigré writer Hermann Kesten. "This is how all writers should live, in a castle by the sea, on a hill, with a view in different directions of the sea and the mountains, twenty rooms, with 11,000 books, among them first editions, Bodoni printings, Aldine editions, etc., with banana, orange, and lemon trees, eucalyptus trees, with a hilly park of two acres, a secretary and a wife who cooks, gardens, rakes, chauffeurs and serves the great poet with devotion." [3] Photographs from the period back Kesten's description, if not his ambivalence. They depict Feucht-wanger in the sunlight before his collection of cactus orchids, exercising on his terrace before a day of dictation, standing in his library in an impeccably tailored suit, lunching in a sun-drenched courtyard. The secretary referred to by Kesten was Hilde Waldo, to whom Feuchtwanger dictated his novels, sometimes at the rate of seven typewritten pages an hour. The novels Feuchtwanger dictated in Pacific Palisades, where he lived until his death in 1958, sold well. The Literary Guild purchased *Simone* (1944) and *Proud Destiny* (1947). *This Is the Hour* (1951), based on the life of the Spanish painter Goya, was bought by the Book-of-the-Month Club and sold six hundred thousand copies in its German edition. Samuel Goldwyn purchased the screen rights for *Simone* at six figures, and there were major screen purchases as well for *Proud Destiny* and *This Is the Hour.*

Thomas Mann, by contrast, derived his prosperity not from Hollywood, with which he never connected, but from the sale of his books in English translation from the publisher Alfred A. Knopf, lecture fees, and a generous stipend from the Library of Congress. A Nobel laureate in literature, the quintessence of upper-middle-class Protestant German civilization, liberal and humanistic — Thomas Mann instantly became the émigré of choice for the New Deal. Mann saw himself especially reflected in the equally patrician Franklin Delano Roosevelt, and Roosevelt in turn treated Mann with the courtesy accorded an exiled head of state. On 14–15 January 1941 Thomas and Katia Mann stayed as guests of the Roosevelts in the White House. Events included cocktails in the President's study (the time, place, and social occasion in which FDR exercised his greatest charm) followed by a companionable dinner. In the preface to *Joseph the Provider* (1944), Mann praised Roosevelt as "an American Hermes, a brilliant messenger of shrewdness whose New Deal is unmistakably reflected in Joseph's administration of the national economy." The New Deal establishment, for its part, returned Thomas Mann's esteem. In September 1940 a generous loan from the Reconstruction Finance Corporation allowed Mann to build a spacious home in Pacific Palisades. In December 1941 Archibald MacLeish, the Harvard poet then serving as Librarian of Congress, appointed Mann Consultant in German Literature, with light duties and a salary of $4,800 a year. When Mann lectured at the library on 17 November 1942, he was introduced by Vice President Henry Wallace as well as by MacLeish. Attorney General Francis Biddle and a raft of New Deal notables sat in the audience.

Mann's brother Heinrich, meanwhile, most likely spent the evening in his shabby apartment in Los Angeles. Not every émigré was as successful as Werfel,

Feuchtwanger, and Thomas Mann. Even at its most comfortable, exile is a bitter thing, and when exile is characterized by poverty, neglect, and alienation, it becomes a terrible ordeal. Many refugees from the Nazis lost hope and destroyed themselves before reaching the United States. Having escaped across France, social philosopher Walter Benjamin poisoned himself on the Spanish frontier on 26 September 1940 when the mayor of a local village threatened to turn his party back. Incarcerated with Feuchtwanger at Les Mille, the poet-novelist Walter Hasenclever grew progressively distraught about his prospects for survival. He asked Feuchtwanger what he thought their chances were for escape. Answering truthfully, Feuchtwanger put them at 5 percent. Shortly thereafter, Hasenclever swallowed a lethal dose of Veronal. For the rest of his life, Feuchtwanger blamed himself for not lying.

Even after reaching safety, certain émigrés reached the decision not to go on living. Expressionist poet and playwright Ernst Toller committed suicide in New York in 1939. In February 1942 writer Stefan Zweig and his wife Lotte, each convinced that civilization as they knew it had come to an end, committed suicide in Rio de Janeiro. The most noted suicide among the Los Angeles émigrés was Heinrich Mann's wife Nelly Kroger Mann. Nelly Mann's suicide was all the more poignant because she, unlike the others, was not an intellectual or an artist committing suicide on a grand stage for heroic reasons of war and peace, Nazism and civilization. Nelly Kroger Mann was a simple woman, a barmaid from Hamburg given to drink. Blonde, blue-eyed, buxom, thirty years younger than her husband, Nelly had been Heinrich Mann's mistress in Nice before the war: a *zaftig* and kind Lola-Lola to Heinrich's Professor Unrat. Heinrich had married Nelly for the sake of love and her German passport. While Lola-Lola brought Unrat to destruction in *The Blue Angel*, Nelly became the loving companion and financial support of her husband as he became progressively more isolated and confused. An outspoken Socialist, earlier and more daringly anti-Nazi than his brother, Heinrich Mann had served as the president of the German Popular Front while living in Nice in the late 1930s.

Known and revered throughout the German-speaking world as a writer and social spokesman, Heinrich Mann was seventy when he reached Hollywood in 1940. For his first year in Los Angeles, Mann had a make-work job as a scriptwriter at Warner Brothers. It paid a comfortable $100 a week. Old, isolated, unfamiliar with English, the author of *The Blue Angel* sat for a year in his office doing nothing, a man lost in time and place, before being discharged in October 1941. Nelly went to work as a practical nurse to support herself and her husband. For three years, she (who might have been First Lady in a Socialist Germany) struggled with a fatiguing hospital schedule and a growing proclivity for alcohol. This being Los Angeles, she had to drive to and from work. Arrested on a number of occasions for drunk driving, Nelly was placed on court probation. Ordered to appear in court for yet another offense, she panicked and took sleeping pills, putting an end, as her friend Salka Viertel put it, "to her constant tussle with the police, her struggle with a language she could never learn, her fear of aging, and her losing battle with liquor."[4]

Taken cumulatively, in success and failure, German-speaking Los Angeles/Hollywood constituted its own distinctive time and place: bonded by language and an unwavering conviction of moral superiority over those prominent intellectuals and artists—actor Emil Jannings, composers Richard Strauss and Franz Lehar (Hitler loved *The Merry Widow* and made Lehar's half-Jewish wife an honorary Aryan), poet Gerhart Hauptmann, poet and critic Gottfried Benn, philosopher Martin Heidegger, Nobel physicist Philipp Lenard, director Gustav Grundgens—who remained behind and cooperated. Whether or not German Los Angeles had become the new Weimar (Thomas Mann claimed that all of German literature had relocated to the United States), it certainly sustained within itself a sense of displaced but defiant caste. "Exile creates a special form of life," Thomas Mann noted, "and the various reasons for banishment or flight make little difference. Whether the cause is leftism or the opposite—the sharing of a common fate and class solidarity are more fundamental than such nuances of opinion, and people find their way to one another."[5]

Mann's remarks were prompted by the mixture of left-wingers and right-wingers he encountered at an émigré party hosted by Count Ostheim, Hohenzollern pretender to the throne of Weimar. Such solidarity also brought together Christian and Jewish émigrés under aristocratic Catholic leadership (a situation that would have been unthinkable in pre-war Germany) when Prince Hubertus zu Loewenstein, a young Catholic nobleman from Bavaria, founded the Anti-Nazi League of Hollywood. A democrat committed to the social philosophy of the papal encyclicals, Prince Hubertus opposed the Nazis not only because they were vulgar but because their social and economic policies were unjust. Fleeing Germany just ahead of the Gestapo, the Prince settled in Los Angeles, where he wrote two books calling for a post-Nazi Fourth Reich based on liberal democratic principles. Unfortunately, not many members of the Catholic center-right followed the Prince to Los Angeles, although a few members of this elite group would attempt to assassinate the Catholic-born Hitler in 1944. Yet for the time being at least, the Prince and his Anti-Nazi League unified Jewish and Christian émigrés.

Another émigré favorite, Prince Max von Hohenlohe, loved to chide the Nazis for their low-born, ambiguously German origins. "I happen to be a member of one of the oldest and most famous families in Germany," the Prince told Erika and Klaus Mann when this brother-and-sister team was researching a book on the émigrés in 1939, "a thing that can hardly be said of that mongrel Austrian, Herr Hitler, whose real name is Schicklgruber, [or] of the 'Deputy of the Fuhrer,' Herr Rudolf Hess, who was born in Egypt, [or] of Dr. Goebbels, with his notoriously un-German looks, or of Herr Rosenberg the Russian."[6]

Aristocratic identities among émigrés, Jewish and Christian alike, reached a high point in a reception given by Emmerich Kalman, composer of such Ruritanian operettas as *The Gypsy Princess* and *Countess Maritza*, for Otto von Hapsburg, who would be sitting on the Austrian throne, had there been one. Hosting the Austro-Hungarian colony to a reception for von Hapsburg in Hollywood, Kalman, the creator of innumerable operettas involving royalty, borrowed a great golden throne from the prop department at MGM and installed it in his living room. "When Otto arrived and saw it," composer Miklos Rozsa later remembered, "he was terrified, refusing not only to sit on the throne but also to sit down at all unless everyone else did. He certainly gave a royal lesson in democracy to his over-solicitous host."[7]

Kalman's party was but one of thousands of émigré gatherings in Los Angeles/ Hollywood before, during, and after the war; for one of the main things the émigrés brought to Southern California was their love of social life. "Where there are good neighbors, good friends, a stimulating circle," noted Katia Mann, "there is life and a feeling of being at home."[8] Central Europeans, given to close quarters and even closer connections of family and caste, loved gossip and festivity, and, as Christopher Isherwood noted (he being an honorary émigré from his longtime residence in Berlin, his fluent German, and his writings), they loved charades and other parlor games. Initially, the eight P.M. curfew directed against enemy aliens, which most of them were, cramped their social style, although they soon got in the habit of gossiping with one another each evening by telephone or giving dinner parties that included an invitation to stay overnight. An inveterate night owl, Bertolt Brecht, Enemy Alien Registration Number 7624464, spent many a night on one or another émigré's couch. Thomas Mann and Albert Einstein appealed directly to President Roosevelt regarding the curfew, and by mid-1943 it had become more honored in the breach than the observance. By 1944 it had become a thing of the past.

With so many émigrés in the area, circles within circles from Europe, old friendships, enmities, and family connections reestablished themselves. As children, Lion Feuchtwanger and Katia Mann had attended school together in Munich. Brecht and Feuchtwanger had known each other for years. Feuchtwanger had profiled Brecht as Caspar Prokl in his novel *Success*, and the two were collaborating through 1941–43 on the play *The Visions of Simone Machard*, based on Feuchtwanger's novel. Erika Mann had studied under Max Reinhardt in Berlin. And besides: almost everyone had been together at Sanary-sur-Mer, and before that in Vienna and Berlin. German-speaking circles, Marta Feuchtwanger later remembered, tended to divide along Austrian and German lines, with the Austrians being more musical and theatrical and the Germans being more literary and academic; yet boundaries were never fixed or precise. Nor did Christians divide themselves from Jews or vice versa. Erika and Klaus Mann described a Westside Los Angeles party in 1939 attended by a mixed group that included actor Peter Lorre, actress Luise Rainer, screenwriter Salka Viertel, composer Franz Waxmann, and directors Fritz Lang, Ernst Lubitsch, and Wilhelm Dieterle. The Franz Werfel circle included conductor Bruno Walter, their next door neighbor in Beverly Hills, the novelist Bruno Frank and his wife, also neighbors, novelist Erich Maria Remarque, Erich and Luizi Korngold (Erich Korngold being the most successful Hollywood composer of them all), the Lion Feuchtwangers, Thomas and Katia Mann, and Gustave Arlt, professor of German at UCLA and Werfel's translator.

Cherubic, child-like, empathetic, Franz Werfel was at the center of a number of circles since his obsession with music, his love of Italian opera, his book on Verdi, and his beautiful singing voice brought him into sympathetic contact with composers and musicians. As a literary man, on the other hand, Werfel also sustained friendships with the Thomas Manns and the Lion Feuchtwangers, although Mann did not consider Werfel (or Feuchtwanger, for that matter) a novelist of the first rank. Werfel became so popular in the Los Angeles area, he was asked to participate in war bond rallies and in 1943 was awarded an honorary doctorate from UCLA. More reserved in their style than Franz and Alma Mahler Werfel, the Thomas Manns tended to entertain German litterateurs such as Werfel, Feuchtwanger, Leonhard Frank, and Bruno Frank, although the Manns also had many friends from the world of music. In July 1942 Lotte Lehmann invited the Manns to her home in Santa Barbara, where they enjoyed tea and German *Lieder*. At literary evenings in Pacific Palisades, Mann would read, after 1945, excerpts from his novel in progress, *Doctor Faustus* (1947).

Ever economical in his writing and amatory life (no assignations until the work day was over), Lion Feuchtwanger arranged his twice-yearly literary evenings for the German-speaking community with the precision of a military campaign. Well in advance of the event, Feuchtwanger's secretary would notify the Brechts, the Dieterles, the Marcuses, both sets of Franks, the Lubitsches, and the others to be at his home at seven-thirty sharp, since Thomas Mann absolutely had to be home by eleven. With everyone gathered, Feuchtwanger would read from a work in progress. If Thomas Mann was present, his would be the first statement of opinion. If there was a second or two of delay before the Kaiser (as Mann was known among the émigrés) spoke, and sometimes there was, as in the case when Feuchtwanger read from *Proud Destiny* [*Waffen fur Amerika*] in early 1946, you could almost hear a sigh of relief when the Kaiser drew a cigarette from his lips and after exhaling in a leisurely manner said: "Well done, Lion."[9] The reading and commentary complete, Marta Feuchtwanger served sherry, Russian salad, and home-made *apfelstrudel* drenched in whipped cream.

A few weeks later, Feuchtwanger would give a similar evening in English for the Charlie Chaplin circle, the English émigrés, and assorted Los Angeles writers and academics. Less conspicuous than these highly stylized events were countless informal gatherings by lesser-known émigrés such as Reinhardt Braun, a novelist and journalist living in a rented apartment in Santa Monica since 1936. The Braun group included a number of German psychiatrists, museum director Karl

With, screenwriter Robert Thoeren, writer Hans Winge, and a bohemian crowd of German- and English-speaking journalists, painters, and sculptors.

Also in Santa Monica, at 165 Mabery Road, just up from the beach, emerged the most interesting and continuous salon of émigré Los Angeles/Hollywood, the Sunday soirees of Salka Viertel. Born in Russia of Polish parents, Salka Viertel had flourished as an actress in Germany before arriving with her husband Berthold in Hollywood in 1927 as part of the first-wave talent drain from Europe in that period. A noted poet as well as director, Berthold Viertel came to Hollywood to work with German-Swedish director F. W. Murnau. At their arrival, Emil Jannings gave the Viertels a welcome party attended by the entire German-language community, including Ernst Lubitsch, Max Reinhardt, and actor Conrad Veidt. Since Berthold had difficulty finding work in Hollywood after Murnau's death, he returned to Europe for long sojourns during the 1930s. And besides: Berthold, a philanderer, preferred to live apart from his wife and three sons for long periods. Hardly at a loss for something to do in either love or work, Salka soon found employment as Greta Garbo's screenwriter at MGM and began holding open house in Santa Monica on Sunday afternoons. By the late 1930s Salka's Sundays had become the most important salon in the émigré community. Regulars included Aldous and Maria Huxley, Charlie Chaplin, Bertrand Russell (then teaching at UCLA), Christopher Isherwood, Charles Laughton and Elsa Lanchester, Greta Garbo (who made an exception to her growing reclusiveness on Salka's behalf), screenwriter Anita Loos, Thomas and Katia Mann and their offspring Erika, Klaus, and Golo, Heinrich and Nelly Mann, Max Reinhardt, his son Gottfried (Salka's acknowledged lover), the Feuchtwangers, the Werfels, Bruno Walter, Erich and Luizi Korngold: virtually the entire spectrum of the creative émigré community, in short, presided over each Sunday by Salka and, after 1941, by Salka and her mother, who had recently escaped across Russia on the trans-Siberian railroad.

Although Salka Viertel's salon continued into the late 1940s, its high point was undoubtedly the black-tie dinner party she hosted for Heinrich Mann's seventieth birthday on 2 May 1941. Everyone came—all the Manns, the Feuchtwangers, the Franks, the Werfels (Alma Mahler Werfel was feuding with Nelly Mann and had to be seated as far from her as possible)—and those who could not be seated were happy to help in the kitchen just to be there. Following the soup course, Thomas Mann rose to his feet, put on his spectacles, and, while the roast beef moved from rare to medium in the oven, read a fifteen-page typewritten tribute to his brother. The roast beef edged into over-done as, following Thomas's tribute, Heinrich rose and answered his brother with what Salka later remembered as a meticulous literary analysis of Thomas Mann's oeuvre as a counter-statement to the Third Reich. Heinrich's speech, Salka Viertel later remembered, "gave one some hope and comfort at a time when the lights of freedom seemed extinguished in Europe, and everything we had loved and valued buried in ruins." As Salka's chocolate cake was being served, Marta Feuchtwanger offered a toast to Nelly

Mann. Nelly, Marta said, had practically carried Heinrich in her arms across the Pyrenees and had remained the courageous emotional center of the émigrés in their flight to the United States. "Nelly hid her face in her hands when we surrounded her to clink glasses," Salka recalled, "and then, screaming with laughter, pointed to her red dress, which had burst open revealing her bosom in a lace bra." [10]

For most of the émigrés, Southern California was at once a problem and a solution. Thomas Mann loved what he termed the Egyptian terrain and climate of the region. "I was enchanted by the light," Mann remembered, "by the special fragrance of the air, by the blue of the sky, the sun, the exhilarating ocean breeze, the spruceness and cleanness of this Southland." [11] Southern California reminded Katia Mann of Israel. For Franz Werfel, it was Tuscany, and he named his Beverly Hills home Tusculum. "The Riviera, " Werfel wrote his parents, "is just trash compared to this." [12] Choreographer George Balanchine could not believe the sunny abundance of the Southland. He would walk through the Farmers Market in Los Angeles just to enjoy the elaborate displays of fruits and produce, which he purchased and arranged in his apartment on North Fairfax Avenue for aesthetic effect. Nor could Balanchine believe the astonishing array of beautiful young women serving as secretaries, waitresses, sales clerks, receptionists—as if all female beauty in America had emigrated to Southern California in the hopes of being discovered by the movies.

Thomas Mann's love of his home in Pacific Palisades is typical of the émigrés' love of their homes and gardens. For screenwriter Vicki Baum the garden of her home in the Santa Monica hills overlooking the city was a metaphor for Southern California itself: the *hortus conclusus*, the enclosed garden of medieval imagination, safe and magical, rediscovered on the shores of the Pacific. Like true southern Californians, the Werfels spent many an hour in their garden, initially at 6900 Los Tilos in the Hollywood Hills, on a slope above the Hollywood Bowl, where they lived before moving to Beverly Hills. On summer evenings, Franz and Alma would sit outdoors and hear the concert from the Bowl below, the night air fragrant with acacia, oleander, and orange blossoms. One of the attractions of the Werfels' second home was its vast enclosed lawn and garden space.

Charles Laughton and Elsa Lanchester, émigrés of sorts, had one of the best-known gardens in the region at their home in Pacific Palisades. A riot of orange and banana trees, fuchsias, camellias, roses, the Laughton garden was especially famous for its night-blooming cereus. Once or twice a year, the Laughtons would give evening parties when the cereus bloomed. Huge perfumed flowers would start to appear at nine in the evening, and by two or so in the morning they had wilted away as guests kept their vigil. Bertolt Brecht wrote a long poem in praise of Laughton's garden when it was threatened by a landslide in August 1944. Entitled "Garden in Progress," Brecht's poem conveys a unique stream of appreciation on his part for at least this small piece of Southern California. For Brecht, the precariousness of this garden, threatened by the collapse of part of Laughton's property to the Pacific Coast Highway below, underscored the precariousness of a world at war, expressed in the thunder of the guns from warships exercising off shore as the night-blooming cereus blooms "with white flowers as big as your fist and as delicate/As a Chinese actor." [13]

Many émigrés were at best indifferent to the constant sunshine. Photographs from the period frequently depict them in dark suits, white shirts, ties, and fedoras as if they were still in *Mitteleuropa*. Novelist Leonhard Frank and the Swiss-German playwright Curt Goetz each claimed that the warmth of Southern California had thinned his blood and made it difficult to write. The Czech writer Joseph Wechsberg believed that the glare of the constant sunlight conferred an over-bright surreality to both the natural and man-made environment. Nearly all of the émigrés missed the change of seasons. Week succeeded week, month succeeded month in an uninterrupted continuum of sunshine. Even Thomas Mann had his reservations. Southern California, he wrote, resisted the touch of his pen. "Here everything blooms in violet and grape colors that look rather made of paper," he noted, "and because one can't appraise them, one can't praise them." Thomas Mann would never find his way to writing a Southern California novel, noted Monica Mann of her father, although he did seriously entertain for a time the idea of writing a novel set in Hollywood. Yet the climate and terrain of Southern California did have an important effect on her father's writing style and literary strategies. "Let me only hint at my belief," she noted, "that the odd elegance of that distant shore, with its almost intangible beauty and worldly barrenness, which surrounded my father for twelve years had a great influence on him and his work. It drove him from his own traditions to stylistic daring and gave him the courage for those linguistic experiments in *The Holy Sinner* and the thoroughly polemic major confession of *Doctor Faustus*. . . . The gleaming emptiness, monotony, and hostility of the landscape ruthlessly threw men—especially those of artistic temper—back on their own resources, so that, mirrored in this almost supernatural setting, the individual essence came to the fore." [14]

Southern California, in short, had an influence on Thomas Mann's German. Given the fact that Mann was one of the most exacting practitioners of literary German, Monica Mann is making a dramatic suggestion. On a number of occasions, Mann stated that his real home was the German language. If so, he must have felt at home in Southern California, where the émigré community was large enough to sustain a complete German-speaking environment. At a Hollywood party, Otto Preminger was alleged to have grown agitated when a number of people began speaking Hungarian. "Don't you guys know you're in Hollywood?" Preminger asked. "Speak German." [15] Living in Hollywood in the early years of the war, Laurence Olivier rented a house on a block where Ernst Lubitsch and others with heavy German accents were serving as blackout wardens. One night, hearing the German accents and even the German conversation of the wardens as they passed down the street making people turn out their lights, Olivier called to a neighbor: "Have we been invaded already? Sounds like the Germans are here."[16] It was so easy to live and work in German in Los Angeles in the early 1940s, Ludwig Marcuse remembered, "I rarely thought there were even Americans here." Only once did Marcuse experience any difficulty by speaking German: a time when he, Bruno Frank, and Alfred Doblin were asked by a restaurant manager to speak English. The three stormed out of the restaurant, but on later reflection Marcuse understood how people who were losing their sons to Germany would be not so eager to hear the German language spoken in a restaurant.[17] By the 1950s some critics were claiming that Lion Feuchtwanger was writing in a German that no longer existed—or existed, rather, as an historical artifact. Feuchtwanger himself worried intensely about being cut off from German as it was going through its post-war changes. Not surprisingly, Southern Californian German stood in danger of becoming a hothouse plant.

By 1941 émigré Los Angeles was as real as any of the other ethnic communities flourishing in the City of the Angels. It even had its own district, the Westside. The more prosperous of the émigrés attached to the entertainment industry—the Werfels, Bruno Walter, Bruno Frank, and others—favored Beverly Hills; less affluent entertainment émigrés settled in the Hollywood Hills and the Fairfax district. The most serious composers—Igor Stravinsky and Arnold Schoenberg most noticeably—formed the core of a Westwood/Brentwood cadre centered on UCLA. Santa Monica, seaside and canyons, nurtured the literary bohemians—Bertolt Brecht, Christopher Isherwood, Salka Viertel—while in nearby Pacific Palisades, serene on the heights, were the Manns and the Feuchtwangers. The arrival of the émigrés accelerated the emergence of the Westside, centered on the movie industry and UCLA, as a flourishing urban Jewish civilization blending characteristics of New York City and pre-Nazi Vienna and Berlin. In and among the palm trees and the creamy-walled, red-roofed bungalows and villas was being consolidated a world center of Jewish civilization electric in intellectual and artistic vitality: its restaurants and cafes packed with convivial crowds, its bakeries and delicatessens overflowing with the wines and foods of Europe, its classrooms dynamic in an atmosphere of upward mobility, its Hillcrest Country Club hilarious with festive talk and show biz schtick.

On the other hand—and this was crucial—while German was spoken in Los Angeles, Los Angeles itself (for the time at least) spoke English as its predominant language. It was, after all, still very much a white Anglo-Saxon Protestant place: from the patricians of Hancock Park, Pasadena, and San Marino to the Folks of Long Beach, to the recycled Dust Bowlers pouring into the defense industry and the staid middle-class establishment in the Downtown. The cops, the firemen, the bartenders, the councilmen, the preachers, the hustlers of every description— in Los Angeles, they spoke English. Novelist Alfred Doblin, for example, author of *Berlin Alexanderplatz* (1929), one of the great urban novels of the century, was a master of the speech, the slang, the jokes, the songs, the headlines, the tough-guy talk of Berlin. Yet he could not hear Los Angeles speaking in English. Los

Angeles German functioned elegantly enough to satisfy the likes of Thomas Mann, Lion Feuchtwanger, Franz Werfel, and the other émigrés; but even in Los Angeles German was the language of another place, another civilization, detached from the feel, pace, energy, and colorful eccentricities of the Southland. So Alfred Doblin bided his time, wrote nothing, envied the success of Thomas Mann, claimed that his name never appeared once in an American magazine or newspaper despite his reputation as a German author, and returned to Germany as soon as he could in 1946.

Even Doblin's *bête noir* Thomas Mann could seem a curiously detached figure from an American perspective: especially the perspective of a precocious teenager named Susan Sontag, aged fourteen, a student at North Hollywood High School who came with her friend Merrill to visit Mann one Sunday afternoon for tea in the fall of 1946. With the intrepidness of youth, Merrill had looked up Mann's number in the phone book and dialed it, and the Kaiser himself had agreed to allow the two high school students to come for tea and an interview. After driving out to Pacific Palisades in Merrill's Chevy, the two were greeted by Katia and ushered into the Kaiser's study. Mann was wearing a bow tie and a beige suit and was sitting behind a long dark table, graced by a small Egyptian funerary votive figure suggestive of the *Joseph in Egypt* tetralogy. As the conversation progressed, Sontag became increasingly intimidated by Mann's high-minded discourse and panicked by her inability to respond on an equal level. The great writer seemed such an Olympian figure, so different from anyone she knew in Los Angeles. During tea, Mann queried the two teenagers regarding their studies at North Hollywood High School.

"Our studies?" Sontag later wrote of the incident. "That was a further embarrassment. I was sure he hadn't the faintest idea what a high school in Southern California was like. Did he know about Drivers' Education (compulsory)? Typing courses? Wouldn't he be surprised by the wrinkled condoms you spotted as you were darting across the lawn for first period (the campus was a favorite nighttime trysting spot)—my own surprise having revealed, the very first week I entered, my being two years younger than my classmates, because I'd witlessly asked someone why there were those little balloons under the trees? And by the 'tea' being sold by a pair of pachukes (as the Chicano kids were called) stationed along the left wall of the assembly building every morning recess? Could he imagine George, who, some of us knew, had a gun and got money from gas-station attendants? Ella and Nella, the dwarf sisters, who led the Bible Club boycott that resulted in the withdrawal of our biology textbook? Did he know Latin was gone, and Shakespeare, too, and that for months of tenth-grade English the visibly befuddled teacher handed out copies of the *Reader's Digest* at the beginning of each period— we were to select one article and write a summary of it—then sat out the hour in silence at her desk, nodding and knitting? Could he imagine what a world away from the Gymnasium in his native Lubeck, where fourteen-year-old Tonio Kroger wooed Hans Hansen by trying to get him to read Schiller's *Don Carlos*, was

North Hollywood High School, alma mater of Farley Granger and Alan Ladd? He couldn't, and I hoped he would never find out. He had enough to be sad about—Hitler, the destruction of Germany, exile. It was better that he not know how really far he was from Europe." [18]

Even more dissonant on the (atonal) scale of connection to Southern California was Arnold Schoenberg. Despite his long residence in Los Angeles, from 1934 to 1951, and his ten years as professor of music at UCLA, Schoenberg remained a figure so detached, so alienated, as to seem not to exist in Los Angeles at all, or at the least, not to derive much satisfaction from his life there, with the exception of movies, ping-pong, and tennis. Schoenberg arrived in Los Angeles with a chip on his shoulder. In November 1934 he refused to attend a banquet in honor of Otto Klemperer, director of the Los Angeles Philharmonic, not because he did not admire Klemperer, which he did, but because, as he wrote in a note to Klemperer: "I consider it unspeakable that these people, who have been suppressing my works in this part of the world for the last twenty-five years, now want to use me as a decoration, to give me a walking-on part on this occasion, because I simply happen, entirely at my own pleasure, to be here." [19]

Hanns Eisler, Ernst Toch, Franz Waxman, Max Steiner, Erich Korngold, Miklos Rozsa, Darius Milhaud, Dimitri Tiomkin, and the other émigré composers, even the legendary Igor Stravinsky, might accommodate themselves to Hollywood, but not Arnold Schoenberg. When Irving Thalberg discussed with Schoenberg the possibility of writing the score for *The Good Earth* in 1936, Schoenberg demanded a fee of $50,000 and total control of the production. Thalberg demurred. Schoenberg's friend (virtually his only friend!) George Gershwin had brought Schoenberg to Thalberg's attention. Schoenberg and Gershwin were tennis fanatics and played on a biweekly basis. Gershwin was one of the few American composers about whom Schoenberg had anything positive to say. Had Gershwin lived, he might have encouraged his older colleague to be more accommodating, but Gershwin died in July 1937, and a genuinely bereft Schoenberg withdrew increasingly into himself both personally and as far as his music was concerned.

While Schoenberg was willing to surrender his German cursive handwriting in favor of standard Latin script and even to make a headlong assault on the English language, which he blended with German to achieve a new tongue, he refused to accommodate either himself or his music to émigré, much less to American, tastes. Miklos Rozsa had the opportunity to watch Schoenberg at a performance of Rozsa's *Sonata for Two Violins* (1933). Whenever a movement ended with a consonant chord, Schoenberg winced, his face contorting in the very same way that ordinary listeners would react to dissonance. Schoenberg, in other words, heard music in reverse.

In this matter of adjustment, as well as musical theory and practice, Arnold Schoenberg offered a complete contrast to Stravinsky. The two composers lived near each other on the Westside but rarely acknowledged each other's presence. Neither had the other to his home. Only now and then would they bump into each other at public events. For all its innovation, Stravinsky's music was mimetic, balletic, theatrical. Stravinsky could write music to which elephants might dance. No elephant, even the brightest, might ever learn to dance to the music of Arnold Schoenberg.

The atonalist was also a terrible snob. With outrageous *chutzpah*, Schoenberg considered the residents of Los Angeles kind and helpful but "most inferior"— which must remain the high point, or better, the low point, of émigré ingratitude.[20] Conventional wisdom has it that Arnold Schoenberg was unhappy in Los Angeles because neither Los Angeles, Southern California, nor indeed the United States recognized his worth as a composer. The fact is: Schoenberg's music had already engendered great controversy in Vienna, and in 1911 Schoenberg had moved to Berlin in search of a more appreciative audience. As late as the 1927 edition, *Grove's Dictionary of Music* did not even have a Schoenberg entry. By and large, Los Angeles, for all its alleged inferiority, treated Schoenberg rather well.

In 1935 UCLA appointed him visiting professor of music at $4,800 a year. The following year, Schoenberg was promoted to professor with tenure at $5,100. Since Schoenberg's music was highly academic, destined never to find a popular audience, the UCLA appointment was appropriate and prestigious. Remarried to a younger woman, and with three young children, Schoenberg needed the money. Among other things, his UCLA appointment allowed him to purchase a commodious Spanish Revival home at 116 North Rockingham in Brentwood near the UCLA campus. Yet Schoenberg was contemptuous of the academy, insisting that he would prefer to live solely by his music. To Schoenberg's credit, he met his classes scrupulously, came well prepared, and taught with exactitude—although, as student Dika Newlin noted, Schoenberg would occasionally arrive with a different shoe on each foot or with his shoelaces untied. At UCLA, Schoenberg acquired a number of disciples, including pianist Leonard Stein, who mastered the Schoenberg canon and later, as professor of music at USC, directed the Arnold Schoenberg Institute, which kept alive the memory and music of the master through the rest of the century. Complain as he might about teaching, Schoenberg went into a state of shock when he was forced to retire from UCLA at age seventy in 1944 on an income of $28.50 a month, his pension after ten years in the system. By March 1945 Schoenberg's meager pension had crept up to $40.38, and he was forced to support himself as a private teacher. He thought seriously of emigrating to New Zealand after the war.

Thank God for ping-pong and tennis, two games in which Schoenberg excelled, tennis especially. A photograph from the period shows Schoenberg walking with his wife and three children. The children are in tennis whites. It is a rare image of satisfaction in the surviving photographs of the period, which show Schoenberg becoming increasingly shrunken in form and cavernous in face, dark

circles under his eyes, the look of a man displaced, haunted, disappointed, suffering progressively bad health as the years go on—diabetes, kidney ailments, hernia,
dropsy, bouts of pneumonia. In 1945, in one of the most stunning rejections in
American foundation history, the Guggenheim Foundation rejected Schoenberg's
application for a grant to finish his opera *Moses and Aron* (compulsively supersti-
tious, Schoenberg insisted that the name Aaron be spelled with one A, lest the
title of his opera contain thirteen letters, an unlucky number) and his oratorio
Jacob's Ladder. In May 1947 the National Institute of Arts and Letters elected
Schoenberg to membership and awarded him $1,000. Schoenberg replied in a rare
English letter that was itself a confused jeremiad of bitterness and self-pity.

There is another side to the story. It is astonishing to see just how well Los
Angeles received Arnold Schoenberg, given his prickly personality and the extraordinarily difficult nature of his music. In May 1937 impresario Merle Armitage
edited a book of tributes to Schoenberg by, among others, Roger Sessions, Franz
Werfel, Leopold Stokowski, Otto Klemperer, and Berthold Viertel. Erica and Klaus
Mann testified to the cult status already accorded Schoenberg by a discriminating
circle of admirers. And there were performances, despite the difficulties of the
music. In May 1935 the Los Angeles Philharmonic, under the direction of Otto
Klemperer, gave a premiere performance of Schoenberg's *Suite for String Orchestra*. Mrs. Elizabeth Sprague-Coolidge subsidized a premiere of Schoenberg's
Fourth String Quartet, which she had commissioned, at Royce Hall on the UCLA
campus in January 1937, followed by further performances of Schoenberg's music
in Pasadena. Throughout the 1930s and 1940s private circles of admirers met for
performances of the master's music. Peter Yates and his wife the pianist Frances
Mullen supported a regular series of private outdoor concerts on the roof of their
Schindler-designed studio in West Los Angeles. More ambitiously, Bruno Walter,
who had his misgivings, conducted Schoenberg's music on 3 and 4 February 1944
in New York. Two days later, Leopold Stokowski premiered Schoenberg's *Concerto
for Piano and Orchestra* in a broadcast by the NBC Symphony Orchestra. That
October, Serge Koussevitzky ended a ten-year boycott and included the music of
Schoenberg in a concert by the Boston Symphony.

It is regrettable that Schoenberg could not take consolation in these moments
of recognition, as intermittent and incomplete as they were. His quarrel with
Thomas Mann over *Doctor Faustus* (1947/1948) shows a mind increasingly under
stress. Friendly with Schoenberg both before and after the quarrel, Mann solidly
supported Schoenberg's music. Salka Viertel remembers a concert at her home
in Santa Monica, with Schoenberg conducting a small group and soprano Erika
Wagner in Schoenberg's *Pierrot Lunaire*. Mann was present, along with Bruno
Walter and Otto Klemperer. "The applause was not unanimous," Viertel notes,
"but it was led by Thomas Mann clapping his hands heartily while Bruno Walter
whispered into his ear, obviously disapproving."[21] The Manns also entertained
the Schoenbergs at their home in Pacific Palisades. In *Doctor Faustus* Mann
attributed the invention of a Schoenberg-like atonalism to his central character,

Adrian Leverkuhn. In the course of writing the novel, Mann consulted extensively with Theodor Adorno, an accomplished musicologist as well as social scientist who had studied music under Alban Berg in Vienna, regarding the musical possibilities of a twelve-tone system. When *Doctor Faustus* appeared, Schoenberg, egged on by Alma Mahler Werfel, who had never liked Katia Mann, crossed the boundaries between fiction and reality. He, Arnold Schoenberg, had invented the twelve-tone system, not Adrian Leverkuhn! Bitterly, Schoenberg sent Mann a mock entry he had written for the *Encyclopedia Americana* of 1988, forty years into the future, in which the invention of the twelve-tone system is attributed to Thomas Mann. Letters flew back and forth, including two of them published in the *Saturday Review of Literature* in January 1949. Alfred A. Knopf agreed to print an insert for its edition of *Doctor Faustus* alerting the reader that this was only a novel and that the real inventor of atonalism was Arnold Schoenberg. In January Schoenberg accepted an offer of reconciliation from Mann, despite the fact that it was Schoenberg who had initiated the attack.

Schoenberg's paranoia, his inability to distinguish fact from fiction, offers evidence of the sense of neglect in which he existed in his bitter final years. Ever successful, Thomas Mann offered many an émigré a convenient scapegoat for bitter disappointments. On the other hand, it is understandable that Schoenberg should be so upset with *Doctor Faustus*. It was not so much that Mann might confuse the public as to who had invented atonalism in real life. A novel, after all, is only make-believe. Frighteningly, Mann had penetrated to the core of what Schoenberg believed he had done: create music anew, as if from nothing. Mann knew that such an act of creation might be considered either an imitation of divinity or a demonically inspired theft. Mann understood that Arnold Schoenberg, like Prometheus, had stolen fire from the gods. Schoenberg, on his part, deeply resented that someone else, even a novelist or a fictional character, might get the credit for the task for which Schoenberg had endangered, if not his immortal soul, then at least his sanity.

Whatever problems Arnold Schoenberg might have with the novel, *Doctor Faustus* represented a heroic effort on Mann's part to employ fiction as a means of diagnosing the sick mind, heart, and soul of Christian Germany. He was, after all, the Kaiser in exile, a not totally facetious designation for the most conspicuous representative of liberal humanistic Christian Germany free to speak his mind, just as Heinrich Mann, for all his present failure, was the President in Exile of an impending German socialist democratic republic. The aura of a monarch, or at least the aura of a quasi-monarchical president in the European style, clung to Thomas Mann during the war years. Deprived of his German citizenship in 1936, Mann had declared that wherever he was, was Germany. When he flew from Los Angeles to San Francisco on 26 March 1941, Mann, a private citizen, was met at the airport by a squad of motorcycle police who escorted him to Berkeley. Thomas Mann's friendship with Roosevelt, his stay in the White House, his affil-

iation with the Library of Congress, his radio addresses to the German people in
which he anointed himself as the conscience of Germany, the political dimension
of so many of his speeches, his honorary doctorates from Berkeley and Harvard,
the establishment of the Thomas Mann archives at Yale: this and much more
reinforced Mann's quasi-official status. A rumor circulated that after the war
Thomas Mann would be installed as president of Germany. When the German-
American theologian Reinhold Niebuhr and others sought to launch a Free Germany Movement as a government in exile, many, including Bertolt Brecht,
wanted Mann to chair the effort and to become the German equivalent of Charles
de Gaulle. Traveling to Washington, Mann asked Assistant Secretary of State
Adolph Berle whether or not he should accept the chairmanship. Berle informed
Mann that the United States would not recognize any German government in
exile, and Mann steered clear of the movement. Later, during the mass bombings
of 1944, Secretary of the Treasury Henry Morgenthau Jr. boasted: "We want to
blast the city of Berlin off the map." [22] Horrified, a number of Los Angeles émigrés
led by Bertolt Brecht and Salka Viertel sought to organize a United Front based
on the premise that not all German people were equally responsible for Naziism
and the war. Once again, Thomas Mann kept his distance.

Mann rejected the theory that there were two Germanys, the one idealistic, the
other demonic, with the evil Germany being temporarily in control. All German
people, Mann believed, shared some measure of guilt for what had happened.
(Did he include himself as well? What about his silence between 1933 and 1936
and the royalties from Germany he continued to collect during this period?)
Meanwhile, Mann lived in elegant comfort in Pacific Palisades, buoyed by the
financial success of *Joseph the Provider* (1944), a Book-of-the-Month Club selection, and the success of the one-volume edition of the four *Joseph* novels in Helen
T. Lowe-Porter's masterful English translation. In Los Angeles and the rest of the
United States, Mann moved exclusively in elite circles: a dignified figure in a
double-breasted suit, his mustache trimmed, his hair combed impeccably, his
shirts starchy white, speaking in a formal literary English or the German of the
upper classes. At a Hollywood party, a producer (believing no doubt that once
you have seen one writer, you have seen them all) slapped him on the back and
called him "Tommy." The Kaiser was not amused. [23]

*Doctor Faustus: The Life of the German Composer Adrian Leverkuhn as Told
by a Friend* (1947/1948) was introduced to its American audience by its English
translator Helen T. Lowe-Porter as "this vast canvas, this cathedral of a book, this
woven tapestry of symbolism." [24] For forty years, Mann had been contemplating a
Faust story. For Mann, as for Goethe, the Faust legend embodied the strengths
and vulnerabilities of German humanism, with its special love-hate relationship
to German theology. From this perspective, Faust and Martin Luther divided the
German world between them. Mann approached this archetypal German story
with the knowledge that, as a contribution to German identity, his proposed novel
could function as his most serviceable book as well as an artistic masterpiece.

Certainly, the Germany of 1943 required spiritual correction. Mann had waited a long time, forty years, before turning to this task, in much the same way that an equally important English author might delay before attempting to write a new version of *Hamlet*. At long last, on 14 March 1943, Mann cleared from his desk the notes and research materials he had gathered for the composition of *Joseph the Provider*. The next morning, he pulled his Faustus file from the shelf and began a new round of research and plot outline. Within two months, he had formulated a new version of the Faust story, equal to Goethe's *Faust* as a probe into the molten magma of the German consciousness.

A more complete explanation takes into consideration not just the German intentions of the novel, as compelling and primary as these are, but its American circumstances and intentions as well. True, *Doctor Faustus* might have been written in Switzerland or Sweden, Canada or Brazil, had Mann sought refuge in these countries. But he did not. He sought refuge in the United States, and after testing Princeton as an environment for two years, he further refined his selection of place, always so important for an artist, in his choice of Southern California. Why? Arguably, because Southern California was, for the time being at least, more German than Germany itself or the German-speaking cantons of Switzerland to which Mann would return toward the end of his life. Southern California, it can be argued, preserved for Mann and his peers not just a safer Germany, free from the ravages of war, but a Germany keeping alive the best possibilities of liberal humanistic Germany: the true free Germany, the Germany of Goethe, whose Faust story Mann was now recasting in twentieth-century terms, in part as his contribution to the war effort. In and through the figure of Adrian Leverkuhn, a modern Faust, Mann advanced his analysis as to why and how Germany had gone wrong—and how it might make atonement and recover itself in the aftermath of defeat. (The novel took Germany into the devastations of the Second World War.) Like Faust, like Germany, Leverkuhn had achieved his triumph, the theory and practice of a revolutionary new mode of music, out of the very flaw—a syphilitic condition over-charging his consciousness—that would likewise bring him to destruction. Did German culture, by analogy, suffer a similar syphilitic strain: the compound virus of Faustianism and anti-Semitism? And if so, could it be eradicated, and by whom? Such were questions Germans had to ask of themselves, Mann believed—and Americans had to ask of the Germans as well, once the war was over and they were responsible for bringing justice and reconstruction to a guilty, shattered, and demoralized nation.

Mann began writing *Doctor Faustus* on 23 May 1943, a sunny Sunday morning. The Santa Monica Bay sparkled blue on the horizon. Three years and eight months later, on the morning of 29 January 1947, he wrote the last lines of the novel, after which he and Katia went for their usual walk along the seashore. The American dimension of *Doctor Faustus* surfaces even more clearly when one considers that when Mann began its composition he had no immediate prospects of a German audience. The Third Reich remained very much in power, and

Mann's books were proscribed throughout much of Europe. As Mann neared the final third of his novel, he had a different problem. Germany lay in ruins. What kind of market could there be in such a devastated environment? The fact is: from the beginning *Doctor Faustus* possessed a dual identity. Long before the manuscript was complete, Helen T. Lowe-Porter of Princeton was busy on its English version. She and Mann worked together, word by word, line by line. Rarely has an important work of art been composed in such a condition of simultaneous translation. Alfred Knopf, meanwhile, Mann's friend and publisher, saw the economics of *Doctor Faustus* in terms of the financial success of its American edition. Given the condition of the German economy, not much could be expected in a financial way from the German edition published by Bermann-Fischer Verlag in Stockholm in 1947. Mann's financial hopes rested on the American edition published by Knopf in 1948.

From the start, Thomas Mann knew that he was writing an American book—and not just in financial terms. He was, after all, an American citizen, with his son Klaus on the Italian front as a staff sergeant in the American Army, and his daughter Erika in uniform, with the rank of captain, as an accredited combat correspondent. On 5 January 1944 Thomas and Katia Mann swore allegiance to the United States of America, with Professor and Mrs. Max Horkheimer serving as character witnesses. Like everyone else, Mann was examined by the clerk of courts on his knowledge of American government. Questioned regarding the authority vested in cities, Mann drew a blank—but then ("since I had to say something") finessed the matter by answering that he was astonished that these governmental entities had so much authority.[25] After the ceremony, the Manns and Horkheimers celebrated with a ceremonial American breakfast of pancakes and maple syrup.

Most émigrés, with the notable exception of Heinrich Mann and Alfred Doblin, made headlong assaults into both American citizenship and the English language, despite the problems of adjusting to a new culture and learning a new language in middle age. ("I've had many difficulties in my life, many sad misadventures," remembered Russian-born composer Dimitri Tiomkin. "I went through two revolutions and suffered many hardships. But the most formidable adversary of all has been the beautiful language of Shakespeare, Byron, and Sam Goldwyn.")[26] Émigré artist George Grosz was so anxious to Americanize himself, he took up chewing gum. When émigré author Frederick Kohner called on Harry Cohn, president of Columbia Pictures, to thank Cohn for hiring him, Cohn snapped: "If you don't produce, you'll be kicked in the pants out the door."[27] Fifteen years later, Kohner was so Americanized he was capable of writing the novel *Gidget* (1957), in which he showed himself the master of Southern California teenage surf culture and slang.

Kohner modeled Gidget on his thoroughly American daughter. Whatever doubts or hesitations an older generation might experience, émigré children (and certainly émigré grandchildren!) were undisputably American, many in the Southern Californian variation of that multi-faceted identity. All four of Thomas Mann's grandchildren were Americans, and two of them, Fridolin (Frido) and Anthony (Tonio), were Californians, the children of Mann's younger son Michael, a violinist with the San Francisco Symphony Orchestra, and his wife Gret Moser, a Swiss. Gret Mann, in fact, went to work in May 1943 as a tank cleaner at Marinship in Sausalito, making Liberty ships. Dominica Borgese, the daughter of Thomas Mann's daughter Elisabeth, married an Italian émigré academic, Antonio Borgese, a noted anti-Fascist, and lived in Chicago. The couple joined the Unitarian Church of Santa Monica when the Borgese family spent the Christmas and winter of 1942–43 in Pacific Palisades. Ronny Schoenberg became a champion tennis player at Loyola High School, and his composer-father was ecstatic. Aldous and Maria Huxley's teenage son Matthew became thoroughly Americanized; he even had an American accent. Salka Viertel's son Peter also excelled at tennis and at the age of nineteen wrote an English-language novel, *The Canyon*, describing his boyhood in the Santa Monica Canyon, which remains a classic of Southern California literature. Slated to enroll at UCLA, Peter Viertel joined the United States Marine Corps instead, qualified for officers' training at Quantico, and saw action in the Pacific before joining the Office of Strategic Service in Europe. Another Viertel son, Oliver, also joined the Marine Corps.

Americanism might come easily to the children, but it took persecutions and war, and eventually a knowledge of the Holocaust, to alert many of the émigrés to their Jewishness. Max Reinhardt, for example, initially believed that all the fuss about being Jewish, either for or against, was a vulgar intrusion into what should be a private matter. After 1933 such liberalism became an impossible stance. Gathered in what Gottfried Reinhardt described as "a ghetto under Pacific palms," the émigrés, so many of them quasi-assimilated in their past lives, were by then very much aware of the perils of their Jewishness.[28] Connections were soon established between the American Jewish community of Los Angeles and the émigrés. Two businessmen, Theo Lowenstein and Lothar Rosenthal, together with a dentist, Bruno Bernstein, founded the German Jewish Club of 1933, which helped refugees find work and overcome their isolation. Under the presidency of Leopold Jessner, a former theatrical producer in Germany, the club launched an ambitious program of cultural events, many of them in conjunction with the European Film Fund, the leading Hollywood organization dealing with refugees. The Viennese Culture Club and the local chapter of B'nai B'rith carried on a similar agenda of social and cultural programs. On its weekly program *Talent in Exile*, radio station KFWB showcased music, plays, and lectures that had been banned by the Nazis or dealt with émigré questions.

While he remained extremely selective in his social life and was not a regular figure in these organizations, Lion Feuchtwanger was also pondering the questions of Jewish identity so evident in the discussions of the Jewish clubs and the artistic performances they sponsored. As a doctoral candidate at the University of Munich, Feuchtwanger wrote his dissertation on Heinrich Heine's Jewish fragment, *The Rabbi of Bacharach* (1840), an early indication of what would become Feuchtwanger's lifelong pursuit of the Jewish question via the historical novel. Taken cumulatively, Feuchtwanger's Jewish novels encompass the history of the Jews in Western Europe. Feuchtwanger burst onto the international scene with the best-selling novel *Judd Suss* (1925), "the Jew Suss," published in English under the title *Power* (1927). In the novel, the Jew Suss rises to prominence in medieval Wurttemberg as a banker and political advisor but remains an outsider, albeit an outsider essential to the preservation of the realm. Suss's condition, the necessary outsider, needed yet rejected, is also reflected in Yehuda, a central figure in Feuchtwanger's final novel, *Raquel, the Jewess of Toledo* (1955).

In the Romanized Jewish soldier, statesman, and historian Flavius Josephus, who lived from 37 to 95 C.E., Feuchtwanger found his most compelling paradigm for the historical destiny of Jews in Western Europe. Born in Jerusalem, Josephus studies with the Essenes, Sadducees, and Pharisees and ultimately joins the Pharisees. As a Jewish patriot, he is appointed governor of Galilee and resists the Romans on the field of battle in the Roman-Jewish war breaking out in 66. Captured by the Roman general Titus Flavius Vespasianus (Vespasian), Josephus wins the favor of his captor, takes his name, and is assimilated into the Roman establishment. In 69 Vespasian becomes emperor, and Josephus finds himself at the center of the Roman establishment. Feuchtwanger began his Josephus trilogy with *Der Judische Krieg* (1932), "the Jewish War," which appeared in English translation as *Josephus* (1932). In 1935 he published *Die Sohne*, translated as *The Jew of Rome* (1936).

He completed the third volume of the trilogy in Pacific Palisades in 1942—yet another émigré masterpiece from Southern California. This time, however, given the war, the Josephus novel appeared in English translation first, as *Josephus and the Emperor* (1942), before appearing in its first German edition under the title *Der Tag wird kommen* in 1945. As Feuchtwanger develops his Josephus character, the historian becomes the archetype of the Jew in the world, in it yet not completely of it, successful yet kept from final assimilation by a certain destiny—the necessary outsider. Josephus is at once a Pharisee, a priest of the temple, and a senator of Rome. He has mastered the Hebrew Scriptures and the Greek and Latin classics. Profoundly aware of the narrow but compelling imperatives of Jewish life, Josephus struggles at the same time to serve the larger secular culture, which eventually accords him its highest honors. He is, in short, the perfect emblem of European Jewry down through the ages, nineteenth- and early twentieth-century German Jewry especially.

Despite his senator's toga, however, his profound identification with Roman civilization and the Empire as an ideal, Josephus is fully aware that Vespasian approves of him—more, adopts him into his very family—only so long as Josephus remains useful to Rome. In *Josephus and the Emperor*, Josephus has put behind him the life of action and has dedicated himself to the writing of Jewish history. The parallel between Josephus and Feuchtwanger is obvious: the Romanized Jew shaping the history of his people according to the highest standards of Roman history, the Bavarian Jew recounting the history of European Jewry through an international empire of multi-translated best-sellers. Called from his retirement and sent back to Judea to deal with an uprising, Josephus is forced to choose between assimilation and his Jewish identity, just as Feuchtwanger, plucked from the center of the German literary establishment, found himself yet another Jew in exile, forced to examine, and perhaps affirm, a special destiny. Josephus, in the end, chooses his Jewishness.

As did Arnold Schoenberg, a former Catholic and, later, a Protestant, who reentered the faith of his ancestors in 1933. In the summer of 1938 Rabbi Jacob Sonderling of Los Angeles commissioned Schoenberg to compose a series of special arrangements of traditional Jewish music from Spain—a rare recognition, Schoenberg believed, from the Jewish community he had reembraced. All during his Los Angeles years, from 1934 to 1951, Schoenberg was working on his *Moses and Aron*, an opera in three acts that he had begun in the late 1920s. Given its premiere in the land of the Holocaust—in Hamburg, Germany, on 12 March 1954—*Moses and Aron* is a masterpiece of Jewish art: a return via the most complex of performance genres, by the most complex composer of the twentieth century, to the most complex of historical questions, Jewish identity. In his final years, Schoenberg had the satisfaction of seeing his work recognized and performed in the newly established State of Israel.

Such recognition proved a balm, a *mitzva*, to Schoenberg's embattled spirit. Blending music with theology, Schoenberg saw in the sacred calling of the Jewish people, which is to say, the maintenance of monotheism amidst affliction, the model for symphonic music in Israel as well. Just as the Jewish people had maintained the highest standards of belief, Schoenberg argued, symphonic music in Israel should maintain the highest standards of selection, performance, and humanism. Brought to near-completion in his Los Angeles years (epics such as this are never fully finished; their power precludes final form), *Moses and Aron* is yet another masterpiece from émigré Los Angeles, however reluctantly Schoenberg held citizenship in this community. Taken together with another creation of Schoenberg's Los Angeles years, the oratorio *A Survivor from Warsaw* (1947), *Moses and Aron* constitutes the deepest possible response via art to the Holocaust as Sacred Event that must never happen again.

What Feuchtwanger saw in terms of culture and history and Schoenberg saw in terms of religion and music, Franz Werfel saw in the more explicitly theological terms of the enduring relationship, the interdependence, of Judaism and Christianity. Growing up in the assimilated environment of Prague at the turn of the century, a city in which bar mitzvahs were called confirmations, Werfel absorbed an appreciation of Catholic piety and practice from his childhood nurse, a Catholic, and from the mixed Jewish-Christian ambience of his family's friendship circle. Later, he attended a Catholic school conducted by the Piarist Fathers, who welcomed Jewish students and exempted them from catechetical instruction. As a young man, Werfel threw himself into the bohemian literary life of Prague, in which Jewish-Christian distinctions were moot. Primarily a poet in temperament and literary outlook, Werfel could by turn empathize with Judaism, Christianity, anarchism, Marxism, conservativism. It all depended upon what subject he was working on. As far as religion was concerned, Werfel understood it primarily in terms of its aesthetic dimension. His was a dreamy mysticism beyond the specifics of any one creed. (As a young man, Werfel attended seances and more than half-believed in what occurred.) "What is religion?" he asked in 1923. "The most ecstatic degree of sensuality. . . . Religion is the erotic of the abstract."[29] No wonder Thomas Mann said that Franz Werfel sometimes resembled an opera singer, sometimes a Catholic priest.

Between 1942 and 1944, Werfel wrote a collection of theological and philosophical aphorisms under the title *Theologumena* [*Thoughts on Theology*], in which he laid out his beliefs that both the Jewish covenant and the Catholic covenant were eternal (the Second Vatican Council would later agree), that the rise of Christianity had a bracing, disciplining effect on Judaism, and, most crucial to Werfel's point of view, that Christianity and Judaism each required the other religion as an essential means of defining itself. "What would Israel be without the Church?" Werfel used to ask. "And what would the Church be without Israel?"[30]

While flourishing as a man and a writer in a distinctive ambience of Judaism laced with strong Catholic sympathies, Werfel insisted that he would never convert, given the current persecution of the Jews in Europe. In *Hearken unto the Voice* (1938), he employed the story of the Babylonian captivity to suggest the darkness descending in Europe. On the other hand, Werfel did marry a Catholic, and two of his closest friends in Southern California were the Viennese Jesuit Georg Moenius, editor of an anti-Nazi journal, and Cyrill Fischer, a Viennese Franciscan assigned to Mission Santa Barbara. In the preface to *The Song of Bernadette*, Werfel explicitly described himself as a Jew, yet many American Catholics and *Time* magazine mistakenly believed that he was a Catholic. To this day, because of *The Song of Bernadette*, Franz Werfel remains a revered figure in American Catholic literature (along with such other non-Catholics as Agnes Repplier and Willa Cather), just as he became a revered figure among Armenians for *The Forty Days of Musadagh*.

Franz Werfel needed all the understanding he could muster, for he was married to a woman who seemed to be, simultaneously, anti- and philo-Semitic. The daughter of the well-known Austrian landscape painter Emile Jacob Schindler, Alma Schindler, a Catholic, was considered the most beautiful young woman in Vienna at the turn of the century. Although she inherited the traditional anti-Semitism of her city and class, the first and third of her three husbands, Gustav Mahler and Franz Werfel, and a number of her many lovers were Jews, and her second husband, architect Walter Gropius, a Christian, was her least favorite. By the early 1940s Alma Mahler Werfel, still statuesque, as imperious as ever, was growing deaf, hence speaking loudly, and consuming a bottle of Benedictine a day. (Gottfried Reinhardt wickedly suggested that it was perhaps the monastic origins of Benedictine that made it so appealing to Alma the ardent Catholic.) Standing side by side, Franz and Alma—the short, dark, Semitic, pudgy Franz a head shorter than his stately Teutonic wife—constituted in and of themselves a *tableau vivant* of the Jewish-Christian dialogue Werfel so ardently promoted.

The complexities of such a relationship speak for themselves. In both his life and his art, Franz Werfel walked a delicate line: a tension revealed in the genesis of the play *Jacobowsky and the Colonel,* which Werfel co-authored with S. N. Behrman between 1943 and 1944. Fleeing the Germans in June 1940, Werfel had been distraught to the point of a near-total breakdown. Hardly more than a year later, he was regaling guests at a dinner party at Max Reinhardt's—among them, Ernst Lubitsch and S. N. Behrman—with humorous anecdotes of his escape. Central to Werfel's monologue was his encounter with a Polish Jewish businessman named Samuel S. Jacobowski, who had escaped from Germany in the company of an anti-Semitic Polish colonel and his mistress. The relationship between Jacobowski and the colonel reflected Werfel's relationship with Alma: a condition of being yoked by necessity—and by grotesque affection—to an anti-Semitic figure who is paradoxically in the Semitic camp. In June 1942 Werfel retired to a bungalow at the Biltmore in Santa Barbara and wrote the play *Jacobowsky and the Colonel: Comedy of a Tragedy in Three Acts [Jacobowsky und der Oberst],* which Viking published in English translation in 1944, for yet another instance of émigré creativity in Southern California during this period. Two years earlier, Ernst Lubitsch had caused a furor by his effort in the film *To Be or Not to Be* (1942) to blend humor with the Nazi invasion of Poland. Werfel was attempting something even more complex: to extract a comedy from a tragedy of apocalyptic proportions. Broadway showed immediate interest in the play, and for a while Werfel played Clifford Odets and S. N. Behrman against each other as collaborators on a performable version of his printed play. Behrman prevailed, and in mid-March 1944 his and Werfel's version of *Jacobowsky and the Colonel* opened at the Martin Beck Theater in a Theatre Guild production, staged by Elia Kazan and starring Louis Calhern as the colonel, the Viennese actor Oscar Karlweis as Jacobowsky, and the French actress Annabella as the colonel's girlfriend.

How to evaluate the success of this play, indeed, how to assess the very fact that it got on Broadway, presents many ambiguities and difficulties. Even as the Nazi killing machine was going into high gear, destroying millions, a cynic might say, Werfel and Behrman, two Jews, were profiting from a comedy whose central joke was anti-Semitism. Were Werfel and Behrman pandering to anti-Semitism by making it seem humorous? And were American audiences lapping up such humor so as to blunt the edge of a disposition that was causing such havoc in Europe and was far from unknown in the United States? Or were Werfel and

Behrman performing a service through their humor? Was not the colonel's anti-Semitism (like Alma's) of a different degree and kind than that of the Nazis from whom both he and Jacobowsky were fleeing? Nonsense! it can be argued in return: anti-Semitism is anti-Semitism in whatever form it takes. Give the colonel an opportunity and he would be persecuting Jacobowsky with relish. How can one differentiate between his anti-Semitism and that of the Nazis?

Meanwhile, in 1944, Fox was bringing bestseller *The Song of Bernadette* to the screen, with Jennifer Jones playing the French peasant girl who saw visions and heard voices. Catastrophe had simultaneously propelled Werfel, Brecht, and Feuchtwanger to the depiction of a young female visionary, a Joan of Arc figure, who in the midst of war and death glimpses the possibilities of transcendence. Earlier, Brecht had employed such a figure in his play *St. Joan of the Stockyards* (1929–30), in which a young Chicago woman belonging to a Salvation Army–like organization seeks to reform working conditions in the stockyards. Brecht returned to a similar figure in the play *Die Gesichte der Simone Machard*, [*The Visions of Simone Machard*], which he and Feuchtwanger jointly wrote during the winter of 1942–43. The play dealt with a young girl who in 1940 becomes a leader in the French Resistance. Brecht, however, wanted Simone to be a more purely mythic figure, an inspired girl of eleven, while Feuchtwanger saw her as a more thoughtful young woman of fifteen, and so the play was left incomplete. Feuchtwanger presented his version in the novel *Simone* (1944). To such imagined Joan of Arc figures, visionary young women in times of war or social stress, must be joined in Werfel's case the real-life figure of Manon Gropius, Alma's daughter by her second husband. A prescient and enchanting young woman, adored by her father Gropius, her stepfather Werfel, and everyone who came in contact with her, Manon Gropius died in her early twenties in Vienna on 22 April 1935. Devastated by her death, Alban Berg dedicated the last work of his life, a violin concerto completed in the summer of 1935, "to the memory of an angel." [31] Werfel likewise dedicated *The Song of Bernadette* to Manon, whose luminous presence shaped his depiction of Bernadette Soubirous.

The success of *The Song of Bernadette*, novel and film, offers a probe into Werfel's motivation and the larger conditions of wartime America as responded to by Hollywood. Just as the Joan of Arc figure reemerged as war broke out in Europe, so too did religiosity reassert itself in wartime America. "There are no atheists in the foxholes," Army chaplain William T. Cummings had stated during the siege of Corregidor and Bataan.[32] The phrase became part of wartime folklore. Along with *The Song of Bernadette*, another religious novel, *The Robe* (1943), a story of early Christianity written by Protestant minister Lloyd C. Douglas, dominated the best-seller lists of 1943, selling more than 250,000 copies. A hit song that year was "Praise the Lord and Pass the Ammunition," based on newspaper reports of an American chaplain in the Pacific who had joined the men on the firing line when their position was being overwhelmed.

Throughout the early and mid-1940s, Hollywood was showing special sensitivity to its Catholic audiences. The divorce and remarriage of George M. Cohan, for example, was tactfully omitted from *Yankee Doodle Dandy* (1942). Toward the end of the war, such solicitude paid off at the box office. *Going My Way* (1944) cost $1 million to make and had grossed $12 million by early 1945. The next year, *The Bells of Saint Mary's* (1945), in which Bing Crosby played yet another priest, became the most profitable film in the history of RKO. Selznick's *The Song of Bernadette* (1943), directed by Henry King, was another blockbuster.

How could such a denominational vehicle—based on apparitions a significant percent of its audience found unbelievable, if not ridiculous—achieve such popularity? First of all, *The Song of Bernadette*, strictly as a novel, was intricate, highly crafted, vivid, and sweeping in its cast of characters, ranging from peasants in the countryside to Emperor Napoleon III. On his publisher's advice, Werfel included a two-page cast of characters with seventy speaking parts. Even Thomas Mann, who deplored what he considered the naive pietism of Werfel's novel, admitted that it was well made. In the figure of Bernadette Soubirous, moreover, Werfel found release for his grief over the death of Manon Gropius as he funded elements of Manon's character and personality into that of the French peasant girl.

The need for spiritual value, of whatever sort, in wartime (so evident in the reemergence of the Joan of Arc figure before, during, and after the war) reinforced the entertainment value of the novel and the film. *The Song of Bernadette* conveyed a message of faith overcoming great obstacles that even a dissenting or disbelieving audience, reading the book or seeing the film, found gratifying in wartime. Werfel's novel functioned as a popular mode of psychological release, tinged with mystical piety: the Catholic counterpart to the Protestant orientation of Douglas's *The Robe*. Both the historical Bernadette Soubirous and Werfel's character remained deliberately vague about the exact identity of the Lady in the apparitions. Novel and film each possessed a generalized spirituality, in dialogue with but not totally dependent upon Catholic doctrine for its psychological power. (The historical Bernadette Soubirous, incidentally, was always a little shaky in catechism class. She became a saint but never a theologian.) When Christopher Isherwood accompanied Swami Prabhavananda and other members of the Vedanta Society of Hollywood to a screening of the film version of *The Song of Bernadette*, he was brought to the verge of tears by the effectiveness of the film and its message of transcendent value in the face of disbelief. One of the Vedanta nuns returned and returned for repeated viewings.

The Song of Bernadette also evoked a Christian European civilization now plunged into the nightmare of war because it had failed to heed the best possibilities of its heritage. Escaping the Nazis, Werfel had knelt and drunk of the waters of Lourdes. Whether he believed or not was beside the point. In drinking at the spring, Werfel—on the verge of emotional collapse, fearing for his life—had experienced renewal and hope. He would get out! He would make it through to Spain and the United States, and he would write about the young woman who first struck these waters from the rock of a Europe that had not yet plunged itself into catastrophe and chaos. Franz Werfel, a Jew fleeing persecution, made at Lourdes—and later kept—a promise that became a covenant.

The covenant had temporarily anchored itself in Southern California, where Jewish and Christian émigrés had escaped from the war and the camps but not from each other. Together, they constituted a saving remnant of a European civilization ravaged by horrors that would only be revealed in the liberation of the death camps and even then might never be fully understood, indeed might represent an evil that was in and of itself dangerous to contemplate, lest one despair of the human condition. What was so brave about the émigrés, Jews and Christians alike, was that by and large they did not despair, despite the dislocation of their lives. They brought with them to Southern California not only their creativity but the rituals and protocols of daily life as they had known it before the catastrophe. Schmoozing of a Sunday at Salka Viertel's in Santa Monica, sipping sherry and nibbling *Apfelstrudel* at Villa Aurora in Pacific Palisades, gossiping by telephone each evening while the alien curfew was in effect, attending concerts and plays after 1943 when the curfew was lifted, they kept close to each other, Jews and Christians alike, and close to the Europe they remembered.

Could such simplicities keep at bay the horrors in their homeland? Of course not, especially after 1945, but coping with catastrophe is so often a matter of small things. Here in Southern California they had rediscovered love and work and the essential goodness of life. Their Southern Californian circumstances might be a reluctant identity. Yet it kept in check the nightmare that was Europe. When the war was over and Europe was rebuilt, they found themselves, most of them, together with their children and their children's children, still sojourning beneath the palm trees of this sunny southern latitude. Why return? They were already home.

Notes

Frequently used citations

CHSQ   *Quarterly of the California Historical Society*
JSDH   *Journal of San Diego History*
NR   *New Republic*
PHR   *Pacific Historical Review*
SCQ   *Southern California Quarterly*
SEP   *Saturday Evening Post*

Chapter One
Good Times on the Coast

1. Farnsworth Crowder, "Where Life Is Better—For What?" *Westways*, 28 (November 1936), 21–24.
2. Larry Engelmann, *The Goddess and the American Girl* (1988), 303.
3. "Why I Live in California," *Sunset*, 61 (October 1928), 20–21.
4. Lucinda Liggett Eddy, "Lillian Jennette Rice: Search for a Regional Ideal," *JSDH*, 29 (Fall 1983), 277.
5. "Southern California: Its Five Contributions to Modern Living," *House and Garden*, 78 (November 1940), 14.
6. *Los Angeles, City of Dreams* (1935), 300.
7. Frank Condon, "Life on the Desert," *SEP* (5 December 1936), 73.
8. "What to Wear in Palm Springs," *Palm Springs Life* (1938), 32.
9. Condon, "Life on the Desert," 13.
10. Max Miller, *It Must Be the Climate* (1941), 225.

Chapter Two
Arcadian Shores

1. "Berkeley in the Age of Innocence," *Atlantic Monthly*, 223 (June 1969), 67.
2. Haakon Chevalier, *Oppenheimer: The Story of a Friendship* (1965), 11.
3. Lawrence Rising, *Proud Flesh* (1924), 129.
4. Miriam Allen deFord, *They Were San Franciscans* (1941), 215.
5. Yehudi Menuhin, *Unfinished Journey* (1977), 25.
6. Rosalind Sharpe Wall, *A Wild Coast and Lonely: Big Sur Pioneers* (1989), 188.

Chapter Three
Unto the Stars Themselves

1. *The Autobiography of Robert A. Millikan* (1950), 240.
2. Ibid., 230.
3. *The Study of Stellar Evolution* (1908), 243.
4. *Signals from the Stars* (1931), 137.
5. Helen Wright, *Explorer of the Universe: A Biography of George Ellery Hale* (1966), 428.

Chapter Four
Gibraltar of the Pacific

1. "The Jumping-Off Place," *The American Jitters: A Year of the Slump* (1932), 259–60.
2. Richard Amero, "San Diego Invites the World to Balboa Park a Second Time," *JSDH*, 31 (Fall 1985), 269, quoting the San Diego *Union* for 10 June 1935.
3. Richard Pourade, *The Glory Years* (1964), 13.
4. Lawrence Lee, "William E. Smyth and San Diego, 1901–1908," *JSDH*, 19 (Winter 1973), 21.
5. Iris Engstrand, *San Diego: California's Cornerstone* (1980), 74.
6. Uldis Ports, "Geraniums vs. Smokestacks: San Diego's Mayoralty Campaign of 1917," *JSDH*, 21 (Summer 1975), 54.
7. Ibid., 55.

Chapter Five
One Man's Family

1. "Sunny Jim Rolph: The First 'Mayor of all the People,' " *CHSQ*, 53 (1974), 172.
2. Matty Simmons and Don Simmons, *On the House* (1955), 193.
3. *With Head and Heart* (1979), 144.
4. *An Autobiographical Novel* (1978), 365.
5. Ibid., 366–67.
6. *The Daring Young Man on the Flying Trapeze* (1934), 53.
7. *An Autobiographical Novel*, 365.

Chapter Six
Pershing Square

1. "The City of Our Lady the Queen of the Angels," *The American Jitters: A Year of the Slump* (1932), 226–27.

2. *A Part of Myself* (1966), 347.

3. Oliver Carlson, *A Mirror for Californians* (1941), 114.

4. "Paradise: Civilization of Southern California," *American Mercury*, 28 (March 1933), 269.

5. John D. Weaver, *Los Angeles: El Pueblo Grande* (1973), 110–11.

6. *Los Angeles: City of Dreams*, 255.

7. Bernadette Soter, *The Light of Learning: An Illustrated History of the Los Angeles Public Library* (1993), 61.

8. Raine Bennett, "The Hawthornes Carry On," *Westways*, 26 (June 1934), 32.

9. *North from Mexico* (1948), 193.

10. Beatrice Griffith, *American Me* (1948), 159.

11. Don Black, "Belles of the Boulevards," *Westways*, 32 (March 1940), 6.

12. *A Loving Gentleman* (1976), 60.

13. Dean Jennings, *We Only Kill Each Other: The Life and Bad Times of Bugsy Siegel* (1967), 17.

14. John D. Weaver, *Warren: The Man, the Court, the Era* (1967), 81.

15. Veronica King, *Problems of Modern American Crime* (1924), 236.

16. Hildegard Hawthorne, *Romantic Cities of California* (1939), 71.

17. W. W. Robinson, *What They Say About the Angels* (1942), 49.

18. Ibid., 64.

19. George Martin, "Cities Are Persons," *Catholic World*, 147 (June 1938), 303.

20. *Los Angeles* (1933), 327.

21. Ibid., 325.

22. Carlson, *Mirror for Californians*, 122.

23. Aubrey Burns, "Regional Culture in California," *Southwest Review*, 17 (July 1932), 383.

24. *What They Say About the Angels*, 57.

25. Ibid., 59.

26. "The Cults of California," *Atlantic Monthly*, 177 (March 1946), 108.

27. Ralph Hancock, *The Forest Lawn Story* (1955), 14.

28. *Southern California: An Island on the Land* (1946), reprinted in 1973 by Peregrine Smith, 375–76.

Chapter Seven
An All-Seeing Eye

1. Ansel Adams, *Autobiography* (1985), 112.

2. *The Daybooks of Edward Weston*, Volume 2, *California*, edited by Nancy Newhall (1966), 203, entry for 21 February 1931.

3. Ibid., 207, entry for 10 March 1931.

4. Ibid., 265, entry for 8 November 1932.

5. Adams, *Autobiography*, 237–38.

6. Ibid., 238–39.

7. Ibid., 9.

8. Ibid., 76.

9. Ibid., 109.

10. Ibid., 241.

11. Charis Wilson, *Edward Weston Nudes* (1977), 3.

12. *Daybooks*, 250–51, entry for 19 March 1934.

13. "My Photographs of California," *Magazine of Art*, 32 (January 1939), 32.

14. Ibid.

15. Weston, *Daybooks*, 154–56, entries for 24, 26, 29 April 1930.

Chapter Eight
Angel's Flight

1. Nancy Boas, *The Society of Six* (1988), 13.
2. Karal Marling, *Wall-to-Wall America* (1982), 41.
3. Bertram Wolfe, *The Fabulous Life of Diego Rivera* (1963), 285.

Chapter Nine
Dreaming Through the Disaster

1. William Dean Howells, "Cinematographic Show," *Harper's*, 125 (September 1912), 634.
2. "Democratic Art," *Nation*, 97 (28 August 1913), 193.
3. William DeMille, *Hollywood Saga* (1939), 274.
4. Sidney Howard, "Hollywood on the Slide," NR, 72 (9 November 1932), 350.
5. "Priests and the Motion Picture Industry," *Ecclesiastical Review*, 90 (1934), 142–43.
6. Ibid., 143–44.
7. Norman Zierold, *The Child Stars* (1965), 76.
8. Howard, "Hollywood on the Slide," 353.
9. Vincent Sheehan, "Hollywood," *Commonweal*, 12 (11 June 1930), 152.
10. Lillian Symes, "The Beautiful and Dumb," *Harper's*, 163 (June 1931), 32.
11. *The Autobiography of Cecil B. DeMille* (1959), 347.
12. David Niven, *Bring on the Empty Horses* (1975), 81.
13. Kenneth Anger, *Hollywood Babylon* (1984), 193–98.
14. Floyd Covington, "The Negro Invades Hollywood," *Opportunity*, 7 (April 1929), 131.

Chapter Ten
The Boys and Girls in the Back Room

1. "The Boys in the Back Room," *Classics and Commercials* (1950), 58, quoting Richard Hallas [Eric Knight], *You Play the Black and the Red Comes Up* (1938), 207–8.
2. Wilson, "Boys," 58.
3. *The Man on the Barge* (1935), 58–59.
4. *Praise the Lord!* (1932), 13, 17.
5. *Ask the Dust* (1939), 13.
6. Ibid., 46.
7. Amy Porter, "Garden of Allah, I Love You!" *Collier's*, 120 (22 November 1947), 19, 102.
8. Dorothy Gardiner and Katherine Sorley Walker, editors, *Raymond Chandler Speaking* (1960), 20, quoting a letter of 1 Janaury 1945 to Charles W. Morton.
9. Ibid., 21; Frank McShane, *The Life of Raymond Chandler* (1976), 1.
10. McShane, *Life of Chandler*, 294.
11. *Little Sister* (1949), reissued by Vintage Books in 1976, 183.
12. Andrew Turnbull, editor, *The Letters of F. Scott Fitzgerald* (1963), 582–83, quoting a letter of 3 May 1939 to Mrs. Frank Case.
13. Budd Schulberg, afterword to Anniversary Edition of *What Makes Sammy Run?* (1990), 322.

Chapter Eleven
War and Peace and the Survival of the Species

1. "Shine, Empire," *The Collected Poetry of Robinson Jeffers*, edited by Tim Hunt (3 vols., 1988–91), III, 17.

2. Robinson Jeffers, *Themes in My Poems* (1956), 28.

3. Ibid., 23–24.

4. Ibid., 31–32.

5. Ibid., 32.

6. "Rock and Hawk," *Collected Poetry*, II, 416.

7. "Shine, Empire," Ibid., III, 17.

8. Theodora Kroeber, *Ishi in Two Worlds* (1961), 218.

9. Ibid., 238.

10. Ibid., 234.

11. See the deluxe illustrated edition of *Ishi in Two Worlds* (1976), 142, for a photograph of Ishi, Kroeber, and others seated in a box at the Orpheum Theater in San Francisco in September 1911.

12. Julian Haynes Steward, editor, *Alfred Kroeber* (1973), 29.

13. *Dedication of the Hoover Library on War, Revolution, and Peace, Stanford University, June 20, 1941* (1941), 38.

Chapter Twelve
Ich Bin ein Südkalifornier

1. *The Muses Flee Hitler*, edited by Jarrell C. Jackman and Carla M. Borden (1983), 105.

2. Bob Thomas, *Clown Prince of Hollywood: The Antic Life and Times of Jack L. Warner* (1990), 127.

3. Niven, *Bring on the Empty Horses*, 119–20.

4. Thomas, *Clown Prince*, 127–28.

5. Charles Higham, *Marlene: The Life of Marlene Dietrich* (1977), 185.

6. Ibid., 70.

7. Ibid., 101.

8. Christopher Isherwood, *My Guru and His Disciple* (1980), 99–100.

9. Jonathan Fryer, *Isherwood* (1978), 203.

10. Jean Renoir, *My Life and My Films* (1974), 218.

11. Man Ray, *Self Portrait* (1963), 335.

Chapter 13
From Catastrophe to Covenant

1. Hans Burgin and Hans Otto Mayer, *Thomas Mann: A Chronicle of His Life* (1969), 153.

2. Lothar Kahn, *Insight and Action: The Life and Work of Lion Feuchtwanger* (1975), 235.

3. Ibid., 299–300, quoting letter of Hermann Kesten to Franz Schonberner, 8 January 1947.

4. Salka Viertel, *The Kindness of Strangers* (1969), 279.

5. Thomas Mann, *The Story of a Novel: The Genesis of "Doctor Faustus,"* translated by Richard and Clara Winston (1961), 149–50.

6. Erika Mann and Klaus Mann, *Escape to Life* (1939), 66.

7. Miklos Rozsa, *Double Life* (1989), 117.

8. Katia Mann, *Unwritten Memories*, translated by Hunter and Hildegarde Hannum (1975), 122–23.

9. Randall Patnode, "Exiles in Paradise," *USC Trojan Family*, 23 (Spring 1991), 16.

10. Viertel, *Kindness of Strangers*, 250–51.

11. Mann, *Story of a Novel*, 64–65.

12. Peter Stephan Jungk, *A Life Torn by History: Franz Werfel*, 1890–1945 (1987), 96.

13. "Garden in Progress," *Bertolt Brecht Poems*, edited by John Willet, Ralph Manheim, and Erich Fried (1976), 395–97.

14. Jarrell C. Jackman, "Exiles in Paradise," *SCQ*, 61 (Summer 1979), 191–92.

15. Anthony Heilbut, *Exiled in Paradise* (1983), 236.

16. Herman Weinberg, *The Lubitsch Touch* (1977), 192.

17. Jackman, "Exiles," 196, 198, 266, 289.

18. Susan Sontag, "Pilgrimage," *New Yorker*, 63 (21 December 1987), 38–54.

19. H. H. Stuckenschmidt, *Schoenberg: His Life, World, and Work*, translated by Humphrey Searle (1977), 403.

20. *Muses Flee Hitler*, 98.

21. Viertel, *Kindness of Strangers*, 259–60.

22. Ronald Hayman, *Brecht: A Biography* (1983), 276.

23. Joseph Wechsberg, *The First Time Around: Some Irreverent Recollections* (1970), 212.

24. Helen T. Lowe-Porter, "Translator's Note," *Doctor Faustus* (1948).

25. Burgin and Mayer, *Mann*, 184–85.

26. Dimitri Tiomkin, *Please Don't Hate Me* (1959), 119.

27. *Muses Flee Hitler*, 101.

28. Gottfried Reinhardt, *The Genius: A Memoir of Max Reinhardt* (1979), 284.

29. Lionel B. Steiman, *Franz Werfel: The Faith of an Exile* (1985), 166.

30. Jungk, *Life Torn by History*, 221.

31. Ibid., 155.

32. *Since You Went Away: World War II Letters from American Women on the Home Front*, edited by Judy Barrett Litoff and David C. Smith (1991), 194.

Bibliographical Essay

Chapter One
Good Times on the Coast

Farnsworth Crowder's three-part series "Where Life Is Better—For What?" appeared in the September, October, and November 1936 issues of *Westways*, volume 28.

Helen Walker Linsenmeyer, *From Fingers to Finger Bowls: A Sprightly History of California Cooking* (1972) is an excellent introduction to the topic. See also Rowena McLean Marks and Betty McDermott, *California Cooks* (1970). Regarding the cookbooks of California, see Philip S. Brown, "Old California Cook Books," *Quarterly News Letter of the Book Club of California*, 20 (Winter 1954), 4–12; and Liselotte and William Glozer, *California in the Kitchen* (1960). Regarding the barbecue in the 1930s, see Edward S. Graham, "Outdoor Grills for the California Home," *Touring Topics*, 28 (November 1933), 28–29; and Sherwood Hall, "Barbecues: An Old California Custom," *Country Life*, 68 (August 1935), 43–47. Regarding ranch-estates, see Kirk Wilkinson, "Return of the Ranch," *Country Life*, 67 (March 1935), 50–54. See also Maynard McFie, *Fifty Distinguished California Wines Selected by the Wine and Food Society of Los Angeles* (1941) and Marcus Crahan, compiler, *The Wine and Food Society of Southern California: A History* (1957).

For excellent descriptions of the Southern California beach towns and cities in the late 1930s, see Hildegarde Hawthorne, *Romantic Cities of California*, illustrated by E. H. Suydam (1939), 1–50. Hawthorne's book also serves as a valuable guide to all urban life in California during this period. Regarding surf culture in the late 1930s, see Helen Morgan, photographer, "Salamanders of the Sea and Sun," *Westways*, 32 (August 1940), 10–11. For the California beach house, see Barbara Lamont, "A House for Pacific Sands," *Westways*, 26 (April 1934), 26–27, 38. Regarding Santa Catalina in its golden era, see Charles N. Barnard, "On Santa Catalina Island, the Kings of Swing Held Sway," *Smithsonian*, 22 (October 1991), 153–67. See also Robin Mastrogeorge and Diann Marsh, *The Golden Promise: An Illustrated History of Orange County* (1986); and Charles Queenan, *Long Beach and Los Angeles: A Tale of Two Ports* (1986).

In the winter of 1984 *California History*, the magazine of the California Historical Society, produced a special issue, *Champions in the Sun*, edited by Frances Ring, relating to the sports history of California. The outdoor articles of Frederick Roland Miner were published by the Times-Mirror Press as *Outdoor Southland of California* (1923). See also

Kenneth Roberts, "California Diversions," SEP, 199 (18 September 1926), 13, 88–89, 92–98. Regarding winter sports in the late 1930s, see, Herbert Warren, "Snow Sports in California," Country Life, 69 (December 1935), 25–26, 66; Joel Hildebrand, A History of Skiing in California (1939); and Robert H. Power, Pioneer Skiing in California (1960).

Printer-writer Jack Stauffacher of San Francisco has shared with me a research file on polo champion Eric Pedley (1896–1986). It includes reprints from the California Polo Annual for 1913–14 and D. A. Raybould's Peninsula Polo Annual for 1912–13. The First Fifty Years, a history of the Monterey Peninsula Country Club at Pebble Beach, appeared in 1976. The story of tennis in Southern California is told by Patricia Henry Yeomans in Southern California Tennis Champions Centennial, 1887–1987 (1987). Regarding Helen Wills, see Larry Engelmann, The Goddess and the American Girl: The Story of Suzanne Lenglen and Helen Wills (1988) and Wills's autobiography, Fifteen-Thirty: The Story of a Tennis Player (1937).

Regarding tourism in the mid-1930s, see Carlson, A Mirror for Californians, 48–62. For the general background of the automobile in Southern California in the 1920s, see Ashleigh Brilliant, The Great Car Craze (1989). See also Don DeNevi and Thomas Moulin, Motor Touring in Old California (1979). Thomas Murphy's On Sunset Highways (1915) was sumptuously reissued in an expanded version in 1921 by L. C. Page & Company of Boston. Regarding the origins of the motel, see John Margolies, The End of the Road: Vanishing Highway Architecture in America (1981).

Regarding the early Sunset, see the anthology edited by Paul C. Johnson, The Early Sunset Magazine, 1898–1928 (1973). See also L. W. Lane Jr., The Sunset Story (1973), a speech first given before the Newcomen Society meeting in San Francisco on 15 May 1969. Regarding the new California look, see "California Creates: New Design on the West Coast," House Beautiful, 76 (November 1934), 36–39; and "Los Angeles Becomes Style Center Built Around Sportswear," Business Week (14 September 1940), 42–43. Also of relevance: the Fashion Group, Inc., California Fashion (1945). See also "Southern California: Its Five Contributions to Modern Living," House and Garden, 78 (November 1940), 12–25. Regarding Gump's, see Carol Green Wilson, Gump's Treasure Trade: A Story of San Francisco (1965).

For early assessments of the California home and lifestyle, see Walter Woehlke, "The Land of Sunny Homes," Sunset, 34 (March 1915), 463–72; and Boardman Pickett, "The Influence of Climate on California Country Homes," Country Life, 44 (October 1923), 52–54. See also "The Patio Is an Essential Part of the California Home," Country Life, 41 (November 1921), 68–69. Kathleen Norris made her home-oriented testimonials in "Here's to California!" American Mercury, 83 (January 1917), 28–29, and " 'Abierta,' My Home in Palo Alto," Arts and Decoration, 44 (March 1936) 12–14, 43. Madame Ernestine Schumann-Heink made her testimony in "Why I Live in California," Sunset, 61 (October 1928), 20–21. See also "If I Could Live Where I Choose in California," Westways, 27 (January 1935), 22–23.

Regarding the International Style, see Esther McCoy, Richard Neutra (1960); and David Gebhard, Schindler (1980). Of special importance is Thomas S. Hines's Richard Neutra and the Search for Modern Architecture (1982/1994). Regarding the design and development of Rancho Santa Fe, see Lucinda Liggett Eddy, "Lillian Jennette Rice: Search for a Regional Ideal," JSDH, 29 (Fall 1983), 262–85. Regarding La Jolla, see Thomas Jamison, "La Jolla Hermosa: A Subdivision Triumph," JSDH, 31 (Summer 1985), 210–26. Barbara Lamont and Jack Courtney covered the Southern California housing scene for Touring Topics/Westways at either end of the 1930s. See especially Lamont's "Designing and Furnishing the Small California Home," Touring Topics, 28 (August 1933), 24–25, 32; "Personality in a Little House," Touring Topics, 28 (September 1933) 28–29, 36; and "California's Castles in the Air," Westways, 26 (May 1934), 28–29, 41. Of importance to this chapter is Courtney's regular column "In and About the House" in *Westways* for February, September, and November 1937 and January 1938. Regarding the bungalow court, see James Curtis and Larry Ford, "Bungalow Courts in San Diego: Monitoring a Sense of Place," *JSDH*, 34 (Spring 1988), 79–92.

Regarding the early days of Palm Springs, see Katherine Ainsworth, *The McCallum Saga: The Story of the Founding of Palm Springs* (1973); and Marjorie Belle Bright, *Nellie's Boardinghouse: A Dual Biography of Nellie Coffman and Palm Springs* (1981). See also the booklet *A Look into Palm Springs Past* by Elizabeth Richards, issued by the Santa Fe Federal Savings and Loan Association in 1961. J. Smeaton Chase wrote the classic *Our Araby: Palm Springs and the Garden of the Sun* (1920). In 1938 Pricilla Chaffey assembled an extensive illustrated guide to Palm Springs under the title *Palm Springs Life*. See also L. Deming Tilton, consultant, *Report on a Master Plan for the City of Palm Springs, Riverside County, California*, issued on 4 March 1941. For a lively view of Palm Springs from the period, see Frank Condon, "Life on the Desert," *SEP* (5 December 1936), 12–13, 72–74). Regarding a famous mountain resort in Southern California during this period, see *Arrowhead* magazine in the California State Library in Sacramento. See also the pioneering leisure magazine *Game and Gossip* in the same collection.

Chapter Two
Arcadian Shores

Regarding UC Berkeley in the 1930s, see *The Golden Book of California* (1937), edited by Robert Sibley for the California Alumni Association, and issues of *Blue and Gold*, the UC Berkeley yearbook, for the period. John Kenneth Galbraith published "Berkeley in the Age of Innocence" in *Atlantic*, 223 (June 1969), 63–68. See also L. Bacon, "Teaching at Berkeley, Recollections," *Harper's*, 178 (March 1939), 416–21. S. Dan Brodie chronicles the football games of the period in *66 Years on the California Gridiron, 1882–1948* (1949). See also *The Stanford Quad* yearbook for the 1930s. The rise and fall of St. Mary's College as a power in football is told by Randy Andrada in *They Did It Every Time: The Saga of the St. Mary's Gaels, the Story of a Vanished College Football Empire* (1975). See also Matthew McDevitt, FSC, *The History of St. Mary's College, 1863–1963* (1963); and Ronald Eugene Isetti, FSC, *Called to the Pacific: A History of the Christian Brothers of the San Francisco District, 1868–1944* (1975).

Kathleen Norris told the story of the Thompson-Norris clan in *Family Gathering* (1959). For Cigi Norris, see Richard Allen Davison, *Charles G. Norris* (1983). Evelyn Wells wrote *Fremont Older* (1936). See also Older's *My Own Story* (1919) and the chapter on Older in Miriam Allen deFord's *They Were San Franciscans* (1941), 212–34. The San Francisco *Chronicle* published Older's obituary on its front page for 4 March 1935. The *Diaries of Mrs. Cora Baggerly Older, 1916–1923* were edited by Donna Harris for the California History Center at Foothill Community College (1971). See also Georgia Hesse, "Mrs. Fremont Older," *Pictorial Living*, San Francisco *Examiner*, 31 December 1961, 2, 4. Of special importance to this section are Edwin Bingham, *Charles Erskine Scott Wood* (1990); and Yehudi Menuhin, *Unfinished Journey* (1977). See also Lionel Menuhin Rolfe, *The Menuhins: A Family Odyssey* (1978). Regarding the Anderson Valley and its special language, see Charles C. Adams, *Boontling: An American Lingo* (1971). Regarding the Skunk, see Spencer Crump, *Redwoods, Iron Horses, and the Pacific: The Story of the California Western "SKUNK" Railroad* (1963).

Regarding life on the Monterey Peninsula in the late 1930s, see *Monterey Peninsula* (1941) in the American Guide Series sponsored by the Writers' Program of the WPA. For the early days of Carmel, see Franklin Walker, *The Seacoast of Bohemia* (1973). For Carmel in the 1920s, see Dorothy Bostick and Dorothea Castelhun, *Carmel—At Work and*

Play (1925). Charles S. Brooks reported on Carmel in the mid-1930s in *A Western Wind* (1935). Also consulted were the bound volumes of the *Carmelite* newspaper for the 1930s. I have depended heavily upon *A Wild Coast and Lonely: Big Sur Pioneers* (1989) by Rosalind Sharpe Wall for my understanding of Big Sur before World War II. Jaime de Angulo wrote and illustrated *Indian Tales* (1953), with a foreword by Carl Carmer. See also de Angulo's *Coyote Man and Old Doctor Loon* (1973) and the excellent *A Jaime de Angulo Reader* (1979) edited with an introduction by Bob Callahan. Van Wyck Brooks chronicled de Angulo in *Scenes and Portraits* (1954). Ella Young entitled her memoirs *Flowering Dusk* (1945). Regarding Hearst Castle, see Thomas Aidala, *Hearst Castle, San Simeon*, photographs by Curtis Bruce (1981); and Sara Holmes Boutelle, *Julia Morgan, Architect*, color photography by Richard Barnes (1988). See also Helaine Kaplan Prentice, *The Gardens of Southern California*, photographs by Melba Levick (1990).

Chapter Three
Unto the Stars Themselves

Helen Wright's well-researched *Explorer of the Universe: A Biography of George Ellery Hale* (1966) has guided all my judgments. Regarding Einstein's visits to Cal Tech, see Roland Clark, *Einstein: The Life and Times* (1971); and Jamie Sayen, *Einstein in America* (1985). For the story of Cal Tech, see Judith Goodstein, *Millikan's School: A History of the California Institute of Technology* (1991) and *The Autobiography of Robert A. Millikan* (1950). Regarding Cal Tech's greatest benefactor, see Rockwell Hereford, *A Whole Man, Henry Mauris Robinson, and a Half Century, 1890–1940* (1985). Regarding the architecture of Cal Tech, see Charles Moore, Peter Becker, and Regula Campbell, *The City Observed: Los Angeles* (1984), 339–43.

For the general history of astronomy, see Giorgio Abetti, *The History of Astronomy*, translated by Betty Burr Abetti (1952); G. Edward Pendray, *Men, Mirrors, and Stars* (rev. ed. 1969); and Dieter B. Herrmann, *The History of Astronomy from Herschel to Hertzsprung*, translated and revised by Kevin Krisciunas (1973), with its valuable chronology on pages 198–201. See also Henry King, *History of the Telescope* (1955). For the powerful affinity between California and astronomy, see Carey McWilliams, "Ladder to the Stars," *California: The Great Exception* (1949), 249–68. Regarding the California Academy of Sciences, see Robert Miller, "The California Academy of Sciences and the Early History of Science in the West," *CHSQ*, 21 (March 1942), 363–71. Oscar Lewis wrote *George Davidson: Pioneer West Coast Scientist* (1954). Regarding the Lick Observatory, see Helen Wright, *James Lick's Monument: The Saga of Captain Richard Floyd and the Building of the Lick Observatory* (1987); and Donald Osterbrock, John Gustafson, and W. J. Shiloh Unruh, *Eye on the Sky: Lick Observatory's First Century* (1988). See also Donald Osterbrock, *James E. Keeler: Pioneer American Astrophysicist and the Early Development of American Astrophysics* (1984). Katherine Bracher has written *The Stars for All: A Centennial History of the Astronomical Society of the Pacific* (1989), which first appeared in the ASP publication *Mercury* in September and October 1989. For the story of the Lowe Observatory, see Eugene Block, *Above the Civil War: The Story of Thaddeus Lowe, Balloonist, Inventor, Railway Builder* (1966).

Crucial to this chapter is the demographic and social study by Stephen Sargent Visher, *Scientists Starred 1903–1943 in "American Men of Science": A Study of Collegiate and Doctoral Training, Birthplace, Distribution, Backgrounds, and Developmental Influences*, published in 1947 by the Johns Hopkins Press.

Regarding the founding of the Mount Wilson Observatory, see Walter Adams, "Early Days at Mount Wilson," *Publications of the Astronomical Society of the Pacific*, 59 (October 1947), 213–31; and Alexander McAdie, George Hale, and Stanley Du Bois, "In Galileo's Footsteps: On This Summit of California's Sierra Madre Today Is Being Solved the Ultimate Problem of the Evolution of the Universe—The World of Science Watching Results," *Sunset*, 22 (February 1909), 133–43. For Pasadena at the time of Hale's arrival, see Bertha Smith's article in *Sunset*, 14 (November 1904), 33–36; and Elizabeth Grinnell, "Pasadena's Rose Tournament," *Sunset*, 12 (February 1904), 331–34. See also Kevin Starr, *Inventing the Dream: California Through the Progressive Era* (1985), 99–127.

In 1908 the University of Chicago Press published George Ellery Hale's *The Study of Stellar Evolution*. In 1915 the Carnegie Institution of Washington issued George Ellery Hale's *Ten Years' Work of a Mountain Observatory*. For the full range of Hale's power as a historian, philosopher, explicator, and interpreter of astrophysics and astronomy, see the series of books from Charles Scribner's Sons that Hale produced upon retiring from Mount Wilson: *The New Heavens* (1922), *The Depths of the Universe* (1924), *Beyond the Milky Way* (1926), and *Signals from the Stars* (1931). Alfred Noyes wrote *The Torch-Bearers: Watchers of the Sky* (1922). Edward Stafford Carlos translated *The Sidereal Messenger of Galileo Galilei*, published by Dawsons of Pall Mall at the turn of the century.

My discussion of Edwin Hubble is based on Bernard Jaffe's "Edwin Powell Hubble" in his *Men of Science in America: The Role of Science in the Growth of Our Country* (1944), 467–504; and the entry "Hubble, Edwin P. (1889–1953)" in Gilbert Satterthwaite's *Encyclopedia of Astronomy* (1970), 176–77. As a non-scientist, I have depended closely on these two sources, and in certain cases I have appropriated technical phrases from them in the interests of maintaining scientific accuracy. I have also read Hubble's *Red Shifts in Spectra of Nebulae* (1934) and *The Observational Approach to Cosmology* (1937) to bolster my understanding. For Hubble as a local hero, see Harold Carew, "A Lawyer Explores the Universe," *Westways*, 29 (September 1937), 28–29. I have also depended upon Fred Hoyle, *The Nature of the Universe* (rev. ed. 1960), which remains a model of elegant exposition for the lay reader.

For early discussion of the two hundred-inch telescope, see Hale's "The Possibility of Large Telescopes," *Harper's*, 156 (April 1928), 639–46; and Walter S. Adams, "A Great Telescope and Its Possibilities," *Science*, 69 (4 January 1929), 1–8. See also Henry Norris Russell's "Where to Put It? Few Realize How Many Factors Will Have to Be Considered in Selecting Scientifically the Best Site for the New 200–inch Telescope," *Scientific American* (January 1929), 20–21. For the full story of Mount Palomar, see David Woodbury, *The Glass Giant of Palomar* (1953); and Helen Wright, *Palomar: The World's Largest Telescope* (1952).

Chapter Four
Gilbraltar of the Pacific

"The Jumping-Off Place" appeared in Edmund Wilson's *The American Jitters: A Year of the Slump* (1932). See also Wilson's *The Thirties, from Notebooks and Diaries of the Period*, edited with an introduction by Leon Edel (1980), 130–32. For further background on poverty in San Diego in the 1930s, see also Chris Ernest Nelson, "The Battle for Ham and Eggs: The 1938–1939 San Diego Campaign for the California Pension Plan," *JSDH*, 39 (Fall 1992), 203–25.

General histories of San Diego include Theodore Strong Van Dyke, *The City and County of San Diego* (1888); William Ellsworth Smythe, *History of San Diego, 1542–1907* (1907); Clarence Alan McGrew, *City of San Diego and San Diego County* (2 vols., 1922); and Carl Heilbron, editor, *History of San Diego County* (1936). Richard Pourade, editor emeritus of the San Diego *Union*, has produced an ambitious, lavishly illustrated seven-volume history of San Diego, of great use to this chapter. The series includes *The Explorers* (1960), *Time of the Bells* (1961), *The Silver Dons* (1963), *The Glory Years* (1964), *Gold in the Sun* (1965), *The Rising Tide* (1967), and *City of the Dream* (1977). Iris H. W. Engstrand has written *San Diego: California's Cornerstone* (1980), also of great value to this chapter. Of special importance as a source of reference is Philip Pryde, editor, *San Diego: An Introduction to the Region* (2d ed., 1984).

Richard Requa, director of architecture for the California-Pacific International Exposition, wrote *Inside Lights on the Building of San Diego's Exposition, 1935* (1937). See also Richard Amero, "San Diego Invites the World to Balboa Park a Second Time," *JSDH,* 31 (Fall 1985), 261–80. Regarding San Diego and La Jolla, Max Carlton Miller has written *I Cover the Waterfront* (1932), *Harbor of the Sun* (1940), *It Must Be the Climate* (1941), and *The Town with the Funny Name* (1948). See also Miller's two San Diego novels, *He Went Away for a While* (1933) and *A Stranger Came to Port* (1938).

For the railroad history of San Diego, see the pamphlet *The Railroad Stations of San Diego County: Then and Now* by James N. Price (1988), based on material previously published in *JSDH.* Regarding the visit of Helen Hunt Jackson, see Evelyn Banning, "Helen Hunt Jackson in San Diego," *JSDH,* 24 (Fall 1978), 457–67. Regarding other arrivees, see Robert Burlison, "Samuel Fox, Merchant and Civic Leader in San Diego, 1886–1939," *JDSH,* 26 (Winter 1980), 1–10; Nicholas Polos, "San Diego's 'Portia of the Pacific': California's First Woman Lawyer," *JDSH,* 26 (Summer 1980), 185–95; and Sally Thornton, " 'An Atmosphere of Friendliness': The Cuyamanca Club," *JSDH,* 29 (Fall 1983), 286–92. For William Smythe's role, see Lawrence Lee, "William E. Smythe and San Diego, 1901–1908," *JSDH,* 19 (Winter 1973), 10–23.

John Baur's *Health-Seekers of Southern California* (1959) is the classic account of the Health Rush. For the San Diego perspective, see Linda Miller, "San Diego's Early Years as a Health Resort," *JSDH,* 28 (Fall 1982), 232–47; and Patricia Schaelchlin, "'Working for the Good of the Community': Rest Haven Preventorium for Children," *JSDH,* 29 (Spring 1983), 96–114. The volume 33 (Spring/Summer 1987) issue of the *JSDH* is devoted entirely to Jesse Shepard and the Villa Montezuma. See especially Clare Crane, "Jesse Shepard and the Spark of Genius," 106–21; and Clare Crane, "The Villa Montezuma as a Product of Its Time," 80–105.

Regarding the Point Loma community, see Paul Kagan and Marilyn Ziebarth, "Eastern Thought on a Western Shore," *CHSQ,* 52 (1973), 4–15; Dale Reynolds, "History of the First Greek Theatre in America at Point Loma, California, 1901–1965," *JSDH,* 12 (April 1966), 17–24; and Bruce Kamerling, "Theosophy and Symbolist Art: The Point Loma Art School," *JSDH,* 26 (Fall 1980), 231–55. Regarding the Scripps Institution, see Elizabeth Shor, "How Scripps Institution Came to San Diego," *JSDH,* 27 (Winter 1981), 161–73. For the San Diego involvements of John D. Spreckels, see H. Austin Adams, *The Man: John D. Spreckels* (1924). For Grant, see Evelyn Banning, "U. S. Grant, Jr., a Builder of San Diego," *JDSH,* 27 (Winter 1981), 1–16.

Regarding Marston, see Nicholas Polos, "George White Marston: The Merchant Prince of San Diego," *JSDH,* 30 (Fall 1984), 252–78; and Gregg Hennessey, "George White Marston and Conservative Reform in San Diego," *JSDH,* 32 (Fall 1986), 230–53. Architect-planner Gregory Montes has written the history of City/Balboa Park in three parts: "San Diego's City Park, 1868–1902: An Early Debate on Environment and Profit," *JSDH,* 23 (Spring 1977), 40–59; "San Diego's City Park, 1902–1910: From Parsons to Balboa," *JSDH,* 25 (Winter 1979), 1–25; and "Balboa Park, 1909–1911: The Rise and Fall of the Olmsted Plan," *JSDH,* 28 (Winter 1982), 46–67. See also Elizabeth MacPhail, *Kate Sessions: Pioneer Horticulturist* (1977). For an illustrated assessment of Irving Gill in the San Diego context, see Bruce Kamerling, "Irving Gill: The Artist as Architect," *JSDH,* 25 (Spring 1979), 151–91. Regarding the Bishop School, see Thomas Mitchell, "The Republican Experiment and the Bishop School," *JSDH,* 30 (Spring 1984), 105–23. Regarding Mission Cliff Gardens, see Beverly Potter, "Mission Cliff Gardens," *JSDH,* 32 (Fall

1977), 1–11; and Elizabeth MacPhail, "A Little Gem of a Park: A Personal Memoir of Mission Cliff Gardens," *JSDH*, 29 (Fall 1983), 295–305. Regarding the San Diego Floral Association, see Sharon Siegan, "From Seed to Center: Seven Decades of Floral Service," *JSDH*, 25 (Summer 1979), 208–220.

Regarding the post-Exposition development of Balboa Park, the following articles have proved of importance: Helen Ellsberg, "The Music Festival San Diego Almost Had," *JSDH*, 28 (Winter 1982), 35–45; Marjorie Betts Shaw, "The San Diego Zoological Garden," *JSDH*, 24 (Summer 1978), 300–310; Beth Mohr, "The Old Globe Theater: Highlights from Fifty Years," *JSDH*, 31 (Fall 1985), 87–120; Peter Mehren, "San Diego's Opera Unit of the WPA Federal Music Project," *JSDH*, 18 (Summer 1972), 12–21. Regarding the 1917 campaign, see Uldis Ports, "Geraniums vs. Smokestacks: San Diego's Mayoralty Campaign of 1917," *JSDH*, 21 (Summer 1975), 50–56. See also James Moss, "For Discovery, Collection, and Preservation: The San Diego Historical Society," *JSDH*, 25 (Spring 1979), 136–50. For further background regarding Madame Schumann-Heink as a San Diegan, see Kathleen Crawford, " 'God's Garden': The Grossmont Art Colony," *JSDH*, 31 (Fall 1985), 298–319.

In chapter 2 of *Fortress California, 1910–1961* (1992), Roger Lotchin describes in detail how San Diego overcame the resistance of the Navy and transformed itself into a naval city. See also the seminal essay by Gregg Hennessey, "San Diego, the U.S. Navy, and Urban Development: West Coast City Building, 1912–1929," *CHSQ* (Summer 1993), 129–49, which commands the subject. For a more antiquarian perspective, see Edward J. P. Davis, *The United States Navy and U.S. Marine Corps at San Diego* (1955). Regarding the USS *Bennington* catastrophe, see Broeck Oder, "San Diego's Naval Disaster: The Explosion of the Bennington," *JSDH*, 22 (Summer 1976), 36–47. Regarding Glenn Curtiss in San Diego, see Gary Kurutz, "The Only Safe and Sane Method . . . The Curtiss School of Aviation," *JSDH*, 25 (Winter 1979), 27–59. Regarding the efforts of Congressman William Kettner to secure the Navy, see Lucille Clark Duvall, "San Diego's Dynamic Congressman," *JSDH*, 25 (Summer 1979), 191–207. Regarding the grounding of the *Asama Gunkan* at Turtle Bay, see Donald Estes, "The Reappraisal of a War Scare," *JSDH*, 24 (Summer 1978), 267–99. For the story of the visit of the Prince of Wales to San Diego in April 1920, see Richard Kurial, "The Prince of Wales Visits San Diego: A Study in Perception," *JSDH*, 38 (Summer 1992), 161–75. See also Benjamin Sacks, "The Duchess of Windsor and the Coronado Legend," Part 1, *JSDH*, 33 (Fall 1987), 165–74; part 2, *JSDH*, 34 (Winter 1988), 1–15.

Chapter Five
One Man's Family

Jerry Flamm's *Good Life in Hard Times: San Francisco's '20s and '30s* (1981) commands the subject, as does Robert Cherny and William Issel's *San Francisco, 1865–1932: Politics, Power, and Urban Development* (1986). Other important surveys include Miriam Allen deFord, *They Were San Franciscans* (1941); Julia Cooley Altrocchi, *The Spectacular San Franciscans* (1949); Robert O'Brien, *This Is San Francisco*, illustrated by Antonio Sotomayor (1948); and Samuel Dickson, *Tales of San Francisco* (1957). Two important reference works are WPA Writers' Program, *San Francisco: the Bay and its Cities*, edited by Gladys Hansen (rev. ed. 1973); and Gladys Hansen, *San Francisco Almanac* (rev. ed. 1980). See also Susan Shephard, *In the Neighborhoods*, photography by Gregg Mancuso (1981).

The obituary of Charles Caldwell Dobie appeared in the *Chronicle* on 12 January 1943. See also Dobie's "Frank Norris; or Up from Culture," *American Mercury* 13 (1928), 412–24. Regarding Timothy Pflueger, see Milton Pflueger, *Time and Tim Remembered* (1985).

Many of Pflueger's drawings and renderings were reproduced in the Butterfield & Butterfield catalog *The John Pflueger Collection of Architectural Renderings, Models, and Photographs*, issued for the sale of 22 March 1990. Regarding Rolph, see Moses Rischin, "Sunny Jim Rolph: The First 'Mayor of All the People,' " *CHSQ*, 53 (1974), 165–72; and David Wooster Taylor, *The Life of James Rolph, Jr.* (1934). Regarding WPA projects in San Francisco in the late 1930s, see the "Report of Clyde E. Healy, Assistant City Engineer, City of San Francisco, and Coordinator of WPA Projects, 10 October 1935 to 31 August 1939," on deposit in the Bancroft Library. Regarding the cemetery removals, see Michael Svanevik and Shirley Burgett, *Pillars of the Past* (1992).

Regarding the ferry boat culture of San Francisco, see George Harlan and Clement Fisher, *Of Walking Beams and Paddle Wheels: A Chronicle of San Francisco Bay Ferryboats* (1951). The *Call-Bulletin* ran "Romantic History of SF Bay Recalled" between 20 and 24 October 1936. See also Jim Walker, *Key System Album* (1978). B. C. Forbes's *Men Who Are Making the West* (1923) contains biographical portraits of Herbert Fleishhacker, Robert Dollar, and A. P. Giannini. Gerald Nash's *A. P. Giannini and the Bank of America* (1992) is a welcomed biography. See also Marquis James and Bessie Rowland James, *Biography of a Bank: The Story of Bank of America* (1954). For further insight into Giannini, see Russell Posner, "The Bank of Italy and the 1926 Campaign in California," *CHSQ*, 37 (September 1958), 267–77, 347–58; Joseph Giovinco, "Democracy in Banking: The Bank of Italy and California's Italians," *CHSQ*, 47 (1968), 195–218; Dwight Clarke, "The Gianninis—Men of the Renaissance," *CHSQ*, 49 (1970), 251–69, 337–51. The obituaries of the Fleishhacker brothers appeared in the *Chronicle* on 14 July 1953 and 3 April 1957. See also *Who's Who in America*, vol. 20, 1938–39. Regarding the retail elite, see Robert Hendrickson, *The Grand Emporiums: The Illustrated History of America's Great Department Stores* (1979). The *Memoirs of Charles Kendrick*, edited and annotated with an introduction by David Warren Ryder, were published in 1972. Relevant business histories include Neill Wilson, *400 California Street: The Story of the Bank of California* (1964); T. Carroll Wilson, *A Background Story of Hills Brothers Coffee, Inc.* (1966); George Koster with E. Elizabeth Summers, *The Transamerica Story: Fifty Years of Service and Looking Forward* (1978); and Michael Nerney, *A History of Wiliams, Dimond & Company Since 1862* (1988). For background to the shipping industry, see Robert Schwendinger, *International Port of Call: An Illustrated Maritime History of the Golden Gate* (1984). Robert Dollar published his *Memoirs* in 1918. His obituary appeared in the *Chronicle* on 16 May 1932.

Regarding the legal culture of San Francisco, see Kenneth M. Johnson, *The Bar Association of San Francisco: The First Hundred Years, 1872–1972* (1972). See also the listings in *The San Francisco Bar* for 1937 and 1938, issued by the San Francisco Bar Association. The obituary of Garrett McEnerney appeared in the *Chronicle* on 4 August 1942. With the assistance of Robert Blair Kaiser, Melvin Belli wrote *My Life on Trial* (1976). See also Brad Williams, *Due Process: The Story of Criminal Lawyer George T. Davis and his Thirty-Year Battle Against Capital Punishment* (1961); and James P. Walsh, *San Francisco's Hallinan, Toughest Lawyer in Town* (1982).

Irena Narrell's *Our City: The Jews of San Francisco* (1981) commands the subject. See also David Dalin, *Public Affairs in the Jewish Community: The Changing Political World of San Francisco Jews* (1977), a Brandeis political science dissertation available from Xerox University Microfilms. Regarding Temple Emanu-El and Irving Reichert, see Fred Rosenbaum, *Architects of Reform, Congregational and Community Leadership, Emanu-El of San Francisco, 1849–1980* (1980). Allan Temko wrote on Temple Emanu-El in *Commentary* for August 1958. See also the very engaging *House of Harmony: Concordia-Argonaut's First 130 Years* (1983) by Bernice Scharlach. Frances Bransten Rothmann wrote the lively memoirs *Coffee, Martinis, and San Francisco* (1978), *The Haas Sisters of Franklin Street*

(1979), and *My Father, Edward Bransten: His Life and Letters* (1982). Regarding Lowell High School, see the Lowell High School Student Association, *Centennial Edition of Red and White*, volume 83 of the *Lowell High School Yearbook*, published in June 1956. Also consulted: *The Red and White*, Lowell, for December 1932; *The Polytechnic*, Polytechnic High School, for the fall of 1939; *The Telescope*, Galileo High School, for December 1938; and *The Heights*, St. Ignatius High School, for 1929—all on deposit in the Bancroft Library.

The institutional life of Roman Catholic San Francisco is documented in *The Official Catholic Directory for the Year of Our Lord 1935* and *The Official Catholic Directory Anno Domini 1940*. Regarding Archibishop Hanna, see the relevant portions of James Gaffey, *Citizen of No Mean City: Archbishop Patrick Riordan of San Francisco* (1976). Nina Bartholomew wrote "A Brief History of the Floods and Their Mansion at 2222 Broadway," a brochure issued in 1977. James P. Walsh wrote *The San Francisco Irish, 1850–1976* (1978). See also *One Hundred Years: The Olympic Club Centennial* (1960). For the Jesuit background, see John Bernard McGloin, SJ, *Jesuits by the Golden Gate, the Society of Jesus in San Francisco, 1849–1969* (1972). Alexander Cody, SJ, wrote *Peddler of Beauty and Other Poems* (1933) and *A Memoir, Richard A. Gleeson, SJ, 1861–1945* (1950). See also St. Dominic's Church, San Francisco, *One Hundredth Anniversary 1873–1973* (1973); and Alessandro Baccari Jr., Vincenza Scarpaci, and Gabriel Zavattaro, SDB, *Saints Peter & Paul Church: The Chronicles of "The Italian Cathedral" of the West 1884–1984* (1985). Of sociological importance is Stewart Perry, *San Francisco Scavengers: Dirty Work and the Pride of Ownership* (1978). Episcopalian San Francisco can be glimpsed through William Bours, *Turning Points in the Evolution of Grace Cathedral, Diocese of California* (1938); and Rosa Lee Baldwin, *The Bells Shall Ring* (1940). For descriptions of places of worship throughout the city, see Ruth Hendricks Willard and Carol Green Wilson, *Sacred Places of San Francisco*, photographs by Roy Flamm (1985).

Regarding the Chinese community, see Thomas W. Chinn, *Bridging the Pacific: San Francisco Chinatown and Its People* (1989). The Chinese-Americans Citizen Alliance issued *San Francisco Lodge 75th Anniversary Souvenir Edition 1912–1987* (1987). Carey McWilliams described the funeral of Mrs. Yick Jung Shee in his "Tides West" column in *Westways*, February 1937. Regarding African-American San Francisco, see Douglas Henry Daniels, *Pioneer Urbanites: A Social and Cultural History of Black San Francisco* (1980). The autobiography of Howard Thurman, *With Head and Heart*, appeared in 1979.

Regarding the restaurants and night life of San Francisco, see Ruth Thompson and Chef Louis Hanges, *Eating Around San Francisco*, illustrated by William Bender (1937); Jack Lord and Jenn Shaw, *Where to Sin in San Francisco*, preface by Beniamino Bufano, drawings by Lloyd Hoff (1939); Edith Shelton and Elizabeth Field, *Let's Have Fun in San Francisco* (1939); and Matty and Don Simmons, *On the House* (1955). See also George Mardikian, *Dinner at Omar Khayyam's* (1944). The story of the St. Francis Hotel is told by David Siefkin in *Meet Me at the St. Francis: The First Seventy-Five Years of a Great San Francisco Hotel* (1979). Dan London's obituary appeared in the *Chronicle* on 20 May 1974. For pleasure spots in the Bay Area hinterlands, see James Lewis, editor, *Doorway to Good Living: Selected Places, Where to Eat and Where to Stay, Where to Fish and Where to Play, Along the Pacific Slope of the Western Wonderland* (1947).

The Atherton Report was published in its entirety in the San Francisco *News* on 16 March 1937. Regarding prostitution in San Francisco, see Jacqueline Barnhart, *The Fair but Frail: Prostitution in San Francisco, 1849–1900* (1986); and Curt Gentry, *The Madams of San Francisco* (3d ed. 1977). The San Quentin Museum Association has issued *San Quentin Inside the Walls* (1991) by Nancy Ann Nichols.

Regarding the literary background of San Francisco, see Lawrence Ferlinghetti and Nancy J. Peters, *Literary San Francisco* (1980). Fremont Older wrote *My Own Story*

(1919). Kathleen Norris told her story in *Family Gathering* (1959). Kenneth Rexroth describes his entrance into San Francisco in 1927 in *An Autobiographical Novel* (1978). For Gertrude Atherton in the 1930s, see Emily Leider's *Gertrude Atherton and Her Times* (1991). Joseph Henry Jackson wrote *Irving Stone and the Biographical Novel* (1954). Stephen Schwartz wrote an extensive obituary of Irving Stone in the *Chronicle* on 28 August 1989. Lawrence Lee and Barry Gifford produced *Saroyan: A Biography* (1984). Saroyan tells his own story, intermittently, of San Francisco in the 1930s in *Letters from 74 rue Taitbout; or, Don't Go but if You Must Say Hello to Everybody* (1969) and *Chance Meetings: A Memoir* (1978). Saroyan was profiled by Richard Donovan in the *Chronicle* for Sunday, 16 February 1941. See also Peter King's obituary in the *Examiner* for 18 May 1981. Regarding Oscar Lewis, see *Oscar Lewis, 1893–1992* (1992), a collection of essays issued by the Book Club of California. In June and July of 1965, Lewis was interviewed by Ruth Teiser and Catheriine Harroun of the Regional Oral History Office of the Bancroft Library; the typed transcript of these tape-recorded interviews, entitled "Literary San Francisco," is on deposit at the Bancroft Library. For the fine print scene in San Francisco in the 1930s, see Gregg Anderson, *Recollections of the Grabhorn Press* (1935); and James D. Hart, *Fine Printing in California* (1960).

Gene Hailey profiled Ralph Stackpole in the *California Art Research Monographs*, vol. 14, first series, 1937, bound mimeographed typescript on deposit at the Bancroft Library. See also William Mahan, *Ralph Stackpole's Fresco at Sacramento City College* (1984), a brochure issued by the Gregroy Kondos Art Gallery in Sacramento. Stackpole was profiled on 29 November 1964, in the *Chronicle*, where his obituary appeared on 12 December 1973. Randolph Falk wrote and photographed *Bufano* (1975). Bufano's former wife, Virginia Lewin, takes a more ambivalent stance in *One of Benny's Faces: A Study of Beniamnio Bufano (1886–1970), the Man Behind the Artist* (1980). Antonio Sotomayor was profiled by Phil Townsend Hanna in "Sotomayor and Happy Valley," *Westways*, 28 (June 1936), 24–25; in the *California Living* supplement for the Sunday *Examiner and Chronicle*, 21 August 1966; the *Chronicle* for 27 September 1978; and the Sunday *Examiner and Chronicle* for 15 October 1978. Sotomayor's obituary appeared in the *Chronicle* on 12 February 1985. Masha Zakheim Jewett wrote the invaluable *Coit Tower, San Francisco: Its History and Art*, color photographs by Don Beatty (1983). Diego River wrote *My Art, My Life* (1960). See also Bertram D. Wolfe, *The Fabulous Life of Diego Rivera* (1963); and Lawrence Hurlburt, *The Mexican Muralists in the United States* (1989).

The musical culture of San Francisco can be traced through: William Huck, "Seventy-Five Years of the San Francisco Symphony," *California History*, 65 (December 1986), 248–62; Arthur Bloomfield, *San Francisco Opera 1922–1978* (1978); and Cobbett Steinberg, *San Francisco Ballet: The First Fifty Years* (1983). See also Francis Gates, *Who's Who in Music in California* (1920); William J. Perlman, compiler, *Music and Dance in California*, edited by José Rodriguez (1940); and Ronald L. Davis, *A History of Opera in the American West* (1965). Leonara Armsby Wood wrote her memoir *Musicians Talk* (1935). See also Robert Magidoff, *Yehudi Menuhin: The Story of the Man and the Musician* (1955). Oscar Lewis wrote *AMB: Some Aspects of His Life and Times* (1941) and *To Remember Albert M. Micky Bender: Notes for a Biography* (1973). Ruth Lewis profiled Bender in "Bachelor of Arts," *Westways* 32 (November 1940), 20–21. There is much information on Charles Templeton Crocker in Ann Holliday's *Theatrical Splendor: Work of Stowitts for Fay Yen Fah, Paris 1926–1927* (1991). Bernice Scharlach's *Big Alma: San Francisco's Alma Spreckels* (1990) is a tour de force. For further treatment of the upper strata, see the profile of Filoli in *Country Life*, 72 (June 1937), 29–40; and *Gabriel Moulin's San Francisco Peninsula: Town & Country Homes 1910–1930* (1990). Also consulted: Pacific Union Club, *Constitution and List of Members*, 1937–38, 1940–41; and Bohemian

Club of San Francisco, *Certificate of Incorporation, Constitution, By-Laws and Rules, Officers and Committees, Members, In Memoriam* (1 January 1939).

Chapter Six
Pershing Square

Essential to any investigation of Los Angeles in any decade is the Los Angeles Metropolitan History Project, *Los Angeles and Its Environs in the Twentieth Century: A Bibliography of a Metropolis*, edited with an introduction by Doyce B. Nunis Jr. (1973). Of central importance to this chapter is the guidebook compiled by the Writers' Program of the Work Projects Administration in Southern California, *Los Angeles: A Guide to the City and Its Environs* (1941). Also of use is *California: A Guide to the Golden State* (1939) in the same series. See also Lanier and Virginia Bartlett, *Los Angeles in Seven Days, Including Southern California* (1932); Richard and Patience Abbe, *Of All Places!* (1937); and Margaret Mackey, *Los Angeles, Proper and Improper* (1938). Morrow Mayo, *Los Angeles* (1933) has not one kind thing to say about the city. Harry Carr's *Los Angeles, City of Dreams*, illustrations by E. H. Suydam (1935), on the other hand, is an uninterrupted paean. Histories of Los Angeles of relevance to the 1930s include Boyle Workman, *The City That Grew* (1936); Marguerite Cameron, *El Pueblo* (1936); Charles Owens and Joseph Seewerker, *Nuestro Pueblo: Los Angeles, City of Romance* (1940); Remi Nadeau, *Los Angeles: From Mission to Modern City* (1968); John Weaver, *Los Angeles: El Pueblo Grande, the Enormous Village* (1973); Lynn Bowman, *Los Angeles, Epic of a City* (1974); W. W. Robinson, *Los Angeles: A Profile* (1968); David L. Clark, *Los Angeles: A City Apart* (1981); Bruce Henstell, *Sunshine and Wealth: L.A. in the Twenties and Thirties* (1984); and Leonard Leader, *Los Angeles and the Great Depression* (1991), a reprint of the author's 1972 UCLA Ph.D. thesis in history. See also Jules Tygiel, *The Great Los Angeles Swindle: Oil, Stocks, and Scandal During the Roaring Twenties* (1994). General surveys with Los Angeles chapters include Margaret Mackey, *Cities in the Sun* (1938); and Hildegarde Hawthorne, *Romantic Cities of California* (1939). W. W. Robinson compiled the anthology *What They Say About the Angels* (1942).

Cultural assessments of importance to this chapter include Aubrey Burns, "Regional Culture in California," *Southwest Review*, 17 (July 1932), 373–97; A. Edward Newton, "The Course of Empire," *Atlantic Monthly*, 150 (September 1932), 298–304; James M. Cain, "Paradise: Civilization of Southern California," *American Mercury*, 28 (March 1933), 266–80; Oswald Garrison Villard, "Los Angeles Kaleidoscope," *Nation*, 138 (21 March 1934), 321; George Marvin, "Cities Are Persons," *Catholic World*, 147 (June 1938), 303–4; and Willard Motley, "Small-Town Los Angeles," *Commonweal*, 30 (30 June 1939), 251–52. Other assessments of use to this chapter include Emory Stephen Bogardus, *Southern California: A Center of Culture* (1938); and Dudley Gordon, *An Entertaining Guide Book to the Cultural Assets of Metropolitan Los Angeles* (1940). See also Raine Bennett, "The Hawthornes Carry On," *Westways*, 26 (June 1934), 18–19, 32.

The most concise interpretive introduction to the architecture of Los Angeles is Thomas Hines's "Los Angeles Architecture: The Issue of Tradition in a Twentieth-Century City," in *American Architecture: Innovation and Tradition*, edited by David De Long, Helen Searing, and Robert A. M. Stern (1986), 112–29. The architectural look of Los Angeles in this period can be best seen in David Gebhard and Harriette von Breton, *L.A. in the Thirties* (1975). See also David Gebhard and Robert Winter, *Architecture in Los Angeles: A Compleat Guide* (1977); and Sam Hall Kaplan, *L.A. Lost & Found: An Architectural History of Los Angeles*, photographs by Julius Shulman (1987). Regarding Art Deco Los Angeles, see Susan Vaughn, "Art Deco: Touching Face of 1920s L.A.," *Los Angeles*

Times, Sunday, 13 October 1991, E16–17; and Alastair Duncan, *American Art Deco* (1988). See also Marjorie Ingle, *The Mayan Revival Style* (1985). Regarding Downtown, see Charles Lockwood, "Los Angeles Exuberant," New York *Times,* Sunday, 3 November 1985, Arts and Leisure, 20; and Carrie Yoshimura, "A Celebration of L.A.'s Movie Palaces," Los Angeles *Times,* 15 July 1987, part VI, 3. Esther McCoy wrote *Richard Neutra* (1960). David Gebhard wrote *R. M. Schindler* (1972). Regarding the two Lovell houses, see "The Demonstration Health House, Los Angeles," *Architectural Record,* 67 (April 1930), 433–39. The roadside architecture of the region can be glimpsed in Karal Ann Marling, *The Colossus of Roads: Myth and Symbol Along the American Highway* (1984); and Jim Heimann and Rip Georges, *California Crazy: Roadside Vernacular Architecture,* introduction by David Gebhard (1985). Regarding the landscaping of Los Angeles, see Charles Henry Rowan, "Ornamental Plants as a Factor in the Cultural Development of Southern California" (M.A. thesis, geography, UCLA, 1957). Edmund Wilson described Los Angeles in "The City of Our Lady the Queen of the Angeles," *The American Earthquake: A Documentary of the Twenties and Thirties* (1958). See also Wilson's *The Thirties, from Notebooks and Diaries of the Period,* edited with an introduction by Leon Edel (1980).

Treatments of more specific locales include Ralph Hancock, *Fabulous Boulevard* (1949); Bernadette Dominique Soter, *The Light of Learning: An Illustrated History of the Los Angeles Public Library* (1933); Dolores Hayden, Gail Dubrow, and Carolyn Flynn, *The Power of Place, Los Angeles* (brochure, no date); Pat Adler, *The Bunker Hill Story* (1963); Leo Politi, *Bunker Hill, Los Angeles* (1964); and *The Story of Griffith Observatory and Planetarium* (1952).

Regarding the traffic of Los Angeles in this period, see E. E. East, "The Traffic Squeeze, a New Menace to Metropolitan Los Angeles," *Westways,* 29 (September 1937), 20–21. See also "Banking by Automobile, First Drive-In Bank in the World, " *Scientific American,* 157 (September 1937), 151. Regarding the clubs of Los Angeles, see Marco R. Newmark, "Pioneer Clubs of Los Angeles Founded During the Nineteenth Century," SCQ, 31 (December 1949), 299–317. Regarding the restaurants of the city, see Automobile Club of Southern California, *Let's Dine Out in Southern California: A Guide to Worthwhile Restaurants, Cafes, Inns, Taverns,* compiled by the staff of *Westways* under the direction of Phil Townsend Hanna (1940).

The weekly news magazine *Los Angeles Saturday Night* issued the supplement *150th Birthday of Los Angeles City and County: A Pre-Olympiad Feature, 1781–1931* (1931). Regarding the Tenth Olympiad, see: *The Games of the Tenth Olympiad, Los Angeles 1932, Official Report* (1933). See also Grace Somerby, "When Los Angeles Was Host to the Olympic Games of 1932," SCQ, 34 (1952), 125–32. Regarding architectural preparations, see "Olympic Stadium in Los Angeles," *Architectural Record,* 70 (December 1931), 419–24. See also Emerson Knight, "Outdoor Theaters and Stadiums in the West," *The Architect and the Engineer,* 78 (August 1924), 53–92. Regarding the neighborhood of the Olympic Village, see the brochure by Warren Rogers, *Mesa to Metropolis: The Crenshaw Area, Los Angeles* (September–October 1957). The well-known German planner Anton Wagner researched *Los Angeles . . . Zweimillionenstadt in Südkalifornien* (1935).

Regarding real estate fraud in Los Angeles, see *Sunshine and Grief in Southern California, Where Good Men Go Wrong and Wise People Lose Their Money, by an Old Promoter Forty Years in the Field of Real Estate* (1931). George Creel chronicled the Clinton investigations in "Unholy City: Los Angeles Is Up to Its Civic Ears in a Fight on Political Corruption and All-Around Sin," *Collier's,* 104 (2 September 1939), 12–13 ff. See also Guy Woodward Finney, *Angel City in Turmoil* (1945); and John Anson Ford, *Thirty Explosive Years in Los Angeles County* (1961). Regarding the Julian oil scandal, see Lorin Lynn Baker, *That Imperiled Freedom* (1932). Harold Carew profiled Chief Davis in "Good Aims for Bad Men," *Westways,* 26 (June 1934), 16–17, 40. Regarding homicide in L.A., see

Nicholas Harris, *Famous Crimes* (1933); Leslie Turner White, *Me, Detective* (1936); and Craig Rice, editor, *Los Angeles Murders* (1947). For an insight into upscale prostitution, see Beverly Davis, *Call House Madam*, as told by Serge Wolsey (1945). When the citizens of Los Angeles got in trouble, which was frequently the case, they turned to Jerry Giesler. See *The Jerry Giesler Story*, as told to Pete Martin (1960). See also Clyde Vedder, "An Analysis of the Taxi-Dance Hall as a Social Institution, with Special Reference to Los Angeles and Detroit" (Ph.D. dissertation, sociology, USC, 1947). See also Tom Griswold, "A Bum's Guide to Los Angeles," *American Mercury*, 51 (December 1940), 408–13.

Agness Underwood's autobiography is *Newspaperwoman* (1949). Regarding Harry Carr, see John Russell McCarthy, "Los Angeles' Bad, Bad Boy," *Westways*, 26 (February 1934), 26–27, 33. Regarding USC in the 1930s, see Manuel Servin and Iris Higbie Wilson, *Southern California and Its University*, foreword by Carey McWilliams (1969). Regarding the Rose Bowl, see Maxwell Stiles, *The Rose Bowl* (1946); Rube Samuelsen, *The Rose Bowl Game* (1951); Edwin Sower, *Tournament of Roses: The Rose Bowl Game* (1959); and Herb Michelson and Dave Newhouse, *Rose Bowl Football Since 1902* (1977).

Regarding the performing arts in Los Angeles in this era, see William Pearlman, compiler, *Music and Dance in California* (1940); Richard Saunders, editor, *Music and Dance in California and the West* (1948); and Howard Swan, *Music in the Southwest, 1825–1950* (1952). Regarding the Hollywood Bowl, see Isabel Morse Jones, *Hollywood Bowl*, foreword by Merle Armitage (1936); George Brookwell, *Saturdays in the Hollywood Bowl* (1940); John Northcutt, *Magic Valley: The Story of Hollywood Bowl* (1967); and Grace Koopal, *Miracle of Music: The History of the Hollywood Bowl* (1972). Of special relevance to this chapter and to the interpretation of Lloyd Wright's shell is Carol Reese's three-part series on the Hollywood Bowl, "The Hollywood Bowl, 1919–1989: The Land, the People, and the Music," in the July, August, and September 1989 issues of *Performing Arts* for the Hollywood Bowl. See also Hollywood Bowl Museum, *A Vision for Music* (1984). David Ewen has written *George Gershwin: His Journey to Greatness* (1970). Meta Carpenter Wilde and Orin Borsten wrote *A Loving Gentleman: The Love Story of William Faulkner and Meta Carpenter* (1976).

Regarding the Mexican-Americans of Los Angeles, see Carey McWilliams, *North from Mexico* (1948); and Beatrice Griffith, *American Me* (1948). Regarding Jewish Los Angeles, see Max Vorspan and Lloyd Gartner, *History of the Jews of Los Angeles* (1970). Regarding the African-Americans of Los Angeles, see Lawrence B. De Graaf, "The City of Black Angels: Emergence of the Los Angeles Ghetto, 1890–1930," *PHR*, 39 (August 1970), 323–53; Robert Williams Jr., "The Negro's Migration to Los Angeles, 1900–1946," *Negro History Bulletin*, 19 (February 1956), 102 ff.; and James Adolphus Fisher, "The Political Development of the Black Community in California, 1850–1950," *CHSQ*, 50 (September 1971), 256–66. Regarding Paul Williams, see Karen Hudson, *Paul R. Williams, Architect: A Legacy of Style*, introduction by David Gebhard (1993). Regarding Crenner Bradley and her family, see J. Gregory Payne and Scott Ratzan, *Tom Bradley: The Impossible Dream* (1986). Also of importance are Delilah Beasley, *The Negro Trailblazers of California* (1919); William Powell, *Black Wings* (1934); Charlotta Bass, *Forty Years* (1960); and Sarah Lifton, "Man of Color: The Incredible Life of John Alexander Somerville," *USC Trojan Family*, 26 (Summer 1994), 35–41. Regarding African-Americans in the workplace, see Charles S. Johnson, "Negro Workers in Los Angeles Industries," *Opportunity: A Journal of Negro Life*, 6 (August 1928), 234–40. Published theses of relevance include J. McFarline Ervin, *The Participation of the Negro in the Community Life of Los Angeles* (M.A. thesis, sociology, USC, 1931, reprinted 1973). Unpublished dissertations of importance to this chapter include J. Max Bond, "The Negro in Los Angeles" (Ph.D. dissertation, history, USC, 1936); and Ruth Mosely, "A Study of the Negro Families in Los Angeles" (M.S. thesis, education, USC, 1938). See also E. Frederick Anderson, *The Development of Leadership and Organization Building in the Black Community of Los Angeles from 1900 Through World War II* (1980). Regarding the segregation of swimming pools in Los Angeles, see "The Race Problem at Swimming Pools," *American City*, 47 (August 1932), 76–77.

Insight into the Folks can be had from Alice Berry, *The Bushes and the Berrys* (1941). See also Gilman Ostrander, *The Prohibition Movement in California, 1848–1933* (1957). Carey McWilliams wrote on religious cults in *Atlantic*, 177 (March 1946), 105–10. See also Diana Serra Cary, "Land of Itching Ears: Southern California, Melting Pot of All Religions," *Catholic World*, 181 (August 1955), 360–65; H. T. Dorman, *California Cult: The Story of Mankind United* (1958); and Arrow Research Institute, *Cults, Sects, Philosophical Groups, and Small Denominations in Los Angeles and Southern California* (1958). Ralph Hancock wrote *The Forest Lawn Story* (1955). Adela Rogers St. Johns wrote *First Step Up Toward Heaven: Hubert Eaton and Forest Lawn* (1959). See also Forest Lawn Memorial Park Association, *Art Guide of Forest Lawn, with Interpretations*, introduction by Bruce Barton (1936). Other relevant interpretations include Horace Sutton, "Ever-Ever Land," *Saturday Review* (5 April 1958), 23–25; Paul Jacobs, "Most Cheerful Graveyard in the World," *Reporter*, 19 (18 September 1958), 26–30; and J. H. Plumb, "De Mortuis: Concerning Forest Lawn," *Horizon*, 9 (Spring 1967), 40–41. Carey McWilliams made his famous tribute to Los Angeles in *Southern California: An Island on the Land* (1946), reprinted by Peregrine Smith in 1973.

Chapter Seven
An All-Seeing Eye

Regarding Watkins, see Peter Palmquist, *Carleton E. Watkins: Photographer of the American West*, foreword by Martha Sandweiss (1983); and *Carleton E. Watkins, Photographs, 1861–1874*; essay by Peter Palmquist, introduction by Jeffrey Fraenkel (1989). Regarding postcards, see Monica Highland, *Greetings from Southern California: A Look at the Past Through Postcards* (1988).

Merle Armitage introduced Edward Weston to the public in his pioneering *The Art of Edward Weston* (1932). See also Armitage's *Fifty Photographs: Edward Weston* (1947). Weston made his own debut in the self-published *Photography* (1934). Edward and Charis Weston produced *California and the West* in 1940. Weston's photographs for *Leaves of Grass* were issued by the Limited Editions Club in 1942, with an introduction by Mark Van Doren. Weston's own statements are most dramatically available in *The Daybooks of Edward Weston*, volume 1, *Mexico* (1961) and volume 2, *California* (1966), edited by Nancy Newhall. Excerpts from *The Daybooks* have found their way into various monographs. These include Edward Weston, *My Camera on Point Lobos* (1950), edited by Ansel Adams; *Edward Weston, Photographer: The Flame of Recognition* (1965), edited by Nancy Newhall; Charis Wilson, *Edward Weston Nudes* (1977); Peter Bunnell, editor, *Edward Weston on Photography* (1983); Amy Conger, *Edward Weston in Mexico, 1923–1926* (1983), foreword by Van Deren Coke; and Beaumont Newhall and Amy Conger, *Edward Weston Omnibus* (1984). Essential criticism of Weston includes Nancy Newhall, *The Photographs of Edward Weston* (1946); *EW: 100, Centennial Essays in Honor of Edward Weston* (1986), edited by Peter Bunnell and David Featherstone, with essays by Robert Adams, Amy Conger, Andy Grundberg, Therese Thau Heyman, Estelle Jussim, Alan Trachtenberg, Paul Vanderbilt, Mike Weaver, and Charis Wilson; and Thomas Buchsteiner, *Edward Cole Kim Weston: Three Generations of American Photography* (1989), in English and German text. Weston defended his California photographs in "My Photographs of California," *Magazine of Art*, 32 (January 1939), 30–33. See also James Enyeart's magisterial *Edward Weston's California Landscapes* (1984). Lawrence Clark Powell discusses

Charis and Edward Weston in *California Classics: The Creative Literature of the Golden State* (1971).

Jonathan Spaulding's *Ansel Adams and the American Landscape* (1996), which appeared while this book was in press, now becomes the authoritative study of this great photographer. *Ansel Adams: An Autobiography* (1985), written with Mary Street Alinder, is more than an autobiography. It is the history of photography in California in the twentieth century. Adams's unfolding career as a photographer can be traced through *The Four Seasons in Yosemite National Park*, edited by Stanley Plumb (1936), *Sierra Nevada, the John Muir Trail* (1938), and the *Illustrated Guide to Yosemite Valley*, with Virginia Adams (1940). See also Nancy Newhall, *The Eloquent Light: Ansel Adams Photographs, 1923–1963* (1963); New York Graphic Society, *Ansel Adams: Images, 1923–1974* (1974); and Andrea Gray, *Ansel Adams: An American Place, 1936* (1982). Adams discussed his techniques in *Making a Photograph: An Introduction to Photography* (1935). See also Steven Gelber, "The Eye of the Beholder: Images of California by Dorothea Lange and Russell Lee," *CHSQ*, 64 (Fall 1985), 264–71.

Chapter Eight
Angel's Flight

All serious research into the history of art in California begins with a monumental achievement of the WPA Federal Art Project, *California Art Research* (20 vols., bound mimeographed, 1937), edited by Gene Hailey, on deposit in the Bancroft Library. Los Angeles *Times* art critic Arthur Millier made a pioneering assessment of artistic taste in California in his essay "Growth of Art in California," included in Frank Taylor, *Land of Homes* (1929), 311–41. See also Eugen Neuhaus, *Painters, Pictures, and the People* (1918), a publication of the Philopolis Press in San Francisco; Paul Mills, editor, *Early Paintings of California* (1956); and *California Design 1910*, edited by Timothy Anderson, Eudorah Moore, and Robert Winter, with photographs by Morely Baer (1974). Artistic taste in California by the end of the 1930s can be discerned in the exhibition programs of the Golden Gate International Exposition held in San Francisco. In this regard, see Department of Fine Arts GGIE, *Contemporary Art, Official Catalogue* (1939) and *Art, Official Catalogue* (1940).

Ruth Lilly Westphal prepared the two-volume survey *Plein Air Painters of California. The Southland* (1982) contains essays by Terry DeLapp, Thomas Kenneth Enman, Nancy Dustin Wall Moure, Martin E. Petersen, and Jean Stern. *The North* (1986) contains essays by Janet Blake Dominik, Harvey L. Jones, Betty Hoag John, Jean Stern, Jeffrey Stewart, and Raymond L. Wilson. I am indebted to these two volumes as a source of reference, images, and interpretations. I am equally indebted to *American Scene Painting, California, 1930s and 1940s* (1991), edited by Westphal and Janet Blake Dominik, with essays by Linda Aldrich, Susan Anderson, Charlotte Berney, Janet Blake Dominik, Donelson Hoopes, Mike McGee, Ted Mills, Robert Perine, Martin Petersen, Jean Stern, and Raymond L. Wilson. Also of relevance is Gordon McClelland and Jay Last, *The California Style: California Watercolor Artists 1925–1955* (1985). See also Laguna Beach Museum of Art, *Southern California Artists, 1890–1940* (1979).

Regarding the artistic map of California, see Stephen Vincent, Paul Mills, and Kevin Starr, *O California! Nineteenth- and Early Twentieth-Century California Landscapes and Observations* (1990). See also Paul Mills, editor, *Early Paintings of California in the Robert B. Honeyman, Jr., Collection*, prepared for the Oakland Museum (1956).

Regarding Theodore Wores, see Joseph Armstrong Baird Jr., *Theodore Wores—The Japanese Years*, an exhibition catalog for the Oakland Museum (1976); *Theodore Wores and the*

Beginnings of Internationalism in Northern California Painting, 1875–1915 (1978), edited by Joseph Armstrong Baird Jr., with essays by William H. Gerdts, Richard West, and participants in Art 288, UC Davis; Huntsville Museum of Art, *Theodore Wores, 1859–1939: A Retrospective Exhibition, 16 March–27 April 1980* (1980), with essays by Joseph Armstrong Baird Jr. and others. See also Helen Brockhoff, *Thad Welch: Pioneer and Painter* (1966); Donald Cleland Whitton, *Percy Gray: The Lyric Landscape* (no date); Katherine Littell, *Chris Jorgensen: California Pioneer Artist* (1988); Martin Petersen, "Maurice Braun: Master Painter of the California Landscape," *JSDH*, 23 (Summer 1977), 20–39; Grace Hartley, *George Demont Otis, 1879–1962: American Impressionist* (no date); Walter Nelson-Rees, *Lillie May Nicholson, 1884–1964: An Artist Rediscovered*, foreword by Joseph Armstrong Baird Jr., (1981) and *John O'Shea, 1876–1956: The Artist's Life as I Know It* (1985). Regarding Maynard Dixon, see *Maynard Dixon: Painter of the West*, introduction by Arthur Millier (1967); Fresno Arts Center, *Maynard Dixon: A Bicentennial Retrospective* (1975), which includes the article "Maynard Dixon, Artist of the West, as Remembered by Edith Hamlin"; and California Academy of Sciences, *Maynard Dixon: Images of the Native American* (1981), with essays by Donald Hagerty, Ansel Adams, Winona Tomanoczy, and Edith Hamlin. Regarding Frank Van Sloun, see John Maxwell Desgrey, "Frank Van Sloun: California's Master of the Monotype and the Etching," *CHSQ*, 54 (Winter 1975), 345–54. Regarding two important San Diego artists, see Bruce Kamerling, "Like the Ancients: The Art of Donal Hord," *JSDH*, 31 (Summer 1985), 164–209; Suzanne Blair Brown, "The Prime of Belle Baranceanu," *San Diego Magazine* (July 1985), 126–31; and Bram Dijkstra and Anne Weaver, *Belle Baranceanu—A Retrospective* (1985). Nancy Boas's *The Society of Six: California Colorists* (1988) is a classic of cultural history and art criticism. See also Oakland Museum, *Society of Six* (1972), with an essay by Terry St. John. For some idea of the attractive painting opportunities around the San Francisco Bay Area, see John Hart, *San Francisco's Wilderness Next Door* (1979).

Regarding the muralists of Mexico, see Alma Reed, *The Mexican Muralists* (1960); and Laurance Hurlburt, *The Mexican Muralists in the United States*, foreword by David Scott (1989). See also Karal Ann Marling, *Wall-to-Wall America: A Cultural History of Post-Office Murals in the Great Depression* (1982). See also Melba Levick and Stanley Young, *The Big Picture: Murals of Los Angeles* (1988). Cited government reports include Public Works of Art Project, *Report of the Assistant Secretary of the Treasury to Federal Emergency Relief Administrator, 8 December 1933–30 June 1934* (1934); and Federal Art Project, Southern California, *Southern California Creates*, foreword by Stanton Macdonald-Wright (1939). See also Orville Clarke Jr., "Social Statements in Art: WPA Murals," *Antiques & Fine Art*, 5 (November–December 1987), 54–59.

Chapter Nine
Dreaming Through the Disaster

John Baxter, *Hollywood in the Thirties* (1968); Andrew Bergman, *We're in the Money: Depression America and Its Films* (1971); and Jerry Vermilye, *The Films of the Thirties* (1982) are crucial to this chapter, as are Thomas Schatz, *Hollywood Genres: Formulas, Filmmaking, and the Studio System* (1981); and Peter Roffman and Jim Purdy, *The Hollywood Social Problem Film: Madness, Despair, and Politics from the Depression to the Fifties* (1981). See also the brilliant essay by Vincent Canby, "Political Premonitions Born of Despair: Films of the Depression," in the New York *Times* for 10 January 1992. Also of importance: Jack Spears, *Hollywood: The Golden Era* (1971); Gavin Lambert, *GWTW: The Making of "Gone with the Wind"* (1973); and Ted Sennett, *Hollywood's Golden Year, 1939: A Fiftieth-Anniversary Celebration* (1989). Regarding the economic recovery of 1937, see Andrew Boone, "Hollywood Business: Facts and Figures of Today's Big Expansion in

Motion Pictures," *California Magazine of Pacific Business*, 27 (January 1937), 7–10 ff.

For the background to the social and cultural importance of horror films, see Siegfried Kracauer, *From Caligari to Hitler* (1947). Regarding gangster films, see John Baxter, *The Gangster Film* (1970); Stephen Karpf, *The Gangster Film, 1930–1940* (1973); John Gabree, *Gangsters, from Little Caesar to the Godfather* (1973); Eugene Rosow, *Born to Lose: The Gangster Film in America* (1978); and Carlos Clarens, *Crime Movies, from Griffith to the Godfather and Beyond* (1980). See also James Parish and Michael Pitts, *The Great Detective Pictures* (1990). Regarding screwball comedy, see Ted Sennett, *Lunatics and Lovers: A Tribute to the Giddy and Glittering Era of the Screen's "Screwball" and Romantic Comedies* (1971); and David Robinson, *The Great Funnies: A History of Film Comedy* (1969). Regarding the Hollywood musical, see Naima Prevots, *Dancing in the Sun: Hollywood Choreographers, 1915–1937* (1987); together with Arlene Croce, *The Fred Astaire & Ginger Rogers Book* (1972); and John Mueller, *Astaire Dancing: The Musical Films* (1985). For the background to Shirley Temple and others, see Norman Zierold, *The Child Stars* (1965). See also Shirley Temple, *My Young Life* (1945) and *Child Star: An Autobiography* (1988). Regarding African-Americans in Hollywood in this era, see Floyd Covington, "The Negro Invades Hollywood," *Opportunity*, 7 (April 1929), 11–13; and Loren Miller, "Hollywood's New Negro Films," *Crisis*, 45 (January 1938), 8–9. See also Donald Bogle, *Blacks in American Films and Television: An Encyclopedia* (1988).

General histories of importance to this chapter include Edwin Obadiah Palmer, *History of Hollywood* (2 vols., 1937); Maurice Bardeche and Robert Brasillach, *The History of Motion Pictures*, translated and edited by Iris Barry (1938); Arthur Knight, *The Liveliest Art: A Panoramic History of the Movies* (1957); Lewis Jacobs, *The Rise of the American Film* (1967); Richard Griffith and Arthur Mayer, *The Movies*, with the assistance of Eileen Bowser (rev. ed. 1970); Robert Stanley, *The Celluloid Empire* (1978); and Joel Finler, *The Hollywood Story* (1988). See also Beth Day, *This Was Hollywood: An Affectionate History of Filmland's Golden Years* (1960); and Ezra Goodman, *The Fifty-Year Decline and Fall of Hollywood* (1961). Also of importance to this chapter is Bob Thomas, *The Heart of Hollywood: A Fifty-Year Pictorial History of the Film Capital and the Famed Motion Picture and Television Relief Fund* (1971). Leo C. Rosten's classic *Hollywood: The Movie Colony, the Movie Makers* (1941) was perceptively reviewed in *Time* on 1 December 1941. See also Hortense Powdermaker, *Hollywood: The Dream Factory* (1950). Annotated reference works of great value include Bosley Crowther, *The Great Films: Fifty Golden Years of Motion Pictures* (1967), *Vintage Films* (1977), and *Reruns: Fifty Memorable Films* (1978); and Pauline Kael, *5001 Nights at the Movies: A Guide From A to Z* (1982). See also Gene Ringgold and DeWitt Bodeen, *The Films of Cecil B. DeMille* (1969).

Of innumerable Hollywood autobiographies and memoirs, the following are of relevance to this chapter: Peggy Hopkins Joyce, *Men, Marriage, and Me* (1930); Elsie Janis, *So Far, So Good!* (1932); Marie Dressler, *My Own Story* (1934); William Churchill DeMille, *Hollywood Saga* (1939); John Nugent, *It's a Great Life* (1940); Oscar Levant, *A Smattering of Ignorance* (1940) and *The Memoir of an Amnesiac* (1965); Ida Alena Ross Wylie, *My Life with George* (1940); J. B. Priestley, *Midnight on the Desert* (1940); Olga Petrova, *Butter with My Bread* (1942); Adolph Zucker, *The Public Is Never Wrong*, with Dale Kramer (1953); King Vidor, *A Tree Is a Tree* (1953); Jesse Lasky, *I Blow My Own Horn*, with Don Weldon (1957); Jessamyn West, *To See the Dream* (1957); *The Autobiography of Cecil B. DeMille*, edited by Donald Hayne (1959); Phil Kouty, *Yes, Mr. DeMille* (1959); Virgil Miller, *Splinters from Holywood Tripods: Memoirs of a Cameraman* (1964); Anita Loos, *A Girl Like I* (1966) and *Kiss Hollywood Good-by* (1974); Adela Rogers St. Johns, *The Honeycomb* (1969) and *Love, Laughter, and Tears: My Hollywood Story* (1978); and Irene Mayer Selznick, *A Private View* (1983). Biographies of relevance to this chapter include John Drinkwater, *The Life and Adventures of Carl Laemmle* (1931); Bosley

420 BIBLIOGRAPHICAL ESSAY

Crowther, *Hollywood Rajah: The Life and Times of Louis B. Mayer* (1960); John Keats, *Howard Hughes* (1966); Bob Thomas, *Thalberg: Life and Legend* (1969) and *Selznick* (1970); Fred Lawrence Guiles, *Marion Davies* (1972) and *Stan: The Life of Stan Laurel* (1980); Lewis Yablonsky, *George Raft* (1974); Vincent Tajiri, *Valentino* (1977); Richard Schickel, *D. W. Griffith: An American Life* (1982); and Bob Thomas, *Clown Prince of Hollywood: The Antic Life and Times of Jack L. Warner* (1990). Regarding Walt Disney, see Richard Schickel, *The Disney Version: The Life, Times, Art, and Commerce of Walt Disney* (1968); and Leonard Mosely, *Disney's World* (1985).

Regarding the writer in Hollywood, see Tom Dardis, *Some Time in the Sun* (1976); Ian Hamilton, *Writers in Hollywood, 1915–1951* (1990); and Nancy Lynn Schwartz, *The Hollywood Writers' Wars* (1982). For the tension between novels and screenplays, see the opening chapter of George Bluestone's *Novels into Film* (1957). Early and important cultural assessments of the film as an art form include William Dean Howells, "Cinematographic Show, Its Essence and Influence," *Harper's*, 125 (September 1912), 634–37; O. H. Dunbar, "Lure of the Films," *Harper's*, 126 (January 1913), 20, 22; "Democratic Art," *Nation*, 97 (28 August 1913), 193–94; Vachael Lindsay, "Photoplay Progress: Professor Munsterberg's Book, *The Photoplay*," NR, 10 (17 February 1917), 76–77; and Virginia Woolf, "The Movies and Reality," NR, 47 (4 August 1926), 308–10.

For valuable insights into the studio system, see James Silke, *Here's Looking at You, Kid: Fifty Years of Fighting, Working, and Dreaming at Warner Brothers* (1976); and Ethan Mordden, *The Hollywood Studios* (1988). Through the courtesy of Dan Garcia, senior vice president of Warner Brothers, and Marvin Taff, AIA, vice president of Gensler and Associates, I was provided with Gensler and Associates/Architects, *Warner Brothers Studio: Historical Resource Report* (February 1993) and Levin and Associates, *Warner Brothers Burbank Studio: Historic Context Statement* (23 April 1993), descriptive inventories of the Warner Brothers facilities from the golden age.

Two important assessments of Hollywood *vis-à-vis* the national culture include Vincent Sheehan, "Hollywood," *Commonweal*, 12 (11 June 1930), 151–52; and Lillian Symes, "The Beautiful and Dumb," *Harper's*, 163 (June 1931), 23–32. Virulently anti-Hollywood assessments include Frances Patterson, "Descent into Hollywood," NR, 65 (14 January 1931), 239–40; and Sidney Howard, "Hollywood on the Slide," NR, 72 (9 November 1932), 350–53.

The fact that Hollywood did not always behave itself is evident from Max Knepper's *Sodom and Gomorrah: The Story of Hollywood*, preface by Upton Sinclair (1935); and Kenneth Anger's *Hollywood Babylon* (1960, 1984). For an opposing viewpoint, see "Churchgoing Hollywood," *Literary Digest*, 121 (14 March 1936), 18. The response to misbehavior on the screen is chronicled in Raymond Moley, *The Hays Office* (1945). See also Gerald Schatz, "Will H. Hays and the Motion Picture Industry, 1919–1922," SCQ, 43 (1961), 316–29. Regarding the response of the American hierarchy, see John J. Cantwell, "Priests and the Motion Picture Industry," *American Ecclesiastical Review*, 90 (1934), 136–46; and Francis Weber, "John J. Cantwell and the Legion of Decency," *American Ecclesiastical Review*, 151 (1964), 237–47. See also Les and Barbara Keyser, *Hollywood and the Catholic Church: The Image of Roman Catholicism in American Movies* (1964). The Jewish dimension of Hollywood is explicated by Neal Gabler in his now classic *An Empire of Their Own: How the Jews Invented Hollywood* (1988). See also Steven Zipperstein, "The Lions of Judah in the Jungle of Hollywood," *Los Angeles Times Sunday Book Review* (5 November 1989), 11.

Regarding the Hollywood lifestyle in the 1930s, see Frank Condon, "What Is a Hollywood Party?" *SEP*, 204 (10 October 1931), 31, 60; Dorothy Speare, "Hollywood Madness," *SEP*, 206 (7 October 1933), 26, 59. See also Helen Patridge, *A Lady Goes to Hollywood* (1941). For couture, on screen and off, see Sylvia Ullback, *Hollywood Undressed* (1931);

and W. Robert LaVine, *In a Glamorous Fashion* (1980). Regarding Hollywood at home, see Charles Lockwood, *Dream Palaces* (1981). *Architectural Digest* for April 1994 is devoted exclusively to Hollywood architecture, interior design, and lifestyle, including the 1930s. For evidence of the effort to make Hollywood seem a stay-at-home kind of place, see W. E. Woodward, "Nine-o'clock Town," *Collier's*, 89 (30 April 1932), 22, 53; and "Hollywood Wives," *SEP*, 205 (21 January 1933), 8–9, 63–64. Contemporary guides to the homes of stars include Ralph Grover, *Royal Homes of the Picture Stars* (1926); Jan and Cora Gordon, *Star-Dust in Hollywood* (1931); Basil Woon, *Incredible Land: A Jaunty Baedeker to Hollywood and the Great Southwest* (1933); and Marcel Rodd, *Souvenir Album: Los Angeles, Hollywood, and the Southland at a Glance* (1942). See also Rubeigh Minney, *Hollywood by Starlight* (1935); and John Swope, *Camera over Hollywood* (1939). See also Charles Lockwood's *The Guide to Hollywood and Beverly Hills* (1984). *House and Garden* featured Norma Shearer's home in Santa Monica on 3 June 1934; George Burns and Gracie Allen's home in Beverly Hills on 3 June 1937; Shirley Temple's home in Santa Monica on 7 August 1938; the homes of George Cukor, Ann Sothern, Constance Bennett, and others in November 1940; and Jimmy Stewart's home in Hollywood in July 1941. Regarding the favorite city of choice for the film industry see Pierce Benedict, editor, *History of Beverly Hills* (1934); William Wilcox Robinson, *Beverly Hills: A Calendar of Events in the Making of a City* (1938); and Fred Basten, *Beverly Hills: Portrait of a Fabled City* (1975).

The emergence of Hollywood as a radio capital can be seen most dramatically in Stuart Blythe, "Hollywood Broadcast: Radio Companies Erect Big New Studios as Many Programs Move to the West Coast," *California Magazine of the Pacific*, 28 (January 1938), 5–8, 35–38. See also Irving Fein, *Jack Benny: An Intimate Biography*, introduction by George Burns (1976); and Milt Josefsberg, *The Jack Benny Show* (1977). Regarding the rise of the gossip industry in this period, see Louella Parsons, *The Gay Illiterate* (1944); Hedda Hopper, *From Under My Hat* (1952) and *The Whole Truth and Nothing But*, with James Brough (1963); Sheilah Graham, *Confessions of a Hollywood Columnist* (1969); and George Eells, *Hedda and Louella* (1972). See also Charles Ray, *Hollywood Shorts* (1935); Edward Holstius, *Hollywood Through the Back Door* (1937); and Grover Jones, "Knights of the Keyhole: Hollywood Gossip Mill," *Collier's*, 101 (16 April 1938), 25–26.

Chapter Ten
The Boys and Girls in the Back Room

Alice Melton lists several hundred novels with California settings in her annotated bibliography *California in Fiction* (1961). Edmund Wilson's "The Boys in the Back Room" was reprinted in *Classics and Commercials: A Literary Chronicle of the Forties* (1950). It was separately issued by the Colt Press of San Francisco in 1941. See also Edmund Wilson, *Letters on Literature and Politics, 1912–1972*, edited by Elena Wilson (1977), and *The Thirties*, edited with an introduction by Leon Edel (1980). Early efforts to plot the possible course of fiction on the Coast include W. T. Fitch, "Is There Literary and Artistic Culture in California," *Overland Monthly*, n.s. 84 (December 1926), 391, 408; Carey McWilliams, "Swell Letters in California," *American Mercury*, 21 (September 1930), 42–47; Aubrey Burns, "Regional Culture in Southern California," *Southwest Review* (July 1932), 373–94; Farnsworth Crowder, "California Is No Sissy!" *Westways*, 28 (February 1936), 14–15; Idwal Jones, "Letters on the Pacific Rim," *Saturday Review of Literature*, 15 (30 January 1937), 3–4 ff.; Sinclair Lewis, "Gold, Inc.," *Newsweek*, 11 (21 February 1938), 21; and Scott O'Dell, "Embarrassing Plenty," *Saturday Review of Literature*, 26 (30 October 1943), 5. Carey McWilliams covered the California literary scene with encyclopedic knowledge in his "Tides West" column in *Westways* in 1936, 1937, and 1938. See also

McWilliams's "Writers of the Western Shore" in *Westways* for November 1978. *Continent's End: A Collection of California Writing*, edited by Joseph Henry Jackson (1944), is an early anthology with pertinent critical commentary. See also Frederick Bracher, "California's Literary Regionalism," *American Quarterly*, 7 (Fall 1955), 275–84; and two fine assessments by Lawrence Clark Powell, *Land of Fiction* (1952) and *California Classics: The Creative Literature of the Golden State* (1971).

The literary background of the Bay Area in this period can be seen in Richard Davison, *Charles G. Norris* (1983); and Emily Leider, *California's Daughter: Gertrude Atherton and Her Times* (1991). Diane Johnson's *Dashiell Hammett: A Life* (1983) and Jackson Benson's *The True Adventures of John Steinbeck, Writer: A Biography* (1984) represent the *de facto* literary history of Northern California during this period. Regarding the background to *Fig Tree John*, see Peter Beidler, *Fig Tree John: An Indian in Fact and Fiction* (1977); and William Pilkington, *My Blood's Country: Studies in Southwestern Literature* (1973).

Regarding the literary scene in Los Angeles, see *Los Angeles in Fiction: A Collection of Original Essays*, edited by David Fine (1984); and Sam Bluefarb, *Set in L.A.: Scenes of the City in Fiction* (1986). Sam Burchell published his seminal assessment "Hard-Boiled L.A." in *Angeles* magazine for January 1989. In *Angel City in Turmoil* (1946), Guy Finney gives excellent background to corruption in L.A. in this period. See also Agness Underwood, *Newspaperwoman* (1949); and Dean Jennings, *We Only Kill Each Other: The Life and Bad Times of Bugsy Siegel* (1968) for further background.

The complex and moody world of Raymond Chandler is thoroughly evident in Frank MacShane's *The Life of Raymond Chandler* (1976). See also the text and commentary of *Selected Letters of Raymond Chandler*, edited by Frank MacShane (1981); *Raymond Chandler Speaking*, edited by Dorothy Gardiner and Katherine Sorley Walker (1962); and *Chandler Before Marlowe: Raymond Chandler's Early Prose and Poetry, 1908–1912*, edited by Matthew Bruccoli, foreword by Jacques Barzun (1973). See also Philip Durham, *Down These Mean Streets a Man Must Go: Raymond Chandler's Knight* (1963); *The World of Raymond Chandler*, edited by Miriam Gross (1977); Al Clark, *Raymond Chandler in Hollywood* (1982); and William Marling, *Raymond Chandler* (1986). See also Matthew Bruccoli, *Raymond Chandler: A Descriptive Bibliography* (1979). Neil Morgan chronicled Chandler's last years in "The Long Good-Bye," anthologized in *The Best of California* (1986), 190–97.

Franklin Walker began the investigation of the Hollywood novel in "Hollywood in Fiction," *Pacific Spectator*, 2 (Spring 1948), 127–33. Regarding Theodore Dreiser in Hollywood, see W. A. Swanberg, *Dreiser* (1965). Regarding Faulkner, see Meta Carpenter Wilde and Orin Borsten, *A Loving Gentleman* (1976); David Minter, *William Faulker: His Life and Work* (1980); and Joseph Blotner, *Faulkner: A Biography* (1984). Budd Schulberg gives a fascinating portrait of Hollywood in *Moving Pictures: Memories of a Hollywood Prince* (1981) and in the introduction and afterword to the 1990 Random House Anniversary Edition of *What Makes Sammy Run?*

Regarding John O'Hara, see Finis Farr, *O'Hara: A Biography* (1973). Regarding Nathanael West, see Stanley Edgar Hyman, *Nathanael West* (1962); Jay Martin, *Nathanael West: The Art of His Life* (1970); Irving Malin, *Nathanael West's Novels*, preface by Harry T. Moore (1972); *Nathanael West: The Cheaters and the Cheated, a Collection of Critical Essays* (1973); Robert Emmet Long, *Nathanael West* (1985); and James Light's undated *Nathanael West: An Interpretive Essay*, a pamphlet issued by Northwestern University Press. David Fine comments brilliantly on West in "Lotus Land or Locust Land?" in the *Los Angeles Times Sunday Book Review* for 31 December 1989.

Charles Bukowski testifies to the power of John Fante as a writer in his preface to *Ask the Dust*, published by the Black Sparrow Press in 1980. Fante's development as a writer in the 1930s and 1940s can be traced through his correspondence with H. L. Mencken, published as *Fante—Mencken: A Personal Correspondence 1930–1952*, edited by Michael Moreau (1989). The Black Sparrow Press has also published *John Fante: Selected Letters, 1932–1981* (1991). Regarding James M. Cain, see Roy Hoopes, *Cain* (1982); and *Sixty Years of Journalism*, edited with introduction by Roy Hoopes (1985). See also Kevin Starr, "It's Chinatown," *NR*, 173 (26 July 1975), 31–32.

Charles Scribner's Sons reissued *The Pat Hobby Stories* in 1962. See also volume 6 of *The Bodley Head Scott Fitzgerald*, edited by Malcom Cowley (1963). *Afternoon of an Author: A Selection of Uncollected Stories and Essays*, with an introduction and notes by Arthur Mizener (1957), reprints other fugitive pieces from this period. Cambridge University Press issued a critical edition of *The Last Tycoon*, edited by Matthew Bruccoli, in 1994. Edmund Wilson edited F. Scott Fitzgerald's *The Crack-Up* in 1945. The poignant last days of F. Scott Fitzgerald in Hollywood can be traced through Arthur Mizener, *The Far Side of Paradise: A Biography of F. Scott Fitzgerald* (1951), reissued in 1972 with 135 illustrations; Aaron Latham, *Crazy Sundays: F. Scott Fitzgerald in Hollywood* (1972); Matthew Bruccoli, *Some Sort of Epic Grandeur: The Life of F. Scott Fitzgerald* (1981); and Jeffrey Meyers, *Scott Fitzgerald: A Biography* (1994). See also Kenneth Eble, *F. Scott Fitzgerald* (1963); and *The Letters of F. Scott Fitzgerald*, edited by Andrew Turnbull (1963). Sheilah Graham wrote *The Garden of Allah* (1970). See also Amy Porter, "Garden of Allah, I Love You," *Collier's*, 120 (22 November 1947), 18–19, 102–3. Also of interest is Frances Ring, "My Boss Scott Fitzgerald," *Los Angeles*, 7 (January 1964), 34–36.

Chapter Eleven
War and Peace and the Survival of the Species

Assessments of Robinson Jeffers begin and end with Lawrence Clark Powell's 1932 doctoral dissertation for the Faculty of Letters of the University of Dijon, France, *An Introduction to Robinson Jeffers*, privately published that year in Dijon and available in a number of California libraries. See also George Sterling's pioneering assessment, *Robinson Jeffers: The Man and the Artist* (1926); Frederic Carpenter's *Robinson Jeffers* (1922); and the very important *Centennial Essays for Robinson Jeffers*, edited by Robert Zaller (1991). Tim Hunt edited *The Collected Poetry of Robinson Jeffers* (3 vols., 1988–91). The Book Club of California published Jeffers's Harvard lectures as *Themes in My Poems* (1956).

Theodora Kroeber published her classic *Ishi in Two Worlds: A Biography of the Last Wild Indian in North America* (1961), with a foreword by Lewis Gannett. See also *Ishi, the Last Yahi: A Documentary History*, edited by Robert Heizer and Theodora Kroeber (1979). Theodora Kroeber also wrote *Alfred Kroeber: A Personal Configuration* (1970). Of Alfred Kroeber's vast output, the following titles are of relevance to this chapter: *Peoples of the Philippines* (1919), *Anthropology* (1923, rev. 1933 with supplement), *Handbook of the Indians of California* (1925), *Cultural and Natural Areas of Native North America* (1939), *The Nature of Culture* (1952), and *An Anthropologist Looks at History* (1963). Kroeber's *A Roster of Civilizations and Culture* (1962) is a posthumously published fragment of what was to have been the culmination of Kroeber's work. Even incomplete, it is a formidable achievement. Regarding Kroeber himself, see *Alfred Kroeber*, edited by Julian Haynes Steward (1973). See also *The Sapir-Kroeber Correspondence: Letters Between Edward Sapir and A. L. Kroeber, 1905–1925*, edited with notes and an index by Victor Golla (1984). Ursula K. Le Guin, the daughter of Alfred and Theodora Kroeber, shows the strong influence of the Ishi story in her *Always Coming Home* (1985), a novel with music by Todd Barton and drawings by Margaret Chodos (1985). While this book was in press, UC Berkeley research archeologist Steven Shackley of the Hearst Museum of Anthropology offered evidence that Ishi made his arrowheads in the style of the Wintu and Nomlaki peoples of Northern California and bore a physical resemblance to them and to the Maidu. Ishi, Shackley argued, was probably of mixed ancestry since the Yahi, well before their final extinction, had most likely been forced to resort to intermarriage with other peoples for their survival. Shackley's argument in no way alters the fact that Ishi considered himself a Yahi, despite what may very well have been his mixed ancestry. See Charles Petit, "Ishi's Famous Legacy Called into Question," San Francisco Chronicle (6 February 1996), A1, A11.

George H. Nash is writing a multi-volume biography of Herbert Hoover. Of importance to this chapter is the second volume, Herbert Hoover and Stanford University (1988). See also The Memoirs of Herbert Hoover (3 vols., 1951–52). Peter Duignan has written The Hoover Institution on War, Revolution, and Peace: Seventy-Five Years of Its History (1989). See also Nina Almond and Harold Fisher, Special Collections in the Hoover Library on War, Revolution, and Peace (1940); and Harold Fisher, A Tower to Peace (1945). Stanford University Press issued Dedication of the Hoover Library on War, Revolution, and Peace, Stanford University, June 20, 1941 (1941).

Chapter Twelve
Ich Bin ein Südkalifornier

For the background of the Hollywood where the émigrés found refuge, see Charles Higham and Joel Greenberg, Hollywood in the Forties (1968); and Otto Friedrich, City of Nets: A Portrait of Hollywood in the 1940s (1986). Regarding the émigrés themselves, see John Russell Taylor, Strangers in Paradise: The Hollywood Émigrés, 1933–1950 (1983); John Baxter, The Hollywood Exiles (1976); and Passport to Hollywood: Film Immigrants Anthology, edited by Don Whittemore and Philip Cecchettini (1976). See also Randall Patnode, "Exiles in Paradise," USC Trojan Family, 23 (Spring 1991), 16–21. For the background of the Hollywood Raj, see Sheridan Morley, Tales from the Hollywood Raj: The British Film Colony On Screen and Off (1983). For even deeper background, see Oscar Winther, "English Migration to the American West, 1865–1900," Huntington Library Quarterly, 27 (February 1964), 159–74. Also of interest: Rupert Hart-Davis, Hugh Walpole: A Biography (1952); Sir Cedric Hardwicke, A Victorian in Orbit (1961); and Maurice Zolotow, Billy Wilder in Hollywood (1977). David Niven chronicled his Hollywood career in Once over Lightly (1951), The Moon's a Balloon (1972), and Bring on the Empty Horses (1975). See also Sheridan Morley, The Other Side of the Moon: The Life of David Niven (1985); and Gerard Garrett, The Films of David Niven (1976). For the career of Charles Laughton, see Charles Higham, Charles Laughton: An Intimate Biography, introduction by Elsa Lanchester (1976); and Simon Callow, Charles Laughton: A Difficult Actor (1987). The use of the Raj to gain support for American entrance into the war is documented in Karol Kulik, Alexander Korda: The Man Who Could Work Miracles (1975). See also Michael Korda, Charmed Lives: A Family Romance (1979). Also of relevance: John Russell Taylor, Hitch: The Life and Times of Alfred Hitchcock (1978).

Aldous Huxley extended the influence of the Raj into both the studios and literature. See Aldous Huxley, 1894–1963: A Memoral Volume, edited by Julian Huxley (1965); and Sybille Bedford, Aldous Huxley: A Biography (1974). See also Charles Rolo, "Aldous Huxley," Atlantic Monthly, 180 (August 1947), 109–15; and Christopher Isherwood, "Aldous Huxley in California," Atlantic Monthly, 213 (September 1964), 44–47. Isherwood told his own story in My Guru and His Disciple (1980). See also Jonathan Fryer, Isherwood

(1978); Brian Finney, *Christopher Isherwood: A Critical Biography* (1979); and John Lehmann, *Christopher Isherwood: A Personal Memoir* (1987). Isherwood published the novel *Prater Violet* in 1945. In *Imagining America* (1980), Peter Conrad conjoins both Huxley and Isherwood, mystics with a taste for drugs, as precursors of the 1960s. Isherwood as homosexual activist prompts a consideration of Charles Laughton and Tyrone Power in this regard. See Hector Arce, *The Secret Life of Tyrone Power* (1979). See also the *Memoirs* of Tennessee Williams (1975); and Roger Austen, *Playing the Game: The Homosexual Novel in America* (1977).

Salka Viertel's *The Kindness of Strangers* (1969) is the most complete and useful émigré memoir from the period. See also Bruno Walter, *Theme and Variation: An Autobiography* (1947); Leonhard Frank, *Heart on the Left*, translated by Cyrus Brooks (1954); Monica Mann, *Past and Present* (1960); Vicki Baum, *I Know What I'm Worth* (1964); Charles Chaplin, *My Autobiography* (1964); Carl Zuckmayer, *A Part of Myself*, translated by Richard and Clara Winston (1966); Hedy Lamarr, *Ecstasy and Me: My Life as a Woman* (1966); Joseph Wechsberg, *The First Time Around: Some Irreverent Recollections* (1970); Erich Maria Remarque, *Shadows in Paradise*, translated by Ralph Manheim (1971); S. N. Behrman, *People in a Diary* (1972); Jean Renoir, *My Life and My Films*, translated by Norman Denny (1974); and Gottfried Reinhardt, *The Genius, A Memoir of Max Reinhardt* (1979).

Biographies of special value to this chapter include Peter Bogdanovich, *Fritz Lang in America* (1967); Gavin Lambert, *On Cukor* (1972); Axel Madsen, *William Wyler: The Authorized Biography* (1973); Maurice Zolotow, *Billy Wilder in Hollywood* (1977); Bernard Taper, *Balanchine* (1984); and Richard Buckle, *George Balanchine: Ballet Master* (1988). See also Herman Weinberg, *The Lubitsch Touch: A Critical Study* (1977); and Frederich Kohner, *The Magician of Sunset Boulevard: The Improbable Life of Paul Kohner, Hollywood Agent* (1977). The rapid adjustment of Man Ray to Los Angeles can be followed through Man Ray, *Self Portrait* (1963); Roland Penrose, *Man Ray* (1975); and Arturo Schwarz, *Man Ray: The Rigour of Imagination* (1977). See also *Man Ray: An Exhibition Organized by the Los Angeles County Museum of Art* (1966). *Casablanca* as an émigré enterprise is chronicled by Howard Koch and others in *Casablanca: Script and Legend* (1973). The central career of Marlene Dietrich, in all its variations, can be traced in Charles Higham, *Marlene: The Life of Marlene Dietrich* (1977); Donald Spoto, *Blue Angel: The Life of Marlene Dietrich* (1992); Steven Bach, *Marlene Dietrich: Life and Legend* (1992); and Maria Riva, *Marlene Dietrich by Her Daughter* (1993). *Vogue* magazine covered Dietrich's tour of the front in its 15 August 1944 edition.

The general background of émigré composers in Hollywood is outlined in Mark Evans, *Soundtrack: The Music of the Movies* (1979). See also Dimitri Tiomkin and Prosper Buranelli, *Please Don't Hate Me* (1959); and Miklos Rozsa, *Double Life*, foreword by Antal Dorati, preface by André Previn (1989). See also Darius Milhaud, *Notes Without Music: An Autobiography* (1952). The joyously adaptive Hollywood career of Igor Stravinsky is evident in Alexandre Tansman, *Igor Stravinsky: The Man and His Music*, translated by Therese and Charles Bleefield (1949); and Eric Walter White, *Stravinsky: The Composer and His Works* (1966). Stravinsky and Robert Craft jointly produced *Conversations with Igor Stravinsky* (1959) and *Memoirs and Commentaries* (1960). See also John Culhane, *Walt Disney's "Fantasia"* (1983). The more torturous Southern California career of Arnold Schoenberg is evident from H. H. Stuckenschmidt, *Schoenberg: His Life, World, and Work*, translated by Humphrey Searle (1977); and Dika Newlin, *Schoenberg Remembered: Diaries and Recollections (1938–76)* (1980). See also *Arnold Schoenberg Letters*, edited by Erwin Stein, translated by Eithne Wilkins and Ernst Kaiser (1965). Regarding the theoretical background to Schoenberg's music, see Theodor Adorno, *Philosophy of Modern Music*, translated by Anne Mitchell and Wesley Blomster (1973). See also Martin Jay, *Adorno* (1984).

Chapter Thirteen
From Catastrophe to Covenant

Jarrell Jackman wrote the seminal essay "Exiles in Paradise: German Émigrés in Southern California, 1933–1950," *SCQ*, 61 (Summer 1979), 183–205. Jackman and Carla Borden edited *The Muses Flee Hitler: Cultural Transfer and Adaptation, 1930–1945* (1983). Of equal importance is Anthony Heilbut, *Exiled in Paradise: German Refugee Artists and Intellectuals in America, from the 1930s to the Present* (1983). See also Laura Fermi, *Illustrious Immigrants: The Intellectual Migration from Europe, 1930–1941* (1968); and Donald Fleming and Bernard Bailyn, editors, *The Intellectual Migration: Europe and America, 1930–1960* (1969). Regarding the intellectual orientation of many émigrés in Southern California, see Martin Jay, *The Dialectical Imagination: A History of the Frankfurt School and the Institute of Social Research, 1923–1950* (1973); and *An Unmastered Past: The Autobiographical Reflections of Leo Lowenthal*, edited with an introduction by Martin Jay (1987).

Regarding Thomas Mann, see Hans Burgin and Hans-Otto Mayer, *Thomas Mann: A Chronicle of His Life* (1969); and Marcel Reich-Ranicki, *Thomas Mann and His Family*, translated from the German by Ralph Manheim (1989). See also the *Letters of Thomas Mann, 1889–1955*, selected and translated by Richard and Clara Winston (1971). Regarding Heinrich Mann, see Nigel Hamilton, *The Brothers Mann: The Lives of Heinrich and Thomas Mann, 1871–1950 and 1875–1955* (1978). Erika and Klaus Mann wrote *Escape to Life* (1939). Katia Mann wrote *Unwritten Memories* (1975). Regarding Klaus Mann, see *Klaus Mann* in the Twayne's World Authors Series (1978). Thomas Mann's introduction to *Joseph and His Brothers*, translated from the German by H. T. Lowe-Porter (1958), contains some significant Southern California references. Of special importance to this chapter is Mann's *The Story of a Novel: The Genesis of "Doctor Faustus,"* translated from the German by Richard and Clara Winston (1961). Susan Sontag described her visit to Mann in "Pilgrimage," *New Yorker*, 63 (21 December 1987), 38–54.

For general background to Lion Feuchtwanger, Franz Werfel, and other German Jewish émigré writers, see Lothar Kahn, *Mirrors of the Jewish Mind: A Gallery of Portraits of European Jewish Writers of Our Time* (1968); and *Protest, Form, Tradition: Essays on German Exile Literature*, edited by Joseph Strelka, Robert Bell, and Eugene Dobson (1979). See also Alfred Doblin, *Destiny's Journey*, edited by Edgar Passler, translated by Edna McCown (1992); and David Dollenmayer, *The Berlin Novels of Alfred Doblin* (1988). Feuchtwanger discussed his situation in "The Working Problems of the Writer in Exile," *Proceedings of the Writers' Congress, Los Angeles 1943* (Berkeley, 1944), 346–47. Feuchtwanger analyzed the historical novel in the posthumously published *The House of Desdemona; or, The Laurels and Limitations of Historical Fiction*, translated from the German by Harold Basilius (1963). Regarding Feuchtwanger, see *Lion Feuchtwanger: The Man, His Ideas, His Work*, a collection of critical essays edited by John Spalek (1972); and Lothar Kahn, *Insight and Action: The Life and Work of Lion Feuchtwanger* (1975).

Biographies of Franz Werfel include Lion Steiman, *Franz Werfel: The Faith of an Exile, from Prague to Beverly Hills* (1985); and Peter Stephan Jungk, *Franz Werfel: A Life in Prague, Vienna, and Hollywood* (1987). Alma Mahler Werfel wrote *And the Bridge Is Love* (1959). Biographies include Karen Monson, *Alma Mahler, Muse to Genius: From Fin-de-Siècle Vienna to Hollywood's Heyday* (1983); and Françoise Giroud, *Alma Mahler; or, The Art of Being Loved*, translated by R. M. Stock (1991).

Biographies of Bertolt Brecht include Martin Esslin, *Brecht: The Man and His Work* (1971); and Ronald Hayman, *Brecht: A Biography* (1983). In 1994 John Fuegi published the revisionist *Brecht and Company: Sex, Politics, and the Making of the Modern Drama*. For the specifics of Brecht's Santa Monica years, see James Lyon, *Bertolt Brecht in America* (1980); Patty Lee Parmalee, *Brecht's America* (1981); Bruce Cook, *Brecht in Exile* (1982); and Eric Bentley, *The Brecht Memoir* (1985). John Willett, Ralph Manheim, and Eric Fried edited *Bertolt Brecht Poems* (1976).

Acknowledgments

This book was researched in the California History Room of the California State Library in Sacramento; the Doe Memorial Library, the Bancroft Library, and the Environmental Design Library of the University of California at Berkeley; the Gleeson Library of the University of San Francisco and the San Francisco Public Library; the Doheny Library of the University of Southern California in Los Angeles, the University Research Library of the University of California at Los Angeles, and the Central Library of Los Angeles Public. Extensive use was made of inter-library loan services, especially from the Gleeson Library in San Francisco. For answering inquiries above and beyond the call of duty, I would especially like to thank the reference staff of the Gleeson Library (Ivan Hudson, Joe Garity, Steve Leary, Vicki Rosen, and Greg Swalley) and the equally dedicated and skilled reference staff, past and present, of the California History Room of the State Library (Kathleen Correia, Mark Cashatt, Anne Clark, John Gonzales, Vickie Lockhart, Richard Terry, and Sibylle Zemitis). I owe a special debt of gratitude to Gary Kurutz, Curator of Special Collections at the State Library and the premier bibliographer of Californiana at work today, for scores of invaluable references and to Rebecca Noonan for her energetic and intelligent research assistance.

Wade and Jane Hughan and Monsignor Steven Otellini of San Francisco have generously helped with proofreading. As usual, Sarah Ereira of London has prepared an excellent index. I owe thanks as well to Thomas F. Andrews, executive director of the Historical Society of Southern California, and Professor Doyce B. Nunis, dean of California historians. For assistance with photographs I would like to thank Dace Taube, curator of the Regional History Collection at the University of Southern California; John Ahouse and Marje Schuetze-Coburn of Special Collections, the University of Southern California Library; R. Wayne Shoaf, archivist of the Arnold Schoenberg Institute; Carolyn Cole, senior librarian, and Roselyn Lee of the Los Angeles Public Library; Gloria Werner, University Librarian at UCLA; Dr. Charlotte E. Erwin, associate archivist of the California Institute of Technology; Annie Brose, coordinator of rights and reproductions at the Los Angeles County Museum of Art; Charles D. Hill, curator of photographs at the San Diego Historical Society; Patricia Akre of the San Francisco History Center of the San Francisco Public Library; Drew Johnson, curator of photography at the Oakland Museum; Gary Kurutz, curator of special collections at the California State Library in Sacramento; and Dianne Nilsen, coordinator of rights and reproductions, Center for Creative Photography at the University of Arizona. Special thanks is acknowledged as well to the Arizona Board of Regents and the Center for Creative Photography for permission to reproduce *Charis, Lake Ediza* 1937 by Edward Weston. Author Jerry Flamm assisted me in portions of the San Francisco background. Writer-historian Mike Davis, economic commentator Joel Kotkin, historian Dr. J. S. Holliday, historian C. Albert Shumate, M.D., and historian Dr. Richard Allison have generously assisted me in matters of selection and interpretation. I owe a special debt to India Cooper and Joellyn M. Ausanka of Oxford University Press.

As in the case of previous volumes, my wife Sheila worked constantly and ably as my primary research assistant. To put the matter simply: there would be no book without her. I am also indebted to my daughters Marian and Jessica for their good-humored support. Literary agent Sandra Dijkstra of Del Mar and her husband, Professor Bram Dijkstra of UC San Diego, bear special responsibility for this book and for the continuing productivity of its author.

Professor Dijkstra first pointed out to me that I was struggling to write two conjoined but distinct books in one volume and that each of these books would be strengthened not by excessive cutting so as to make the mass of the material manageable, but by a dramatic separation into two volumes, *Endangered Dreams* and *The Dream Endures*. I am most grateful to Professor Dijkstra for his simple but elegant solution to a problem that had been bedeviling me for at least two years and for his assistance in the rearrangement of the material.

The dedication of this book to Sheldon Meyer, senior vice president of Oxford University Press in New York, makes but a faint return on the debt I owe to one of the most accomplished editors in the long history of the publishing house he continues to serve with such distinction. For more than three decades, the name Sheldon Meyer and American studies have been near-synonymous in these United States. Twenty years ago, Sheldon Meyer encouraged me to make a series out of my initial *Americans and the California Dream* study. With patience and friendship, he has guided into completion four subsequent volumes of the series, despite the many other engagements of their author. It was Sheldon Meyer, the consummate New Yorker, who more than any other person persuaded me that chronicling California might be the worthy work of a lifetime. One of the primary benefits of this journey has been the gift of Sheldon Meyer's intellectual influence, good company, and friendship. Would that I could remain forever young, and forever at my desk, and forever hearing Sheldon Meyer on the telephone or over dinner in the course of his yearly visits to California urging me with the urbane insistence of a polished Princetonian to get on with my task and meet my deadline!

Los Angeles, San Francisco, Sacramento   K.S.
October 1996

Index

National Institute of Arts and Letters, 384
National Labor Relations Act, 183
National Origins Law, 136
National Park Service, 33
National Recovery Administration (NRA), 258, 262, 263
National Research Council, 80
Native Son, 314
Native Sons of the Golden State, 136
Native Sons of the Golden West, 136
Natoma, 121
Natomas Company, 127
Naval Affairs Committee, 112
Naval Air Station, 112
Naval Amphibious Base, 112
Naval Hospital, 112
Naval Radio Stations, 112
Naval Training Station, 112, 210
Navy, 12, 38, 68, 91, 93–94, 109–14, 152
Navy Ball, 12
Nazimova, Alla, 300
NBC, 35, 38, 115, 155, 266, 269–70, 339
NBC Symphony Orchestra, 384
Negri, Pola, 266
Negro Trailblazers of California, The, 177
Nelson, Albert, 301
Neptune Baths, 122
Neutra, Richard, 21–22, 158, 265
Nevada County, 207
New Deal, 48, 224, 259, 263, 278, 372
New Heavens, The, 79
New Hope Baptist Church, 180
New Jersey, 18
New Masses, 48
New Republic, 44, 90, 249, 268
New Science, 323
New Yorker, 226
Newberry, Perry, 51
Newhall, Beaumont, 217, 218
Newhall, Nancy Parker, 217

Newlin, Dika, 383
Newport Beach, 10
Newsom, William, 144
Newsweek, 285
Nez Perce, 47
Nibelungen, The, 347
Nicholson, Lillie May, 229
Niebuhr, Reinhold, 386
Night at the Opera, A, 263
Night Court, 277
Night Sun—Abandoned Playground, 360
Ninotchka, 343
Nipomo Hills, 240
Niven, David, 13, 274, 281, 282, 349
No Place to Go, 233
No Pockets in a Shroud, 308
Nob Hill, 44, 135, 238
Nobel, Alfred, 80
Nobel Prize, 63, 80, 85, 125
Nolen, John, 106, 112, 113
Nolen Report (1908), 106, 107, 108
Normal Heights, 107
Norris, Charles Gilman (Cigi), 20, 34, 42, 43–44, 146, 285, 288–89
Norris, Frank, 20, 34, 43, 132, 141, 145, 147, 148, 285, 286, 292, 344
Norris, Kathleen, 6, 20, 42–44, 48, 145, 146, 288, 289
North Bay, 230
North Beach, 133, 134, 149
North Hollywood, 67
North Hollywood High School, 381–82
North Island, 110, 112
North Park, 107
North Rossmore, 23
Nosferatu, 345
Noskowiak, Sonya, 205, 219
Not All Rivers, 289, 290
Notre Dame, 36–37, 130, 174
November Grass, 293
Now, Voyager, 351
Now and Forever, 259
Noyes, Alfred, 82–83
Noyes, Arthur, 80, 85–86